ORDNANCE SURVEY

STREET ATLAS
Staffordshire

Contents

PHILIP'S

First edition published 1995 by

Ordnance Survey   and   Philip's
Romsey Road   an imprint of Reed Books
Maybush   Michelin House, 81 Fulham Road, London, SW3 6RB
Southampton SO16 4GU   and Auckland, Melbourne, Singapore and Toronto

ISBN 0-540-06134-4 (Philip's, hardback)
ISBN 0-540-06135-2 (Philip's, softback)
ISBN 0-319-00568-2 (Ordnance Survey, hardback)
ISBN 0-319-00569-2 (Ordnance Survey, softback)

To the best of the Publishers' knowledge, the information in this atlas was correct at
the time of going to press. No responsibility can be accepted for any errors or their
consequences.

The representation in this atlas of a road, track or path is no evidence of the existence
of a right of way.

Printed and bound in Great Britain by
Bath Press, Bath

Key to map symbols

⇌	**British Rail station**
🚂	**Private railway station**
⬤	**Bus or coach station**
Ⓗ	**Heliport**
◆	**Police station** (may not be open 24 hours)
✚	**Hospital with casualty facilities** (may not be open 24 hours)
☐	**Post office**
✢	**Place of worship**
▬	**Important building**
P	**Parking**
174	**Adjoining page indicator**
⨯	**No adjoining page**
▬▬▬	**Motorway**
══	**Dual carriageway**
───	**Main or through road**
A27	**Road numbers** (Department of Transport)
─┬─	**Gate or obstruction to traffic** (restrictions may not apply at all times or to all vehicles)
- - - - -	**All paths, bridleways, BOAT's, RUPP's, dismantled railways, etc.**
══	**Track**

The representation in this atlas of a road, track or path is no evidence of the existence of a right of way

Amb Sta	**Ambulance station**	LC	**Level crossing**
Coll	**College**	Liby	**Library**
FB	**Footbridge**	Mus	**Museum**
F Sta	**Fire station**	Sch	**School**
Hospl	**Hospital**	TH	**Town hall**

0	¼	½	¾	1 mile
0	250m	500m	250m	1 Kilometre

The scale of the maps is 3½ inches to 1 mile (1:18103)

The small numbers around the edges of the maps identify the 1 kilometre National Grid lines

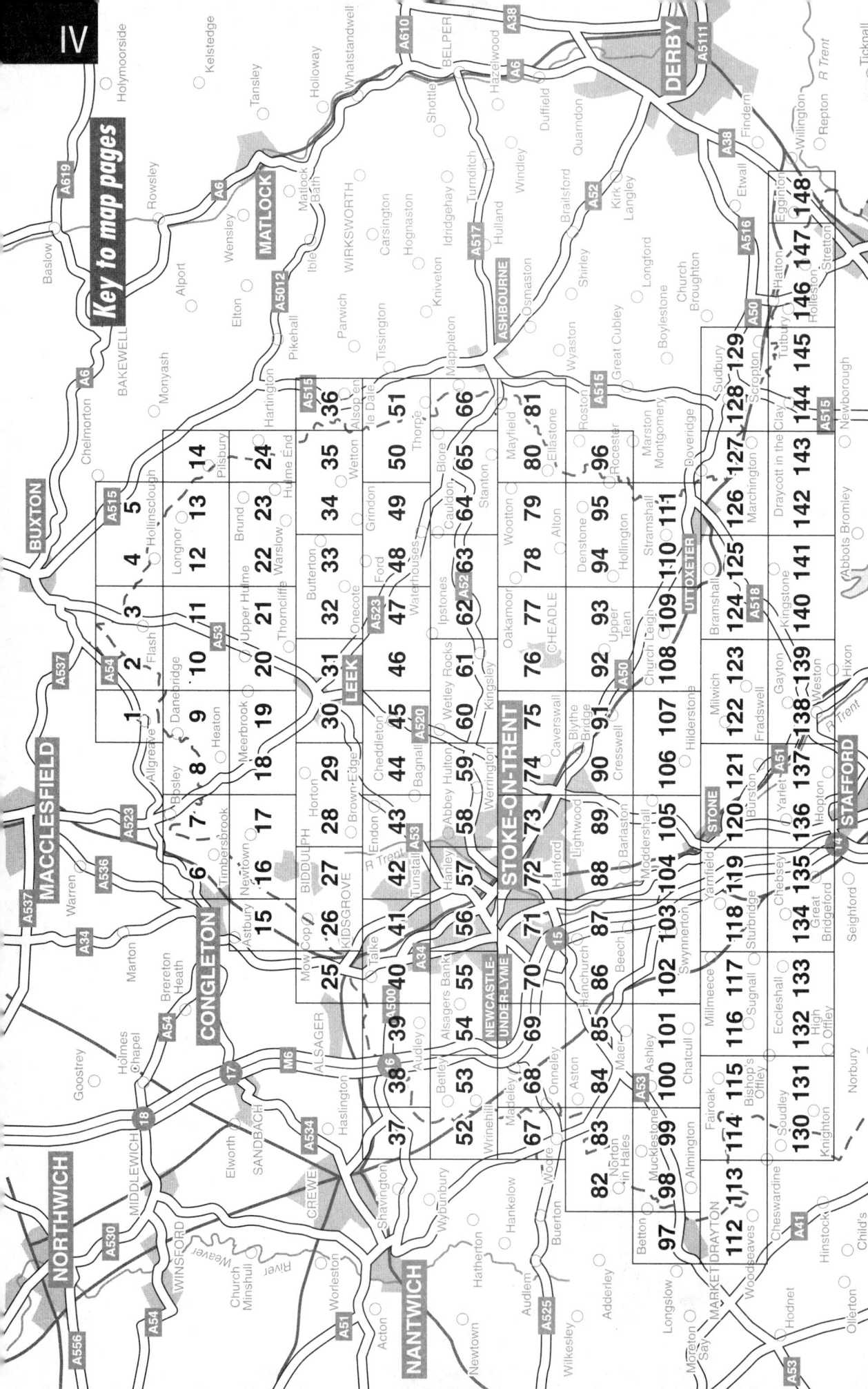

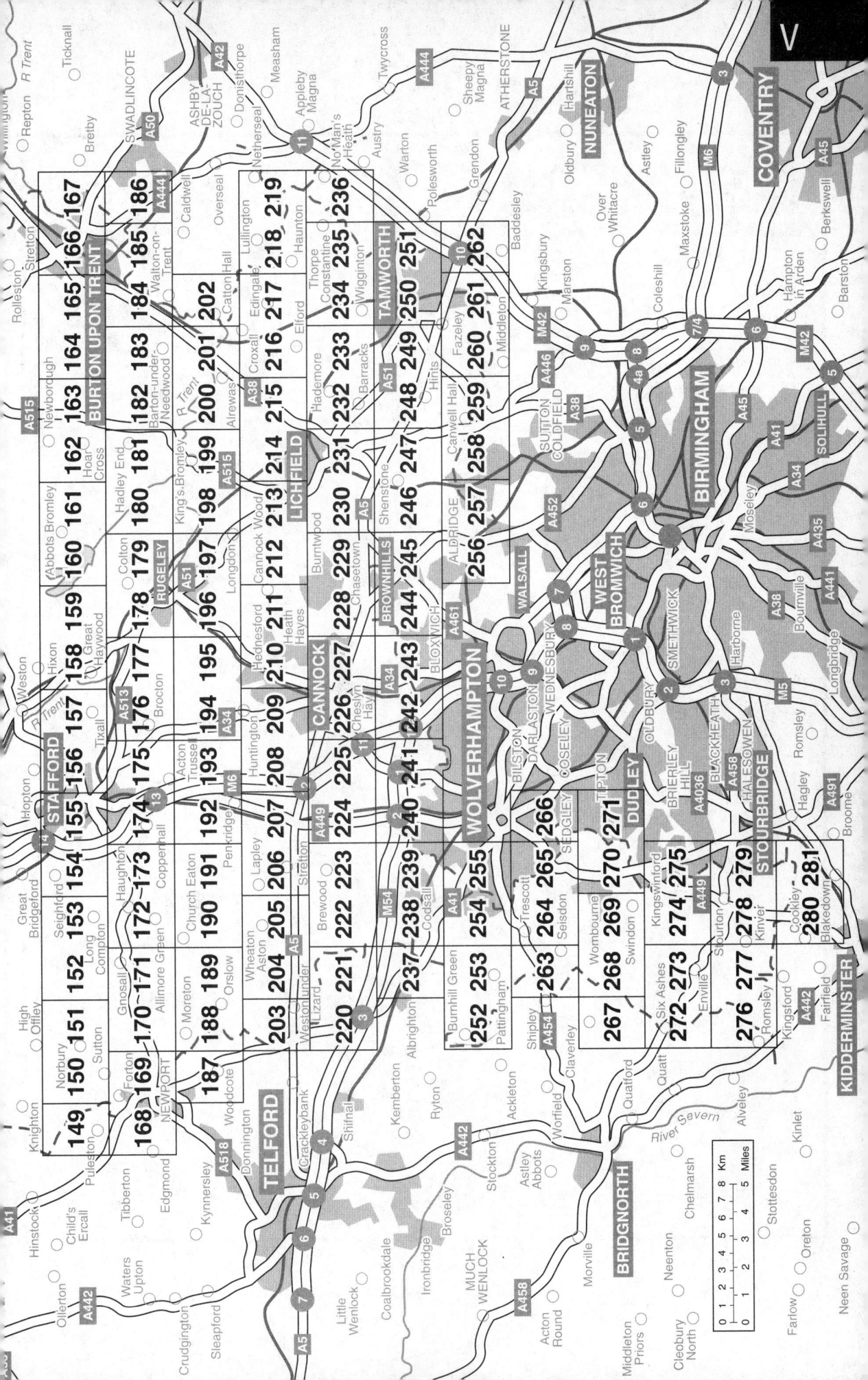

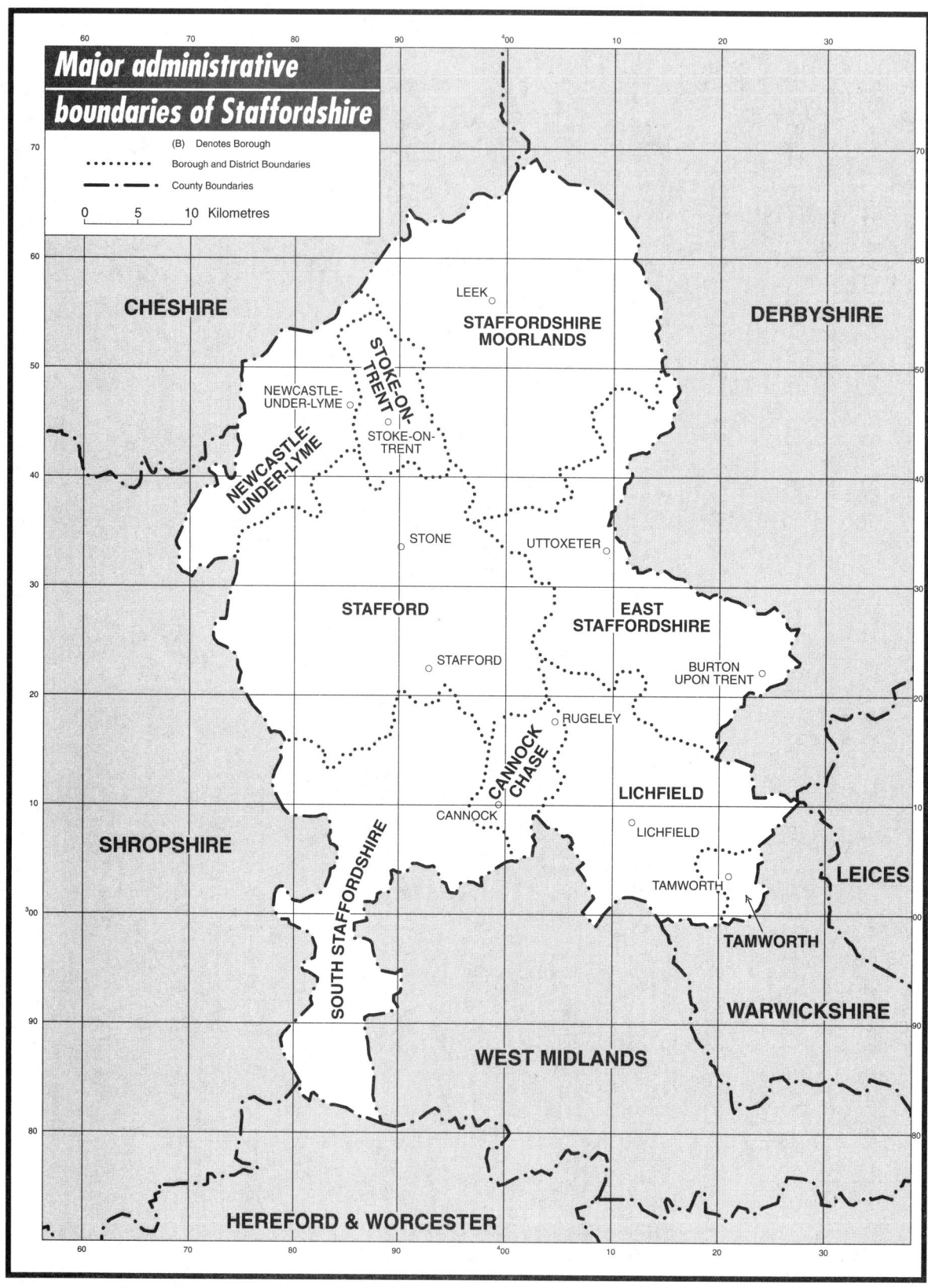

Major administrative boundaries of Staffordshire

(B) Denotes Borough

.... Borough and District Boundaries

—·—·— County Boundaries

0   5   10   Kilometres

CHESHIRE

DERBYSHIRE

LEEK

STAFFORDSHIRE MOORLANDS

STOKE-ON-TRENT

NEWCASTLE-UNDER-LYME

NEWCASTLE-UNDER-LYME

STOKE-ON-TRENT

STONE

UTTOXETER

STAFFORD

EAST STAFFORDSHIRE

STAFFORD

BURTON UPON TRENT

RUGELEY

CANNOCK CHASE

LICHFIELD

CANNOCK

LICHFIELD

SHROPSHIRE

SOUTH STAFFORDSHIRE

TAMWORTH

LEICES

TAMWORTH

WARWICKSHIRE

WEST MIDLANDS

HEREFORD & WORCESTER

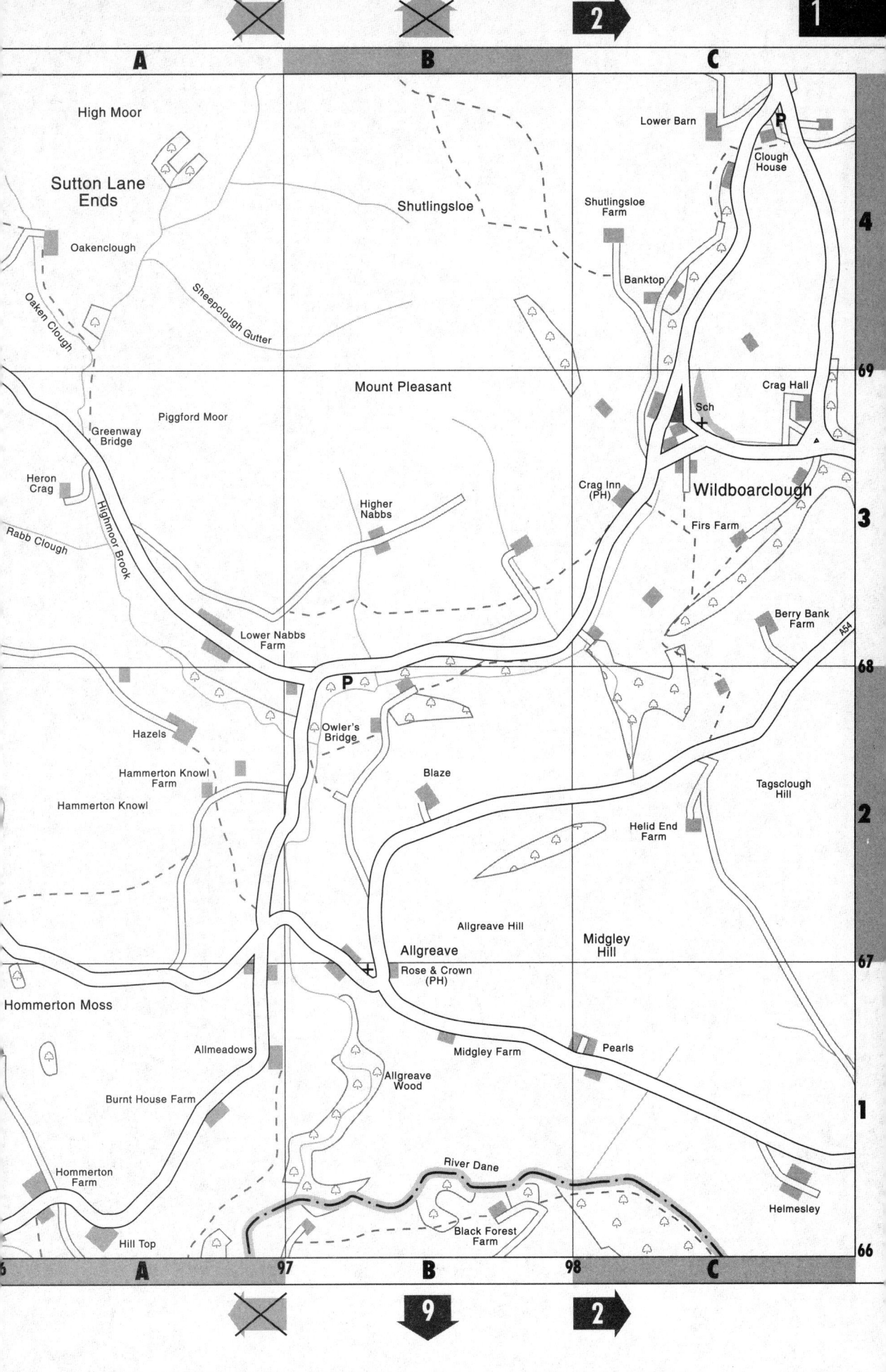

A
B
2 →
C

High Moor

Sutton Lane
Ends

Oakenclough

Oaken Clough

Sheepclough Gutter

Shutlingsloe

Lower Barn

Clough
House

P

Shutlingsloe
Farm

Banktop

4

Greenway
Bridge

Piggford Moor

Mount Pleasant

Crag Hall

69

Sch

Heron
Crag

Highmoor Brook

Rabb Clough

Higher
Nabbs

Crag Inn
(PH)

Wildboarclough

Firs Farm

3

Lower Nabbs
Farm

Berry Bank
Farm

A54

68

Hazels

P

Owler's
Bridge

Blaze

Helid End
Farm

Tagsclough
Hill

2

Hammerton Knowl
Farm

Hammerton Knowl

Allgreave Hill

Allgreave

Midgley
Hill

67

Rose & Crown
(PH)

Hommerton Moss

Allmeadows

Midgley Farm

Pearls

1

Burnt House Farm

Allgreave
Wood

Hommerton
Farm

River Dane

Helmesley

Hill Top

Black Forest
Farm

66

6
A
97
B
98
C

9

2 →

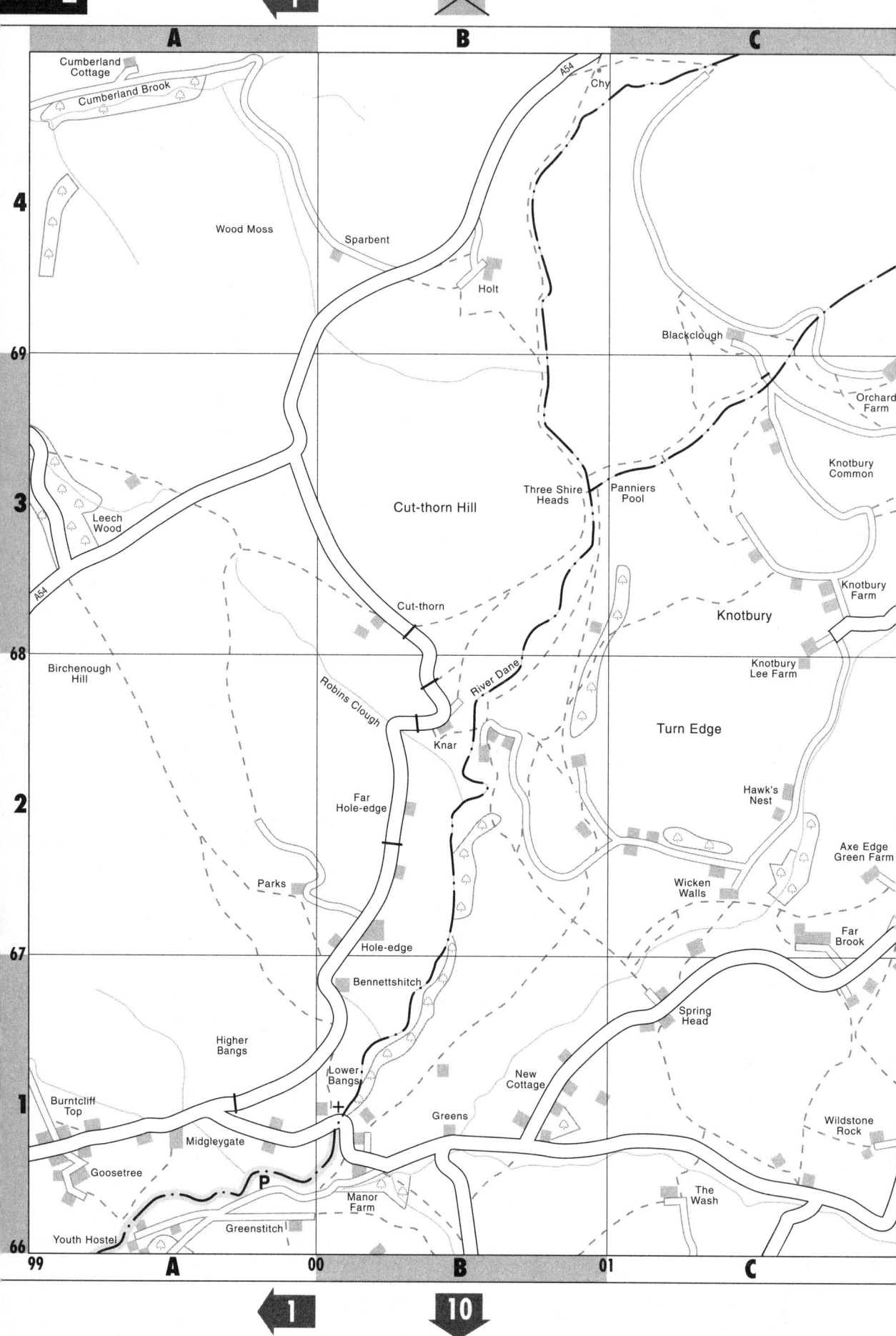

A

B

C

Cumberland
Cottage

Cumberland Brook

Wood Moss

Sparbent

A54

Chy

Holt

Blackclough

Orchard
Farm

4

69

Leech
Wood

Knotbury
Common

A54

Cut-thorn Hill

Three Shire
Heads

Panniers
Pool

Knotbury
Farm

3

Cut-thorn

Knotbury

Birchenough
Hill

Knotbury
Lee Farm

68

Robins Clough

River Dane

Knar

Turn Edge

Far
Hole-edge

Hawk's
Nest

Axe Edge
Green Farm

2

Parks

Wicken
Walls

Far
Brook

Hole-edge

67

Bennettshitch

Spring
Head

Higher
Bangs

New
Cottage

Burntcliff
Top

Lower
Bangs

Greens

Wildstone
Rock

1

Midgleygate

P

Goosetree

Manor
Farm

The
Wash

Youth Hostel

Greenstitch

66

99

A

00

B

01

C

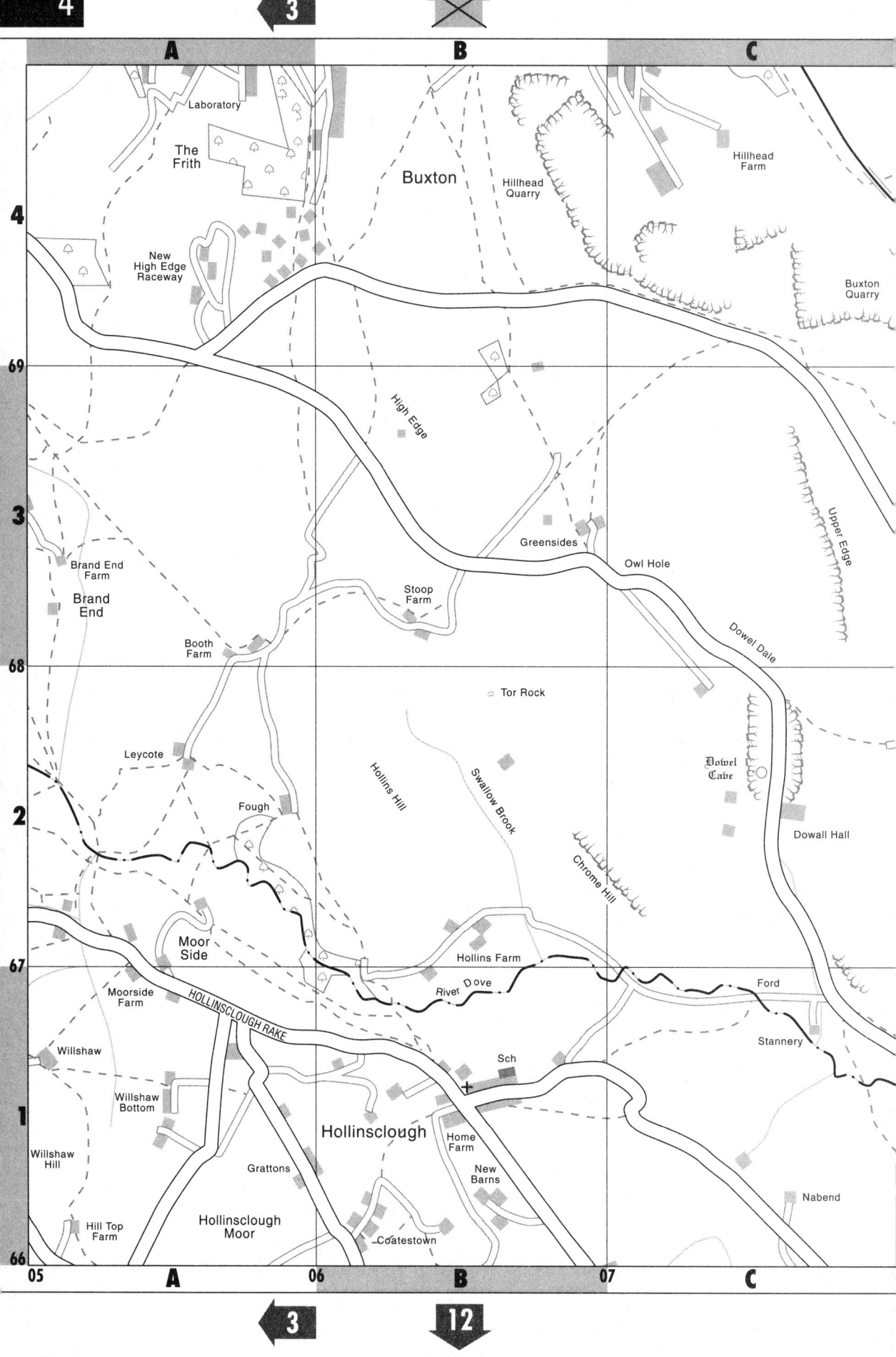

A
B
C

4

69

3

68

2

67

1

66

05
A
06
B
07
C

Laboratory

The Frith

Buxton

Hillhead Quarry

Hillhead Farm

New High Edge Raceway

Buxton Quarry

High Edge

Brand End Farm

Brand End

Greensides

Owl Hole

Upper Edge

Stoop Farm

Booth Farm

Dowel Dale

Tor Rock

Leycote

Hollins Hill

Swallow Brook

Dowel Cave

Fough

Dowall Hall

Chrome Hill

Moor Side

Hollins Farm

Moorside Farm

HOLLINSCLOUGH RAKE

River Dove

Ford

Stannery

Willshaw

Sch

Willshaw Bottom

Hollinsclough

Home Farm

Willshaw Hill

Grattons

New Barns

Nabend

Hill Top Farm

Hollinsclough Moor

Coatestown

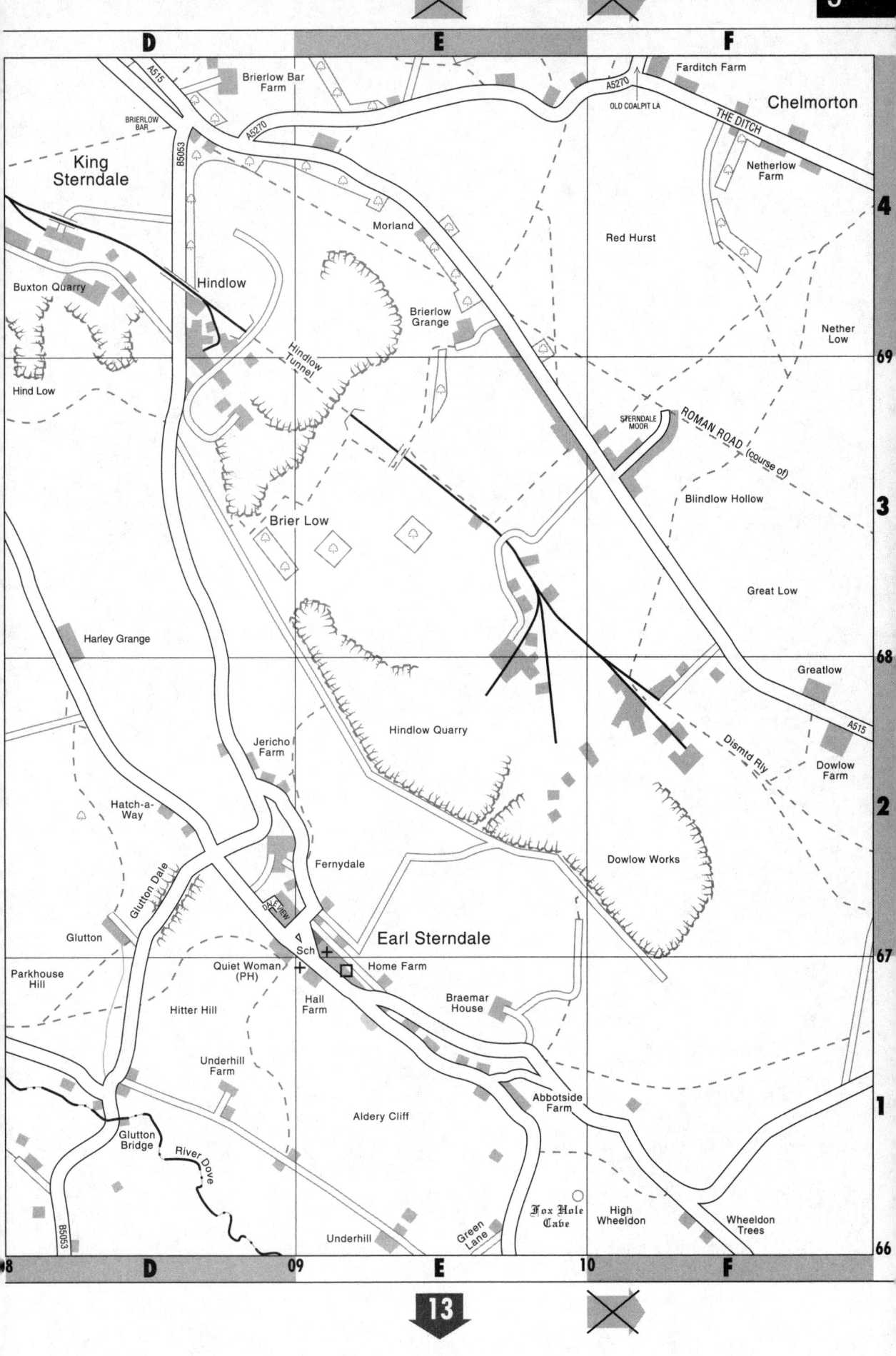

King
Sterndale

Buxton Quarry

Hindlow

Hind Low

BRIERLOW
BAR

A515

B5053

A5270

Brierlow Bar
Farm

Morland

Brierlow
Grange

Hindlow
Tunnel

Brier Low

Harley Grange

Jericho
Farm

Hatch-a-
Way

Glutton

Glutton Dale

Parkhouse
Hill

Hitter Hill

Underhill
Farm

Glutton
Bridge

River Dove

Underhill

Hindlow Quarry

Fernydale

Sch

Quiet Woman
(PH)

Hall
Farm

Aldery Cliff

Green
Lane

Fox Hole
Cave

Earl Sterndale

Home Farm

Braemar
House

Abbotside
Farm

High
Wheeldon

Farditch Farm

Chelmorton

OLD COALPIT LA

THE DITCH

Netherlow
Farm

Red Hurst

Nether
Low

STERNDALE
MOOR

ROMAN ROAD (course of)

Blindlow Hollow

Great Low

Greatlow

Dismtd Rly

Dowlow
Farm

A515

Dowlow Works

Wheeldon
Trees

A5270

4

69

3

68

2

67

1

66

D

E

F

8

09

10

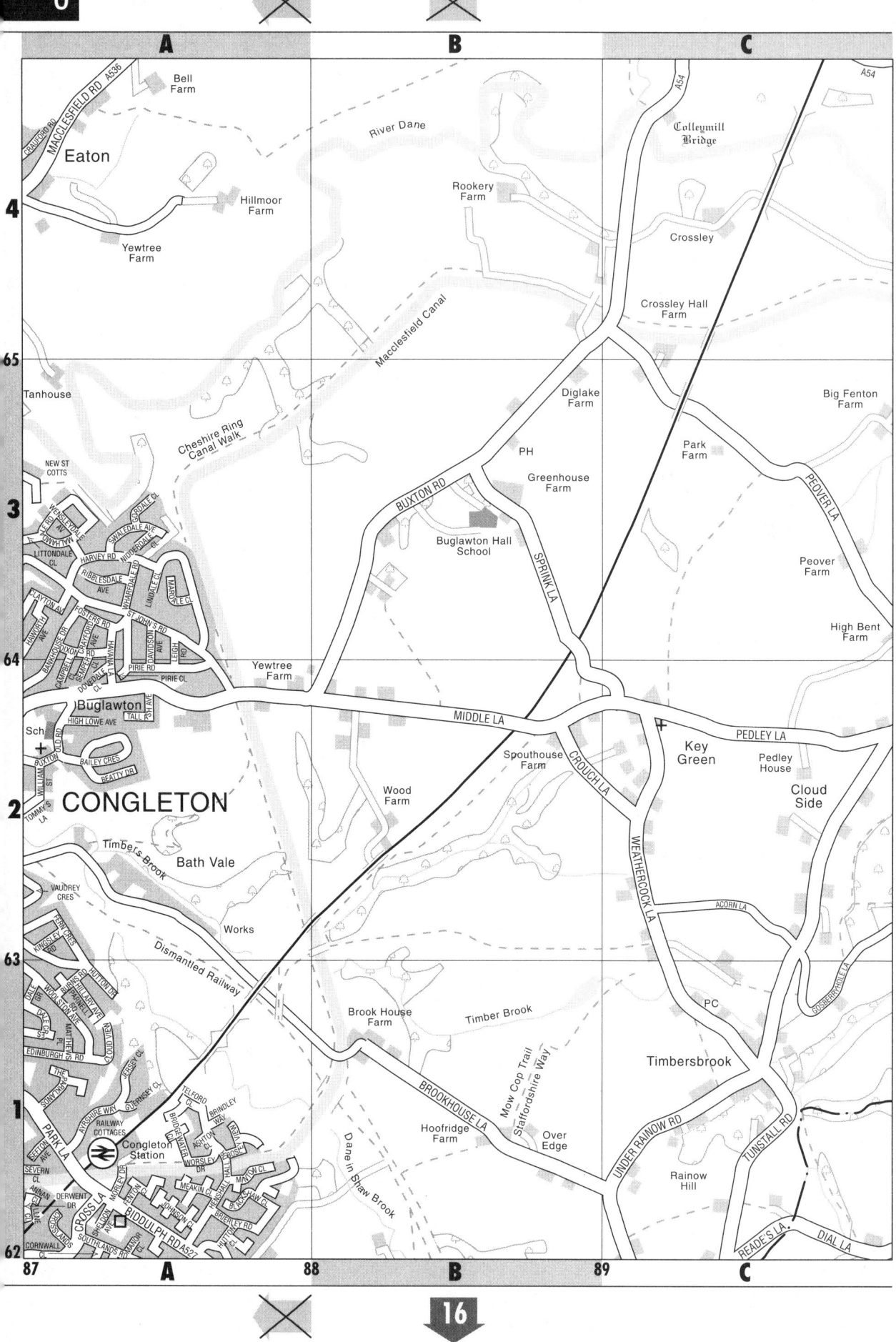

A
B
C

4

River Dane

Macclesfield Rd A536
Cranford Rd

Bell Farm

Eaton

Hillmoor Farm

Yewtree Farm

Colleymill Bridge

A54

Rookery Farm

Crossley

Crossley Hall Farm

65

Tanhouse

Cheshire Ring Canal Walk

Macclesfield Canal

Diglake Farm

PH

Greenhouse Farm

Big Fenton Farm

Park Farm

Peover La

3

New St Cotts

Wensleydale Rd

Swaledale Ave
Garsdale Cl
Nidderdale Cl

Harvey Rd

Littondale Cl
Ribblesdale Ave
Fosters Rd

St John's Rd
Marvel Cl
Linnidale Cl

Clayton Av
Hanover Ave
Bankhouse Dr
Dixon Cl
Campbell Cl
Craxford Rd
Satterley Cl
Dovedale Cl
Davidson Ave
Tynwald
High Rd

Buxton Rd

Sprink La

Buglawton Hall School

Peover Farm

High Bent Farm

64

Yewtree Farm

Buglawton

Tall St
High Lowe Ave

Pirie Rd
Pirie Cl

Middle La

Crouch La

Key Green

Pedley La

Pedley House

Sch

Buxton Rd
William St
Tommy's La

Bailey Cres
Beatty Dr

Spouthouse Farm

Cloud Side

2

CONGLETON

Timbers Brook

Bath Vale

Wood Farm

Weathercock La

Acorn La

Vaudrey Cres

Fern Cres
Kingsley Rd

Works

Dismantled Railway

63

Hutton Dr
Dale
Delf
Burns Cl
Railway Ave
Cross Cl
Oak Cl

Matthew Cl
Milne Cl

Edinburgh Rd

Edward
Severn
The Parkway

Jersey Cl
Guernsey Way

Brook House Farm

Timber Brook

PC

Telford Cl
Brindley Cl
Bridge Dale
Ashton Cl
Neath Cl
Frobisher Cl

Timbersbrook

1

Park La
Ayrshire Way
Railway Cottages
Worsley Dr

Brookhouse La

Mow Cop Trail
Staffordshire Way
Over Edge

Under Rainow Rd

Tunstall Rd

Congleton Station

Meakin Cl
Johnson Cl
Kendal Cl
Ferndale Cl
Bamford Cl

Hoofridge Farm

Rainow Hill

Severn Cl
Annan Cl
Cleethorpe

Derwent Dr
Cross La

Dane in Shaw Brook

Southlands Cl

Biddulph Rd A527

Cornwall Cl

Reade's La
Dial La

62

87
A
88
B
89
C

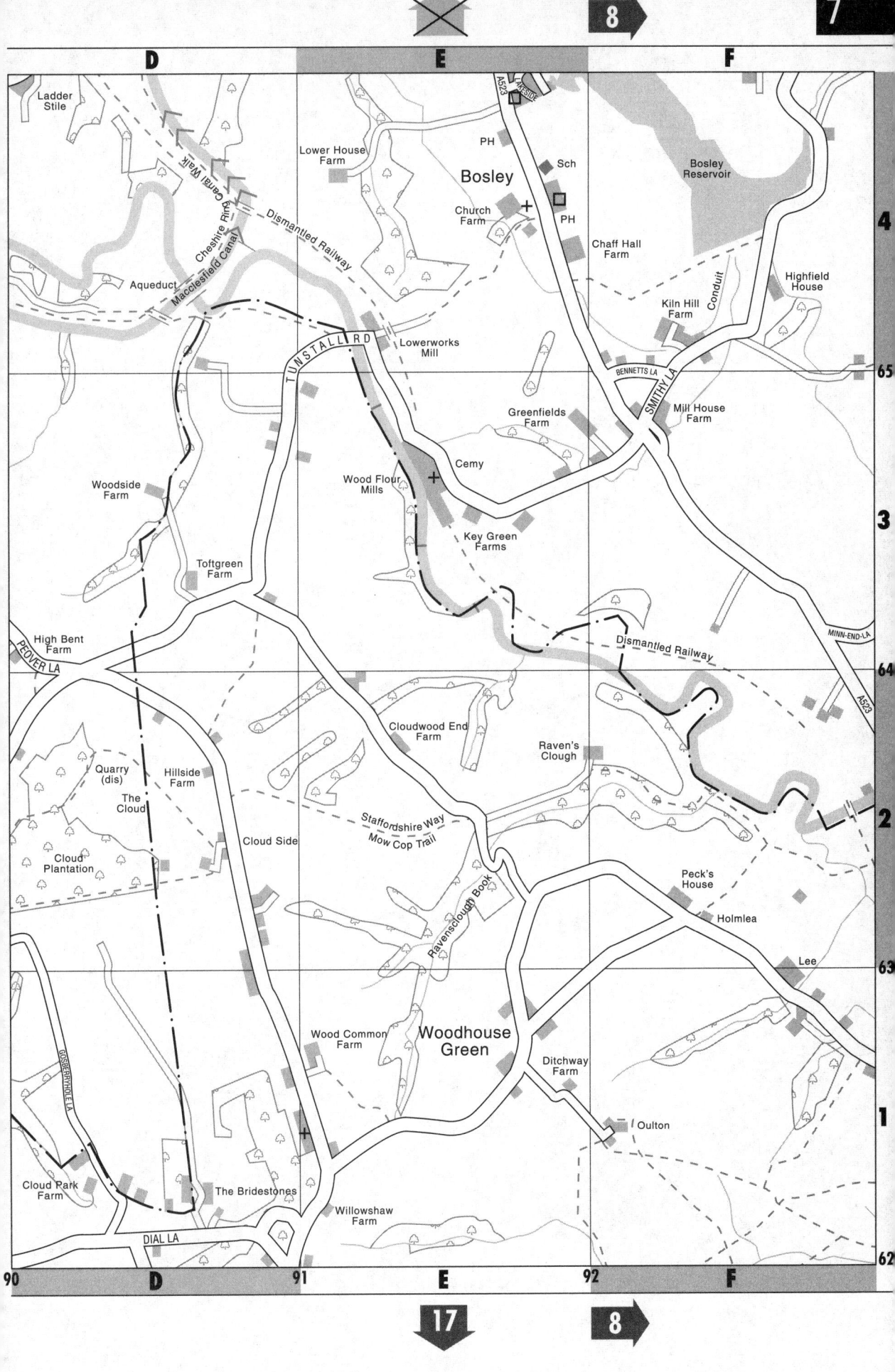

D   E   F

Ladder
Stile

Lower House
Farm

Bosley

PH

Sch

Bosley
Reservoir

Church
Farm

PH

Chaff Hall
Farm

4

Cheshire Ring Canal Walk

Dismantled Railway

Aqueduct

Macclesfield Canal

Conduit

Highfield
House

Kiln Hill
Farm

TUNSTALL RD

Lowerworks
Mill

BENNETTS LA

65

SMITHY LA

Mill House
Farm

Greenfields
Farm

Woodside
Farm

Wood Flour
Mills

Cemy

Key Green
Farms

MINN-END-LA

3

Toftgreen
Farm

A523

High Bent
Farm

PEOVER LA

Dismantled Railway

64

Cloudwood End
Farm

Raven's
Clough

Quarry
(dis)

Hillside
Farm

The
Cloud

Cloud Side

Staffordshire Way
Mow Cop Trail

Peck's
House

2

Cloud
Plantation

Ravensclough Book

Holmlea

Lee

63

Wood Common
Farm

Woodhouse
Green

Ditchway
Farm

BOSLEYBROOKE LA

Oulton

1

Cloud Park
Farm

The Bridestones

DIAL LA

Willowshaw
Farm

62

7

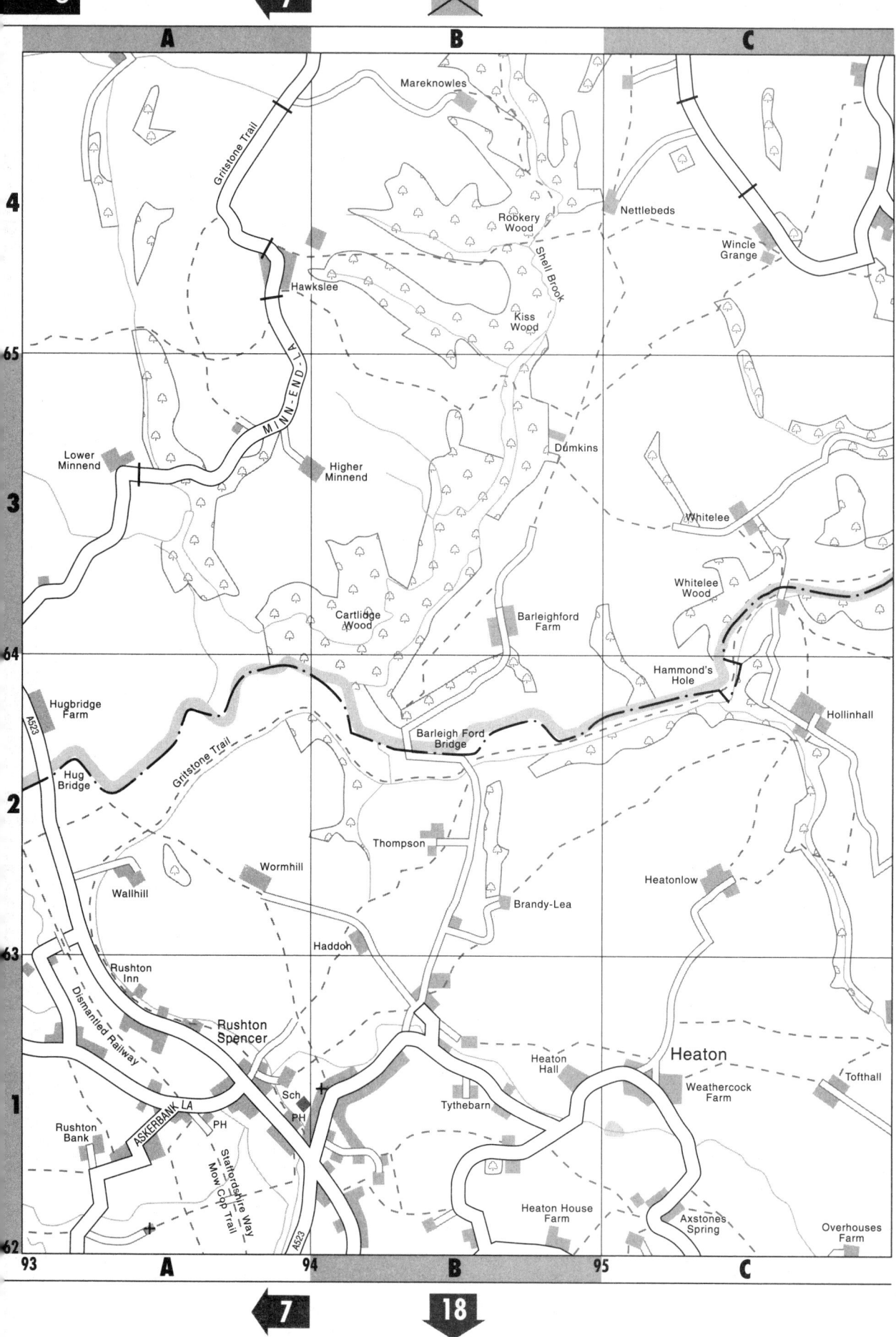

A

B

C

4

Mareknowles

Rookery Wood

Shell Brook

Kiss Wood

Nettlebeds

Wincle Grange

Gritstone Trail

MINN-END-LA

Hawkslee

65

Lower Minnend

Higher Minnend

Dumkins

Whitelee

3

Whitelee Wood

Cartlidge Wood

Barleighford Farm

Hammond's Hole

64

Hugbridge Farm

A523

Gritstone Trail

Barleigh Ford Bridge

Hollinhall

Hug Bridge

2

Thompson

Heatonlow

Wormhill

Wallhill

Brandy-Lea

63

Haddon

Rushton Inn

Dismantled Railway

Rushton Spencer

Heaton

Heaton Hall

Weathercock Farm

Tofthall

1

Sch

PH

Tythebarn

ASKERBANK LA

PH

Rushton Bank

Staffordshire Way
Mow Cop Trail

A523

Heaton House Farm

Axstones Spring

Overhouses Farm

62

93

A

94

B

95

C

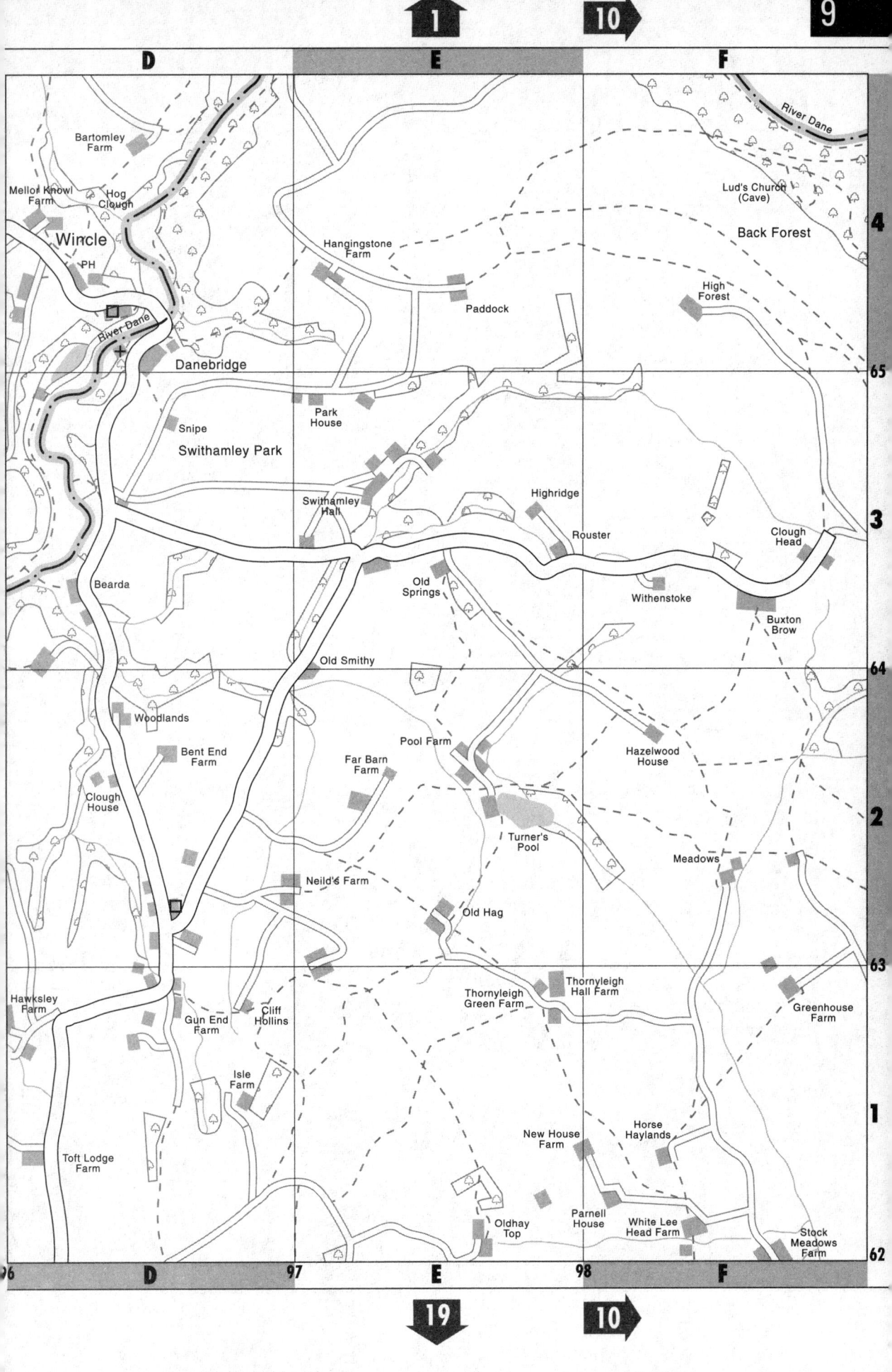

D
E
F

Bartomley Farm

Mellor Knowl Farm

Hog Clough

Wincle

PH

River Dane

Danebridge

4

Hangingstone Farm

Paddock

Lud's Church (Cave)

Back Forest

High Forest

65

Snipe

Park House

Swithamley Park

Swithamley Hall

Highridge

Rouster

Clough Head

3

Bearda

Old Springs

Withenstoke

Buxton Brow

Old Smithy

64

Woodlands

Bent End Farm

Far Barn Farm

Pool Farm

Hazelwood House

Clough House

Turner's Pool

Meadows

2

Neild's Farm

Old Hag

Hawksley Farm

Gun End Farm

Cliff Hollins

Thornyleigh Green Farm

Thornyleigh Hall Farm

Greenhouse Farm

63

Isle Farm

Horse Haylands

1

Toft Lodge Farm

New House Farm

Parnell House

White Lee Head Farm

Stock Meadows Farm

Oldhay Top

62

96

D
97
E
98
F

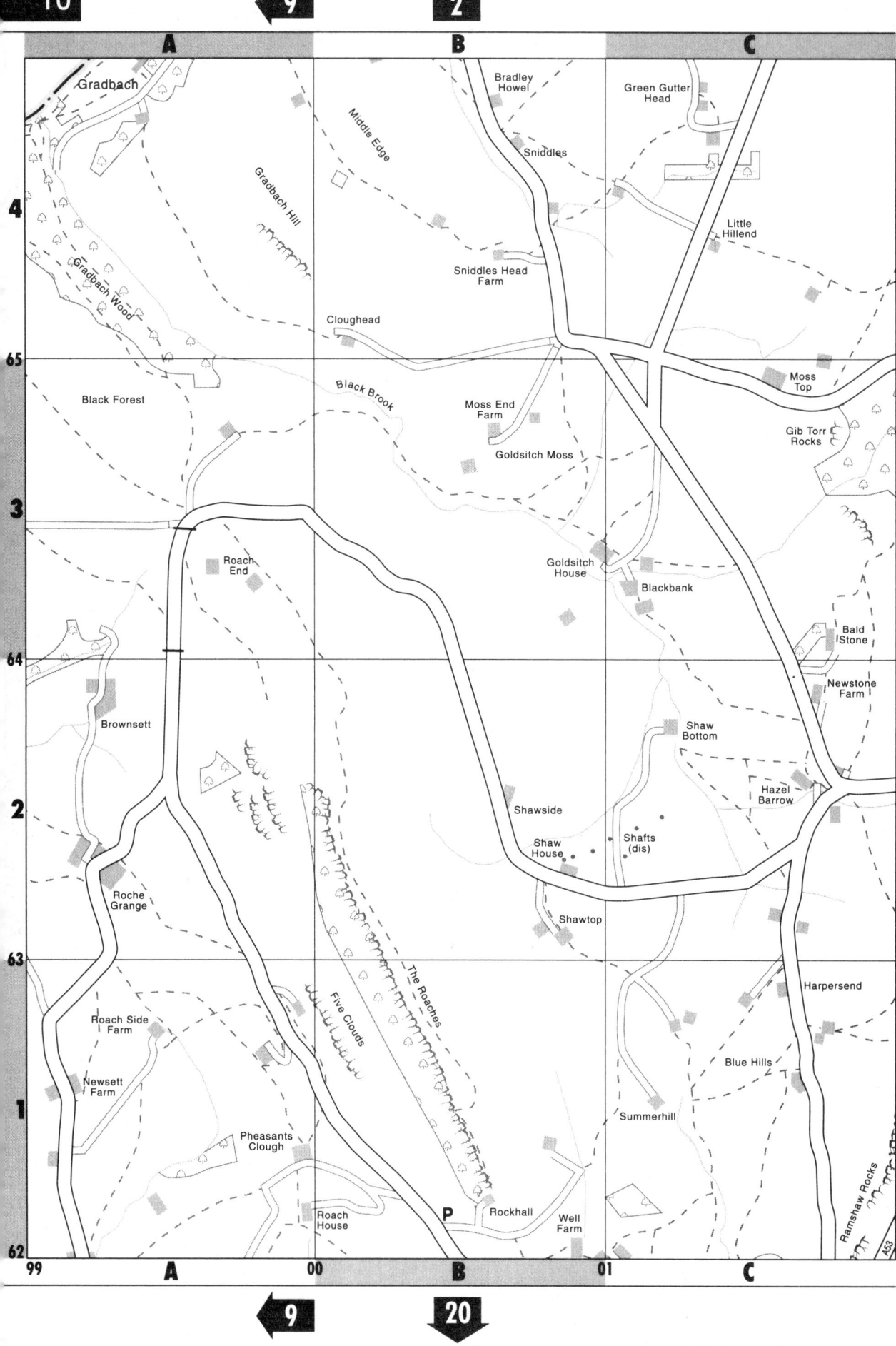

Gradbach

Middle Edge

Gradbach Hill

Gradbach Wood

Bradley Howel

Sniddles

Green Gutter Head

Little Hillend

4

Sniddles Head Farm

Cloughead

Black Brook

Moss Top

65

Black Forest

Moss End Farm

Goldsitch Moss

Gib Torr Rocks

3

Roach End

Goldsitch House

Blackbank

Bald Stone

64

Brownsett

Newstone Farm

Shaw Bottom

Hazel Barrow

2

Shawside

Shaw House

Shafts (dis)

Roche Grange

Five Clouds

The Roaches

Shawtop

63

Harpersend

Roach Side Farm

Blue Hills

Newsett Farm

1

Summerhill

Pheasants Clough

Ramshaw Rocks

P

Roach House

Rockhall

Well Farm

62

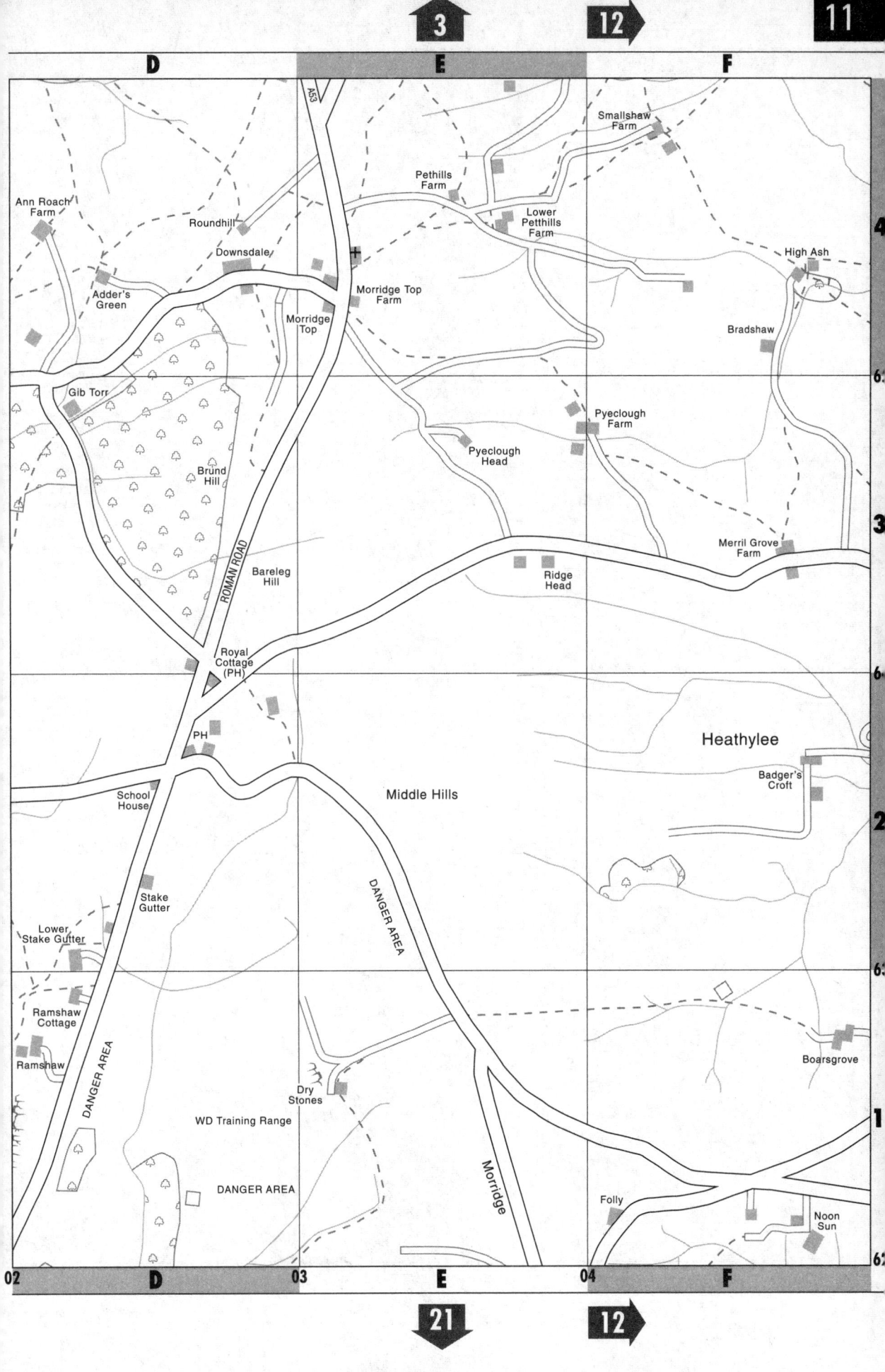

D
E
F

A53

Smallshaw
Farm

Pethills
Farm

Lower
Petthills
Farm

Ann Roach
Farm

Roundhill

Downsdale

High Ash

Adder's
Green

Morridge Top
Farm

Bradshaw

Morridge
Top

Gib Torr

Pyeclough
Farm

Pyeclough
Head

Brund
Hill

Merril Grove
Farm

Bareleg
Hill

Ridge
Head

ROMAN ROAD

Royal
Cottage
(PH)

Heathylee

Badger's
Croft

PH

School
House

Middle Hills

DANGER AREA

Stake
Gutter

Lower
Stake Gutter

Ramshaw
Cottage

Boarsgrove

DANGER AREA

Ramshaw

Dry
Stones

WD Training Range

Morridge

DANGER AREA

Folly

Noon
Sun

02
D
03
E
04
F

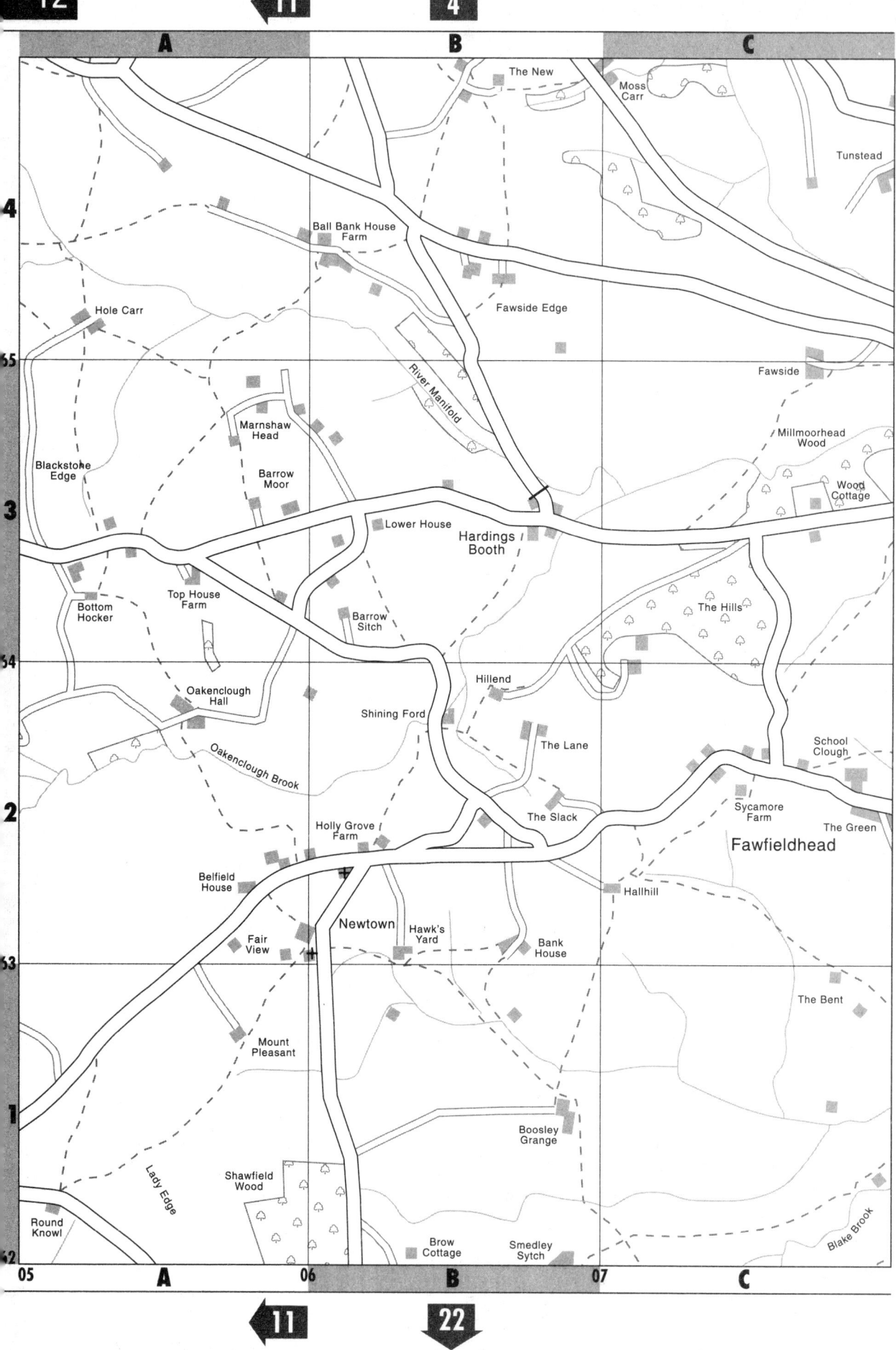

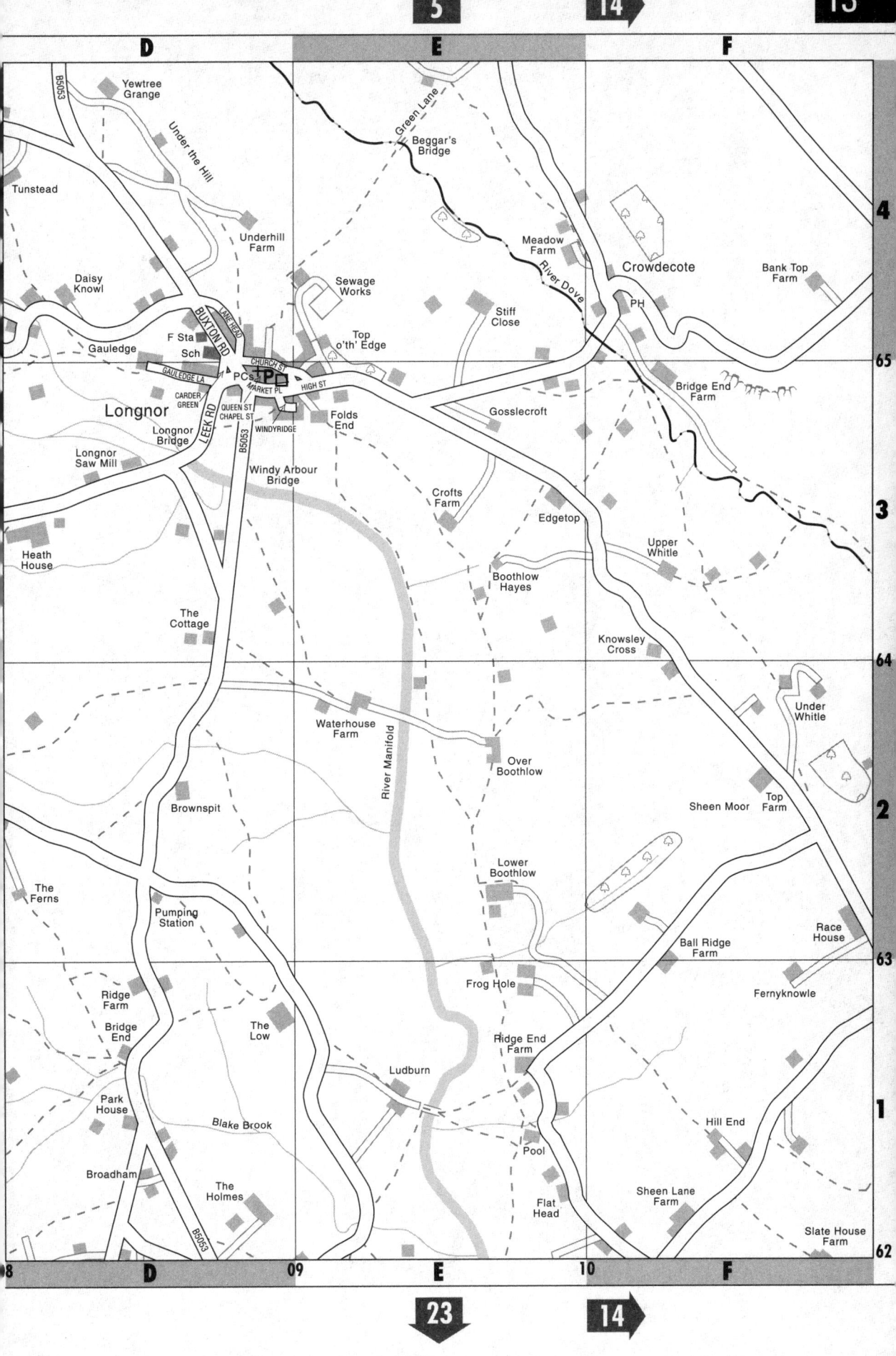

5
14

D   E   F

4

B5053

Yewtree Grange

Under the Hill

Tunstead

Green Lane

Beggar's Bridge

Meadow Farm

River Dove

Crowdecote

Bank Top Farm

Underhill Farm

Daisy Knowl

Sewage Works

Stiff Close

PH

Gauledge

LANE HEAD

F Sta
Sch

BUXTON RD

Top o'th' Edge

CHURCH ST

65

Bridge End Farm

PCs

MARKET PL

HIGH ST

Longnor

CARDER GREEN

QUEEN ST

GAULEDGE LA

Gosslecroft

Longnor Bridge

LEEK RD

CHAPEL ST

Folds End

WINDYRIDGE

B5053

Longnor Saw Mill

Windy Arbour Bridge

Crofts Farm

Edgetop

Upper Whitle

3

Heath House

Boothlow Hayes

The Cottage

Knowsley Cross

64

Under Whitle

Waterhouse Farm

River Manifold

Over Boothlow

Sheen Moor

Top Farm

2

Brownspit

Lower Boothlow

The Ferns

Ball Ridge Farm

Race House

Pumping Station

63

Ridge Farm

Frog Hole

Fernyknowle

Bridge End

The Low

Ridge End Farm

Park House

Ludburn

Hill End

1

Blake Brook

Broadham

The Holmes

Pool

Sheen Lane Farm

B5053

Flat Head

Slate House Farm

62

8   D   09   E   10   F

23
14

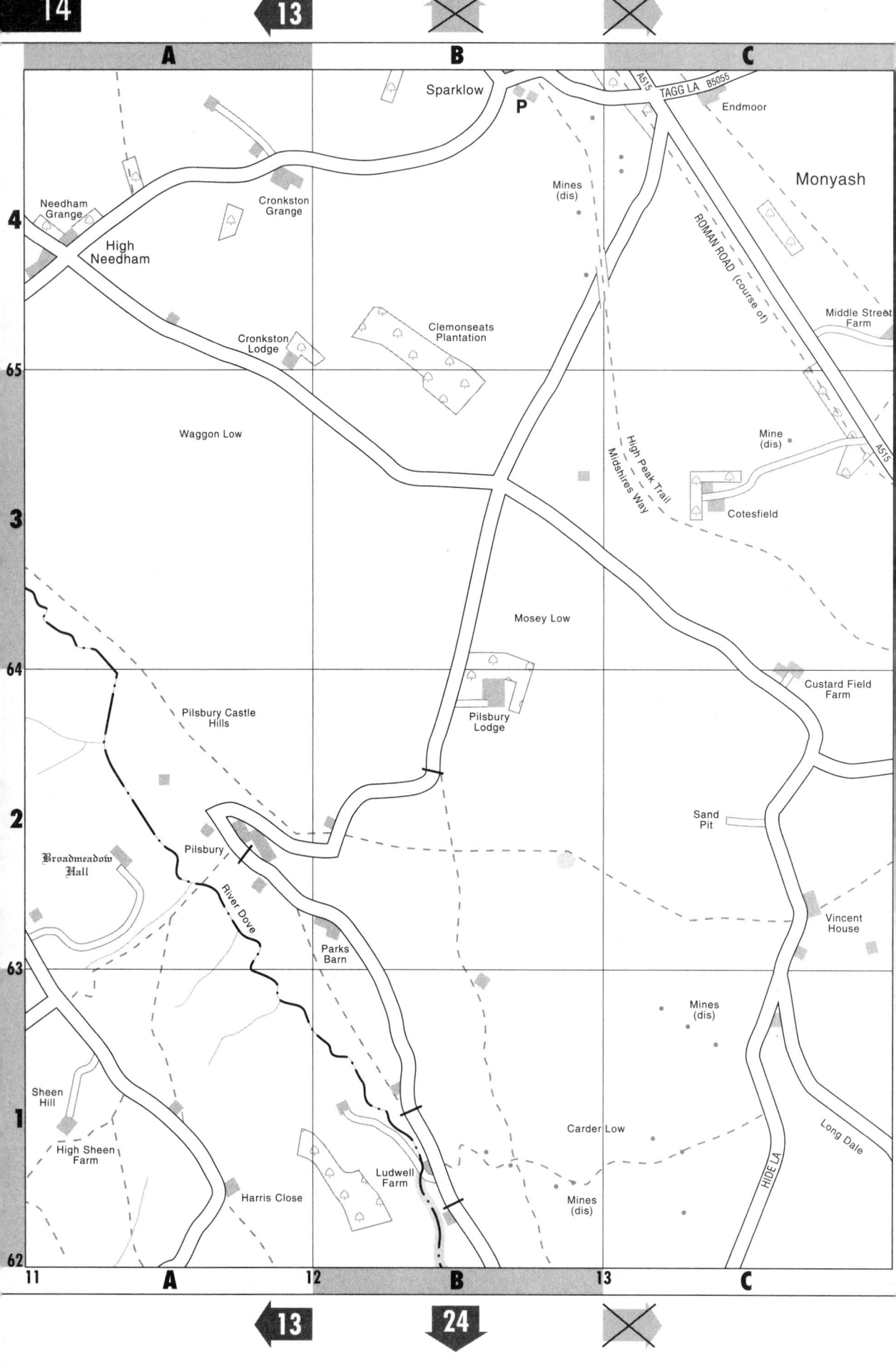

A   B   C

Sparklow
P

A515 TAGG LA B5055
Endmoor

Mines
(dis)

Monyash

4
Needham
Grange
Cronkston
Grange

High
Needham

ROMAN ROAD (course of)

Middle Street
Farm

Cronkston
Lodge

Clemonseats
Plantation

65

Waggon Low

High Peak Trail
Midshires Way

Mine
(dis)

Cotesfield

A515

3

Mosey Low

64
Pilsbury Castle
Hills

Pilsbury
Lodge

Custard Field
Farm

2
Broadmeadow
Hall

Pilsbury

Sand
Pit

River Dove

Vincent
House

63
Parks
Barn

Sheen
Hill

Mines
(dis)

1
High Sheen
Farm

Carder Low

Long Dale

HIDE LA

Harris Close

Ludwell
Farm

Mines
(dis)

62

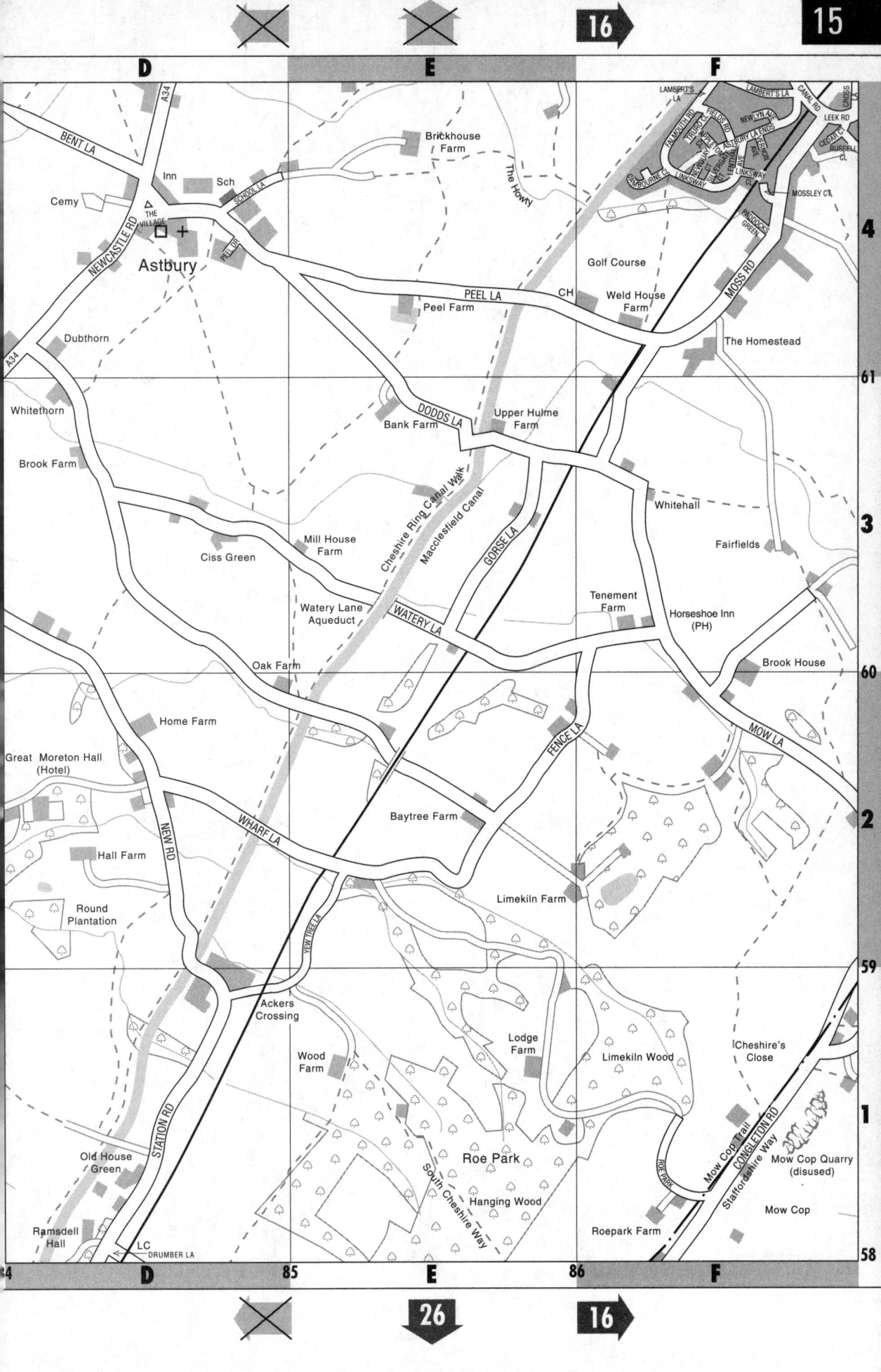

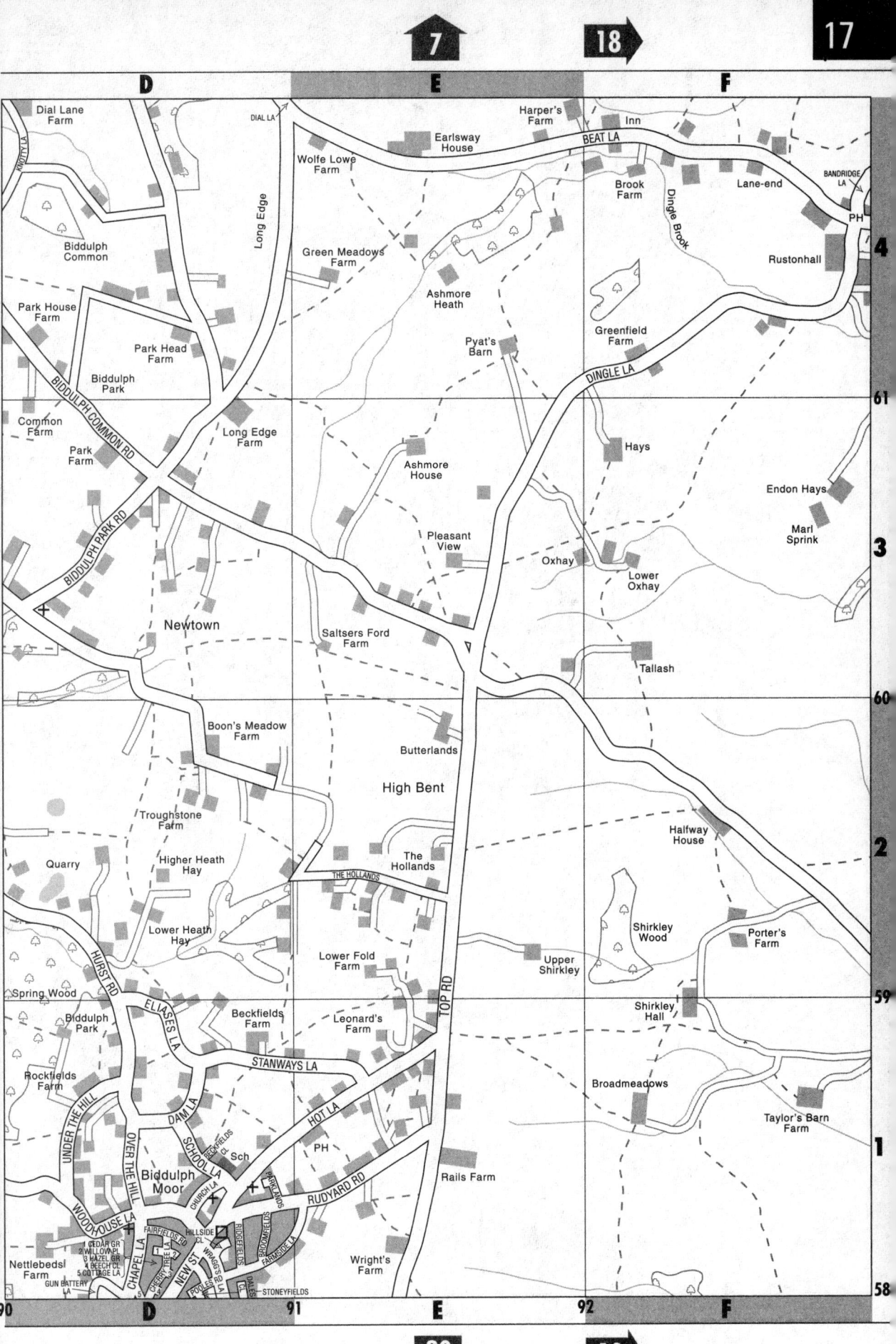

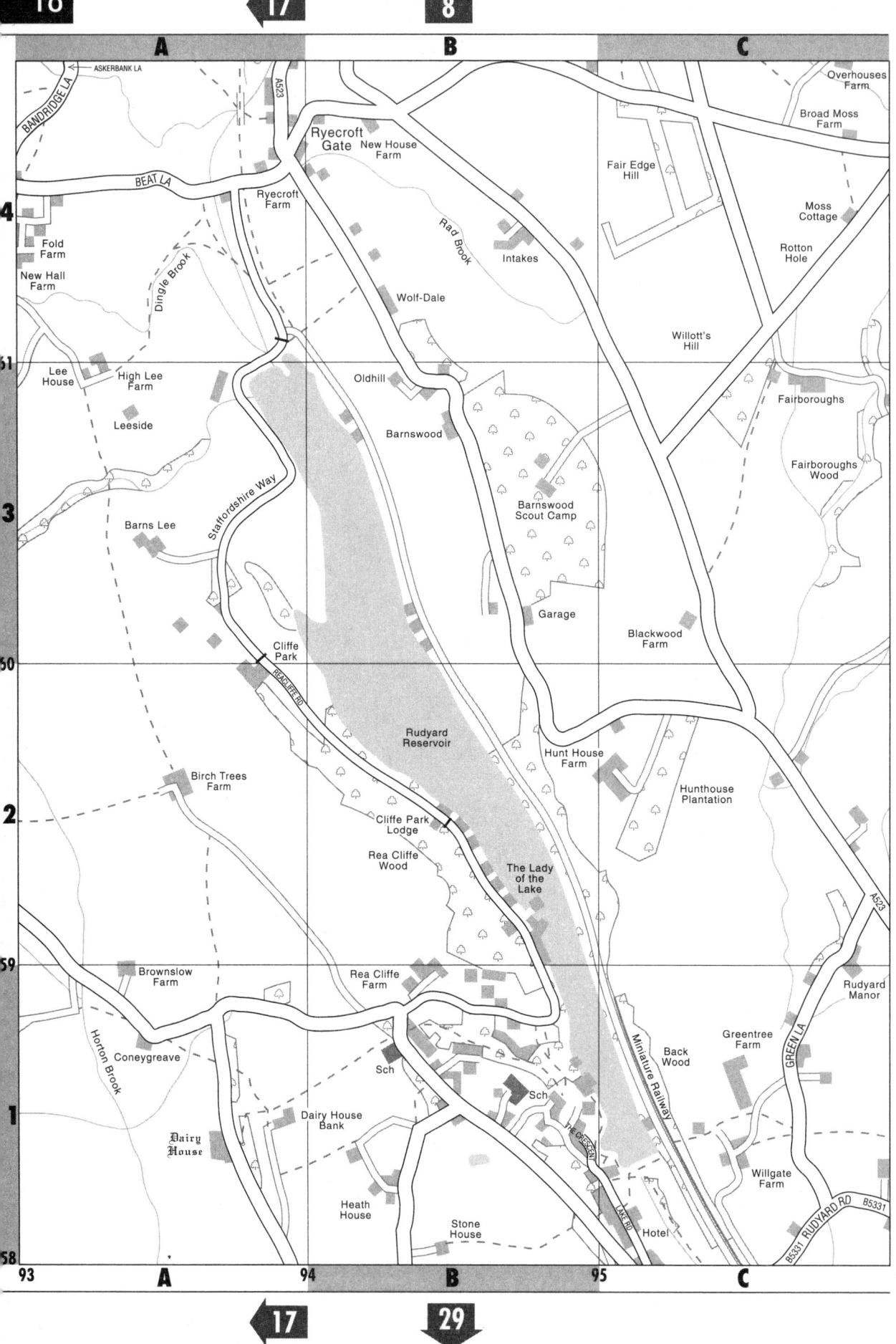

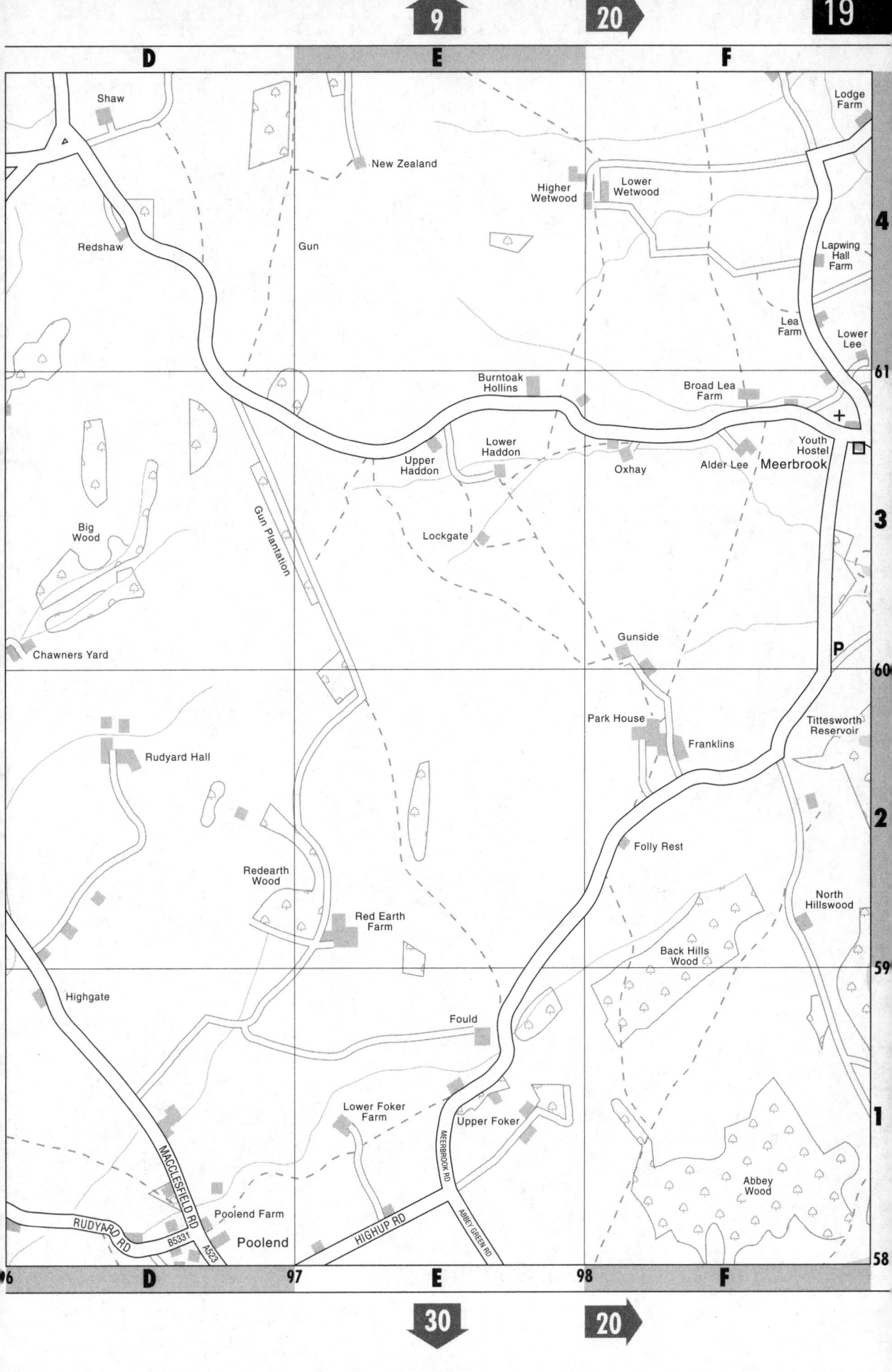

A **B** **C**

4

Greenlane

Lodge Farm

Rose Cottage

Windygates

Far House

Hen Cloud

Ramshaw Rocks

Ferny Khowl

The Roaches House

Naychurch

Frith Bottom

Paddock Farm

Dains Mill

Cat Tor

Knowles

61

Benthead

The Prospect

Homestead Farm

The Rock (PH)

Wks

WHITTY LA

Upper Hulme

The Angry Trout (PH)

Nether Hay

Marsh Farm

WHITTY LA

BRIDGE TERR

3

Middle Hulme

River Churnet

Stoney Cliffe

P

PC

P

New Cottage

The Hollies

Caravan Site

Sch

60

Three Horse Shoes Inn

TITTESWORTH GATE

Blackshawmoor Reservoirs

Tittesworth Reservoir

Resr

Lower Blackshaw Farm

Birchtree Farm

Hawthorne House

Blackshaw Moor

2

The Coppice

Blackshaw Grange Caravan Park

Anzio Camp

59

Troutsdale Farm

Resr

Underbank Farm

Ley Fields

Thorncliffe

1

Upper Tittesworth

Red Lion (PH)

Lower Farm

Clough House Farm

Grove Bank Farm

Water Works

River Churnet

Oaks Plantation

South Hillswood Farm

Solomon's Hollow

Edge End Wood

A53

BUXTON RD

58

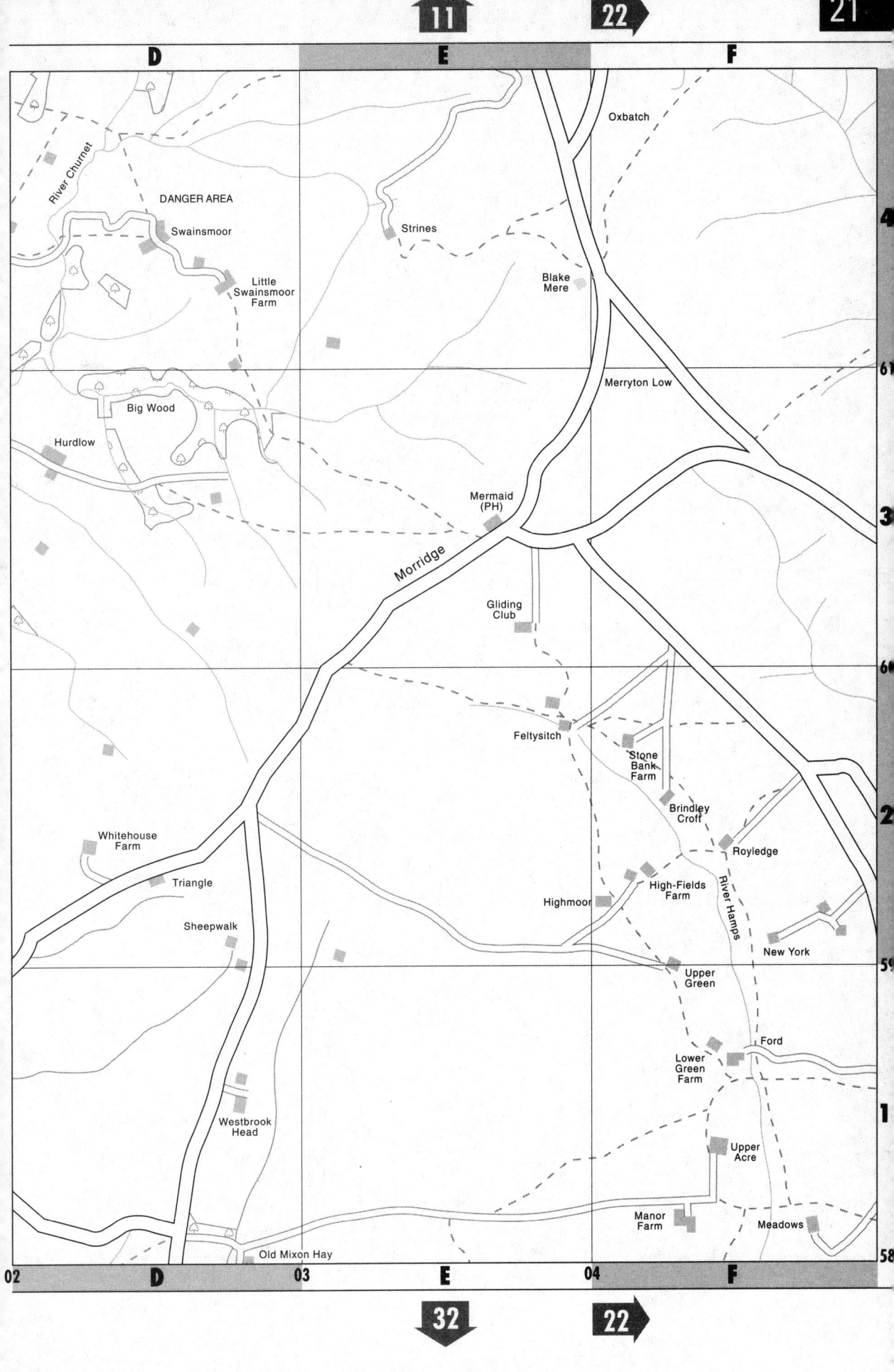

D E F

DANGER AREA

River Churnet

Swainsmoor

Little
Swainsmoor
Farm

Strines

Oxbatch

Blake
Mere

Merryton Low

Big Wood

Hurdlow

Mermaid
(PH)

Morridge

Gliding
Club

Feltysitch

Stone
Bank
Farm

Brindley
Croft

Royledge

Whitehouse
Farm

Triangle

Sheepwalk

Highmoor

High-Fields
Farm

River Hamps

New York

Upper
Green

Ford

Lower
Green
Farm

Westbrook
Head

Upper
Acre

Manor
Farm

Meadows

Old Mixon Hay

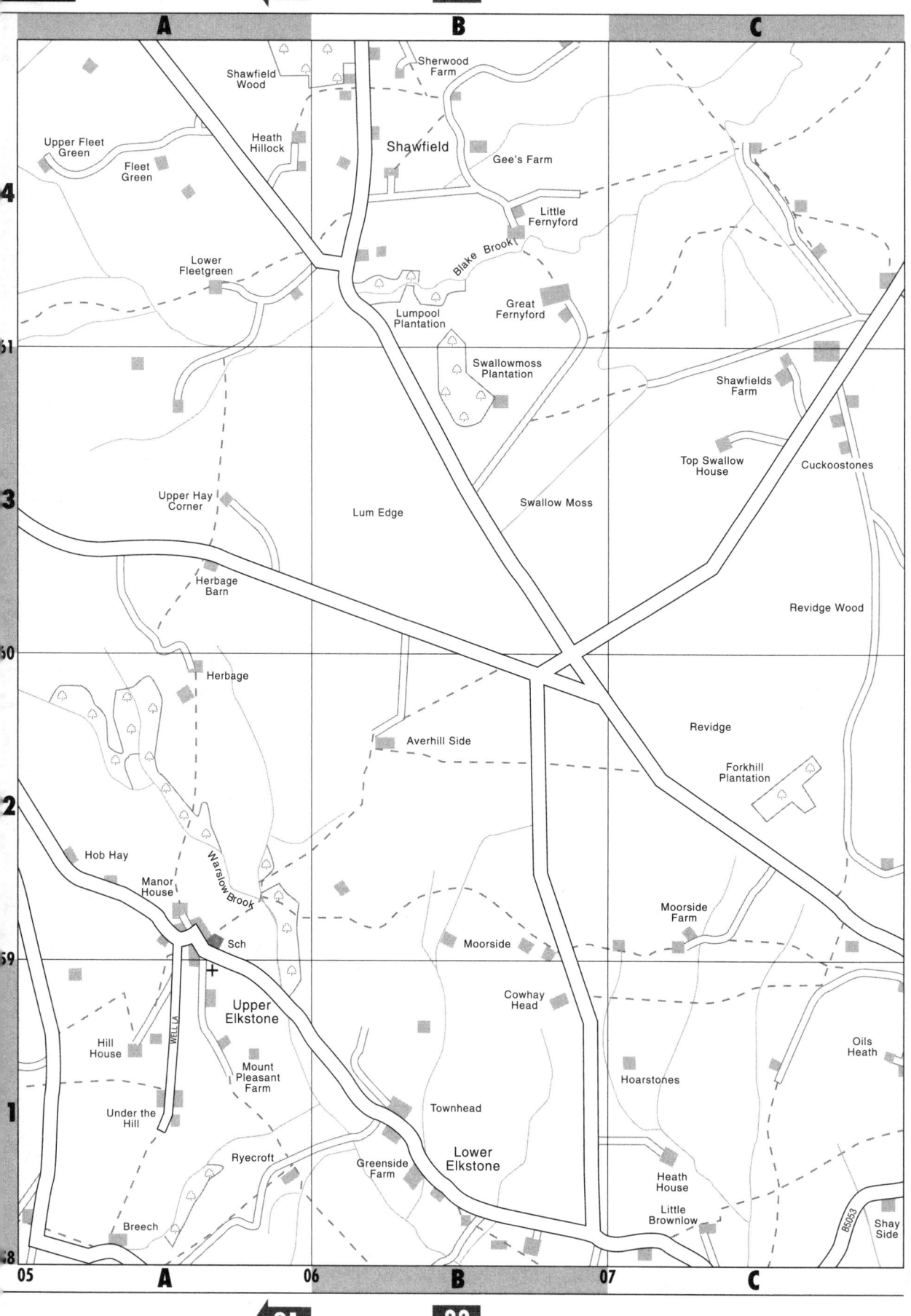

21

33

A B C

4

1

05 A 06 B 07 C

Shawfield Wood
Sherwood Farm
Heath Hillock
Shawfield
Gee's Farm
Little Fernyford
Upper Fleet Green
Fleet Green
Lower Fleetgreen
Blake Brook
Great Fernyford
Lumpool Plantation
Swallowmoss Plantation
Shawfields Farm
Top Swallow House
Cuckoostones
Upper Hay Corner
Lum Edge
Swallow Moss
Herbage Barn
Revidge Wood
Herbage
Averhill Side
Revidge
Forkhill Plantation
Hob Hay
Warslow Brook
Manor House
Sch
Moorside Farm
Moorside
Upper Elkstone
Cowhay Head
Oils Heath
Hill House
WELL A
Mount Pleasant Farm
Hoarstones
Under the Hill
Townhead
Ryecroft
Lower Elkstone
Greenside Farm
Heath House
Breech
Little Brownlow
B5053
Shay Side

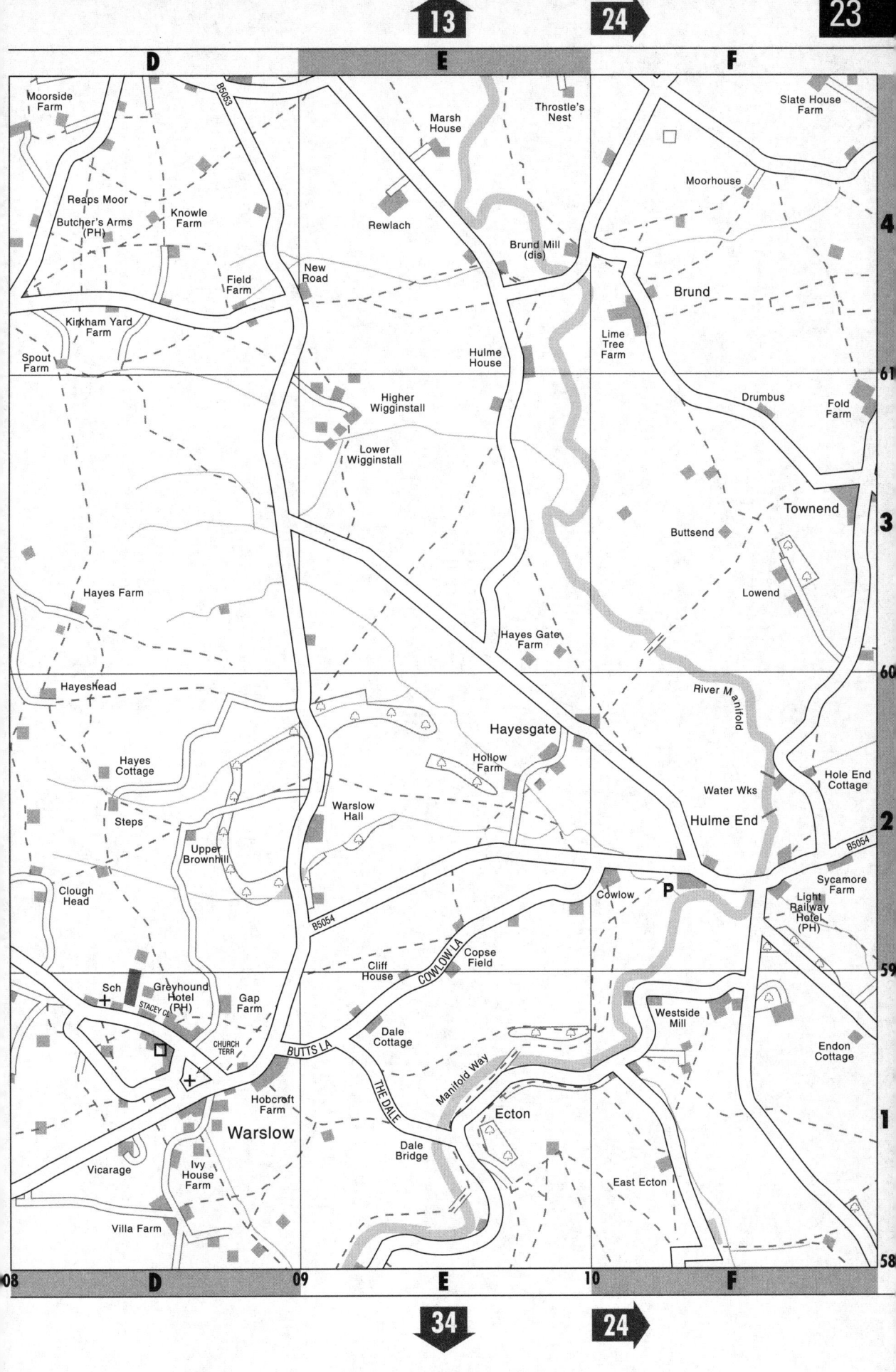

Moorside Farm

Slate House Farm

Marsh House

Throstle's Nest

Moorhouse

Reaps Moor

Butcher's Arms (PH)

Knowle Farm

Rewlach

Brund Mill (dis)

Brund

4

Field Farm

New Road

Kirkham Yard Farm

Hulme House

Lime Tree Farm

Drumbus

Fold Farm

Spout Farm

61

Higher Wigginstall

Lower Wigginstall

Townend

3

Buttsend

Lowend

Hayes Farm

Hayes Gate Farm

60

Hayeshead

River Manifold

Hayesgate

Hayes Cottage

Hollow Farm

Water Wks

Hole End Cottage

Steps

Warslow Hall

Hulme End

2

Upper Brownhill

B5054

Sycamore Farm

Clough Head

Cowlow

P

Light Railway Hotel (PH)

B5054

Cliff House

COWLOW LA

Copse Field

59

Sch

Greyhound Hotel (PH)

STACEY CL

Gap Farm

Westside Mill

Endon Cottage

CHURCH TERR

Dale Cottage

Manifold Way

BUTTS LA

Hobcroft Farm

THE DALE

Ecton

1

Warslow

Vicarage

Ivy House Farm

Dale Bridge

East Ecton

Villa Farm

58

A | B | C

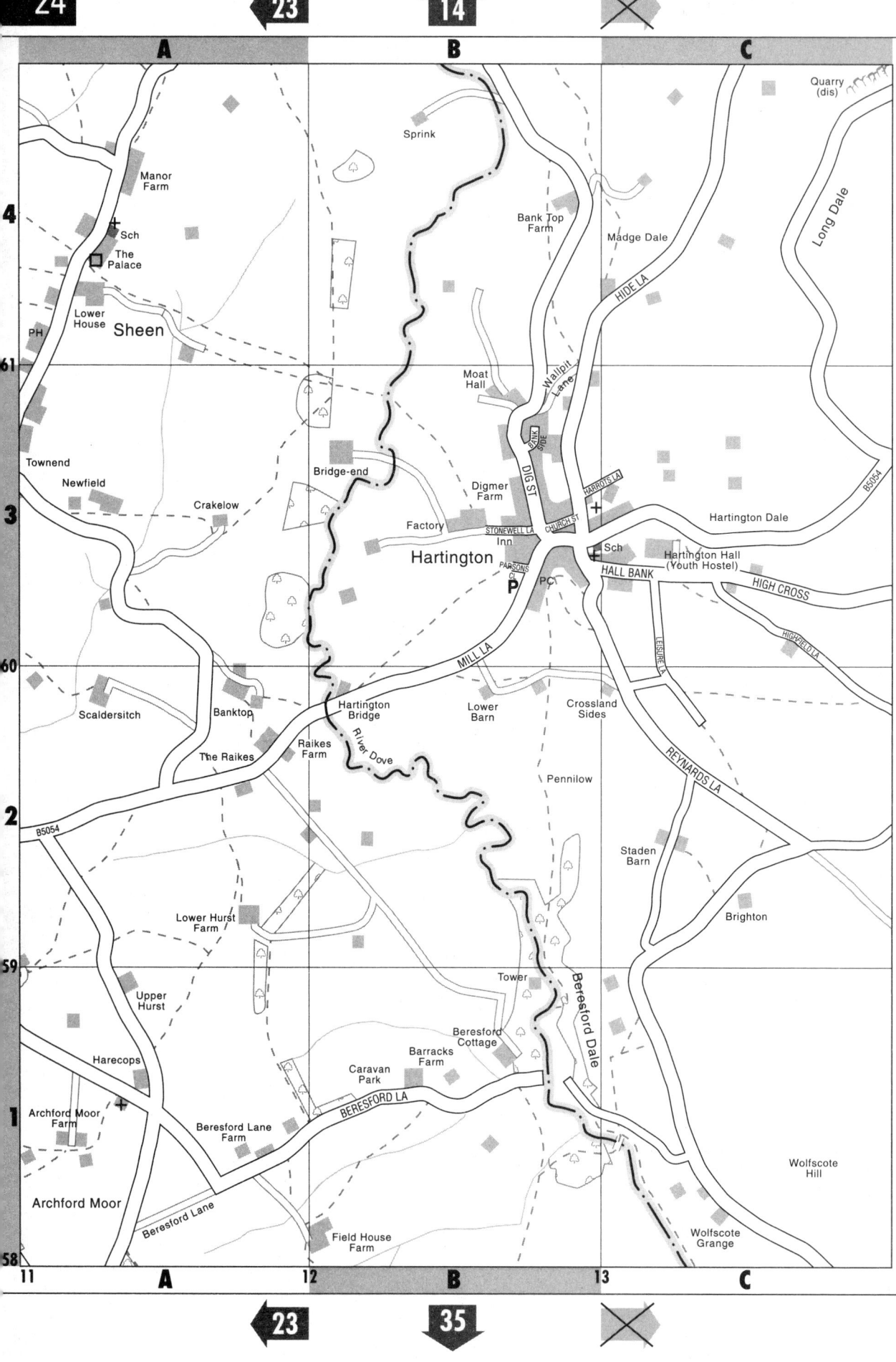

Quarry (dis)

Long Dale

4

Manor Farm

Sch
The Palace

Sprink

Bank Top Farm

Madge Dale

HIDE LA

B5054

PH
Lower House
Sheen

61

Moat Hall

Wallpit Lane

BANK SIDE

DIG ST

HARROTS LA

Townend

Newfield

Crakelow

Bridge-end

Digmer Farm

Hartington Dale

3

Factory

STONEWELL LA

Inn

CHURCH ST

Sch

Hartington Hall (Youth Hostel)

HIGH CROSS

Hartington

PARSONS CL

P

PC

HALL BANK

HIGHFIELD LA

60

MILL LA

LEISURE LA

Scaldersitch

Banktop

Hartington Bridge

Lower Barn

Crossland Sides

The Raikes

Raikes Farm

River Dove

Pennilow

REYNARDS LA

2

B5054

Staden Barn

Brighton

Lower Hurst Farm

59

Upper Hurst

Tower

Beresford Dale

Harecops

Beresford Cottage

Barracks Farm

1

Archford Moor Farm

Caravan Park

Beresford Lane Farm

BERESFORD LA

Wolfscote Hill

Archford Moor

Beresford Lane

Field House Farm

Wolfscote Grange

58

D **E** **F**

CHANCE HALL LA →

Townsend Farm

TOWNSEND LA

POOL SIDE

Rode Pool

Old Wood

Rode Hall

Rode Mill

Holehouse Farm

CHURCH LA

HOLEHOUSE LA

A34

Works

Scholar Green

Kent Green Farm

BARLEYCROFT TERR

STATION RD

FOUNDRY LA

HOLLINSHEAD CL

MOORSIDE AVE

BARNBRIDGE CL

STONE CHAIR LA

WAINTREE AVE

BARBER DR

MEAD AVE

ORCHILL RD

CINDER MILL LA

MARGERY AVE

ALMA CL

THE MOUNT

4

57

Bank Farm

Big Barr

Lunts Moss Farm

Brick House Farm

Bratt's Wood

Snape's Aqueduct

A50

Sch

CONGLETON RD N

PORTLAND DR

Little-moss

NURSERY RD

Cheshire Ring Canal Walk

Macclesfield Canal

3

Brattswood Dr

CHERRY TREE AVE

WOODGATE AVE

Sch

LAWTONGATE ESTATE

Ashbank Farm

Hall Green

BLEEDING WOLF LA

CROSS CL

MOSS LA

Summer House Plantation

Lawton Hall (Sch)

Mill Lane Plantation

WOODSIDE

LAWTON HEATH RD

THE SPINNEY

Moss House Farm

56

Lawton-gate

THE GREEN

GROVE AVE

CREWE RD

THE GROVE

GROVE PARK AVE

ELMWOOD CL

CROSSWAYS

DERWENT RD

LIVERPOOL RD W

Bridge Farm

Church Lawton

KNOWSLEY LA

2

A5011

LINLEY GR

FODEN AVE

LC

Cheshire Ring Canal Walk

Trent and Mersey Canal

LAWTON AVE

Red Bull

Red Bull Aqueduct

Works

CONGLETON RD S

Playing Field

LINLEY RD

Rye Low

LIVERPOOL RD E

Training Centre

Pool-lock Aqueduct

Works

GLOUCESTER RD

WHITEHALL AVE

VICTORIA AVE

SOMERSET AVE

55

LINLEY LA

Toll Gate Farm

Slum Wood

WEST AVE

TOWNFIELD CL

OLD BUTT LA

OLD BUTT LA

SLACKLANE

PICKFORD LA

WOODSHUTTS ST

LIME KILN LA

Harding's Wood

HARDINGSWOOD RD

LIVERPOOL RD

WHITE HALL RD

STATION RD

A50

HEATHCOTE ST

B5371

Kidsgrove Sta

Liby

MEADOWS RD

Sch

St JOHN'S WOOD

MILL RISE

1

Dismantled Railway

Golf Course

A5011

Linley Hall

Nelson Ind Est

St SAVIOUR'S ST 1

UNITY WAY 2

HIGHER ASH RD 3

Sch

Butt Lane

CHURCH ST

SKELLERN ST

TERR

CONGLETON RD

MILLSTONE AVE

Sch

B5371

SECOND AVE

THIRD AVE

CEDAR AVE

BANBURY ST

MITCHELL DR

PRIORY RD

BRINDLEY CL

HOLLINS CRES

HARECASTLE AVE

TOWER HILL RD

GROVE AVE

FIRST AVE

CORONATION CRES

Woodshutts

St JOHN'S WOOD Sch

B5371

54

Linley Trading Estate

A34

FIFTH AVE

FOURTH AVE

D 82 **E** 83 **F**

D E F

Hayhill

Moodystreet Farm

AKESMOOR LA

Woodside Farm

BIDDULPH

Newpool Farm

Newpool

NEWPOOL RD

Knowle Style
Sch

TOWER HILL RD

Brown Lees

BROWN LEES RD

Brown Lees Farm

Stadmorslow Farm

STADMORSLOW LA

Lane Ends

Brindley Ford

BULL LA

Playing Fields

Dismantled Railway

COOPERS WAY
FORRESTER CL
CROFTER CL
MASON DR
THATCHER CT
HUNTERS CT
DUCIE ST
BANBURY GR
HAVELOCK GR
BELLRINGER CL
HAMS CL
WHARF SOUTH
HIGH ST
KING ST
DIAMOND ST
STANLEY ST
Mkt
Liby
P
PC
WEST ST
SLATER ST
SHAW ST
COLE ST
CASTLE VIEW
KNOWLE RD
WARWICK ST
VILLA CL
LYNMOUTH CL
JOHN ST
Sch
Sch
PC
Sch
CROSSFIELD AVE
TURNLEA CL
LANCHESTER CL
Knypersley
THE SPINNEY
CONWAY RD
DENBIGH CL
BARDELL
FARNWORTH
HENLEY AVE
BIRCH AVE
JAMES AVE
KESTREL
LOTUS AVE
LOUIS AVE
MANSFIELD CL
LYNSIDE RD
LAGONDA CL
LANCIA CL
HAMBLETON CL
NEWPOOL COTTS
CORONATION AVE
STILE CL
ROYCE AVE
FRITHMARSH DR
MINERVA CL
GILFERN
BATEMAN AVE
NEWPOOL TERR
HEANLEY
BROOK ST
COWLISHAW CL
GARDENERS CL
TUNSTALL RD
TUNSTALL RD IND EST
FORGE WAY
Ind Est
VICTORIA ROW

MEADOW SIDE

MASON DR

COOPERS WAY
STATION RD
WALLEY DR
STRINGER ST
CONGLETON RD
EAST DR
MOORLAND RD
PALMERSTON WAY
GLADSTONE ST
HUMBER DR
SEVERN CL
RIBBLE DR
REDWAR
DEVON
LINNET WAY
TORVALE DR
GOLDCREST WAY
CHAFFINCH DR
Firwood House
The Nursery
Wickenstones Farm
Wicken Stones
Rock End
NEW ST
CROWBOROUGH RD

ALBERT ST
CHARLES ST
PRINCESS
COMDENE
ST JOHN'S RD
ST JOHN'S PL
LORD ST
CHURCH RD
SPRINGFIELD
EDGELEY RD
APPLETON CL
SWALLOW ST
QUEEN'S RD
WHITMORE ST
Greenfield
TRENT GR
CHURCH CL
MAYFIELD RD
PARK LA
Sch
MEADOW
GWYN LA
ORME AVE
CONWYN DR
SQUIRREL HAYES AVE
LODGE BARN RD

Braddocks Hay
Sch
RUPERT ST
CROMWELL ST
KINGSFIELD RD W
HIGHFIELD RD E
JUBILEE
LAWTON ST
MOORLAND RD
SPEDDING WAY
THAMES DR
CHAMBERLAIN WAY
ROSSERY
WHITBREAD DR
Amb and F/Sta
BRAMBLES CT
WELL ST
BELLRINGER
Biddulph Brook
BLUEBELL
CORNFIELD RD

3
4
57
56
55
2
1
54

Knypersley Park
Knypersley End
Knypersley Wood
Greenway Bank Country Park
Knypersley Reservoir
Gawton's Well

MILL HAYES RD
Mill Hayes

Greenway Bank
GREENWAY BANK
Dallows Wood

NEW BLDGS
CHILDERPLAY RD
PH
FORGE WAY

Knypersley Mill
JUDGEFIELD LA

Tongue Lane Farm
TONGUE LA

Head of Trent

MELLOR ST
JASMIN WAY
WOODRUFF CL
SANDY ST
BEATRICE WLK
TERENCE WLK
PATRICK PL
HANDLEY PL
LALLY PL
FINCH PL
FISHER ST
BRIDGE ST
OUTCLOUGH RD
HUGH BOURNE PL
BARMOUTH GR
FINCH ST
PECK MILL LA
BIDDULPH RD
A527
Brook House

Bemersley Green
BEMERSLEY RD
Stanley Fields

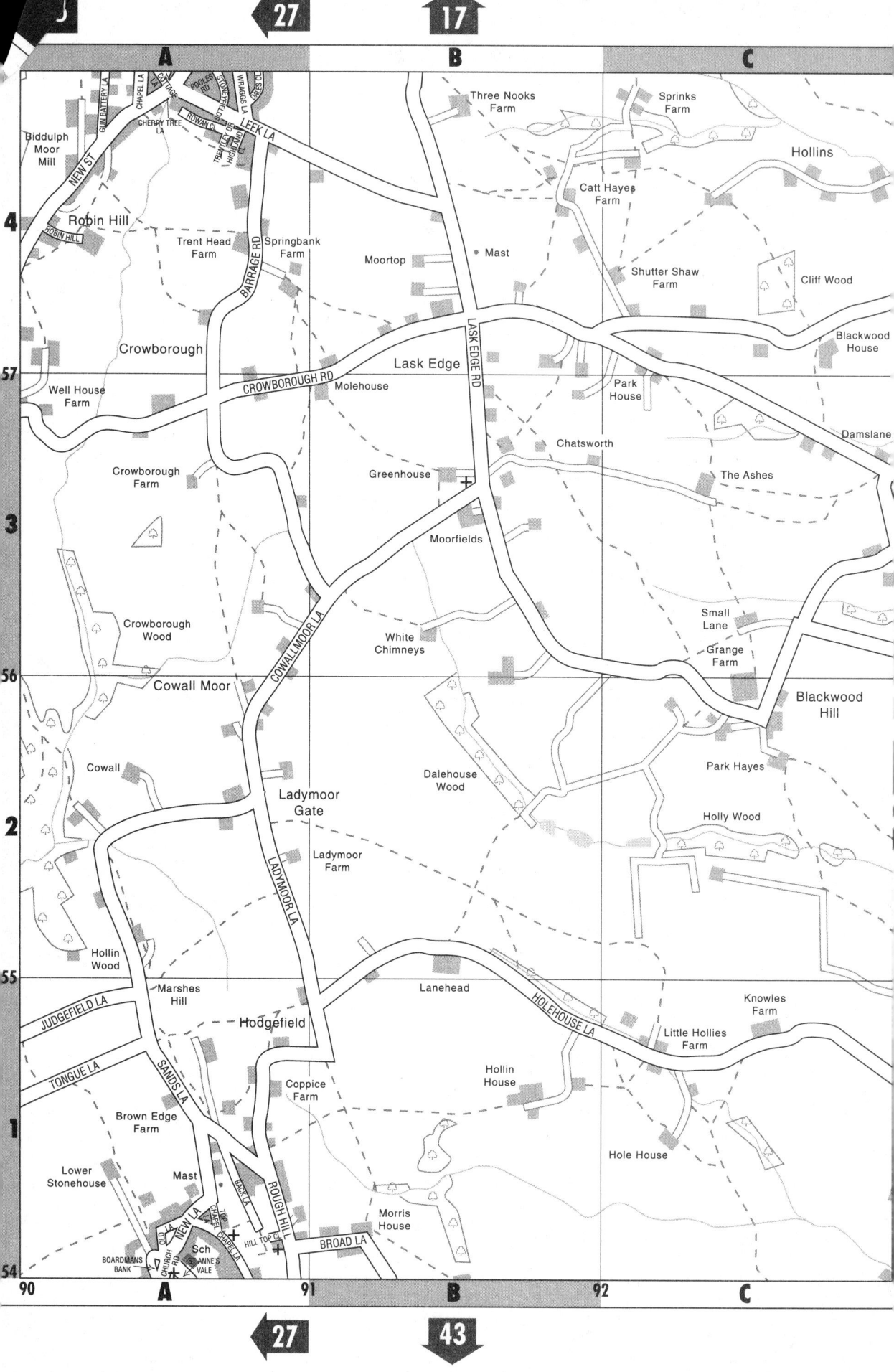

A   **B**   **C**

Biddulph Moor Mill

NEW ST

GUN BATTERY LA

CHAPEL LA

SCH

COTTAGE

POOLEY RD

STONEYFIELDS

WRAGGS CL

SPIRES CL

CHERRY TREE LA

ROWAN CL

TREBLE LOW

HIGH LA

LEEK LA

Robin Hill

ROBIN HILL

Trent Head Farm

Springbank Farm

BARRAGE RD

Moortop

• Mast

4

Three Nooks Farm

Sprinks Farm

Catt Hayes Farm

Hollins

Shutter Shaw Farm

Cliff Wood

Blackwood House

57

Crowborough

CROWBOROUGH RD

Lask Edge

Molehouse

LASK EDGE RD

Park House

Damslane

Well House Farm

Chatsworth

The Ashes

Crowborough Farm

Greenhouse

✝

Moorfields

3

Crowborough Wood

White Chimneys

COWALLMOOR LA

Small Lane

Grange Farm

56

Cowall Moor

Blackwood Hill

Cowall

Dalehouse Wood

Park Hayes

Ladymoor Gate

Holly Wood

2

LADYMOOR LA

Ladymoor Farm

Hollin Wood

Lanehead

HOLEHOUSE LA

Knowles Farm

55

Marshes Hill

JUDGEFIELD LA

Hodgefield

Little Hollies Farm

TONGUE LA

SANDS LA

Coppice Farm

Hollin House

Brown Edge Farm

1

Lower Stonehouse

Mast

BACK LA

ROUGH HILL

HILL TOP CL

CHAPEL CHAPEL LA

Morris House

Hole House

OLD LA

NEW LA

CHURCH RD

Sch

ST ANNE'S VALE

BROAD LA

✝

BOARDMANS BANK

✝

54

90   **A**   91   **B**   92   **C**

D   E   F

Wardle Barn Farm
Haregate Wood
Sch
HAREGATE RD
PRIORY AVE
ROCHE AVE
THORNCLIFFE VIEW
PRINCESS AVE
HORSECROFT
FARNSWORTH WAY
ARGYLES RD
FURNISTON PL
WINDSOR RD
PAINTON CHASE
Sch
PC
Haregate
WESTMINSTER RD
HALL AVE
PROVOST
HARE RD
ABBOTS RD
NOVI LA
MILNER TERR
HAIG RD
CARLTON
BEATTY RD
THE CRESCENT
ASHDALE
WESTON ST
VICTORIA ST
ASHLEA VIEW
WOODLEIGH
A53
SPRINGFIELD DR
Sch
Sch
PARKER ST
FOUNTAIN ST
SHIRBURN ST
EAST ST
Sch
A523
SPRINGFIELD RD
F Sta
KNIVEDEN LA
LOCKERBIE CL
LOWTHER
TRAFFORD
MOORLAND RD
THORNFIELD VIEW
WHITFIELD
MACNASH
Hosp
PICKWOOD
Peak View
PROSPER RD
FAIR VIEW RD
ASHBOURNE RD
SHERBORNE DR

A53
BUXTON RD
Edge End Farm
Moss Rose Inn (PH)
THORNCLIFF RD
Easing Villa
Hollystones
Cartledge
Freshwinds
Dee Bank Farm
MOUNT RD
Sch
Mast
Kniveden

Leek Moorside
Ankers Lane Farm
Easing Moor Farm
EASING LA
Ashes Farm
Easing Farm
Coltsmoor Farm
Lark Hall
Hare House
Holly House
Stile House Farm
Beeley Barn

Pickwood Cottage
Padwick Farm
Poolhall
Twillow Heath
Holly Dale
Ballington Grange Farm
Home Farm
Lowe Hill Farm
Wildgoose Farm
Buckley Farm
DOUSE LA
Brook Farm
SCHOOL LA
Sch
Bradnop
PORTERS LA
Meadow View
Lowe Hill
Cliff Farm
Hollybush
Ashenhurst Cottages
Ivy Cottage
Fairfield
Middle Cliff
Birchall Wood
Ashenhurst Mill
Throstle Nest
Longshaw
COOK'S LA
A523
Jackfield Plantation
Ashenhurst
Egg Well

4
57
3
56
2
55
1
54

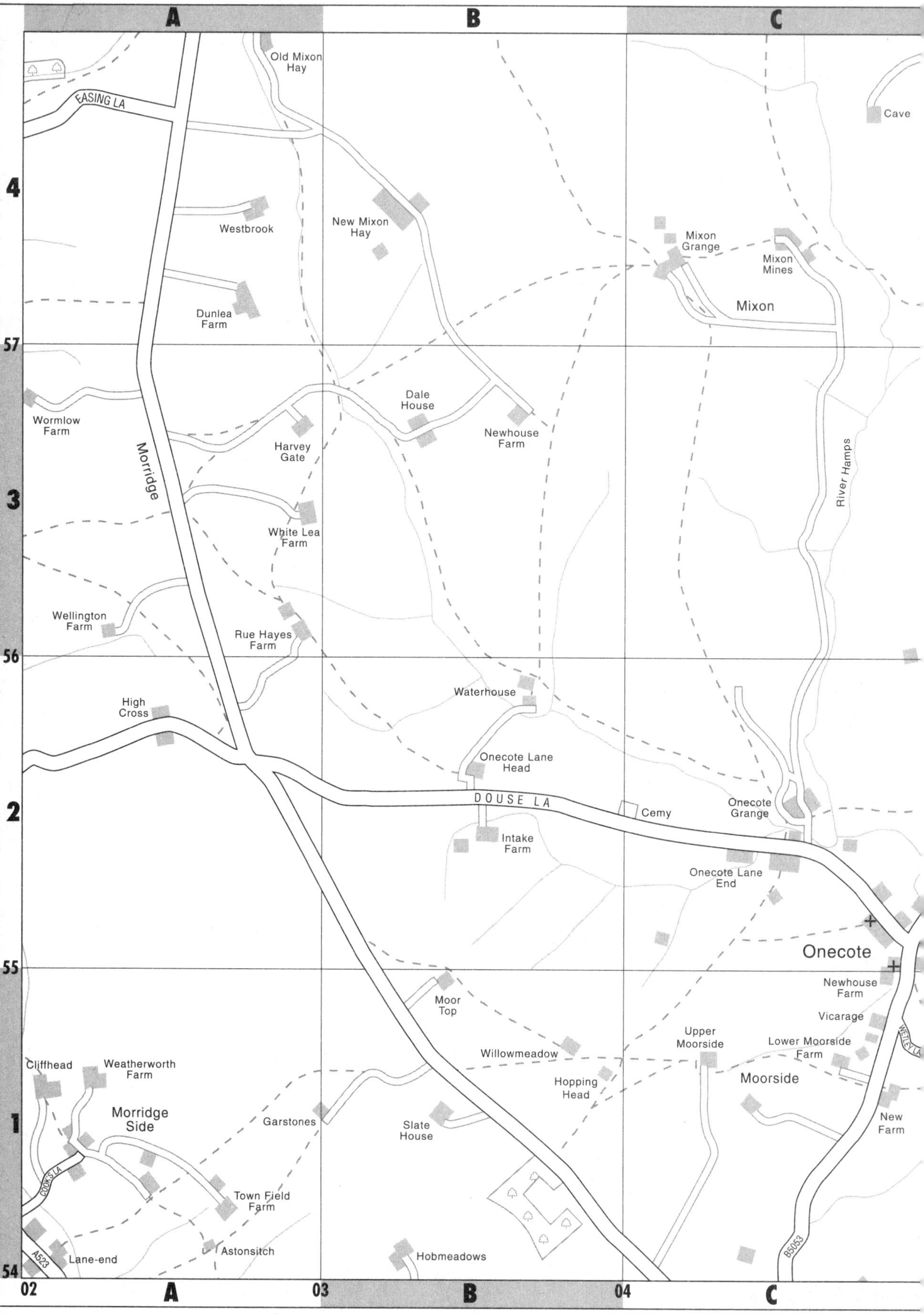

A   B   C

EASING LA

Old Mixon
Hay

Cave

4

Westbrook

New Mixon
Hay

Mixon
Grange

Mixon
Mines

Dunlea
Farm

Mixon

57

Wormlow
Farm

Dale
House

Harvey
Gate

Newhouse
Farm

River Hamps

Morridge

3

White Lea
Farm

Wellington
Farm

Rue Hayes
Farm

56

Waterhouse

High
Cross

Onecote Lane
Head

DOUSE LA

Cemy

Onecote
Grange

2

Intake
Farm

Onecote Lane
End

Onecote

55

Newhouse
Farm

Moor
Top

Willowmeadow

Vicarage

Upper
Moorside

Lower Moorside
Farm

Cliffhead

Weatherworth
Farm

Hopping
Head

Moorside

1

Morridge
Side

Garstones

Slate
House

New
Farm

COOK'S LA

Town Field
Farm

B5053

A523

Lane-end

Astonsitch

Hobmeadows

54

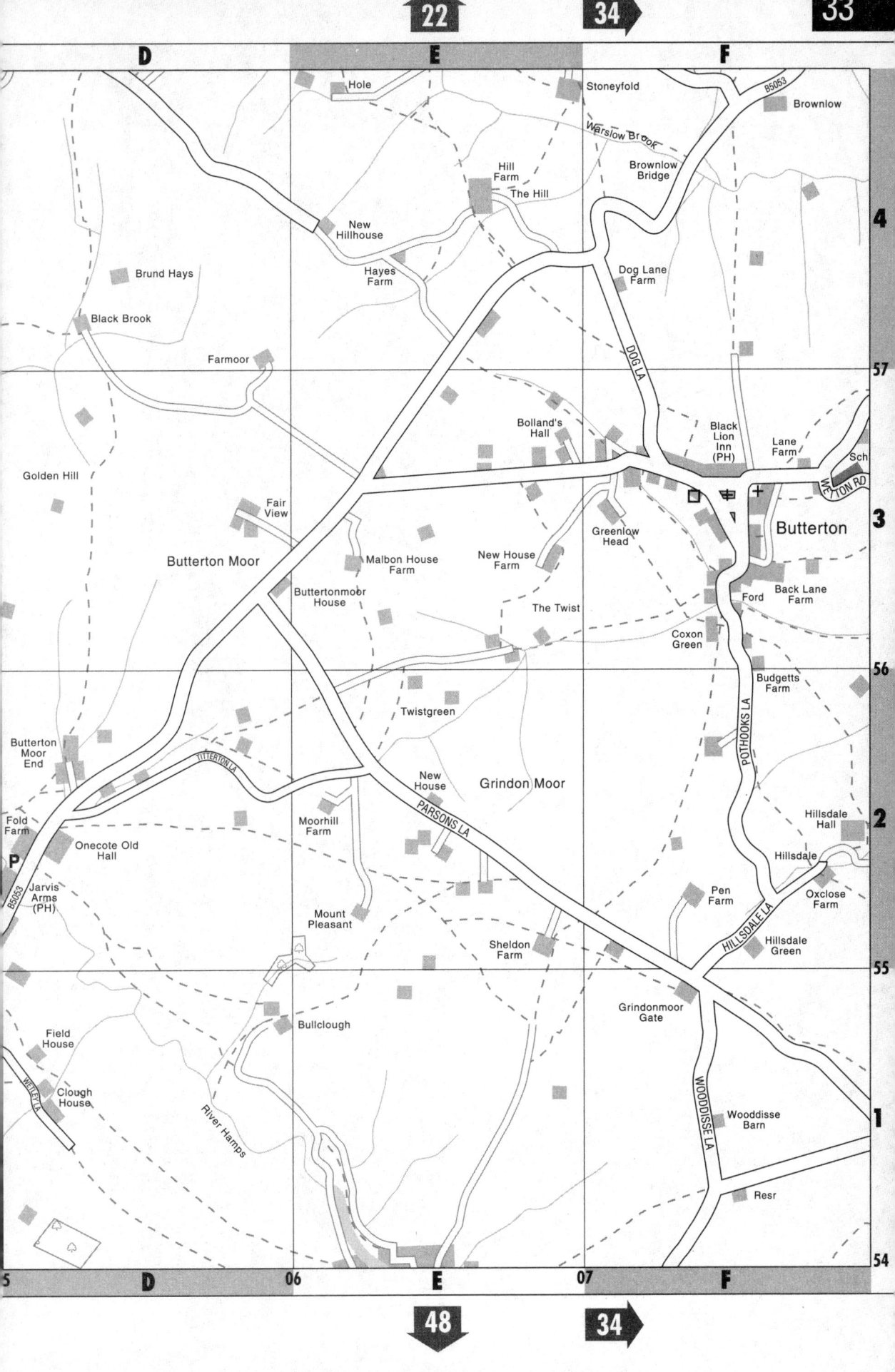

D   E   F

Hole
Stoneyfold
B5053
Brownlow
Warslow Brook
Brownlow
Bridge
Hill
Farm
The Hill
Dog Lane
Farm
4
New
Hillhouse
Brund Hays
Hayes
Farm
57
Black Brook
Black
Lion
Inn
(PH)
Lane
Farm
Sch
Farmoor
Bolland's
Hall
WETTON RD
Golden Hill
Fair
View
Greenlow
Head
Butterton
3
Butterton Moor
Malbon House
Farm
New House
Farm
Back Lane
Farm
Ford
Buttertonmoor
House
The Twist
Coxon
Green
56
Budgetts
Farm
Twistgreen
POTHOOKS LA
Butterton
Moor End
New
House
Grindon Moor
Hillsdale
Hall
2
Fold
Farm
TITTERTON LA
Moorhill
Farm
Hillsdale
Onecote Old
Hall
PARSONS LA
Pen
Farm
Oxclose
Farm
P
HILLSDALE LA
Jarvis
Arms
(PH)
B5053
Mount
Pleasant
Hillsdale
Green
Sheldon
Farm
55
Field
House
Bullclough
Grindonmoor
Gate
WELLEY LA
Clough
House
River Hamps
WOODDISSE LA
Wooddisse
Barn
1
Resr
5   D   06   E   07   F   54

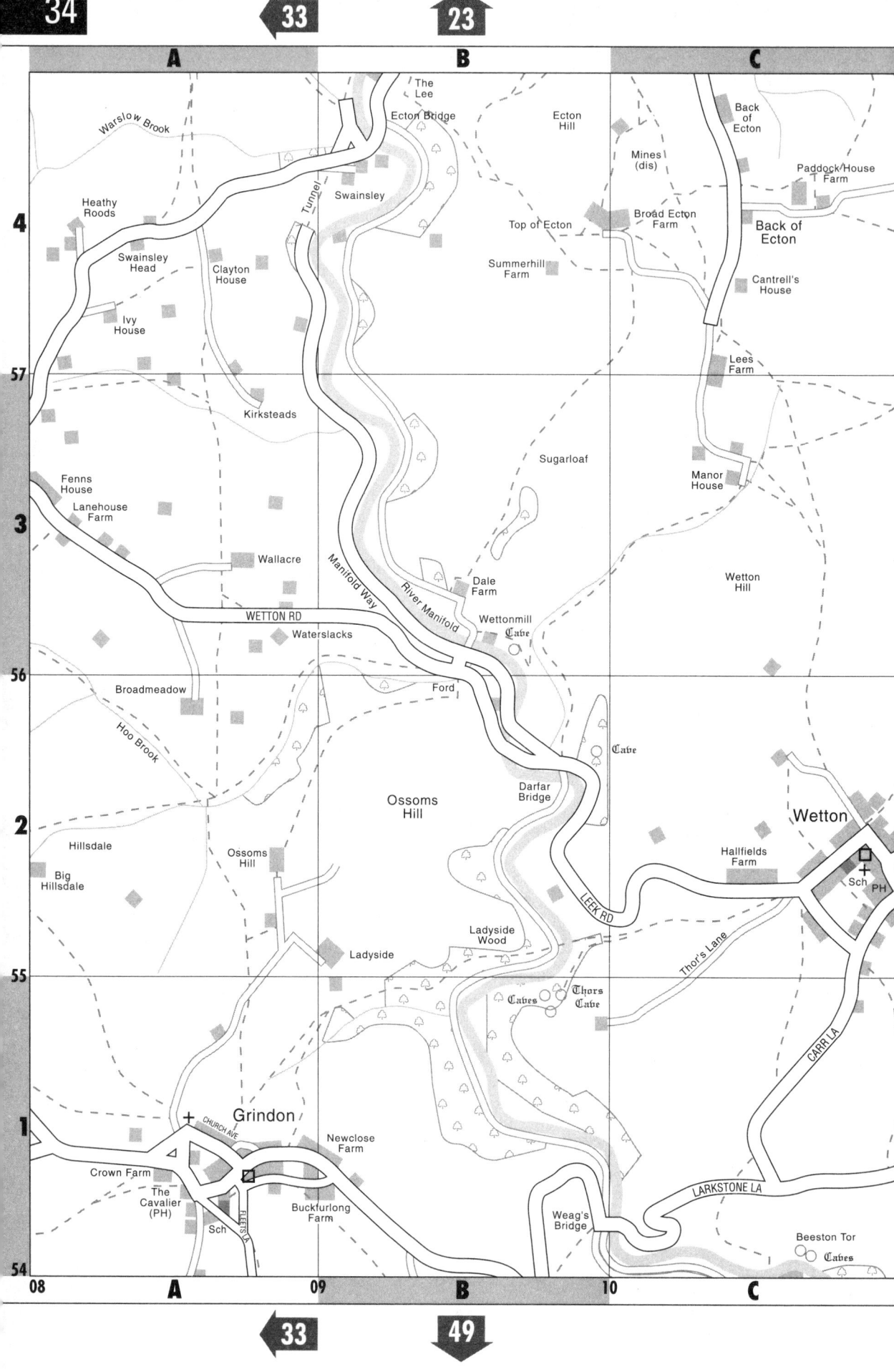

33
23

A
B
C

Warslow Brook

The Lee

Ecton Bridge

Ecton Hill

Back of Ecton

Swainsley

Mines (dis)

Paddock House Farm

Heathy Roods

4

Top of Ecton

Broad Ecton Farm

Back of Ecton

Swainsley Head

Clayton House

Summerhill Farm

Cantrell's House

Ivy House

57

Lees Farm

Kirksteads

Sugarloaf

Manor House

Fenns House

3

Wetton Hill

Lanehouse Farm

Wallacre

Manifold Way

River Manifold

Dale Farm

WETTON RD

Wettonmill Cave

Waterslacks

56

Broadmeadow

Ford

Cave

Hoo Brook

Darfar Bridge

Wetton

Ossoms Hill

2

Hillsdale

Hallfields Farm

Big Hillsdale

Ossoms Hill

LEEK RD

Sch
PH

Ladyside Wood

Ladyside

Thor's Lane

55

Caves

Thors Cave

CARR LA

Grindon

CHURCH AVE

1

Newclose Farm

Crown Farm

The Cavalier (PH)

FLEETS LA

Sch

Buckfurlong Farm

Weag's Bridge

LARKSTONE LA

Beeston Tor

Caves

54

08
A
09
B
10
C

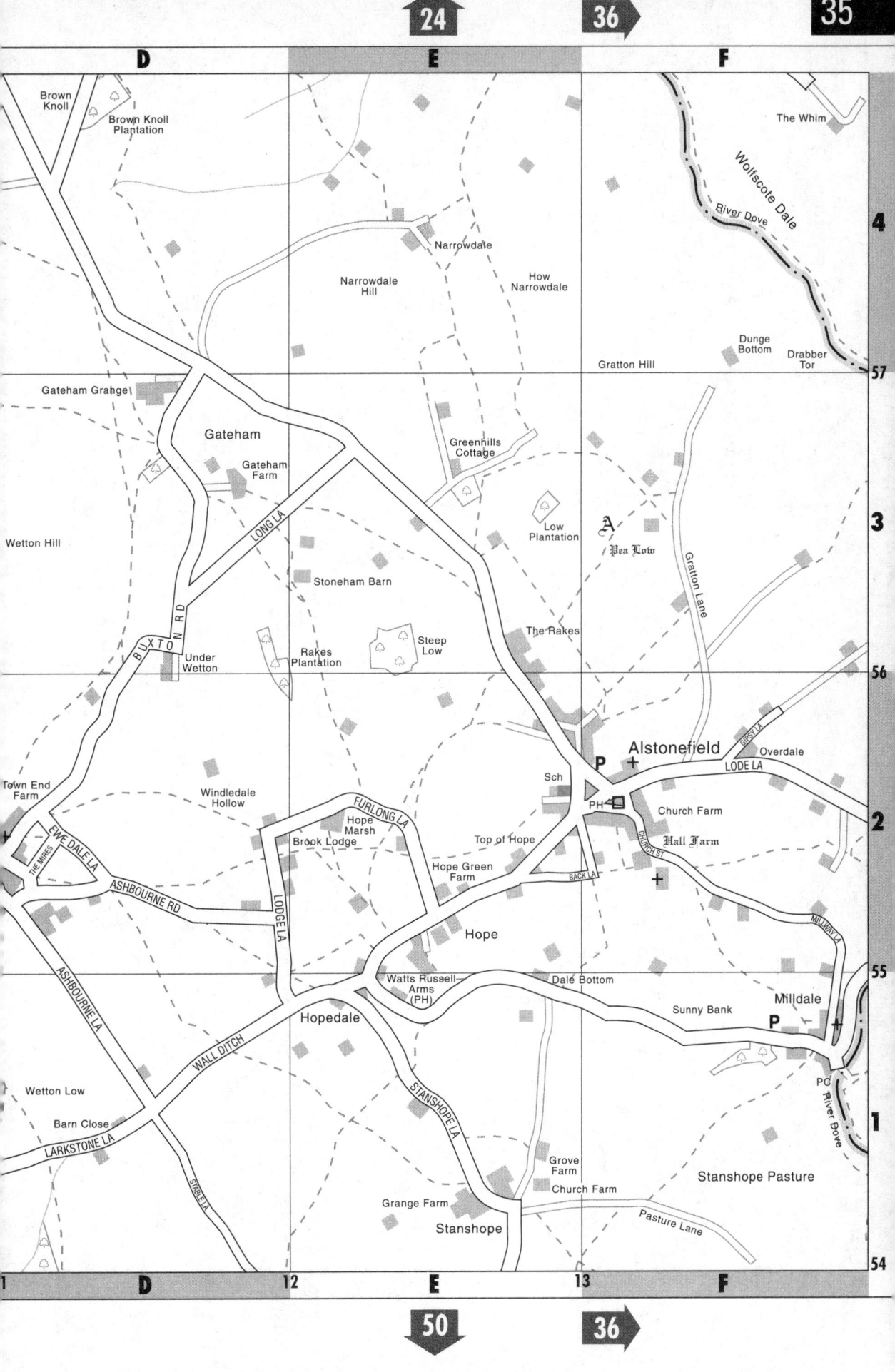

D   E   F

Brown
Knoll

Brown Knoll
Plantation

The Whim

Wolfscote Dale

River Dove

4

Narrowdale

Narrowdale
Hill

How
Narrowdale

Dunge
Bottom

Drabber
Tor

Gratton Hill   57

Gateham Grange

Gateham

Greenhills
Cottage

Gateham
Farm

LONG LA

Wetton Hill

Low
Plantation

Pea Low

Gratton Lane

3

Stoneham Barn

BUXTON RD

Rakes
Plantation

Steep
Low

The Rakes

Under
Wetton   56

Alstonefield

GIPSY LA

Overdale

LODE LA

Town End
Farm

Windledale
Hollow

FURLONG LA

P

Sch

PH

Church Farm

2

THE MIRES

EWE DALE LA

Hope
Marsh

Brook Lodge

Top of Hope

PH

Hall Farm

CHURCH ST

ASHBOURNE RD

LODGE LA

Hope Green
Farm

BACK LA

MILLWAY LA

Hope

ASHBOURNE LA

WALL DITCH

Watts Russell
Arms
(PH)

Dale Bottom

55

Sunny Bank

Milldale

P

Hopedale

STANSHOPE LA

Wetton Low

PO

River Dove

1

Barn Close

LARKSTONE LA

Grove
Farm

Stanshope Pasture

STABLE LA

Church Farm

Grange Farm

Pasture Lane

Stanshope

54

D   12   E   13   F

A

B

C

4

57

3

56

2

55

1

54

14

15

16

Biggin Dale

Biggin

The Liffs

Greenrake Plantation

Johnson's Knoll

A515

Alsop Moor Plantation

LIFFS RD

Cave

Coldeaton

Gipsy Bank

Dove Top Farm

Lees Barn

Gipsy Lane

Iron Tors

Coldeaton Bridge

Nettly Knowe

Tissington Trail

Oulds Barn

Alsop Moor Cottages

CROSLOW LA

Oxdales Farm

Dismantled Railway

Pine View

Oxdales House

Eatondale Wood

River Dove

Pinelow Plantation

Crosslow Bank Farm

Lode House

Greenlowfield

Cross Low

Lode Plantation

Manor Farm

LODE LA

Alsop en le Dale Hall

Alsop en le Dale

DAM LA

Church Farm

Shining Tor

THE PINCH

OXCLOSE LA

Stonepit Plantation

Mill Dale

P

GREEN LA

New Inns Hotel

New Hanson Grange

GAG LA

A515

Baley Hill

Moat Low

A   B   C

LC

Top End Farm

Valley Brook

Walnut Tree Farm

Bridge House Farm

Mill Farm

MILL LA

M6

RADWAY GREEN RD

B5078

Foxley Farm

Toad Hole Farm

4

Smith Green Farm

Smith's Green

BARTHOMLEY RD

Daisy Bank Farm

SMITHY LA

New Farm

Flash House

Monneley Farm

53

Cherrytree Farm

A 500

Churchfield Farm

SMITHY LA

Bluemire Farm

RADWAY GREEN RD

Barthomley

White Lion (PH)

Motel

B5078

A 500

3

Englesea Brook

Town House Farm

Old Hall Farm

Junction 16

Glebe Farm

Valley Farm

Domvilles Wood

52

AUDLEY RD

SNAPE LA

Manor Farm

Englesea-brook

ENGLESEA BROOK LA

DEANS LA

Dean Rough

Basford Coppice

Bayley-Lane Farm

Domvilles Farm

BARTHOMLEY RD

The Limes Farm

Dean Brook

Knowl End

2

Balterley Green Farm

51

Balterley Green

Mill Dale Farm

Spring Farm

B5500

Pear Tree Lake Farm

Mill Dale

Shortfields Farm

1

Pear Tree Farm

Black Mere

Balterley

Hall o' th' Wood

BACK LA

Bell Farm

Waggon and Horses (PH)

B5500

NANTWICH RD

LIMBRICK RD

M6

50

75   A   76   B   77   C

40

Bank Top

Audley Rd

Alsager

D

E

F

4

Lower Foxley

Mosshouse

Foxley

Eardleyend Rd

Foxley Farm

Foxley Drumble

Foxley Gorse

53

Brockwood Hill Farm

High Foxley Farm

Wrench's Coppice

Eardleyend

Park Manor Farm

Eardley Hall

3

Brockwood Hill

The Fields

Millend

Alsager Rd

Millend La

Hullock's Pool Rd

Cross La

A500

Cress Farm

52

Brook Farm

Pool House

Hullock's Pool

Great Oak Farm

Park Lane Farm

Wks

Greatoak Rd

Yewtree Farm

New Farm

Park La

Park End

2

Park Farm

Moat Farm

Townhouse

Bignall End Rd

Sch

Edward St

Woods St

Albert St

Bignall End

Firs Farm

Moat La

Pear Tree Farm

Ravens Cl

Chapel La

Old Rd

Woods St

B5500

RAVEN'S LA

51

PCI

New Rd

Watlands Rd

Georges Row

Benjamins Way

Kent Hill Farm

Wilbraham's Wlk

Riley's Way

Gresley Way

New Peel Farm

P

Chester Rd

Dean Hollow

Liby

McKellin Cl

Boyles Hall Rd

Westlands

Monument View

Barthomley Rd

Audley

Chapel La

Church St

Church Bank

P

Cherry Tree Rd 1

Cedar Cres 2

Wedgewood Ave 3

Boon Hill Rd

The Quarry

Westfield Ave

Vernon Ave

Nantwich Rd

Vernon Cl

Booth St

Peel Hollow

Meadow Croft Ave

Kent Hall Way

Outwer Cl

Hougher Wall Rd

Grassygreen La

Dismtd Rly

Hawthorne Ave

Old Peel Farm

Wereton

New King St

Princess Ave

Queen St

King St

Mellard St

Geoffrey St

Maddock St

Rye Hills

Ryehills

Boon Hill

B3367

Quarry New Farm

Greenbutts House

Wereton Rd

Ryehill Farm

Grange Farm

Carr La

Limerick Rd

Shraleybrook

Tom Fields Sch

8

D

79

E

80

F

50

54

40

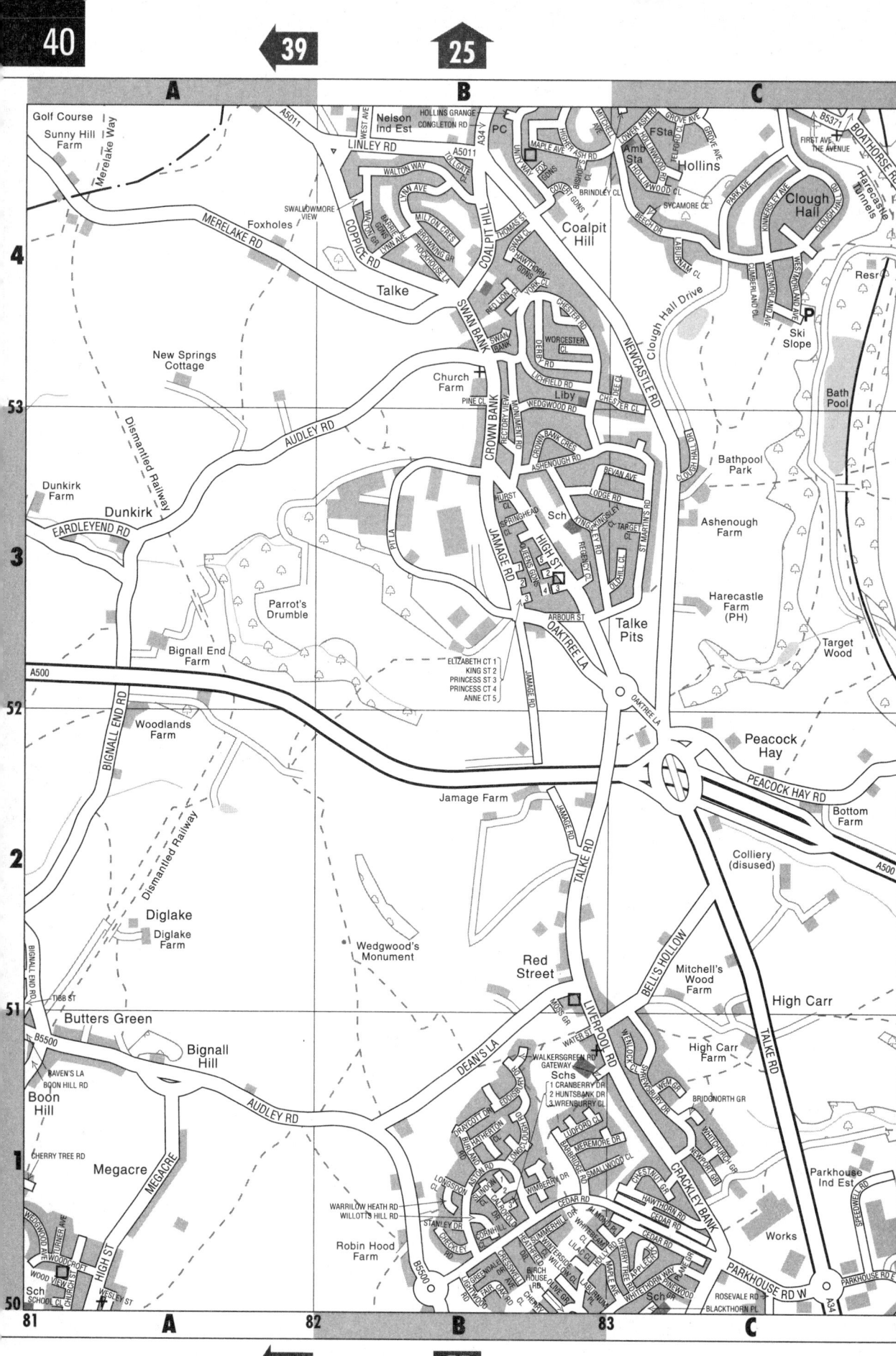

A   B   C

4

53

3

52

2

51

1

50

Golf Course
Sunny Hill
Farm
Merelake Way
MERELAKE RD
Foxholes
Talke
New Springs
Cottage
Dismantled Railway
Dunkirk
Farm
Dunkirk
EARDLEYEND RD
Parrot's
Drumble
Bignall End
Farm
A500
Woodlands
Farm
Dismantled Railway
BIGNALL END RD
Diglake
Diglake
Farm
Wedgwood's
Monument
BIGNALL END RD
TIBB ST
Butters Green
B5500
Bignall
Hill
RAVEN'S LA
BOON HILL RD
Boon
Hill
CHERRY TREE RD
Megacre
MEGACRE
AUDLEY RD
HIGH ST
WEDGWOOD AVE
TURNER AVE
WOODCROFT
WOOD VIEW
CHURCH ST
WESLEY ST
Sch
SCHOOL CL
Robin Hood
Farm
WARRILOW HEATH RD
WILLOTTS HILL RD
STANLEY DR
CHECKLEY
CORNHILL
B5500
DEAN'S LA

NELSON IND EST
LINLEY RD
A5011
WALTON WAY
LYNN AVE
COPPICE RD
SWALLOWMORE VIEW
MILTON CRES
BROWNING GR
ROCKHOUSE LA
COPPICE RD
Talke
SWAN BANK
SWAN BANK
CROWN BANK
AUDLEY RD
Church
Farm
PINE CL
RECTORY VIEW
MONUMENT
JAMAGE RD
HURST CL
SPRINGHEAD
PIT LA
HIGH ST
QUEENS GDNS
ARBOUR ST
OAKTREE LA
Talke
Pits
JAMAGE RD
Jamage Farm
COAL PIT HILL
THOMAS CL
SWAN CL
HAWTHORN GDNS
DERBY RD
WORCESTER CL
LICHFIELD RD
DEE CL
WEDGWOOD RD
CROWN BANK CRES
ASHENOUGH RD
Sch
KINGSLEY
RECENCY CL
CAHILL CT
ST MARTIN'S RD
BEVAN AVE
LODGE RD
TARGET CL
Liby
CHESTER CL
CHESTER CL
Coalpit
Hill
NELSON
CONGLETON RD
MAPLE AVE
MITCHELL
ASH RD
ASH RD
UNITY WAY
COVERT GDNS
BRINDLEY CL
SHALLOWWOOD CL
FOX EGDNS
Hollins
PARK AVE
BIRCH DR
LABURNAM CL
SYCAMORE CL
HAZEL DR
NEWCASTLE RD
Clough Hall Drive
CUMBERLAND DR
WESTMORLAND AVE
WESTMORLAND AVE
P
Ski
Slope
Clough
Hall
Bath
Pool
Bathpool
Park
Ashenough
Farm
Harecastle
Farm
(PH)
Target
Wood
Peacock
Hay
PEACOCK HAY RD
Bottom
Farm
Colliery
(disused)
A500
High Carr
Mitchell's
Wood
Farm
BELL'S HOLLOW
Red
Street
TALKE RD
TALKE RD
High Carr
Farm
LIVERPOOL RD
WATER ST
WENLOCK CL
NEW GR
High Carr
BRIDGNORTH GR
Schs
1 CRANBERRY DR
2 HUNTSBANK DR
3 WRENBURY CL
WALKERSGREEN RD
GATEWAY
LUDFORD CL
MEREMORE DR
WIMBERRY DR
CRACKLEY BANK
NEWPORT CL
WHITCHURCH RD
CEDAR RD
CEDAR RD
CHERRY TREE
Parkhouse
Ind Est
SPEEDWELL DR
Works
ROSEVALE RD
BLACKTHORN PL
PARKHOUSE RD W
PARKHOUSE RD E
A34
Sch
BIRCH HOUSE RD
LILAC GR
WHITETHORN WAY
SUMMERHILL
GREENHILL
CHESTNUT AVE

ELIZABETH CT 1
KING ST 2
PRINCESS ST 3
PRINCESS CT 4
ANNE CT 5

HOLLINS GRANGE
CONGLETON RD
PC
F Sta
Amb
Sta
GROVE AVE
GROVE AVE
FIRST AVE
THE AVENUE
BOATHORSE RD
B5371
Harecastle
Tunnels
Resr
A34

81   A   82   B   83   C

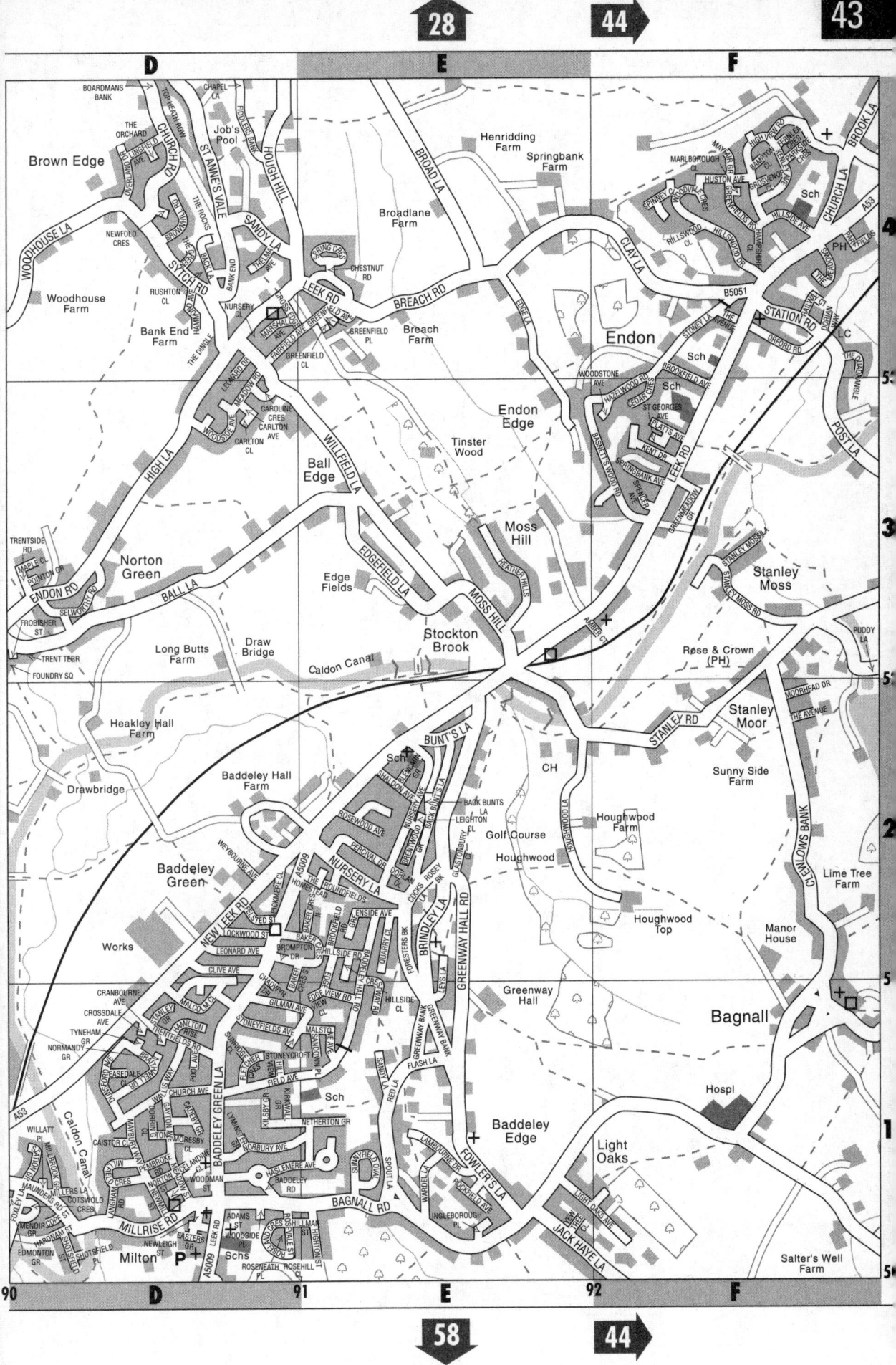

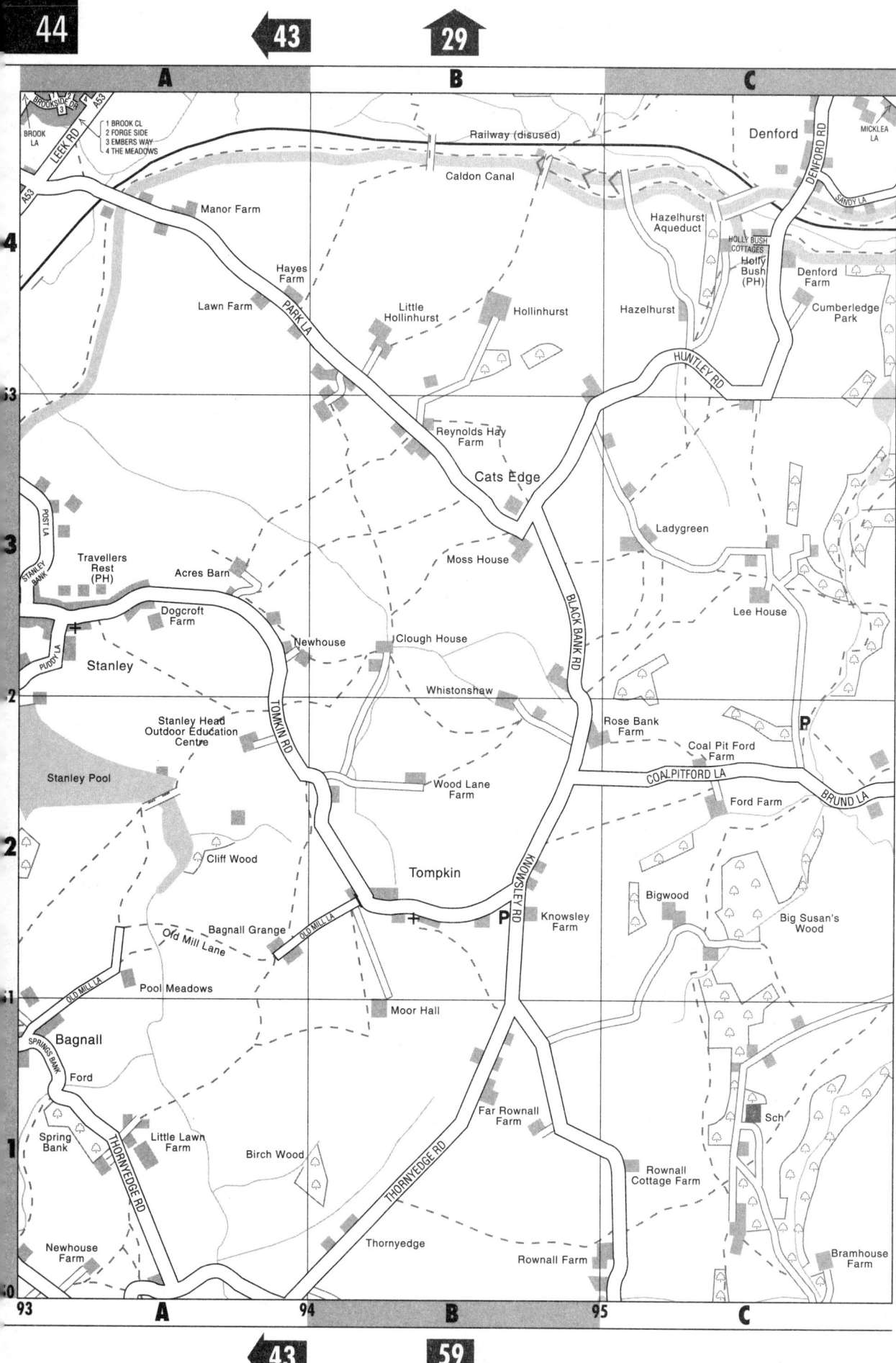

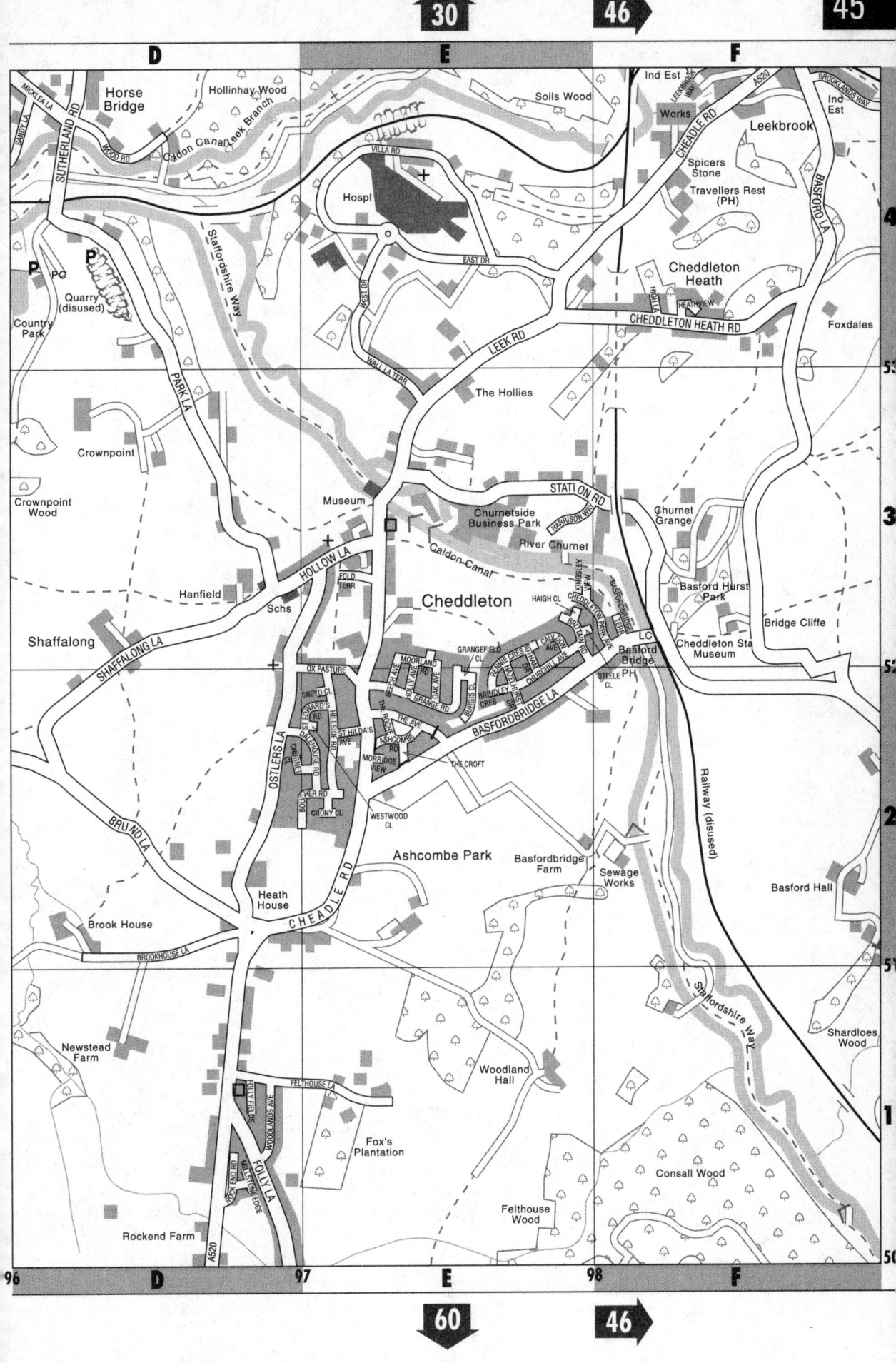

D   **E**   **F**

MICKLEA LA
SANDY LA
SUTHERLAND RD
WOOD RD

Horse Bridge

Hollinhay Wood

Caldon Canal Leek Branch

Soils Wood

Ind Est
LEEKBROOK WAY
A520
BROOKLANDS WAY
Ind Est

Works

CHEADLE RD

BASFORD LA

Leekbrook

VILLA RD

Hospl

Spicers Stone

Travellers Rest (PH)

4

Staffordshire Way

EAST DR

Cheddleton Heath

HIGH LA

P   P
PC

Quarry (disused)

WEST DR

LEEK RD

WALL LA TERR

HEATHVIEW

CHEDDLETON HEATH RD

Foxdales

Country Park

PARK LA

53

Crownpoint

The Hollies

Crownpoint Wood

Museum

STATION RD

Churnetside Business Park

HARRISON WAY

Churnet Grange

3

River Churnet

HOLLOW LA

Caldon Canal

AYLESBURY DR

Basford Hurst Park

Hanfield

Schs

FOLD TERR

Cheddleton

HAIGH CL

CHEDDLETON PARK AVE
BASFORDBRIDGE

Bridge Cliffe

Shaffalong

SHAFFALONG LA

GRANGEFIELD CL

MOORLAND RD

BEECH AVE

HOLLY AVE

CALVIN AVE

RENNIE CRES

BRITTAIN AVE

CHURCHILL AVE

STEELE CL

LC

Basford Bridge

Cheddleton Sta Museum

52

OX PASTURE

SNEYD CL

OAK AVE

GRANGE RD

BRINDLEY CRES

PH

OSTLERS LA

ST EDWARD'S RD

HILLSIDE AVE

ST HILDA'S AVE

DALEHOUSE RD

THE AVE

BASFORDBRIDGE LA

CHAPEL LA

THE ROCHE

ASHCOMBE RD

THE CROFT

Railway (disused)

BRUND LA

BOON HILL
ARCHER RD

CRONY CL

MORELIDGE VIEW

WESTWOOD CL

2

Heath House

Ashcombe Park

Basfordbridge Farm

Sewage Works

Basford Hall

Brook House

CHEADLE RD

BROOKHOUSE LA

51

Staffordshire Way

Shardloes Wood

Newstead Farm

FELTHOUSE LA

FOLLY FIELDS

WOODCOCK AVE

Woodland Hall

ROCK END DR

MILLSTONE EDGE

FOLLY LA

Fox's Plantation

1

A520

Rockend Farm

Felthouse Wood

Consall Wood

50

A B C

BROOKLANDS WAY

Roost Hill

Revedge

Fynneylane Farm

Yew Tree Farm

Ballfields

Sixoaks Farm

Apesford

Crowholt

Roughstone Hole

Barnfield

Ringehay

Ferny Hill

Nature Reserve

Cloughmeadow Cottage

Sixoaks Wood

Oldfield

Combes Brook

Padwick

Padwick Wood

The Combes

Spiritholes Wood

Blackhill Wood

Lower House Farm

Upper Fernyhill Farm

Sharpcliffe Hall

Home Farm

Basford Grange

Sneyd Arms Farm

The Ridge

Low Wood

Whitehough Wood

Little Rocks Plantation

Basford Green

Crab Tree Farm

Whitehough

Mill Wood

Mosslee Mill Farm

Brockholes

Mosslee Barn

Collyhole

The Clough

Hills Farm

Mosslee Hall Farm

Blackbank Wood

Coltstone

Stakebank Wood

Collyhole Brook

CHURCH LA

Middle Farm

Turner's Knipe

Railway (disused)

Intake

Stocks Green

CHURCH MEADOW

River Churnet

Rough Intake

Oddo Hall

F Sta

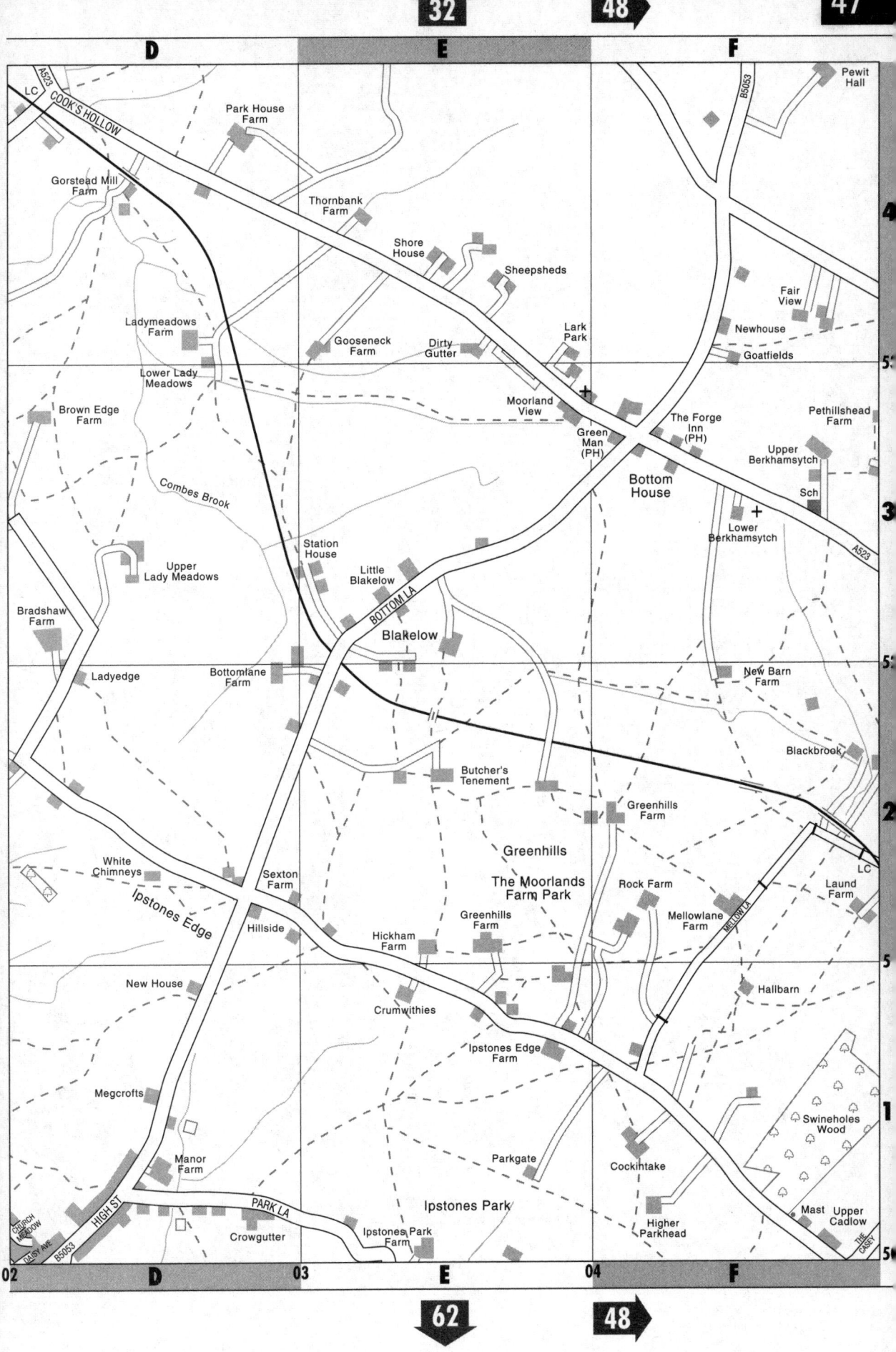

D
E
F

LC
A523
COOK'S HOLLOW

Park House
Farm

Gorstead Mill
Farm

Thornbank
Farm

Shore
House

Sheepsheds

Lark
Park

Fair
View

Newhouse

Goatfields

Ladymeadows
Farm

Gooseneck
Farm

Dirty
Gutter

Lower Lady
Meadows

Moorland
View

Green
Man
(PH)

The Forge
Inn
(PH)

Pethillshead
Farm

Brown Edge
Farm

Upper
Berkhamsytch

Sch

Combes Brook

Bottom
House

Station
House

Little
Blakelow

Lower
Berkhamsytch

A523

Upper
Lady Meadows

BOTTOM LA

Bradshaw
Farm

Blakelow

Ladyedge

Bottomlane
Farm

New Barn
Farm

Blackbrook

Butcher's
Tenement

Greenhills
Farm

White
Chimneys

A523

Greenhills

Sexton
Farm

The Moorlands
Farm Park

Rock Farm

Laund
Farm

LC

Ipstones Edge

Hillside

Greenhills
Farm

Mellowlane
Farm

MELLOW LA

New House

Hickham
Farm

Hallbarn

Crumwithies

Ipstones Edge
Farm

Megcrofts

Swineholes
Wood

Manor
Farm

Parkgate

Cockintake

Mast

Upper
Cadlow

CHURCH
MEADOW

DAISY AVE

HIGH ST

B5053

PARK LA

Crowgutter

Ipstones Park
Farm

Ipstones Park

Higher
Parkhead

THE CASEY

4

5²

3

5²

2

5

1

5⁰

02
D
03
E
04
F

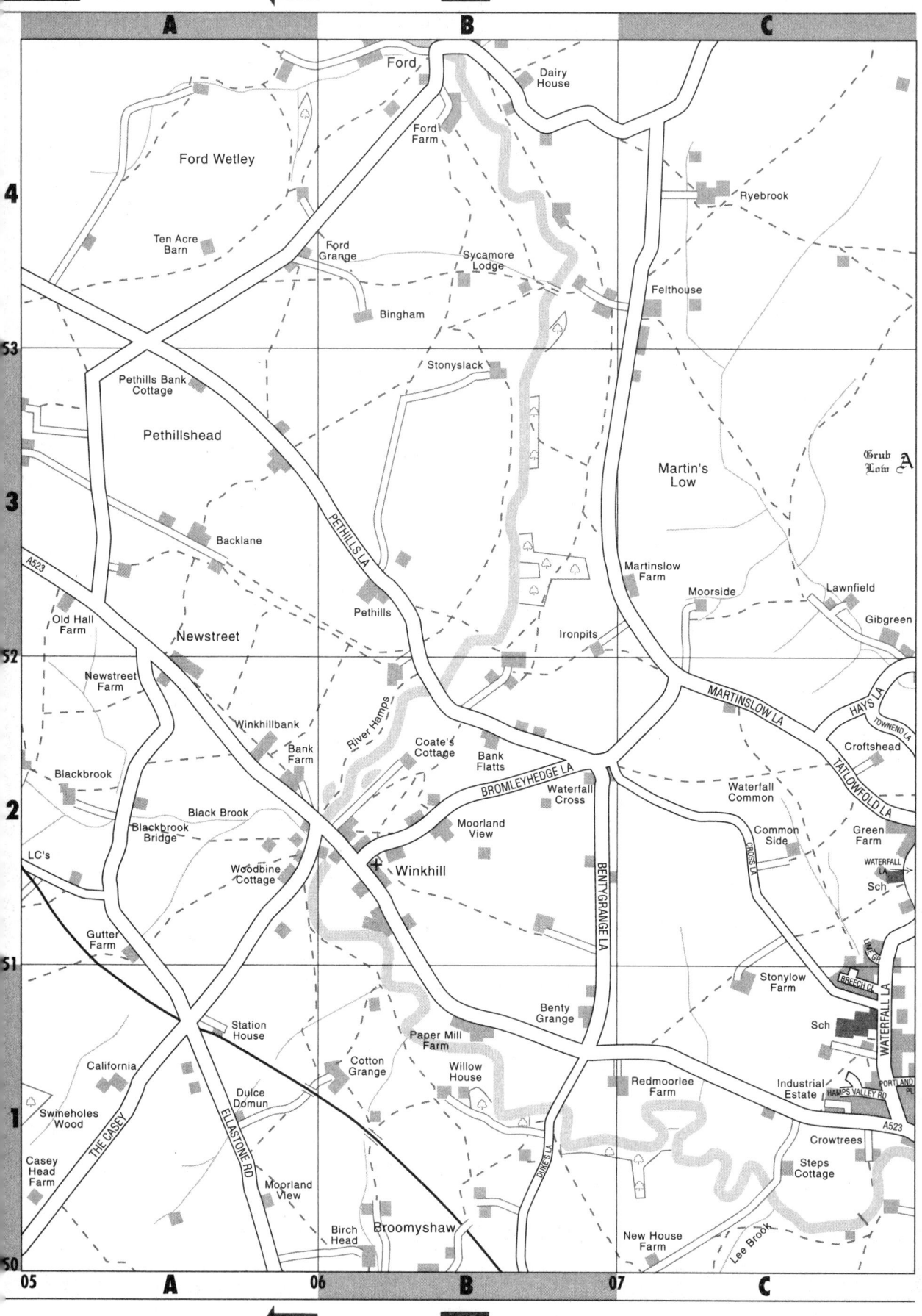

A   B   C

Ford

Dairy House

Ford Farm

4

Ryebrook

Ten Acre Barn

Ford Grange

Sycamore Lodge

Felthouse

Bingham

53

Stonyslack

Pethills Bank Cottage

Martin's Low

Grub Low

Pethillshead

3

Backlane

Martinslow Farm

Moorside

Lawnfield

Old Hall Farm

Newstreet

Pethills

Gibgreen

Ironpits

52

Newstreet Farm

MARTINSLOW LA

HAYS LA

TOWNEND LA

Croftshead

Winkhillbank

River Hamps

Coate's Cottage

Bank Flatts

Waterfall Common

TATLOWFOLD LA

Blackbrook

Bank Farm

Black Brook

BROMLEYHEDGE LA

Waterfall Cross

Common Side

Green Farm

2

Blackbrook Bridge

Moorland View

WATERFALL LA

Sch

Woodbine Cottage

Winkhill

BENTYGRANGE LA

CROSS LA

LC's

Stonylow Farm

BEECH CL

Gutter Farm

51

Sch

Station House

Benty Grange

WATERFALL LA

California

Paper Mill Farm

Industrial Estate

HAMPS VALLEY RD

PORTLAND PL

Dulce Domun

Cotton Grange

Willow House

Redmoorlee Farm

A523

1

Swineholes Wood

ELLASTONE RD

THE CASEY

Crowtrees

Casey Head Farm

Moorland View

DUKE'S LA

Steps Cottage

Birch Head

Broomyshaw

New House Farm

Lee Brook

50

05   A   06   B   07   C

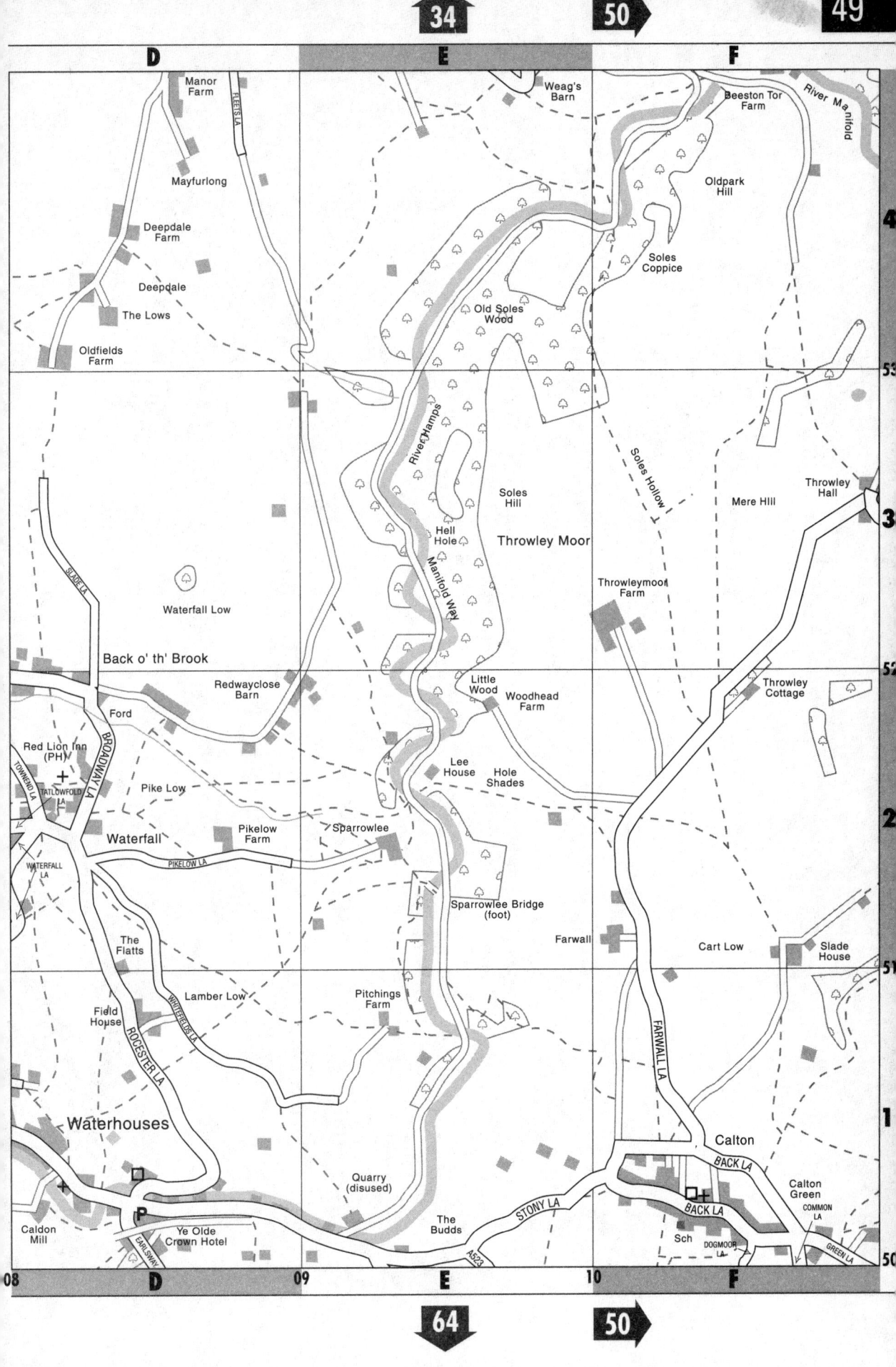

D
E
F

Manor Farm

Weag's Barn

Beeston Tor Farm

River Manifold

Mayfurlong

Oldpark Hill

Deepdale Farm

Soles Coppice

Deepdale

The Lows

Old Soles Wood

4

Oldfields Farm

53

River Hamps

Soles Hill

Soles Hollow

Throwley Hall

Mere Hill

3

Waterfall Low

Hell Hole

Throwley Moor

Throwleymoor Farm

Manifold Way

Back o' th' Brook

Little Wood

Throwley Cottage

52

Redwayclose Barn

Woodhead Farm

Ford

Red Lion Inn (PH)

BROADWAY LA

TATLOWFOLD LA

TOWNEND LA

Lee House

Hole Shades

Pike Low

Pikelow Farm

Sparrowlee

2

Waterfall

PIKELOW LA

WATERFALL LA

Sparrowlee Bridge (foot)

Farwall

Cart Low

Slade House

The Flatts

51

Lamber Low

Pitchings Farm

FARWALL LA

Field House

WHITFIELDS LA

ROCESTER LA

1

Waterhouses

Calton

BACK LA

Calton Green

Quarry (disused)

Caldon Mill

P

EARLS WAY

Ye Olde Crown Hotel

The Budds

STONY LA

Sch

BACK LA

DOGMOOR LA

COMMON LA

GREEN LA

50

08
D
09
E
10
F

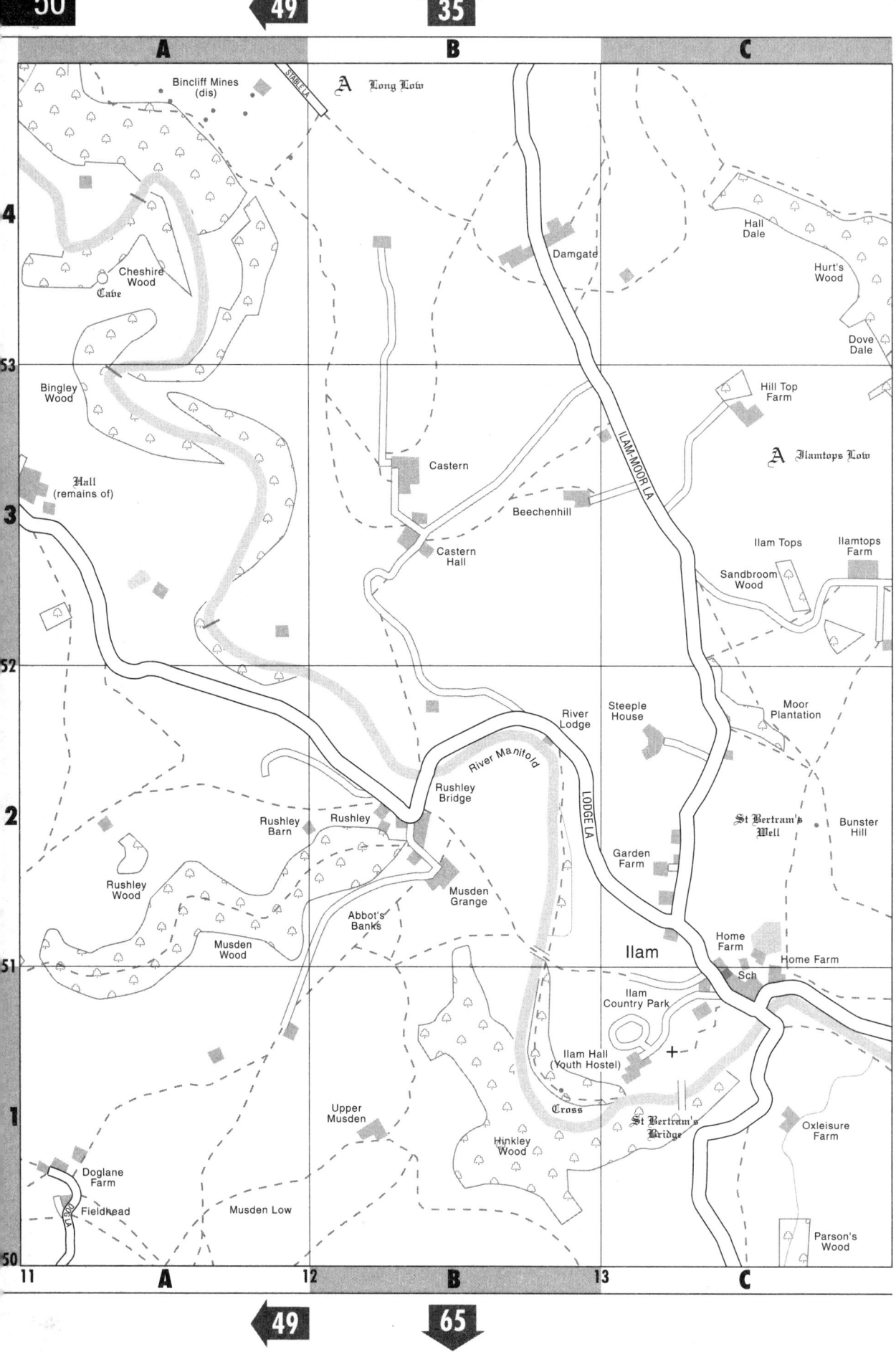

A

B

C

4

Bincliff Mines
(dis)

Long Low

Damgate

Hall
Dale

Hurt's
Wood

Cheshire
Wood
Cave

Dove
Dale

53

Bingley
Wood

Hill Top
Farm

Ilamtops Low

Hall
(remains of)

Castern

Beechenhill

ILAM-MOOR LA

Ilam Tops

Ilamtops
Farm

3

Castern
Hall

Sandbroom
Wood

52

River
Lodge

Steeple
House

Moor
Plantation

Rushley
Bridge

River Manifold

LODGE LA

2

Rushley
Barn

Rushley

Garden
Farm

St Bertram's
Well

Bunster
Hill

Rushley
Wood

Musden
Grange

Home
Farm

Home Farm

Abbot's
Banks

Ilam

Sch

Musden
Wood

Ilam
Country Park

51

Ilam Hall
(Youth Hostel)

Upper
Musden

Cross

St Bertram's
Bridge

Oxleisure
Farm

1

Hinkley
Wood

Doglane
Farm

Fieldhead

Musden Low

Parson's
Wood

50

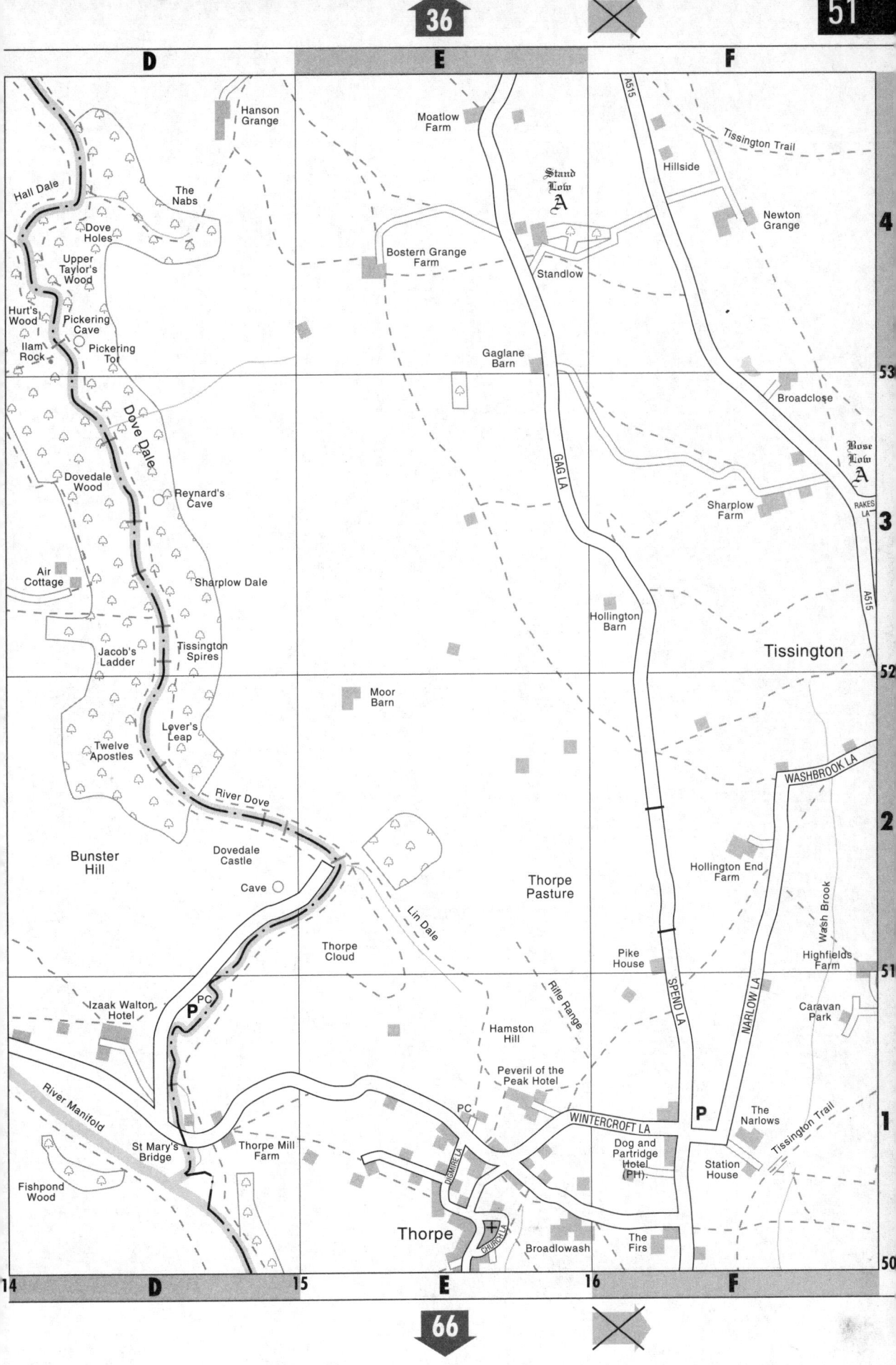

D

E

F

4

Hanson Grange

Moatlow Farm

A515

Tissington Trail

Hillside

Stand Low A

Newton Grange

Hall Dale

The Nabs

Dove Holes

Bostern Grange Farm

Standlow

Upper Taylor's Wood

53

Hurt's Wood

Pickering Cave

Gaglane Barn

Broadclose

Ilam Rock

Pickering Tor

Dove Dale

GAG LA

Bose Low A

RAKES LA

Dovedale Wood

Reynard's Cave

Sharplow Farm

3

Tissington

Hollington Barn

A515

Air Cottage

Sharplow Dale

Jacob's Ladder

Tissington Spires

Moor Barn

52

Lover's Leap

Twelve Apostles

WASHBROOK LA

Wash Brook

River Dove

Bunster Hill

Dovedale Castle

Hollington End Farm

2

Thorpe Pasture

Highfields Farm

Cave

Lin Dale

51

Thorpe Cloud

Pike House

Izaak Walton Hotel

PC
P

Rifle Range

Hamston Hill

Caravan Park

SPEND LA

NARLOW LA

The Narlows

Tissington Trail

Peveril of the Peak Hotel

P

River Manifold

St Mary's Bridge

Thorpe Mill Farm

PC

WINTERCROFT LA

Dog and Partridge Hotel (PH)

Station House

1

Fishpond Wood

DIGMINE LA

CHURCH LA

Thorpe

Broadlowash

The Firs

50

14

D

15

E

16

F

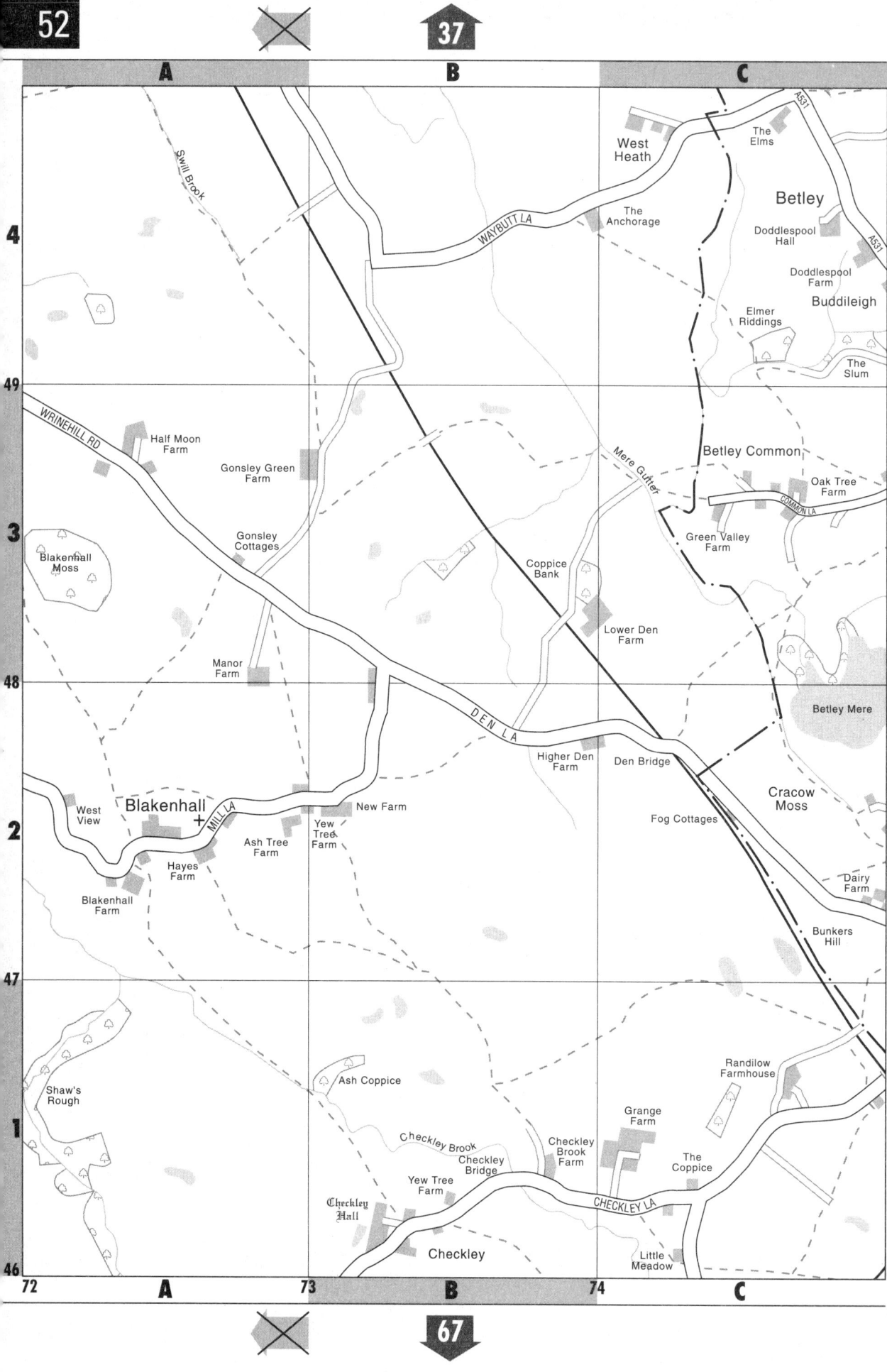

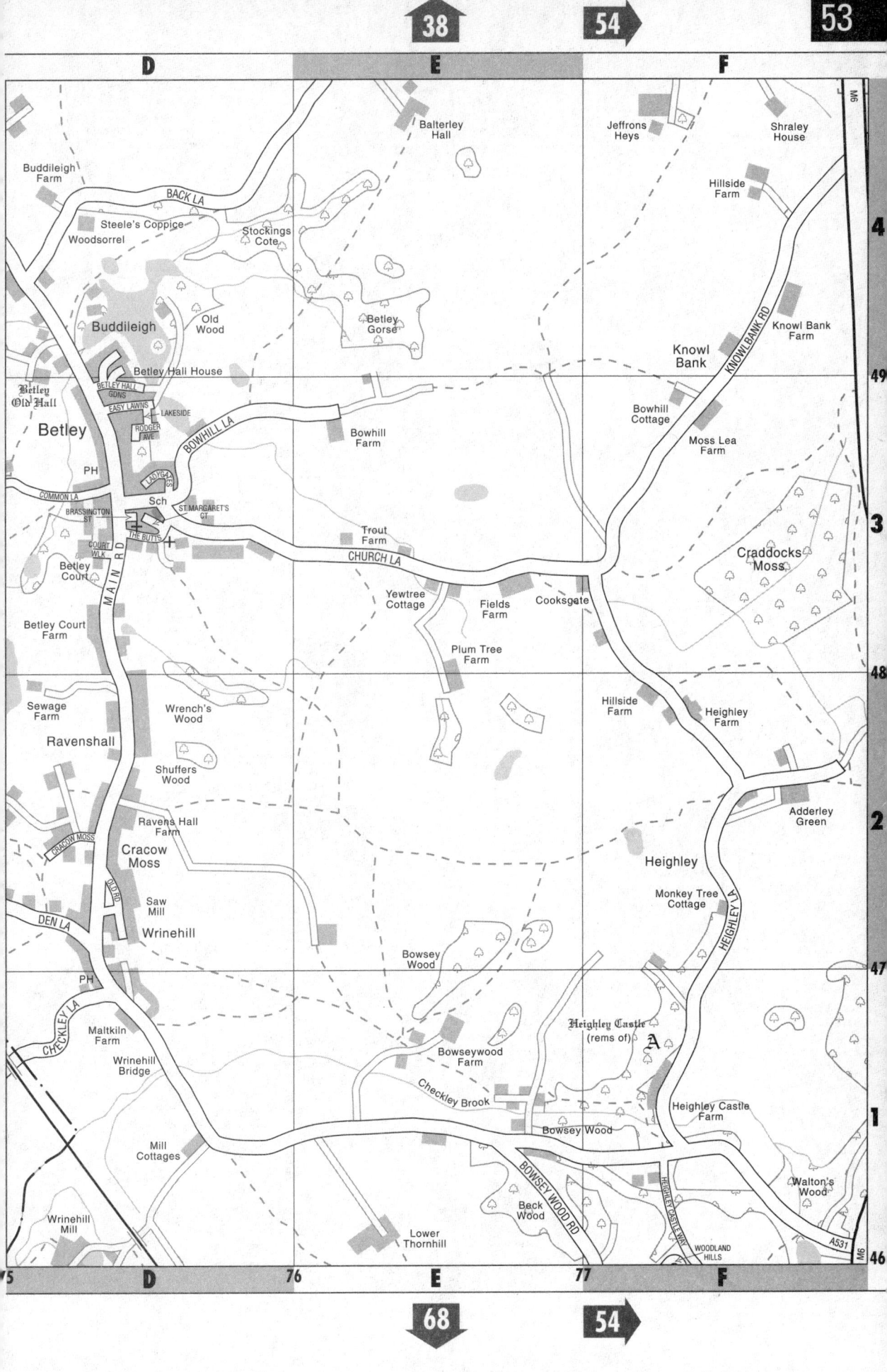

D
E
F

M6

Balterley Hall

Jeffrons Heys

Shraley House

Buddileigh Farm

BACK LA

Steele's Coppice
Woodsorrel

Stockings Cote

Hillside Farm

4

Buddileigh

Old Wood

Betley Gorse

Knowl Bank

Knowl Bank Farm

KNOWL BANK RD

Betley Hall House

Bowhill Cottage

49

Betley Old Hall

BETLEY HALL GDNS
EASY LAWNS   LAKESIDE
RODGER AVE

Bowhill Farm

BOWHILL LA

Moss Lea Farm

Betley

PH

COMMON LA

LADY GATES

Sch

ST MARGARET'S CT

THE BUTTS

Trout Farm

CHURCH LA

Cooksgate

Craddocks Moss

3

BRASSINGTON ST

COURT WLK

Betley Court

MAIN RD

Yewtree Cottage

Fields Farm

Plum Tree Farm

Betley Court Farm

Sewage Farm

Wrench's Wood

Hillside Farm

Heighley Farm

48

Ravenshall

Shuffers Wood

CRACOW MOSS

Ravens Hall Farm

Adderley Green

2

Cracow Moss

OLD RD

Saw Mill

Heighley

Monkey Tree Cottage

HEIGHLEY LA

DEN LA

Wrinehill

Bowsey Wood

47

PH

CHECKLEY LA

Maltkiln Farm

Heighley Castle (rems of)

Wrinehill Bridge

Bowseywood Farm

Checkley Brook

Heighley Castle Farm

1

Mill Cottages

Bowsey Wood

HEIGHLEY CASTLE WAY

Walton's Wood

BOWSEY WOOD RD

Wrinehill Mill

Lower Thornhill

Beck Wood

WOODLAND HILLS

A531

M6

46

5
D
76
E
77
F

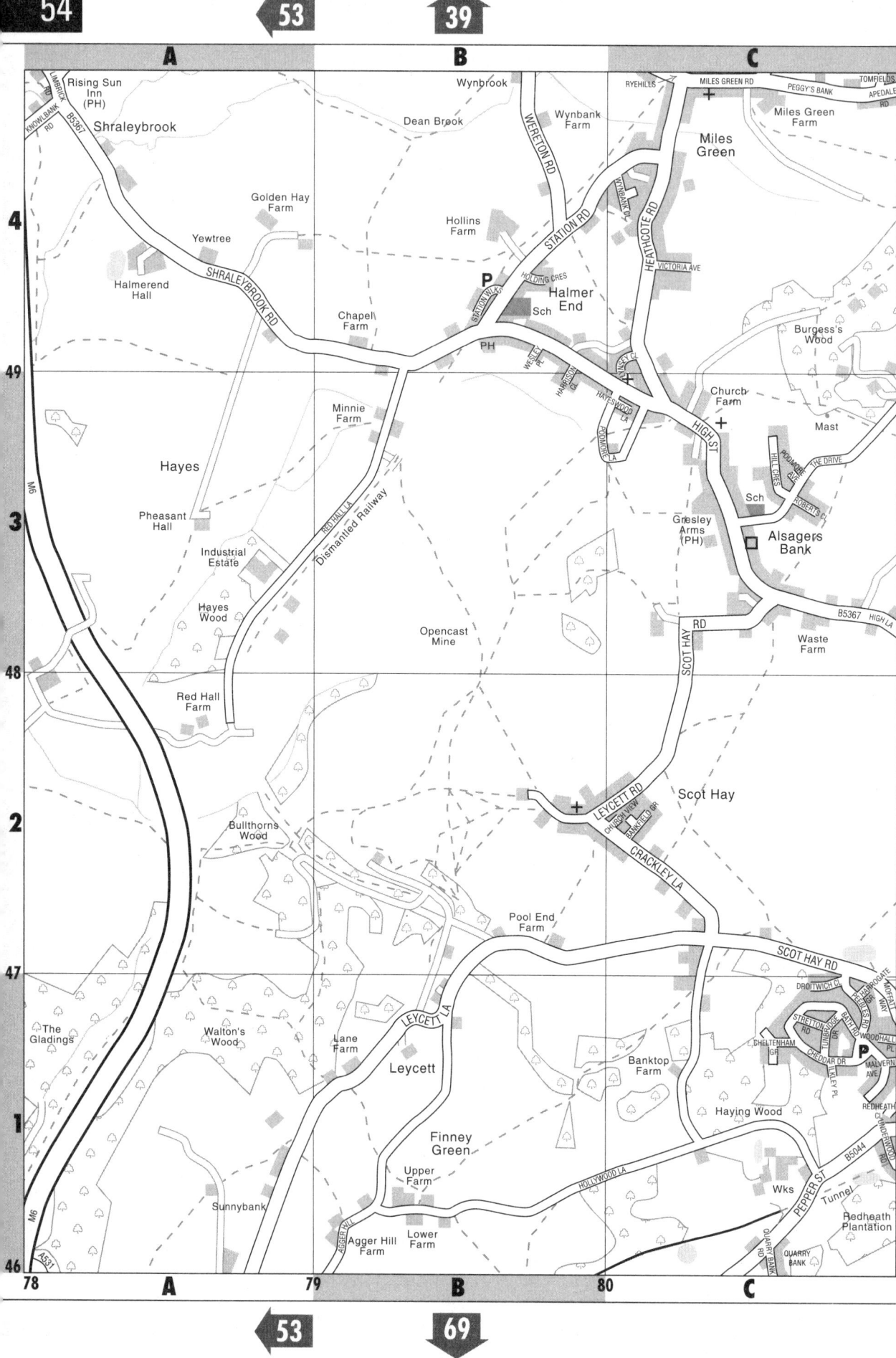

A
B
C

Rising Sun
Inn
(PH)

Shraleybrook

Wynbrook

Dean Brook

Wynbank
Farm

RYEHILLS

MILES GREEN RD

PEGGY'S BANK

TOMFIELDS
APEDALE RD

Miles Green
Farm

4

Golden Hay
Farm

Yewtree

Hollins
Farm

STATION RD

WERETON RD

WYNBANK CT

HEATHCOTE RD

VICTORIA AVE

Miles
Green

Halmerend
Hall

SHRALEYBROOK RD

Chapel
Farm

P

STATION WLK

HOLDING CRES

Sch

Halmer
End

Burgess's
Wood

49

Minnie
Farm

PH

WESLEY PL

HARRISON CL

HAYESWOOD LA

POLMORE LA

KINSEY CT

HIGH ST

Church
Farm

Mast

HILL CRES

POLMORE AVE

THE DRIVE

ROBERT'S CL

Hayes

Pheasant
Hall

RED HALL LA

Dismantled Railway

Sch

Gresley
Arms
(PH)

Alsagers
Bank

3

Industrial
Estate

Hayes
Wood

Opencast
Mine

SCOT HAY RD

B5367 HIGH LA

Waste
Farm

48

Red Hall
Farm

Scot Hay

2

Bullthorns
Wood

LEYCETT RD

CHURCH VIEW
TANKFIELD GR

CRACKLEY LA

Pool End
Farm

SCOT HAY RD

47

The
Gladings

Walton's
Wood

LEYCETT LA

Lane
Farm

Leycett

Banktop
Farm

Haying Wood

DROITWICH CL

STRETTON SIDE RD

BATFORD

CHELTENHAM GR

LIMBRIDGE RD

CRACKLEY PL

TURNBRIDGE

CHEDDAR DR

WOODHALL RD

NORTHGATE PL

MOFFATT WAY

REDHEATH CL

MALVERN AVE

P

1

Finney
Green

Upper
Farm

HOLLYWOOD LA

Wks

PEPPER ST

B5044

Tunnel

INGLEWOOD

Redheath
Plantation

Sunnybank

AGGER HILL

Agger Hill
Farm

Lower
Farm

QUARRY BANK RD

QUARRY
BANK

46

M6

A531

78

A

79

B

80

C

D
E
F

APEDALE RD
CHURCH ST 1
HIGH ST 2
Wood Lane
Woodhouse Farm
Springwood
Crackley
Industrial Estate
Miry Wood
Saw Mill
Apedale
Home Farm
Burley Farm
APEDALE BUSINESS PARK
Wks
Chesterton
Park CT
Sch
Beasley
Hospl
Watermills Farm
Industrial Estate
Broad Meadow
Church Fields
Off Depot
Stadium
HIGH LA
Mast
HIGH LA
BLACKBANK RD
Black Bank
Wks
Gorsty Bank
Cemy
Sch
Colliery
SCOT HAY RD
PEPPER ST
Marl Pit
Dismantled Railway
Wks
Knutton
CHURCH ST
SNEYD TERR
CHURCH LA
Tunnel
UNDERWOOD RD
HIGH ST
NEWCASTLE ST
MILL ST
Sch
Silverdale
SILVERDALE RD
Cemy
Allot Gdns
Foundry
CEMETERY RD
Sewage Works
Golf Course
MILLBANK PL 1
HEDLEY PL 2

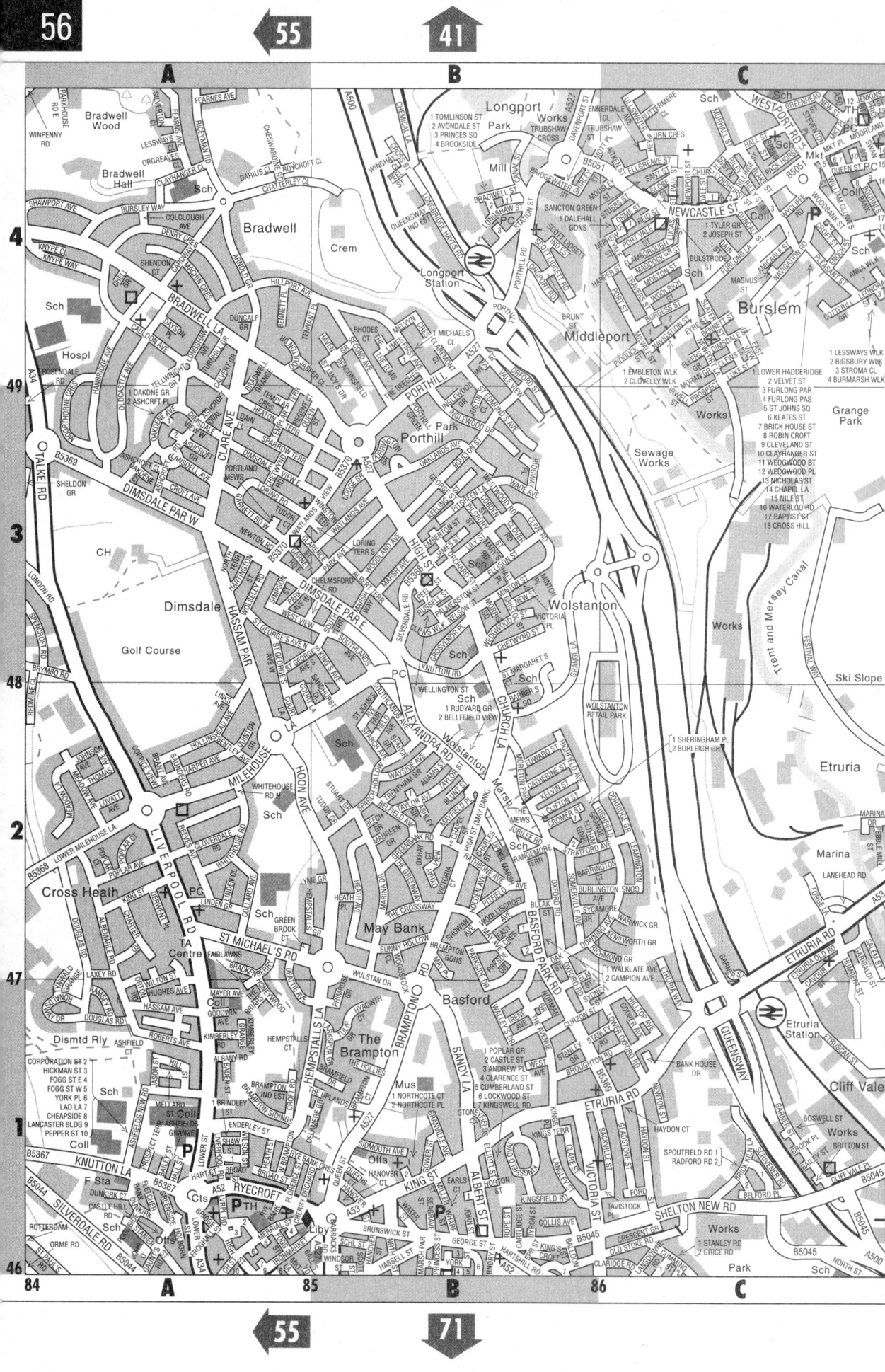

A | B | C

Works

Carmountside
Cemy
Crem
Carmounthead
Woodhead
WOODHEAD RD
Mast
Jack Hayes
JACK HAYE LA
Jack Hayes Farm
Greenfields Farm

Abbey Farm
BIRCHES HEAD RD
PH
REDHILLS RD
LEEK RD
Abbey Hulton
Holehouse Farm
Kerry Hill Farm
Kerry Hill

49
River Trent
Caldon Canal
Abbey St
GRANTHAM PL
GREASLEY RD
Little Eaves
Moorside Farm

3
ELGAR CRES
PERIVALE CL
AVONWICK GR
HANDEL GR
A5009
WHITEHOUSE RD
SOUTH RD
NEWSTEAD RD
Sch
MALCOLM DR
EAVES LA
Great Eaves
Firtree Farm Nursery
Launders Bank
Wetley Moor

48
CHAPTER WLK
ABBEY LA
Bucknall
Heath House La
Hospl
Brookhouse Wood
Heather View

Bucknall Park
PC
Off
TURNOCK ST
DEAN ST
GLADWYN ST
BIRCHGATE
BROOKHOUSE LA
Hanley Hayes Farm

2
A52
WERRINGTON RD
Ruxley Rd
ROBERTVILLE RD
MULLINER CL
Stewart's Farm
Ash Hall

Townsend
Brookhouse
ASH BANK RD
Ash Bank
A52
PH

47
1 BREWESTER RD
2 BROUGHTON RD
KEYWORTH WLK
1 HOLBEACH AVE
2 DRAYTON GN
3 LONGFORD WLK
Sch
DIVIDY RD
SUNDORNE PL
LEICESTER
BEVERLEY DR
Bentilee
Simfields

1
WALCOT GR
GLENROYD AVE
KETTERING DR
HOVERINGHAM DR
BURFORD WAY
Berry Hill
Berry Hill Greenway
Sch
WINSLOW GN
WENDLING CL
DEREHAM WAY
GRISTHORPE WAY
Widow Fields Farm
Ford Hayes
DRIFFIELD CL
FORD HAYES LA

46
WHIMPLE SIDE
MANIFOLD WLK
Ubberley
B5040
TYSON GR

90 | A | 91 | B | 92 | C

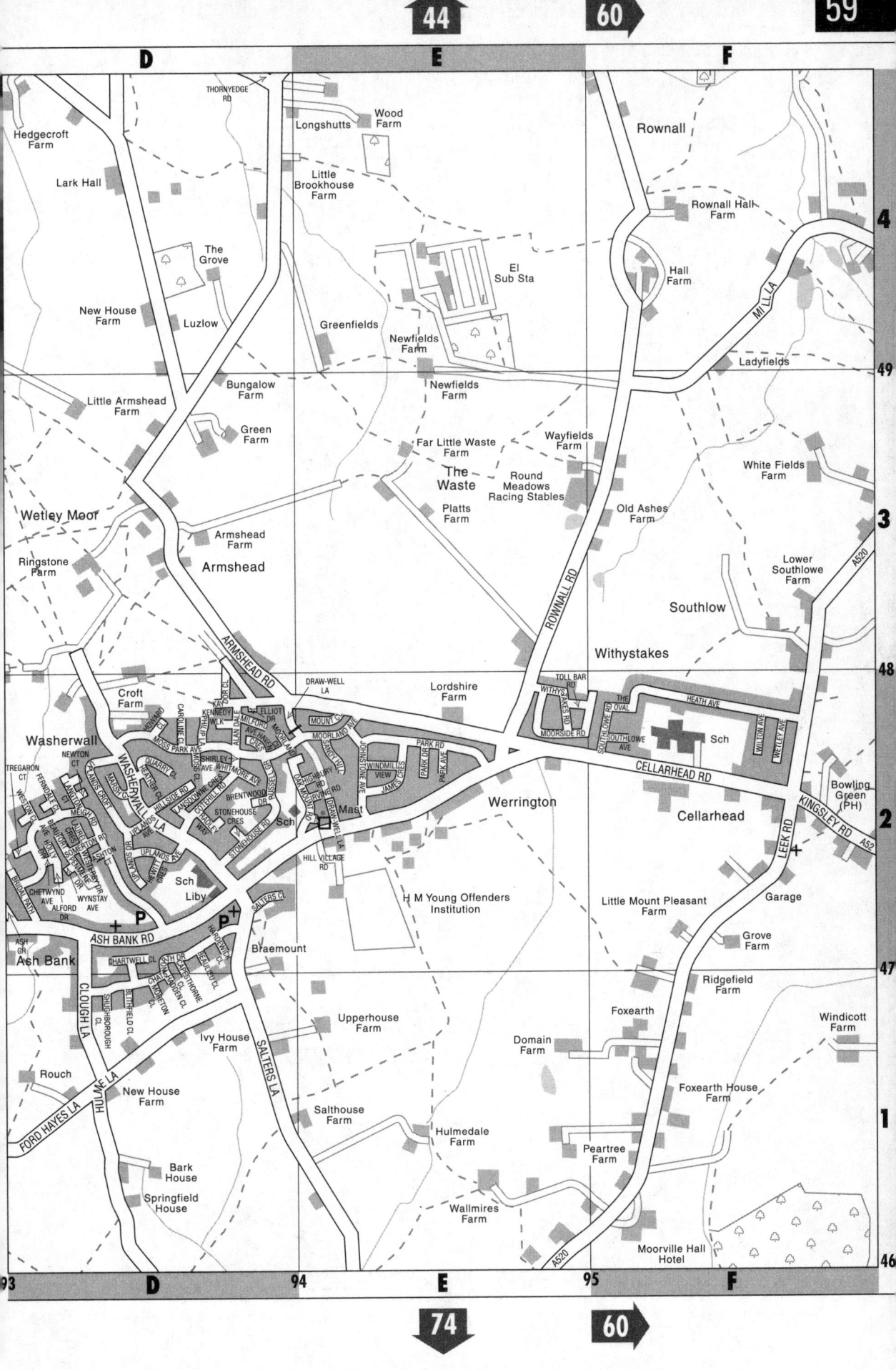

D E F

THORNYEDGE RD

Hedgecroft Farm

Lark Hall

Longshutts

Wood Farm

Little Brookhouse Farm

Rownall

The Grove

New House Farm

Luzlow

El Sub Sta

Greenfields

Rownall Hall Farm

Hall Farm

4

MILL LA

Newfields Farm

Ladyfields

49

Bungalow Farm

Newfields Farm

Little Armshead Farm

Green Farm

Far Little Waste Farm

The Waste

Wayfields Farm

White Fields Farm

Round Meadows Racing Stables

Old Ashes Farm

ROWNALL RD

Lower Southlowe Farm

A520

Wetley Moor

Platts Farm

Armshead Farm

Armshead

Southlow

3

Ringstone Farm

Withystakes

ARMSHEAD RD

48

Croft Farm

DRAW-WELL LA

Lordshire Farm

TOLL BAR WITHYS- TAKES RD

THE OVAL

HEATH AVE

Sch

Washerwall

TREGARON CT

NEWTON CT

FERNDELE CT

WESSON RD

WASHERWALL LA

KENNEDY WLK

KAYSOR CL

ELLIOT AVE

MILFORD AVE

MOUNT AVE

MOORLAND RD

SALTERS HILL

HIGHBURY RD

WINDMILLS VIEW

PARK RD

PARK DR

PARK AVE

JAMES

MOORSIDE RD

SOUTHLOWE AVE

THE

WILTON AVE

WETLEY AVE

Sch

Cellarhead

Bowling Green (PH)

KINGSLEY RD

A52

2

Mast

CELLARHEAD RD

Werrington

Little Mount Pleasant Farm

LEEK RD

Garage

Sch Liby

HILL VILLAGE RD

H M Young Offenders Institution

Grove Farm

P

ASH BANK RD

P

Braemount

47

ASH GR

Ash Bank

CLOUGH LA

CHARTWELL CL

Ridgefield Farm

Windicott Farm

HUME LA

SALTERS LA

Upperhouse Farm

Foxearth

Domain Farm

Rouch

Ivy House Farm

New House Farm

Salthouse Farm

Foxearth House Farm

1

Bark House

Springfield House

Hulmedale Farm

Peartree Farm

FORD HAYES LA

Wallmires Farm

A520

Moorville Hall Hotel

46

93 D 94 E 95 F

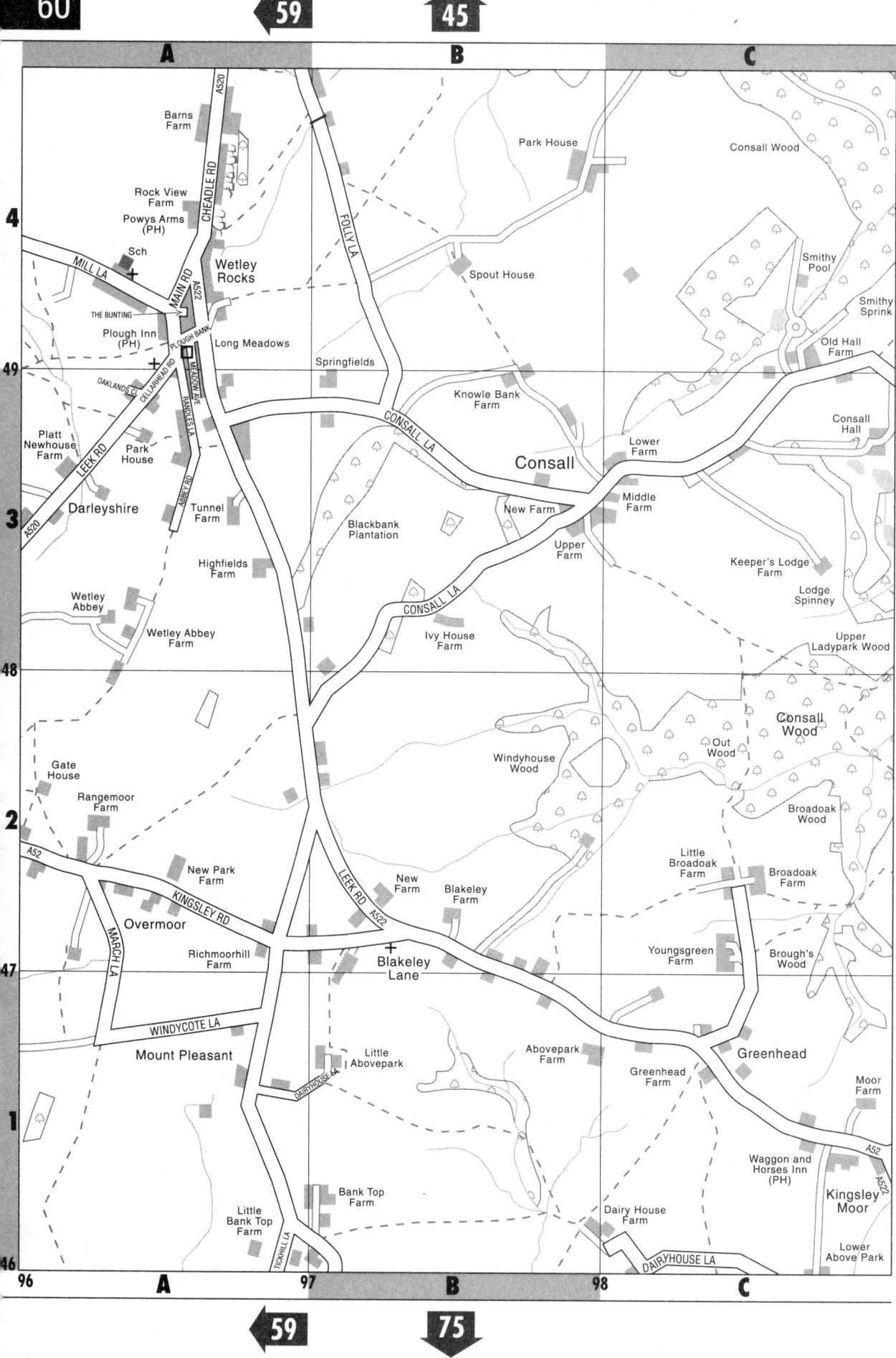

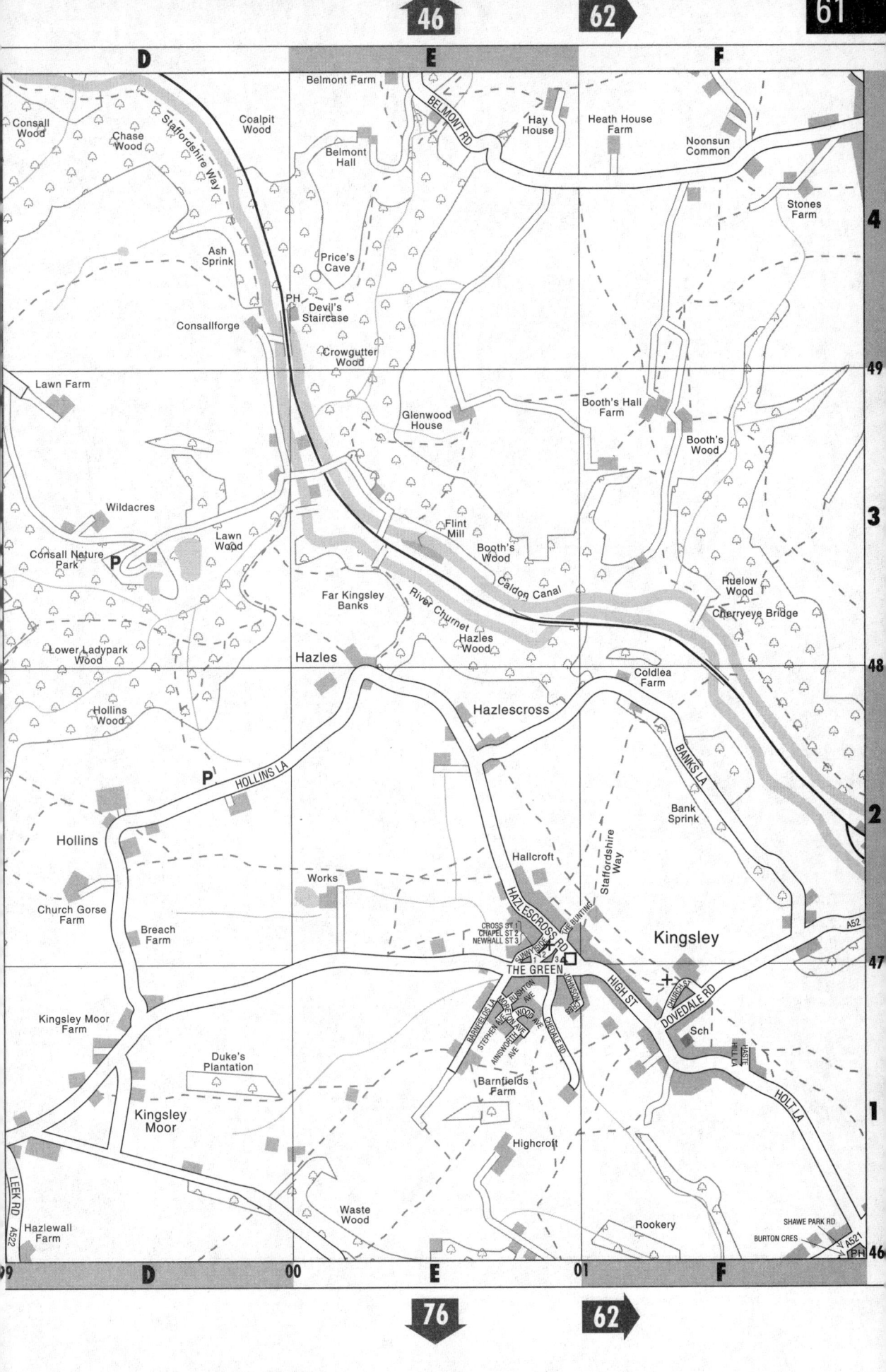

D
E
F

Consall
Wood

Chase
Wood

Coalpit
Wood

Belmont Farm

Staffordshire Way

Hay
House

Heath House
Farm

Noonsun
Common

Belmont
Hall

BELMONT RD

4

Stones
Farm

Price's
Cave

Ash
Sprink

PH

Devil's
Staircase

Consallforge

Crowgutter
Wood

49

Lawn Farm

Glenwood
House

Booth's Hall
Farm

Booth's
Wood

Wildacres

3

Lawn
Wood

Flint
Mill

Booth's
Wood

Ruelow
Wood

P

Consall Nature
Park

Far Kingsley
Banks

River Churnet

Caldon Canal

Cherryeye Bridge

Lower Ladypark
Wood

Hazles
Wood

Hazles

48

Coldlea
Farm

Hollins
Wood

Hazlescross

P

HOLLINS LA

BANKS LA

Hollins

Bank
Sprink

2

Church Gorse
Farm

Works

Hallcroft

Staffordshire Way

A52

Breach
Farm

CROSS ST 1
CHAPEL ST 2
NEWHALL ST 3

THE BUNTING

HAZLESCROSS RD

Kingsley

47

Kingsley Moor
Farm

THE GREEN

BARNFIELDS LA
STEPHEN AV
AINSWORTH
AVE
RUSHTON
WOOD AVE
CHEADLE RD
JOHNSON ST

HIGH ST

CHURCH ST

DOVEDALE RD

Sch

CASTLE
HILL LA

Duke's
Plantation

Barnfields
Farm

Kingsley
Moor

1

Highcroft

HOLT LA

Waste
Wood

Rookery

SHAWE PARK RD

LEEK RD
A522

Hazlewall
Farm

BURTON CRES

A521

PH

99
00
01
46

D
E
F

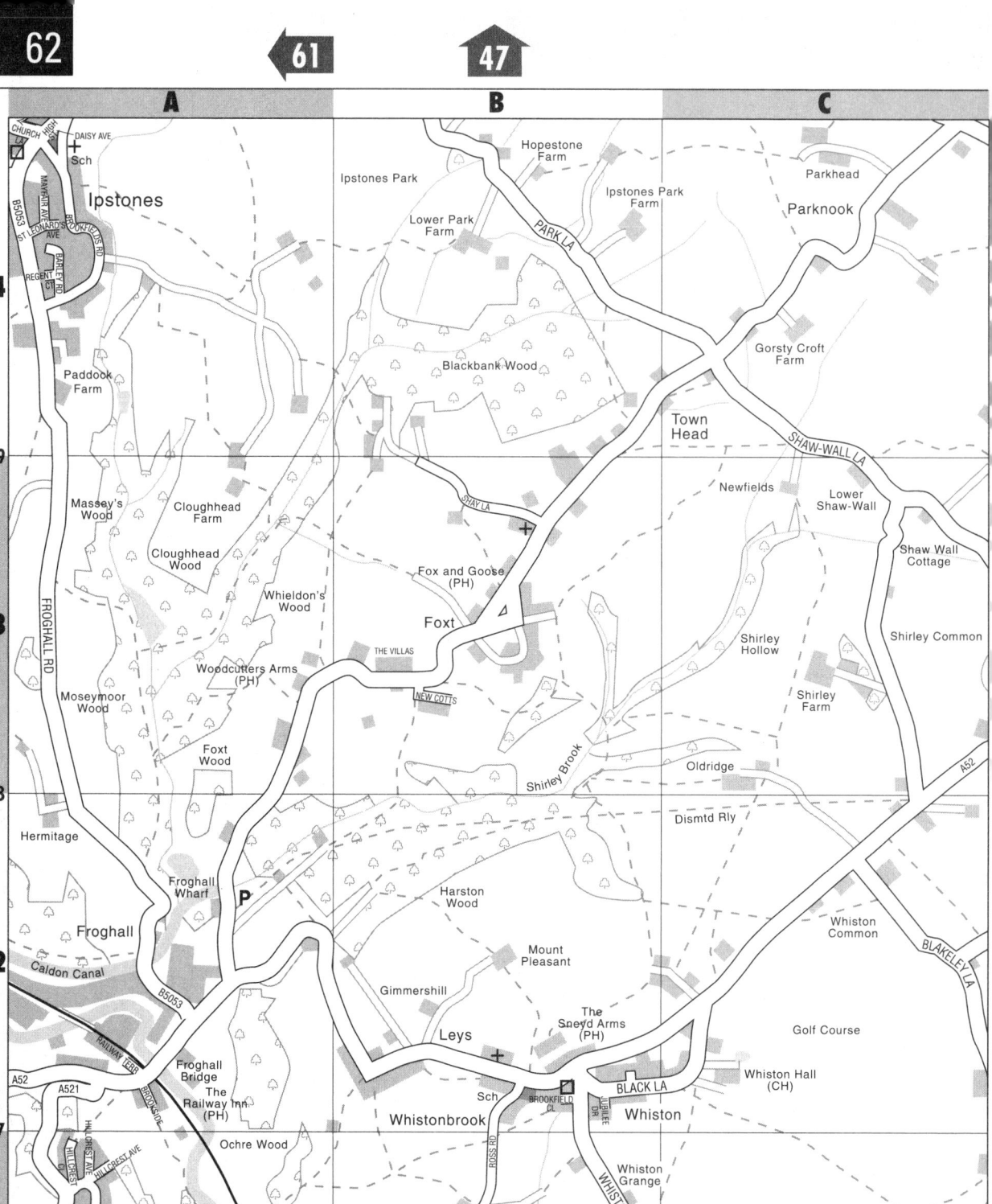

A B C

4

49

3

48

2

47

1

46

02 A 03 B 04 C

CHURCH HIGH
DAISY AVE
Sch
Ipstones
MAYFAIR RD
B5053
ST LEONARD AVE
BROOKFIELDS RD
BARLEY RD
REGENT CT
Paddock Farm
FROGHALL RD

Massey's Wood
Cloughhead Farm
Cloughhead Wood
Whieldon's Wood
Woodcutters Arms (PH)
Moseymoor Wood
Foxt Wood

Ipstones Park
Lower Park Farm
Hopestone Farm
Ipstones Park Farm
PARK LA
Blackbank Wood
Town Head
SHAY LA
Fox and Goose (PH)
Foxt
THE VILLAS
NEW COTTS
Shirley Brook

Parkhead
Parknook
Gorsty Croft Farm
SHAW-WALL LA
Newfields
Lower Shaw-Wall
Shaw Wall Cottage
Shirley Hollow
Shirley Common
Shirley Farm
Oldridge
A52

Hermitage
Froghall Wharf
P
Froghall
Caldon Canal
B5053
RAILWAY TERR
A52
A521
BROOKSIDE
Froghall Bridge
The Railway Inn (PH)
HILLCREST AVE
HILLCREST AVE
HILLCREST
SIDNEY AVE
CHURNET VALLEY RD
A521
LOCKWOOD CL
LOCKWOOD RD
Bank Top
Kingsley Holt
Staffordshire Way
Whiston Bridge
Banktop Woods
River Churnet
Hag Wood
Well Wood
Ochre Wood

Harston Wood
Mount Pleasant
Gimmershill
Leys
Sch
BROOKFIELD CL
Whistonbrook
ROSS RD
Ross Lane
Eavesford
Heath House
Littleheath Houses

The Sneyd Arms (PH)
BLACK LA
Whiston Hall (CH)
Whiston
JUBILEE DR
WHISTON EAVES LA
Whiston Grange
Whiston Eaves

Dismtd Rly
Whiston Common
Golf Course
BLAKELEY LA
Whiston Barn
Black Plantation
Moneystone Quarry
EAVES LA

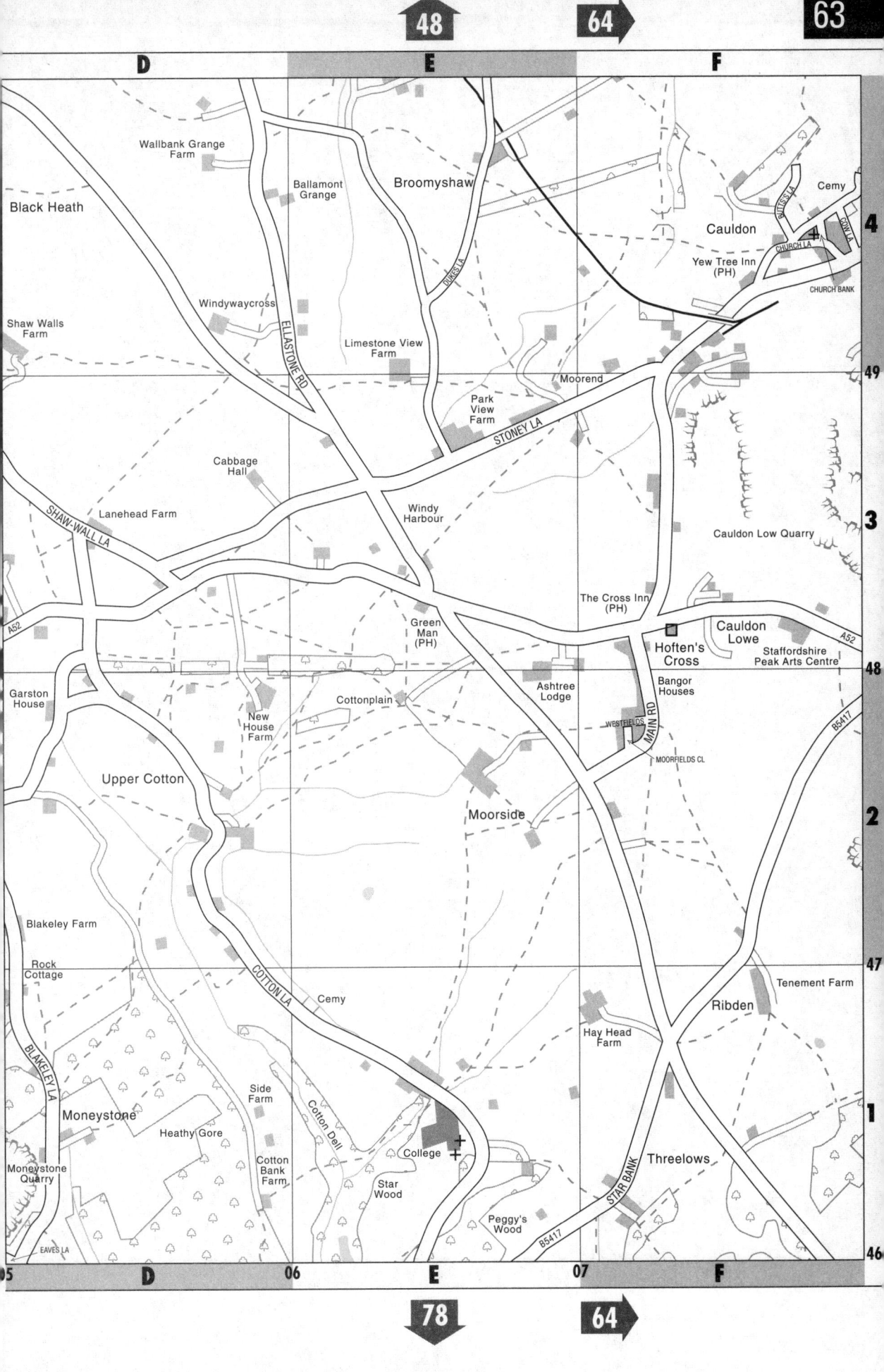

D E F

Wallbank Grange Farm

Ballamont Grange

Broomyshaw

Cemy

Cauldon

Black Heath

4

Yew Tree Inn (PH)

CHURCH LA

CHURCH BANK

Windywaycross

ELLASTONE RD

Limestone View Farm

Moorend

49

Shaw Walls Farm

DUKES LA

Park View Farm

STONEY LA

Cabbage Hall

Lanehead Farm

Windy Harbour

Cauldon Low Quarry

3

SHAW-WALL LA

The Cross Inn (PH)

Green Man (PH)

Cauldon Lowe

A52

Staffordshire Peak Arts Centre

48

Garston House

Hoften's Cross

Cottonplain

Ashtree Lodge

Bangor Houses

WESTFIELDS

MAIN RD

B5417

New House Farm

MOORFIELDS CL

Upper Cotton

Moorside

2

Blakeley Farm

Rock Cottage

47

Cemy

COTTON LA

Ribden

Tenement Farm

BLAKELEY LA

Side Farm

Hay Head Farm

Moneystone

Cotton Dell

Heathy Gore

Moneystone Quarry

Cotton Bank Farm

College

Star Wood

STAR BANK

Threelows

1

EAVES LA

Peggy's Wood

B5417

46

05

D 06 E 07 F

GREEN LA

A

B

C

Works

Middlehills Farm

EARLSWAY

Cauldon

Stoney Rock Farm

Broadhurst Farm

Milk Hill

A523

Field House Farm

Heath House

COMMON LA

Daisy Bank Farm

4

Huddale Lane

Huddale Farm

Miles Knoll

49

A523

Caldon Low

Quarry

Quarry

The Dale

Dale Lane

Walker's Barn

3

Quarry

Dale Farm

Dale Tor

Stanton Dale Farm

Dale Abbey Farm

A52

48

A52

B5417

Rue Hill

DALE LA

Red House

Wardlow

Quarry

2

Walk Farm

Wetside Lane

47

Quarry

Wredon

Weaver Farm

Softlow Wood

1

The Walk

Weaver Hills

46

Raddlepits

08

A

09

B

10

C

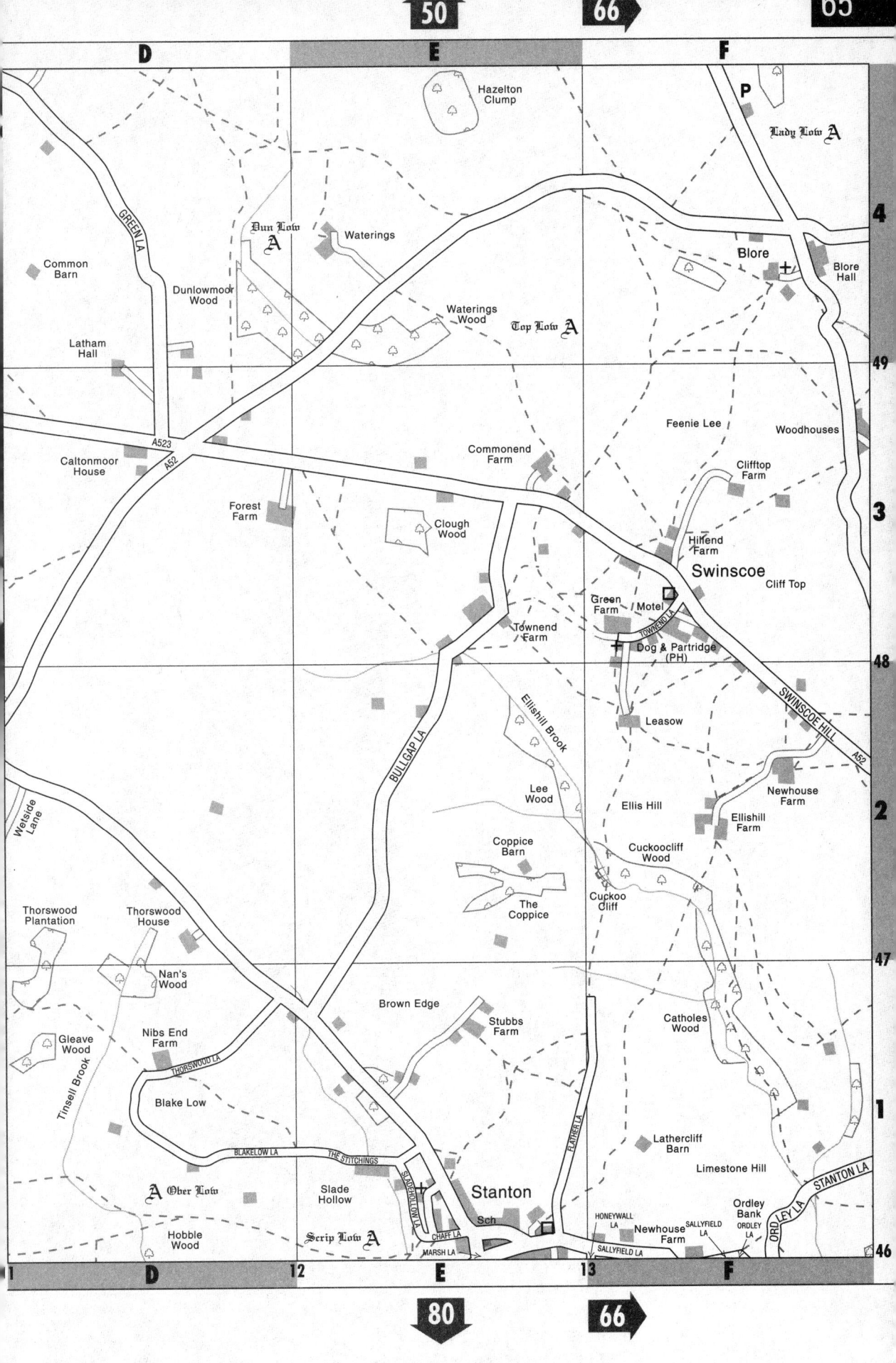

D E F

P

Lady Low A

Hazelton
Clump

Dun Low
A

Waterings

Blore

Blore
Hall

4

Common
Barn

Dunlowmoor
Wood

GREEN LA

Waterings
Wood

Top Low A

Feenie Lee

Woodhouses

49

Latham
Hall

Clifftop
Farm

Caltonmoor
House

A523

A52

Commonend
Farm

Hilfend
Farm

Swinscoe

Cliff Top

3

Forest
Farm

Clough
Wood

Green
Farm

Motel

Townend
Farm

Dog & Partridge
(PH)

SWINSCOE HILL

A52

48

Ellishill Brook

Leasow

BULLGAP LA

Lee
Wood

Ellis Hill

Newhouse
Farm

2

Wetside
Lane

Coppice
Barn

Cuckoocliff
Wood

Ellishill
Farm

Thorswood
Plantation

Thorswood
House

Nan's
Wood

The
Coppice

Cuckoo
Cliff

47

Brown Edge

Stubbs
Farm

Catholes
Wood

Gleave
Wood

Nibs End
Farm

THORSWOOD LA

Tinsell Brook

Blake Low

RATHER LA

Latherscliff
Barn

1

BLAKELOW LA

THE STITCHINGS

SLADEHOLLOW LA

Limestone Hill

A Ober Low

Slade
Hollow

Stanton

Sch

HONEYWALL
LA

Newhouse
Farm

SALLYFIELD
LA

Ordley
Bank

ORDLEY
LA

STANTON LA

Hobble
Wood

Scrip Low A

CHAFF LA

MARSH LA

SALLYFIELD LA

ORDLEY

46

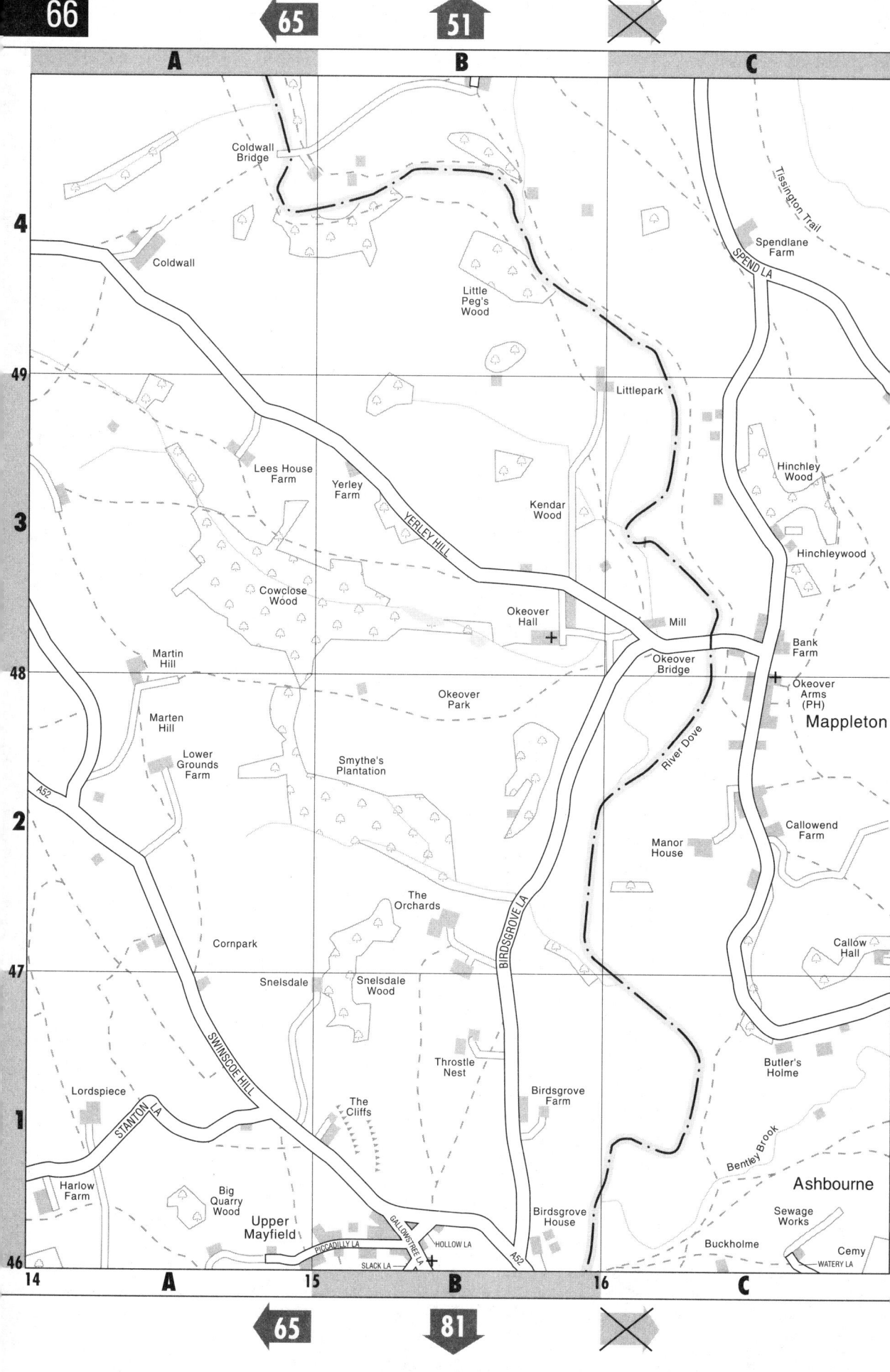

65
51

A   B   C

Coldwall Bridge

4

Coldwall

Little Peg's Wood

Spendlane Farm

SPEND LA

Tissington Trail

49

Littlepark

Hinchley Wood

Lees House Farm

Yerley Farm

YERLEY HILL

Kendar Wood

Hinchleywood

3

Cowclose Wood

Okeover Hall

Mill

Bank Farm

Martin Hill

Okeover Bridge

Okeover Arms (PH)

48

Marten Hill

Okeover Park

River Dove

Mappleton

Lower Grounds Farm

Smythe's Plantation

Manor House

Callowend Farm

2

Cornpark

The Orchards

BIRDSGROVE LA

Callow Hall

47

Snelsdale

Snelsdale Wood

Throstle Nest

Butler's Holme

Lordspiece

The Cliffs

Birdsgrove Farm

Bentley Brook

1

STANTON LA

SWINSCOE HILL

Ashbourne

Harlow Farm

Big Quarry Wood

Upper Mayfield

GALLOWSTREE LA

PICCADILLY LA

HOLLOW LA

SLACK LA

Birdsgrove House

A52

Buckholme

Sewage Works

Cemy
WATERY LA

46

14   A   15   B   16   C

A52

A
B
C

Wrinehill
Hall

River Lea

Higher
Thornhill

BOWSEY WOOD RD

WOODLAND
HILLS

WOODLAND HILLS

Madeley
Manor

HIGHLEY CASTLE WAY

PARK CL

Manor Park
Farm

COLLEGE CL

Little
Madeley

Park
House

A525

4

Windy
Arbour

Lowermill
House

Grafton's
Wood

The Lum

NEW RD

WOODSIDE

THORNHILL
DR

HOLLY OAK DR

ROSEBERRY WAY

CINDERS WAY

PETTOM

SALISBURY
WAY

KINGSTON

BECK RD

ZINGFISHER

NEWCASTLE RD

Wrinehill
Wood

ARBOUR CL

CEDAR GR

MEADOWS RD

Middle
Madeley

45

Bowerend

THE HILL PATH

PEAR TREE
DR

APPLECROFT

HEATHER DENE

FERN DENE

BRAMBLE

THE
CLOSE

FURNACE LA

BEVAN PL

RIVER LEA
MEWS

Sch

Moss House
Farm

PRIMROSE
DELL

CLOVER
PL

PLUM CROFT

CHARLES

PLUMTREE

POOLSIDE

PH

45

Beechfields

BOWER END LA

MOSS LA

JOHN OFFLEY RD

MERLIN
GREEN

CHERRY
TREE

GRAYLING

WILLOWS

Madeley

3

Wood
Farm

Moor Hall
Farm

MAYPOLE ST

BRAMBLE
LEA

BIRCH DALE

LAVEROCK

PASTORAL CT

KNIGHTLEY

HUNGERFORD LA

3

Beech Wood

ISAAC WALTON
WAY

Sch

THE HOLBORN

VICARAGE
LA

CASTLE LA

POST OFFICE
SQ

Birches
Farm

44

ONNELEY LA

Yewtree
Farm

Barhill
Wood

Sandfield
House

Monument

STATION RD

NETHERSET HEY LA

Works

44

Field
House

Bar Hill

Bar Hill
House Farm

River Lea

2

Golf Course

Bar Hill
Farm

BAR HILL

Red Lane

MANOR RD

Cemy

2

Wheatsheaf Inn
(PH)

CH

Hey House

NEWCASTLE
RD

A525

Upper Bitterns
Wood

43

Onneley

Manor
Farm

43

Peak's Farm

STATION RD

Lower Bitterns
Wood

Onneley Hall
Farm

New
Terrace

1

1

Dismantled Railway

Old Madeley
Manor
(remains of)

Lea Head
Manor

Aston Cliff

42

42

75
A
76
B
77
C

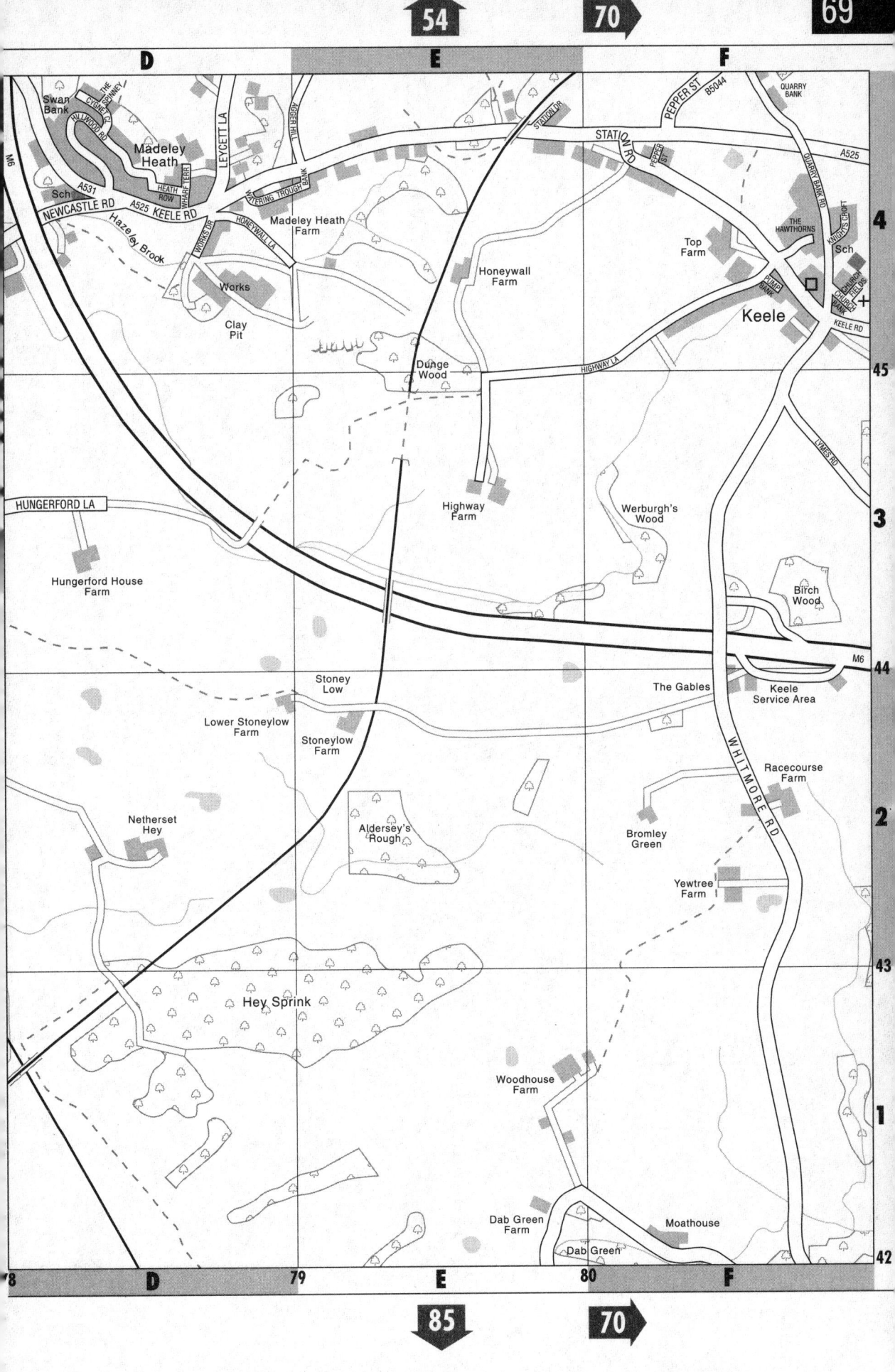

D
E
F

Swan Bank

THE SPINNEY

Madeley Heath

M6

HILLWOOD RD

CYGNET CT

LEYCETT LA

AGGER HILL

STATION DR

STATION RD

PEPPER ST

B5044

QUARRY BANK

A525

Sch

A531

HEATH ROW

WHARF TERR

KEELE RD

A525

NEWCASTLE RD

WATERING TROUGH BANK

Madeley Heath Farm

Honeywall Farm

PEPPER ST

Top Farm

THE HAWTHORNS

QUARRY BANK RD

Sch

KNIGHTS COURT

CHURCH FIELDS

4

Haze ley Brook

WORKS DR

HONEYWALL LA

Keele

PUMP BANK

CHURCH BANK

KEELE RD

+

Works

Clay Pit

Dunge Wood

HIGHWAY LA

45

LYMES RD

HUNGERFORD LA

Highway Farm

Werburgh's Wood

3

Hungerford House Farm

Birch Wood

M6

44

Stoney Low

The Gables

Keele Service Area

Lower Stoneylow Farm

Stoneylow Farm

WHITMORE RD

Racecourse Farm

Netherset Hey

Aldersey's Rough

Bromley Green

2

Yewtree Farm

43

Hey Sprink

Woodhouse Farm

1

Dab Green Farm

Moathouse

Dab Green

42

8
D
79
E
80
F

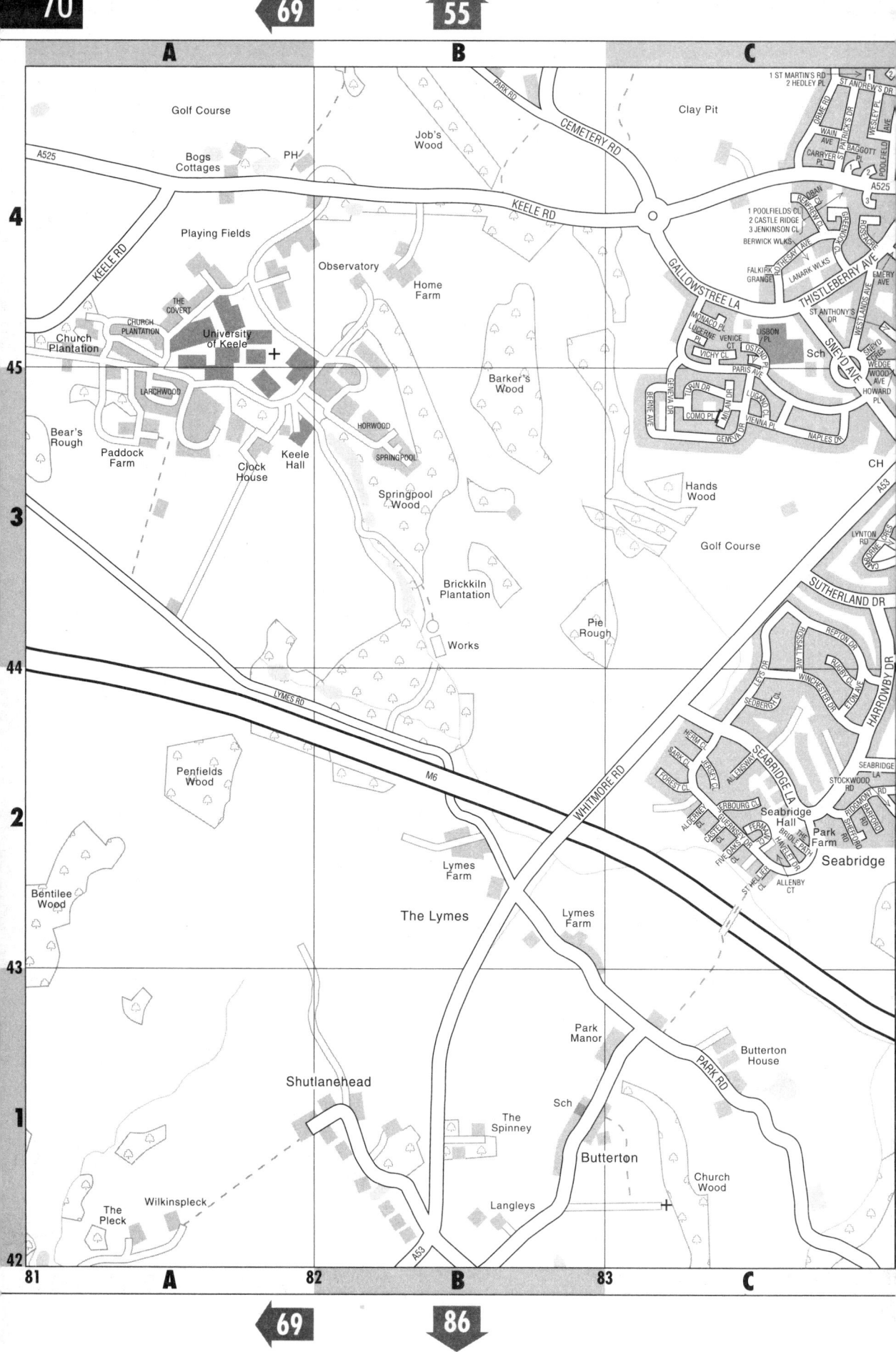

A   B   C

Golf Course

Clay Pit

1 ST MARTIN'S RD
2 HEDLEY PL

ST ANDREW'S DR

CEMETERY RD

Job's
Wood

PARK RD

Bogs
Cottages

PH

A525

KEELE RD

1 POOLFIELDS CL
2 CASTLE RIDGE
3 JENKINSON CL

BERWICK WLKS

4

Playing Fields

Observatory

Home
Farm

FALKIRK
GRANGE

GALLOWSTREE LA

THISTLEBERRY AVE

EMERY
AVE

THE
COVERT

CHURCH
PLANTATION

University
of Keele

St ANTHONY'S DR

Sch

WESTLANDS AVE

SNEYD AVE

Church
Plantation

45

LARCHWOOD

+

Barker's
Wood

PARIS AVE

VICHY CL

HOWARD
PL

WEDGE
WOOD
AVE

Bear's
Rough

HORWOOD

GENEVA DR

BERNE AVE

COMO PL

VIENNA PL

NAPLES DR

CH

Paddock
Farm

Clock
House

Keele
Hall

SPRINGPOOL

Springpool
Wood

GOLF Course

LYNTON
RD

3

SUTHERLAND DR

Brickkiln
Plantation

Pie
Rough

Hands
Wood

REPTON DR

HARROWBY DR

Works

44

LYMES RD

SEDBERGH

WINCHESTER DR

SEABRIDGE
LA

SEABRIDGE
LA

Penfields
Wood

M6

STOCKWOOD
RD

2

Lymes
Farm

Seabridge
Hall

Park
Farm

Seabridge

Bentilee
Wood

WHITMORE RD

The Lymes

Lymes
Farm

ST HELIER

ALLENBY
CT

43

A53

Park
Manor

Butterton
House

PARK RD

Shutlanehead

The
Spinney

Sch

1

Butterton

Church
Wood

+

The
Pleck

Wilkinspleck

Langleys

A53

42

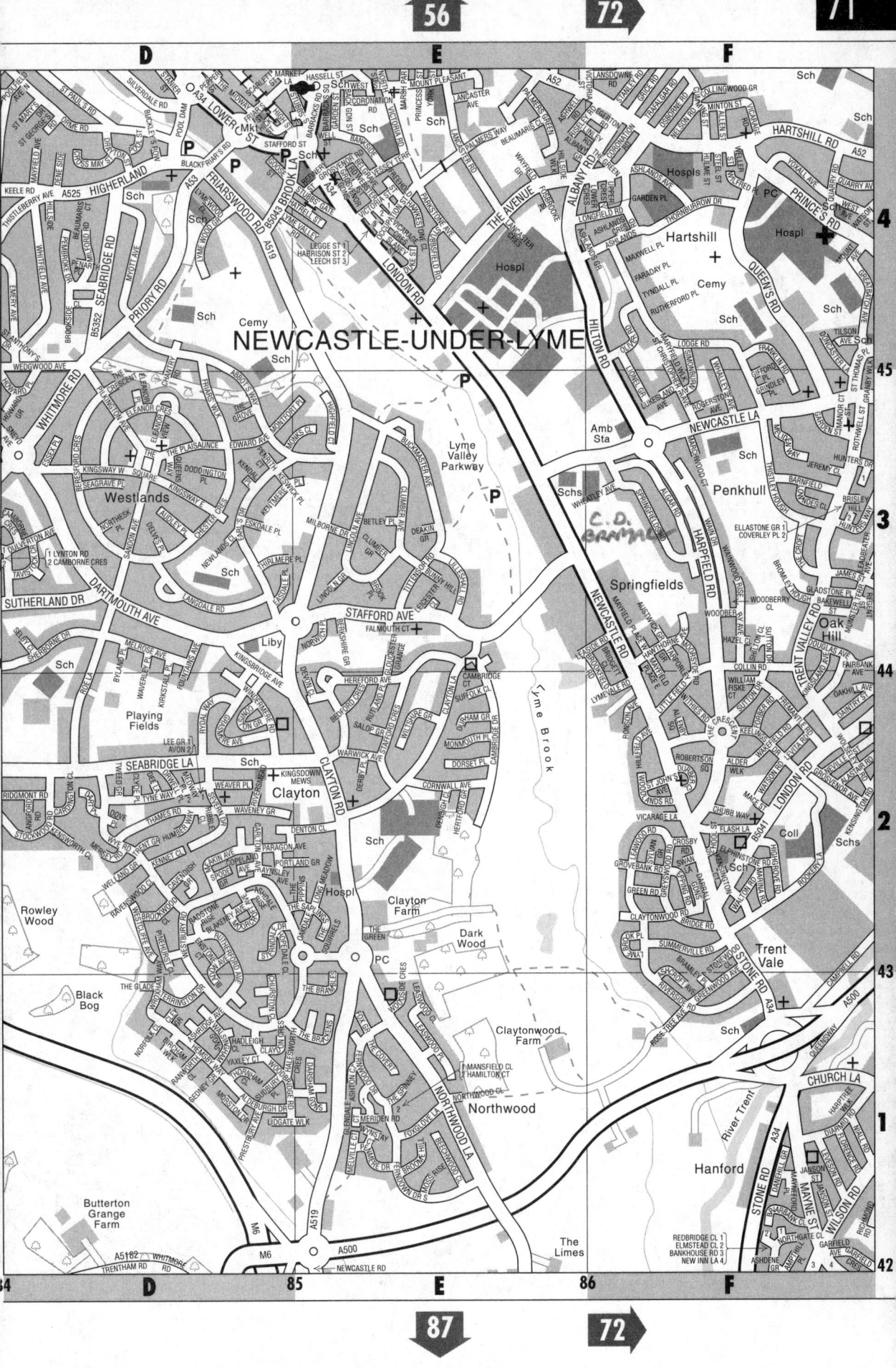

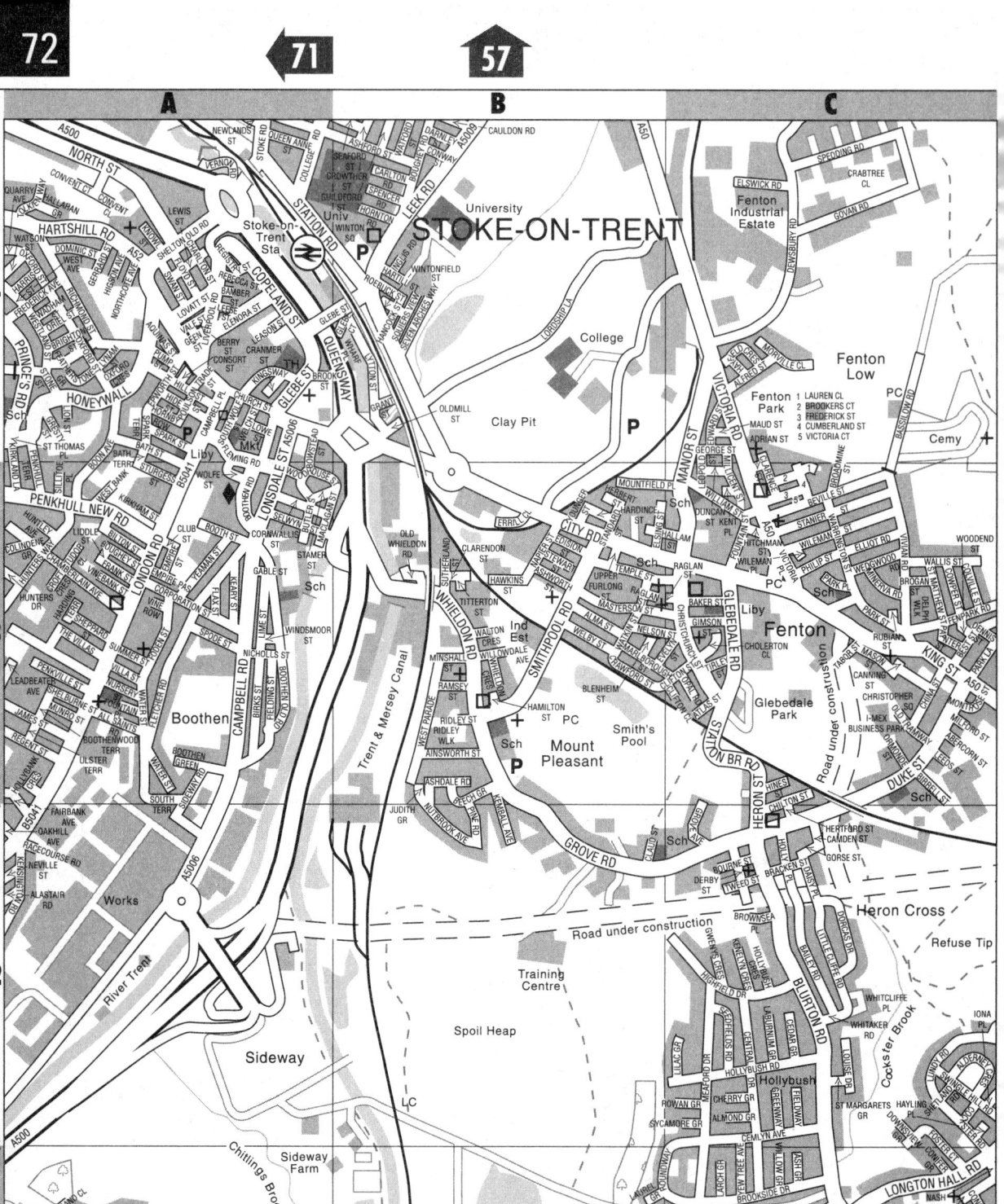

A **B** **C**

Stonehouse Farm

HULME LA

Hulme

The Candlesticks (PH)

HULME RD

Hall Farm

4

Winterfield Farm

WINTERFIELD LA

MALTHOUSE LA

SALTERS LA

Malthouse Farm

A520

Captain's Barn

Creswell's Piece

Smallbrook Farm

LEEK RD

Blythe Lea

Ford

Sheepwash Farm

Sheepwash

45

Ward Hill Farm

PC

P

Boltongate Farm

PC

Parkhall Country Park

3

P

Roughcote

Tickhill Farm

Hardiwick Farm

CARNATION CL

DAHLIA CL

ASTER CL

EAST ST

LYNN ST

SEL BY ST

COALVILLE PL

FERN FA GR

COUPE DR

HORTON DR

ENGLESEA AVE

OSWALD AVE

FLINT ST

IRIS CL

LILAC CL

LIME CL

LAVENDER CL

River Blithe

ROUGHCOTE LA

Caverswall Common

Cocking Farm

TICKHILL LA

HANDLEY BANKS

FOXGLOVE CL

WEST ST

DIMMELOW ST

CAT ST

Sch

THE CLOSE

Weston Coyney

PARK HALL RD

B5040

HEATHCOTE

WELDON AVE

STRATFORD RD

HAYCHEAD CRES

Heysham Cl

44

PARK HALL RD

TAME WLK

Sch

MANNIN GR

ROSS RD

IBSEN RD

GEOFFREY

PARK HALL CRES

WESTON DR

THE MOAT

HALL DR

CAVERSWALL RD

HAYNER GR

FITZGERALD CL

PALAZ

NEW KINGSWAY

QUEENS WLK

FIELD VIEW

CRES

AVE

Intakes Farm

Green Farm

2

WESTON COYNEY RD

Parkhead Gr

Weston Sprink

PARTON GR

PARKHEAD DR

PADWORTH ST

PARKNAME CRES

COYNEY GR

SPRINKWOOD

WESTON RD

MACDONALD CRES

Sch

PRINCESS WAY

DALE VIEW

DAWN VIEW

VALLEY

KINGS CRES

YORK RD

TERRY CL

MICHAEL CL

BRINDON CL

MYRTLE AVE

LANSBURY GR

Cookshill

THE GREEN

HALL DEARN

HONG

NATHAN CL

MILL CL

Cookshill Hall

TREVOR DR

VICARAGE

Yewtree Farm

Tunstall Sytch

43

WHITCOMBE RD

THE GRANGE

DENEHURST CL

BROADWAY

CHERRY HILL

OAK PL

BROOKHOUSE

BROWNFIELD ROAD

WESTWOOD ROAD

HARV CL

TILLET GREEN

GOODWIN RD

BRD

SNOWDEN

HENDERSON

COMBER

BURNS

BONDFIELD ROW

BLATCHFORD

WOOD CL

STANSMORE RD

MAPLE

THE SQUARE

LEA PL

MAXTON WAY

BROOKWOOD DR

MONTGOMERY

TAWNEY

BEVERIDGE

THE WOOD

SCHOOL LA

HIGH ST

THE SQUARE

THE DAMS

Castle

Caverswall

Sch

CHURCH TERR

DILHORNE LA

The Red House PH

1

OAK PL

TONMARSH

GIBSON RD

BRIGHT ST

CORNELIUS ST

EAST GR

YARFIELD PL

ROWNALL PL

ROWNALL

PEMBER

KINGSLEY

SOUTH WAY

TIPPING

BERCHT

OAKWOOD CL

MEADWAY

PINEWOOD CL

BRIARWOOD PL

GREENWOODS PL

Sch

Wood House Farm

Caverswall Park

WILLOWOOD GR

CAVERSWALL LA

BLYTHE BRIDGE RD

Foxfield Steam Railway

Meir

UTTOXETER RD

GEORGE AVE

LYME RD

A50

LC

42

P

PICKFORD PL

SARACEN WAY

PC

P

EDNAM

GRANGEWOOD

CARTWRIGHT

HARDWOOD CL

BROADWOOD

PEMBERTON

STANTON RD

1 CHATSWORTH PL
2 CROSSLAND PL W
3 COBHAM PL

APPLEWOOD CRES

RAVENHURST AVE

A50

93 **A** **94** **B** **95** **C**

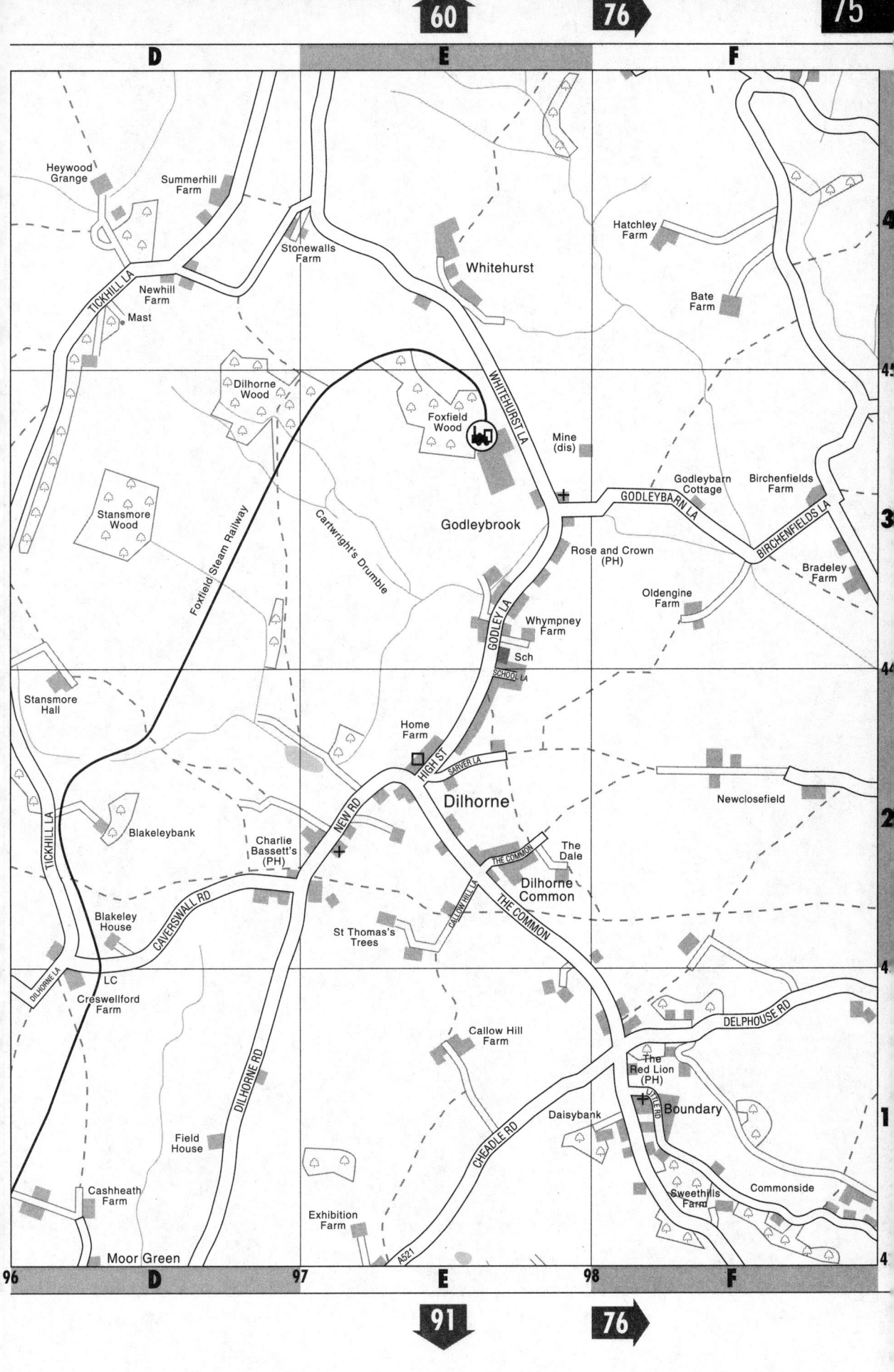

D
E
F

Heywood
Grange

Summerhill
Farm

TICKHILL LA

Newhill
Farm

Mast

Stonewalls
Farm

Whitehurst

Hatchley
Farm

Bate
Farm

Dilhorne
Wood

Foxfield
Wood

WHITEHURST LA

Mine
(dis)

Godleybarn
Cottage

Birchenfields
Farm

Stansmore
Wood

Cartwright's Drumble

Godleybrook

GODLEYBARN LA

BIRCHENFIELDS LA

Foxfield Steam Railway

Rose and Crown
(PH)

Bradeley
Farm

Oldengine
Farm

GODLEY LA

Whympney
Farm

Sch

SCHOOL LA

Stansmore
Hall

Home
Farm

HIGH ST

SARVER LA

Newclosefield

TICKHILL LA

Blakeleybank

Charlie
Bassett's
(PH)

NEW RD

Dilhorne

The
Dale

THE COMMON

Dilhorne
Common

CALLOW HILL LA

Blakeley
House

CAVERSWALL RD

St Thomas's
Trees

THE COMMON

DELPHOUSE RD

DILHORNE LA

LC

Creswellford
Farm

Callow Hill
Farm

DILHORNE RD

The
Red Lion
(PH)

WHITE RD

Boundary

Daisybank

Commonside

Field
House

CREADLE RD

Sweethills
Farm

Cashheath
Farm

Moor Green

Exhibition
Farm

A521

96
D
97
E
98
F

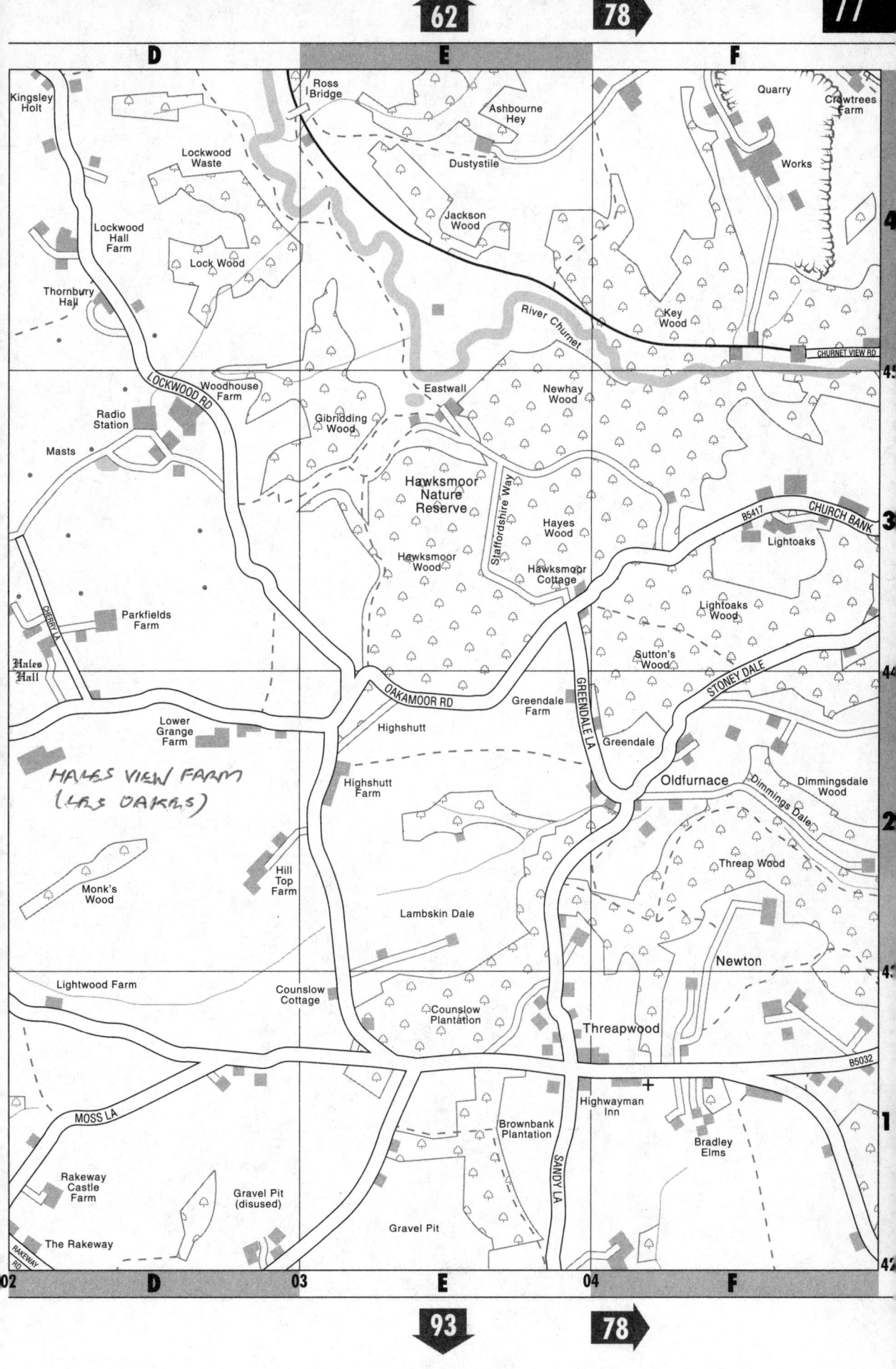

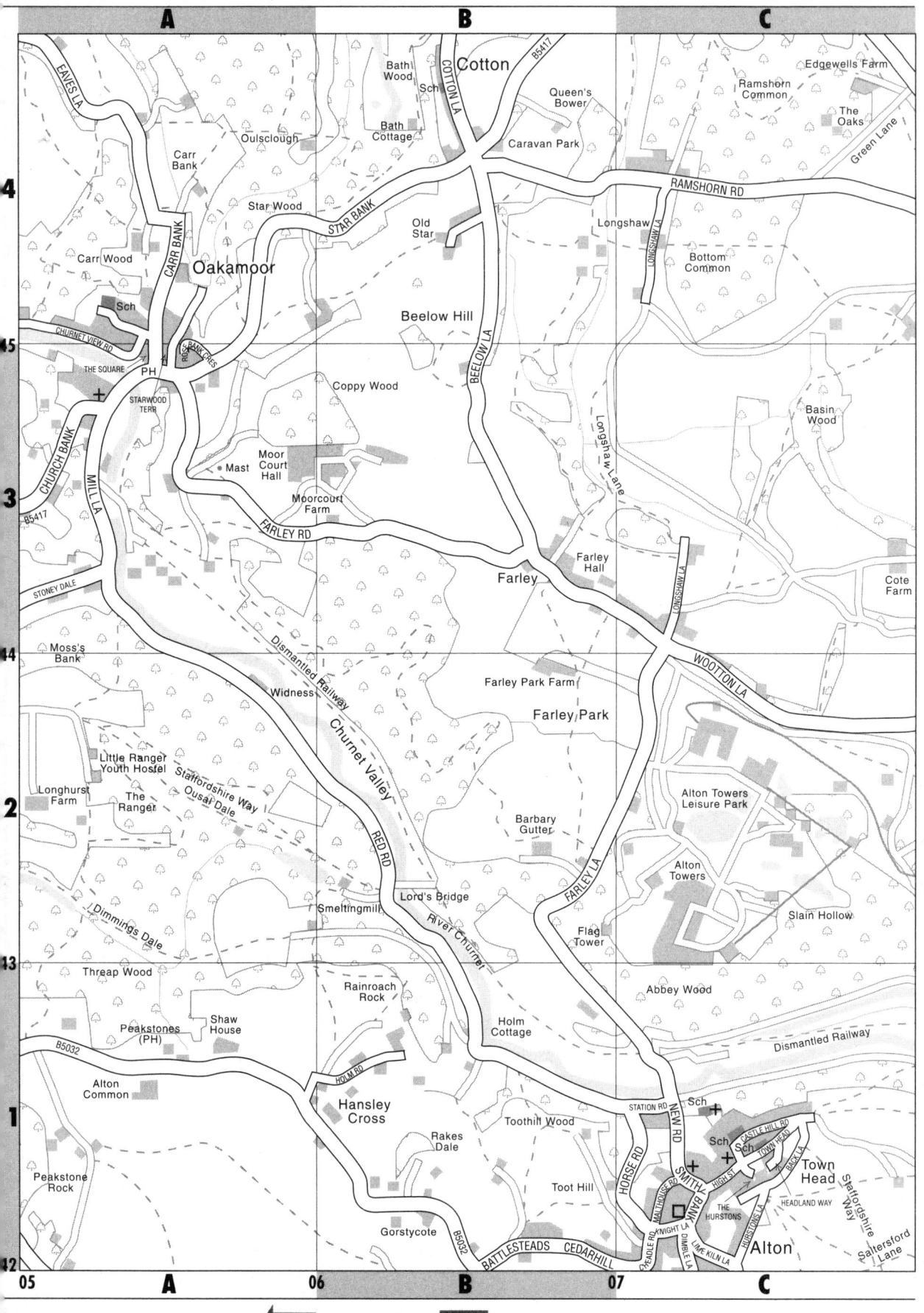

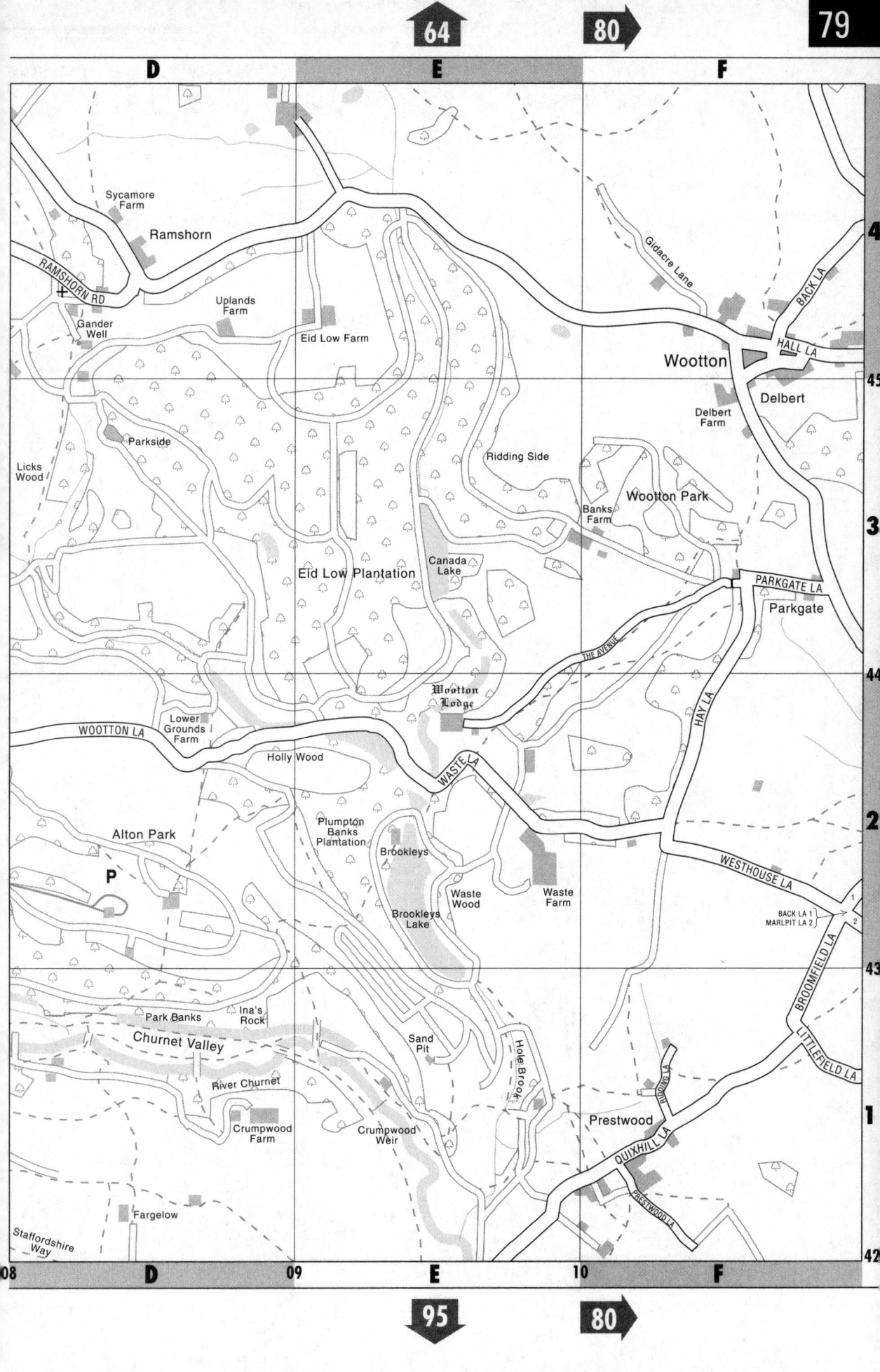

D E F

Sycamore Farm

Ramshorn

RAMSHORN RD

Gander Well

Uplands Farm

Eid Low Farm

Gidacre Lane

BACK LA

Wootton

HALL LA

Delbert

Delbert Farm

Licks Wood

Parkside

Ridding Side

Wootton Park

Banks Farm

Eid Low Plantation

Canada Lake

PARKGATE LA

Parkgate

THE AVENUE

Wootton Lodge

HAY LA

WOOTTON LA

Lower Grounds Farm

Holly Wood

WASTE LA

Plumpton Banks Plantation

Brookleys

Waste Wood

Waste Farm

WESTHOUSE LA

BACK LA 1
MARLPIT LA 2

Alton Park

P

Brookleys Lake

BROOMFIELD LA

LITTLEFIELD LA

Park Banks

Ina's Rock

Churnet Valley

River Churnet

Sand Pit

Hole Brook

RIDDING LA

Prestwood

QUIXHILL LA

Crumpwood Farm

Crumpwood Weir

PRESTWOOD LA

Fargelow

Staffordshire Way

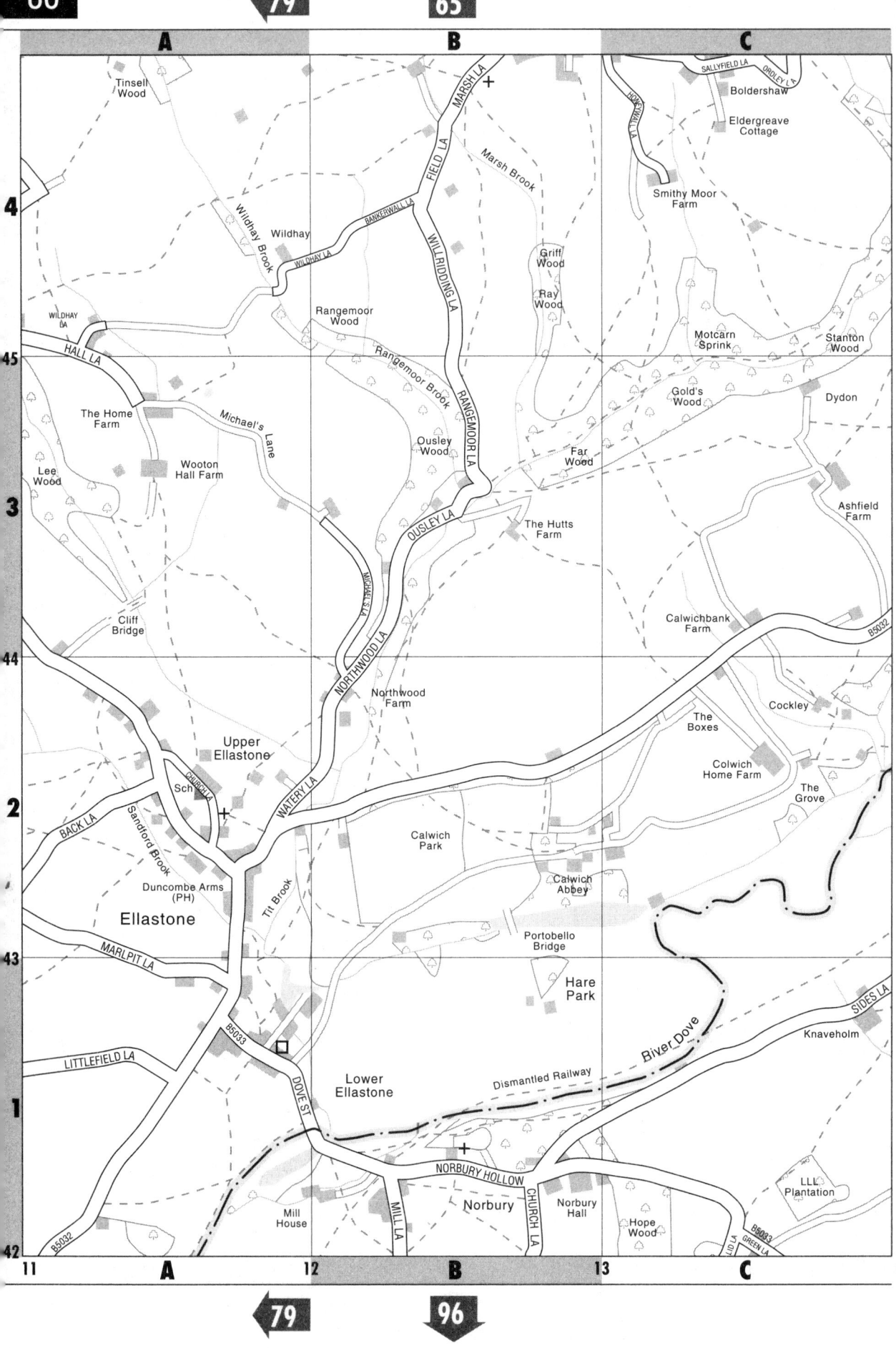

A

B

C

Tinsell Wood

MARSH LA

SALLYFIELD LA

ORDLEY LA

Boldershaw

HOPE WALL LA

Eldergreave Cottage

4

Wildhay Brook

FIELD LA

Marsh Brook

Smithy Moor Farm

BANKERWALL LA

Wildhay

Wildhay

WILDHAY LA

WILRIDDING LA

Griff Wood

Motcarn Sprink

Stanton Wood

Rangemoor Wood

Ray Wood

45

WILDHAY LA

HALL LA

Rangemoor Brook

Gold's Wood

Dydon

The Home Farm

Michael's Lane

Ousley Wood

RANGEMOOR LA

Far Wood

Ashfield Farm

Lee Wood

Wooton Hall Farm

OUSLEY LA

The Hutts Farm

B5032

3

MICHAEL'S LA

Cliff Bridge

Calwichbank Farm

44

NORTHWOOD LA

Northwood Farm

Cockley

The Boxes

Upper Ellastone

Colwich Home Farm

The Grove

2

BACK LA

CHURCH LA

Sch

WATERY LA

Calwich Park

Duncombe Arms (PH)

Sandford Brook

Tit Brook

Calwich Abbey

Ellastone

Portobello Bridge

43

MARLPIT LA

Hare Park

River Dove

SIDES LA

Knaveholm

B5033

Dismantled Railway

LITTLEFIELD LA

DOVE ST

Lower Ellastone

LLL Plantation

1

NORBURY HOLLOW

MILL LA

Norbury

CHURCH LA

Norbury Hall

Hope Wood

B5033

B5032

Mill House

LID LA

GREEN LA

42

11

A

12

B

13

C

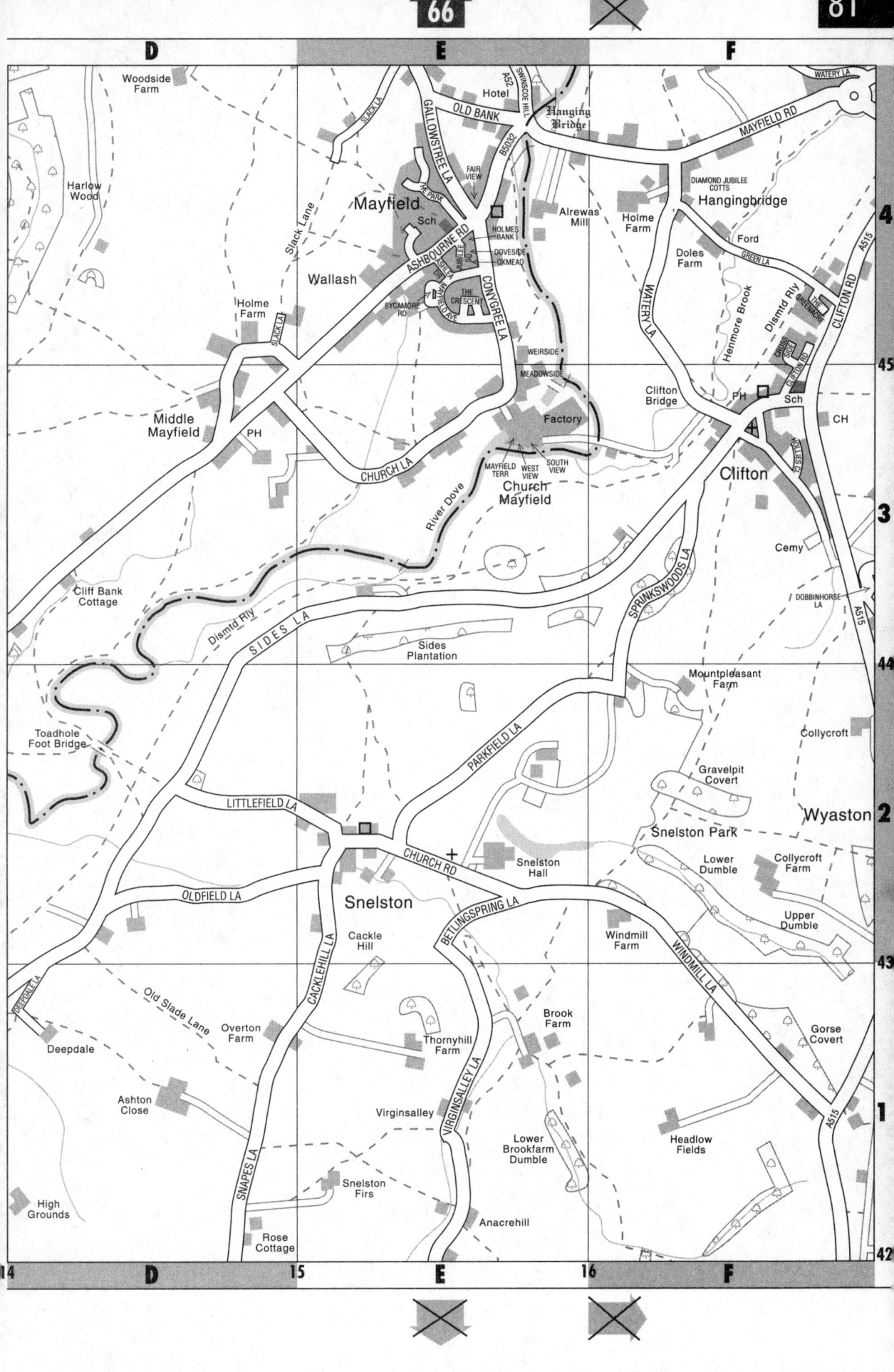

D

Woodside Farm

Harlow Wood

SLACK LA

Slack Lane

Holme Farm

SLACK LA

Middle Mayfield

PH

CHURCH LA

River Dove

Cliff Bank Cottage

Dismtd Rly

SIDES LA

Toadhole Foot Bridge

LITTLEFIELD LA

OLDFIELD LA

DEEPDALE LA

Old Slade Lane

Deepdale

Overton Farm

Ashton Close

SNAPES LA

High Grounds

E

Hotel

GALLOWSTREE LA

OLD BANK

A52

SWINSIDE HILL

B5032

THE PARK

Hanging Bridge

FAIR VIEW

Mayfield

Sch

ASHBOURNE RD

HOLMES BANK

Alrewas Mill

DOVESIDE

OXMEAD

Wallash

JUBILEE

SYCAMORE RD

THE CRESCENT

MAYFIELD DRIVE

CONYGREE LA

WEIRSIDE

MEADOWSIDE

Factory

MAYFIELD TERR

WEST VIEW

SOUTH VIEW

Church Mayfield

Sides Plantation

PARKFIELD LA

CACKLEHILL LA

CHURCH RD

Snelston

Cackle Hill

Snelston Hall

BETLINGSPRING LA

Thornyhill Farm

VIRGINSALLEY LA

Virginsalley

Snelston Firs

Rose Cottage

Anacrehill

Brook Farm

Lower Brookfarm Dumble

F

WATERY LA

MAYFIELD RD

DIAMOND JUBILEE COTTS

Hangingbridge

Holme Farm

Ford

Doles Farm

GREEN LA

Henmore Brook

Dismtd Rly

THE GREENMOR

CLIFTON RD

CROSS SIDE

CLIFTON RD

WATERY LA

Clifton Bridge

PH

Sch

CH

Clifton

FOYLES ST

Cemy

DOBBINHORSE LA

A515

SPRINKSWOODS LA

Mountpleasant Farm

Collycroft

Gravelpit Covert

Wyaston

Snelston Park

Lower Dumble

Collycroft Farm

Upper Dumble

Windmill Farm

WINDMILL LA

Gorse Covert

Headlow Fields

A515

4

45

3

44

2

43

1

42

14   **D**   15   **E**   16   **F**

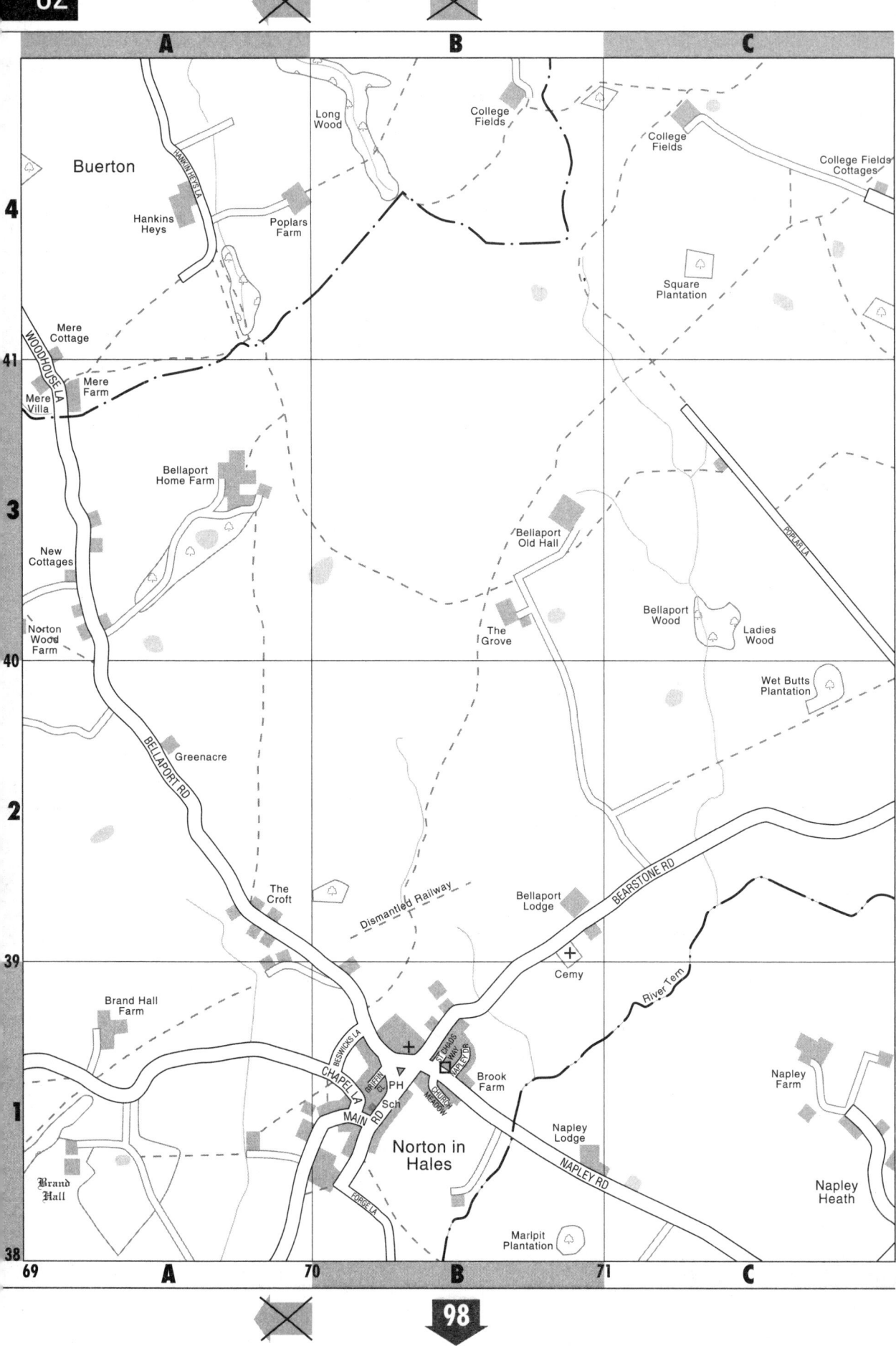

A   B   C

Buerton

Long Wood

College Fields

College Fields

College Fields Cottages

4

Hankins Heys

Poplars Farm

Square Plantation

Mere Cottage

WOODHOUSE LA

HANKINS LA

41

Mere Farm

Mere Villa

Bellaport Home Farm

POPLAR LA

3

New Cottages

Bellaport Old Hall

Bellaport Wood

Ladies Wood

Norton Wood Farm

The Grove

Bellaport Wood

40

Wet Butts Plantation

Greenacre

BELLAPORT RD

2

The Croft

Dismantled Railway

Bellaport Lodge

BEARSTONE RD

39

Cemy

River Tern

Brand Hall Farm

BESWICKS LA

CHAPEL LA

MAIN RD

FORGE LA

PH
Sch

ST CHADS WAY

CHURCH MEADOW

Brook Farm

Napley Farm

1

Napley Lodge

Brand Hall

Norton in Hales

NAPLEY RD

Napley Heath

38

Maripit Plantation

69   A   70   B   71   C

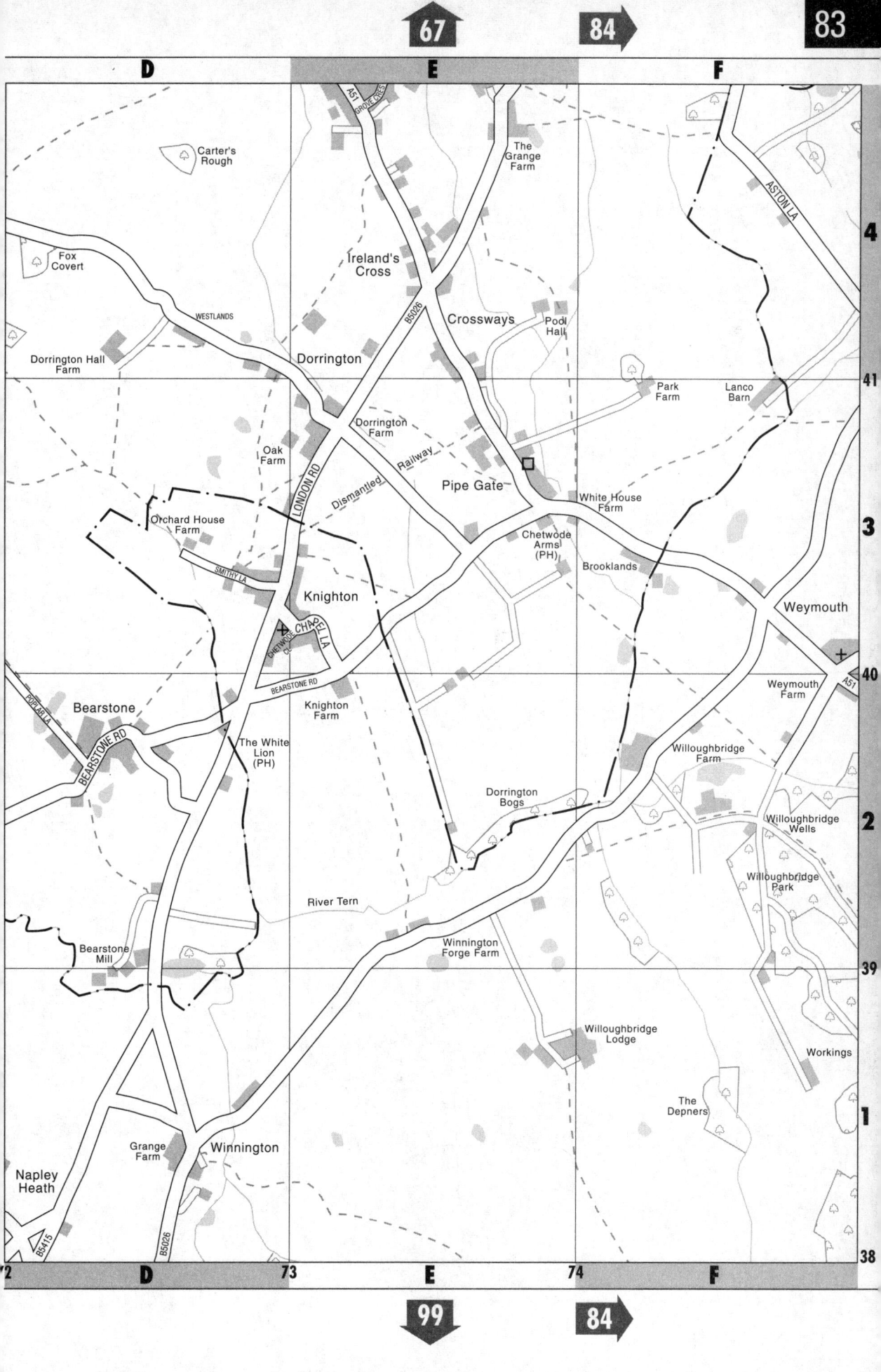

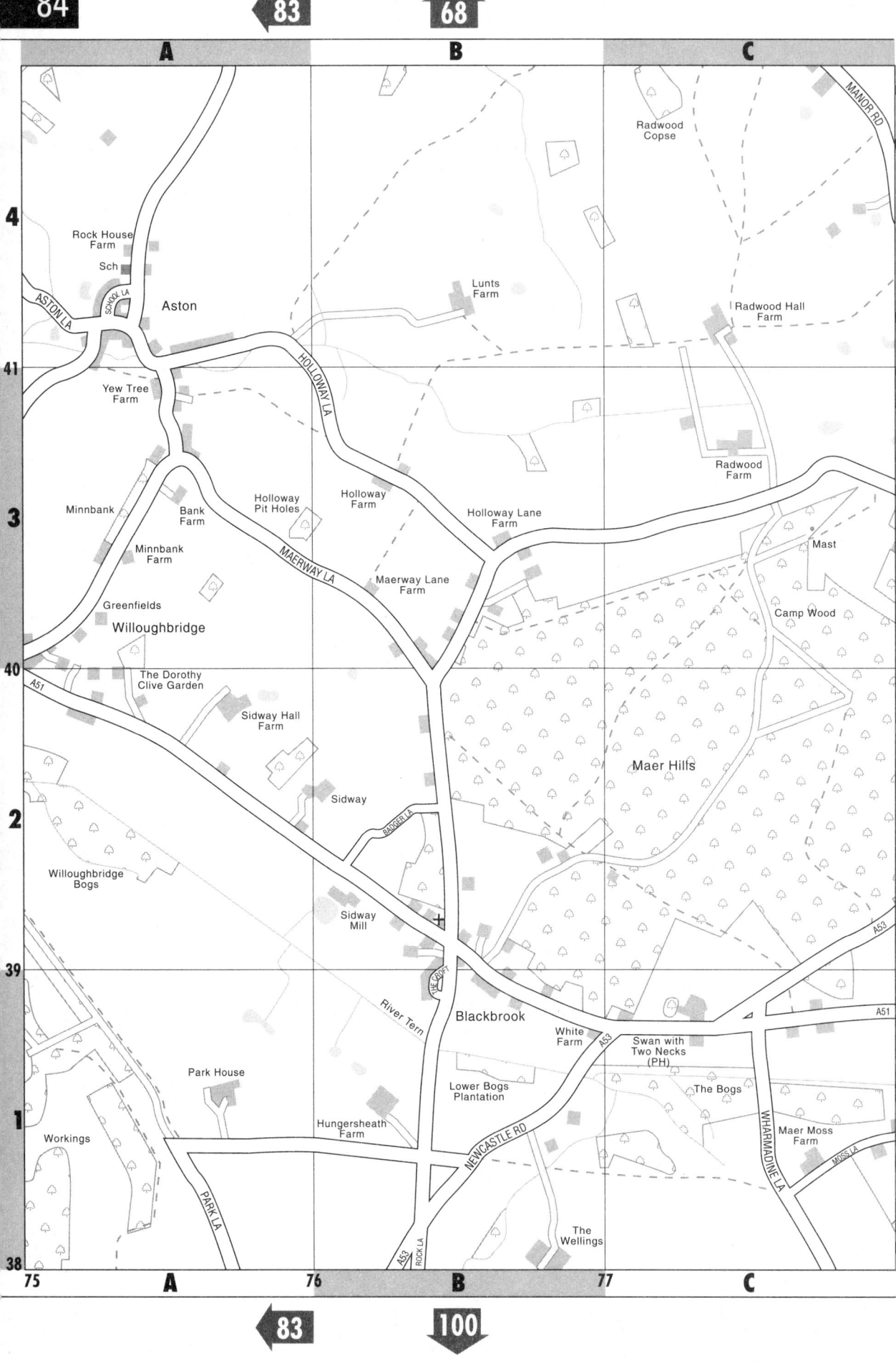

A   B   C

MANOR RD

Radwood
Copse

4

Rock House
Farm

Sch

ASTON LA

SCHOOL LA

Aston

Lunts
Farm

Radwood Hall
Farm

41

Yew Tree
Farm

HOLLOWAY LA

Radwood
Farm

3

Minnbank

Bank
Farm

Holloway
Pit Holes

Holloway
Farm

Holloway Lane
Farm

Mast

Minnbank
Farm

MAERWAY LA

Maerway Lane
Farm

Camp Wood

Greenfields

Willoughbridge

40

A51

The Dorothy
Clive Garden

Maer Hills

Sidway Hall
Farm

A53

2

Sidway

BADGER LA

Willoughbridge
Bogs

Sidway
Mill

A51

A53

39

THE CROFT

River Tern

Blackbrook

White
Farm

A53

Swan with
Two Necks
(PH)

Park House

Lower Bogs
Plantation

The Bogs

WHARMADINE LA

1

Workings

Hungersheath
Farm

NEWCASTLE RD

Maer Moss
Farm

MOSS LA

PARK LA

The
Wellings

A53

ROCK LA

38

75   A   76   B   77   C

D
E
F

Meat Wood

WHITMORE RD

Whitmore Wood

Hillside Lodge

Limepits

Hillside Farm

4

EASTWOOD RISE
PARK WOOD DR
SOUTH WOOD
MANOR GLADE

Madeley Park Farm

Snapehall Farm

SNAPE HALL RD

BIRCH TREE LA

Whitmore Heath

HEATH RD

WHITMORE RD

Sch

SANTRY LA

A53

41

Madeley Park Wood

Rectory

MANOR RD

New House Farm

White House

The Hill

Swallow Hill

Whitehouse Wood

Coney Greave

Meece Brook

3

Camp Hall

PH

STATION DRIVE

SPROT AVE

GATEWAY AVE

CONEYGREAVE LA

APPLETON DR

White House

Slymansdale

Sandyfields Estate

TOLLGATE AVE

MEADOW WAY

Sch

Shropshire's Wood

DALE CL

MOSS LA

40

Baldwin's Gate

Works

Chorlton Moss

Moss Farm

Maer Hills

WOODSIDE

SANDY LA

Bungalow Farm

2

Red Hill

Berry Hill

War Hill

Hill Chorlton

39

Berth Hill Fort

Maerfield Gate Farm

A51

Coombesdale

Coombe's Rough

Little Lane

MOSS LA

Maer Pool

HADDON LA

Broughton Plantation

1

The Ridding

Maer Hall

Maer

The Old Rectory

Bates Farm

38

85
70

A   B   C

PARK RD

A53

A5182

Holbrook's
Wood

New Hayes
Farm

Rock Hall
Farm

A5182

Acton Hall
Farm

TRENTHAM RD

4

Acton

WHITMORE RD

Whitmore
Hall

The
Rookery

WHISPER LA

Actonhill
Farm

Model
Farm

41

A53

Whitmore

Little
Paddocks

Hobgoblin
Gate

3

Newhouse
Farm

Hanchurch
Hills

Hanchurch
Heath

40

HARLEY THORN LA

Swynnerton
Old Park

Water
Tower

DRAYTON RD

Shelton under
Harley
Farm

P

2

Cloud
End

Byatt's
Common

Keepers
Cottage

Shelton
under
Harley

Springfields

Harley Thorns

DOG LA

39

Stableford
Bridge

Nursery
Common

A51

Cock Inn
(PH)

Stableford

STABLEFORD BANK

1

Common Lane

Rowe
Farm

Little
Lane

The Rowe

Hatton
Common

Hatton Rough

Bluebell
Bank

A51

38

TRENTHAM RD
A5182
M6
Junc 15
NEWCASTLE RD
NORTHWOOD LA
Turbine Farm
A34
BANKHOUSE RD
BRANDON GR
NEW INN LA
Cliff's Rough
B5038
WHITMORE RD
PLV.GR.
MORETON AVE
ASHENDEN GR 1
APLEY PL 2
JUBILEE RD
89 AVE
MARGARET AVE
ROMA RD
Sch
TURNBERRY DR

PEACOCK LA
HANCHURCH LA
Golf Course
Hargreaves Wood
FAIRWAY
THE GREENWAY
CHURCHILL WAY 1
TRENTHAM GARDENS CL 2
WESTERHAM CL 3
CONISTON PL 4
SWANTON PL 5
ROBINSON RD
PARKWOOD AVE
ALLERTON RD
Sch

4

Hanchurch Plantation
Hanchurch
A519
RIDDING BANK
Hargreaves Pool
THE PARKWAY
PKWAY
STONE RD
B5038
PERTHY GR
CHURCHILL AVE
WEMBLEY GR
WENGER CRES
TRENTLEY RD

Park Cottage
CH
Park Brook
TRENTHAM CT
PARK DR
5
S
41

+
PC
River Trent
A34

Hanchurch Pools
PC

3

Kingswoodbank
DRAYTON RD
Kingswood Bank
Caravan Park
Trentham Lake

Underhills
Drayton Road Cottage

40

The Toft
Trentham Park

Hanchurch Hills
Black Lake
King's Wood
P

2

Hanchurch Hills Plantation
Fernybank
Jervis Wood

Harley Thorn Farm
HARLEY THORN LA
Knowl Wall

The Sheepcotes
Beechcliff
Beech Cliff Farm
The Oaks
Mon
Tittensor Hill

39

BEECH LA

1

Old Waste Plantation
HARLEY LA
Beech
A519
OLD LA
TOP LA
Caves
Beech Farm
BEECH DALE RD
M6
Beechcliff Cottages
WINGHOUSE LA

38

SCHOOL LA
TRENTHAM RD A5035
MEADOW DR

Queen's Park

Blurton Grange Farm

Colliery

CHAPEL LA
FAIRFIELD AVE
A5005
ACORN RISE
FIR TREE RD
WOODPARK LA

A-CRANWORTH GR
ASHWOOD GR
STARWOOD RD
SANDWELL PL
DOVECOTE PL
CORNWOOD PL
SEDDON RD
RYDER RD
A520
BUXTON AVE
HAWTHORN ROW
1 HAWTHORN PL
2 LABURNUM PL
SPOURTNEY RD
CASTLETON RD
DALEGATE
FAIRLAWN
SEALEN CL
CLIFTON RD
ELMBROOK CL
ANSON RD
MARTINDALE CL
Sch
STOCKFIELD RD
NORMACOT GRANGE RD
CREST RD
HARROWBY RD
DALEHEAD
LOXLEY
SANDON OLD RD
DISCOUNT PK
4

Lightwood

PH
FAREHAM GR
QUEENSWAY
LONGE
KINGSMEAD RD
SHERWOOD RD
RIDGE WK
GRAVELLY BANK
LIGHTWOOD RD
SANDON RD

Cocknage Farm

Copshurst

Marl Pit

GRANGEWOOD AVE
GRANGE RD
41

Coldriding Farm

COCKNAGE RD

Cocknage Wood

CHERRYWOOD RD
WINYARD GR
ROSEACRE GR
FIELD GR
RIDGE CRES
BIRCH CL
3

BARLASTON RD

South Cocknage Farm

Lodge Farm

Rough Close Farm

BRACKENS CL
HEATHERLANDS CL
GRINDLEY LA
HILDERSTONE RD
B5029

Glazleyfield

The Woodlands

Sch
COMMON LA
Sch
WINDMILL HILL
WINDMILL CL
WARD GR
ANTHONY
NEBB
40

EDGWOOD DR

The Cedars

Woodend Farm

Barlaston Common

A5005
LITTLE LA

PH

Rough Close

2

BLURTON RD

Woodeaves

LONGTON RD

Hartwell Farm

Leadendale

Leyden House

LEADENDALE LA
39

HARTWELL LA

Wastebarn

Hurden Hall

Hartwell Cottage

Little Hartwell

Great Hartwell Farm

Hartwell

LONGTON RD

Hillberry

Hartwell Hall

1

Hartwellhall Farm

Berry Hill Farm

Lower Hartwell Farm

Lower Cullamoor

Middle Cullamoor

OLD RD A520

Far Croft

38

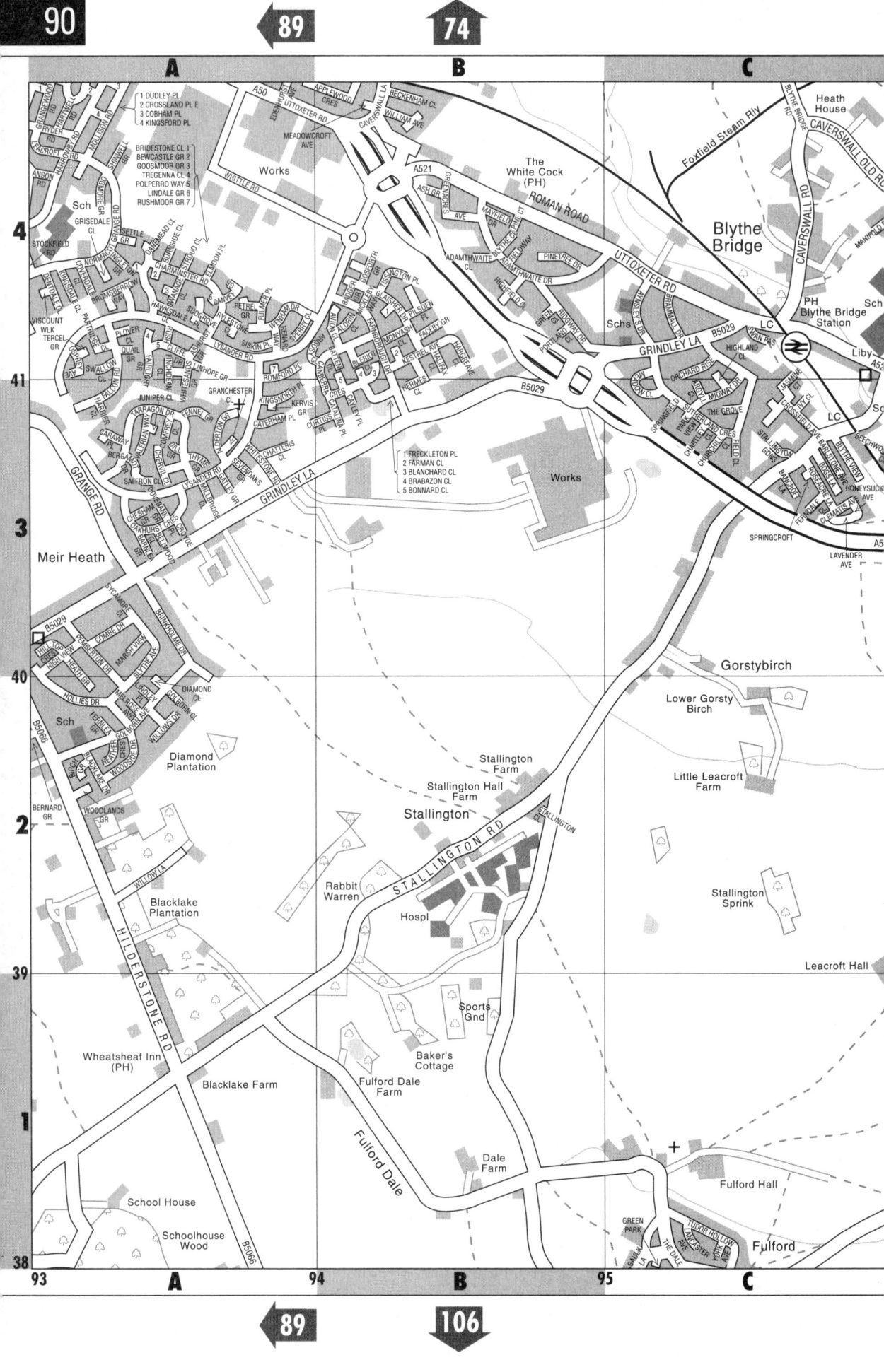

75
92

D   E   F

Moor
Green

1 MANIFOLD RD
2 STRATFORD CL

SPRING
GDNS
NEW CLOSE
BROOKGATE
PORTLAND
DR

Cemy

A521

Mount Pleasant
Farm

Wayside
Farm

Newhouse
Farm

The Fields

Draycott
Cross

DRAYCOTT CROSS RD

CAVERSWALL OLD RD
HILLSIDE AVE
BEVERLEY
SPRINGFIELD CL
CHAPEL ST
GREENWD
PARK WY
EAST BANK RIDE
YORK
DR

4

Sch

CHEADLE RD

Forsbrook

Lyndhurst

PC

BLYTHE MOUNT
PARK
WESLEY ST
THE AVENUE

Blythe Marsh

DRAYCOTT OLD RD

Cairneycroft

Dismd Rly

41

Sch

BEECHWOOD
CL
ELMWOOD
ASHWOOD
PINEWOOD

OAKDENE

A521

A521

The Grange

CHEADLE RD

Grange
Farm

Stonehouses

STUART AVE
MANOR CL
NEW AVE

Hawthorne
Farm

Hollow
Farm

3

A50

Marsh
House

UTTOXETER RD

Sch

Draycott in
the Moors

ROMAN ROAD

CHURCH LA

Woodlands

Hill Top
Farm

40

CRESSWELL LA

2

River Blithe

Isaac Walton
(PH)

CRESSWELL OLD LA

A50

Cresswell

LC

Works

SANDON RD

Saverley House
Farm

Saverley Green
Farm

SANDON CL

39

The Hollows
Farm

ROOKERY CRES

Newton

Saverley
Green

MEADOWSIDE
BLYTHE VIEW

The Hunter
(PH)

Leese House
Farm

1

Wastegate
Farm

Paynsley
Hall

38

6   D   97   E   98   F

107
92

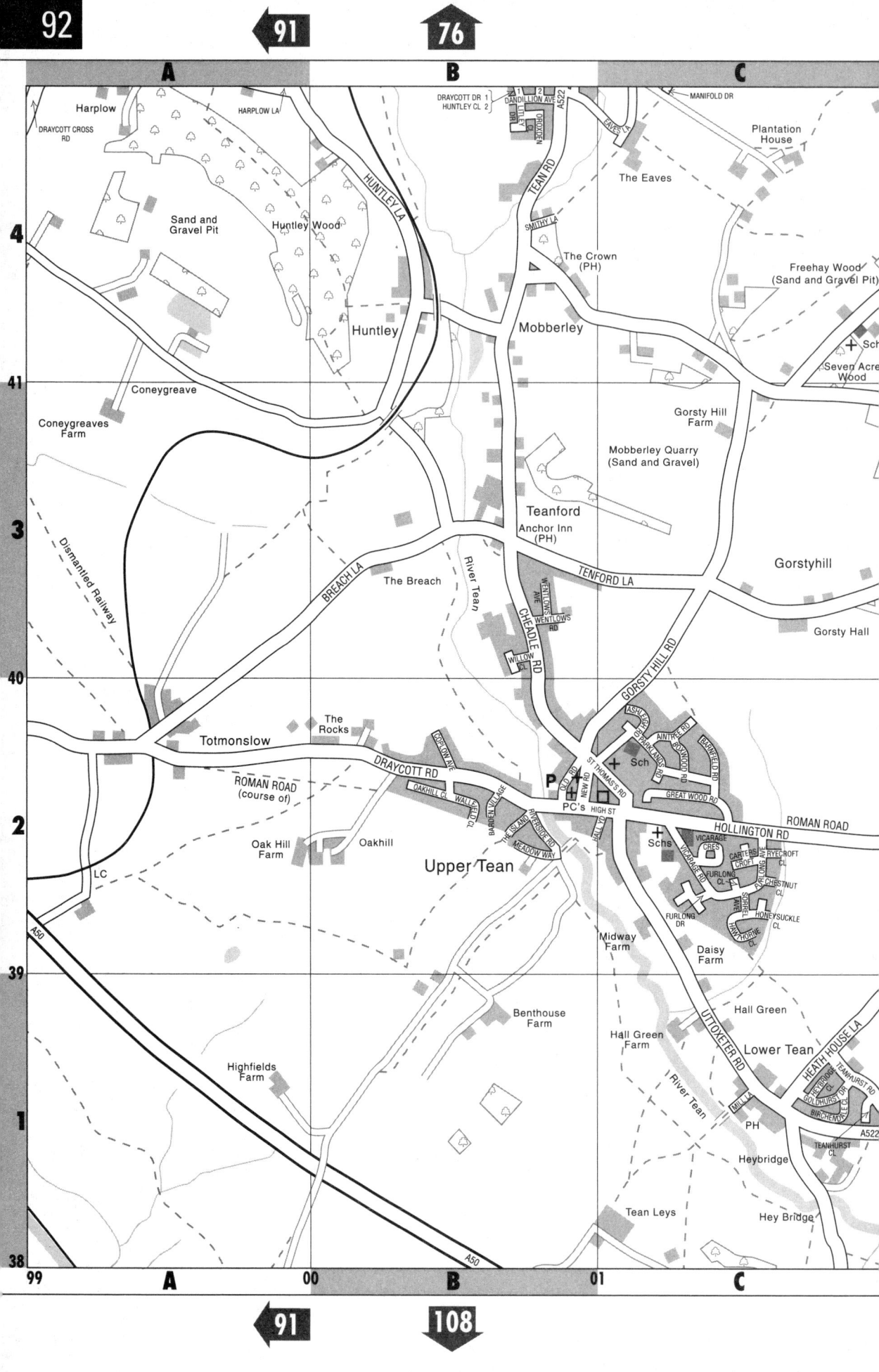

91
76

A   B   C

DRAYCOTT DR 1
HUNTLEY CL 2
DANDILLION AVE
MANIFOLD DR

Harplow
HARPLOW LA
Plantation
House

DRAYCOTT CROSS
RD

Sand and
Gravel Pit
Huntley Wood
TEAN RD
A522

SMITHY LA
The Eaves

4
The Crown
(PH)
Freehay Wood
(Sand and Gravel Pit)

HUNTLEY LA

Huntley
Mobberley
Seven Acre
Wood
Sch

41
Coneygreave
Gorsty Hill
Farm

Coneygreaves
Farm
Mobberley Quarry
(Sand and Gravel)

Gorstyhill

3
Teanford
Anchor Inn
(PH)
TENFORD LA

BREACH LA
The Breach
River Tean
WENTLOWS AVE
WENTLOWS RD
Gorsty Hall

Dismantled Railway
CHEADLE RD
GORSTY HILL RD

WILLOW CL

40
The Rocks
ASHLEY
PARK LANE
BOXWOOD RD
AINTREE RD
BARNFIELD RD

Totmonslow
DRAYCOTT RD
LOCK ON AVE
WAL RD
ST THOMAS'S RD
NEW RD
Sch
GREAT WOOD RD

ROMAN ROAD
(course of)
OAKHILL CL
WALLE
P
PC's
HIGH ST
HOLLINGTON RD
ROMAN ROAD

2
Oak Hill
Farm
Oakhill
BARDEN VILLAGE
THE ISLAND
RIVERSIDE RD
MEADOW WAY
HALL
Schs
VICARAGE
CRES
CARTERS
CROFT
RYECROFT
CL
CHESTNUT
CL

LC
Upper Tean
FURLONG
CL
HONEYSUCKLE
CL
SORREL
HAWTHORNE

Midway
Farm
FURLONG
DR
Daisy
Farm

39
Benthouse
Farm
Hall Green

A50
Hall Green
Farm
UTTOXETER RD
Lower Tean
HEATH HOUSE LA

Highfields
Farm
River Tean
MILL LA
PH
A522

1
Heybridge
TEANHURST
CL

Tean Leys
Hey Bridge

38
99   A   00   B   01   C

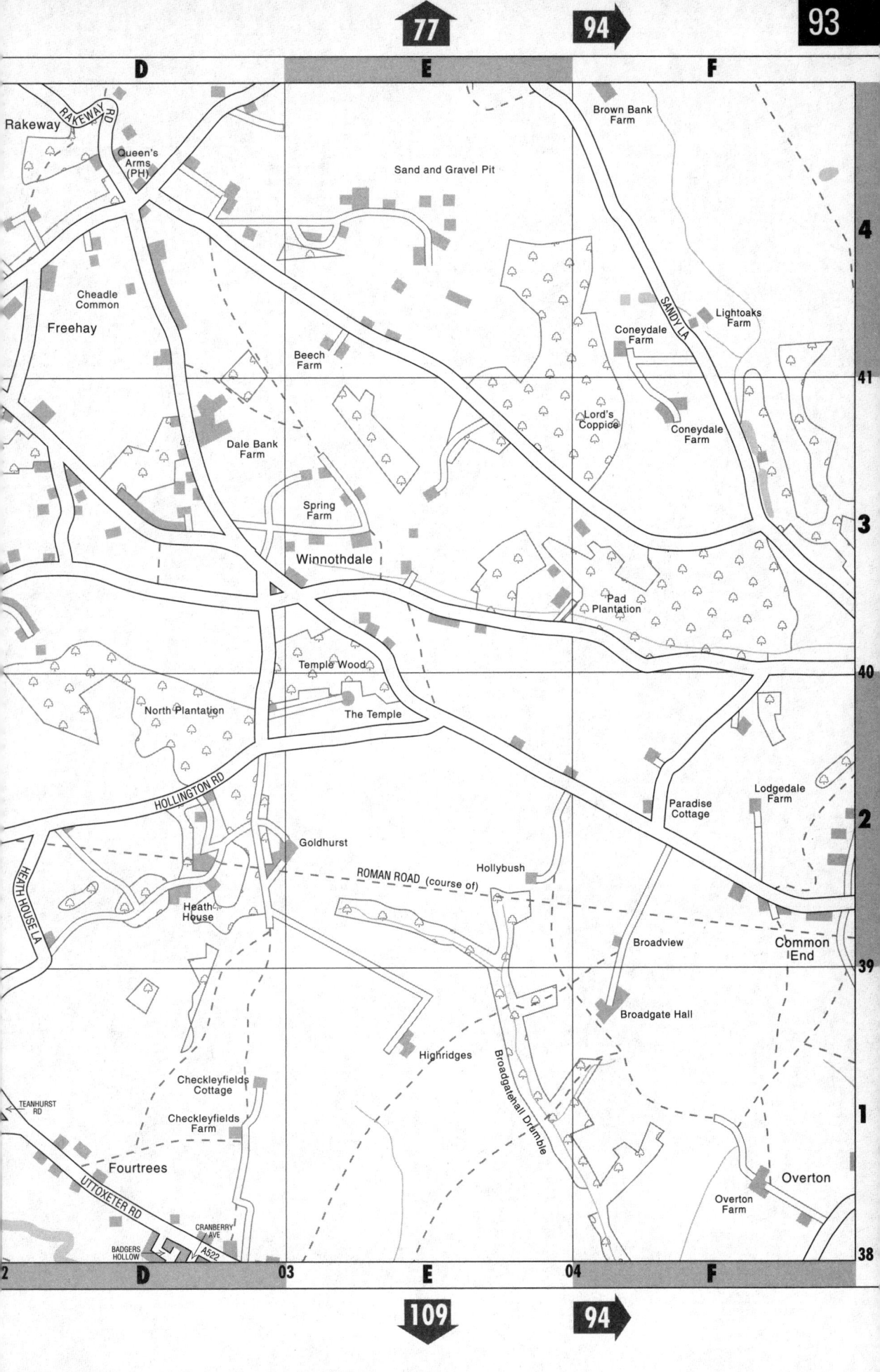

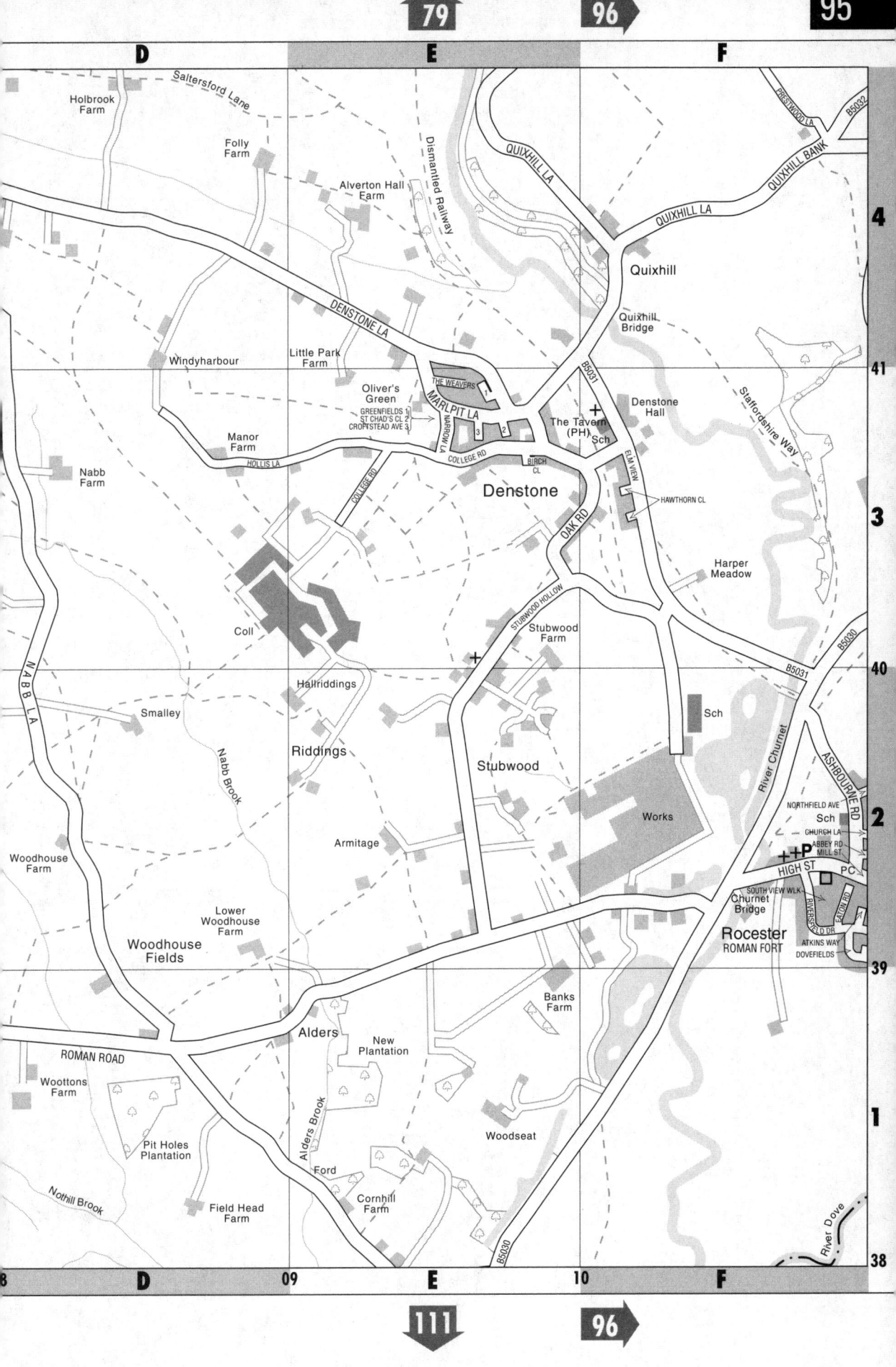

79
96

D   E   F

Saltersford Lane

Holbrook
Farm

Folly
Farm

Alverton Hall
Farm

Dismantled Railway

QUIXHILL LA

PRESTWOOD LA

QUIXHILL BANK

B5032

4

Quixhill

QUIXHILL LA

Quixhill
Bridge

DENSTONE LA

Windyharbour

Little Park
Farm

Oliver's
Green

THE WEAVERS

MARLPIT LA

NARROW LA

GREENFIELDS 1
ST CHAD'S CL 2
CROFTSTEAD AVE 3

Denstone
Hall

Staffordshire Way

41

Manor
Farm

HOLLIS LA

COLLEGE RD

COLLEGE RD

3   2

The Tavern
(PH)

Sch

B5031

ELM VIEW

Nabb
Farm

Denstone

BIRCH
CL

OAK RD

HAWTHORN CL

3

Harper
Meadow

Coll

NABB LA

Hallriddings

STUBWOOD HOLLOW

Stubwood
Farm

Sch

B5031

B5030

40

Smalley

Nabb Brook

Riddings

Stubwood

River Churnet

ASHBOURNE RD

NORTHFIELD AVE
Sch
CHURCH LA
ABBEY RD
MILL ST

Works

2

Woodhouse
Farm

Armitage

Lower
Woodhouse
Farm

Woodhouse
Fields

HIGH ST

P

PC

SOUTH VIEW WLK

Churnet
Bridge

RIVERSFIELD DR

EATON RD

Rocester
ROMAN FORT

ATKINS WAY
DOVEFIELDS

Banks
Farm

39

Alders

New
Plantation

ROMAN ROAD

Woottons
Farm

Alders Brook

Pit Holes
Plantation

Ford

Cornhill
Farm

Field Head
Farm

Nothill Brook

Woodseat

B5030

River Dove

1

38

D   09   E   10   F

111
96

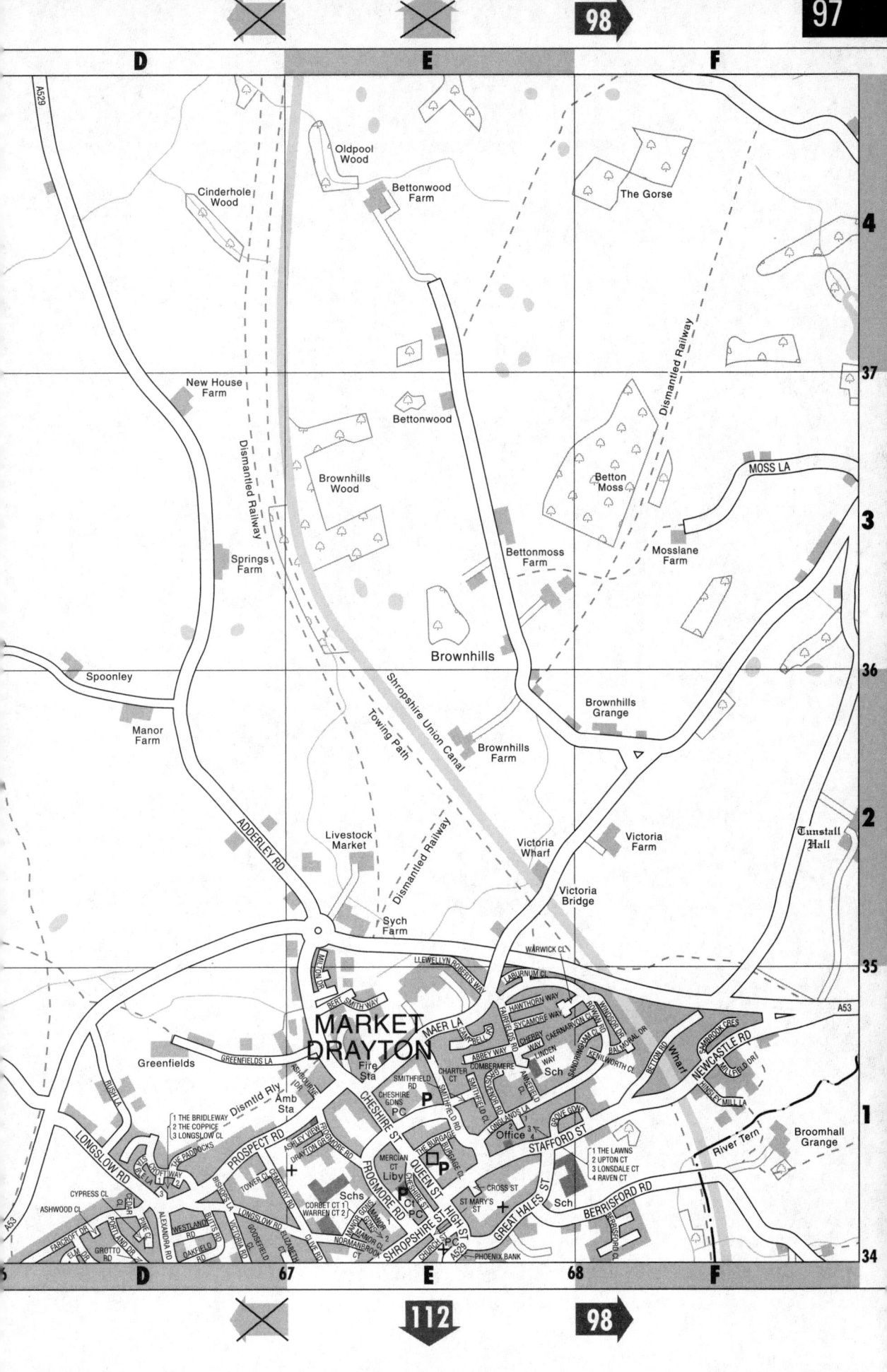

D   E   F

A529

Oldpool
Wood

Cinderhole
Wood

Bettonwood
Farm

The Gorse

4

Dismantled Railway

New House
Farm

Bettonwood

37

Brownhills
Wood

Betton
Moss

MOSS LA

Dismantled Railway

Springs
Farm

Bettonmoss
Farm

Mosslane
Farm

3

Brownhills

Shropshire Union Canal

Towing Path

Spoonley

36

Brownhills
Grange

Manor
Farm

Brownhills
Farm

ADDERLEY RD

Livestock
Market

Dismantled Railway

Victoria
Wharf

Victoria
Farm

Tunstall
Hall

2

Victoria
Bridge

Sych
Farm

WARWICK CL

LLEWELLYN ROBERTS WAY

LABURNUM CL

35

A53

BEM SMITH WAY

HAWTHORN WAY
SYCAMORE WAY
FAIRFIELDS
CHERRY
WAY
LINDEN
WAY
WINDSOR CL
BALMORAL DR
KENILWORTH CL
SANDBROOK CRES
NEWCASTLE RD
BELLFIELD DRI

MARKET
DRAYTON

MAER LA

ABBEY WAY
COMBERMERE
CAERMARYON CL
SANDOWN RD
Sch

BETTON RD
Wharf

KINSLEY MILL LA

Greenfields

GREENFIELDS LA

Fire
Sta

CHARTER
CT

SMITHFIELD CL

Broomhall
Grange

1 THE BRIDLEWAY
2 THE COPPICE
3 LONGSLOW CL

Dismtld Rly

Amb
Sta

CHESHIRE ST

SMITHFIELD
RD
CHESHIRE
GDNS
P
PC

LONGLANDS RD
Office
1
2 3
4

River Tern

1 THE LAWNS
2 UPTON CT
3 LONSDALE CT
4 RAVEN CT

RUSH LA

PROSPECT RD

ASHLEY VIEW
DRAYTON GROVE
FROGMORE RD
MERCIAN
CT
Liby
QUEEN ST
P

GROVE GDNS
STAFFORD ST

Sch
GREAT HALES ST

Longslow
RD

THE PADDOCKS

TOWER CT
CEMETERY RD
Schs
CORBET CT 1
WARREN CT 2
P
PC
CROSS ST
ST MARY'S
ST

BERRISFORD RD

BERRISFORD CL

CYPRESS CL

ASHWOOD CL

A53

FAIRCROFT DR

GROTTO
RD

WESTLANDS
RD
ALEXANDRA RD
OAKFIELD
BUTTER LA
GOOSEFIELD
LONGSLOW RD
ELIZABETH
MANOR CL
NORMANBROOK
CT
FROGMORE RD
SHROPSHIRE ST
HIGH ST
CHURCH ST
CHURCH LA
A529
PHOENIX BANK

Sch

D   67   E   68   F

34

97

82

A

B

C

Greenhill Farm

FORGE LA

Norton Forge Farm

Devil's Ring & Finger

The Arbour

NAPLEY RD

B5415

Napley

Betton Hall Farm

Oakley Park

The Haven

4

Betton Hall

Park House

37

Betton

Oakley Hall

Oakley Park Farm

Bache Pool

Old Pool Plantation

Oakley Folly

Betton Farm

River Tern

3

Marlpit Wood

The Folly

36

Drayton Spinney

Oakley Lodges

Daisy Lake

Audley's Cross Farm

A53

Tunstall Hall

The Rough

2

Shiffords Grange

SANDY LA

Red Bull

1459

Audley's Cross

The Park

Boreheath

B5415

Boreheath Farm

35

Shifford's Bridge

Clod Hall

PINFOLD LA

A53

NEWCASTLE RD

NEW COUNCIL HOUSES

Blore Heath Farm

Almington

Sand Pit

BLORE RD

1

Upper House Farm

Little Heath Green

Almington Hall

FLASH LA

Coal Brook

Hales Farm

Hales

34

69

A

70

B

71

C

D
E
F

Buckley's Drumble

Cowleasow

Lordsley End Farm

Lordsley

Mucklestone

Sch

4

Rectory Farm

The Forty Acres

37

Beasley Bank

ROCK LA

Eccleshall Road Farm

White House Farm

ECCLESHALL RD

MUCKLESTONE WOOD LA

GRAVELLY HILL

A53

Copthorne Cottage

Tadgedale

MARTIN DALE

ST MARY'S RD

QUEEN MARGARET'S

BADGER BROW RD

BROOM HOLLOW

PINEWOOD

NEWCASTLE RD

3

MUCKLESTONE RD

BROOKFIELD

ROWLANDS

BROCKHILL

BRACKEN

FOX HOLLOW

Ashley Heath

The Folly

Loggerheads

PRICE CL

HADDERDALE AVE

ROWNEY CL

BIRKS DR

36

Wickeytree

MARKET DRAYTON RD

Inn

Sch

Mast

HEATH TOP

Westfields Farm

Rowney Farm

THE GREENS

KESTREL DR

PARTRIDGE RIDE

PINEWOOD DR

TOWER RD

OAKLEY FOLLY

WREN VIEW

GOLDFINCH VIEW

WOODPECKER VIEW

PHEASANT WLK

CHEASANT WLK

ECCLESHALL RD

BIRCH RISE

HEA THOOTLE AVE

Hookgate

LOWER RD

2

Oaklands Farm

B5026

CHAPEL LA

35

Blore

Parkhill Farm

FLASH LA

Blore Farm

PARK LA

Parkhill Cottage

Burnt Wood

1

34

2
73
74

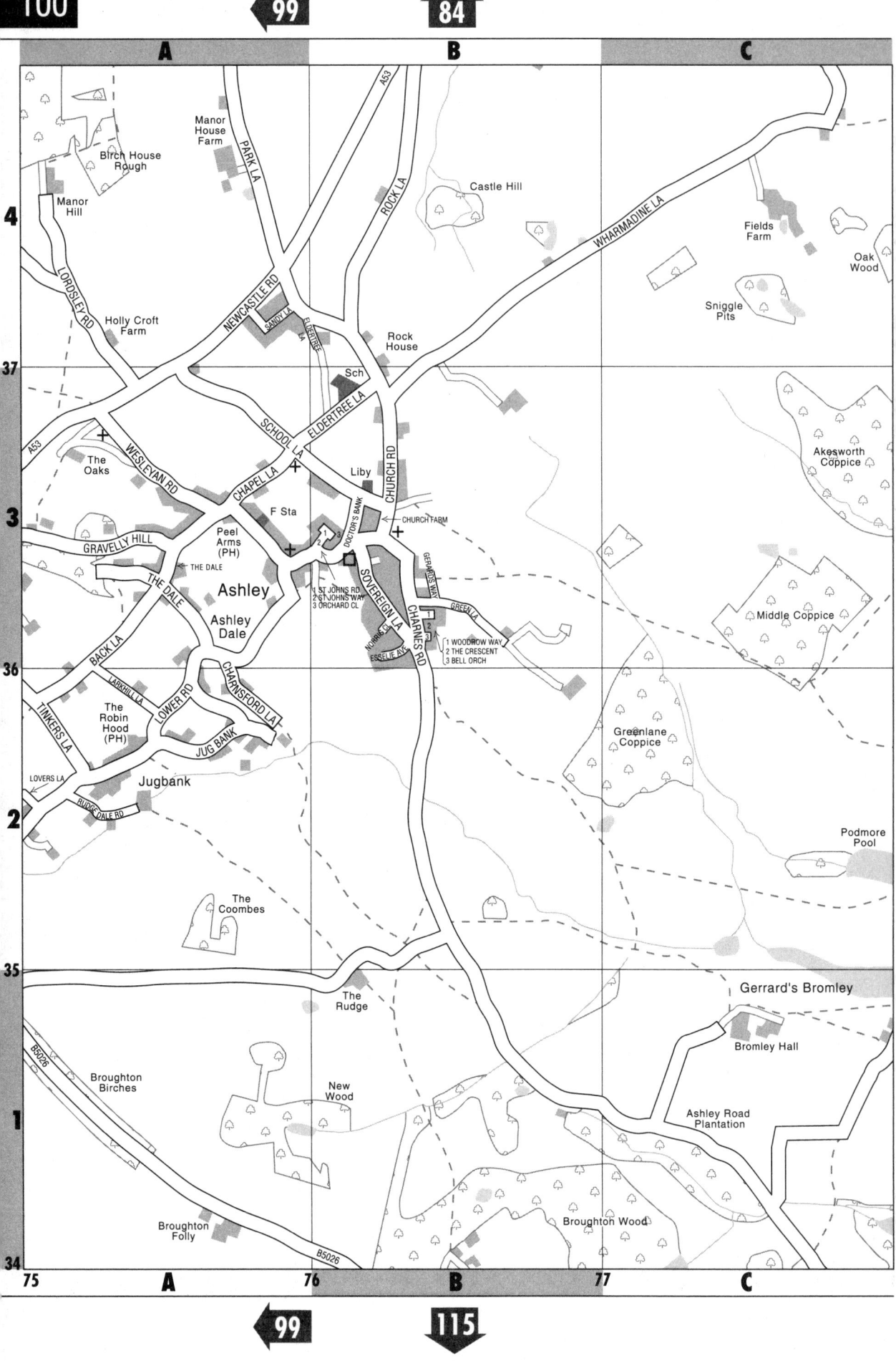

A   B   C

Birch House Rough

Manor House Farm

PARK LA

A53

ROCK LA

Castle Hill

WHARMADINE LA

Fields Farm

Oak Wood

Manor Hill

4

Sniggle Pits

Akesworth Coppice

LORDSLEY RD

Holly Croft Farm

NEWCASTLE RD

SANDY LA

FR. DERME

Rock House

37

Sch

A53

The Oaks

WESLEYAN RD

SCHOOL LA

ELDERTREE LA

CHURCH RD

Liby

CHURCH FARM

3

CHAPEL LA

F Sta

DOCTOR'S BANK

Peel Arms (PH)

THE DALE

Ashley

1 ST JOHNS RD
2 ST JOHNS WAY
3 ORCHARD CL

GERARDS WAY

GREEN LA

Middle Coppice

GRAVELLY HILL

THE DALE

Ashley Dale

SOVEREIGN LA

CHARNES RD

1 WOODROW WAY
2 THE CRESCENT
3 BELL ORCH

BACK LA

NORRIS CH

ESSELIE AVE

36

LARKHILL LA

The Robin Hood (PH)

LOWER RD

CHARNSFORD LA

Greenlane Coppice

TINKERS LA

JUG BANK

LOVERS LA

Jugbank

2

RUDGE DALE RD

The Coombes

Podmore Pool

35

The Rudge

Gerrard's Bromley

B5026

Broughton Birches

New Wood

Bromley Hall

1

Ashley Road Plantation

Broughton Folly

B5026

Broughton Wood

34

75   A   76   B   77   C

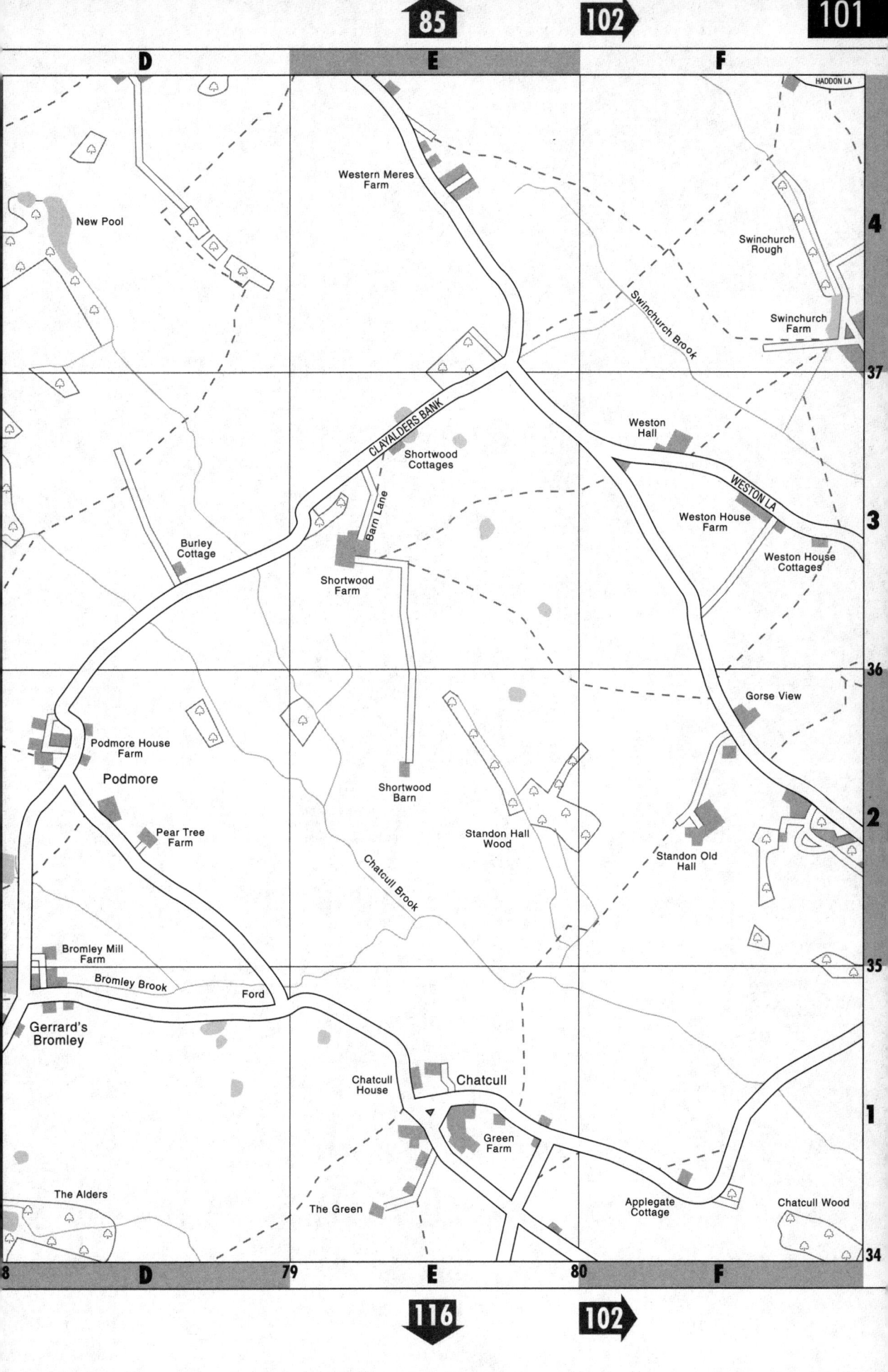

HADDON LA

New Pool

Western Meres
Farm

Swinchurch
Rough

4

Swinchurch
Farm

Swinchurch Brook

37

CLAYALDERS BANK

Shortwood
Cottages

Weston
Hall

Burley
Cottage

Barn Lane

WESTON LA

Weston House
Farm

3

Shortwood
Farm

Weston House
Cottages

36

Gorse View

Podmore House
Farm

Podmore

Shortwood
Barn

Standon Old
Hall

2

Pear Tree
Farm

Standon Hall
Wood

Chatcull Brook

Bromley Mill
Farm

35

Bromley Brook

Ford

Gerrard's
Bromley

Chatcull
House

Chatcull

1

The Alders

Green
Farm

Applegate
Cottage

Chatcull Wood

The Green

34

101
86

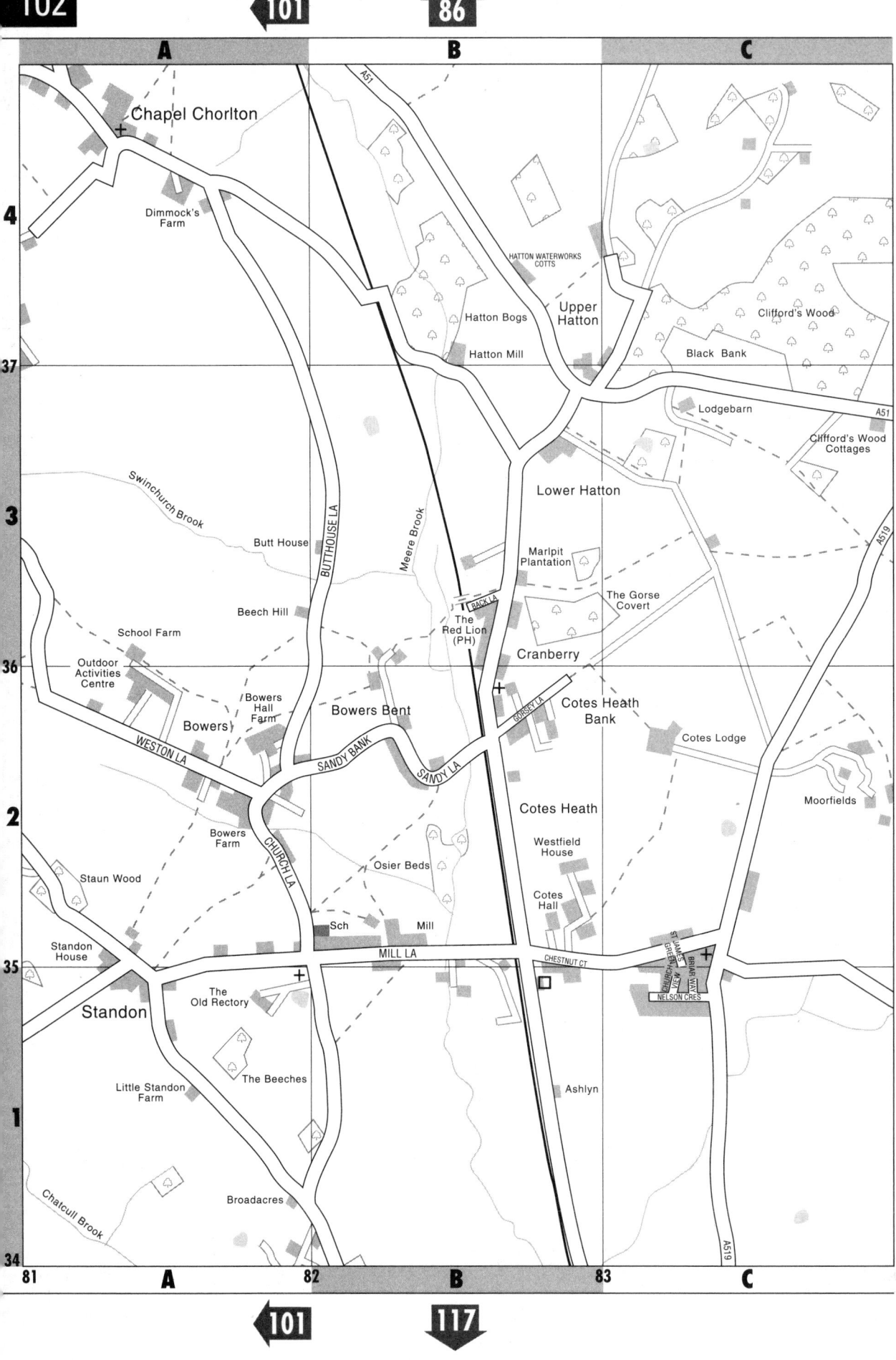

A B C

Chapel Chorlton

Dimmock's Farm

A51

Hatton Waterworks Cotts

Upper Hatton

Clifford's Wood

Hatton Bogs

Black Bank

Hatton Mill

A51

Lodgebarn

Clifford's Wood Cottages

Swinchurch Brook

Lower Hatton

BUTTHOUSE LA

Meere Brook

Butt House

A519

Marlpit Plantation

Beech Hill

The Gorse Covert

BACK LA

The Red Lion (PH)

School Farm

Cranberry

Outdoor Activities Centre

Cotes Heath Bank

Bowers Hall Farm

Bowers Bent

GORSEY LA

Cotes Lodge

Bowers

WESTON LA

SANDY BANK

SANDY LA

Moorfields

Bowers Farm

CHURCH LA

Cotes Heath

Staun Wood

Osier Beds

Westfield House

Cotes Hall

Standon House

Sch

Mill

ST JAMES GREENCHURCH A519

BRIAR WAY

MILL LA

CHESTNUT CT

NELSON CRES

Standon

The Old Rectory

The Beeches

Little Standon Farm

Ashlyn

Chatcull Brook

Broadacres

A519

81 A 82 B 83 C

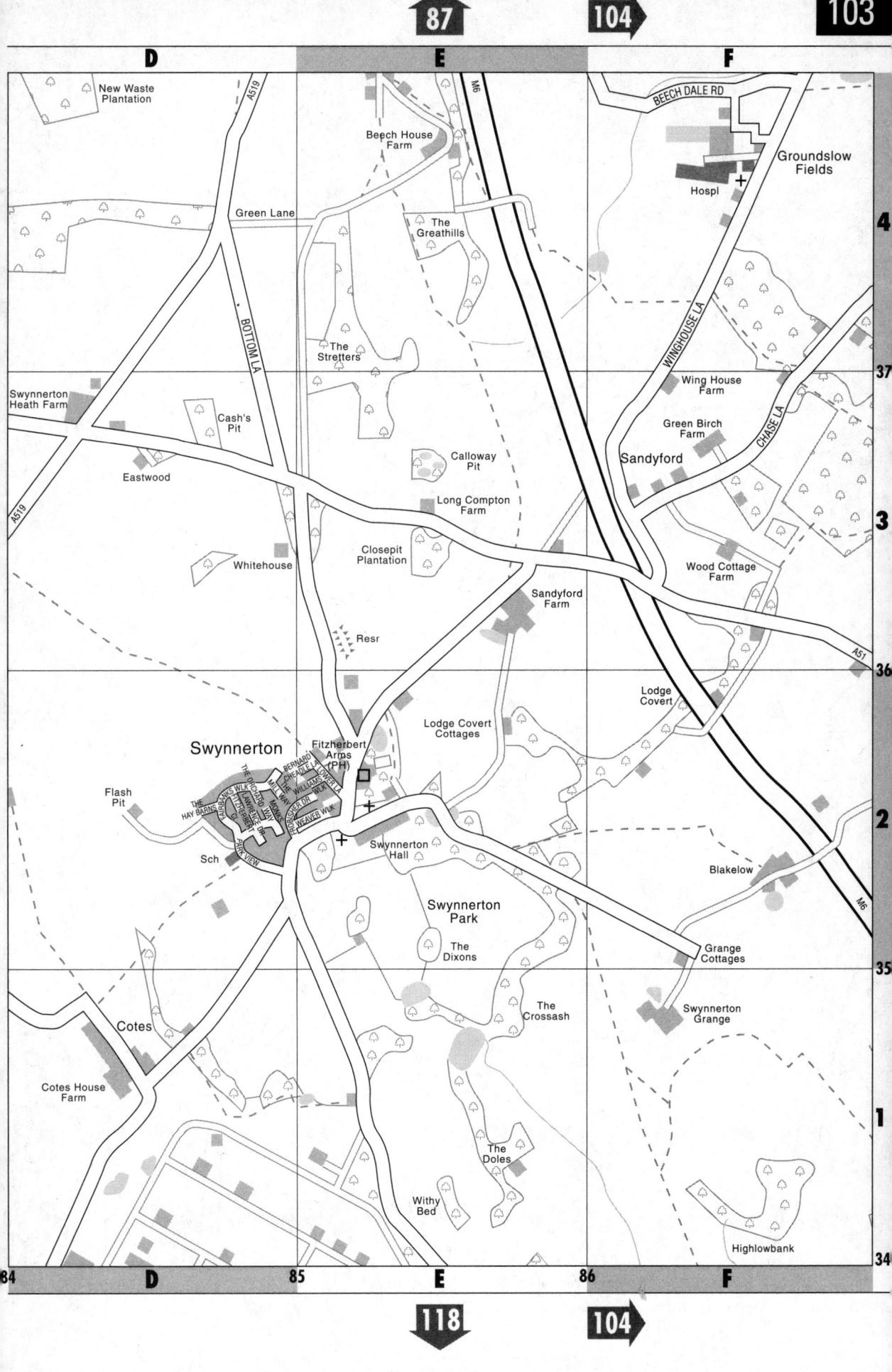

D E F

New Waste
Plantation

BEECH DALE RD

Groundslow
Fields

Hospl

Green Lane

Beech House
Farm

4

The
Greathills

WINGHOUSE LA

Wing House
Farm

37

The
Stretters

BOTTOM LA

Green Birch
Farm

CHASE LA

Sandyford

Swynnerton
Heath Farm

Cash's
Pit

Calloway
Pit

A519

Eastwood

Long Compton
Farm

Wood Cottage
Farm

3

Whitehouse

Closepit
Plantation

A519

Resr

Sandyford
Farm

A51

36

Lodge
Covert

Swynnerton

Fitzherbert
Arms
(PH)

Lodge Covert
Cottages

Flash
Pit

THE HAY BARNS

FERNBANK'S WLK

THE DIXON'S WLK

CHEADLE LA

BERNARD LA

LOWER LA

MILL WK

MOSS'S

FITZHERBERT

LAWRENCE DR

FLETCHER'S DR

WEAVER WLK

WILLIAMS

PARK VIEW

Sch

Swynnerton
Hall

Blakelow

2

Swynnerton
Park

The
Dixons

Grange
Cottages

M6

35

Cotes

The
Crossash

Swynnerton
Grange

Cotes House
Farm

1

The
Doles

Withy
Bed

Highlowbank

34

84

D

85

E

86

F

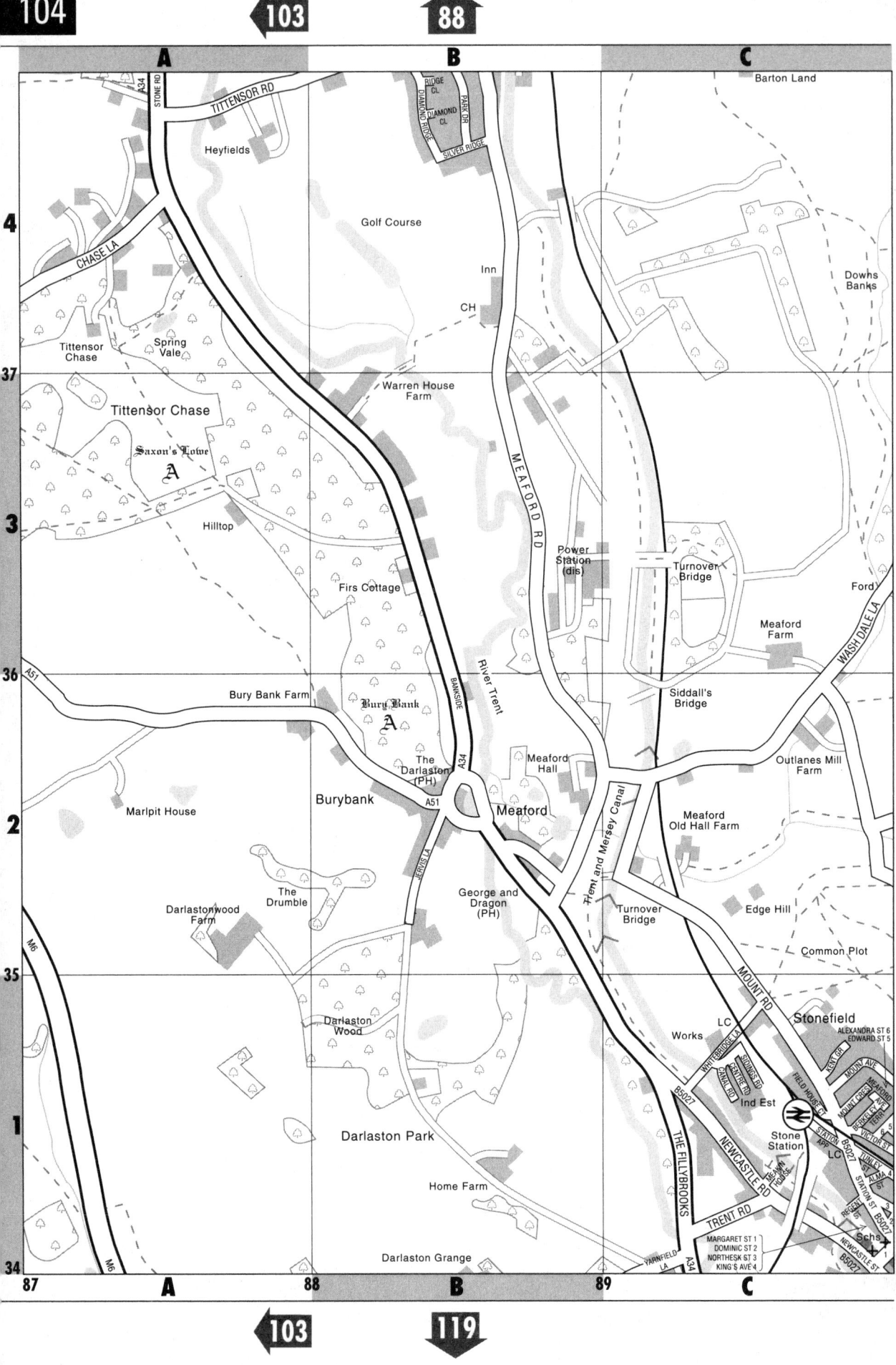

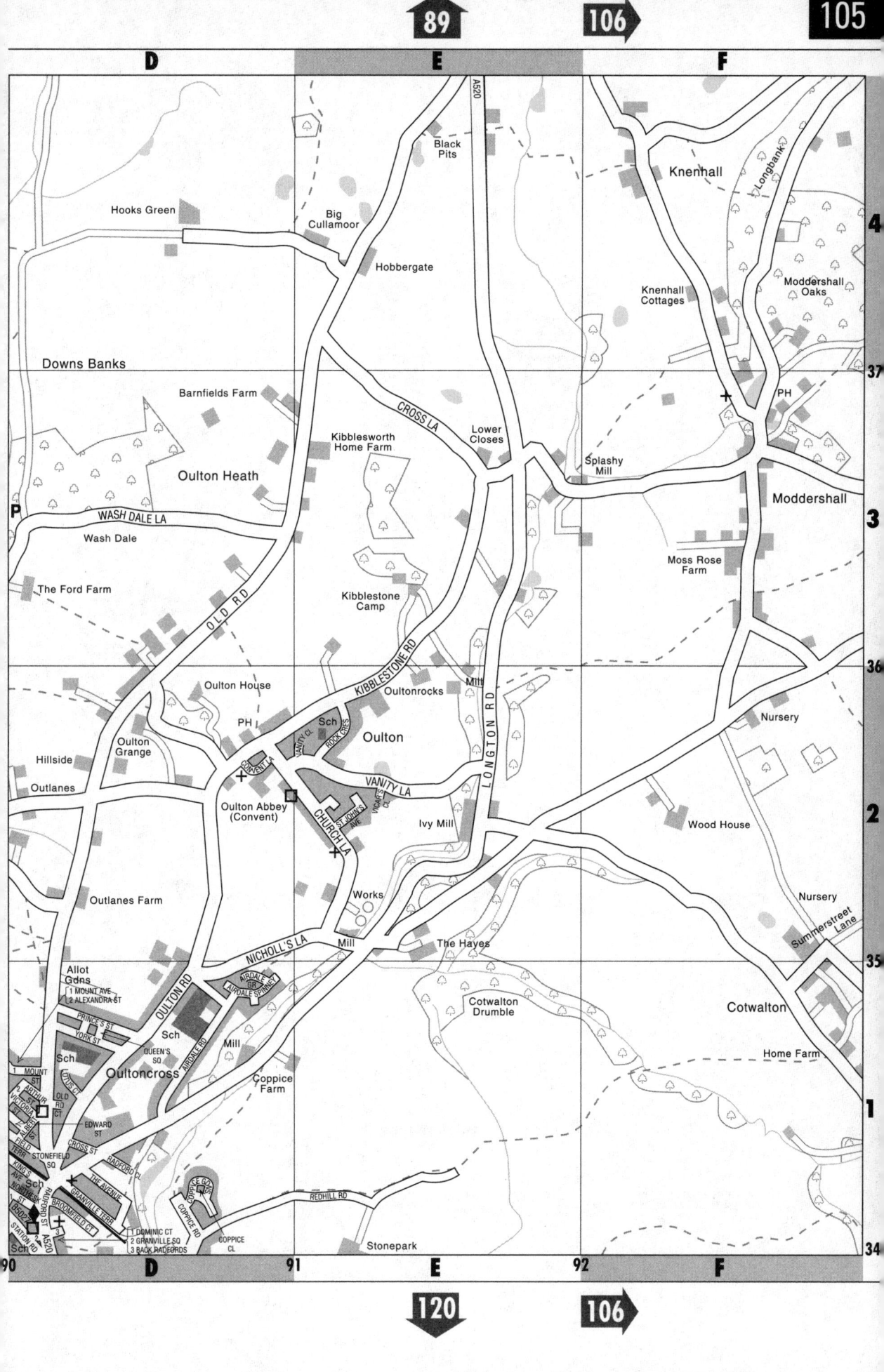

D
E
F

Black Pits

Knenhall

Longbanks

Hooks Green

Big Cullamoor

Hobbergate

Knenhall Cottages

Moddershall Oaks

4

Downs Banks

37

Barnfields Farm

CROSS LA

Lower Closes

PH

Kibblesworth Home Farm

Splashy Mill

Moddershall

Oulton Heath

P

WASH DALE LA

3

Wash Dale

Moss Rose Farm

The Ford Farm

OLD RD

Kibblestone Camp

36

Oulton House

Oultonrocks

Mill

Nursery

PH

Sch

Rock Cres

VANITY CL

CARPENTER LA

Oulton

LONGTON RD

KIBBLESTONE RD

Hillside

Oulton Grange

Wood House

Outlanes

VANITY LA

2

Oulton Abbey (Convent)

CHURCH LA

ST JOHN'S AVE

VICAR'S CL

Ivy Mill

Nursery

Outlanes Farm

Works

Mill

The Hayes

Summerstreet Lane

NICHOLL'S LA

35

Allot Gdns

1 MOUNT AVE
2 ALEXANDRA ST

AIRDALE CRES

AIRDALE SPINNEY

OULTON RD

Cotwalton Drumble

Cotwalton

PRINCE'S ST

YORK ST

Sch

QUEEN'S SQ

Sch

AIRDALE RD

Mill

Home Farm

1 MOUNT ST

Sch

Oultoncross

ARTHUR ST

VICTORIA ST

VICTORIA RD

KING'S CL

OLD RD CT

Coppice Farm

EDWARD ST

1

FIELD TERR

STONEFIELD SQ

CROSS ST

KING'S AVE

Sch

THE AVENUE

RADFORD PL

NORTH ST

RADFORD ST

BROOMFIELD ST

GRANVILLE TERR

COPPICE RD

THE GATES

REDHILL RD

A520

STATION RD

Sch

1 DOMINIC CT
2 GRANVILLE SQ
3 BACK RADFORDS

COPPICE CL

Stonepark

34

90
D
91
E
92
F

A B C

Moddershall
Grange

Fulford

THE DALE
CHERRY CL

MEADOW LA

SAVERLEY GREEN RD

HILLSIDE CL

Townend

Stallington
Heath

Broom's
Farm

BAULK LA

KINGSFISHER CRES

TOWNEND

FULFORD RD

Sch

Longlane
Head
Farm

4

Idlerocks
Farm

Idlerocks

Crossgate

Greensitch
Farm

Idlerocks

Spot
Acre

Spot Acre
Spinney

B5066

Mossgate

Flats

37

Nurseries

Spotgate Inn
(PH)

Mosslane

MOSS LA

BALAAM'S LA

HILDERSTONE RD

Nursery

Rushlade

3

The Spot

Spot
Farm

The
Leasows

Farthings

Bird in Hand
(PH)

36

Spot
Grange

The Hurstage

High Elms

2

Home Farm

Manor House
Farm

35

Hilderstone
Hall

Sewage
Works

BARNES
CROFT

THE
MEADOWS

Crossgate
Barn

Newfields

Hall Wood

1

Hilderstone

Roebuck Inn
(PH)

Hall Farm

Wooliscroft

Peakshill
Wood

EASTHOLME

WHITESYCHE LA

B5066

34

93 A 94 B 95 C

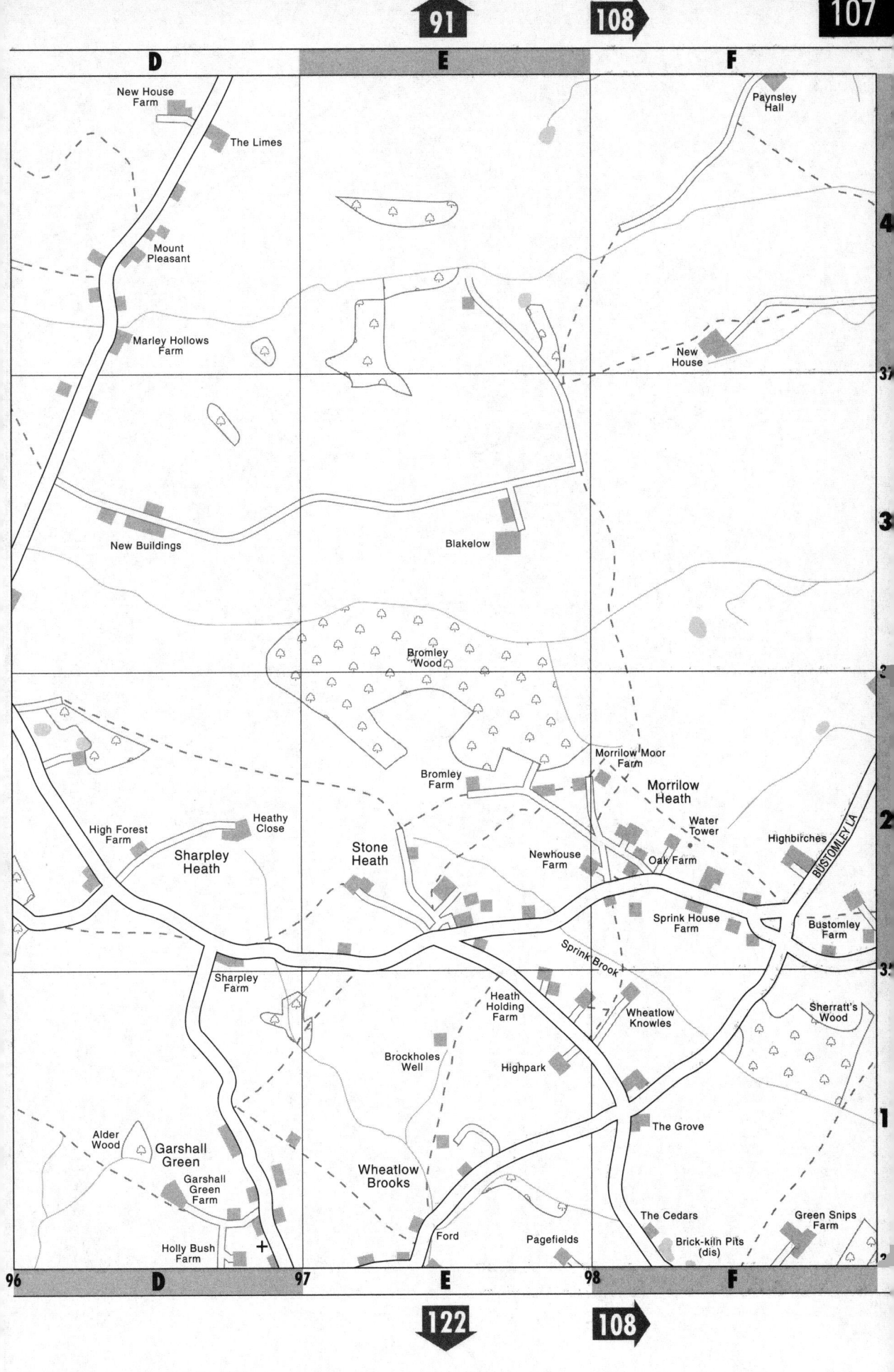

D E F

New House Farm

The Limes

Mount Pleasant

Marley Hollows Farm

New Buildings

Blakelow

Paynsley Hall

New House

Bromley Wood

Morrilow Moor Farm

Morrilow Heath

Bromley Farm

High Forest Farm

Heathy Close

Sharpley Heath

Stone Heath

Newhouse Farm

Water Tower

Oak Farm

Highbirches

BUSTOMLEY LA

Sprink House Farm

Bustomley Farm

Sharpley Farm

Sprink Brook

Heath Holding Farm

Wheatlow Knowles

Sherratt's Wood

Brockholes Well

Highpark

Alder Wood

Garshall Green

The Grove

Garshall Green Farm

Wheatlow Brooks

Holly Bush Farm

Ford

Pagefields

The Cedars

Brick-kiln Pits (dis)

Green Snips Farm

4

37

3

2

3½

2

1

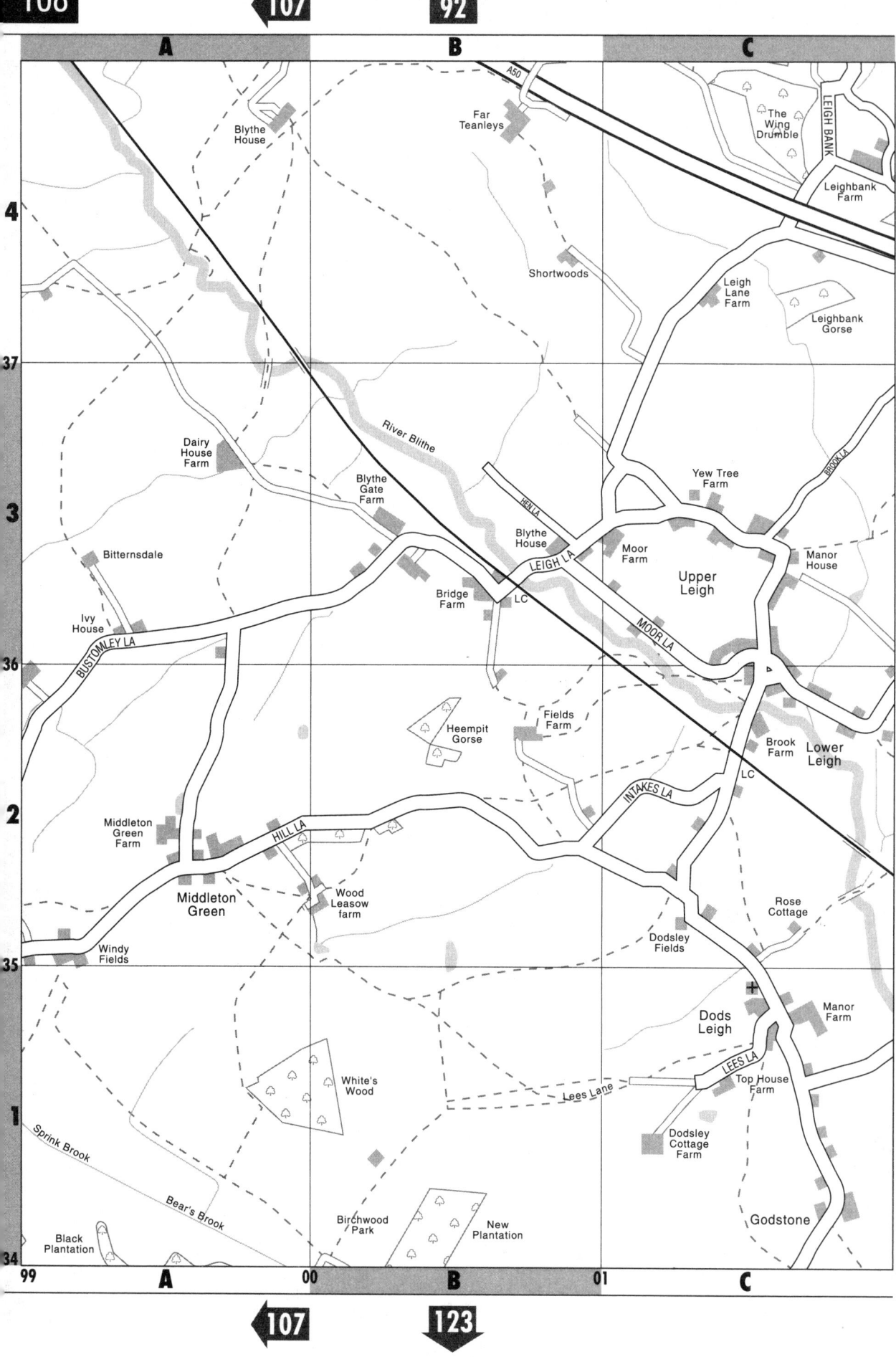

A B C

4

37

3

36

2

35

1

34

A B C

99 00 01

The Wing Drumble

LEIGH BANK

Leighbank Farm

Far Teanleys

A50

Blythe House

Shortwoods

Leigh Lane Farm

Leighbank Gorse

River Blithe

Dairy House Farm

Blythe Gate Farm

Yew Tree Farm

BROOK LA

Bitternsdale

Blythe House

HEN LA

Moor Farm

Upper Leigh

Manor House

Ivy House

Bridge Farm

LEIGH LA

LC

BUSTOMLEY LA

MOOR LA

Heempit Gorse

Fields Farm

Brook Farm

Lower Leigh

LC

Middleton Green Farm

HILL LA

INTAKES LA

Rose Cottage

Middleton Green

Wood Leasow farm

Dodsley Fields

Windy Fields

Dods Leigh

Manor Farm

LEES LA

Top House Farm

White's Wood

Lees Lane

Sprink Brook

Dodsley Cottage Farm

Bear's Brook

Birchwood Park

New Plantation

Godstone

Black Plantation

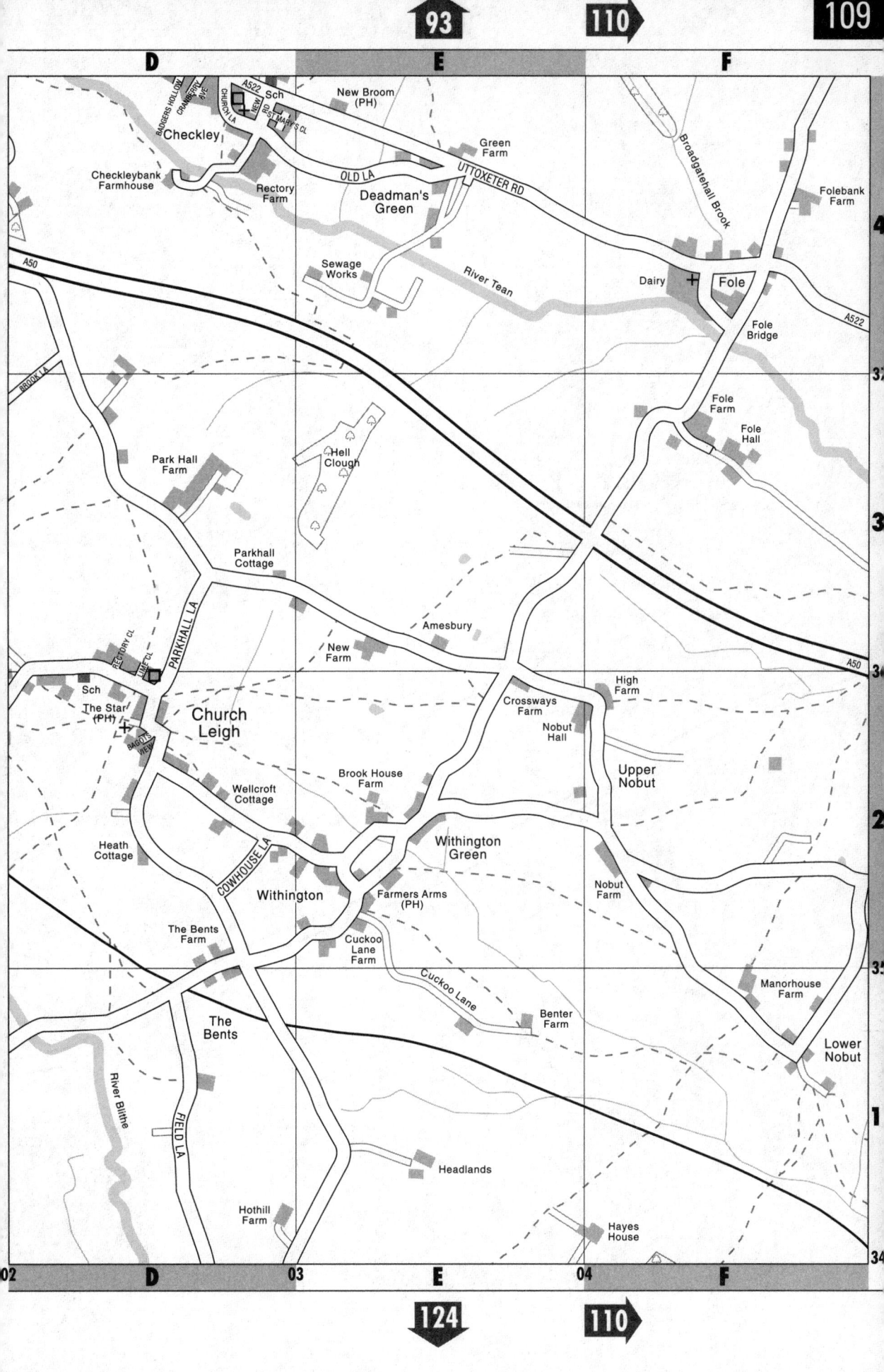

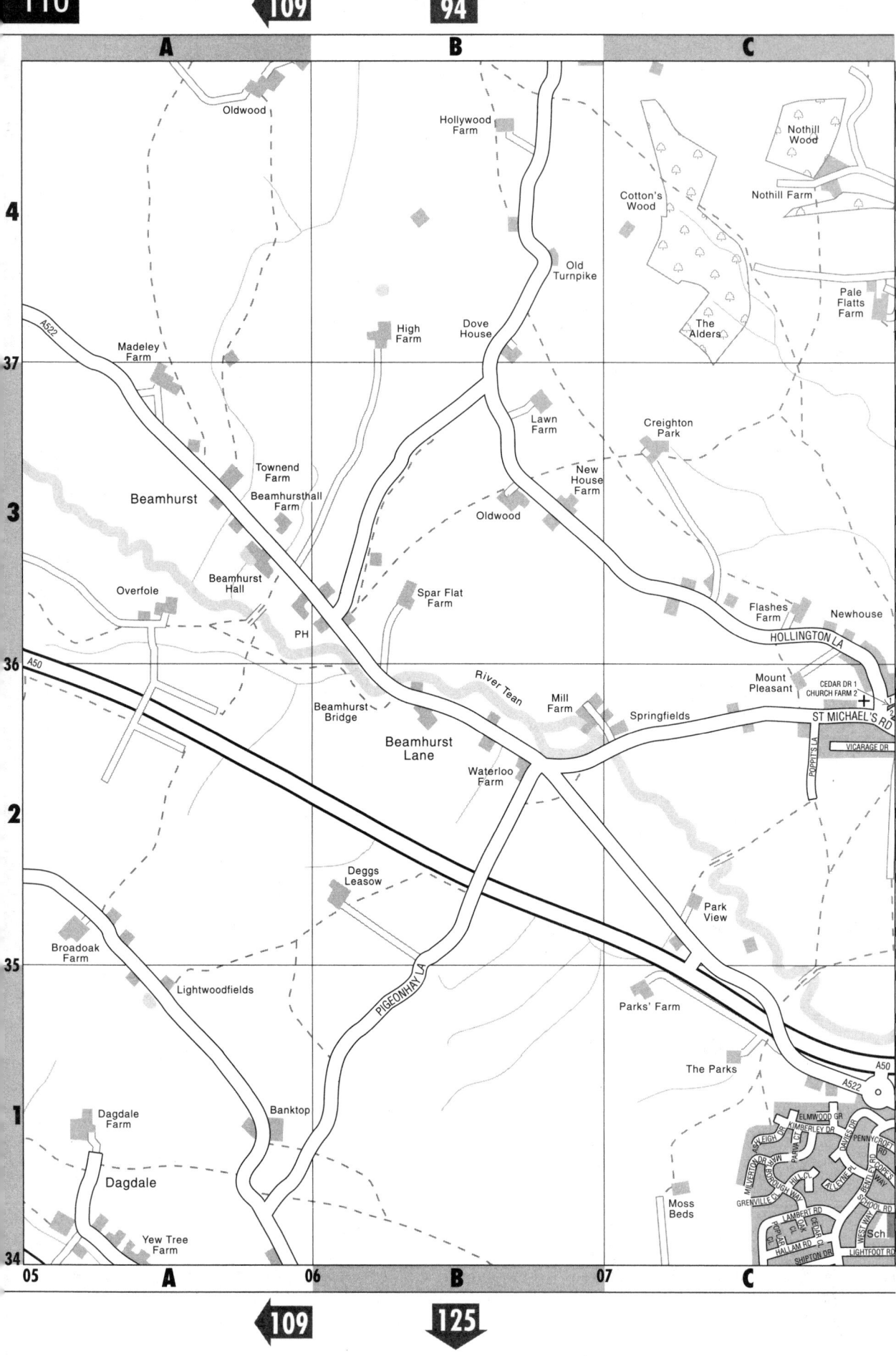

A   B   C

4

37

3

36

2

35

1

34

Oldwood

Hollywood Farm

Nothill Wood

Cotton's Wood

Nothill Farm

Pale Flatts Farm

Old Turnpike

The Alders

A522

Madeley Farm

High Farm

Dove House

Lawn Farm

Creighton Park

New House Farm

Townend Farm

Beamhurst

Beamhursthall Farm

Oldwood

Overfole

Beamhurst Hall

Spar Flat Farm

Flashes Farm

Newhouse

HOLLINGTON LA

PH

River Tean

Mount Pleasant

CEDAR DR 1
CHURCH FARM 2

A50

Beamhurst Bridge

Mill Farm

Springfields

ST MICHAEL'S RD

Beamhurst Lane

Waterloo Farm

POPPITS LA

VICARAGE DR

Deggs Leasow

Park View

Broadoak Farm

Lightwoodfields

PIGEONHAY LA

Parks' Farm

The Parks

A50

A522

Dagdale Farm

Banktop

ELMWOOD GR
KIMBERLEY DR
PENNYCROFT

Dagdale

Moss Beds

GRENVILLE CL
LAMBERT RD
HALLAM RD

Sch

SHIPTON DR
LIGHTFOOT RD

Yew Tree Farm

05   A   06   B   07   C

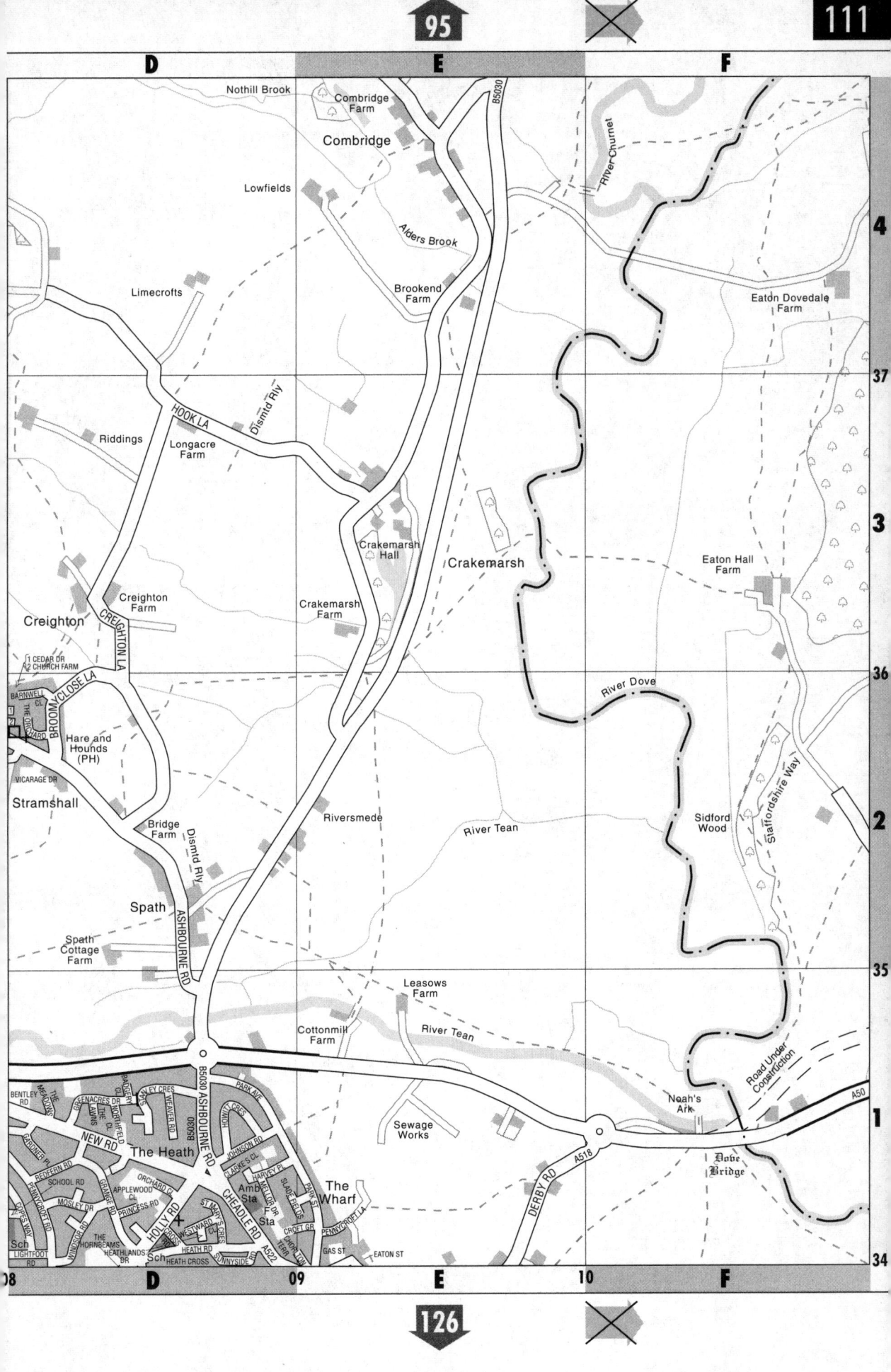

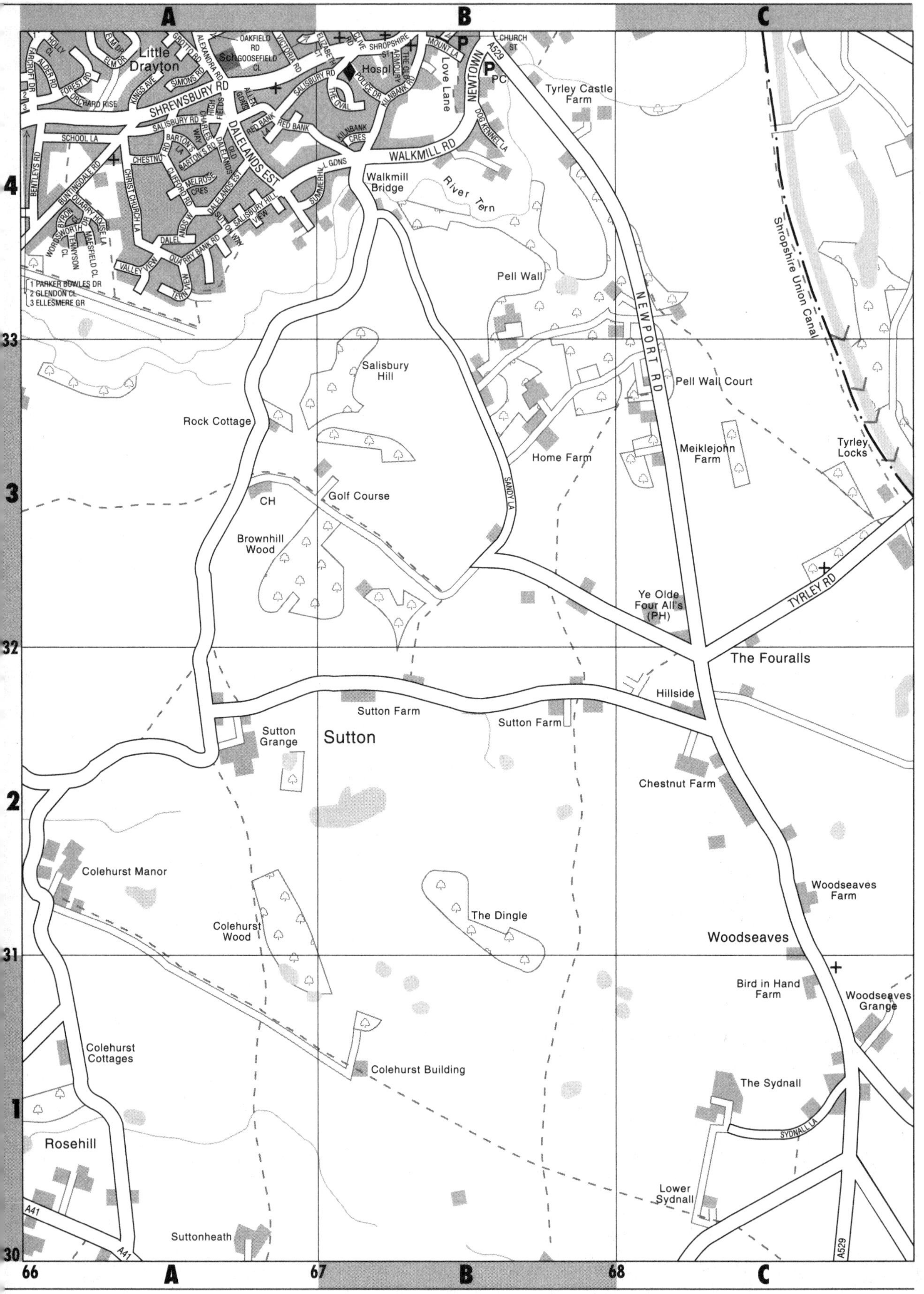

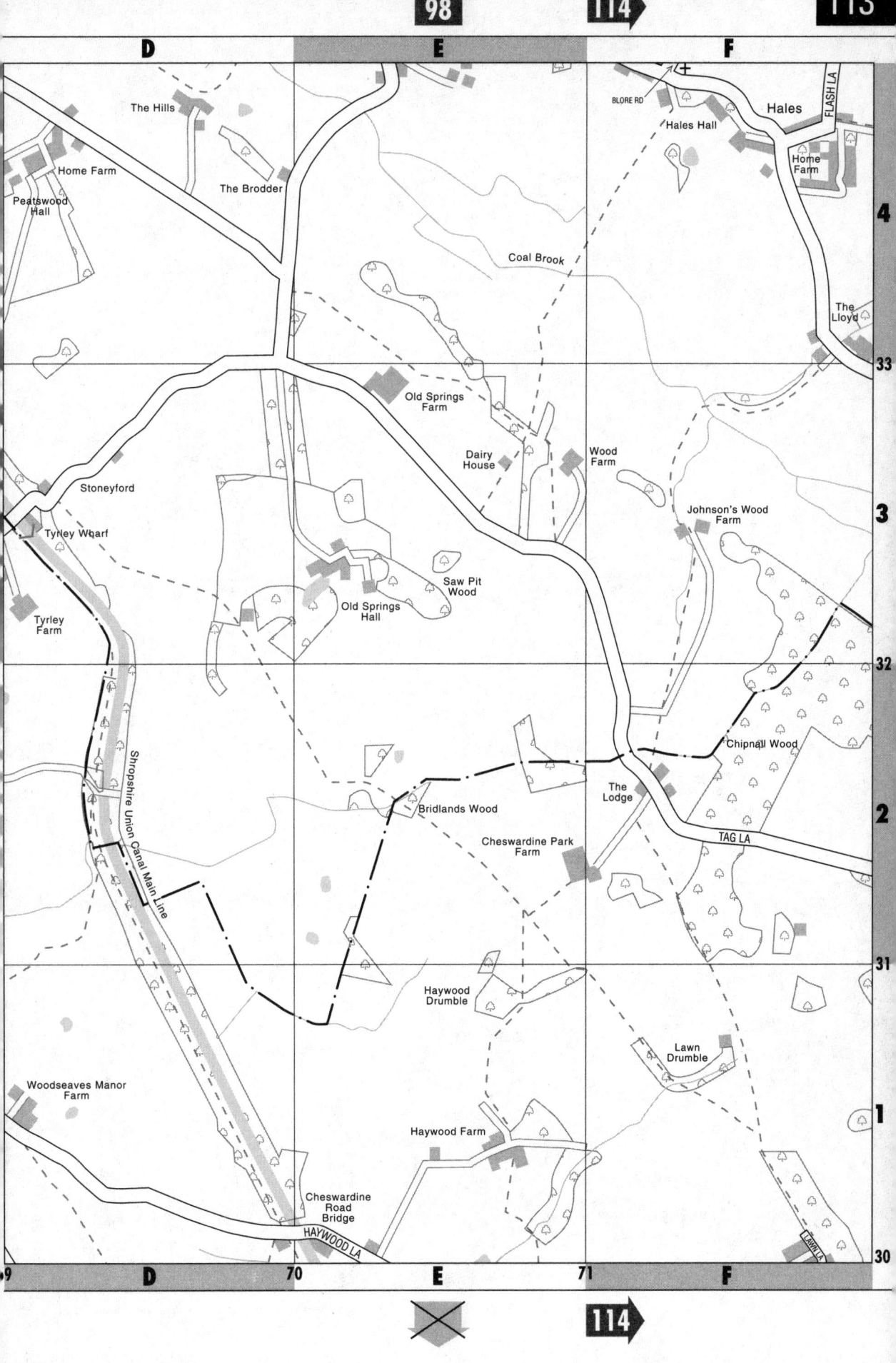

D
E
F

The Hills

Home Farm

Peatswood
Hall

The Brodder

BLORE RD

Hales Hall

Hales

FLASH LA

Home
Farm

4

The
Lloyd

Coal Brook

33

Old Springs
Farm

Stoneyford

Dairy
House

Wood
Farm

Johnson's Wood
Farm

3

Tyrley Wharf

Tyrley
Farm

Old Springs
Hall

Saw Pit
Wood

32

Shropshire Union Canal Main Line

Chipnall Wood

The
Lodge

2

Bridlands Wood

Cheswardine Park
Farm

TAG LA

Haywood
Drumble

31

Woodseaves Manor
Farm

Lawn
Drumble

1

Haywood Farm

Cheswardine
Road
Bridge

HAYWOOD LA

LWN LA

30

D
70
E
71
F

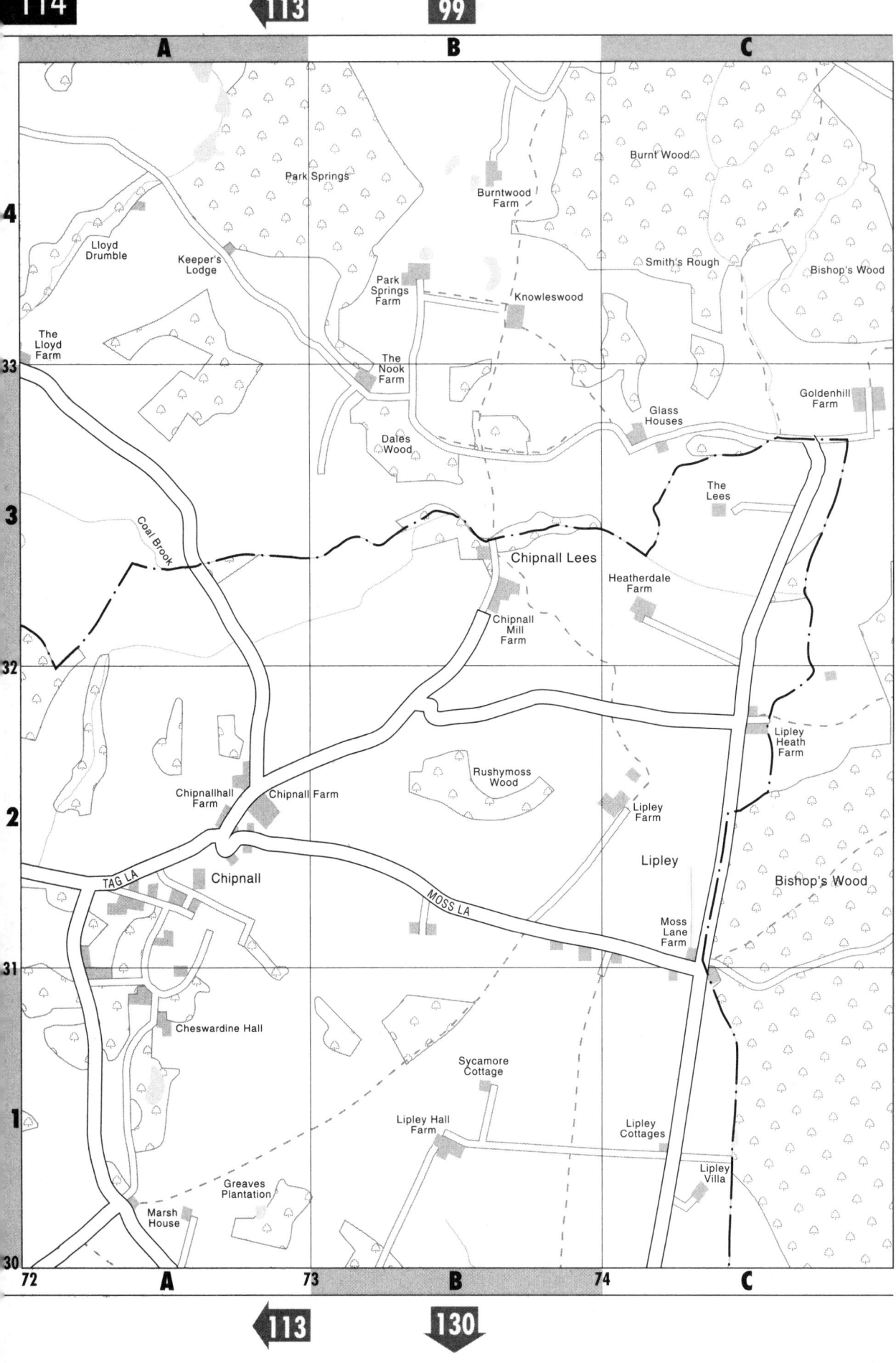

Park Springs

Burnt Wood

Burntwood
Farm

Lloyd
Drumble

Keeper's
Lodge

Smith's Rough

Bishop's Wood

Park
Springs
Farm

Knowleswood

The Lloyd
Farm

The
Nook
Farm

Goldenhill
Farm

Glass
Houses

Dales
Wood

Coal Brook

Chipnall Lees

The
Lees

Heatherdale
Farm

Chipnall
Mill
Farm

Lipley
Heath
Farm

Chipnallhall
Farm

Chipnall Farm

Rushymoss
Wood

Lipley
Farm

Lipley

Bishop's Wood

TAG LA

Chipnall

MOSS LA

Moss
Lane
Farm

Cheswardine Hall

Sycamore
Cottage

Lipley
Cottages

Lipley Hall
Farm

Lipley
Villa

Greaves
Plantation

Marsh
House

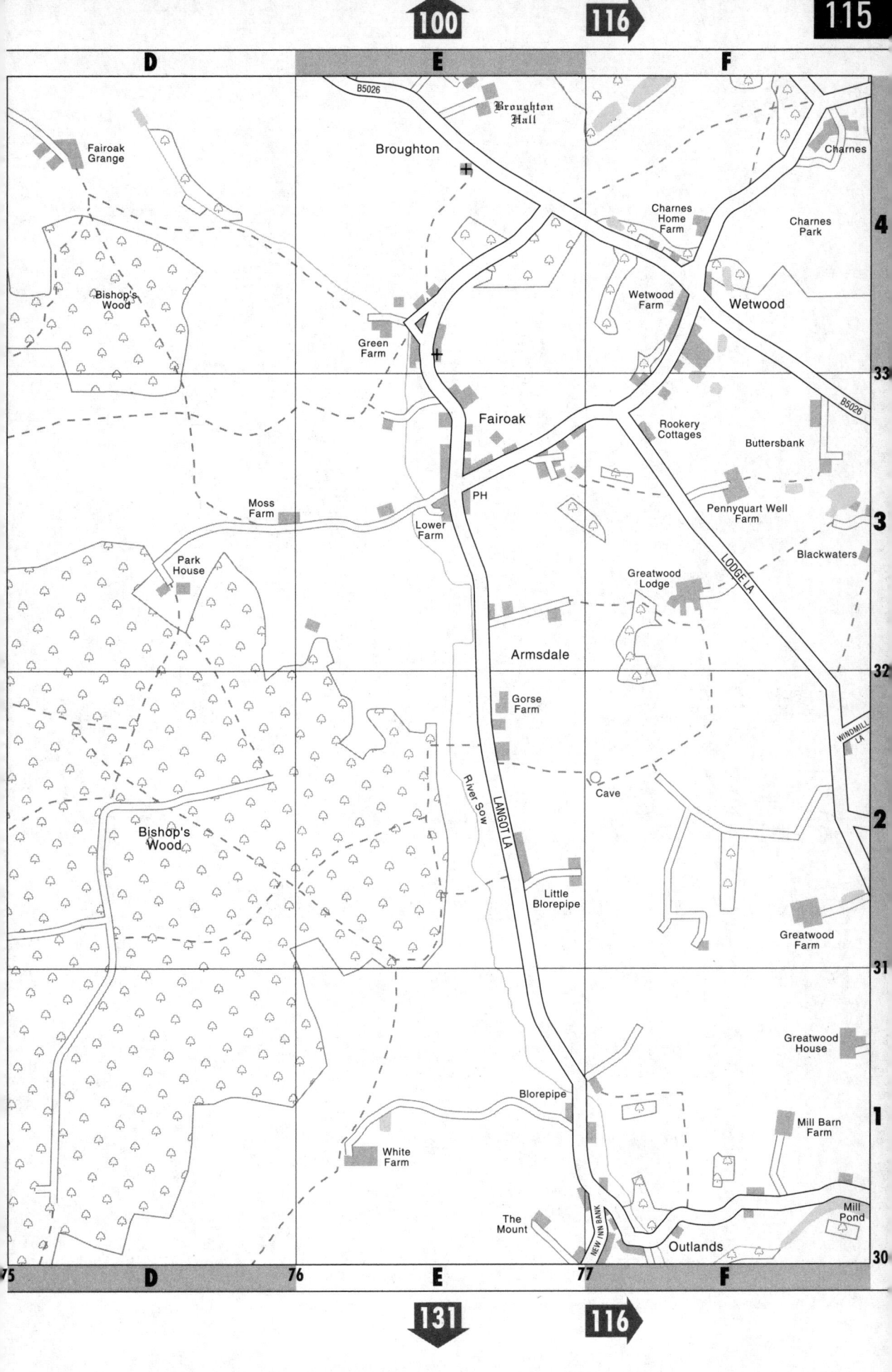

115
101

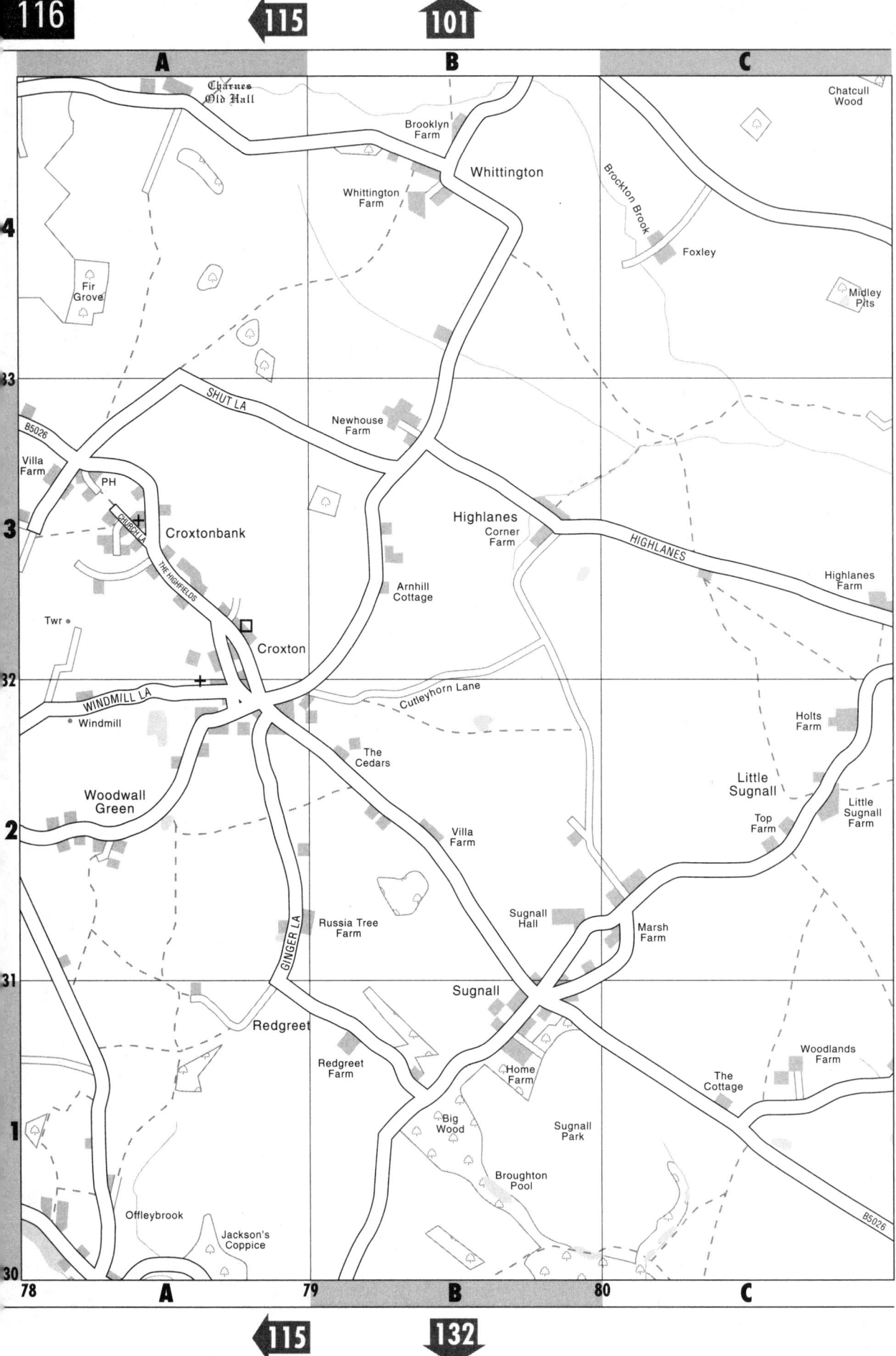

115
132

D   E   F

Walford Hall
Walford
Marlpits

Pumping Station

A519

Walford House

Woodhill Villa

Chatcull Brook

Millmeece
4

Brown's Bridge

Brownsbridge Farm

Camp Site (dis)

Aspley Farm

Aspley

Aspley House Farm

Meece Brook

PH

33

The Brooms

Slindon House

The Villa Farm

Slindon

3

Eastfields Bungalow

Brockton Brook

HIGHLANES

Brockton Farm

Red Lion Farm

32

Brockton Villa

Brockton

Brockton Hall

Parks Wood

Ankerton

PATERSON AVE

Drake Hall (HM Prison)

HILTON DR

BRADY CRES

2

BROCKTON LA

Brockton Rookery

Cat's Hill

Little Ankerton

Lower House Farm

Brockton Bank

Underwood Farm

31

New House Farm

The Rough

Cat's Hill Cross

Raleigh Hall

SMITHY LA

Old Sturbridge Farm

1

Spring Lane

Spring Fields

The Ashtons Farm

Sturbridge

Sturbridge Farm

Green Farm

B5026

Pool House

A519

30

D   82   E   83   F

A B C

4

33

3

32

2

1

30

New Birch House

Swynnerton
Training
Area

Sewage
Works

Pilstones
Wood

Meece
House

Works

Coldmeece

Post Office
Technical Training
College

Eastfields

Hill
Farm

Baden Hall
Lodge

HILTON DR

Baden Hall Cottages

Drake Hall
(HM Prison)

The Rookery

Baden Hall

Pool
Plantation

Hilcote
Cottages

Hilcote
Farm

The Highlows

Mast

Beatty
Hall

British
Telecom
Technical
College

High Lows Lane

Howard
Hall

SUMMERFIELDS

FIELDSIDE

TIMBERFIELDS

HOLLY FIELDS

HIGH LOWS LA

Yarnfield

Sch

POTTERS

THE
WILLOWS

CALVELEY CL

MEADOWWAY

FORD DR

COLLEGE
FIELDS

PADDOCKS

SOPWITH CL

YARNFIELD LA

MEECE RD

BATTEN
WLK

THE FURLONG

ASHDALE PARK

DE HAVILLAND
DR

GREENSIDE

ASH LA

MAPLE
CL

COBHAM CL

MITCHELL RISE

DE HAVILLAND DR

NORTH RD

SOUTH RD

STATION RD

MEECE RD

The Broom

Dismantled Railway

Meece Brook

Middle
Heamies

Upper
Heamies
Cottages

Upper
Heamies

Lower Heamies

Lower
Heamies
Wood

Magpie
Wood

B5026

Oxleasows

Norton Bridge

STATION RD

SCAMMELL LA

B5026

84 A 85 B 86 C

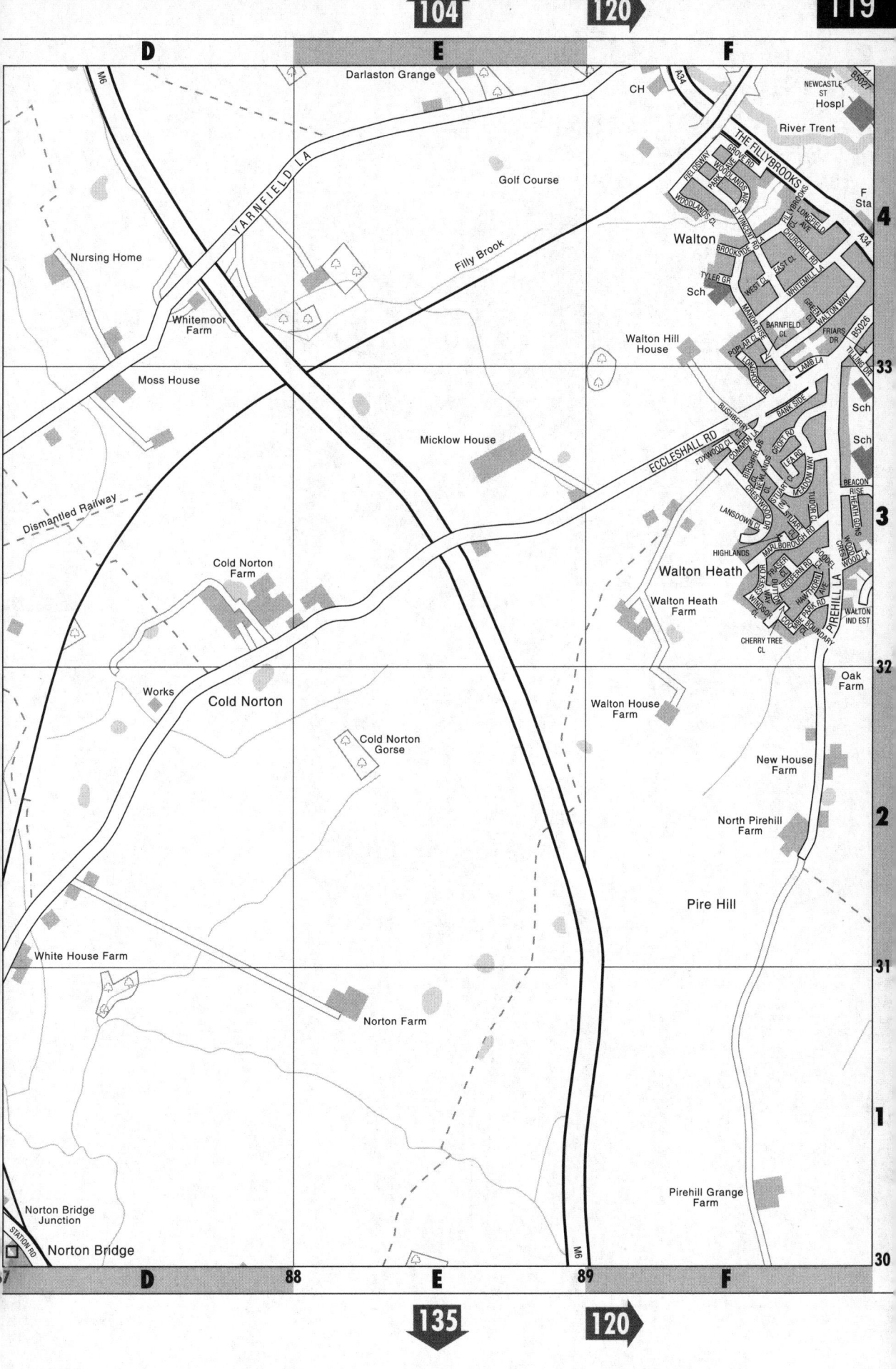

D E F

NEWCASTLE
ST
Hospl

Darlaston Grange

CH

A34

River Trent

M6

THE FILLYBROOKS

GROVE RD

HELDSWAY

WOODLANDS AVE

WOODLANDS CL

FILLYBROOK

LONGFIELD AVE

F
Sta

F

4

Golf Course

ST ANDREWS DR

BROOKSIDE

CHURCHILL RD

WALTON WAY

A34

Walton

YARNFIELD LA

Filly Brook

WEST CL

WEST CL

WHITEHILL LA

TYLER GR

Sch

GREY

Nursing Home

MANOR RISE

BARNFIELD
CL

FRIARS
DR

B5026

TILLING DR

POPLAR CL

Walton Hill
House

LONGHORE DR

LAMB LA

33

Whitemoor
Farm

BUSHBERRY

PARK SIDE

Sch

ECCLESHALL RD

FOXWOOD
CL

COMMON

BELCHFIELD

GROUP RD

TEA RD

Sch

Moss House

THE AVENUE

TUDOR RD

BEACON
RISE

HEATH GDNS

WOODLAND

CRESSWOOD LA

Micklow House

LANSDOWNE

MARLBOROUGH

HIGHLANDS

FRASER

REDFERN RD

SOREL

PIREHILL LA

3

Dismantled Railway

WILLSOR

HAWTHORN

PARK RD

Walton Heath

Cold Norton
Farm

Walton Heath
Farm

CHERRY TREE
CL

WALTON
IND EST

Works

32

Cold Norton

Oak
Farm

Walton House
Farm

Cold Norton
Gorse

New House
Farm

North Pirehill
Farm

2

White House Farm

Pire Hill

31

Norton Farm

1

M6

Norton Bridge
Junction

Pirehill Grange
Farm

STATION RD

Norton Bridge

30

D 88 E 89 F

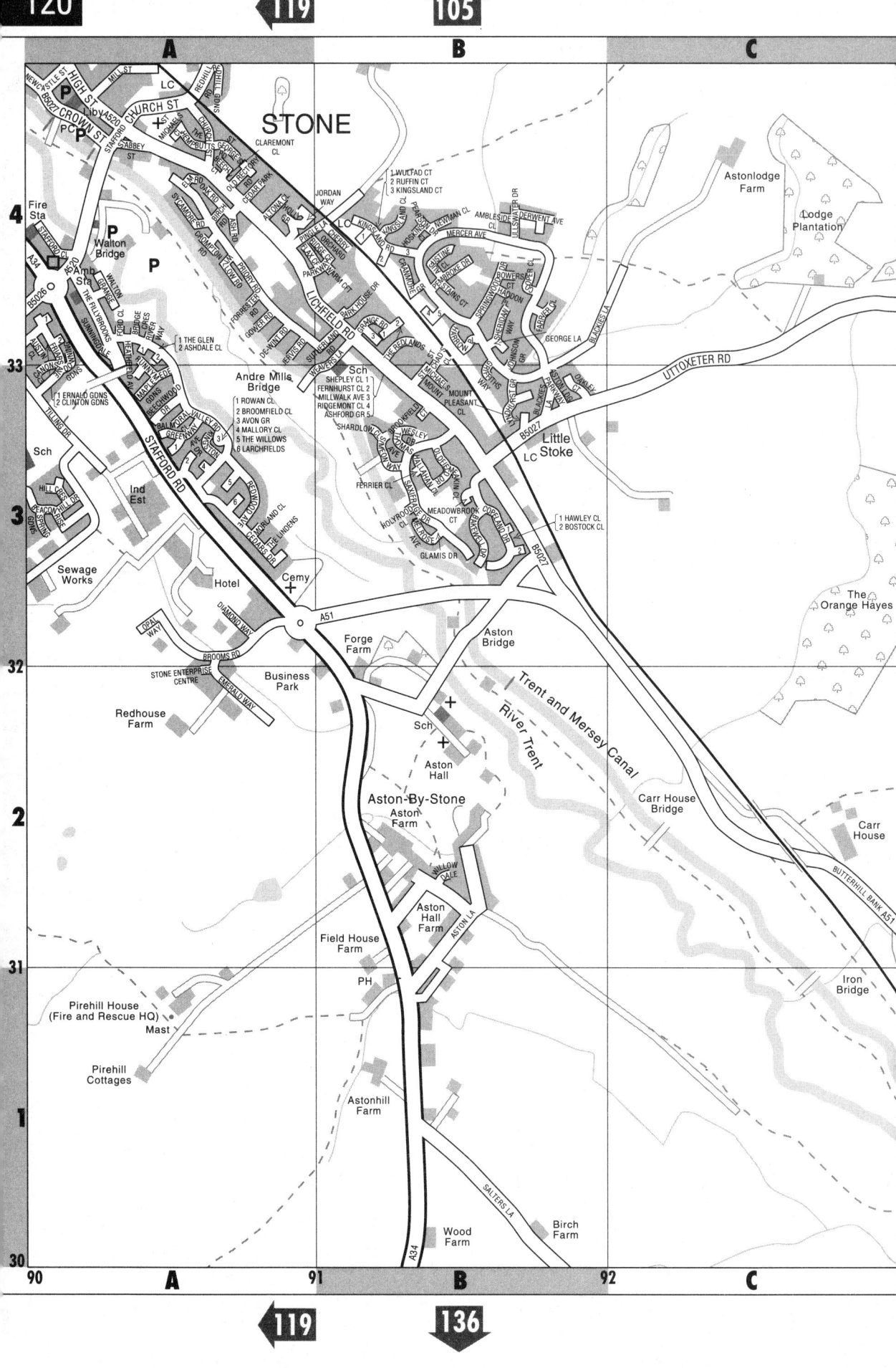

119

105

STONE

A   B   C

Newcastle ST
HIGH ST
B5027
CROWN ST
CHURCH ST
MILL ST
LC
REDHILL
P
P
PC
P
Lib A520
STAFFORD ST
ABBEY ST
MIDDLE ST
CHURCHILL RD
CRUMBUTTS ST
GEORGE ST
OLDCROFT
CLAREMONT CL

1 WULFAD CT
2 RUFFIN CT
3 KINGSLAND CT

JORDAN WAY
LC
AMBLESIDE DR
DERWENT AVE
ULLSWATER DR
Astonlodge Farm
Lodge Plantation

Fire Sta
A34
A520
B5026
P
Walton Bridge
WALTON CL
GRANGE
THE FAIRBROOKS
SUNNINGDALE
Amb Sta
P
SYCAMORE RD
HOMETON DR
LLOYD RD
FORRESTER RD
GOWER RD
JERVIS RD
ASH RD
PRIORY RD
PIREHILL LA
CHETWYND DR
KINGS RD
KINGS RD
MERCER AVE
GEORGE LA
BLACKIES LA
UTTOXETER RD

1 THE GLEN
2 ASHDALE CL

Andre Mills Bridge

1 ROWAN CL
2 BROOMFIELD CL
3 AVON GR
4 MALLORY CL
5 THE WILLOWS
6 LARCHFIELDS

Sch
SHEPLEY CL 1
FERNHURST CL 2
MILLWALK AVE 3
RIDGEMONT CL 4
ASHFORD GR 5
SHARDLOW

Little Stoke
LC
B5027

1 ERNALD GDNS
2 CLINTON GDNS

Sch
HILL CREST GDNS
BEACON HILL GDNS
Ind Est
STAFFORD RD
BALMORAL VALLEY RD
GREENWAY
MAPLE
BEECHWOOD
REDWOODS
CEDARS DR
THE LINDENS
MORLAND CL

FERRIER CL
MEADOWBROOK CT
GLAMIS DR

1 HAWLEY CL
2 BOSTOCK CL
B5027

Sewage Works
Hotel
Cemy
DIAMOND WAY
OPAL WAY
BROOMS RD
A51
Forge Farm
Aston Bridge

Redhouse Farm
Stone Enterprise Centre
EMERALD WAY
Business Park
Sch
Aston Hall

Trent and Mersey Canal
River Trent
Carr House Bridge
The Orange Hayes

Aston-By-Stone
Aston Farm
Carr House
BUTTERHILL BANK A51

WILLOW DALE
Aston Hall Farm
ASTON LA

Field House Farm
Iron Bridge

PH
Pirehill House (Fire and Rescue HQ)
Mast

Pirehill Cottages
Astonhill Farm

SALTERS LA
A34
Wood Farm
Birch Farm

4   33   3   32   2   31   1   30

90   A   91   B   92   C

119   136

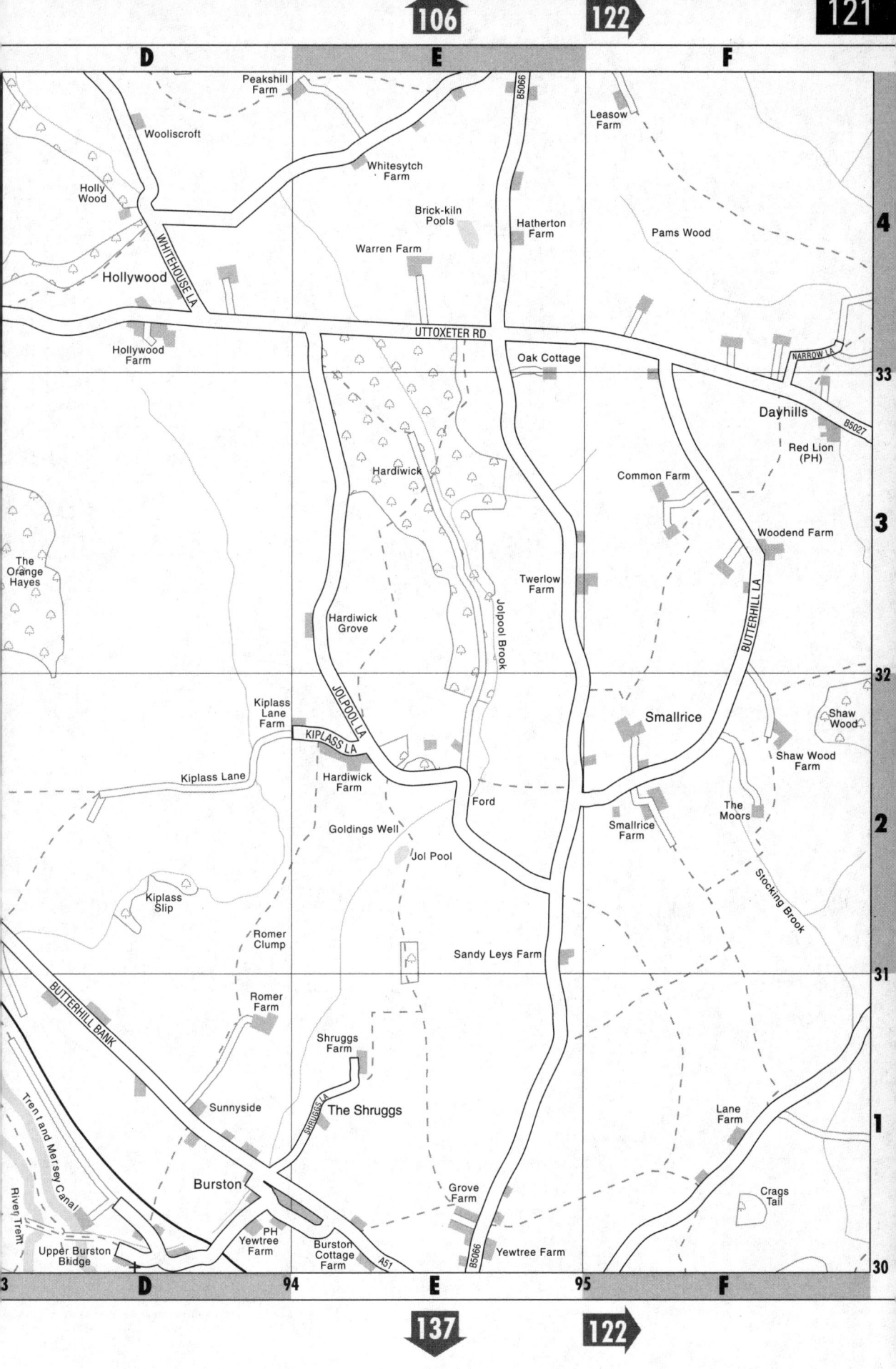

D
E
F

Peakshill Farm

Wooliscroft

Leasow Farm

Whitesytch Farm

Holly Wood

Brick-kiln Pools

Hatherton Farm

Pams Wood

4

Warren Farm

Hollywood

WHITEHOUSE LA

B5066

Hollywood Farm

UTTOXETER RD

Oak Cottage

NARROW LA

33

Dayhills

B5027

Red Lion (PH)

Hardiwick

Common Farm

3

The Orange Hayes

Woodend Farm

Hardiwick Grove

Twerlow Farm

Jolpool Brook

BUTTERHILL LA

32

Shaw Wood

Kiplass Lane Farm

JOLPOOL LA

KIPLASS LA

Smallrice

Shaw Wood Farm

Kiplass Lane

Hardiwick Farm

Ford

The Moors

2

Stocking Brook

Goldings Well

Smallrice Farm

Kiplass Slip

Jol Pool

Romer Clump

Sandy Leys Farm

31

BUTTERHILL BANK

Romer Farm

Shruggs Farm

Trent and Mersey Canal

Lane Farm

Sunnyside

SHRUGGS LA

The Shruggs

1

River Trent

Burston

Grove Farm

Crags Tail

PH Yewtree Farm

Upper Burston Bridge

Burston Cottage Farm

A51

B5066

Yewtree Farm

30

3
D
94
E
95
F

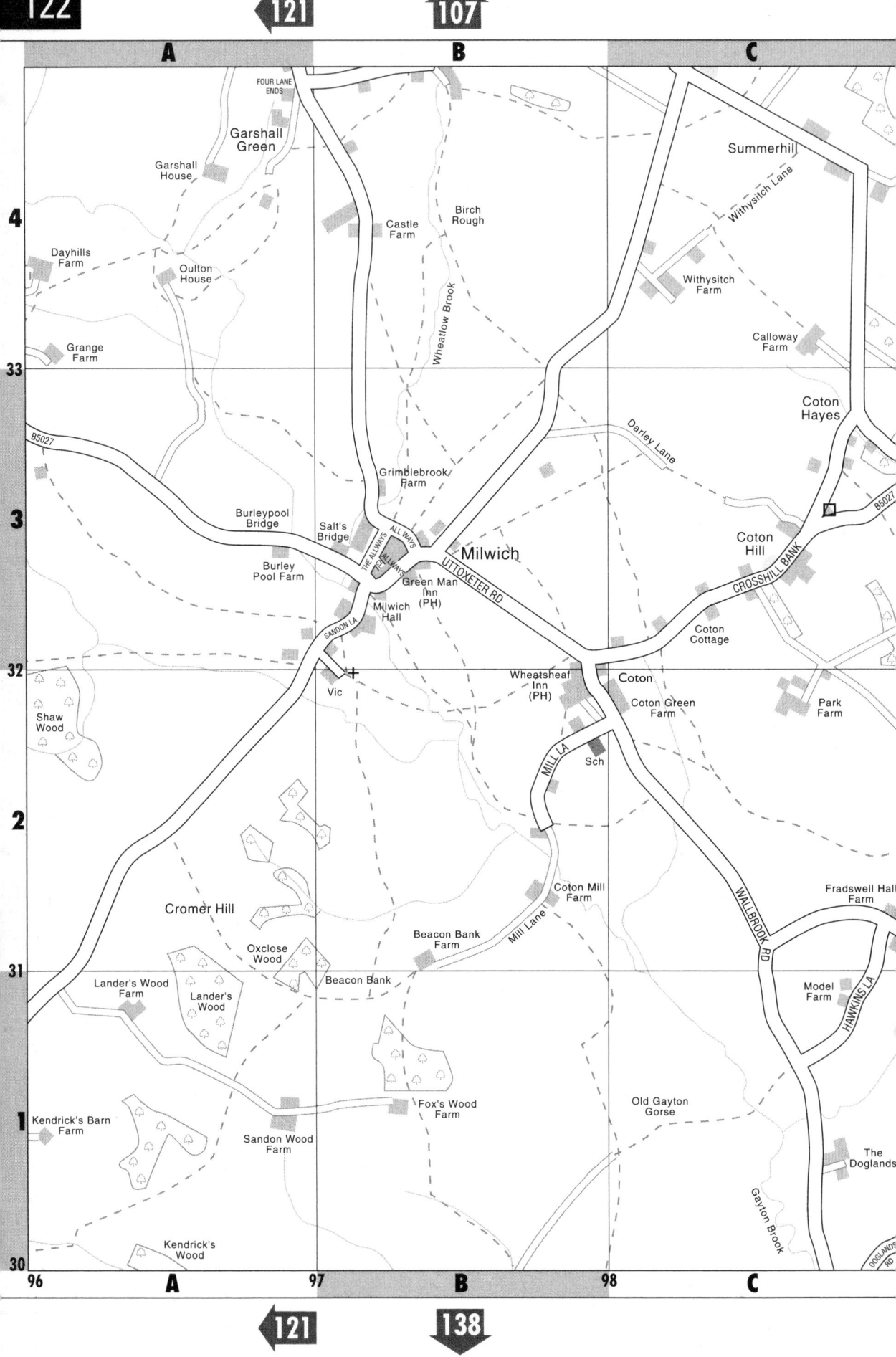

4

Garshall
Green

Garshall
House

FOUR LANE
ENDS

Castle
Farm

Birch
Rough

Summerhill

Withysitch Lane

Withysitch
Farm

Dayhills
Farm

Oulton
House

Wheatlow Brook

Calloway
Farm

33

Grange
Farm

Coton
Hayes

B5027

Darley Lane

B5027

3

Burleypool
Bridge

Salt's
Bridge

Grimblebrook
Farm

Coton
Hill

Burley
Pool Farm

THE ALLWAYS
ALL WAYS
ALL WAYS

Milwich

Coton
Hill

CROSSHILL BANK

Green Man
Inn
(PH)

UTTOXETER RD

Milwich
Hall

SANDON LA

Coton
Cottage

32

Vic

Wheatsheaf
Inn
(PH)

Coton

Coton Green
Farm

Park
Farm

Shaw
Wood

MILL LA

Sch

2

Cromer Hill

Oxclose
Wood

Coton Mill
Farm

Beacon Bank
Farm

Mill Lane

WALLBROOK RD

Fradswell Hall
Farm

HAWKINS LA

31

Lander's Wood
Farm

Lander's
Wood

Beacon Bank

Model
Farm

Kendrick's Barn
Farm

Fox's Wood
Farm

Old Gayton
Gorse

The
Doglands

1

Sandon Wood
Farm

Gayton Brook

DOGLANDS RD

Kendrick's
Wood

30

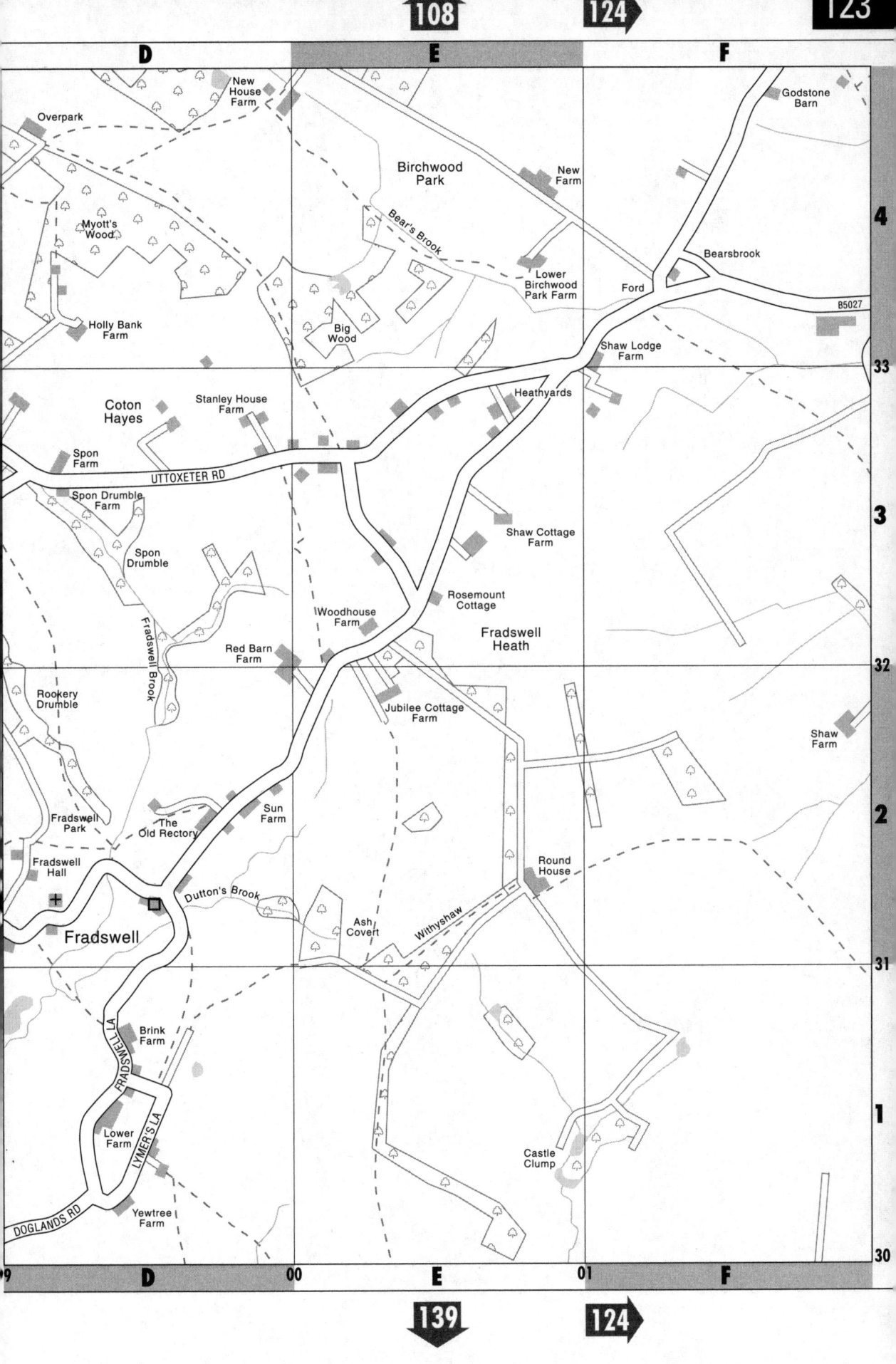

D E F

4

Overpark
New House Farm
Myott's Wood
Birchwood Park
Bear's Brook
New Farm
Godstone Barn
Bearsbrook
Lower Birchwood Park Farm
Ford
B5027

33

Holly Bank Farm
Big Wood
Shaw Lodge Farm

Coton Hayes
Stanley House Farm
Heathyards

3

Spon Farm
UTTOXETER RD
Spon Drumble Farm
Shaw Cottage Farm

Spon Drumble
Fradswell Brook
Woodhouse Farm
Rosemount Cottage
Fradswell Heath

32

Red Barn Farm

Rookery Drumble
Jubilee Cottage Farm
Shaw Farm

2

Fradswell Park
The Old Rectory
Sun Farm
Round House

Fradswell Hall
Dutton's Brook
Ash Covert
Withyshaw

31

Fradswell

Fradswell La
Brink Farm

1

Lymer's La
Lower Farm
Castle Clump

Doglands RD
Yewtree Farm

30

D 00 E 01 F

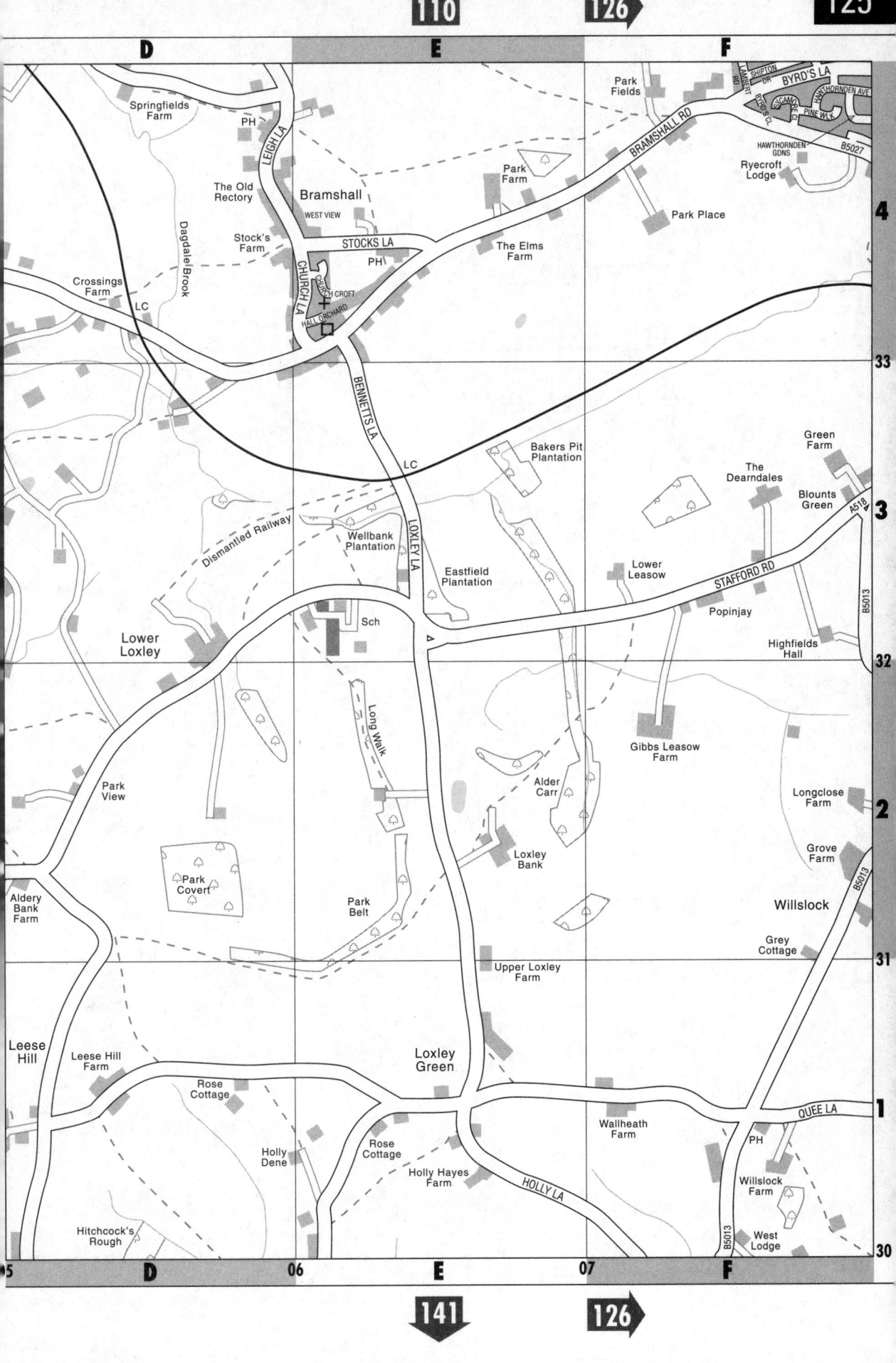

D
E
F

Springfields
Farm

PH

LEIGH LA

The Old
Rectory

Bramshall

WEST VIEW

Stock's
Farm

STOCKS LA

PH

CHURCH LA

CHURCH CROFT

HALL ORCHARD

Crossings
Farm

LC

Dagdale Brook

Park
Fields

BRAMSHALL RD

SHIPTON
DR

LAMBERT RD

BYRD'S LA

PINE WLK

HAWTHORNDEN AVE

ESCAMORE CL

BURTON CL

B5027

HAWTHORNDEN
GDNS

Ryecroft
Lodge

Park Place

Park
Farm

The Elms
Farm

4

33

BENNETTS LA

LC

Dismantled Railway

Wellbank
Plantation

LOXLEY LA

Bakers Pit
Plantation

Eastfield
Plantation

Green
Farm

The
Dearndales

Blounts
Green

A518

Lower
Leasow

STAFFORD RD

Popinjay

Highfields
Hall

B5013

3

32

Lower
Loxley

Sch

Long Walk

Gibbs Leasow
Farm

Longclose
Farm

Grove
Farm

B5013

2

Park
View

Park
Covert

Park
Belt

Alder
Carr

Loxley
Bank

Willslock

Grey
Cottage

31

Aldery
Bank
Farm

Leese
Hill

Leese Hill
Farm

Rose
Cottage

Holly
Dene

Rose
Cottage

Loxley
Green

Upper Loxley
Farm

Holly Hayes
Farm

HOLLY LA

Wallheath
Farm

QUEE LA

PH

1

B5013

Willslock
Farm

West
Lodge

30

Hitchcock's
Rough

D
06
E
07
F

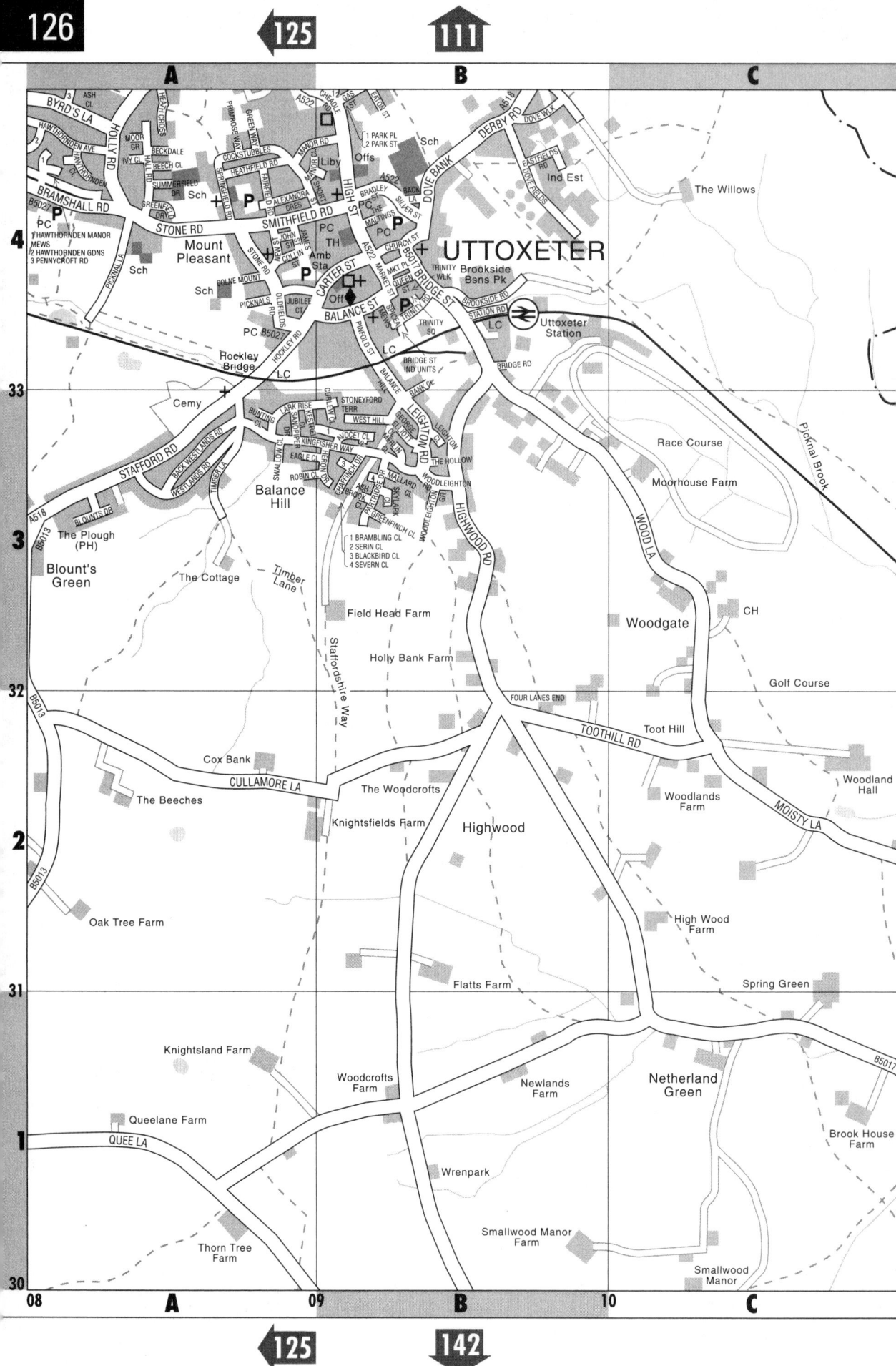

128

Somersal Herbert

Road
Under
Construction

Manor
House

CHAPEL
GREEN

Sch

Old
Hall

Sewage
Works

Doveridge

Deepmoor
Farm

Yelt Farm

Brocksford
Bridge

Ley-Hill
Farm

Palmer Moor
Farm

Palmer Moor

Brocksford Hall
School

Brocksford
Cottages

A50

Brocksford Brook

Brocksford
Gorse

Holtwood
Cottages

Herepark

Holtwood

The
Breach

Woodford
Rough

Woodford

River Dove

Railway
Cottages

Green
Acres

Riddings
Farm

Slade's
Farm

MOISTY LA

Hall
Croft

Marchington

THE SQUARE
Sch

PH

Pear Tree
Farm

Field
Farm

HALL RD

Church
Farm

Upper Brook
House

Birch Cross

Brookside
Farm

PH

Brickhill
Hill

Field
House
Stables

Lower Brook
House

HODGE LA

STOCK LA

The
Vicarage

Marchington
Ind Est

Small Silver
Green

Hound
Hill

Carrig

A   B   C

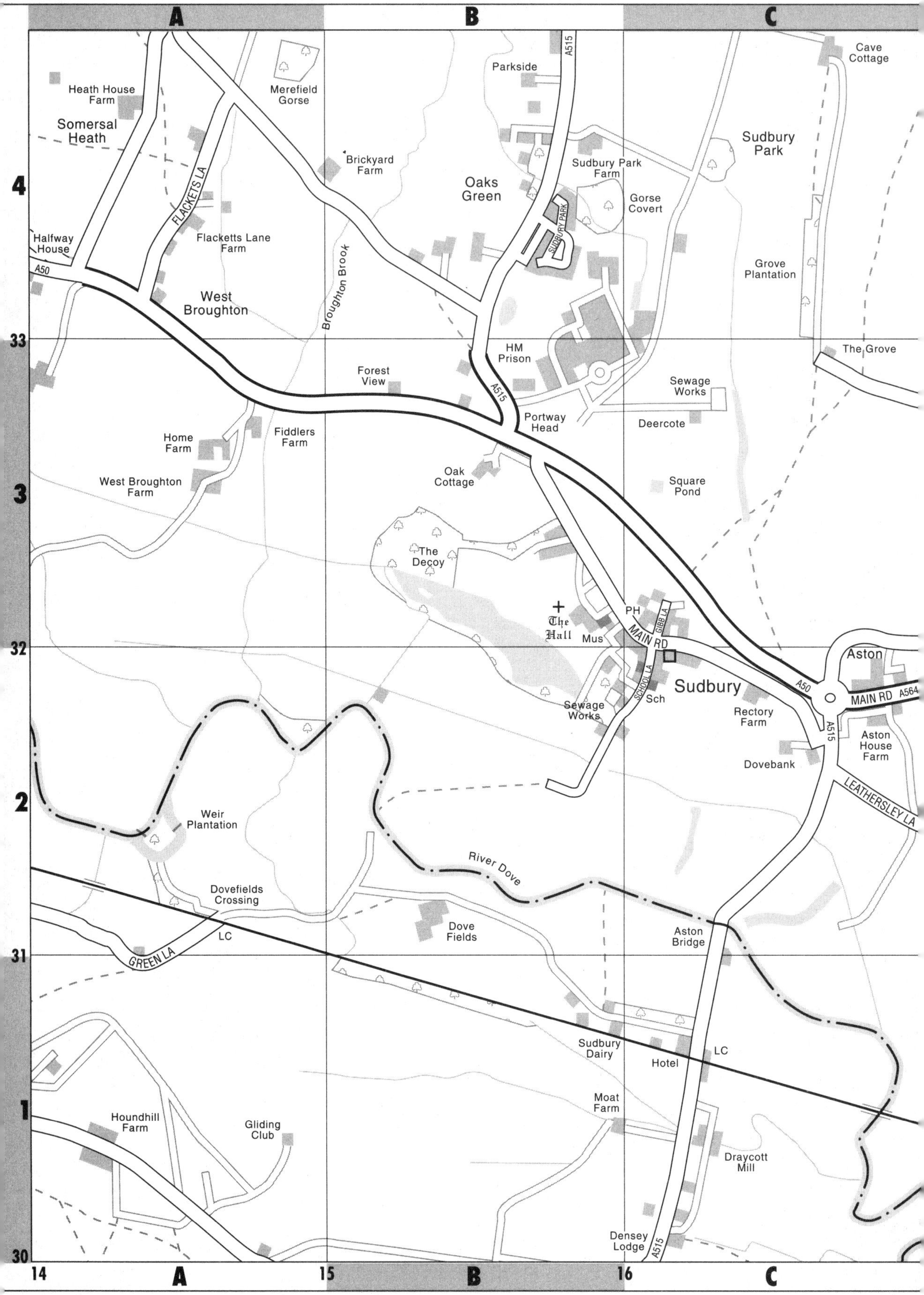

4

Heath House Farm

Somersal Heath

Merefield Gorse

Parkside

Sudbury Park

Cave Cottage

Halfway House

A50

FLACKETTS LA

Flacketts Lane Farm

West Broughton

Brickyard Farm

Oaks Green

Broughton Brook

Sudbury Park Farm

Gorse Covert

Grove Plantation

33

Forest View

HM Prison

Portway Head

Sewage Works

Deercote

The Grove

Home Farm

Fiddlers Farm

3

West Broughton Farm

A515

Oak Cottage

Square Pond

The Decoy

The Hall

Mus

PH

GIBB LA

MAIN RD

32

Sewage Works

Sch

SCHOOL LA

Sudbury

A50

A515

Aston

MAIN RD   A564

Rectory Farm

Dovebank

Aston House Farm

LEATHERSLEY LA

2

Weir Plantation

River Dove

Dovefields Crossing

LC

GREEN LA

Dove Fields

Aston Bridge

31

Sudbury Dairy

Hotel

LC

1

Houndhill Farm

Gliding Club

Moat Farm

Draycott Mill

Densey Lodge

A515

30

14   A   15   B   16   C

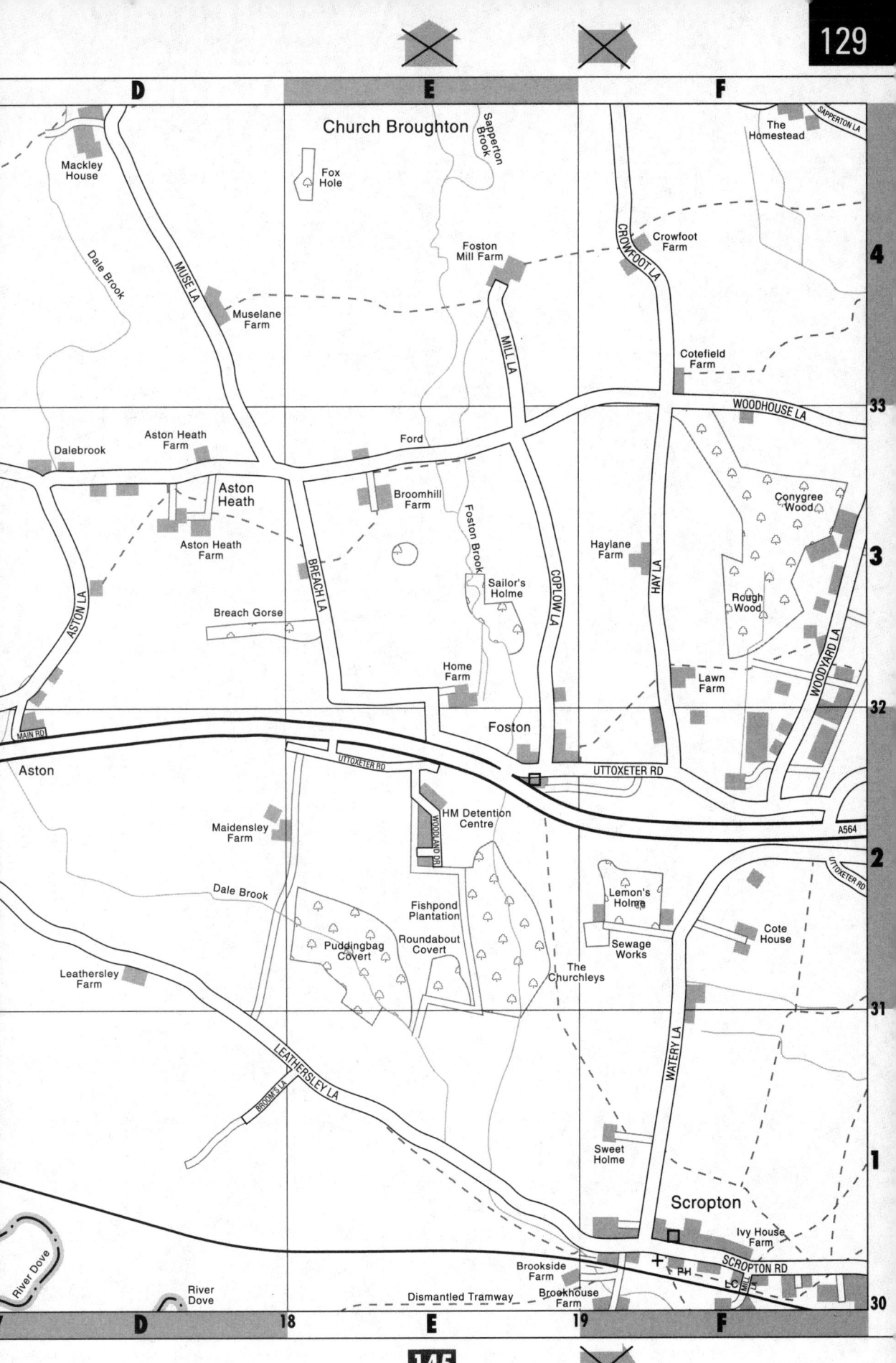

Church Broughton

Fox Hole

Mackley House

Dale Brook

MUSE LA

Muselane Farm

Sapperton Brook

The Homestead

SAPPERTON LA

CROWFOOT LA

Crowfoot Farm

Foston Mill Farm

MILL LA

Cotefield Farm

WOODHOUSE LA

Dalebrook

Aston Heath Farm

Aston Heath

Aston Heath Farm

ASTON LA

Breach Gorse

BREACH LA

Ford

Broomhill Farm

Foston Brook

Sailor's Holme

COPLOW LA

Home Farm

Foston

Conygree Wood

Haylane Farm

HAY LA

Rough Wood

Lawn Farm

WOODYARD LA

MAIN RD

Aston

UTTOXETER RD

UTTOXETER RD

A564

UTTOXETER RD

Maidensley Farm

WOODLAND DR

HM Detention Centre

Dale Brook

Fishpond Plantation

Puddingbag Covert

Roundabout Covert

Lemon's Holme

Sewage Works

Cote House

The Churchleys

Leathersley Farm

LEATHERSLEY LA

BROOM'S LA

WATERY LA

Sweet Holme

River Dove

River Dove

Scropton

Ivy House Farm

Brookside Farm

Dismantled Tramway

Brookhouse Farm

PH

LC

SCROPTON RD

A B C

THE COMPTONS
Sch
GLEBE CH
Cheswardine Farm
MARSH LA
4
HIGH ST
Cheswardine
WESTCOTT LA
Doorway Farm

Cheswardine Marsh

Doley Farm

Doley Manor

Doleymill

Doley

Old House Farm

29
MOSSFIELD
Soudley
PH
Robin Hood House

Hanwood Farm

3
Hopshort
Knighton Reservoir

The Drumble

Adbaston Farm

Shawbroom

Soudley Park

28
Canal Feeder

Knighton Wood

Knighton Grange

2
Towing Path
Shropshire Union Canal

Knighton

Park Heath Farm
Park Heath
Palins Farm

27
Works

The Rookery

Thorneypits

1
Waggs Brook

Stone Plantation

Kingswell Cottages

26
72 A 73 B 74 C

D
E
F

Lower Wood Corner Farm

Doley Cottages

Four Lane Ends Farm

Outlands

Bishop's Offley

FOURLANE ENDS

NEW INN BANK

Manor Farm

4

pper Wood Corner Farm

Wood Farm

29

Adbaston Grange

LERRIDGE LA

MAIN RD

3

Sch

Lea House Farm

The Lea

28

Adbaston Hall Farm

ST. MICHAEL'S CL

CHURCH VIEW

Adbaston

THE BUNGALOWS

Haberdasher's Arms (PH)

Marsh Meadow

Tunstall Hall

2

Adbaston House

Tunstalls Farm

Tunstall

Knighton Hall

Offleygrove Farm

27

Lonco Brook

Offley Grove

1

Shropshire Union Canal Main Line

Batchacre Park

The Claylands

TUNSTALL LA

Shebdon Farm

Wharf Inn (PH)

26

D
76
E
77
F

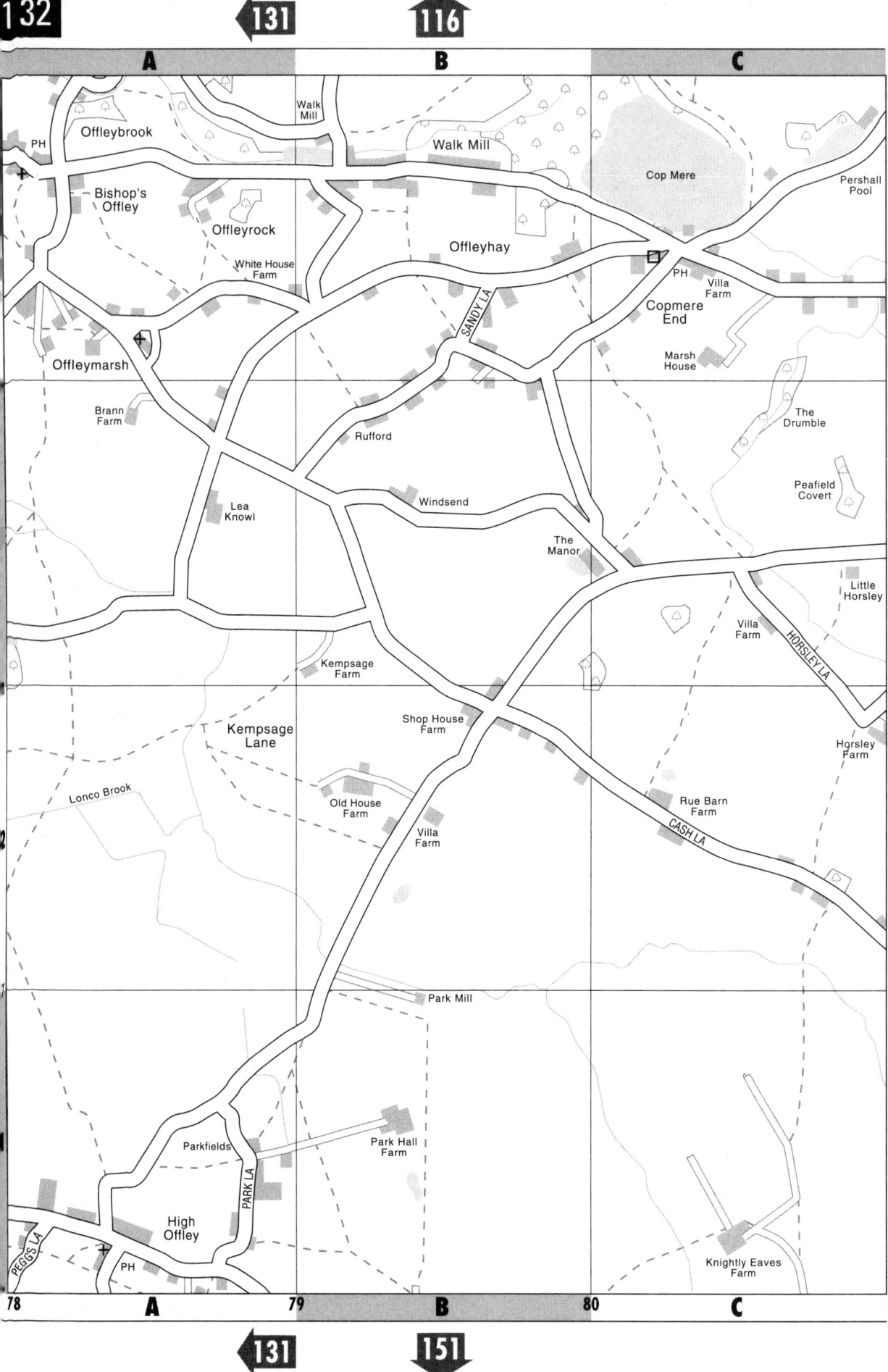

Offleybrook
Walk Mill
Walk Mill
PH
Cop Mere
Pershall Pool
Bishop's Offley
Offleyrock
Offleyhay
SANDY LA
PH
Villa Farm
Copmere End
White House Farm
Offleymarsh
Marsh House
Brann Farm
The Drumble
Rufford
Peafield Covert
Lea Knowl
Windsend
The Manor
Little Horsley
Villa Farm
HORSLEY LA
Kempsage Farm
Kempsage Lane
Shop House Farm
Horsley Farm
Lonco Brook
Old House Farm
Rue Barn Farm
CASH LA
Villa Farm
Park Mill
Parkfields
Park Hall Farm
PARK LA
High Offley
PEGGS LA
PH
Knightly Eaves Farm

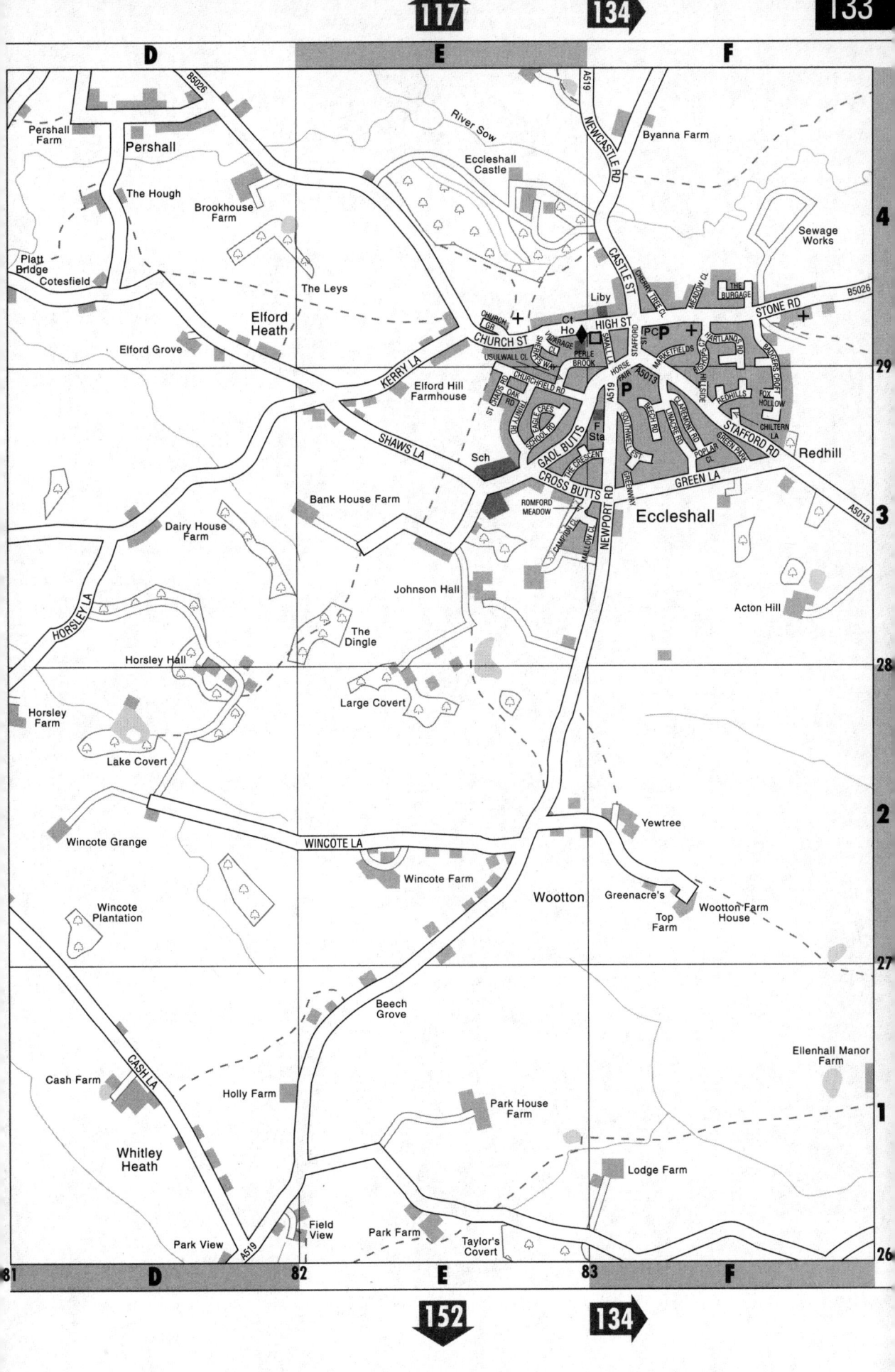

D
E
F

B5026

Pershall Farm

Pershall

River Sow

Eccleshall Castle

A519

NEWCASTLE RD

Byanna Farm

The Hough

Brookhouse Farm

Sewage Works

4

Platt Bridge
Cotesfield

The Leys

CASTLE ST

CHERRY TREE CL

THE BURGAGE

STONE RD

B5026

Elford Heath

Elford Grove

KERRY LA

Liby

CHURCH GR

Ct Ho

HIGH ST

PC P

MEADOW CL

HARTLANDS

29

Elford Hill Farmhouse

CHURCH ST

USULWALL CL

SHERRATTS WAY

STAFFORD ST

PERLE BROOK

STAFFORD

SHALLS

MARKETFIELDS

ST CHADS RD

P

HORSE FAIR

A5013

HILLSIDE

REDHILLS

FOX HOLLOW

BARGERS CROFT

SHAWS LA

CHURCHFIELD RD

OAK RD

CASTLE CRES

A519

SCHOOL RD

ELLENHALL RD

BEECH RD

CLAREMONT RD

MOOR RD

CREAMONT RD

GREEN PARK

CHILTERN LA

Sch

GAOL BUTTS

F Sta

SOUTHWELL ST

POPLAR CL

STAFFORD RD

Redhill

Bank House Farm

THE CRESCENT

A5013

3

Dairy House Farm

CROSS BUTTS

NEWPORT RD

GREEN LA

Eccleshall

HORSLEY LA

ROMFORD MEADOW

CAMPION CL

MALLOW CL

Johnson Hall

Acton Hill

Horsley Hall

The Dingle

28

Horsley Farm

Large Covert

Lake Covert

2

Wincote Grange

WINCOTE LA

Yewtree

Wincote Farm

Greenacre's

Wootton

Wootton Farm House

Top Farm

Wincote Plantation

27

Beech Grove

CASH LA

Ellenhall Manor Farm

Cash Farm

Holly Farm

Park House Farm

1

Whitley Heath

Lodge Farm

A519

Field View

Park Farm

Park View

Taylor's Covert

26

81
D
82
E
83
F

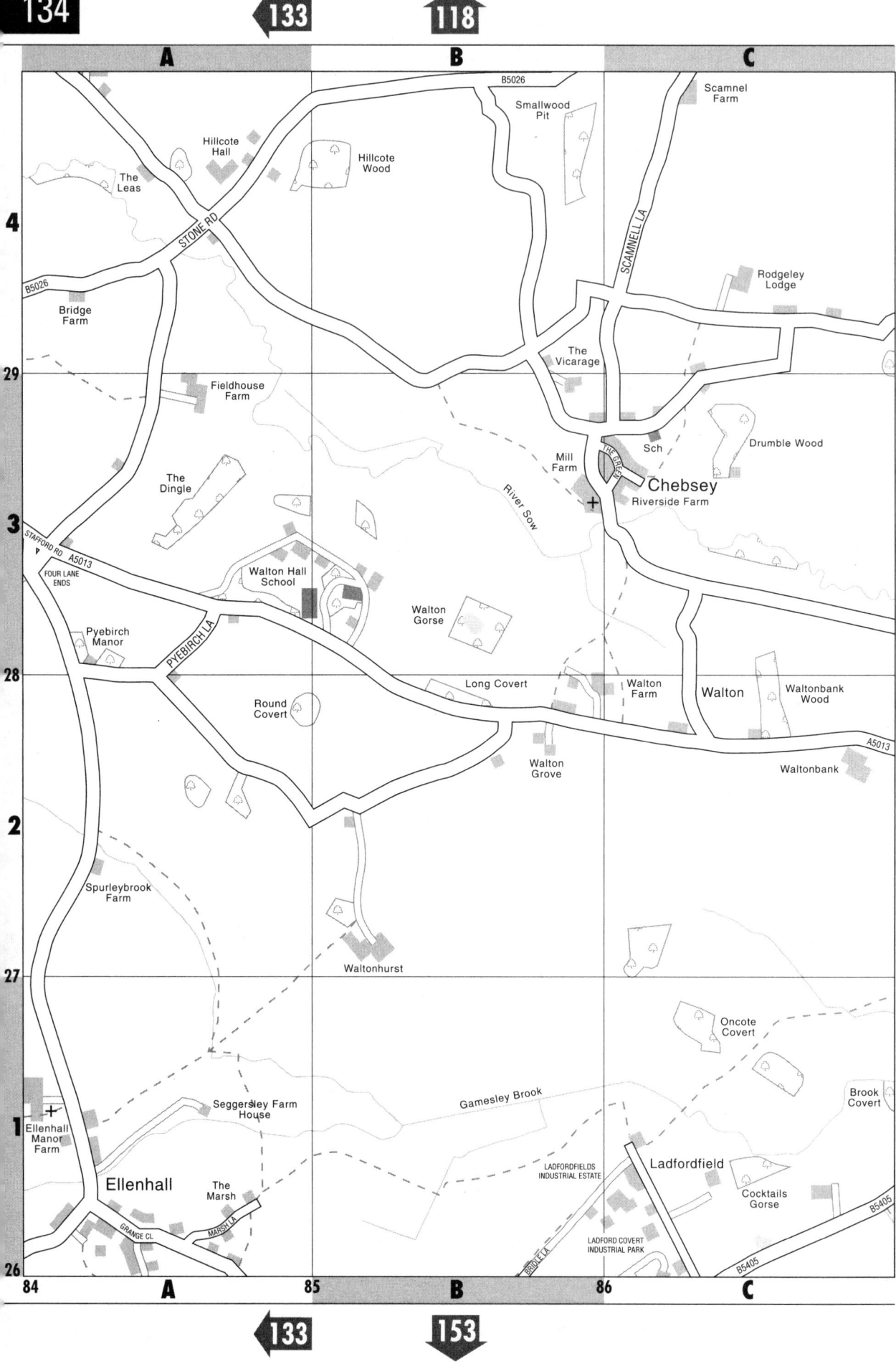

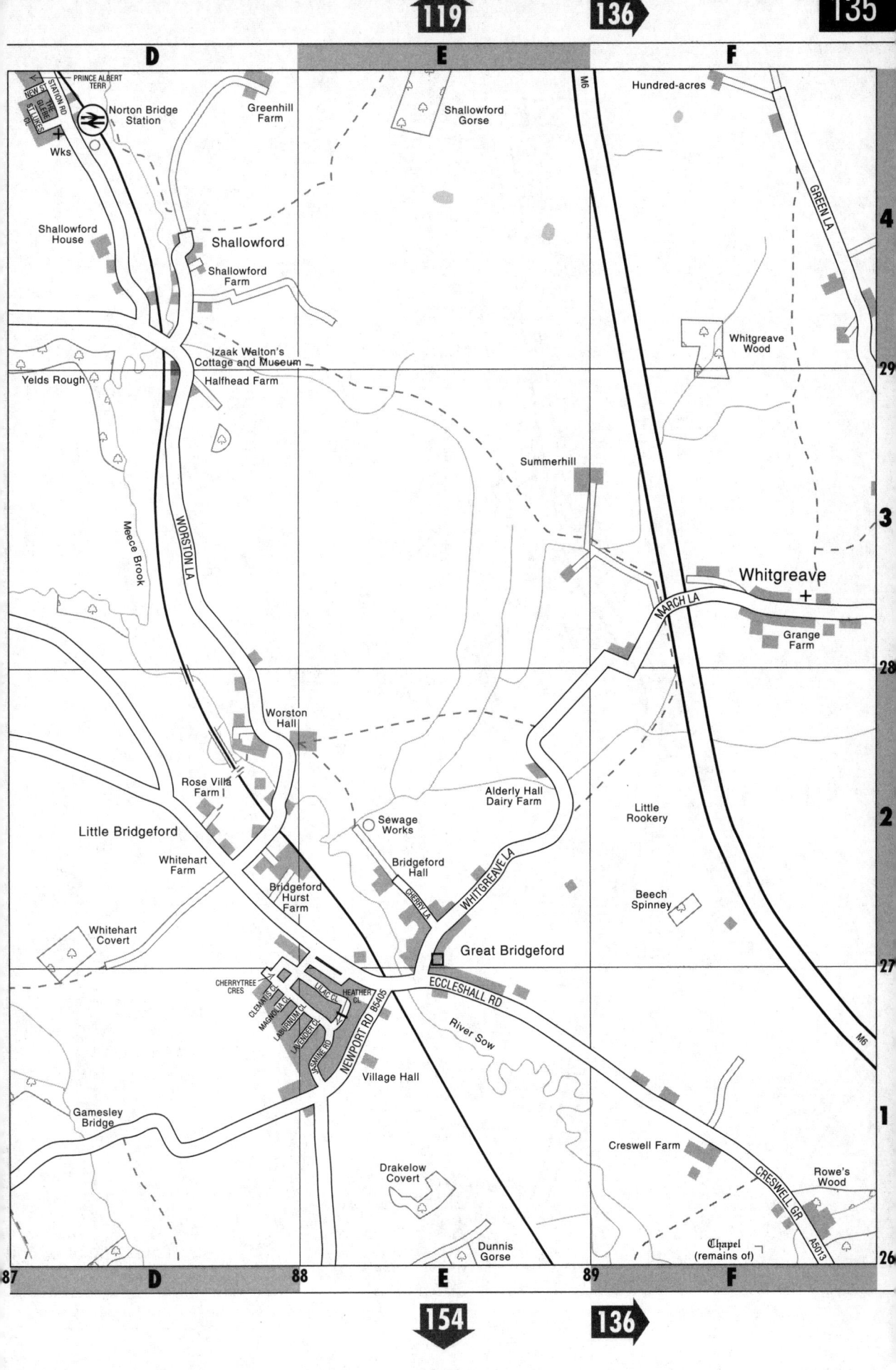

D

E

F

PRINCE ALBERT TERR

NEW ST
GLEBE
ST LUKES
STATION RD

Norton Bridge Station

Wks

Greenhill Farm

Shallowford Gorse

Hundred-acres

GREEN LA

4

Shallowford House

Shallowford

Whitgreave Wood

Shallowford Farm

Izaak Walton's Cottage and Museum

Halfhead Farm

29

Yelds Rough

Summerhill

3

Meece Brook

WORSTON LA

MARCH LA

Whitgreave

Grange Farm

28

Worston Hall

Rose Villa Farm

Little Bridgeford

Alderly Hall Dairy Farm

Little Rookery

2

Whitehart Farm

Sewage Works

WHITGREAVE LA

Beech Spinney

Bridgeford Hall

Bridgeford Hurst Farm

CHERRY LA

Whitehart Covert

Great Bridgeford

27

CHERRYTREE CRES

CLEMATIS CL
MAGNOLIA CL
LILAC CL
LABURNUM CL
LAVENDER CL
JASMINE RD
HEATHER CL
NEWPORT RD B5405

ECCLESHALL RD

River Sow

M6

Gamesley Bridge

Village Hall

1

Creswell Farm

CRESWELL GR

Rowe's Wood

Drakelow Covert

A5013

Dunnis Gorse

Chapel (remains of)

26

87

D

88

E

89

F

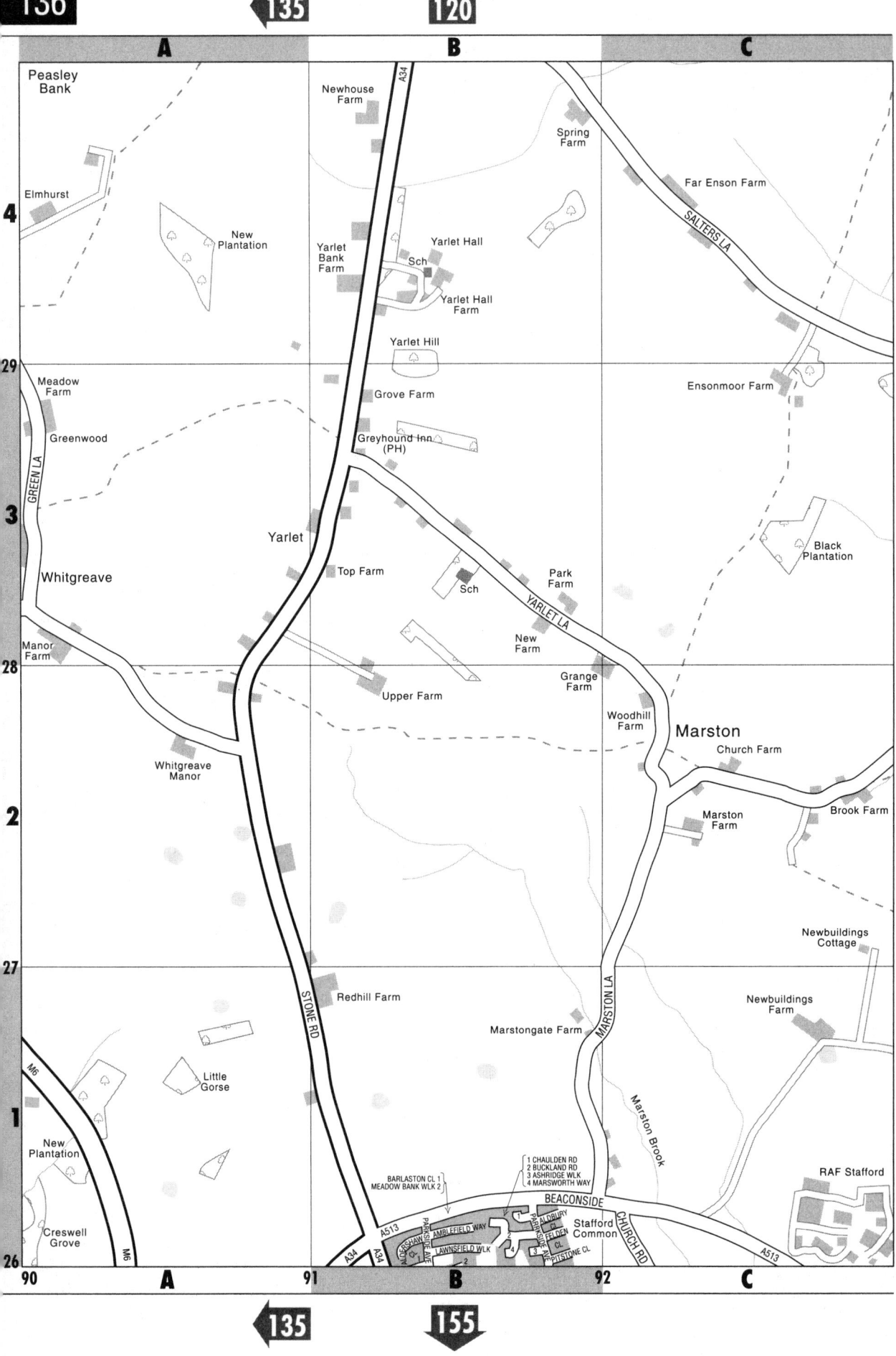

135
120

A   **B**   **C**

Peasley Bank

Elmhurst

New Plantation

4

Newhouse Farm

Spring Farm

Far Enson Farm

SALTERS LA

Yarlet Bank Farm

Yarlet Hall

Sch

Yarlet Hall Farm

Yarlet Hill

29

Meadow Farm

Grove Farm

Ensonmoor Farm

Greenwood

Greyhound Inn (PH)

GREEN LA

3

Yarlet

Top Farm

Park Farm

Black Plantation

Whitgreave

Sch

YARLET LA

New Farm

Grange Farm

Manor Farm

28

Upper Farm

Woodhill Farm

Marston

Church Farm

Whitgreave Manor

Marston Farm

Brook Farm

2

Newbuildings Cottage

27

MARSTON LA

Redhill Farm

Newbuildings Farm

STONE RD

Marstongate Farm

Marston Brook

1

M6

Little Gorse

RAF Stafford

New Plantation

1 CHAULDEN RD
2 BUCKLAND RD
3 ASHRIDGE WLK
4 MARSWORTH WAY

BARLASTON CL 1
MEADOW BANK WLK 2

BEACONSIDE

Creswell Grove

M6

A513

A34

AMBLEFIELD WAY

LAWNSFIELD WLK

ALDBURY

FELDEN CL

PITSTONE CL

Stafford Common

CHURCH RD

A513

26

90   **A**   91   **B**   92   **C**

135
155

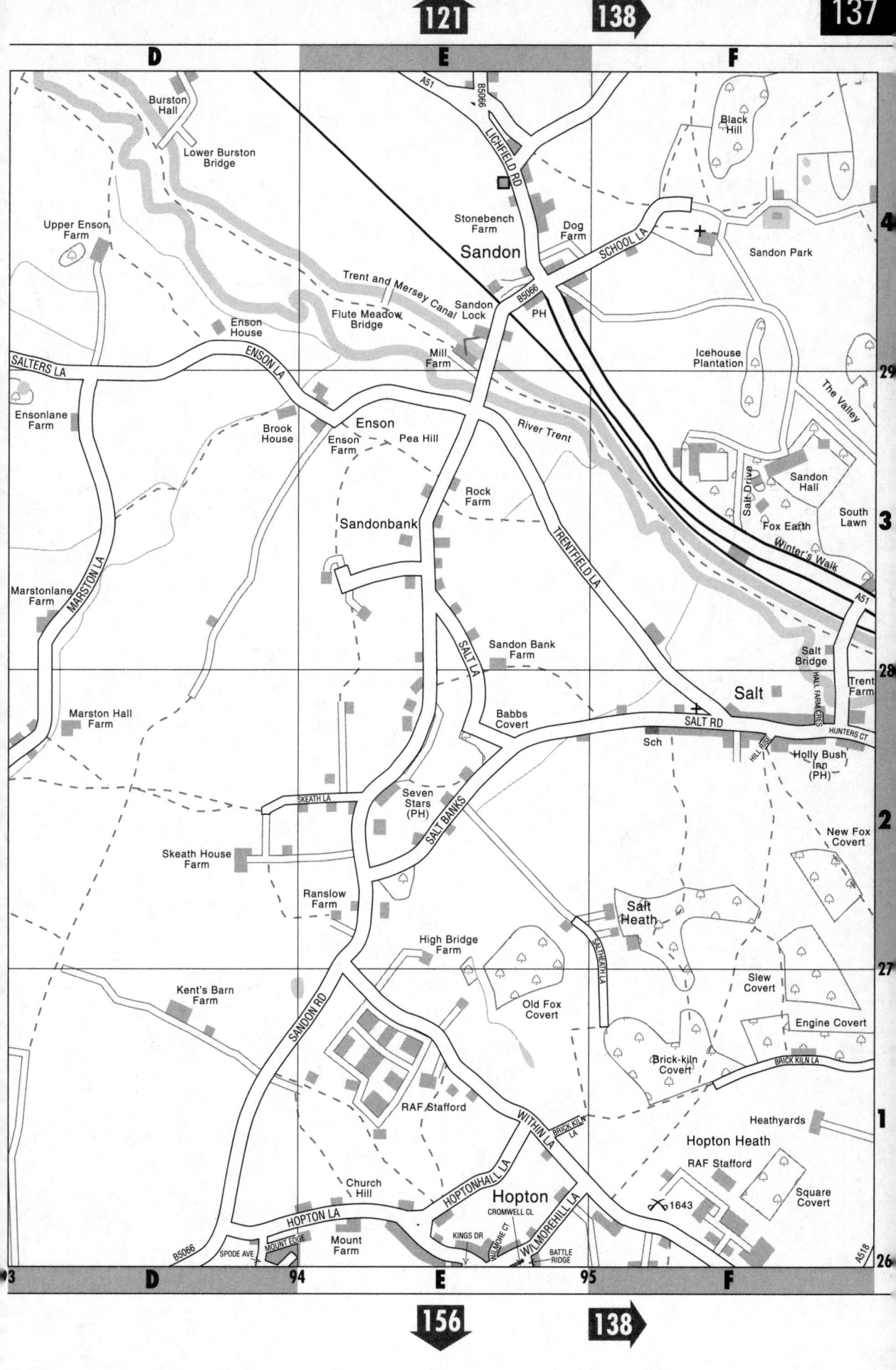

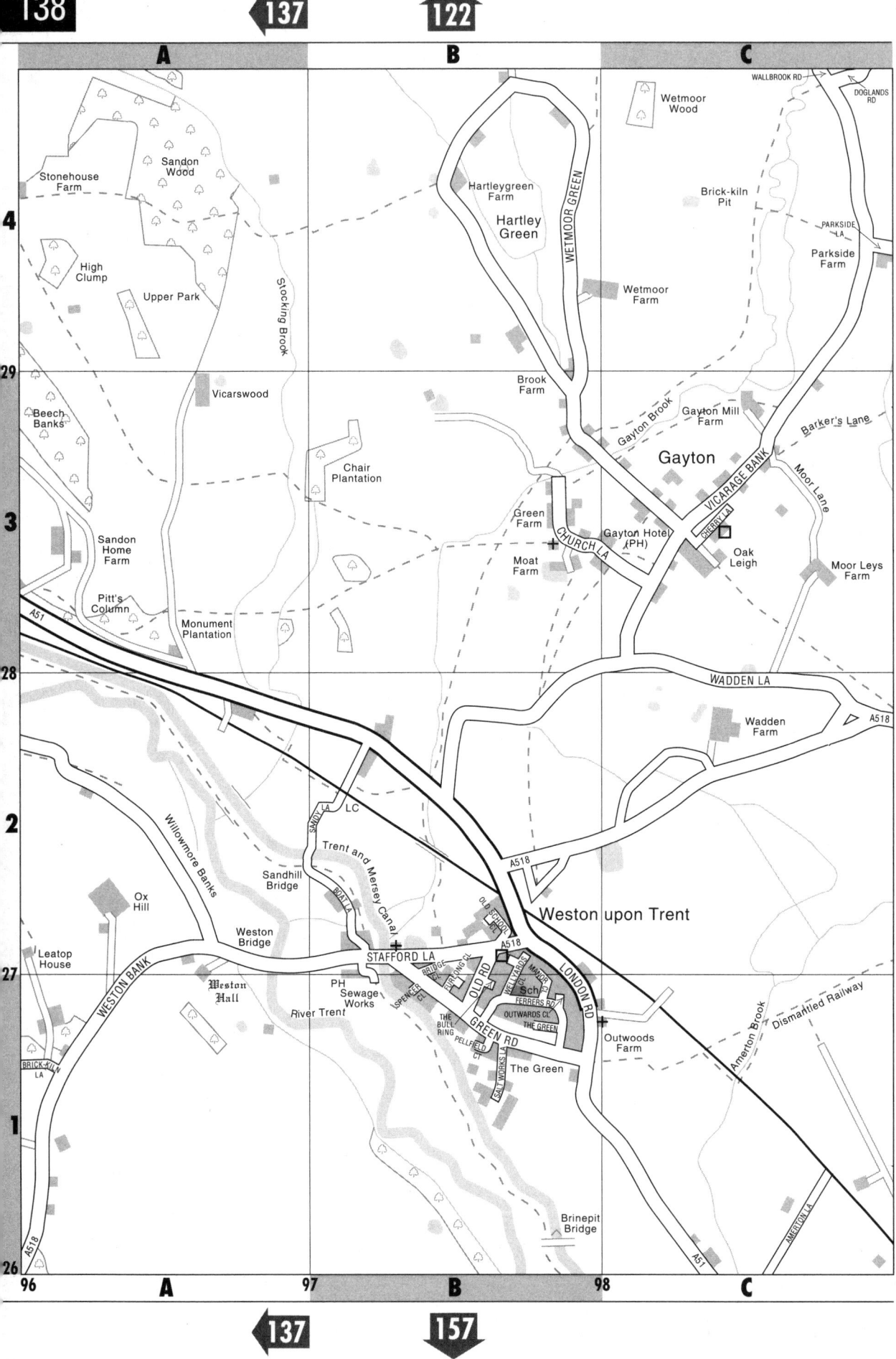

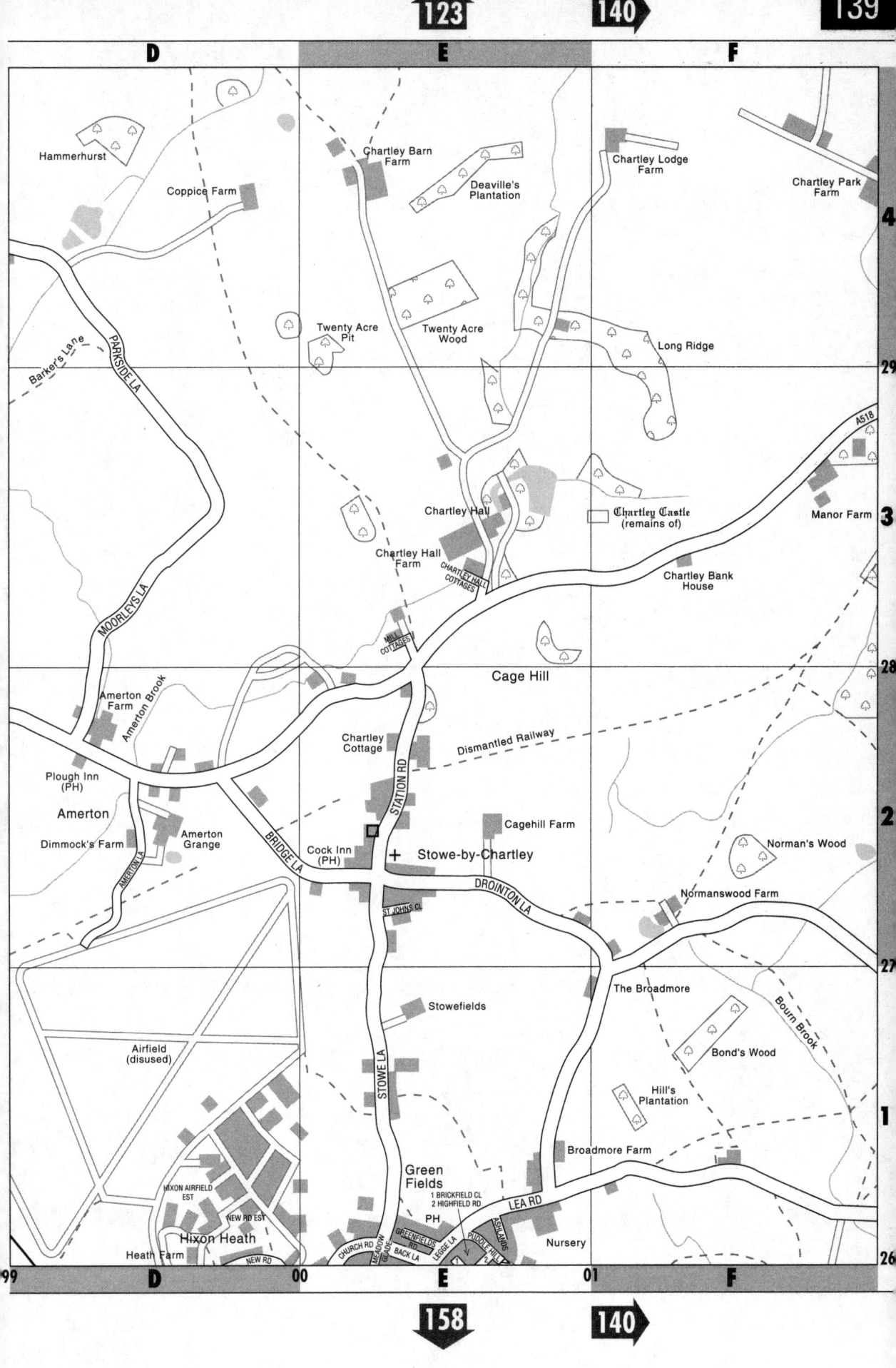

D
E
F

Hammerhurst

Coppice Farm

Chartley Barn Farm

Deaville's Plantation

Chartley Lodge Farm

Chartley Park Farm

4

Barker's Lane

PARKSIDE LA

Twenty Acre Pit

Twenty Acre Wood

Long Ridge

29

A518

MOORLEYS LA

Chartley Hall

Chartley Castle (remains of)

Manor Farm

3

Chartley Hall Farm

CHARTLEY HALL COTTAGES

Chartley Bank House

MILL COTTAGES

Cage Hill

28

Amerton Brook

Amerton Farm

Chartley Cottage

Dismantled Railway

Plough Inn (PH)

STATION RD

2

Amerton

Cagehill Farm

Norman's Wood

Dimmock's Farm

Amerton Grange

BRIDGE LA

Cock Inn (PH)

Stowe-by-Chartley

AMERTON LA

DROINTON LA

Normanswood Farm

ST JOHNS CL

27

The Broadmore

Bourn Brook

Airfield (disused)

STOWE LA

Stowefields

Bond's Wood

Hill's Plantation

1

HIXON AIRFIELD EST

Broadmore Farm

NEW RD EST

Green Fields

1 BRICKFIELD CL
2 HIGHFIELD RD

LEA RD

Hixon Heath

Heath Farm

NEW RD

PH

GREENFIELDS RD

CHURCH RD

MEADOW GLADE

BACK LA

LEGGE LA

PUDDLE HILL

ASHLANDS

Nursery

26

99

D

00

E

01

F

	A	B	C

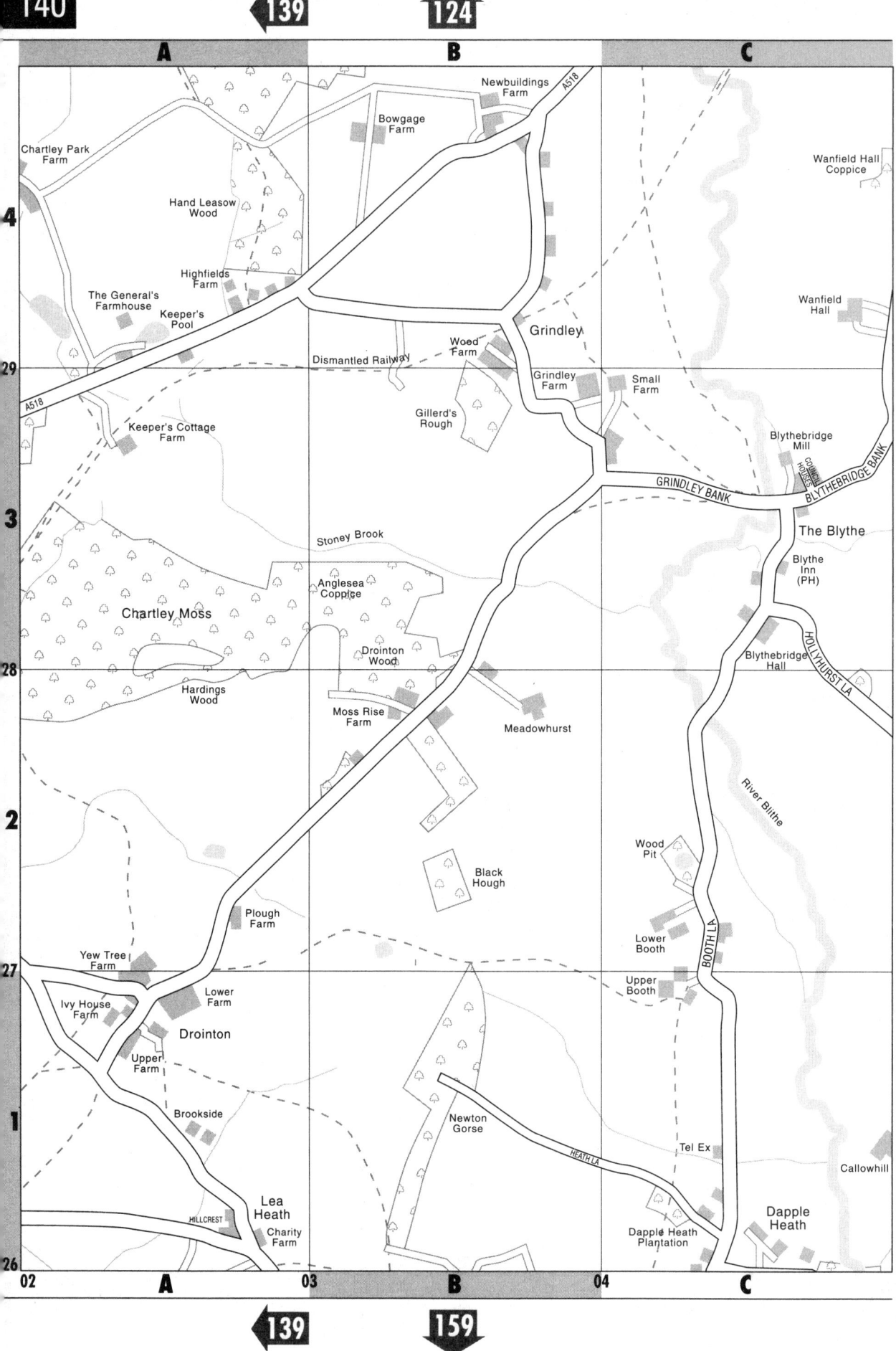

Chartley Park Farm

Hand Leasow Wood

4

Highfields Farm

The General's Farmhouse

Keeper's Pool

Bowgage Farm

Newbuildings Farm

A518

Grindley

Woed Farm

Dismantled Railway

29

Keeper's Cottage Farm

Gillerd's Rough

Grindley Farm

Small Farm

Wanfield Hall Coppice

Wanfield Hall

Blythebridge Mill

A518

COLWALL HOUSES

GRINDLEY BANK

BLYTHEBRIDGE BANK

The Blythe

3

Stoney Brook

Anglesea Coppice

Chartley Moss

Drointon Wood

Blythe Inn (PH)

HOLLYHURST LA

Blythebridge Hall

28

Hardings Wood

Moss Rise Farm

Meadowhurst

River Blithe

2

Black Hough

Wood Pit

Plough Farm

Lower Booth

BOOTH LA

Yew Tree Farm

27

Ivy House Farm

Lower Farm

Drointon

Upper Booth

Upper Farm

Brookside

1

Newton Gorse

HEATH LA

Tel Ex

Callowhill

Lea Heath

HILLCREST

Charity Farm

Dapple Heath Plantation

Dapple Heath

26

02	A	03	B	04	C

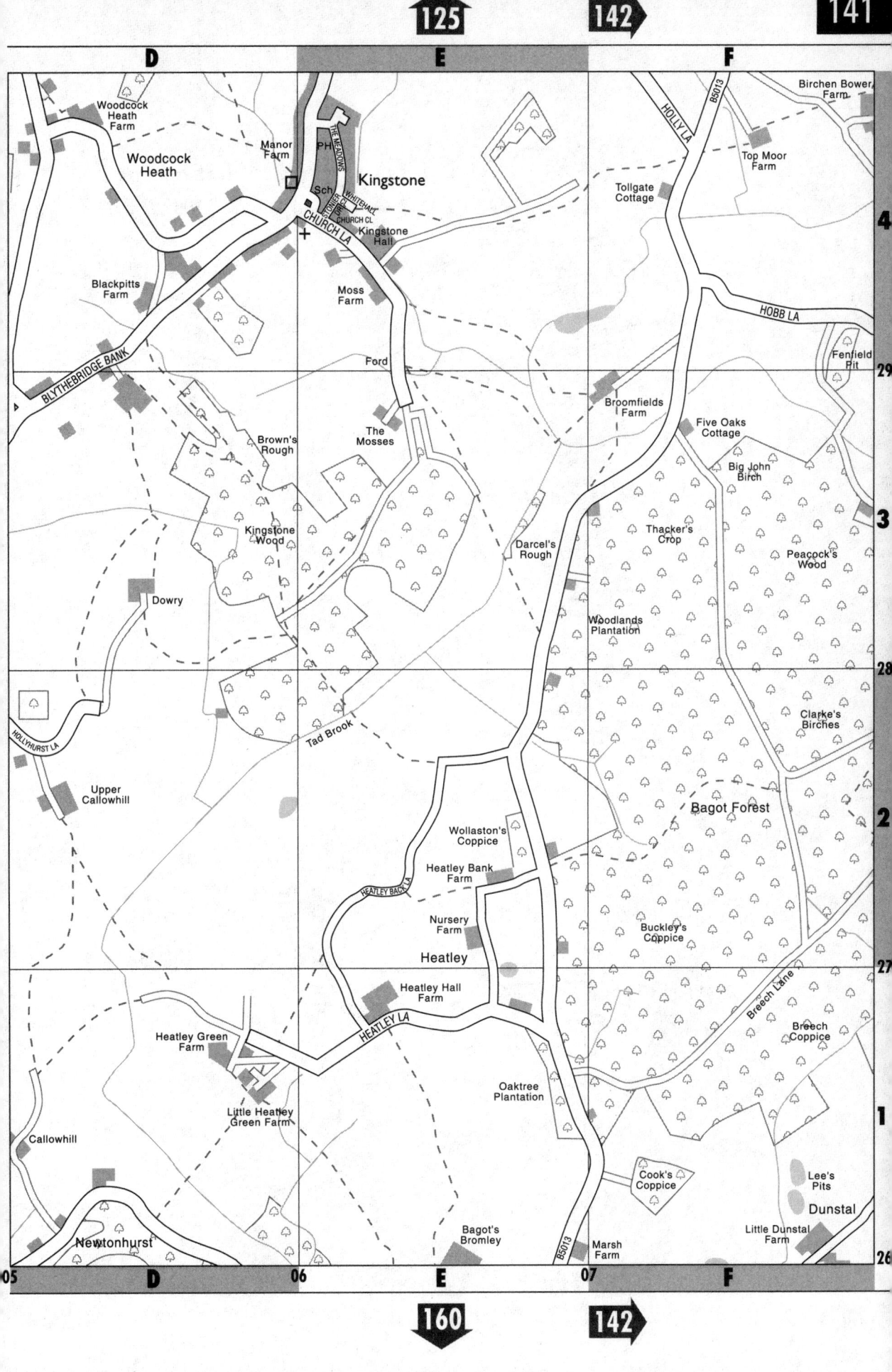

Birchen Bower Farm

B5013

HOLLY LA

Woodcock Heath Farm

Top Moor Farm

Manor Farm

PH

THE MEADOWS

Kingstone

Tollgate Cottage

Woodcock Heath

Sch

WHITEHALL

CHURCH CL

CHURCH CL

HOBB LA

4

Kingstone Hall

CHURCH LA

+

Blackpitts Farm

Moss Farm

Fenfield Pit

BLYTHEBRIDGE BANK

Ford

Broomfields Farm

29

Five Oaks Cottage

Brown's Rough

The Mosses

Big John Birch

Thacker's Crop

Peacock's Wood

3

Darcel's Rough

Kingstone Wood

Woodlands Plantation

Dowry

28

Clarke's Birches

Tad Brook

HOLLYHURST LA

Bagot Forest

Upper Callowhill

2

Wollaston's Coppice

Heatley Bank Farm

HEATLEY BACK LA

Buckley's Coppice

Nursery Farm

Heatley

Breech Lane

27

Heatley Hall Farm

Heatley Green Farm

HEATLEY LA

Breech Coppice

Little Heatley Green Farm

Oaktree Plantation

1

Callowhill

Cook's Coppice

Lee's Pits

Dunstal

Newtonhurst

Little Dunstal Farm

Bagot's Bromley

B5013

Marsh Farm

26

141
126

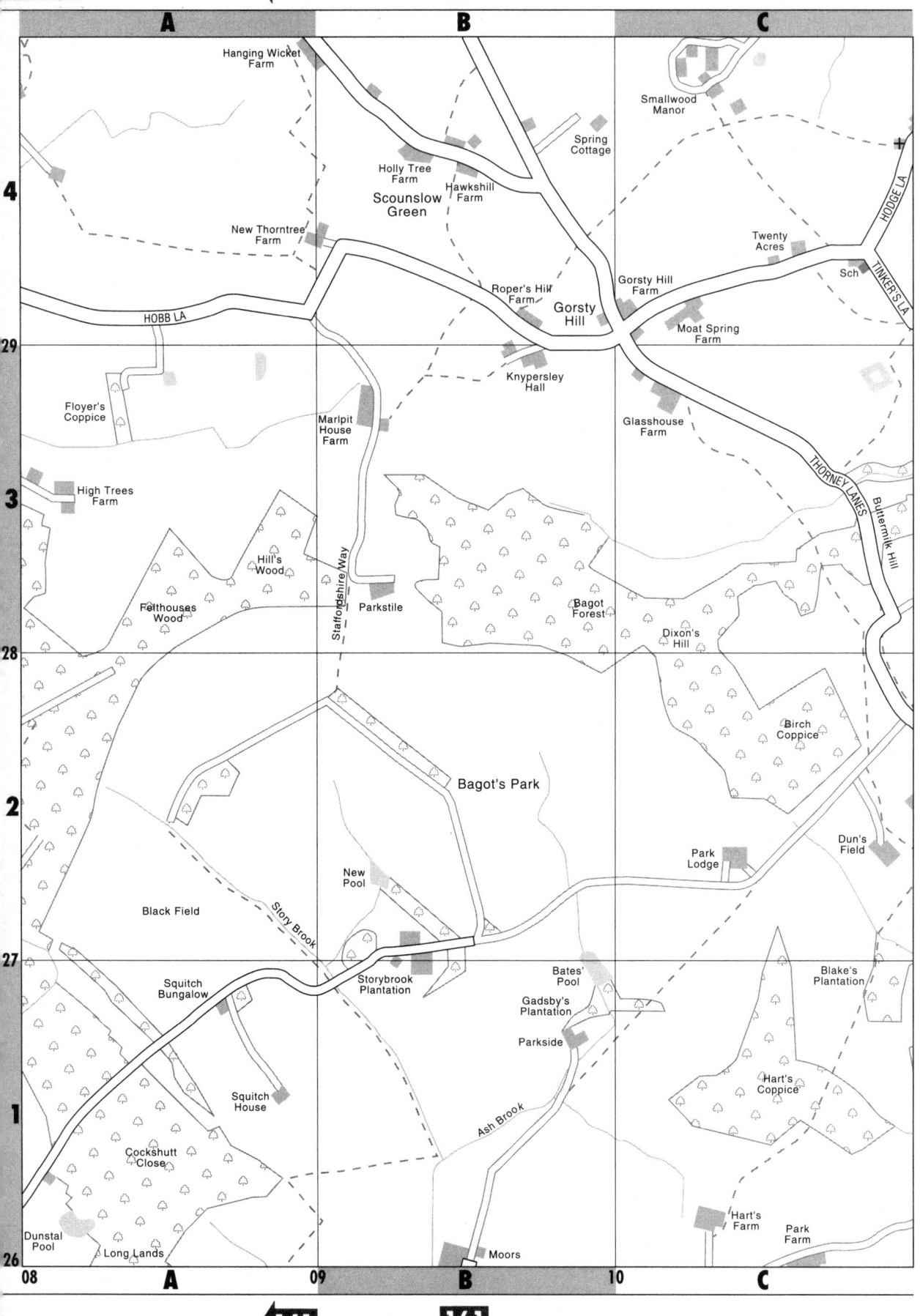

	A	B	C

4

Hanging Wicket Farm

Smallwood Manor

Spring Cottage

Holly Tree Farm

Hawkshill Farm

Scounslow Green

Twenty Acres

New Thorntree Farm

Roper's Hill Farm

Gorsty Hill Farm

Sch

HODGE LA

TINKER'S LA

29

HOBB LA

Gorsty Hill

Moat Spring Farm

Floyer's Coppice

Knypersley Hall

Marlpit House Farm

Glasshouse Farm

THORNEY LANES

Buttermilk Hill

3

High Trees Farm

Hill's Wood

Felthouses Wood

Staffordshire Way

Parkstile

Bagot Forest

Dixon's Hill

28

Birch Coppice

2

Bagot's Park

Park Lodge

Dun's Field

Black Field

Story Brook

New Pool

Bates' Pool

Blake's Plantation

27

Squitch Bungalow

Storybrook Plantation

Gadsby's Plantation

Parkside

Hart's Coppice

1

Squitch House

Ash Brook

Cockshutt Close

Hart's Farm

Park Farm

Dunstal Pool

Long Lands

Moors

26

08	A	09	B	10	C

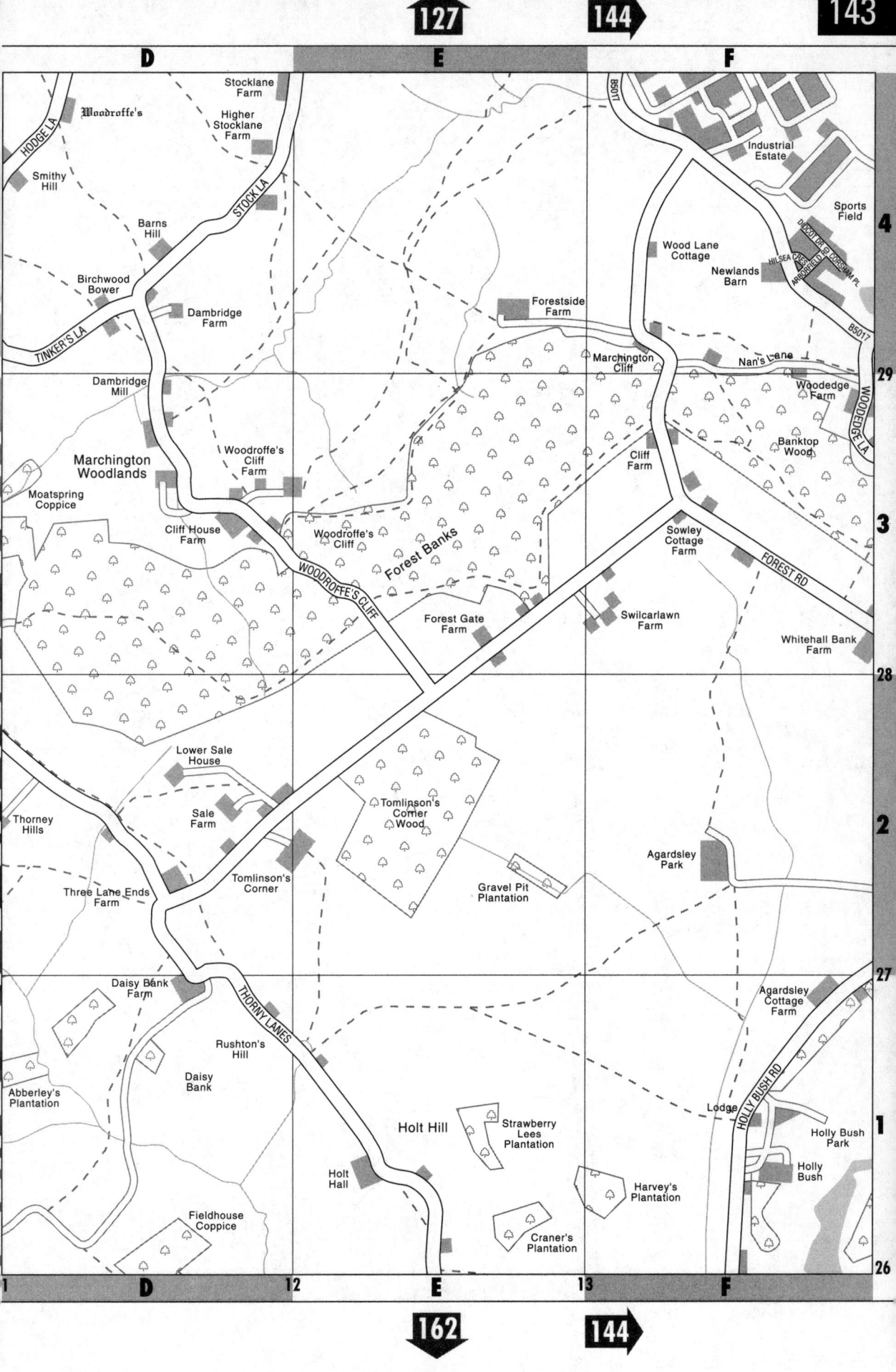

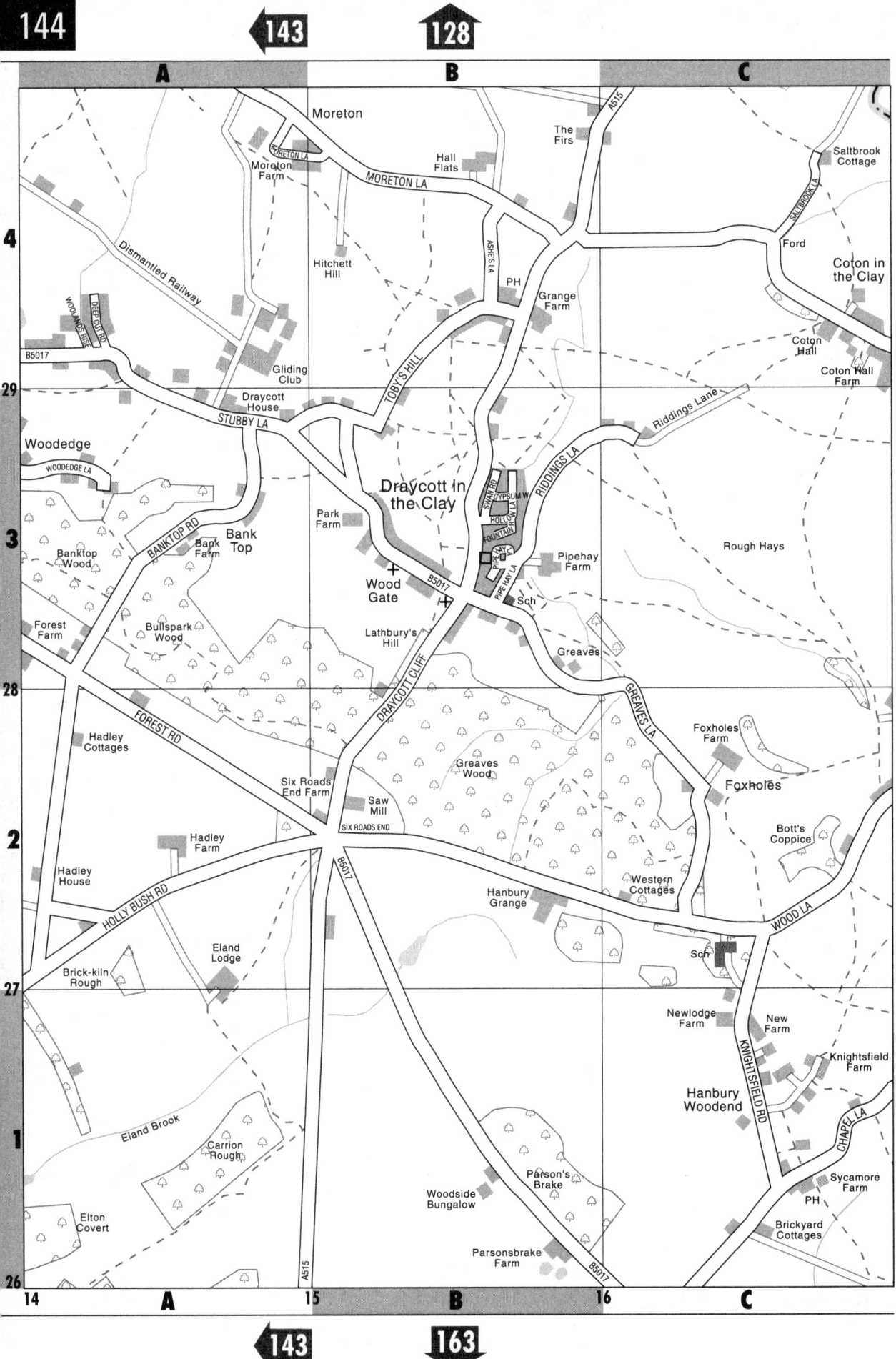

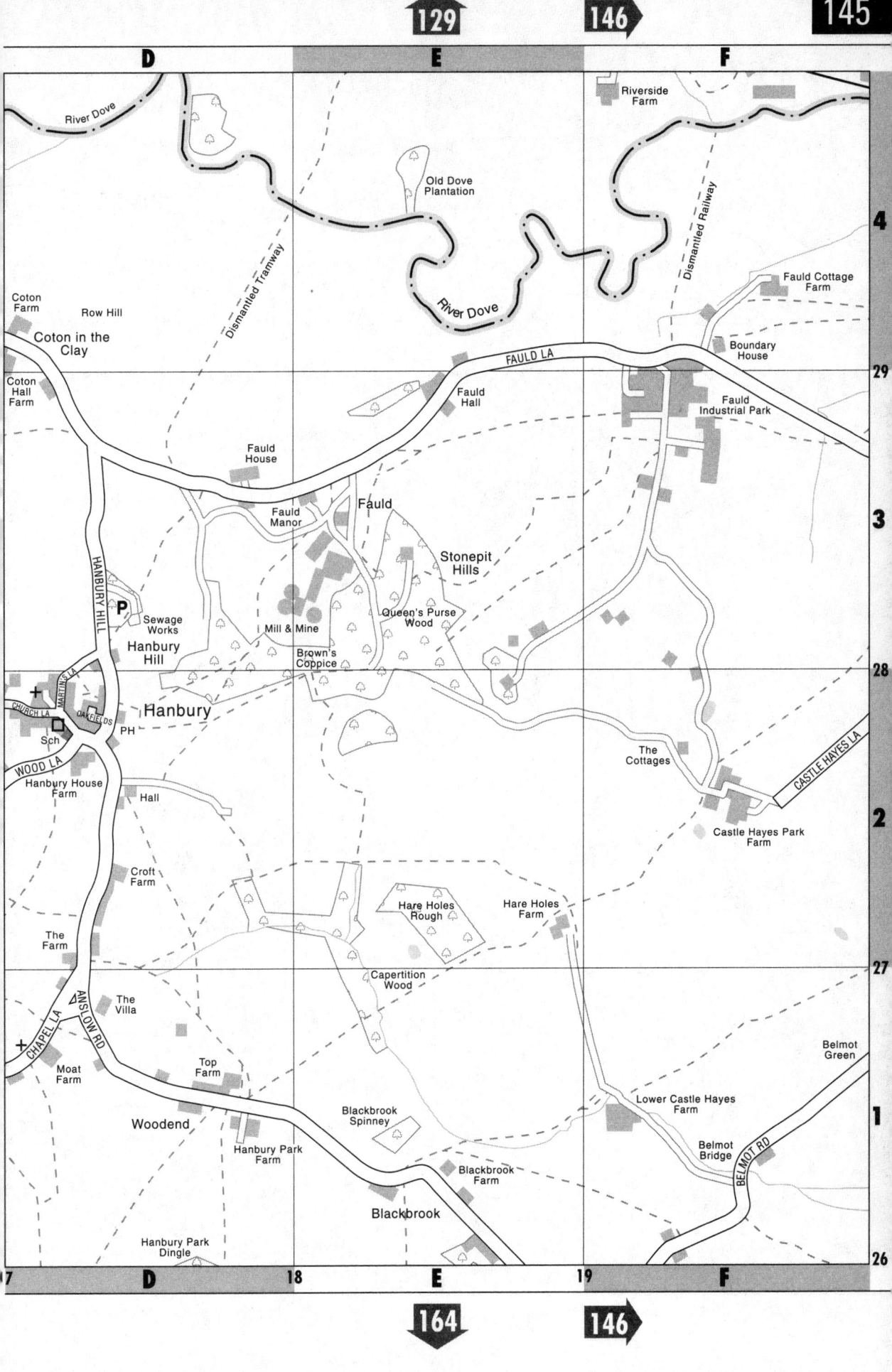

D
E
F

River Dove

Old Dove
Plantation

Dismantled Tramway

Dismantled Railway

Riverside
Farm

River Dove

4

Coton
Farm

Row Hill

Coton in the
Clay

Fauld Cottage
Farm

Boundary
House

FAULD LA

29

Coton
Hall
Farm

Fauld
Hall

Fauld
Industrial Park

Fauld
House

HANBURY HILL

Fauld
Manor

Fauld

3

Stonepit
Hills

P

Sewage
Works

Mill & Mine

Queen's Purse
Wood

Hanbury
Hill

Brown's
Coppice

28

CHURCH LA

MARTIN'S LA

OAKFIELDS

Hanbury

PH

The
Cottages

CASTLE HAYES LA

WOOD LA

Hanbury House
Farm

Hall

2

Castle Hayes Park
Farm

Croft
Farm

Hare Holes
Rough

Hare Holes
Farm

The
Farm

27

Capertition
Wood

CHAPEL LA

ANSLOW RD

The
Villa

Belmot
Green

Moat
Farm

Top
Farm

Lower Castle Hayes
Farm

1

Woodend

Blackbrook
Spinney

Belmot
Bridge

BELMOT RD

Hanbury Park
Farm

Blackbrook
Farm

Blackbrook

26

Hanbury Park
Dingle

7
D
18
E
19
F

A B C

Green End Lane

SCROPTON RD

FOSTON CL
FIELD AVE
HEATHWAY
STATION RD
CHURCH AVE
CHURCH MEWS
MERVAL CL
HOON RD

Hatton

Sewage Works

Hoonhay

Ind Est

MARSTON LA

Scropton Old Rd

LC

PH

Tutbury Bridge

DOVE SIDE

MARSTON OLD LA

River Dove

4

Mill Fleam

Picnic Area

F Sta

BRIDGE ST

Mill Farm

A50

Castle Hill

Castle

CASTLE CT. PCs

CASTLE ST
CHURCH ST
MONK ST
HIGH ST
LOWER HIGH ST

Mill Fleam

Tutbury Mill

29

THE CLOSE

HILLSIDE ST
PCs
DUKE ST
SILK MILL LA
KEEP

P

P

1
2

CORNMILL LA

Hoblands Farm

Owen's Bank

PARK LA
WAKEFIELD AVE
HALLS LA
QUEENS RISE
NORMAN
NEEDWOOD
LUDGATE ST
OAKS VIEW
WILD DR
Sch
BURTON ST

1 CLOSE BANK
2 DOVE VIEW

FAULD LA

Woodhouse Farm

3

THE PARK PARK RD
HAWTHORN

BURTON RD

New Farm

Shotwood Hill

REDHILL LA

FERRERS AVE
PRIORY CL
HILLCREST
LANCASTER DR
PINFOLD CT
PORTWAY DR
BARRINGTON CL
CROMWELL CL

Tutbury

IRONWALLS LA

SHOTWOODHILL LA

BELMOT RD

GREEN LA

ROLLESTON LA

Green Lane Farm

Lane End Farm

28

CASTLE HAYES LA

Green Lane

BURTON RD

Woodside Farm

Cemy

HALL RD

Chapel House Farm

Falling Pit Plantation

ROOLEY LA

Moorfield Hill

The Lawn

2

BELMOT RD

Northwood

Bleak House Farm

Hoblands Farm

Grange Farm

Mayfield

Matthew's Big Plantation

Alder Moor

LODGE HILL

27

Deer Park Plantation

Rolleston Park

Lower Covert

Alder Moor Plantation

TUTBURY RD A50

Bushton

Piltons Farm

BUSHTON LA

1

LOUNT LA

Lount Farm

LONGHEDGE LA

Bushton Bridge

Whitestone Lane

Newgatefield Lane

The Bungalow

26

20 A 21 B 22 C

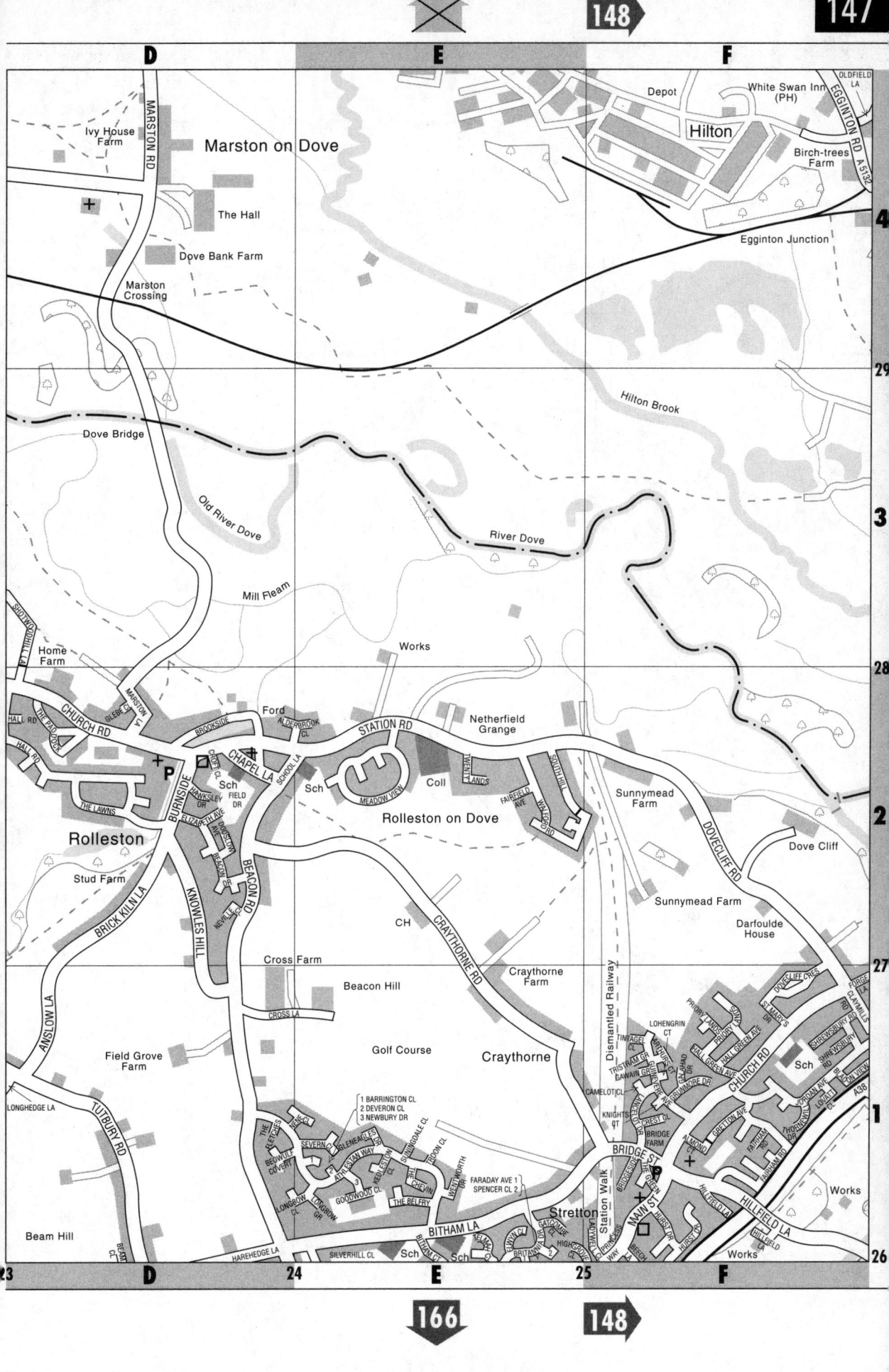

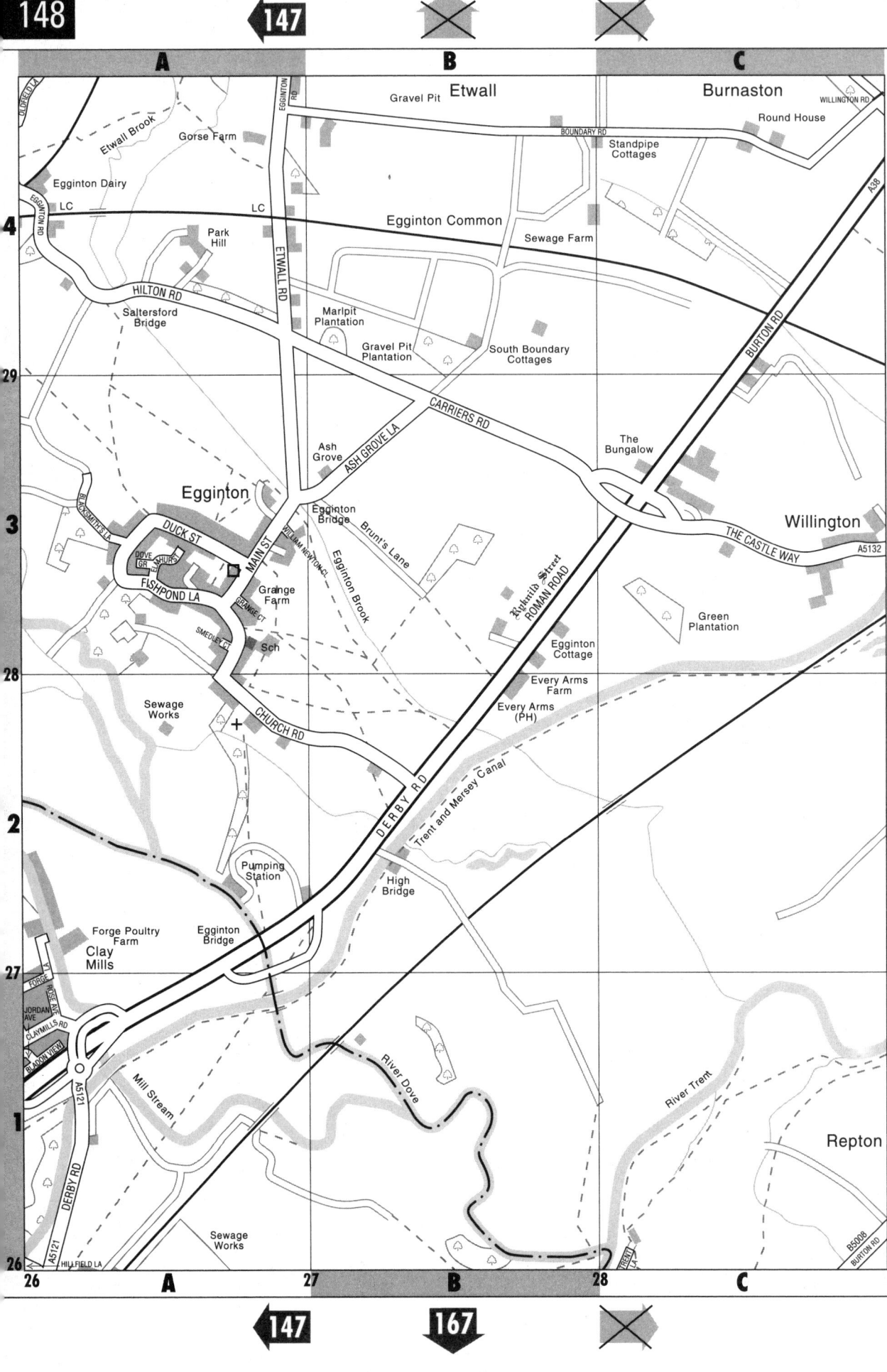

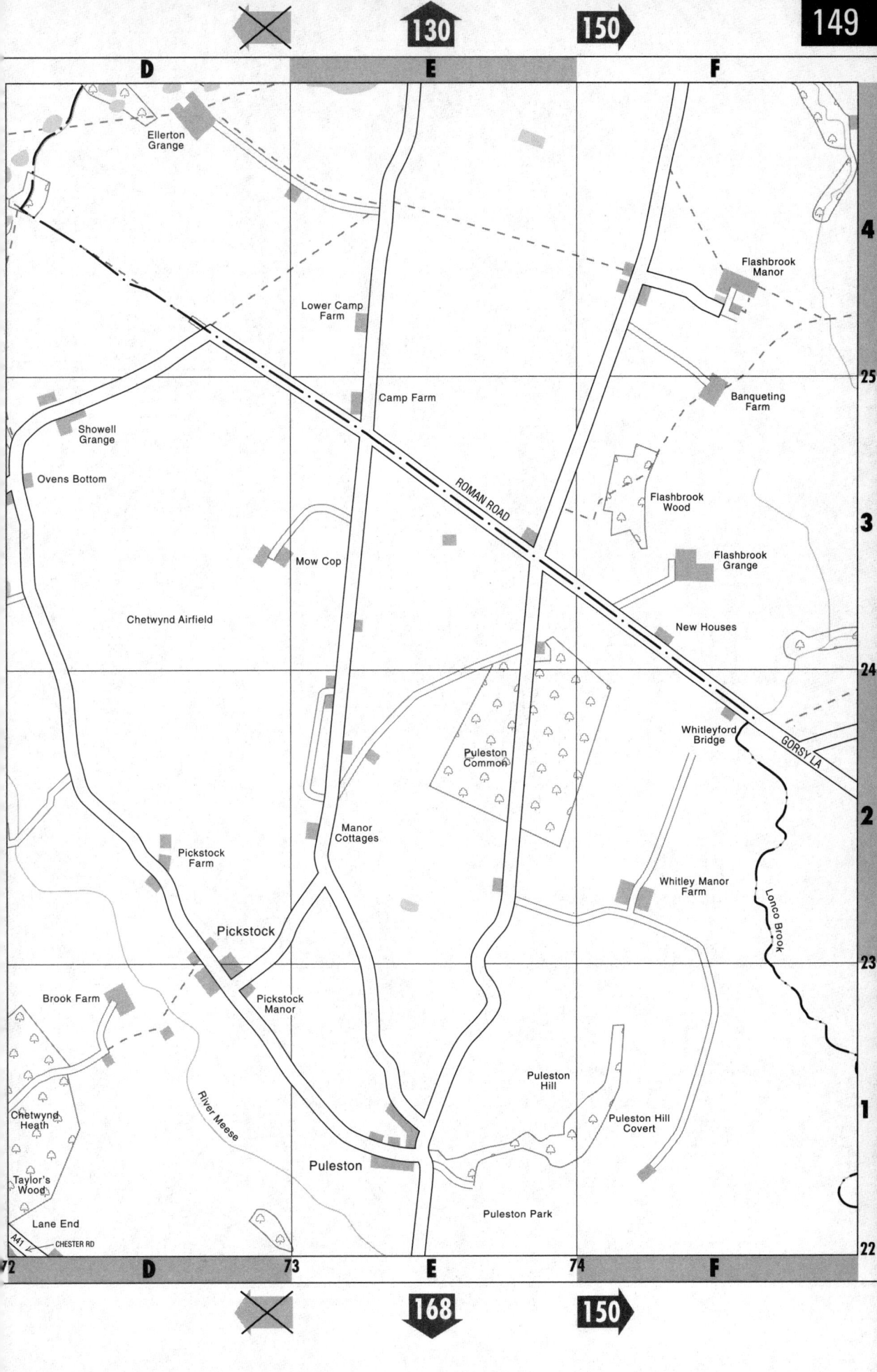

D
E
F

4

Ellerton
Grange

Flashbrook
Manor

25

Lower Camp
Farm

Camp Farm

Banqueting
Farm

Showell
Grange

ROMAN ROAD

Flashbrook
Wood

3

Ovens Bottom

Mow Cop

Flashbrook
Grange

Chetwynd Airfield

New Houses

24

Puleston
Common

Whitleyford
Bridge

GORSY LA

Manor
Cottages

Lonco Brook

2

Pickstock
Farm

Whitley Manor
Farm

Pickstock

23

Brook Farm

Pickstock
Manor

Chetwynd
Heath

River Meese

Puleston
Hill

1

Taylor's
Wood

Puleston Hill
Covert

Lane End

A41

CHESTER RD

Puleston

Puleston Park

22

72

D

73

E

74

F

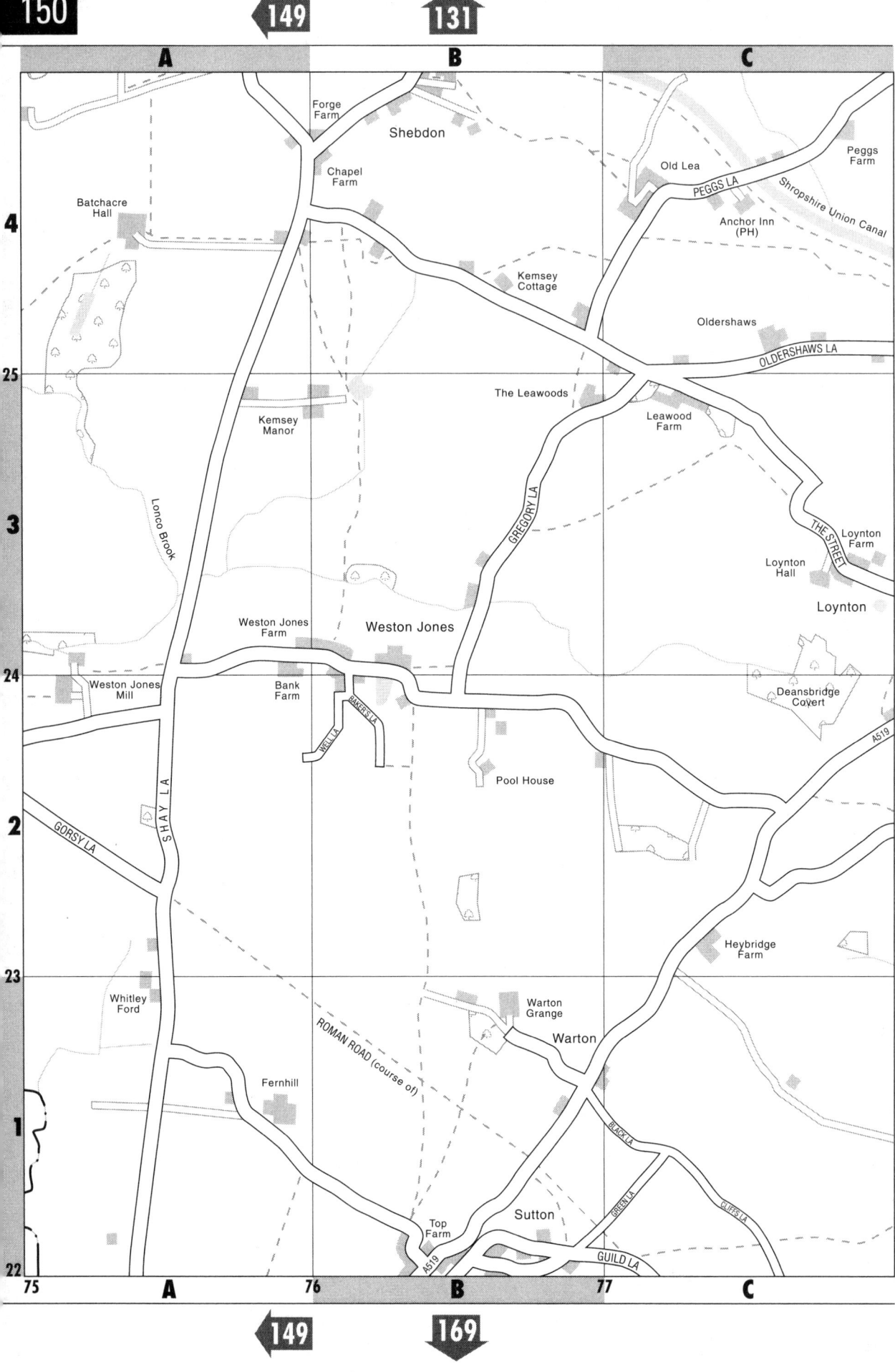

A B C

4

25

3

24

2

23

1

22

75 A 76 B 77 C

Batchacre
Hall

Forge
Farm

Shebdon

Chapel
Farm

Old Lea

Peggs
Farm

PEGGS LA

Shropshire Union Canal

Anchor Inn
(PH)

Kemsey
Cottage

Oldershaws

OLDERSHAWS LA

The Leawoods

Leawood
Farm

Kemsey
Manor

Lonco Brook

GREGORY LA

THE STREET

Loynton
Farm

Loynton
Hall

Loynton

Weston Jones
Farm

Weston Jones

Deansbridge
Covert

Weston Jones
Mill

Bank
Farm

WELL LA

BAKER'S LA

SHAY LA

A519

GORSY LA

Pool House

Heybridge
Farm

Whitley
Ford

ROMAN ROAD (course of)

Fernhill

Warton
Grange

Warton

BLACK LA

GREEN LA

CLIFFS LA

Top
Farm

Sutton

A519

GUILD LA

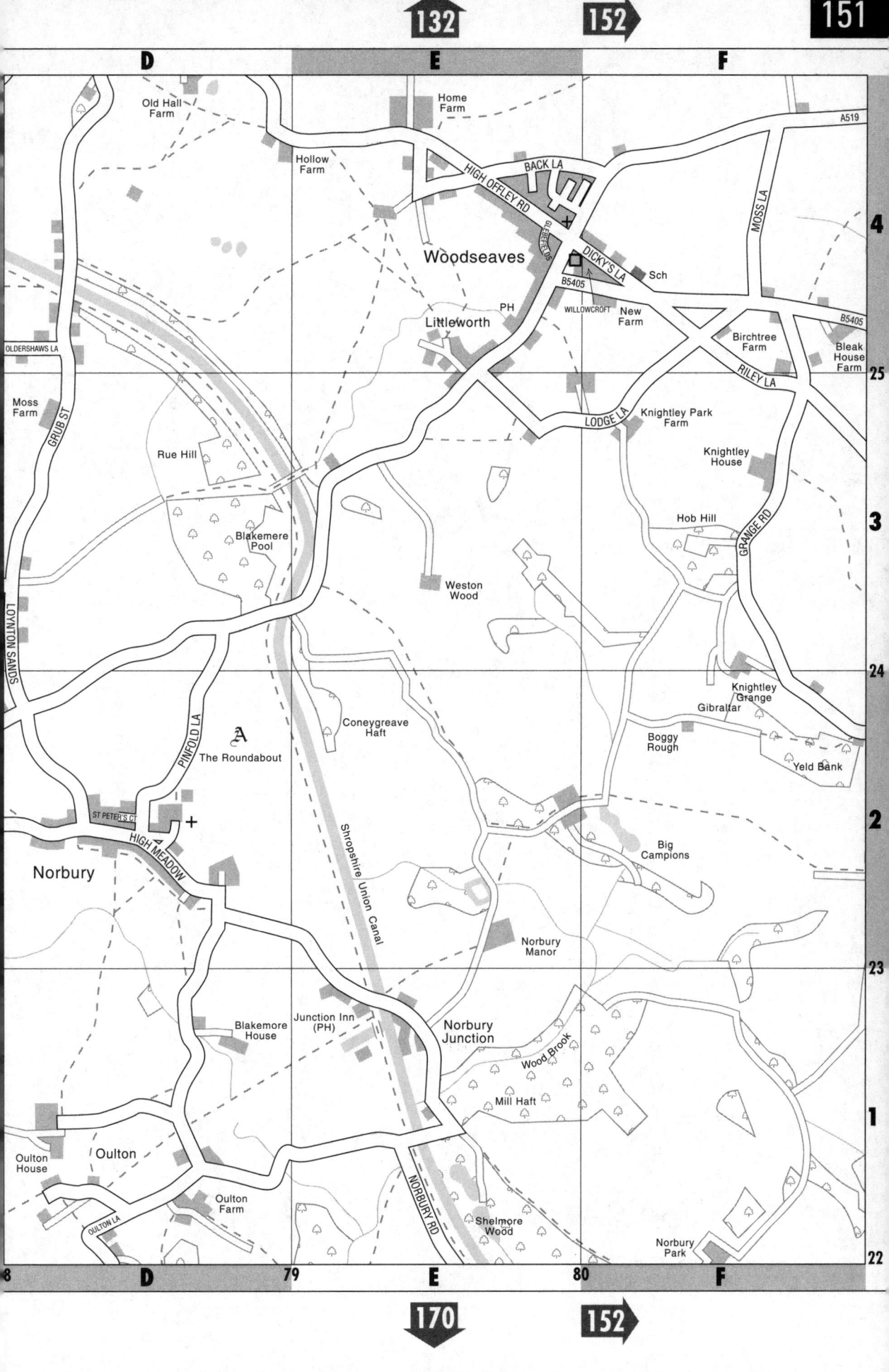

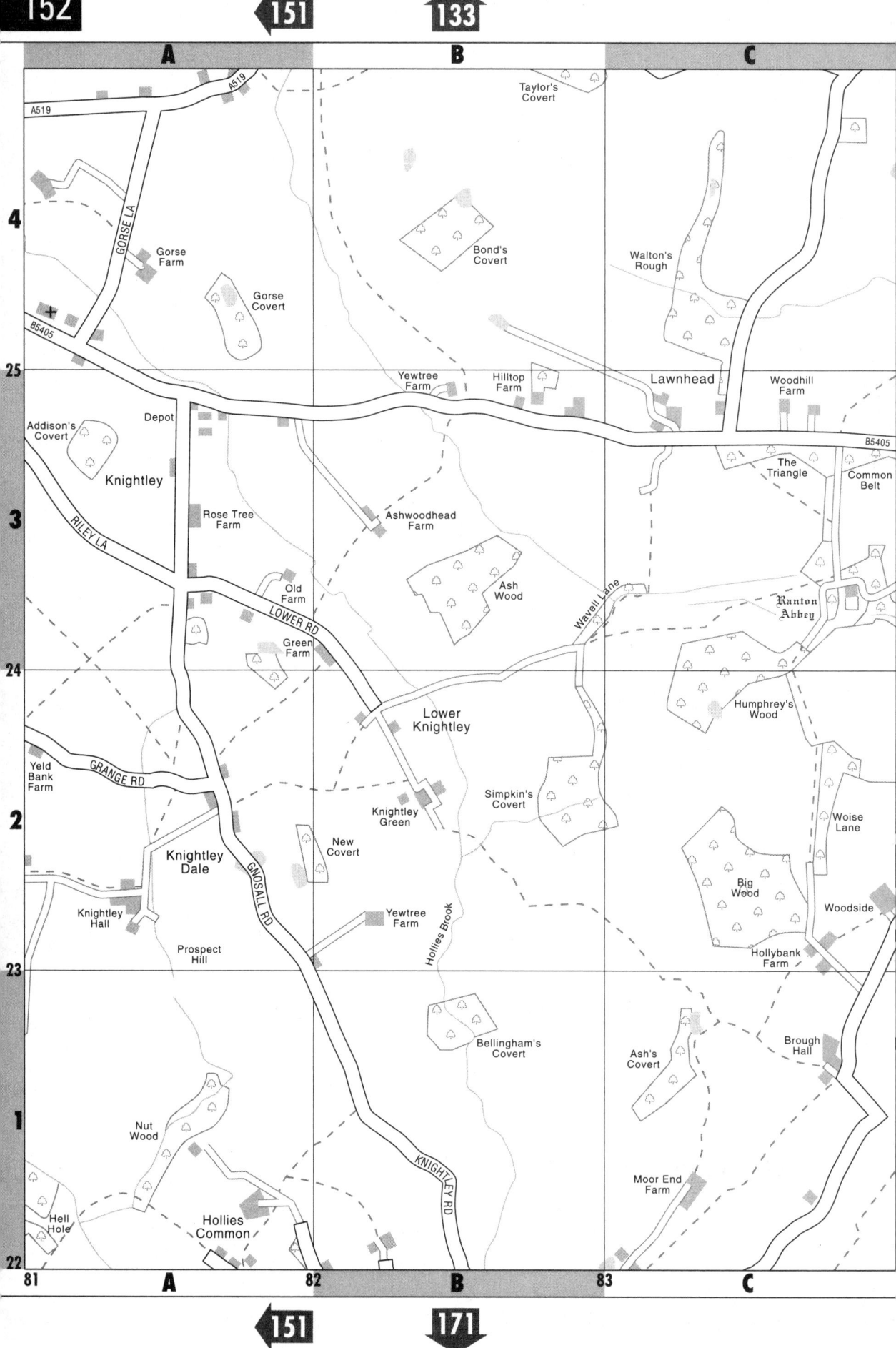

A

B

C

Taylor's Covert

4

Gorse Farm

Gorse Covert

Walton's Rough

Woodhill Farm

B5405

25

Yewtree Farm

Hilltop Farm

Lawnhead

Addison's Covert

Depot

The Triangle

Common Belt

Knightley

Rose Tree Farm

Ashwoodhead Farm

3

RILEY LA

Old Farm

Ash Wood

Wavell Lane

Ranton Abbey

LOWER RD

Green Farm

24

Lower Knightley

Humphrey's Wood

Yeld Bank Farm

GRANGE RD

Knightley Green

Simpkin's Covert

Woise Lane

2

New Covert

Big Wood

Woodside

Knightley Dale

GNOSALL RD

Knightley Hall

Prospect Hill

Yewtree Farm

Hollies Brook

Hollybank Farm

23

Bellingham's Covert

Ash's Covert

Brough Hall

1

Nut Wood

KNIGHTLEY RD

Moor End Farm

Hell Hole

Hollies Common

22

81   A   82   B   83   C

D
E
F

Sewage Works

BRIDLE LA

Broad Heath

Five Lanes End

FOUR LANES END

B5405

CLANFORD RD

ABBERLEYFIELDS NO PARK

4

Broad Heath Farm

Hextall Covert

Stubbs' Wood

The Wicket

Hextall

25

HEXTALL LA

Anne's Well Wood

Hextall Brook

William's Wood

Lodge Belt

3

Clanford Brook

Ranton Hall

STOCKING LA

Sch

BOURNE AVE

JOHNSON CL

ABBEYSIDE

Gap Pool Wood

Church Farm

CHUR

Ranton

BROOKSIDE

24

WHITE'S MEADOW

Parknook

Coton House Farm

COTON LA

Brook House Farm

DOG LA

Ranton House

BACK LA

BROOK LA

2

Green Farm

Chapel House Farm

Vicarage Farm

Ranton Green

23

The Rookery

PH

PH

Long Compton

Barts Farm

Long Compton Farm

1

Home Farm

BUTT LA

STOCKING-GATE LA

Buttlane Farm

HOLLY LA

WOODHOUSE LA

LONG LA

Wood Knowle Farm

Whitecross Farm

Whitecross

22

4

D

85

E

86

F

A5013 CRESWELL GR

Bullockcroft Brook

Creswell

WILKE'S RD

CRESWELL DR

Wilke's
Wood

The
Mount

M6

Lower
Cooksland
Farm

Edwards
Covert

Floss
Bridge

The
Grove

Love Lane

Cooksland
Hall
Farm

Cooksland

Seighford
Hall

Ashpit
Covert

Ansell's
Covert

MOOR LA

CLANFORD RD

Ford

Moor
Covert

Millian Brook

Seighford

BRAMHALL CL
SMITHS LA

THE
CUMBERS

THE PADDOCK

Ashes
Covert

Holly Bush
(PH)

Clanford
Covert

Haynes's
Covert

SEIGHFORD RD

GRASSMERE
HOLLOW

CLANFORD LA

Clanford Hall
Farm

Oldford
Covert

DOXEY
FIELDS

Clanford
Bridge

Oldford
Farm

Wassage
Covert

Ashton Hill
Farm

ASTON BK

Aston

Aston
Bank
Farm

OLDFORD LA

Coton
Clanford

Presford Brook

Barn
Farm

Sunnyside
Farm

ASTON HILL

Aston Hall
Farm

COTON LA

CORSTY LA

Little Aston
Farm

Glen
Farm

Holly Bush
Farm

Hill
Farm

Coton Hall
Farm

Green
Farm

Presford
Bribge

Doxey Brook

Works

BUTTER BK

Butterbank
Bridge

Mill
Farm

STOCKING-GATE
LA

Presford House
Farm

BUTTERBANK LA

Oak
Farm

BLACKHOLE LA

TWEMLOW
CL

ST MATTHEWS DR

+

Villa
Farm

Butterbank Brook

Red Lion
(PH)

CHESTNUT DR
RUSKIN DR
CHURCH LA

MOUNT PLEASANT

WILLOW
BROOK

The
Handfords

CROSSING LA

Stallbrook
Hall

St Matthews
Dr

CASTLE VIEW

Derrington

Dismantled Railway

MAPLE DR
YEW TREE CL

Mount
Pleasant

Castle View
Estate

Bungalow
Farm

LONG LA

DERRINGTON LA

Boons
Industrial
Estate

Longlane
Farm

DALE LA

M6

A   B   C

SANDON RD   B5066
Hopton
farm
Barracks

Dismtd Rly

RAF
Stafford

4

SANDON RD

A513

Beaconside

BEACONSIDE

CORONATION RD
FONTHILL RD
CHARNLEY RD

25

3

BLWORTH CT

EMBRY
AVE
DOUGLAS
AVE
SLESSOR
DR
PROSPECT RD
BYRD ST
CAMBRIDGE ST
JOHN ST
TITHE BARN RD

Littleworth

SMALLMAN ST
TITHE
BARN
CT
ARMSTRONG
AVE
KNIGHT
AVE
PRESCOTT
AVE

24

Sch

PORTAL RD
GARROD
NEWALL
TEDDER DR
HELENS
 ALDRIN
CAIRNS DR
ELLINGTON DR

MELBOURNE CRES
TASMAN DR

KINGSTON BROOK

University

Depots

2

MYNORS
BEDFORD
ST THOMAS
GILL AVE
WESTHEAD AVE
ST JOHN'S AVE
HATHERTON CL
WEST CL
GREENWAY
DARTMOUTH ST
HARROWBY ST
CROSSWAY

Works

Kingston Hill

23

River Sow

Works

Sch
ST GEORGE'S RD
ST LEONARD'S AVE
QUEENSVILLE AVE
CHRISTOPHER TERR

1

LICHFIELD RD A34
HAWTHORN WAY

Works

QUEENSVILLE BRIDGE

Hough Drain

MALVERN CL
BENENDEN CL
AMPLEFORTH DR
CHARTERHOUSE DR
WHINSTONE AVE
ETON CL
ARDINGLEY AVE

22

93   A   94   B   95   C

Lowerhouse
Farm

KINGS RD
BATTLE RIDGE

Beacon
Hill

Beacon
Farm

SHERINGHAM DR
SALISBURY DR
SALISBURY RD
CANBERRA DR
LYMINGTON DR

A513

WESTON RD

Kingston Pool
Covert

Recn Gd

Pool
Farm
Hopton
Pools

Hopton
Pools
Covert

County Show
Ground
Berryhill

Upper
Berryhill

Lower
Berryhill

Brick House
Farm

Stafford
Lodge

WITHIN LA
A518

Park
Farm

Blackheath
Covert

Sch

Crem
+
Cemy

BLACKHEATH LA

King's
Low

HANYARDS LA

Crab
Covert

TIXALL RD

ST THOMAS LA

St Thomas
Priory Farm

Staffordshire and Worcestershire Canal

Brancotegorse
Covert

Sewage
Works

Baswich
Bridge

River Penk

TILCON AVE

Works

Baswich

KESTREL CL
DOLPHIN
+

BASWICH LA

COMPTON RD

WOODSTOCK
RD

BALMORAL
RD
BASWICH CREST
ST MAWES
SIDMOUTH AVE

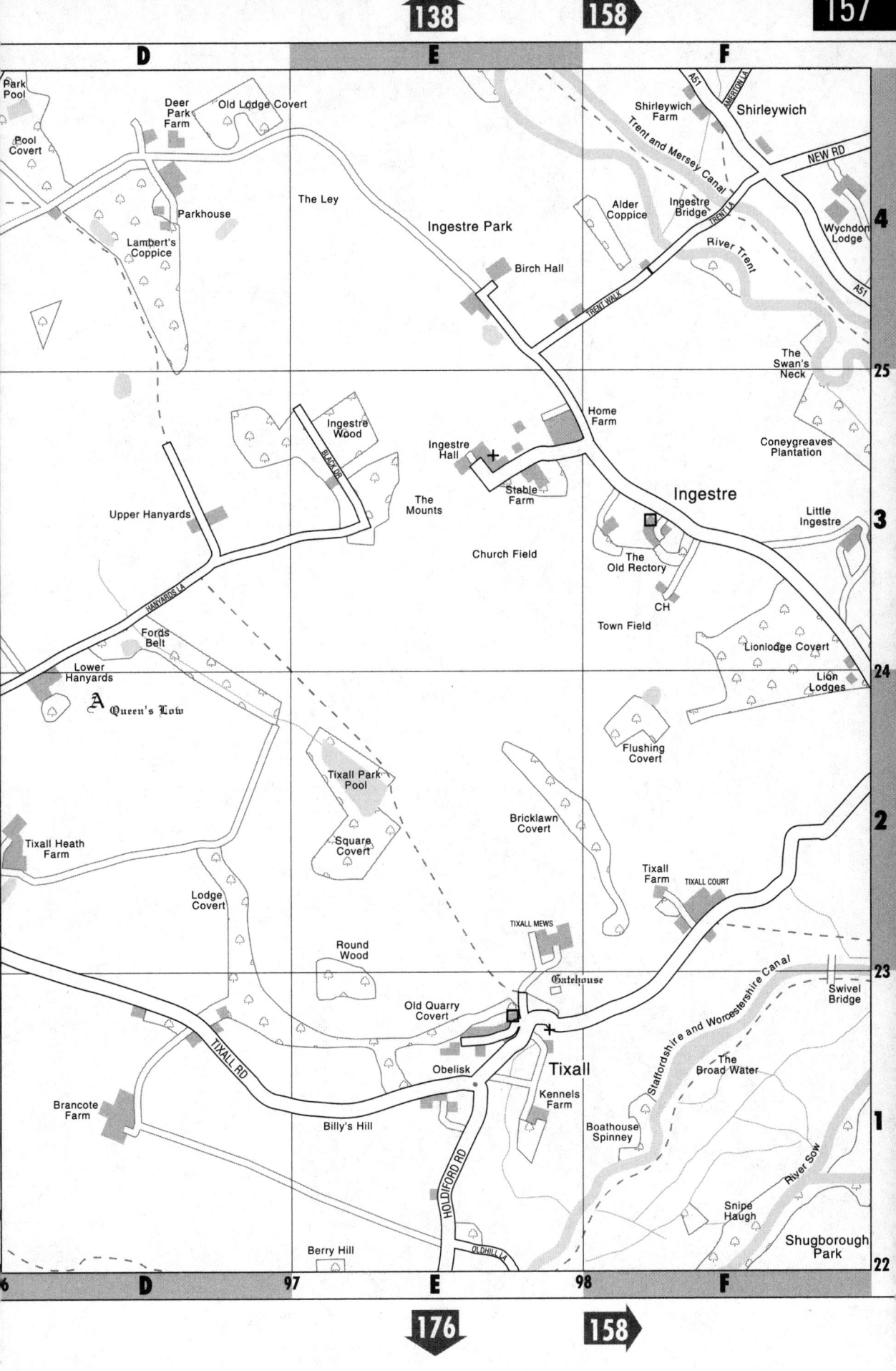

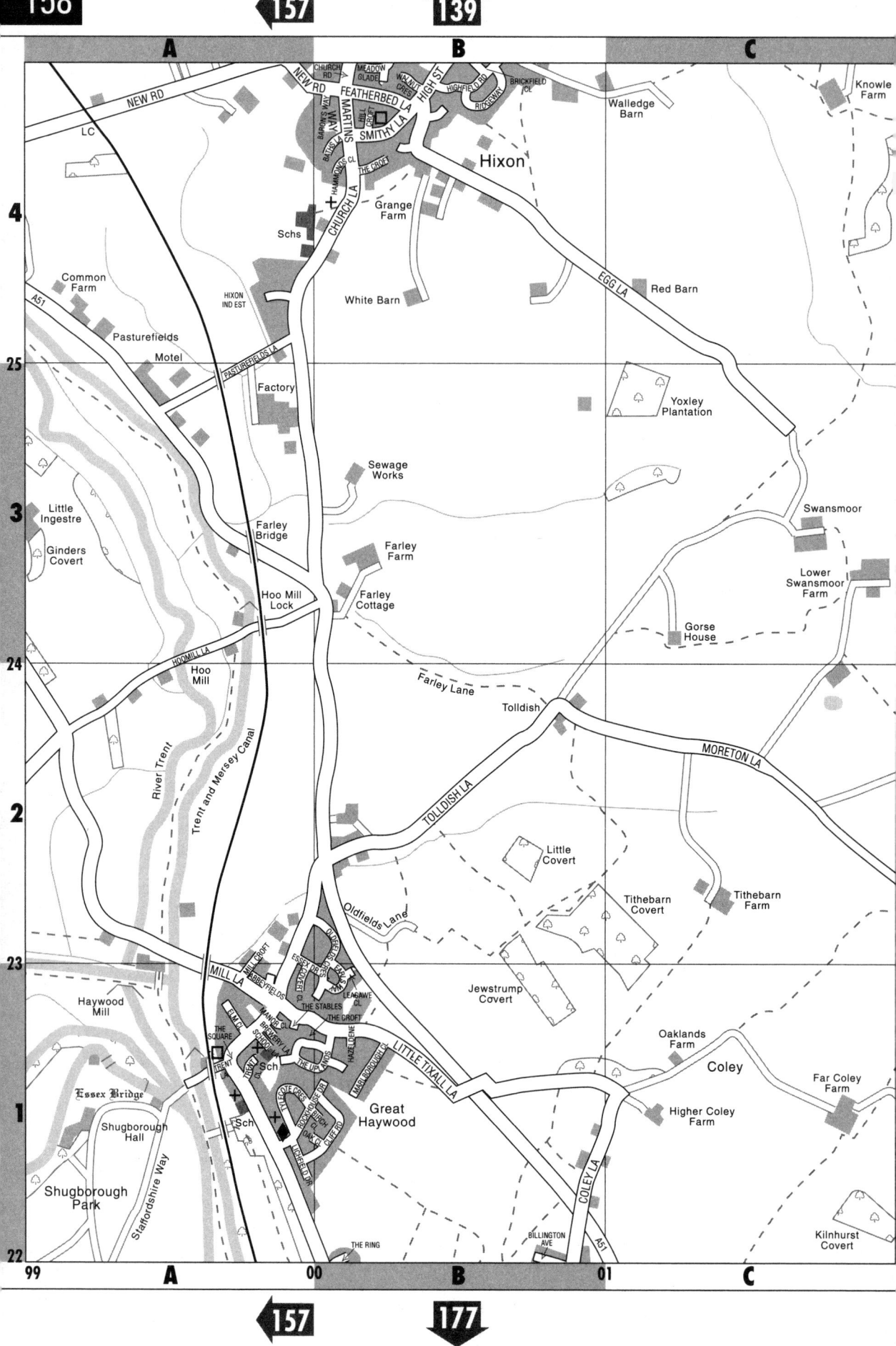

A B C

New Rd

Church Rd

Meadow Glade

New Rd

High St

Highfield Rd

Brickfield Pce

Walledge Barn

Knowle Farm

Martins Way

Battsol Cl

Featherbed La

Wallnut Cres

Ridgeway

Smithy La

The Croft

Hammonds Cl

Church La

Schs

Grange Farm

Hixon

4

Common Farm

Hixon Ind Est

White Barn

Egg La

Red Barn

Pasturefields

Motel

Pasturefields La

Factory

Yoxley Plantation

25

Sewage Works

A51

Little Ingestre

Ginders Covert

Farley Bridge

Farley Farm

Swansmoor

3

Lower Swansmoor Farm

Hoo Mill Lock

Farley Cottage

Gorse House

Hoomill La

Hoo Mill

Farley Lane

Tolldish

Moreton La

24

River Trent

Trent and Mersey Canal

Tolldish La

Little Covert

Tithebarn Covert

Tithebarn Farm

2

Oldfields Lane

Mill La

Mill Croft

Abbeyfields

Essex Dr

Leasowe La

The Stables

The Croft

Jewstrump Covert

Oaklands Farm

Coley

23

Haywood Mill

Manor Cl

Brewery La

The Square

Elm Cl

The Lands

Hazeldene

Little Tixall La

Coley La

Far Coley Farm

Trent

Sch

The Uplands

Marshbrook Cl

Great Haywood

Higher Coley Farm

Essex Bridge

Sch

Shugborough Hall

Staffordshire Way

Shugborough Park

The Ring

Billington Ave

A51

Kilnhurst Covert

1

22

99 A 00 B 01 C

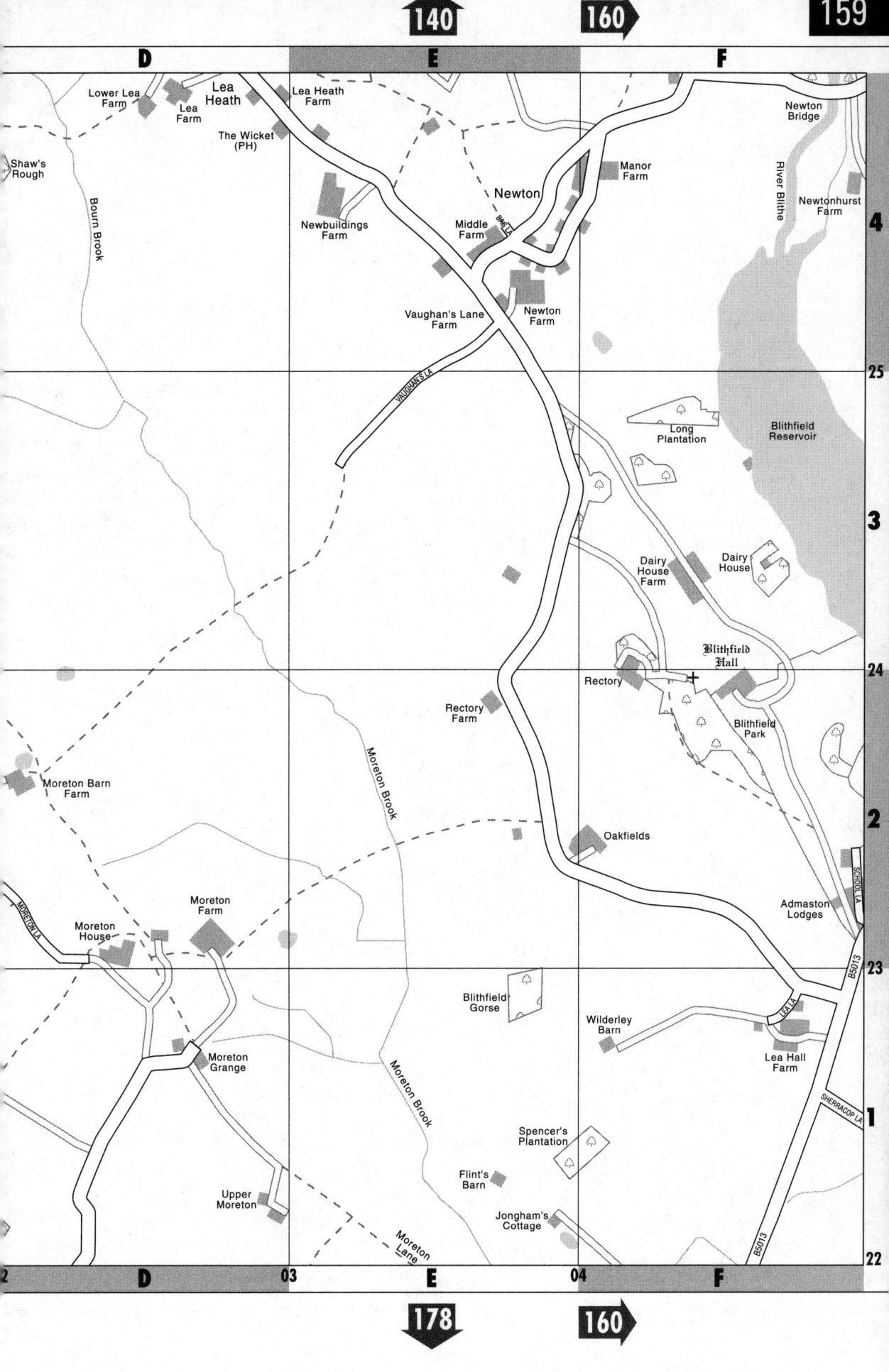

D E F

Lower Lea
Farm

Lea Farm

Lea
Heath

The Wicket
(PH)

Lea Heath
Farm

Shaw's
Rough

Bourn Brook

Newbuildings
Farm

Newton

Middle
Farm

Manor
Farm

Newton
Bridge

River Blithe

Newtonhurst
Farm

4

Vaughan's Lane
Farm

Newton
Farm

VAUGHAN'S LA

Long
Plantation

Blithfield
Reservoir

25

3

Dairy
House
Farm

Dairy
House

Rectory
Farm

Moreton Brook

Rectory

Blithfield
Hall

Blithfield
Park

24

Moreton Barn
Farm

Oakfields

2

Admaston
Lodges

SCHOOL LA

Moreton
Farm

MORETON LA

Moreton
House

Blithfield
Gorse

Wilderley
Barn

Lea Hall
Farm

B5013

LEA LA

23

Moreton
Grange

Moreton Brook

B5013

SHERRACOP LA

1

Upper
Moreton

Spencer's
Plantation

Flint's
Barn

Jongham's
Cottage

Moreton
Lane

B5013

22

D 03 E 04 F

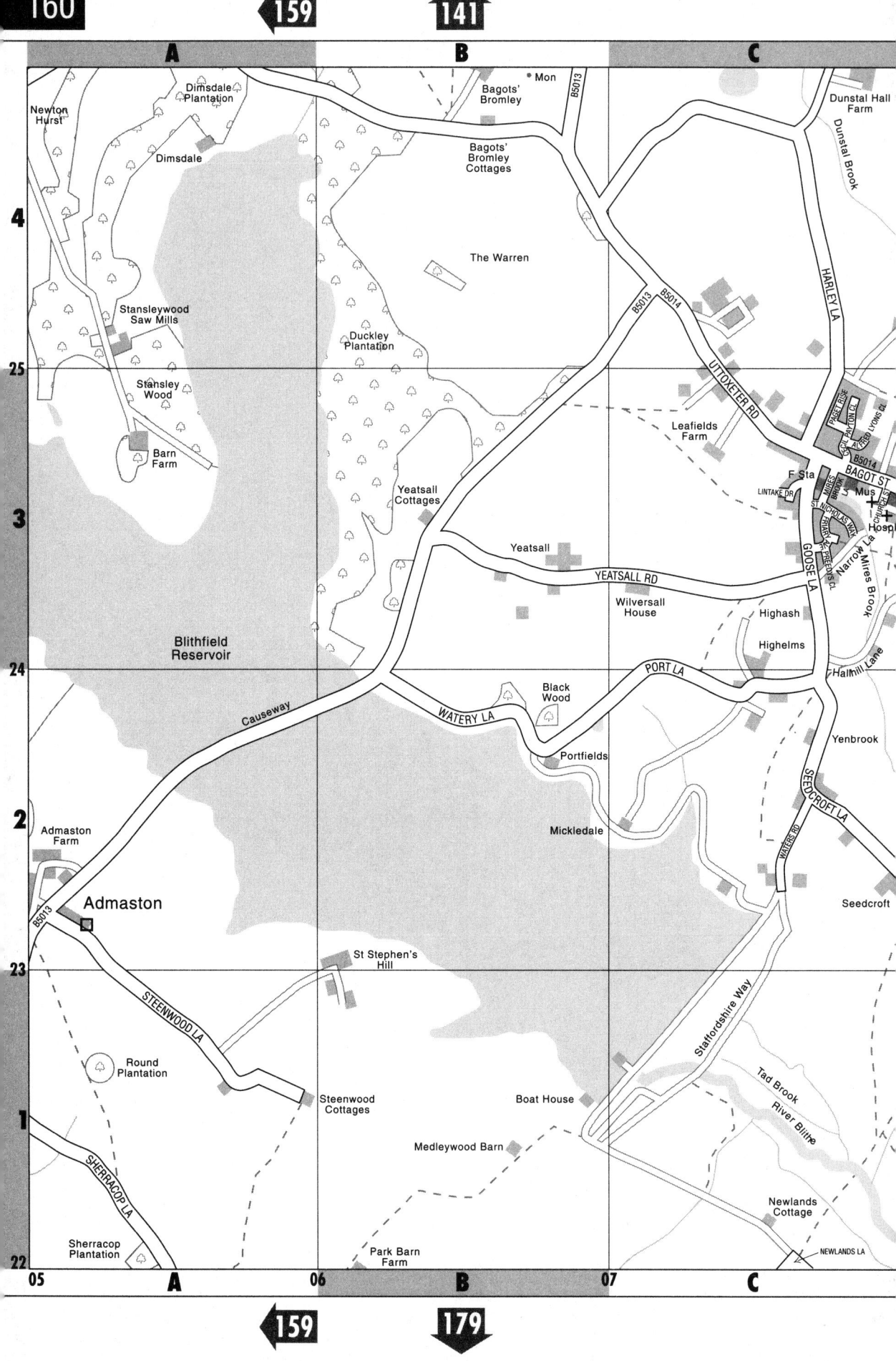

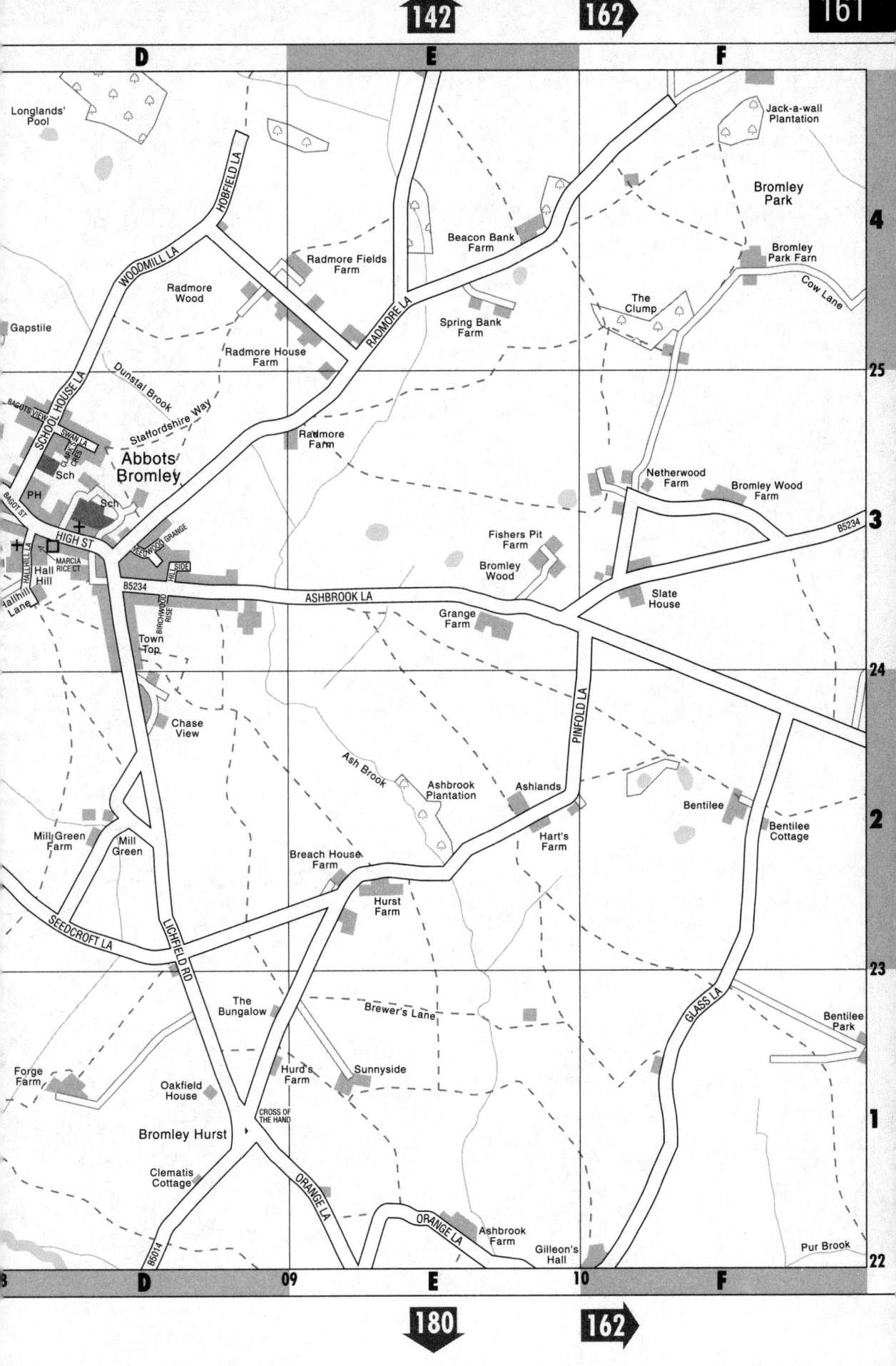

D
E
F

Longlands' Pool

Jack-a-wall Plantation

Bromley Park

4

HOBFIELD LA

Radmore Fields Farm

Beacon Bank Farm

Bromley Park Farm

Cow Lane

WOODMILL LA

Radmore Wood

RADMORE LA

Spring Bank Farm

The Clump

Gapstile

Radmore House Farm

25

SCHOOL HOUSE LA

Dunstal Brook

Staffordshire Way

Radmore Farm

Netherwood Farm

Bromley Wood Farm

BAGOTS VIEW

SWAN LA

CLARK'S CT

Sch

Abbots Bromley

B5234

PH

Sch

Fishers Pit Farm

3

BAGOT ST

HIGH ST

KEEDWOOD GRANGE

MARCIA RICE CT

Bromley Wood

HALLHILL LA

Hall Hill

HILL SIDE

Slate House

Hallhill Lane

B5234

BIRCHWOOD RISE

ASHBROOK LA

Grange Farm

Town Top

PINFOLD LA

24

Chase View

Ash Brook

Ashbrook Plantation

Ashlands

Bentilee

2

Mill Green Farm

Mill Green

Breach House Farm

Hart's Farm

Bentilee Cottage

SEEDCROFT LA

LICHFIELD RD

Hurst Farm

23

The Bungalow

Brewer's Lane

GLASS LA

Bentilee Park

Forge Farm

Oakfield House

Hurd's Farm

Sunnyside

CROSS OF THE HAND

1

Bromley Hurst

Clematis Cottage

ORANGE LA

B5014

ORANGE LA

Ashbrook Farm

Gilleon's Hall

Pur Brook

22

D
09
E
10
F

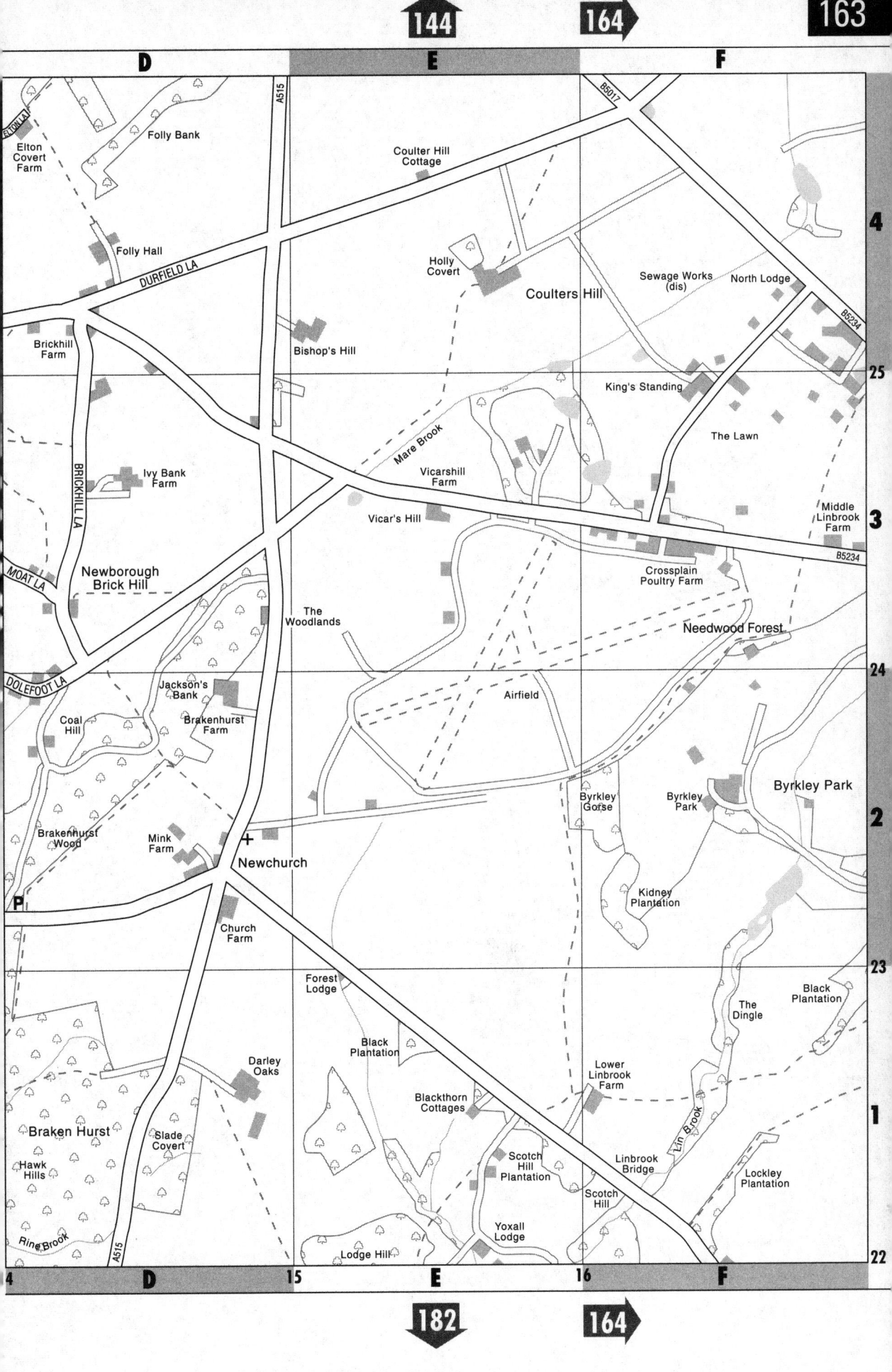

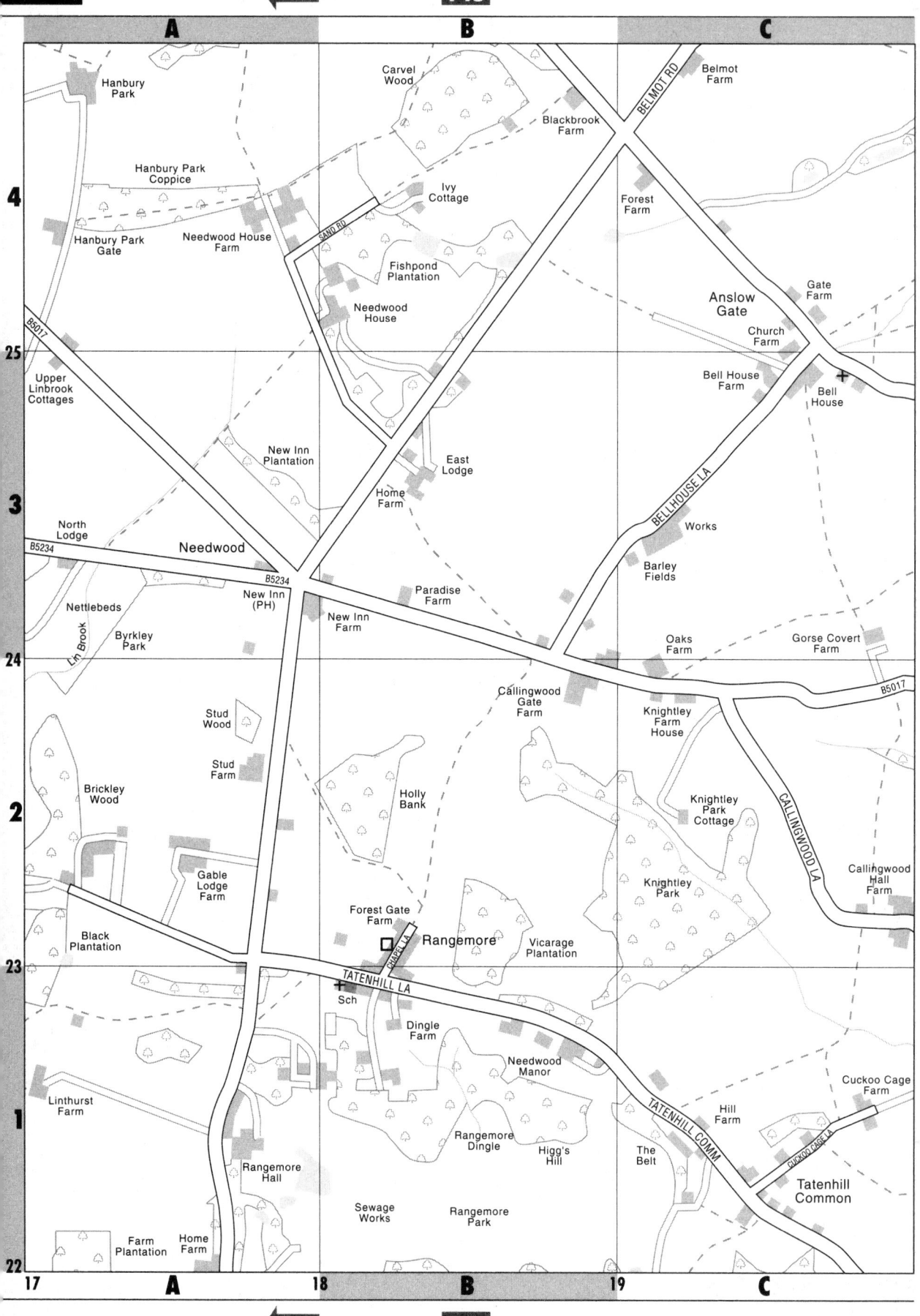

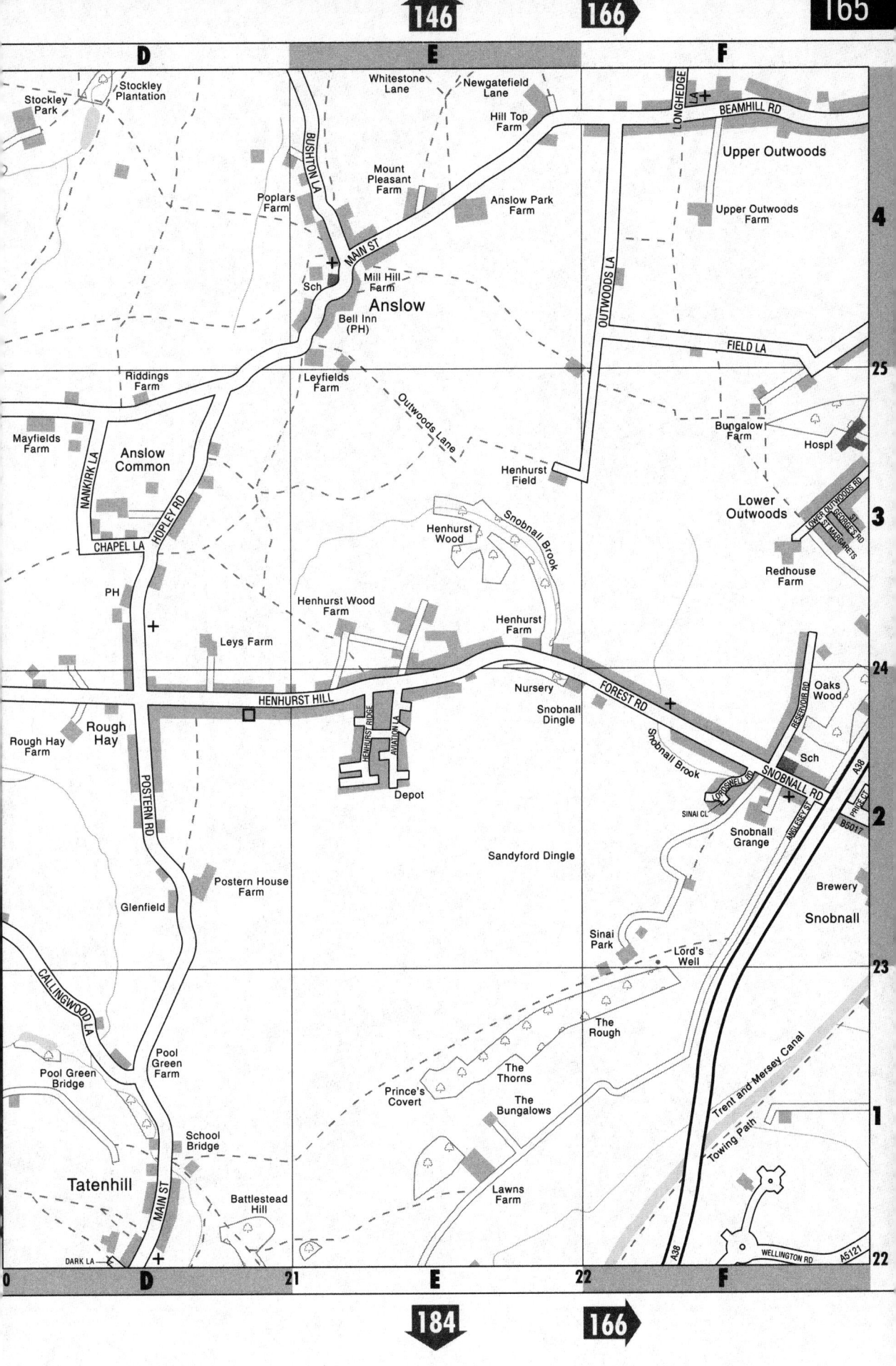

D   E   F

Stockley
Park

Stockley
Plantation

Whitestone
Lane

Newgatefield
Lane

Hill Top
Farm

BUSHTON LA

Poplars
Farm

Mount
Pleasant
Farm

Anslow Park
Farm

LONGHEDGE LA

BEAMHILL RD

Upper Outwoods

Upper Outwoods
Farm

4

MAIN ST

Sch

Mill Hill
Farm

Anslow

Bell Inn
(PH)

OUTWOODS LA

FIELD LA

25

Riddings
Farm

Leyfields
Farm

Outwoods Lane

Mayfields
Farm

NANKIRK LA

Anslow
Common

Henhurst
Field

Bungalow
Farm

Hospl

Lower
Outwoods

LOWER OUTWOODS RD

ST GEORGES ST

ST MARGARETS

3

HOPLEY RD

CHAPEL LA

Henhurst
Wood

Snobnall Brook

Redhouse
Farm

PH

Henhurst Wood
Farm

Henhurst
Farm

Leys Farm

RESERVOIR RD

Oaks
Wood

24

Rough Hay
Farm

Rough
Hay

HENHURST HILL

HENHURST RIDGE

AVALON LA

Nursery

Snobnall
Dingle

FOREST RD

Snobnall Brook

Sch

CRESSWELL RD

SNOBNALL RD

A38

PRINCE CT

B5017

Depot

Sandyford Dingle

SINAI CL

Snobnall
Grange

ANGLESEY ST

Snobnall

2

POSTERN RD

Postern House
Farm

Glenfield

Sinai
Park

Lord's
Well

Brewery

23

CALLINGWOOD LA

Pool Green
Bridge

Pool Green
Farm

Prince's
Covert

The
Rough

The
Thorns

The
Bungalows

Trent and Mersey Canal

Towing Path

1

School
Bridge

Tatenhill

MAIN ST

Battlestead
Hill

Lawns
Farm

A38

WELLINGTON RD

A5121

22

DARK LA

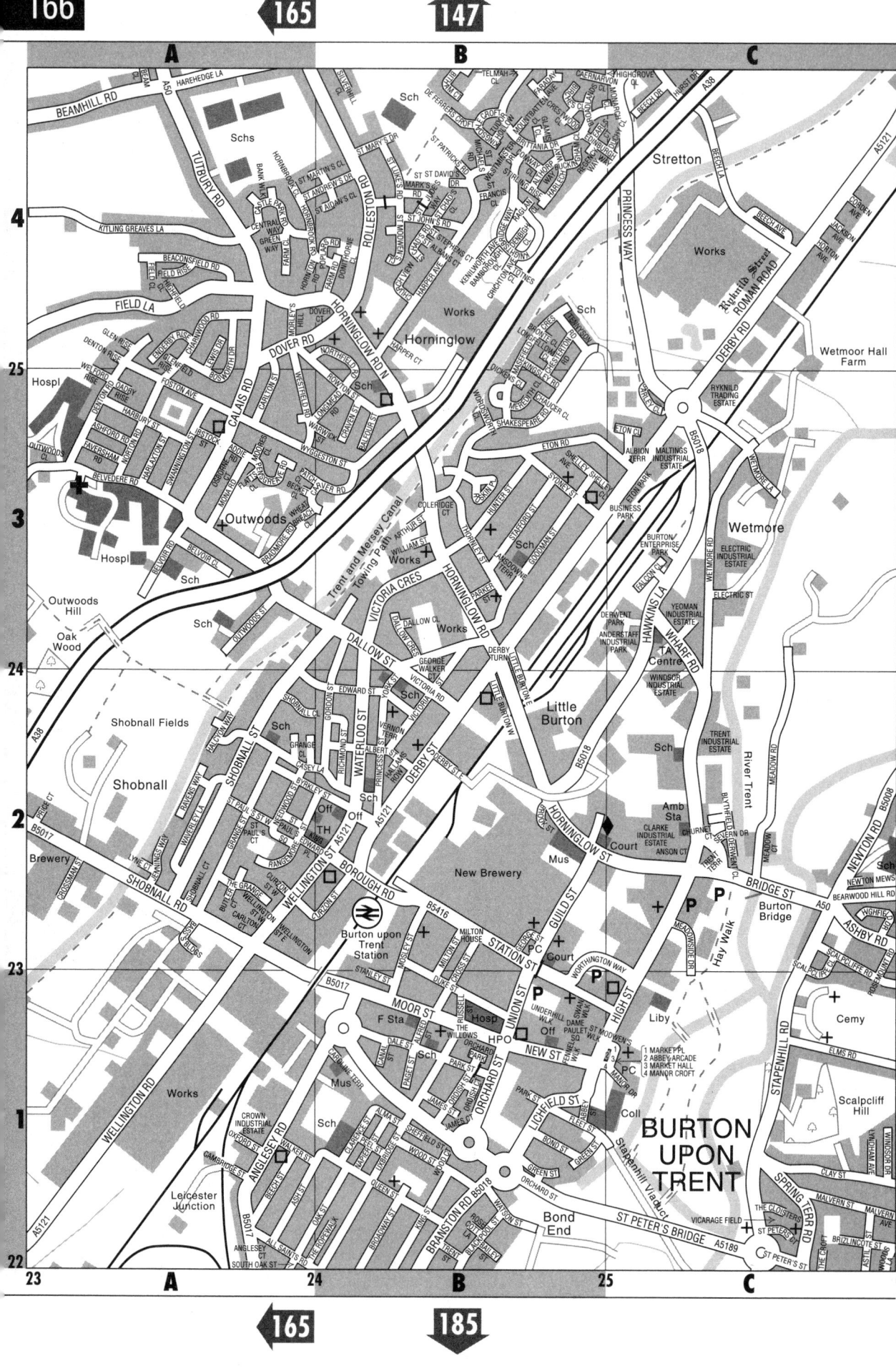

165
147

BURTON UPON TRENT

1 MARKET PL
2 ABBEY ARCADE
3 MARKET HALL
4 MANOR CROFT

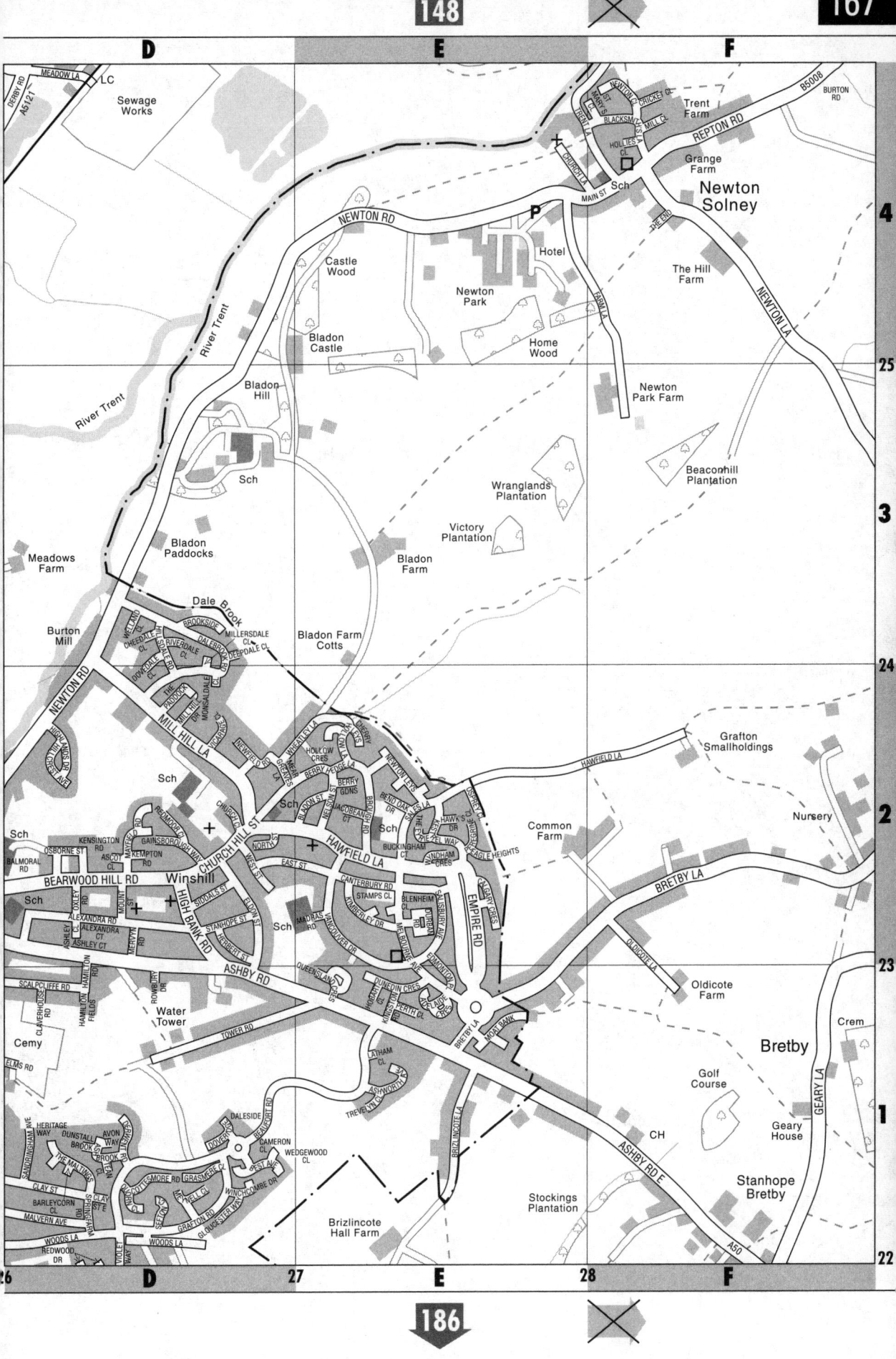

A   B   C

A41
Lane End Farm
CHESTER RD
River Meese
Lonco Brook

4

CHETWYND PARK
Chetwynd Park
New House Farm
Chetwynd
Chetwynd Manor

21

CHETWYND RD
Middle Lodge

WATERLOO RD
Waterloo
Edgmond Marsh
A41
A519

3

Chetwynd Park Deer Park
The Scaur
Park Pool
Islington
PLOUGH

New Inn Farm
FORTON RD
KINGFISHER
SWANMERE
HENRY WAY
BEECHFIELD

B5062

20

Lamb Hotel (PH)
WOODRIDGE CL
PLAYDALE
SILVERDALE
SHREWSBURY RD
CHETWYND RD
Blue House Farm
BLUE HOUSE BARNS
MASON'S
CHETWYND RD
FAIR OAK
ISLINGTON CL
VINEYARD
BRACKEN WAY
MAYNARDS
CFT
CALDERCROFTS

Flatt Pit Farm
Egremont House
Sch
Lion Inn PH
Cherry Hill Farm
Summerhill
EDGMOND RD
B5062
Sch
Canal (dis)
Victoria Park
FISHERS CRT
SUMMERFIELD
WATERSFORD

2

STACKYARD LA
PIPER'S LA
MANOR RD
HIGHFIELD
ROBIN LA
TURNERS
CONNERS LA
BRATLEY MILLS
NEWPORT RD
NEWPORT
Ticketthouse Lock
Wrekin View Farm
HAVISHAM CT
CHETWYND END
BROOK HOUSE
Off
WATER LA
Liby
PC
LAUREL
A518
STAFFORD RD
CORNMELL
MEADOW RD
UNDERHILL CL

Edgmond
SCHOOL RD
Sch
PIPER'S LODGE
Sewage Works
BROOMFIELD
NFIELD
BROOMFIELD RD
GREENACRES
HALLCROFT GDNS
SALTER'S LA
F Sta
Sch
HIGH ST
Sch
SALTER'S CT
PC
P
BEAUMARIS RD
P

19

BADDELY'S CT
P
AUDLEY
AVE
AVENUE RD
GRANVILLE
Sch

Vauxhall
Lower Farm
Vauxhall Farm
MOORFIELD CL
ADAMS CL
GRAVELLY DR
SANDIFORD CRES
RODDAM CT
Sch
BLAKEMERE
Hosp
UPPER BAR

Strine Brook
SHREWSBURY WAY
BLACKMERE
DUNBAR
INGESTRE
JORDAN
BOUGHEY RD
STETTON
HAWKSTONE AVE
WELLOCK DR
GRANVILLE RD
Sch

1

LONGFORD RD
Sunnyholme Farm
Longford
GILBERT
VIKING CL
TALBOT
FORD RD
THE LANCHER
WATERFORD DR
MOORFIELD LA
ASPEN
ELM CL
SPRINGFIELDS INDUSTRIAL ESTATE
PRINCESS GDNS
STATION CT
STATION RD

Brook Cottage
Home Farm
Longford Hall
Pool Covert
Grove Farm
Aston Grove Pinewoods
ST ANDREWS WY
NEWTOWN
A518
PRIMROSE
RICHMOND
Millwood Mere
Baddely's Well

18

72   A   73   B   74   C

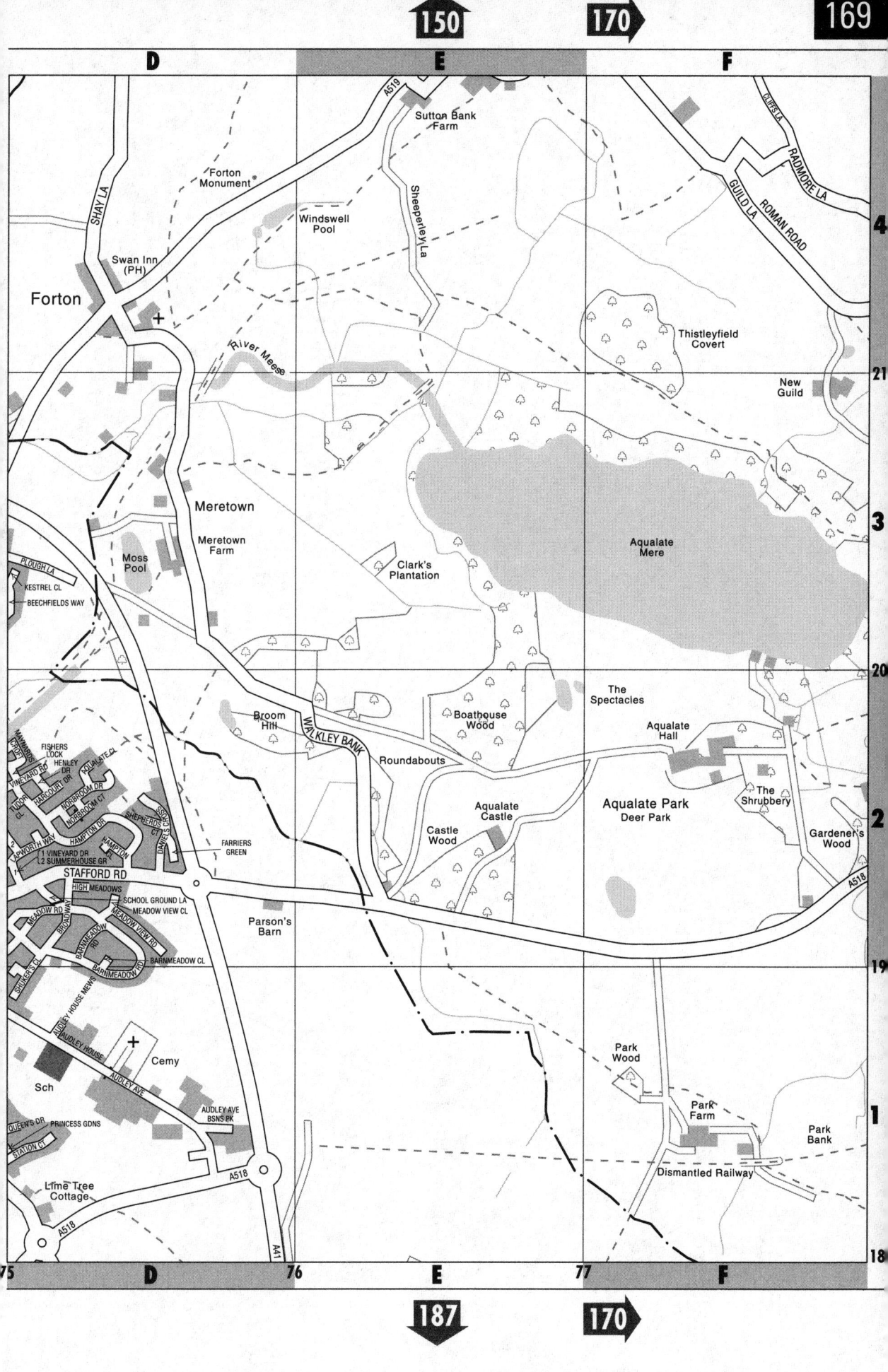

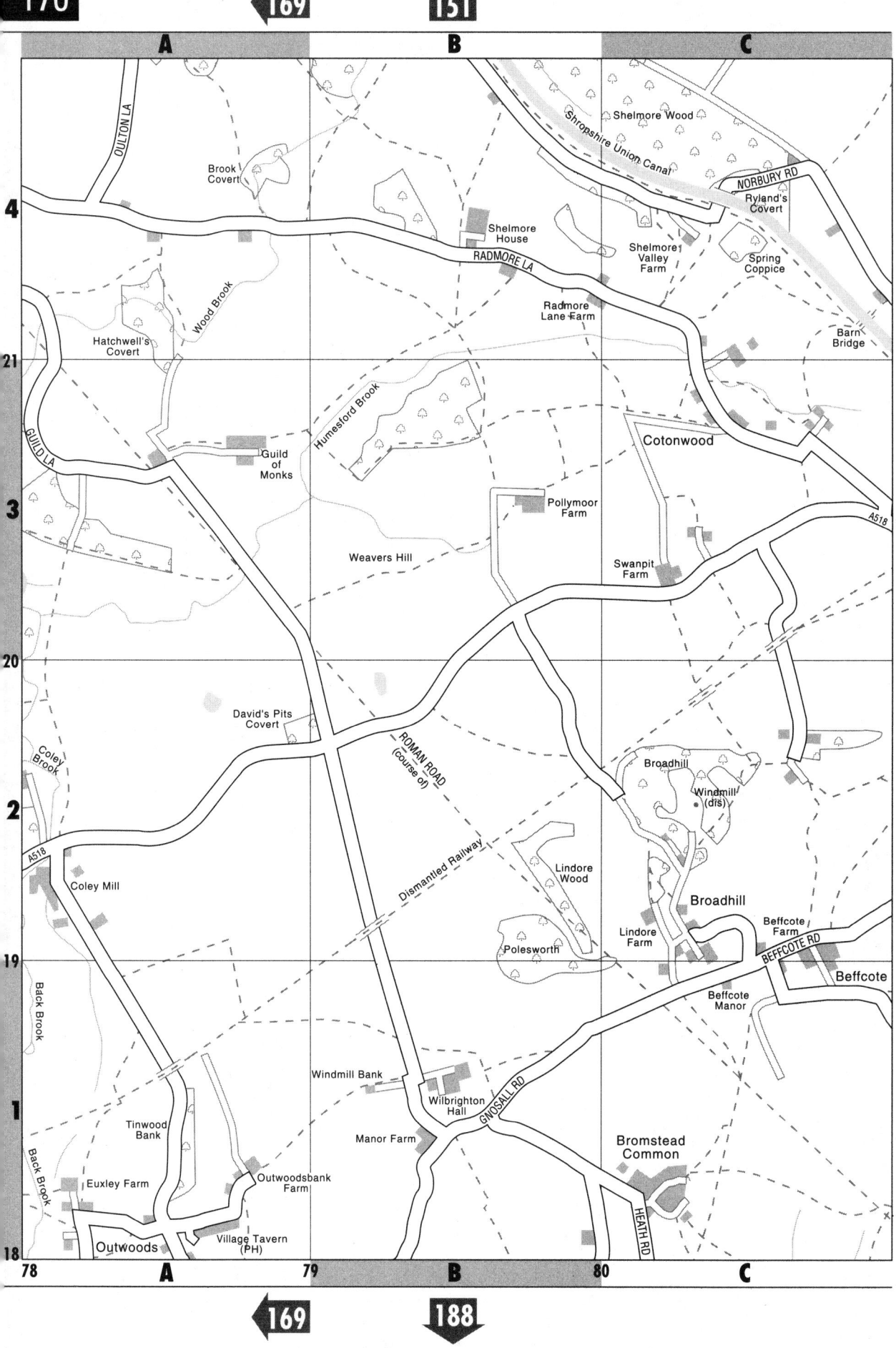

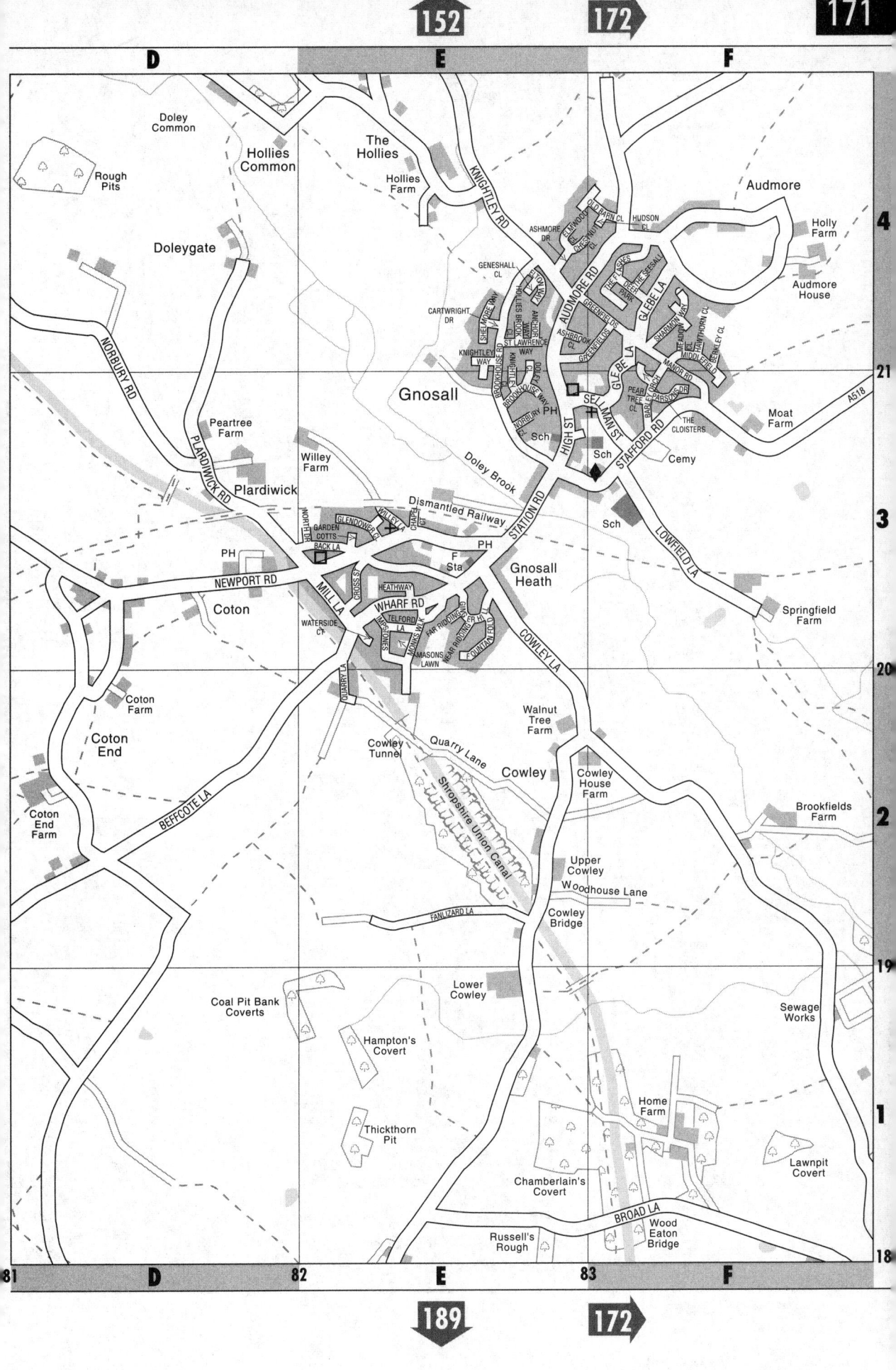

D   E   F

Doley Common

Rough Pits

Hollies Common

The Hollies

Hollies Farm

Doleygate

Audmore

Holly Farm

Audmore House

NORBURY RD

KNIGHTLEY RD

OLD BARN CL
HUDSON CL

ASHMORE DR
EASTWOOD RD
CHESTNUT CL

THE ASHES
DEEPHAYES
THE SESSAIL
PARK

GENESHALL CL

AUDMORE RD

GLEBE LA

4

Peartree Farm

CARTWRIGHT DR

ASHBROOK CL
GREENFIELDS

GREENFIELD DR

SHARMAN WAY

THE DOWN

HAWTHORN CL

BRETHLEY CL

21

PLARDIWICK RD

Willey Farm

SHELMORE TWY

ST LAWRENCE WAY

KNIGHTLEY WAY

Gnosall

NORBURY WAY

BROOKHOUSE RD
KNIGHTLEY RD
BROOKHOUSE WAY

HIGH ST

PH

Sch

GLEBE LA

SELLMAN ST

PEAR TREE CL
PEARSON DR

STAFFORD RD

MAJOR RD
MIDDLEFELL

THE CLOISTERS

Moat Farm

A518

Plardiwick

Doley Brook

Sch

Cemy

Dismantled Railway

STATION RD

Sch

LOWFIELD LA

3

PH

GARDEN COTTS

GLENDOWER CT

WILLEY LA

CHAPEL LA

Sch

PH

F Sta

PH

Gnosall Heath

Springfield Farm

Coton

NEWPORT RD

NORTH END

BACK LA

CROSS ST

HEATHWAY

WHARF RD

MILL LA

MASONS LAWN

TELFORD LA

MASONS WLK

FAR RIDDINGS

NEAR RIDDINGS

FER HL

FOUNTAIN CL

COWLEY LA

20

WATERSIDE CT

QUARRY LA

Coton Farm

Coton End

Walnut Tree Farm

Cowley Tunnel

Quarry Lane

Cowley

Cowley House Farm

Brookfields Farm

2

Coton End Farm

BEFFCOTE LA

Shropshire Union Canal

Upper Cowley

Woodhouse Lane

Cowley Bridge

FANLIZARD LA

19

Coal Pit Bank Coverts

Lower Cowley

Sewage Works

Hampton's Covert

Home Farm

1

Thickthorn Pit

Chamberlain's Covert

Lawnpit Covert

BROAD LA

Wood Eaton Bridge

Russell's Rough

18

81   D   82   E   83   F

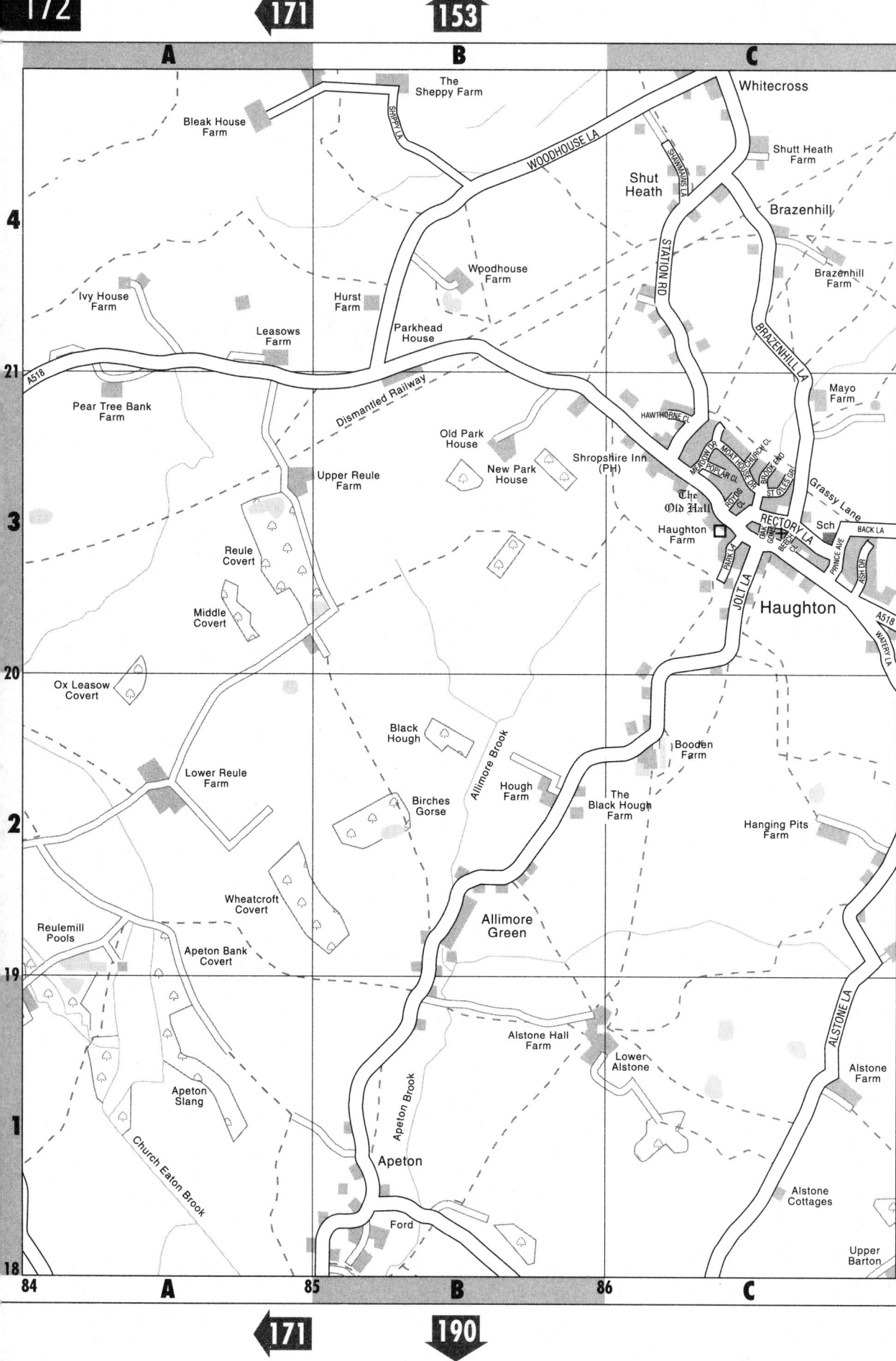

The Sheppy Farm

Bleak House Farm

WOODHOUSE LA

Whitecross

Shutt Heath Farm

Shut Heath

Brazenhill

Woodhouse Farm

Brazenhill Farm

Ivy House Farm

Hurst Farm

STATION RD

SPEPPY LA

STANMANS LA

BRAZENHILL LA

Leasows Farm

Parkhead House

Mayo Farm

A518

Pear Tree Bank Farm

Dismantled Railway

HAWTHORNE CL

Old Park House

New Park House

Shropshire Inn (PH)

MEADOW DR

MOAT HOUSE DR

POPLAR CL

CHURCH CL

BROOK END

ST GILES GDN

Grassy Lane

The Old Hall

Haughton Farm

RECTORY LA

Sch

BACK LA

Upper Reule Farm

Reule Covert

REDES

BEECH CL

PRINCE AVE

ASH DR

Haughton

PARK LA

JOLT LA

Middle Covert

A518

WATERY LA

Ox Leasow Covert

Black Hough

Booden Farm

Allimore Brook

Hough Farm

The Black Hough Farm

Hanging Pits Farm

Lower Reule Farm

Birches Gorse

Wheatcroft Covert

Allimore Green

Reulemill Pools

Apeton Bank Covert

ALSTONE LA

Alstone Hall Farm

Lower Alstone

Alstone Farm

Apeton Slang

Church Eaton Brook

Apeton Brook

Apeton

Ford

Alstone Cottages

Upper Barton

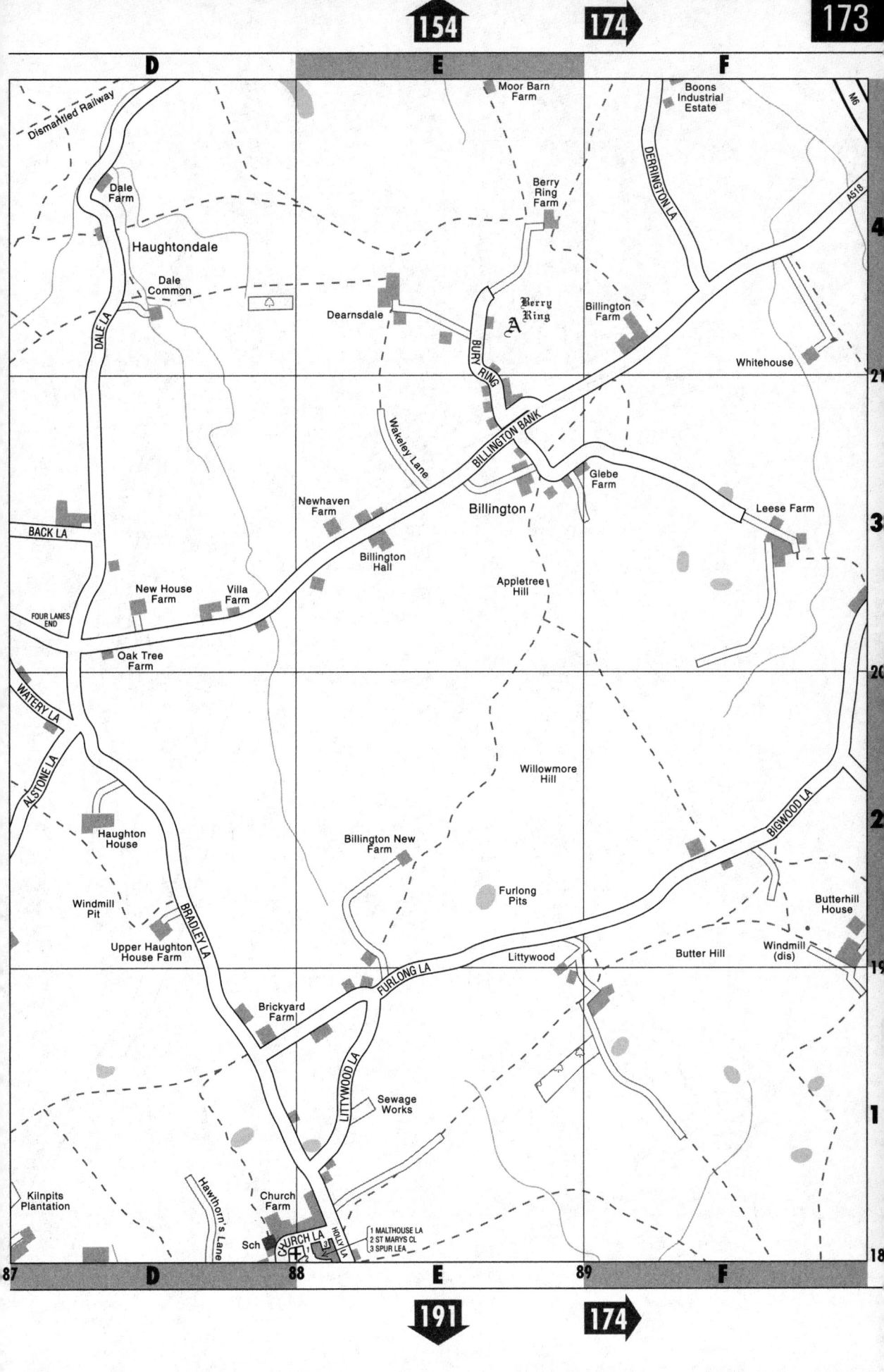

D E F

4

Dismantled Railway

Dale Farm

Haughtondale

Dale Common

DALE LA

Haughtondale

Moor Barn Farm

Boons Industrial Estate

Berry Ring Farm

Dearnsdale

BURY RING

Berry Ring

A

Billington Farm

Whitehouse

DERRINGTON LA

A518

M6

BACK LA

Wakeley Lane

BILLINGTON BANK

Billington

Glebe Farm

Leese Farm

Newhaven Farm

Billington Hall

Appletree Hill

New House Farm

Villa Farm

FOUR LANES END

Oak Tree Farm

WATERY LA

ALSTONE LA

Haughton House

Willowmore Hill

BIGWOOD LA

Billington New Farm

Butterhill House

Windmill Pit

BRADLEY LA

Upper Haughton House Farm

Furlong Pits

FURLONG LA

Littywood

Butter Hill

Windmill (dis)

Brickyard Farm

LITTYWOOD LA

Sewage Works

Kilnpits Plantation

Hawthorn's Lane

Church Farm

Sch

CHURCH LA

HOLLY LA

1 MALTHOUSE LA
2 ST MARYS CL
3 SPUR LEA

4

21

3

20

2

19

1

18

87 D 88 E 89 F

LEXINGTON GR 1
LETHERIDGE GDNS 2
LINCOLN MEADOW 3
DENVER FOLD 4
DOWNDERRY CL 5
DEXTON RISE 6
KESWICK GR 7
KELD AVE 8
KENTMERE CL 9
DART AVE 10
CRANBROOK WALK 11
CLEVELAND WALK 12
CLAREMONT GR 13
BONINGDALE WAY 14
BURLINGTON DR 15

EDMUND AVE 16
BURNS AVE 17
HELFORD GR 18
LINDEN CL 19
DUNSTER CL 20
KENDAL CL 21
BEESTON RIDGE 22
MELROSE AVE 23
KIRKSTALL AVE 24
MASEFIELD DR 25
WEST WAY 26
SHAKESPEARE RD 27
THACKERAY WALK 28
AUDEN WAY 29
TAYLOR WALK 30
GREY WALK 31
OWEN WALK 32

LONGSHORE CL 1
ELSDON RD 2
TURNHILL CL 3
CRINAN GR 4
SHENLEY GR 5

1 ROWLEY HALL CL
2 ROWLEY HALL DR

CLANFORD CL 1

1 HUNTERS RISE
2 CRAFTDOWN CL
3 WOODBERRY CL

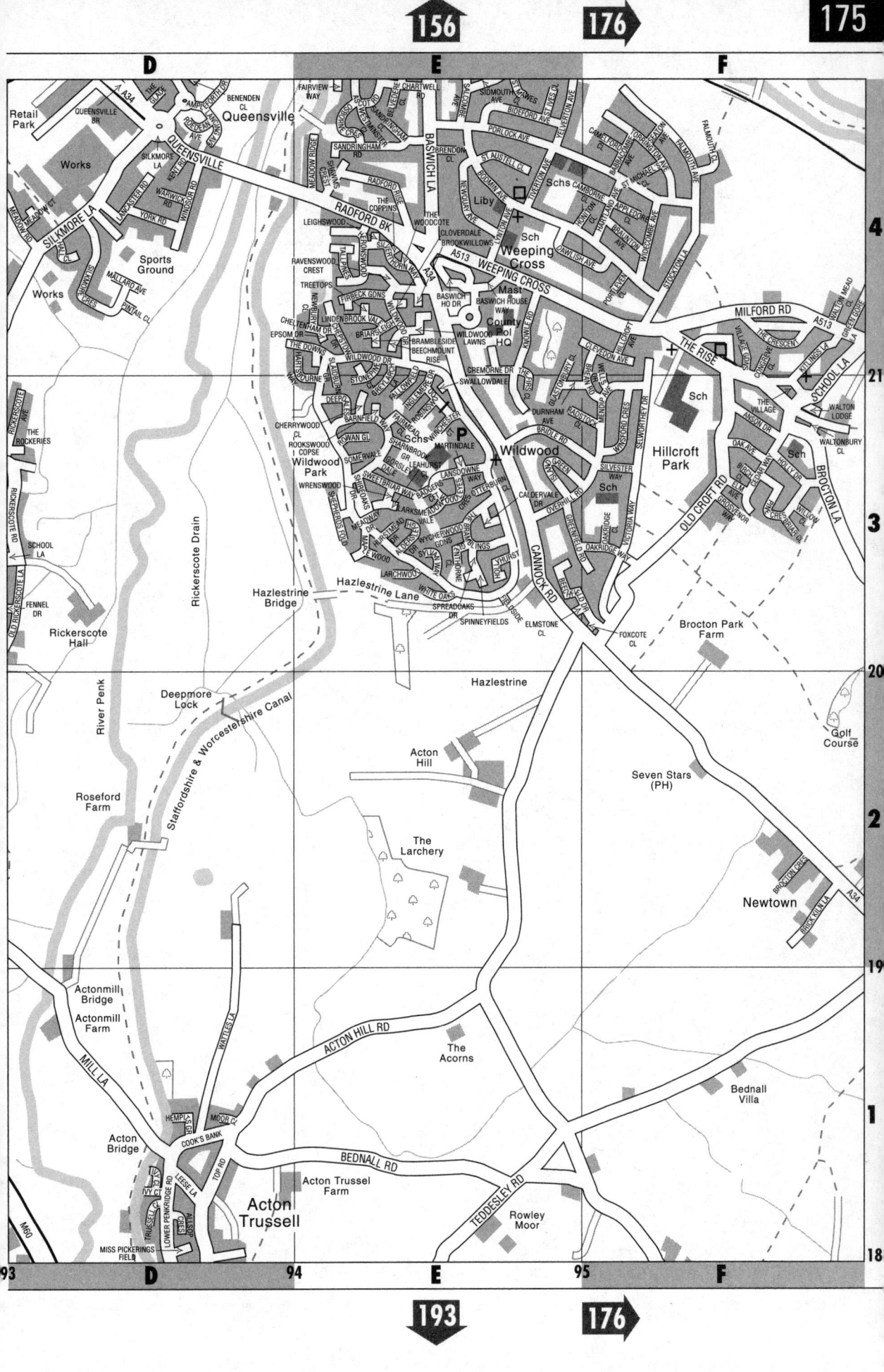

D E F

Retail Park

THE BLACK PATH

A34

Queensville

Works

Works

QUEENSVILLE BR

SILKMORE LA

QUEENSVILLE

Sports Ground

BENENDEN CL
AMPLEFORTH PK

ROEDEAN AVE
SILKMORE LA

LANCASTER RD
WARWICK RD
WINDSOR RD
YORK RD

MALLARD AVE
PINTAIL CL
MEADOW CT
NESTLE CT
BROOKLYN DR

SILKMORE CRES

FAIRVIEW WAY
CHARTWELL RD
CAWES

SALCOMBE
SIDMOUTH AVE

BASWICH LA

RADFORD BK

LEIGHSWOOD

RAVENSWOOD CREST

TREETOPS

CHELTENHAM DR
EPSOM DR
THE DOWNS
LINDENBROOK VAL
FIRBECK GDNS
WILDWOOD DR
BRIARS

WILDWOOD DR
STONERIVE

HAREBOURNE

DEEP

CHERRYWOOD CL
ROOKSWOOD COPSE

Wildwood Park

WRENSWOOD

SOMERVALE
BARNFIELD WAY
ROWAN GL

SHEPHERDS FOLD
SWEETBRIAR WAY
SYLVAN WAY
LARKWOOD

RIVERSIDE
SPREADOAKS DR

PORLOCK AVE
BIDEFORD AVE
BODMIN WAY

ST AUSTELL CL

TIVERTON AVE

NEWQUAY WAY

A34

A513

WEEPING CROSS

BASWICH HO DR
BASWICH HOUSE WAY

County Hall HQ

CLOVERDALE
BROOKWILLOWS

Weeping Cross

Sch

Liby

St AUSTELL CL

CAMBORNE

St MICHAEL AVE
APPLEDORE AVE

HORTON AVE

DARTMOUTH AVE
BODINGTON AVE

CAWLISH AVE

Schs

Mast

WILDWOOD LAWNS

BRAMBLESIDE
BEECHMOUNT RISE

CREMORNE DR
SWALLOWDALE

KNOWLE RD

DURNHAM AVE

CLEVEDON AVE

HILLCROFT AVE

THE RISE

Sch

Schs

SHARNGROVE GR
LEAHURST
MARTINDALE

P

Wildwood

WINCHESTER CL
BRIDLE RD

CALDERVALE DR

CAMEL DON AVE
TORRINGTON AVE
FALMOUTH CL

St MICHAEL AVE

WIDECOMBE AVE

PORT HOLE

VERATON AVE

STOCKTON LA

MILFORD RD
A513

WALTON MEAD
GREENACRE

THE CRESCENT

VILLAGE GRANGE
CANKERDINE LA

THE RISE

THE VILLAGE
ANSON DR

KILLINGHALL

SCHOOL LA

WALTON LODGE

WALTONBURY CL

Sch

OAK AVE
HIGH AVE
ELM AVE
HOLLY DR
WILLOW

BROCTON LA

Sch

BROSTERFIELD WAY

GROVE NOR WAY

CRESFIELD CL

Hillcroft Park

BLASTON
BRENT HILL

GREENE CT

OLD CROFT RD

VICTORIA WAY

OAKRIDGE WAY

OVERHILL RD

OAKBRIDGE

SILVESTER WAY

SELWORTHY DR

CANNOCK RD

WYCHERWOOD GDNS

CATHORNE

WHITE OAKS

SPINNEYFIELDS

Hazlestrine Bridge

Hazlestrine Lane

FOXCOTE CL

ELMSTONE CL

Brocton Park Farm

Hazlestrine

RICKERSCOTE AVE
THE ROCKERIES

OLD RICKERSCOTE LA

SCHOOL LA
FENNEL DR

Rickerscote Hall

Rickerscote Drain

River Penk

Staffordshire & Worcestershire Canal

Deepmore Lock

Roseford Farm

Acton Hill

Golf Course

The Larchery

Seven Stars (PH)

BROCTON CRES

BRICK KILN LA

A34

Newtown

Actonmill Bridge

Actonmill Farm

MILL LA

M60

WATLING LA

TOP RD

HEMPLA
MOOR CL
COOK'S BANK

ACTON HILL RD

The Acorns

Acton Bridge

TRUSSELL RD
IVY CT
LEESE LA
ALLSOP CRES

LOWER PENKRIDGE RD

Acton Trussell Farm

BEDNALL RD

Acton Trussell

TEDDESLEY RD

Rowley Moor

Bednall Villa

MISS PICKERINGS FIELD

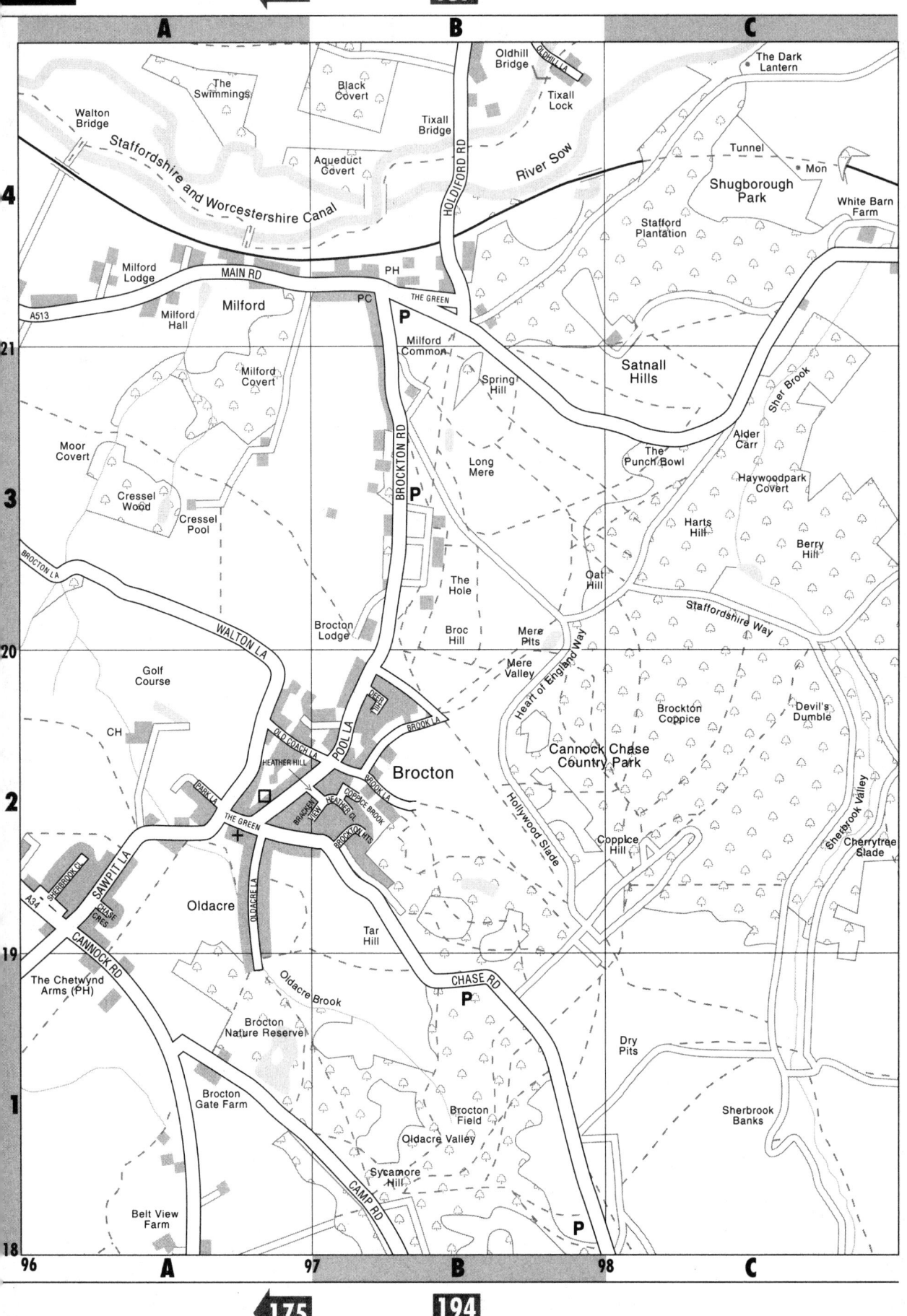

175
157

A   B   C

4

The Swimmings

Walton Bridge

Black Covert

Oldhill Bridge

OLDHILL LA

Tixall Lock

Tixall Bridge

HOLDIFORD RD

River Sow

The Dark Lantern

Tunnel

Mon

Shugborough Park

White Barn Farm

Stafford Plantation

Staffordshire and Worcestershire Canal

Aqueduct Covert

Milford Lodge

MAIN RD

PH

THE GREEN

PC

A513

Milford Hall

Milford

21

Milford Common

P

Satnall Hills

Sher Brook

Milford Covert

Spring Hill

Moor Covert

BROCTON RD

Long Mere

The Punch Bowl

Alder Carr

Haywoodpark Covert

3

Cressel Wood

P

Harts Hill

Berry Hill

Cressel Pool

BROCTON LA

The Hole

Oat Hill

Staffordshire Way

Brocton Lodge

Broc Hill

Mere Pits

WALTON LA

20

Golf Course

DEER HILL

Mere Valley

Heart of England Way

Brockton Coppice

Devil's Dumble

CH

OLD COACH LA

POOL LA

BROOK LA

Cannock Chase Country Park

Sherbrook Valley

HEATHER HILL

Brocton

2

PARK LA

BROCTON VIEW

COPPICE BROOK

HEATHER CL

BROCTON HTS

Coppice Hill

Cherrytree Slade

THE GREEN

Hollywood Slade

SHERBROOK RD

A34

CHASE CRES

CANNOCK RD

Oldacre

OLDACRE LA

SAWPIT LA

Tar Hill

19

The Chetwynd Arms (PH)

Oldacre Brook

CHASE RD

P

Dry Pits

Brocton Nature Reserve

Brocton Gate Farm

1

Brocton Field

Sherbrook Banks

Oldacre Valley

Belt View Farm

Sycamore Hill

CAMP RD

P

18

96   A   97   B   98   C

175
194

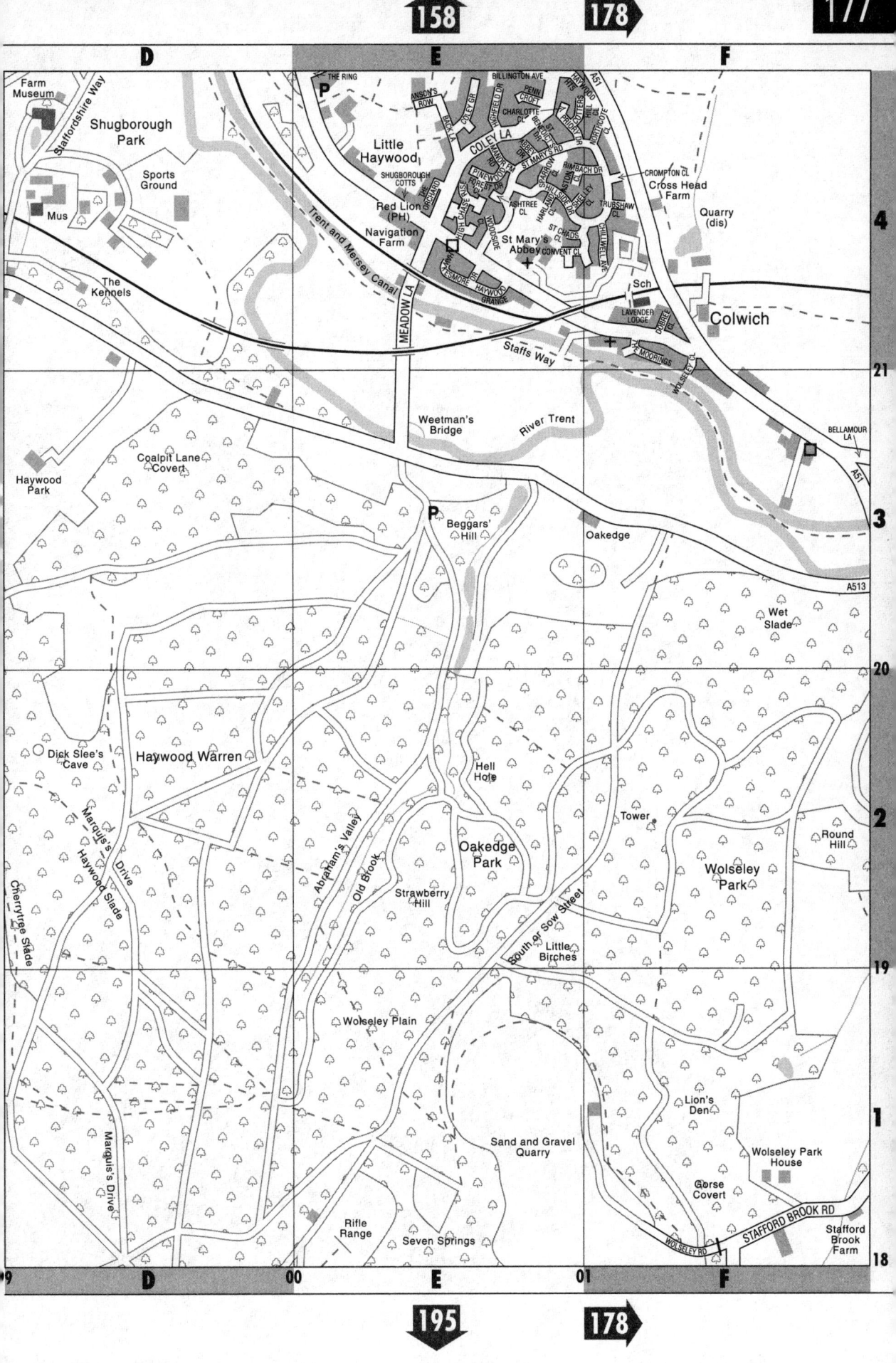

Farm Museum

Staffordshire Way

Shugborough Park

Sports Ground

THE RING

P

ANSON'S ROW

COLEY GR

BILLINGTON AVE
PENN CROFT
CHARLOTTE

COLEY LA

Little Haywood

SHUGBOROUGH COTTS

Red Lion (PH)

Navigation Farm

THE ORCHARD

PINEWOOD

FORESTRY

ASHTREE CL

HIGH CHASE RISE

WOODSIDE

St Mary's Abbey

CONVENT CL

ST MARY'S RD

ST CHADS

CROMPTON CL
Cross Head Farm

TRUBSHAW CL

Quarry (dis)

Sch

HILLWELL AVE

Colwich

LAVENDER LODGE

DOBBLE

THE MOORINGS

WOLSELEY CL

4

Mus

The Kennels

Trent and Mersey Canal

MEADOW LA

Staffs Way

21

Weetman's Bridge

River Trent

BELLAMOUR LA

A51

Haywood Park

Coalpit Lane Covert

P Beggars' Hill

Oakedge

3

Wet Slade

A513

20

Dick Slee's Cave

Haywood Warren

Marquis's Drive

Haywood Slade

Cherrytree Slade

Abraham's Valley

Old Brook

Hell Hole

Oakedge Park

Strawberry Hill

Little Birches

South or Sow Street

Tower

Wolseley Park

Round Hill

2

19

Wolseley Plain

Marquis's Drive

Lion's Den

Sand and Gravel Quarry

Wolseley Park House

1

Gorse Covert

Rifle Range

Seven Springs

WOLSELEY RD

STAFFORD BROOK RD

Stafford Brook Farm

18

A   **B**   **C**

4

21

Bishton Farm

Bishton Lane Farm

Moreton Lane

Lount Farm

Hamley Cottage Farm

Hamleyheath

MOOR LA

Bellamour

3

Bishton

Bishton Hall (Sch)

Taft Farm

Taft Bridge

BELLAMOUR LA

Trent and Mersey Canal

Staffordshire Way

Colwich Lodge

Wilmour Farm

Bellamour Lodge Farm

Boughey Hall Farm   Sch

BELLAMOUR WAY

A51
BISHTON LA

A513

PH

Wolseley Garden Park

Wharf Cottage

20

Chapel Hill

Sewage Works

River Trent

COLTON RD

Rydal Farm

2

Long Covert

Stafford Brook

Bower House

Highland Way

Pumping Station

Rugeley Trent Valley Station

Trent Farm

TRENT VALLEY TRADING EST

19

BOWER LA

THE BEECHES

SHUGBORO FIELD

Allen Birt Wlk

Watson

Playing Field

Old Chancel Rd

WOLSELEY RD

COLTON RD

1

STAFFORD BROOK RD

ETCHING HILL RD

MOUNT RD

Etchinghill

OAKFIELD CL

HENLEY GRANGE

LARGHOLME CL

OAKWOOD CL

WEST BUTTS RD

EAST BUTTS RD

PEAKS RD

CHURCH LA

Sch

Sch

HORSESHOE DR 1
HUTCHINSON CL 2
DAFFODIL WLK 3
LANSDOWNE WAY 4
HURSTBOURNE CL 5
REDMOND CL 6

P REDMOND CL

Pump Lane

SHERINGHAM DR

WAVERLEY GDNS

Arthur Wood

Chapelside Schs

WESTERN SPRINGS RD

Sch

Millington St

Station Rd

P   P

F Sta

P   Off

Liby

Sneydlands

18

SHOOTING BUTTS RD

STONEHOUSE RD

CHASELEY RD

HAGLEY RD

PENKRIDGE BANK

A51

CROSSLEY STONE

BEES LA

A   **B**   **C**

02   03   04

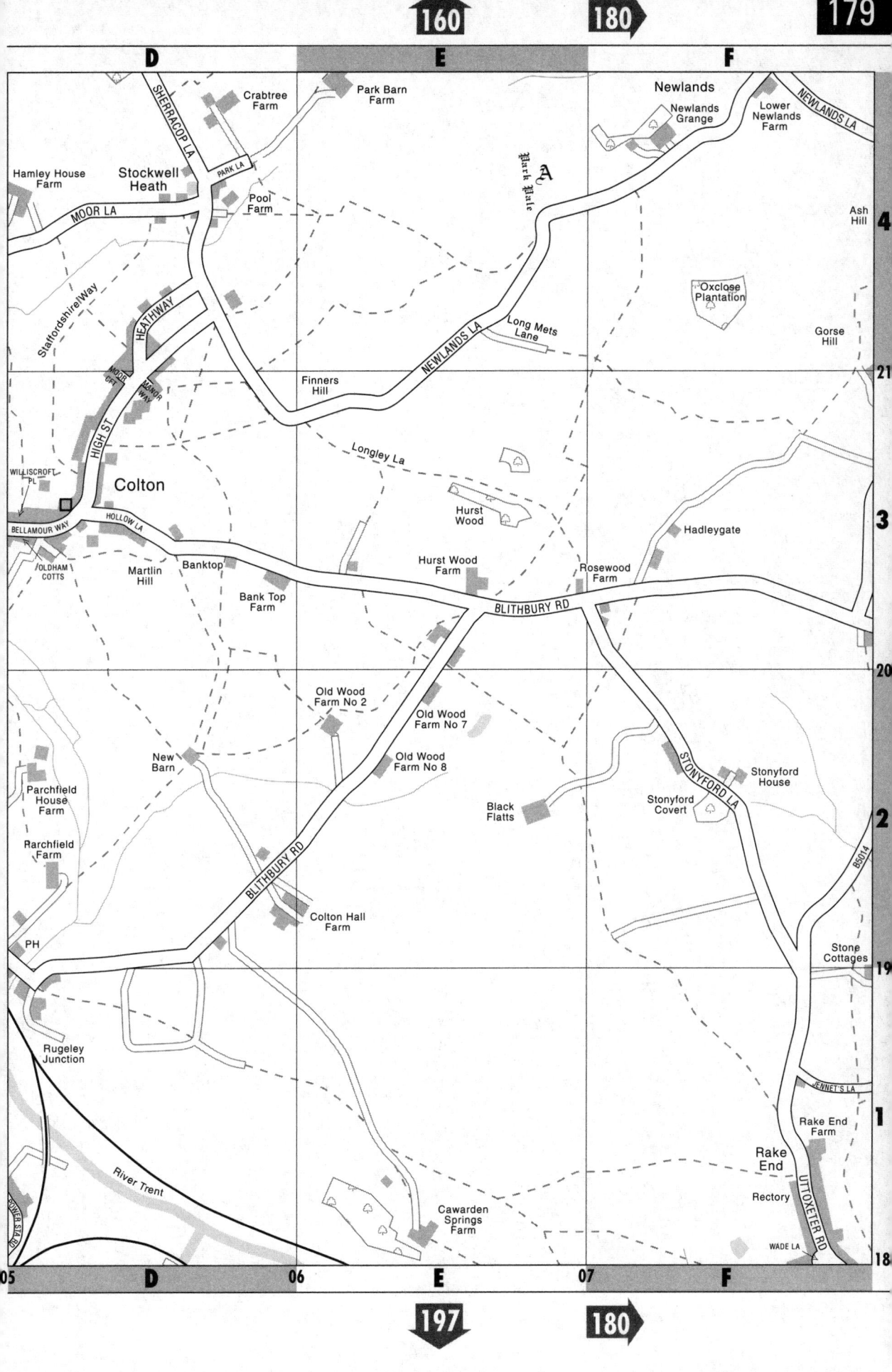

D
E
F

Crabtree Farm
Park Barn Farm
Newlands
Newlands Grange
Lower Newlands Farm
NEWLANDS LA

SHERRACOP LA
PARK LA
Hamley House Farm
Stockwell Heath
Pool Farm
MOOR LA

Park Hale A

Ash Hill
4

Oxclose Plantation
Gorse Hill

StaffordshireWay
HEATHWAY
NEWLANDS LA
Long Mets Lane

MOOR LA
MANOR WAY
Finners Hill
21

HIGH ST
Longley La
Hurst Wood

WILLISCROFT PL
Colton
Hadleygate
3

BELLAMOUR WAY
HOLLOW LA
Hurst Wood Farm
Rosewood Farm

OLDHAM COTTS
Martlin Hill
Banktop
BLITHBURY RD

Bank Top Farm
20

Old Wood Farm No 2
Old Wood Farm No 7

New Barn
Old Wood Farm No 8
Stonyford House

Parchfield House Farm
Black Flatts
Stonyford Covert
STONYFORD LA
2

Rarchfield Farm
BLITHBURY RD

B5014

PH
Colton Hall Farm
Stone Cottages
19

Rugeley Junction

JENNET'S LA
1
Rake End Farm

River Trent
Rake End
UTTOXETER RD

Rectory
Cawarden Springs Farm
WADE LA

BOWER SIDE RD

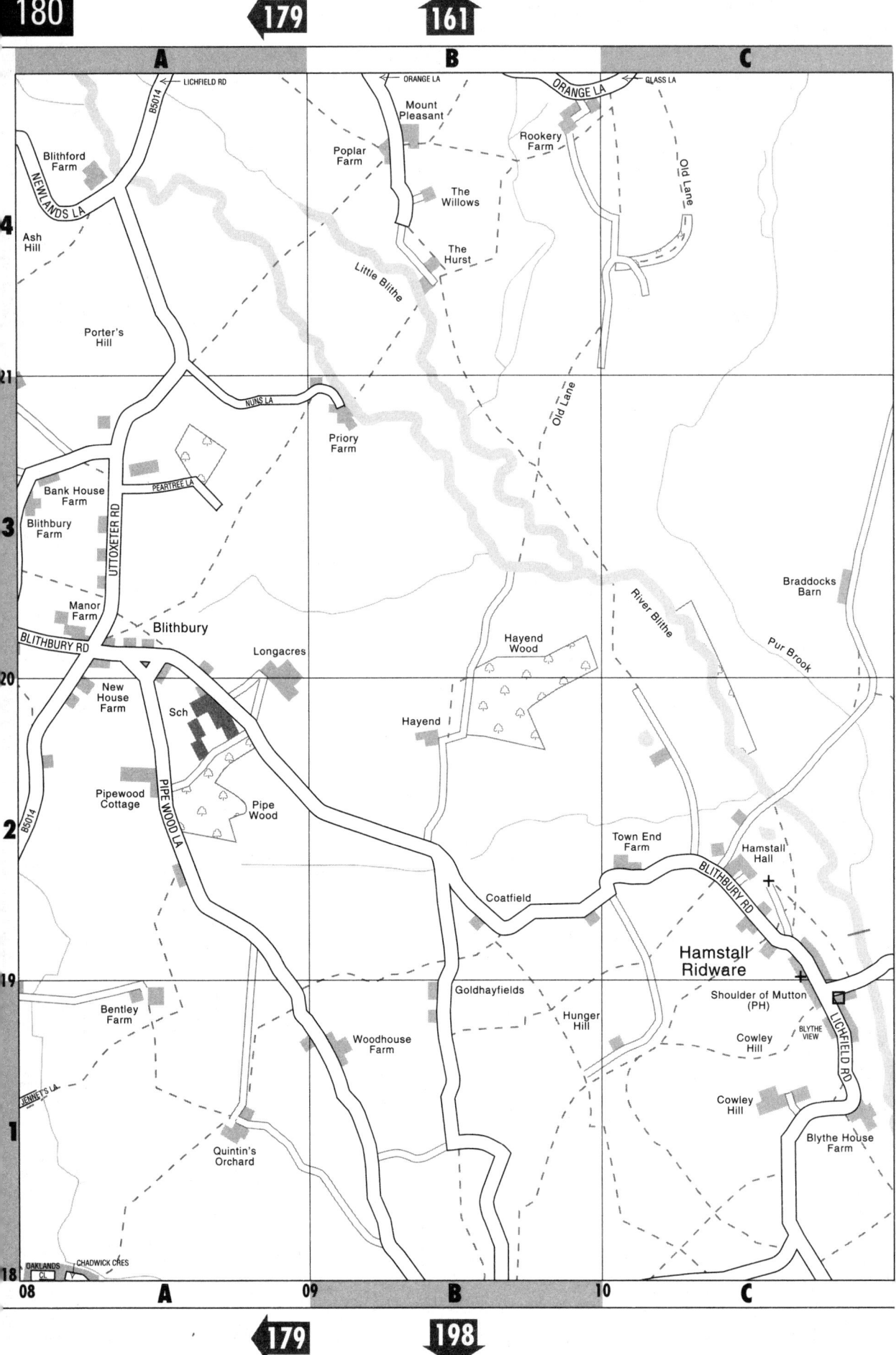

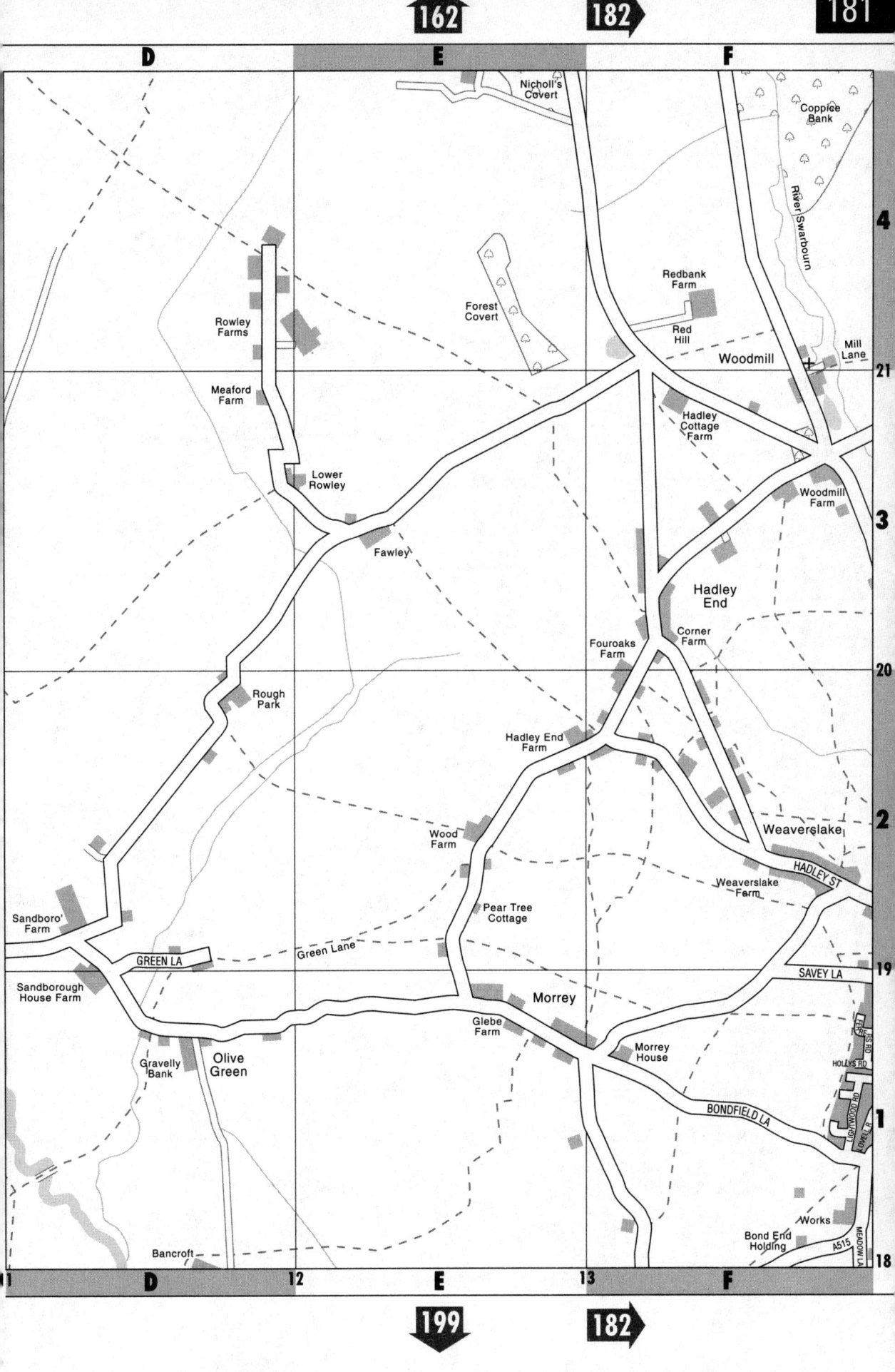

D
E
F

4

Nicholl's
Covert

Coppice
Bank

Forest
Covert

Redbank
Farm

Red
Hill

Mill
Lane

Woodmill

21

Rowley
Farms

Meaford
Farm

Hadley
Cottage
Farm

Woodmill
Farm

Lower
Rowley

Fawley

Hadley
End

3

Corner
Farm

Fouroaks
Farm

Rough
Park

20

Hadley End
Farm

Weaverslake

2

HADLEY ST

Wood
Farm

Weaverslake
Farm

Sandboro'
Farm

Pear Tree
Cottage

Green Lane

GREEN LA

SAVEY LA

19

Sandborough
House Farm

Morrey

Gravelly
Bank

Olive
Green

Glebe
Farm

Morrey
House

HOLLYS RD

BONDFIELD LA

1

Works

Bond End
Holding

A515

MEADOW LA

Bancroft

D
12
E
13
F
18

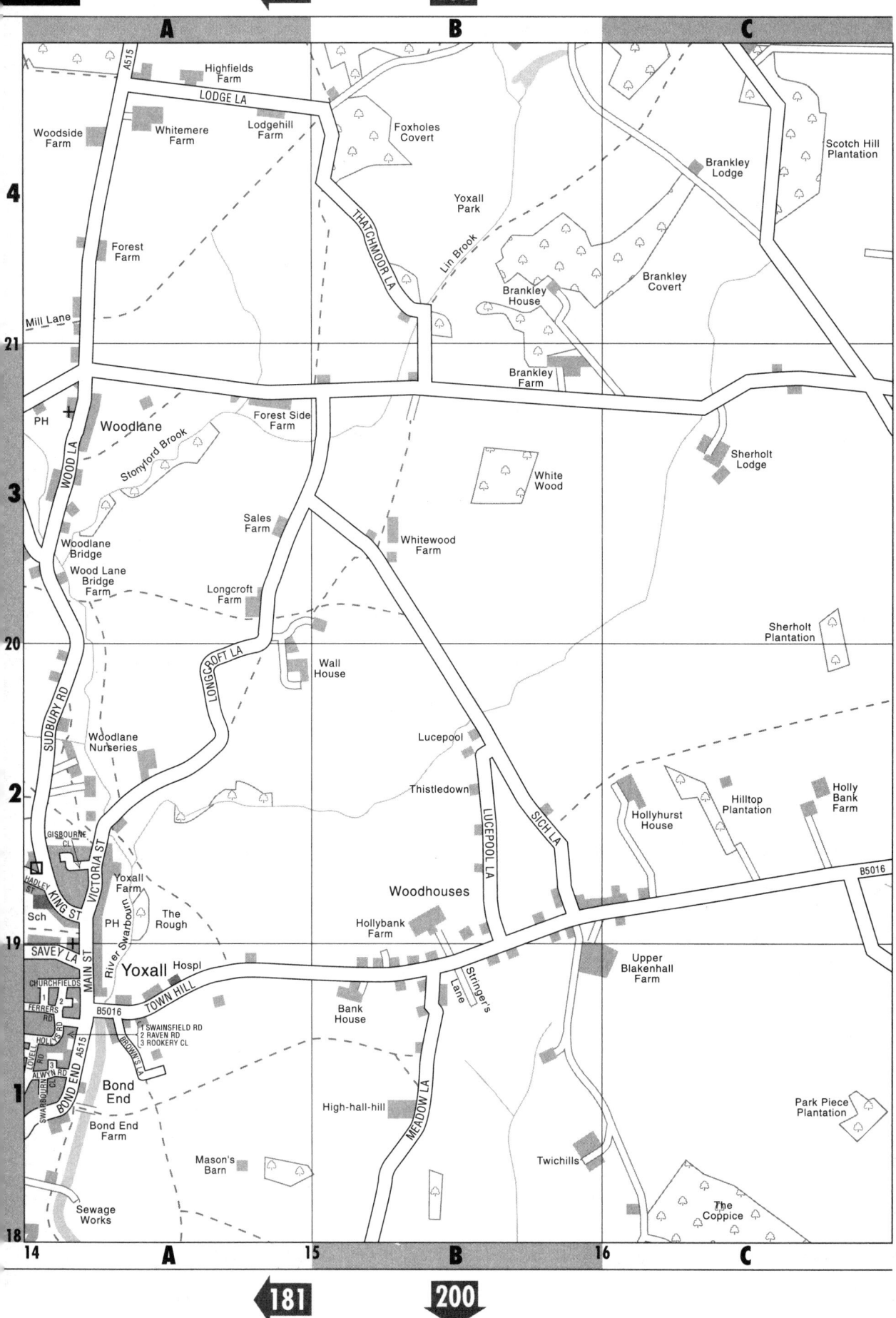

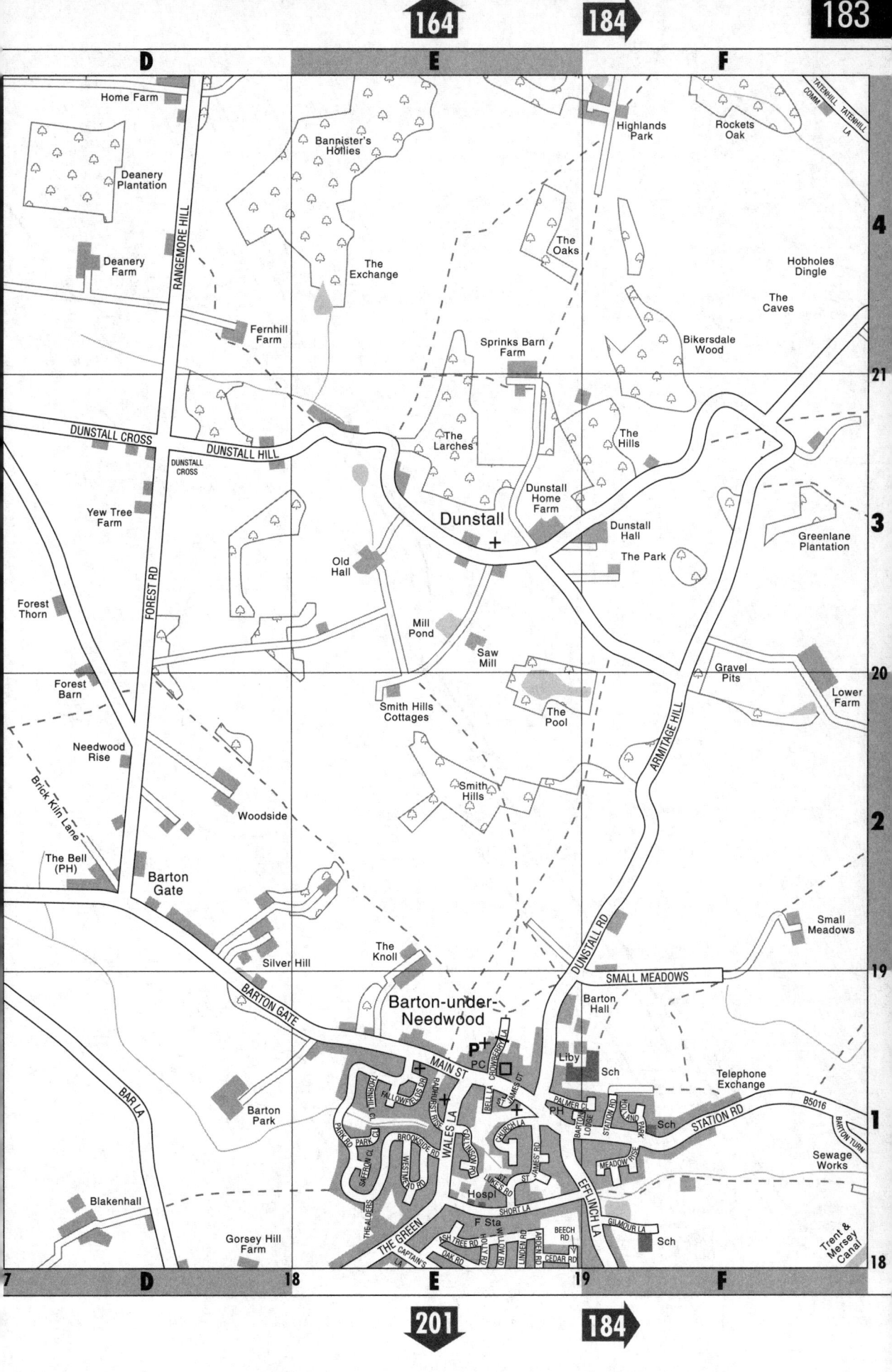

D
E
F

Home Farm

Deanery Plantation

RANGEMORE HILL

Deanery Farm

Bannister's Hollies

The Exchange

Fernhill Farm

The Oaks

Highlands Park

Rockets Oak

TATENHILL COMM
TATENHILL LA

4

Hobholes Dingle

The Caves

Sprinks Barn Farm

Bikersdale Wood

21

DUNSTALL CROSS

DUNSTALL HILL

DUNSTALL CROSS

The Larches

Dunstall Home Farm

The Hills

Yew Tree Farm

Dunstall

Dunstall Hall

FOREST RD

Old Hall

The Park

Greenlane Plantation

3

Forest Thorn

Mill Pond

Saw Mill

Gravel Pits

Lower Farm

Forest Barn

Smith Hills Cottages

The Pool

ARMITAGE HILL

20

Brick Kiln Lane

Needwood Rise

Smith Hills

Woodside

2

The Bell (PH)

Barton Gate

The Knoll

DUNSTALL RD

Small Meadows

Silver Hill

SMALL MEADOWS

19

BARTON GATE

Barton-under-Needwood

Barton Hall

BAR LA

P
PC

Liby

Sch

Telephone Exchange

MAIN ST

Barton Park

THIRNBURY
FALLOWS CL
PROMBRISE
WALES LA
CROWBERRY LA
BELL
JAMES CT
CHURCH LA
PALMER CL
BARTON
STATION RD
HOLLAND PARK
Sch
STATION RD

B5016

BARTON TURN

1

PARK RD
SAFFRON CL
BROOKSIDE RD
WESTWAY
RD
HOLST RD
CHURCHILLA
ST JAMES RD
PH
MEADOW RISE

Sewage Works

Blakenhall

THE ALDERS
Hospl
LINK'S RD
SHORT LA

Gorsey Hill Farm

THE GREEN
CAPTAIN'S
F Sta
ASH TREE RD
OAK RD
OR MOTTRAM
LINDEN RD
ARDEN RD
CEDAR RD
BEECH RD
GILMOUR LA
EFFLINCH LA

Sch

Trent & Mersey Canal

18

7
D
18
E
19
F
18

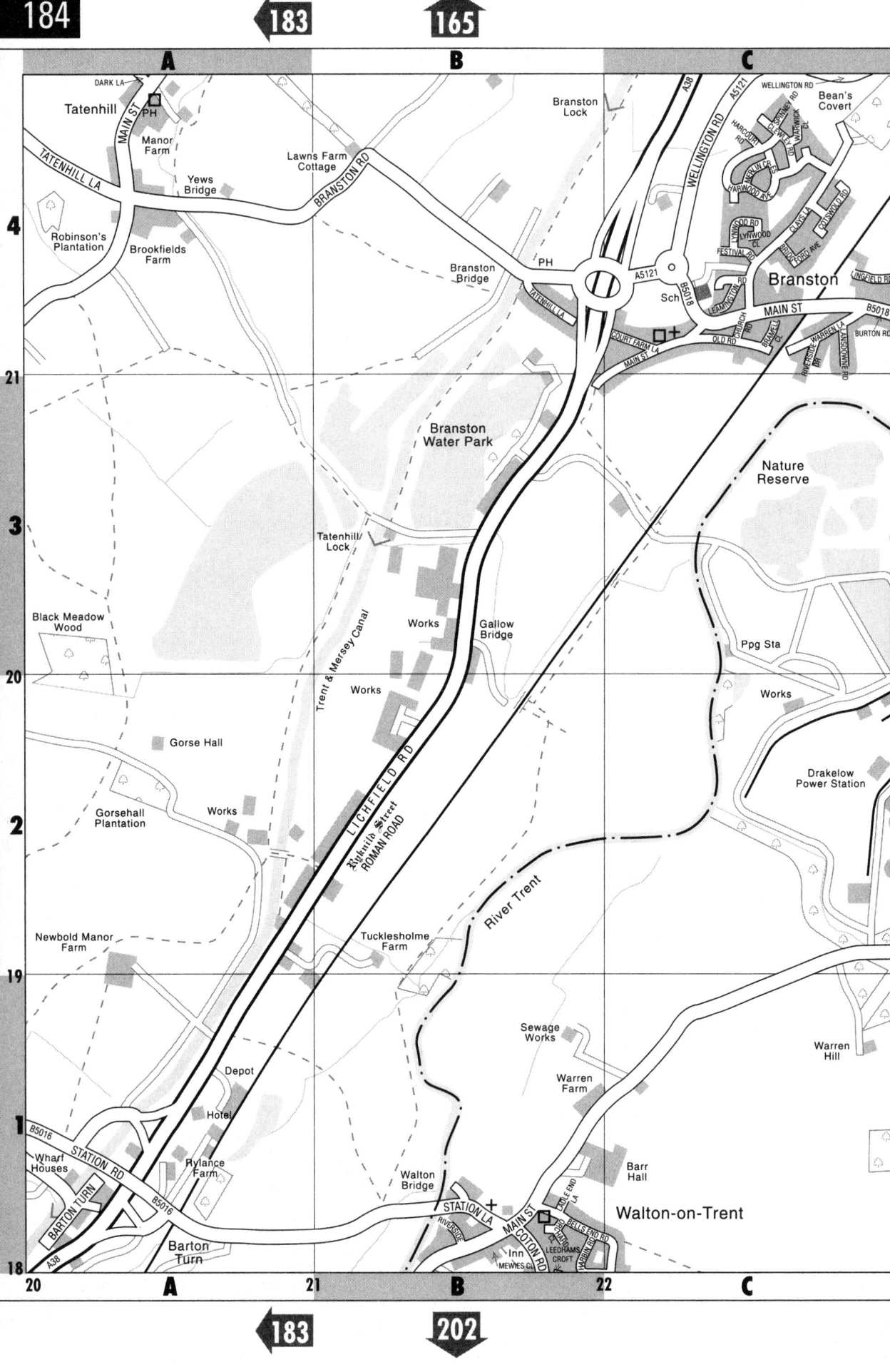

183
165

A
B
C

DARK LA
Tatenhill
PH
Manor
Farm
Yews
Bridge
TATENHILL LA
MAIN ST
Robinson's
Plantation
Brookfields
Farm

Lawns Farm
Cottage
BRANSTON RD

Branston
Bridge
Branston
Lock

PH
TATENHILL LA

A38
A5121
WELLINGTON RD
Bean's
Covert
WELLINGTON RD
HARCOURT RD
WARWICK
LYNWOOD CL
HARWOOD PK
MERLIN CR
CLAYS LA
RYKNELD RD
LORD AVE
FESTIVAL ST
LEAMINGTON
CHURCH RD
Branston
INGFIELD RD

A5121
Sch
MAIN ST
B5018
BURTON RD
COURT FARM LA
OLD RD
RIVERSIDE DR
WARREN LA
RANSOME RD
B5018
MAIN ST
BRANSELL CL

4

21

Branston
Water Park

Nature
Reserve

3

Tatenhill
Lock

Works
Gallow
Bridge

Ppg Sta

Black Meadow
Wood

Trent & Mersey Canal

20

Works

Works

Gorse Hall

LICHFIELD RD

Works
Ryknild Street
ROMAN ROAD

Drakelow
Power Station

Gorsehall
Plantation
Works

2

River Trent

Newbold Manor
Farm

Tucklesholme
Farm

Sewage
Works

Warren
Hill

19

Depot

Hotel

Warren
Farm

1

B5016
STATION RD
Wharf
Houses
BARTON TURN
B5016
Rylance
Farm

Walton
Bridge

STATION LA
RIVERSIDE
MAIN ST
COTON RD
Barr
Hall
BELLS END RD
CASTLE END
HARIN RD
CROFT
LEEDHAMS
MEWSE CL

Walton-on-Trent

18

Barton
Turn
A38

Inn

20
A
21
B
22
C

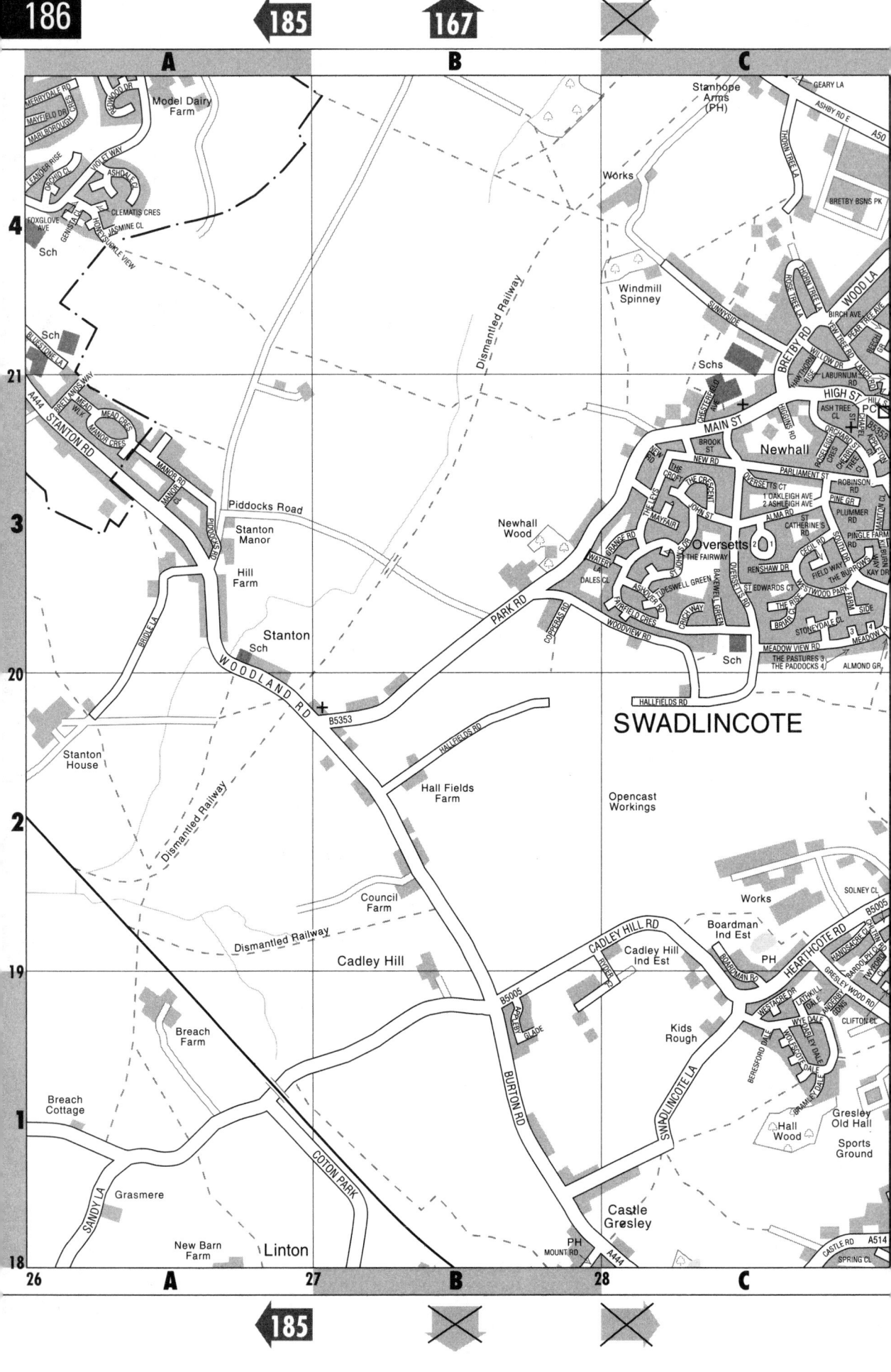

A   B   C

MERRYDALE RD
MAYFIELD
MARLBOROUGH
RICHWOOD DR

Model Dairy
Farm

LEANDER RISE
ORCHID CL
VIOLET WAY
ASHOAK CL
GENISTA CL
HONEYSUCKLE VIEW
CLEMATIS CRES
JASMINE CL
FOXGLOVE AVE
4
Sch

Stanhope
Arms
(PH)

GEARY LA
ASHBY RD E
A50

Works

BRETBY BSNS PK

Windmill
Spinney

LINDEN TREE LA
ROSE TREE LA
YEW TREE LA
BIRCH AVE
PEAR TREE AVE
WOOD LA
BRETBY RD
SUNNYSIDE

BLUESTONE LA
Sch
21
A444
STANTON RD
FIELDS WAY
MEAD WLK
MANOR CRES
MEAD CRES
MANOR RD
MANOR

Piddocks Road

Stanton
Manor
3
Hill
Farm

PIDDOCKS RD
BRIDLE LA

Stanton
Sch

Schs
CHESTERFIELD
HIGH ST
PO
A353
ASH TREE CL
MAIN ST
BROOK ST
NEW ST
NEW RD
Newhall
THE CROFT
THE CRESCENT
JOHN ST
OVERSETTS CT
PARLIAMENT ST
1 OAKLEIGH AVE
2 ASHLEIGH AVE
ROBINSON RD
PINE GR
PLUMMER RD
PINGLE FARM
ALMA RD
ST CATHERINE'S RD
CECIL RD
SOUTH DR
FIELD WAY
WESTWOOD PARK
THE BURROWS
KAY DR

Newhall
Wood
WATERY LA
DALES CL
GRANGE RD
THE LEYS
MAYFAIR
Oversetts
THE FAIRWAY
RENSHAW DR
TIDESWELL GREEN
BAKEWELL GREEN
THE RISE
ASHOVER RD
PARFIELD CRES
CROXALL WAY
ST EDWARDS CL
BRIARS
STONEYDALE CL
SIDE
MEADOW

WOODVIEW RD
COPPERAS RD
PARK RD

20
WOODLAND RD
B5353
HALLFIELDS RD
MEADOW VIEW RD
THE PASTURES 3
THE PADDOCKS 4
ALMOND GR
Sch

SWADLINCOTE

Stanton
House

HALLFIELDS RD
Hall Fields
Farm

Opencast
Workings

Dismantled Railway

2

Council
Farm

Dismantled Railway

Cadley Hill

CADLEY HILL RD
Cadley Hill
Ind Est
BOARDMAN RD

Works
SOLNEY CL
B5005
Boardman
Ind Est
PH
HEARTHCOTE RD
HANDSACRE
GRESLEY WOOD RD
BARROW
CLIFTON CL

19
B5005
RIVER
GLADE
WESTACRE DR
LATHKILL DALE
DOVE DALE
WOLFSCOTE DALE
BERESFORD DALE
WYE DALE
Kids
Rough
BRAMLEY DALE
SWADLINCOTE LA

Breach
Farm

BURTON RD

Breach
Cottage
1

Hall
Wood
Gresley
Old Hall
Sports
Ground

SANDY LA
Grasmere

COTON PARK

Castle
Gresley
PH
MOUNT RD
A444

CASTLE RD
A514
SPRING CL

New Barn
Farm
Linton
18
26   A   27   B   28   C

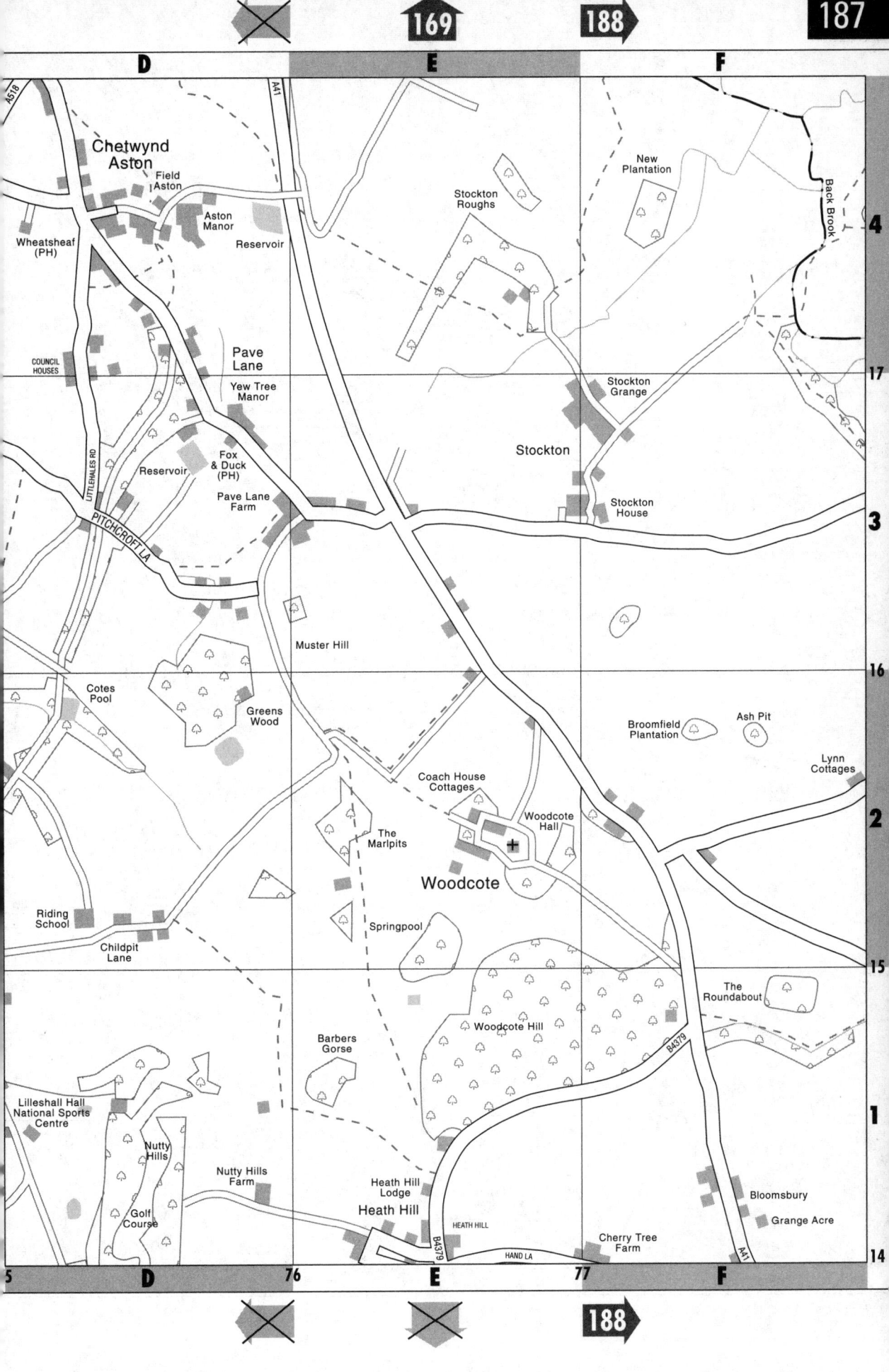

169

188

D
E
F

Chetwynd
Aston

Field
Aston

Aston
Manor

Wheatsheaf
(PH)

Reservoir

A518

A41

4

COUNCIL
HOUSES

Pave
Lane

Yew Tree
Manor

Stockton
Roughs

New
Plantation

Back Brook

Stockton
Grange

Stockton

17

LITTLEHALES RD

Fox
& Duck
(PH)

Reservoir

Pave Lane
Farm

Stockton
House

PITCHCROFT LA

3

Muster Hill

Cotes
Pool

Greens
Wood

16

Broomfield
Plantation

Ash Pit

Lynn
Cottages

Coach House
Cottages

Woodcote Hall

The
Marlpits

Woodcote

2

Riding
School

Childpit
Lane

Springpool

15

The
Roundabout

Barbers
Gorse

Woodcote Hill

B4379

Lilleshall Hall
National Sports
Centre

Nutty
Hills

1

Nutty Hills
Farm

Heath Hill
Lodge

Heath Hill

HEATH HILL

Cherry Tree
Farm

Bloomsbury

Grange Acre

A41

Golf
Course

B4379

HAND LA

14

5
D
76
E
77
F

188

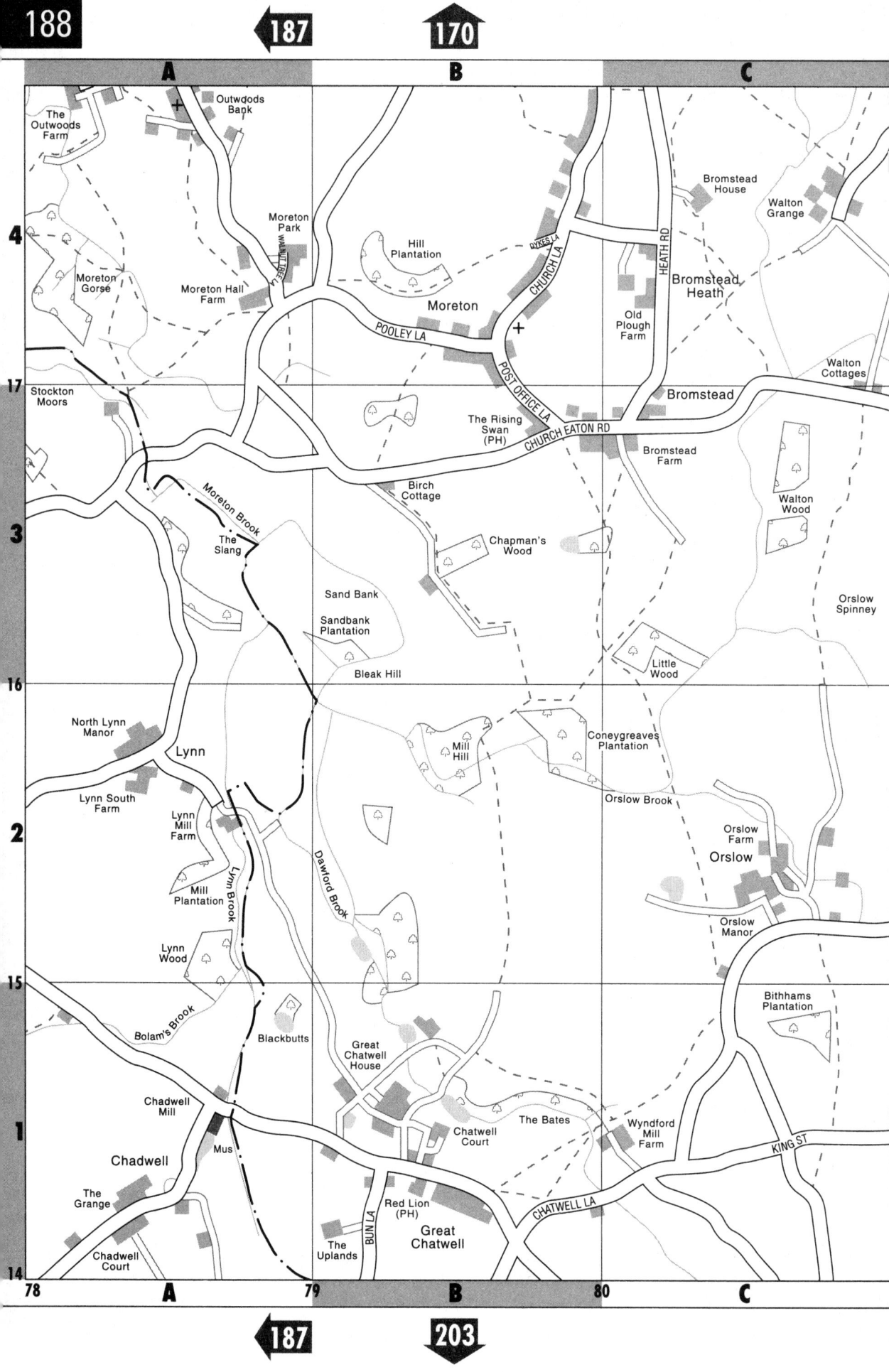

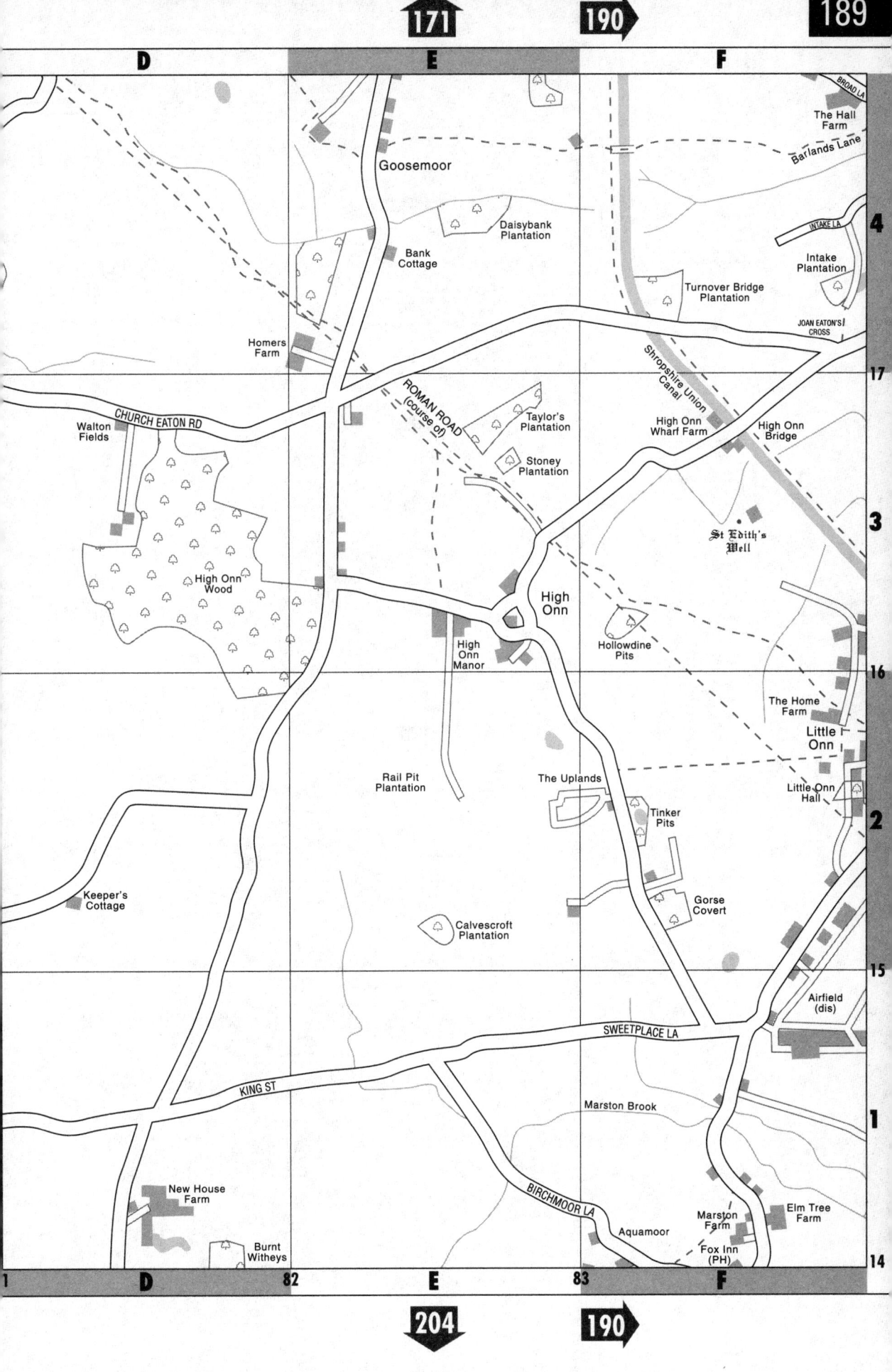

D
E
F

Goosemoor

Daisybank
Plantation

Bank
Cottage

BROAD LA

The Hall
Farm

Barlands Lane

INTAKE LA

Intake
Plantation

Turnover Bridge
Plantation

4

Homers
Farm

JOAN EATON'S
CROSS

Shropshire Union
Canal

17

Walton
Fields

CHURCH EATON RD

ROMAN ROAD
(course of)

Taylor's
Plantation

Stoney
Plantation

High Onn
Wharf Farm

High Onn
Bridge

St Edith's
Well

3

High Onn
Wood

High
Onn

Hollowdine
Pits

16

High
Onn
Manor

The Home
Farm

Little
Onn

Rail Pit
Plantation

The Uplands

Tinker
Pits

Little Onn
Hall

2

Keeper's
Cottage

Calvescroft
Plantation

Gorse
Covert

15

Airfield
(dis)

SWEETPLACE LA

King St

Marston Brook

1

New House
Farm

BIRCHMOOR LA

Aquamoor

Marston
Farm

Elm Tree
Farm

Burnt
Witheys

Fox Inn
(PH)

14

1
D
82
E
83
F

189
172
189
205

A   B   C

ALSTONE LA

Brookhouse Farm
Wood Eaton
BROAD LA
Barlands Lane
INTAKE LA

Church Eaton

Sch
Barton Covert

4

HIGH ST
The Oaklands
ALLEY'S LA
ASHLEY
PERKINS CL
WOOD EATON RD
TO WMO
PH

Middle Covert

Greenfields Farm

Church Eaton Common

LITTLE ONN RD

Church Eaton Green

17

Green Farm

Shredicote Wood

Park Hall Farm

Church Eaton Brook

3

Stafford Lane

Woollaston Farm

Red House Farm

Wollaston Cottages

16

Rusty Pits

Little Onn

Woollaston

Shropshire Union Canal

2

Bagnallditch

Upper Woollaston Covert

Airfield (disused)

ROMAN ROAD (course of)

SLAB LA
Ryehill Bridge

15

Little Onn Gorse

Longnor Gorse Farm

Gorse Lane

Mitton Lodge Farm

Port Coppice

Barn Cottage

1

The Rookery

Shushions Manor

Wheaton Aston Brook

Stonyford Bridge

Longnor Brook

Longnor

Longnor Hall

14

84   A   85   B   86   C

D

E

F

Bradley

BARTON LA

Old Lane

Spring Farm

CHAPEL LA

ALMSHOUSE LA

ELM DR

HOLLY LA

WELLS LA

Whitehouse Farm

LEVEDALE RD

OAK LA

4

Pigstockheys Covert

SHREDICOTE LA

Hayes Farm

MITTON RD

Willow Farm

Levedale

17

Bradley Hall

Levedale Farm

Shredicote Hall Farm

Field House Farm

3

Priory Farm

Down House Farm

Shredicote Farm

New House Farm

16

Spion Kop

2

Upper Mitton Farm

Church Eaton Brook

Staffordshire Way

Mitton

Lower Mitton Farm

15

Mitton Manor

Whiston Brook

Whiston Hall

1

Bickford

The Swan (PH)

Ivy House Farm

Pear Tree Farm

Whiston

Longnor Farm

14

7

D

88

E

89

F

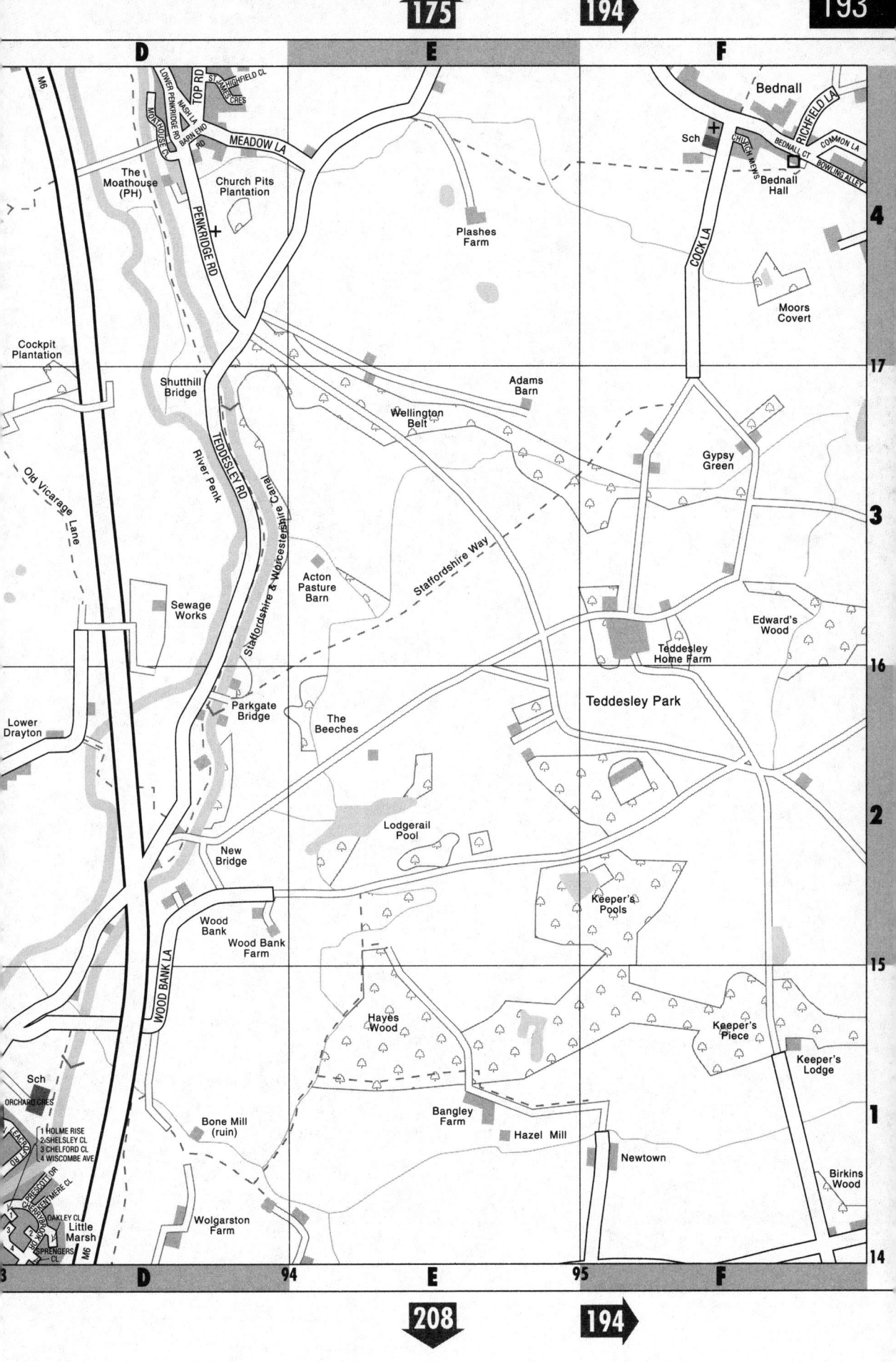

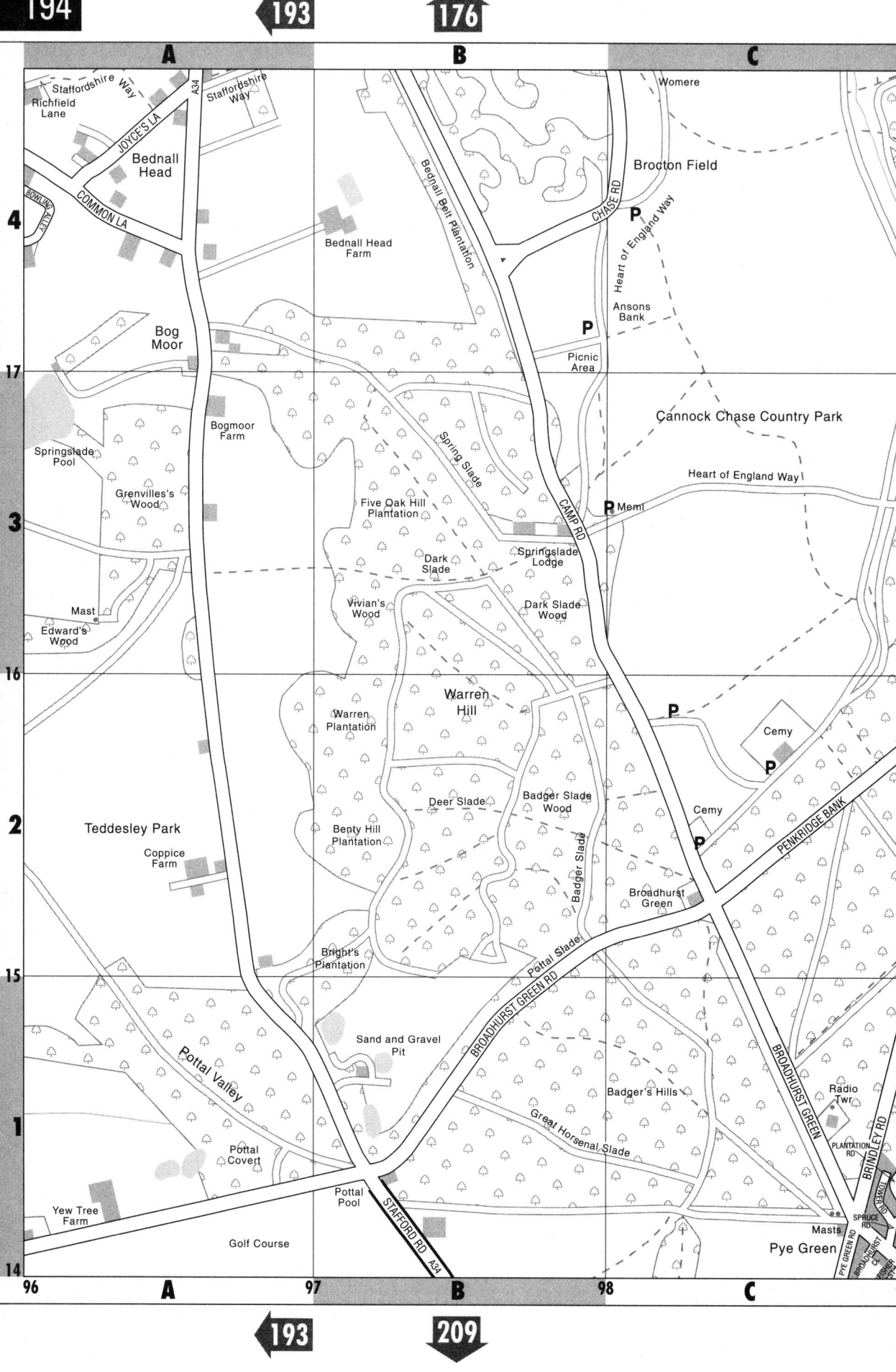

Staffordshire Way

Richfield
Lane

Staffordshire Way

JOYCE'S LA

A34

Bednall
Head

BOWLING ALLEY

COMMON LA

Womere

Brocton Field

CHASE RD

P

Heart of England Way

Bednall Head
Farm

Bednall Belt Plantation

Ansons
Bank

4

P

Bog
Moor

Picnic
Area

Cannock Chase Country Park

17

Bogmoor
Farm

Spring Slade

Springslade
Pool

Heart of England Way

Grenvilles's
Wood

Five Oak Hill
Plantation

CAMP RD

P Meml

Springslade
Lodge

3

Dark
Slade

Mast

Vivian's
Wood

Dark Slade
Wood

Edward's
Wood

16

Warren
Hill

Warren
Plantation

P

Cemy

P

Teddesley Park

Deer Slade

Badger Slade
Wood

Cemy

Coppice
Farm

Benty Hill
Plantation

PENKRIDGE BANK

2

Badger Slade

P

Broadhurst
Green

Bright's
Plantation

Pottal Slade

BROADHURST GREEN RD

BROADHURST GREEN

15

Pottal Valley

Sand and Gravel
Pit

Badger's Hills

Radio
Twr

BRINDLEY RD

Great Horsenal Slade

PLANTATION
RD

1

Pottal
Covert

Pottal
Pool

STAFFORD RD

SPRUCE
RD

Yew Tree
Farm

A34

Masts

Pye Green

PYE GREEN RD

BROADHURST
C

Golf Course

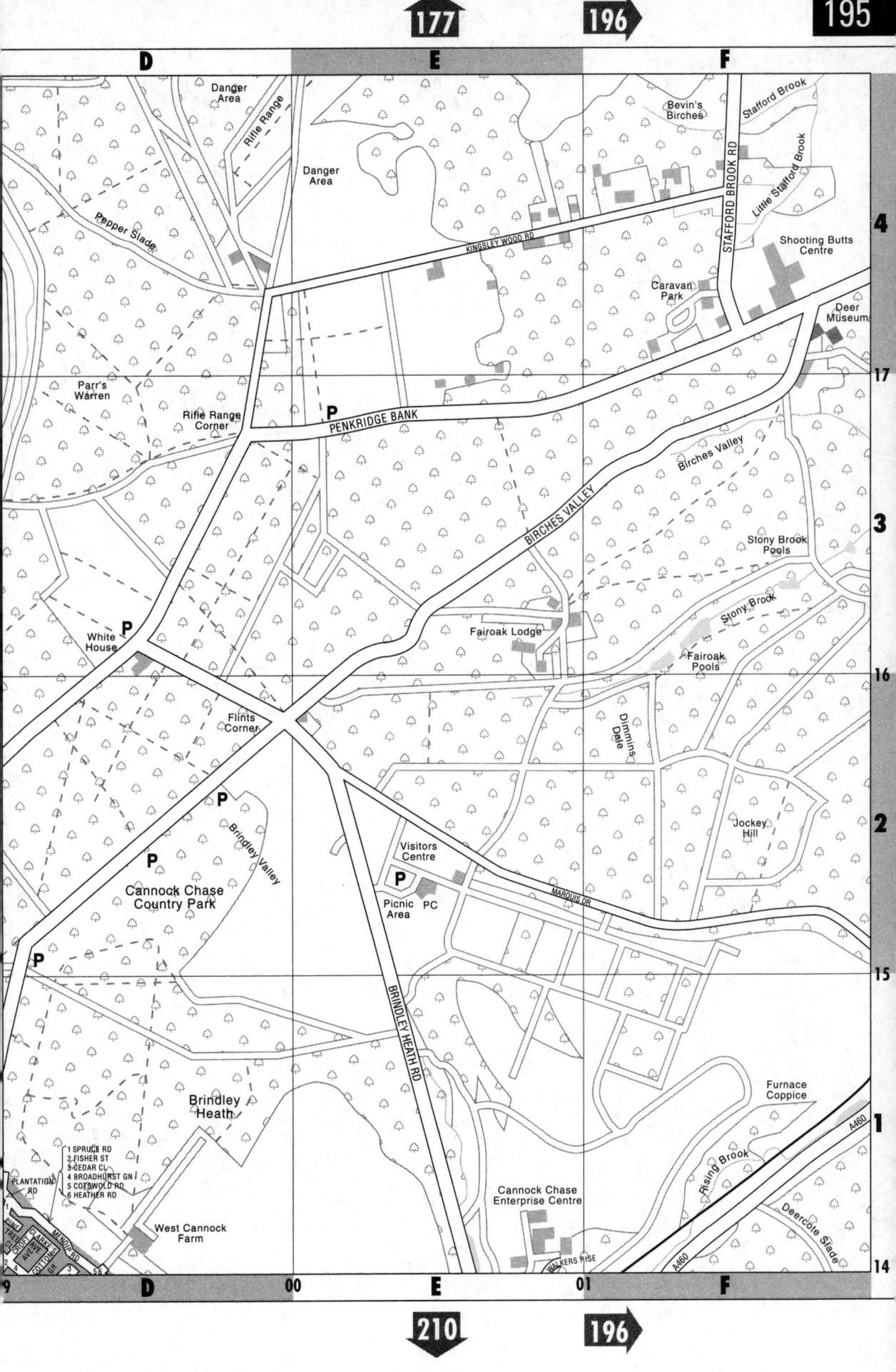

D   E   F

4

Danger Area
Rifle Range
Danger Area
Bevin's Birches
Stafford Brook
STAFFORD BROOK RD
Little Stafford Brook
Shooting Butts Centre
Pepper Slade
KINGSLEY WOOD RD
Caravan Park
Deer Museum

17

Parr's Warren
Rifle Range Corner
P
PENKRIDGE BANK
Birches Valley
BIRCHES VALLEY

3

Stony Brook Pools
Stony Brook
P
White House
Fairoak Lodge
Fairoak Pools

16

Flints Corner
Dimmins Dale

2

P
Brindley Valley
P
Visitors Centre
Jockey Hill
P
Cannock Chase Country Park
P
Picnic Area
PC
MARQUIS DR

P

15

BRINDLEY HEATH RD
Furnace Coppice
A460

1

Brindley Heath
Rising Brook
1 SPRUCE RD
2 FISHER ST
3 CEDAR CL
4 BROADHURST GN
5 COTSWOLD RD
6 HEATHER RD
PLANTATION RD
Cannock Chase Enterprise Centre
Deercote Slade
West Cannock Farm
WALKERS RISE
A460

14

9   D   00   E   01   F

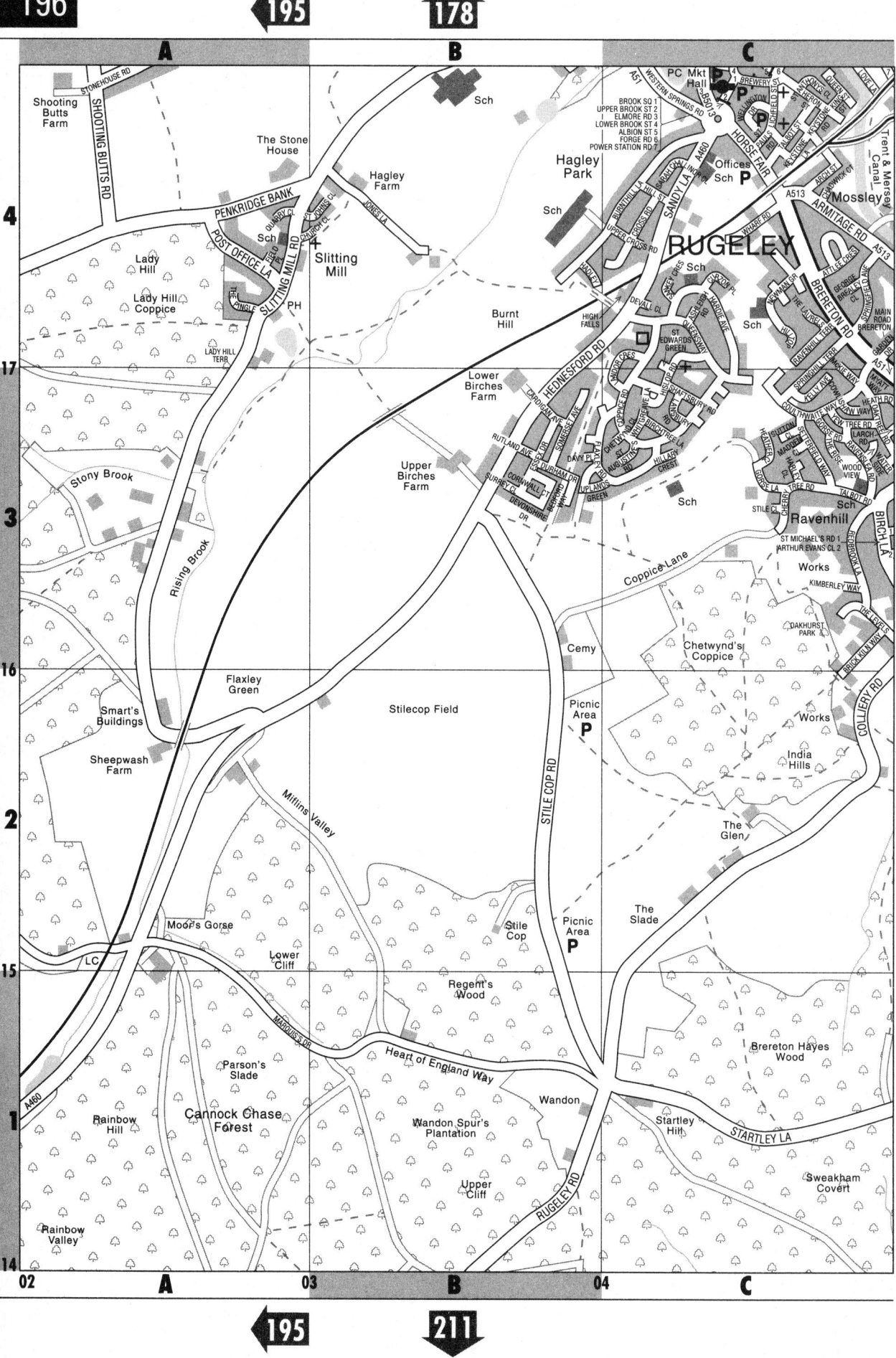

179
198

D

E

F

Power Stations

River Trent

Wade Lane House

UTTOXETER RD

WADE LA

B5014

Ridware Hall

Lawnmeadow Covert

4

17

Manor Farm

TRENT VIEW CT

GARDEN DR

AS1

Colliery (disused)

Glover's Hill

REGENCY CT

ARMITAGE RD

GARRICK RISE

ARMITAGE GDNS

Hawkesyard Lane

The Plum Pudding (PH)

Ash Tree Inn (PH)

3

BEECHES RD

REDBROOK

OAK RD

FOLEY CT

SYCAMORE CRES

ASHTREE

The MEADOWS

BANK RD

COALWAY RD

LEES

DANE LEES

HILL ST

The SHRUBBERY

RUGELEY RD

CHURCH LA

Upper Lodge Farm

CHAPEL RD

ST MICHAEL'S

ARTHUR EVANS CL

ST MICHAEL'S RD

Sch

WALNUT DR

PRIORY

WALKER CT

LEA HALL LA

ABBOTS WLK

HOLLY BANK VIEW

HOBBS VIEW

Trent and Mersey Canal

Hawkesyard Priory (Dominican)

Caravan Park

Armitage

A513

MAIN RD BRERETON

Liby

Sch

CEDAR CRES

SWAN CL

CHURCH VIEW

BRERETON

ARMITAGE LA

Sch

Hobs Hill

Park Farm

LODGE RD

DAWE CT

16

BIRCH LA

Brereton

P

COALPIT LA

WATFIELD CT

BRERETON HILL

RECTORY LA

RUNNING HILLS

WESTFIELDS RD

The Springs Farm

Birchen Fields

BATESWAY

Breretonhill

Gorsy Bank

West Fields

2

The Springs

MAIN RD

BARDY LA

Foley Farm

Brereton Cross

New House Farm

AS1

Bradley Lakes

Hawcroft Grange

HOOD LA

15

Dark Lane

Windmill Cottage

BRERETONHILL LA

Dump's Covert

Russell's Bank

Upper Longdon

STOCKINGS LA

HIGH ST

SWAN CT

BROOK END

THE CSE

Sch

1

STARTLEY LA

SHAWER'S LA

UPPER WAY

THE GRANGE

LOWER WAY

Lodge Farm

CATKEADOWL LA

BARDY LA

GIDDYWELL LA

Longdon

AS1

Hare Hills

Shropshire Covert

HORSEY LA

Red Hill

Rookery Farm

BOROUGH LA

Moat Farm

Beaudesert Old Park

14

05

D

06

E

07

F

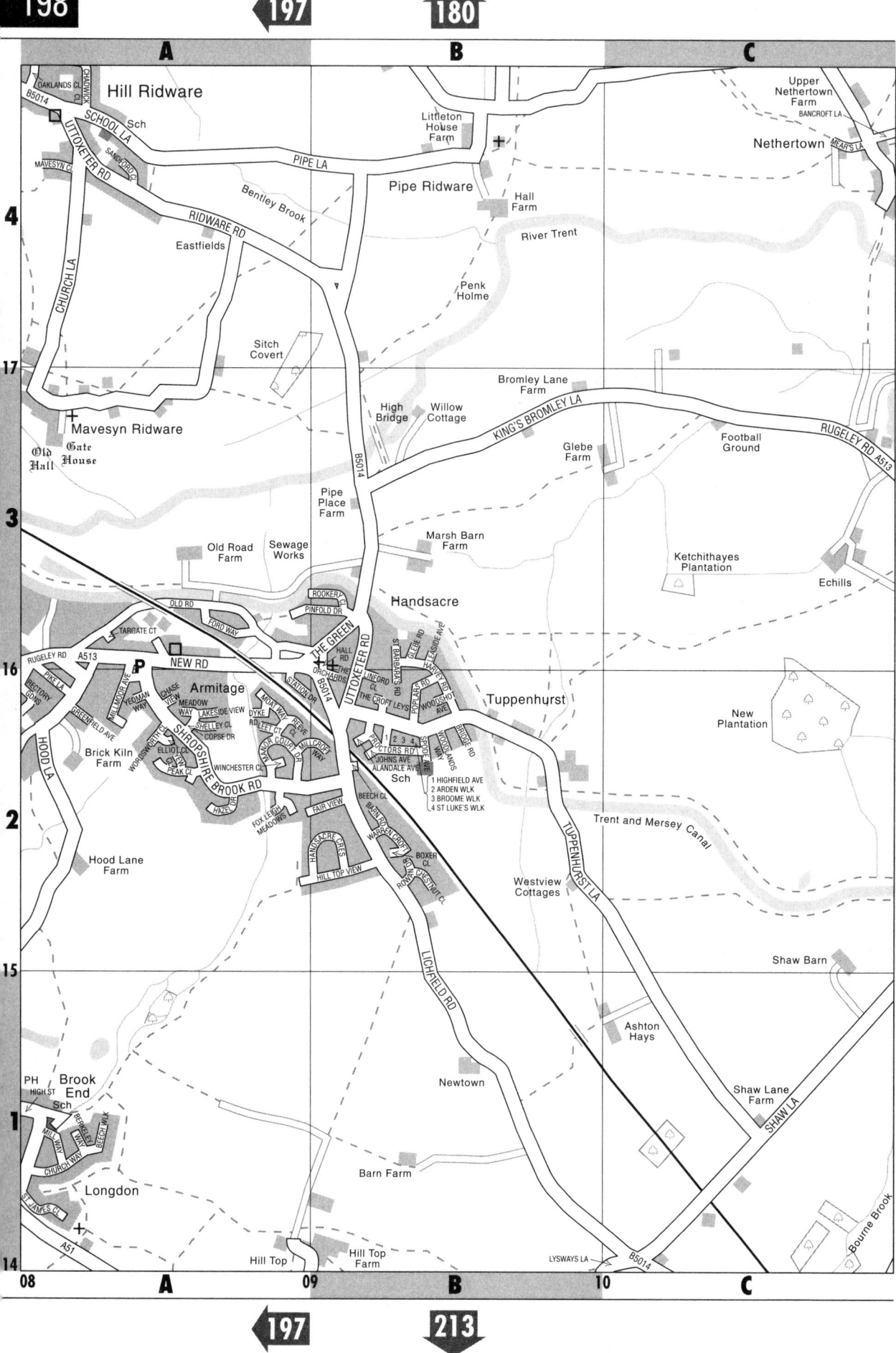

A   B   C

Oaklands Cl
B5014
CHADWICK CL

Hill Ridware

School La
Sch

Uttoxeter Rd
Mavesyn Cl
Sandford

Pipe La

Littleton House Farm

Pipe Ridware

Upper Nethertown Farm
Bancroft La

Nethertown

Mears La

4

Bentley Brook

Ridware Rd

Eastfields

Hall Farm

River Trent

Penk Holme

Church La

Sitch Covert

17

Bromley Lane Farm

Mavesyn Ridware
Gate House

High Bridge

Willow Cottage

King's Bromley La

Glebe Farm

Football Ground

Rugeley Rd A513

Old Hall

B5014

Pipe Place Farm

3

Marsh Barn Farm

Ketchithayes Plantation

Echills

Old Road Farm

Sewage Works

Rookery Cl
Pinfold Dr

Handsacre

Old Rd

Ford Way

The Green
The Orchards
Hall Rd

St Barbara's Rd
Glebe Rd
Lakeside Ave

16

Rugeley Rd   A513
Pike La
Rectory Cl

P

New Rd

Station Dr

Armitage

Hall Rd
Linford Cl

Uttoxeter Rd

The Croft Leys

Poplar Rd
Hasler Rd
Woodshot Ave

Tuppenhurst

New Plantation

Greenfield Ave
Millmoor Ave
Chase View
Yeoman Way
Meadow Way
Lakeside View
Shelley Cl
Copse Dr

Moat Way
Dyke Rd
Lee Ct Cl
Manor Court Dr
Hillcroft Way
Winchester Cl

Doctors Rd
1 2 3 4
Spode Ave
Johns Ave
Alandale Ave
Sch

Woodlands Way
Broome Rd

1 HIGHFIELD AVE
2 ARDEN WLK
3 BROOME WLK
4 ST LUKE'S WLK

Brick Kiln Farm

Woodsworth Cl
Elliot Cl
Peak Cl
Hazel Rise

Shropshire Brook Rd

Fox Le Gate
Meadows

Fair View

Beech Cl

Hood La

2

Hood Lane Farm

Handsacre Cres

Hill Top View

Warren Croft
Ronal Cl

Boxer Cl

Chestnut Cl

Westview Cottages

Trent and Mersey Canal

Tuppenhurst La

Shaw Barn

15

Lichfield Rd

Ashton Hays

Shaw Lane Farm

Shaw La

1

PH
High St
Brook End
Sch

Newtown

Longdon
Mill Way
Brereley Way
Beech Wlk
Church Way
St James Cl

Barn Farm

Bourne Brook

14

08

A

Hill Top

09

Hill Top Farm

B

Lysways La

10

B5014

C

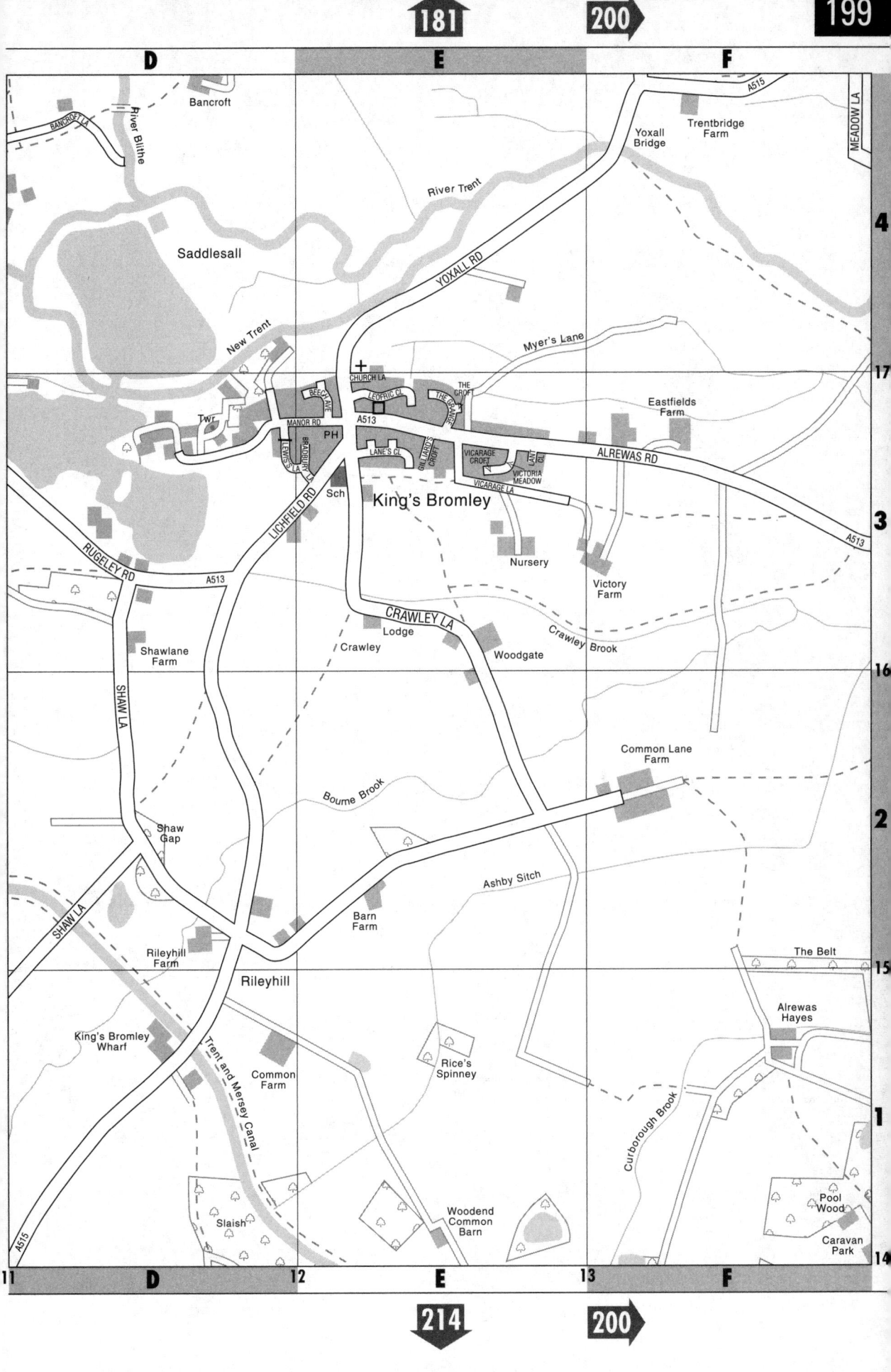

199
182

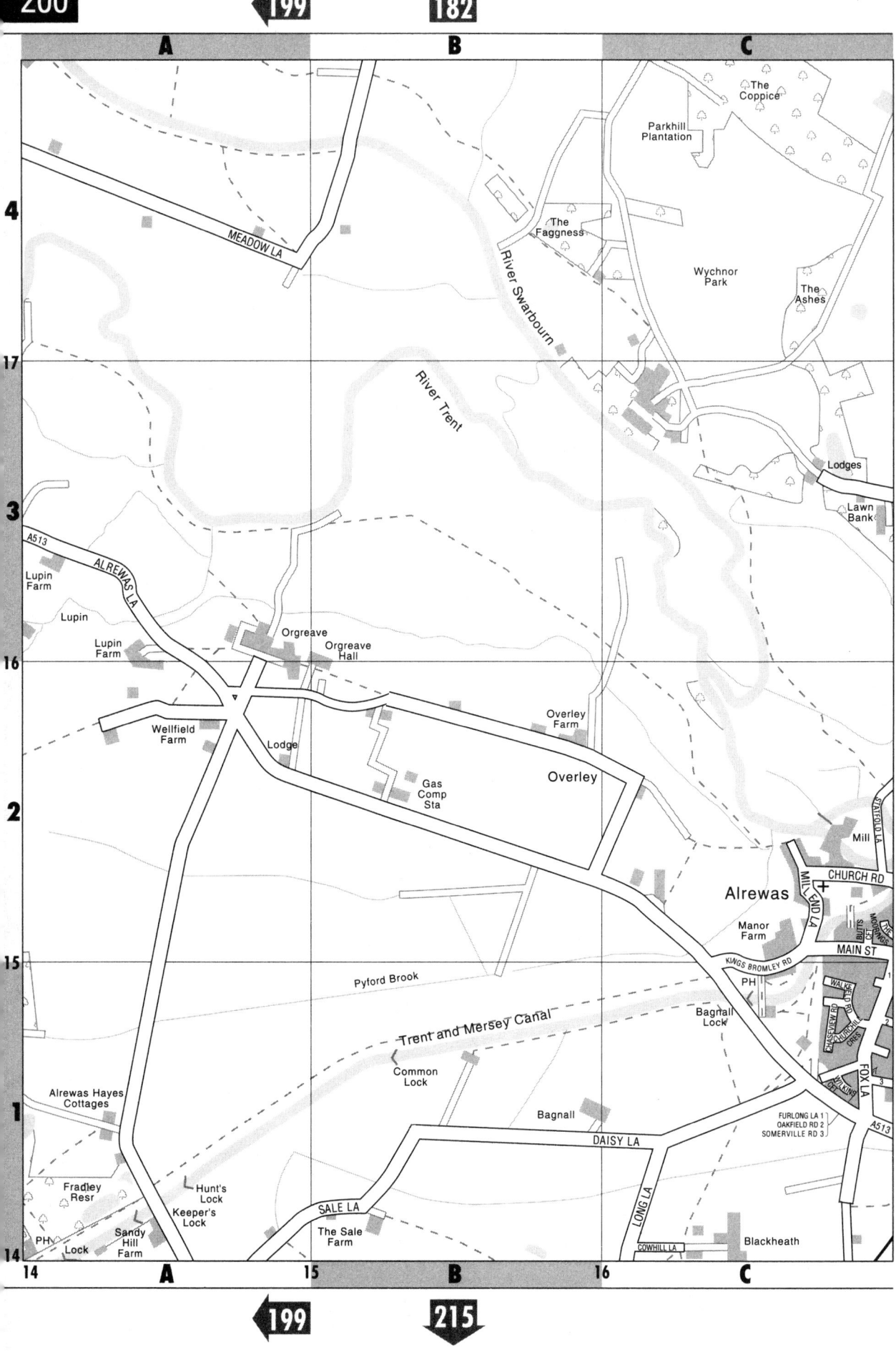

A

B

C

4

The Coppice

Parkhill Plantation

The Faggness

Wychnor Park

The Ashes

River Swarbourn

17

River Trent

Lodges

3

Lawn Bank

A513

ALREWAS LA

Lupin Farm

Lupin

Lupin Farm

Orgreave

Orgreave Hall

16

Overley Farm

Wellfield Farm

Lodge

Gas Comp Sta

Overley

2

Mill

STAFFOLD LA

CHURCH RD

Alrewas

Manor Farm

MILL END LA

BUTTS CT

THE MOORINGS

MAIN ST

15

Pyford Brook

KINGS BROMLEY RD

PH

Bagnall Lock

CHASEVIEW RD

MILLHILL CRES

WALKER RD

Trent and Mersey Canal

Common Lock

Bagnall

FOX LA

WELKINS RD

Alrewas Hayes Cottages

DAISY LA

FURLONG LA 1
OAKFIELD RD 2
SOMERVILLE RD 3

A513

1

Fradley Resr

Hunt's Lock

Keeper's Lock

LONG LA

Sandy Hill Farm

SALE LA

COWHILL LA

Blackheath

PH

Lock

The Sale Farm

14

14

A

15

B

16

C

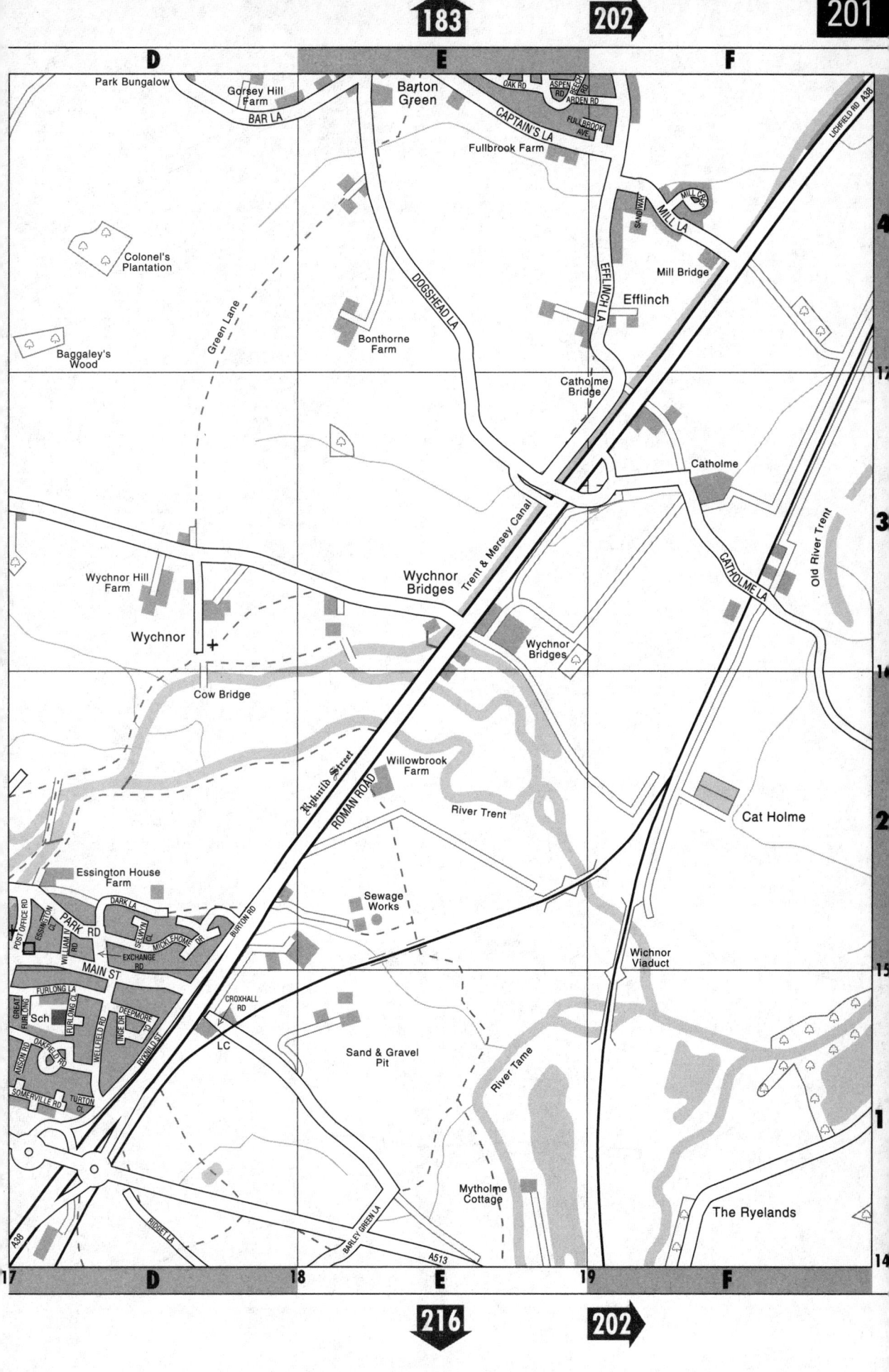

183
202

D   E   F

Park Bungalow

Gorsey Hill Farm

Barton Green

BAR LA

OAK RD
ASPEN RD
ARDEN RD
FULLBROOK AVE

CAPTAIN'S LA

Fullbrook Farm

LICHFIELD RD A38

4

Colonel's Plantation

SANDWAY

MILL CRES

MILL LA

Mill Bridge

Efflinch

EFFLINCH LA

Baggaley's Wood

Green Lane

Bonthorne Farm

DOGSHEAD LA

Catholme Bridge

12

Catholme

3

Wychnor Bridges

Wychnor Hill Farm

Trent & Mersey Canal

CATHOLME LA

Old River Trent

Wychnor

Wychnor Bridges

+

Cow Bridge

16

Ryknild Street

ROMAN ROAD

Willowbrook Farm

River Trent

Cat Holme

2

Essington House Farm

DARK LA

BURTON RD

PARK RD

POST OFFICE RD

ESSINGTON CL

MICKLEHOME DR

SELWYN

WILLIAM IV RD

EXCHANGE RD

MAIN ST

Sewage Works

Wichnor Viaduct

CROXHALL RD

15

Sch

GREAT FURLONG

FURLONG LA

FURLONG CL

WELLFIELD RD

DEEPMORE RD

TINGE DR

RYKNILD ST

LC

Sand & Gravel Pit

River Tame

NIXON RD

OAKFIELD RD

SOMERVILLE RD

TURTON CL

1

A38

RIDGE LA

BARLEY GREEN LA

A513

Mytholme Cottage

The Ryelands

17   D   18   E   19   F

216
202

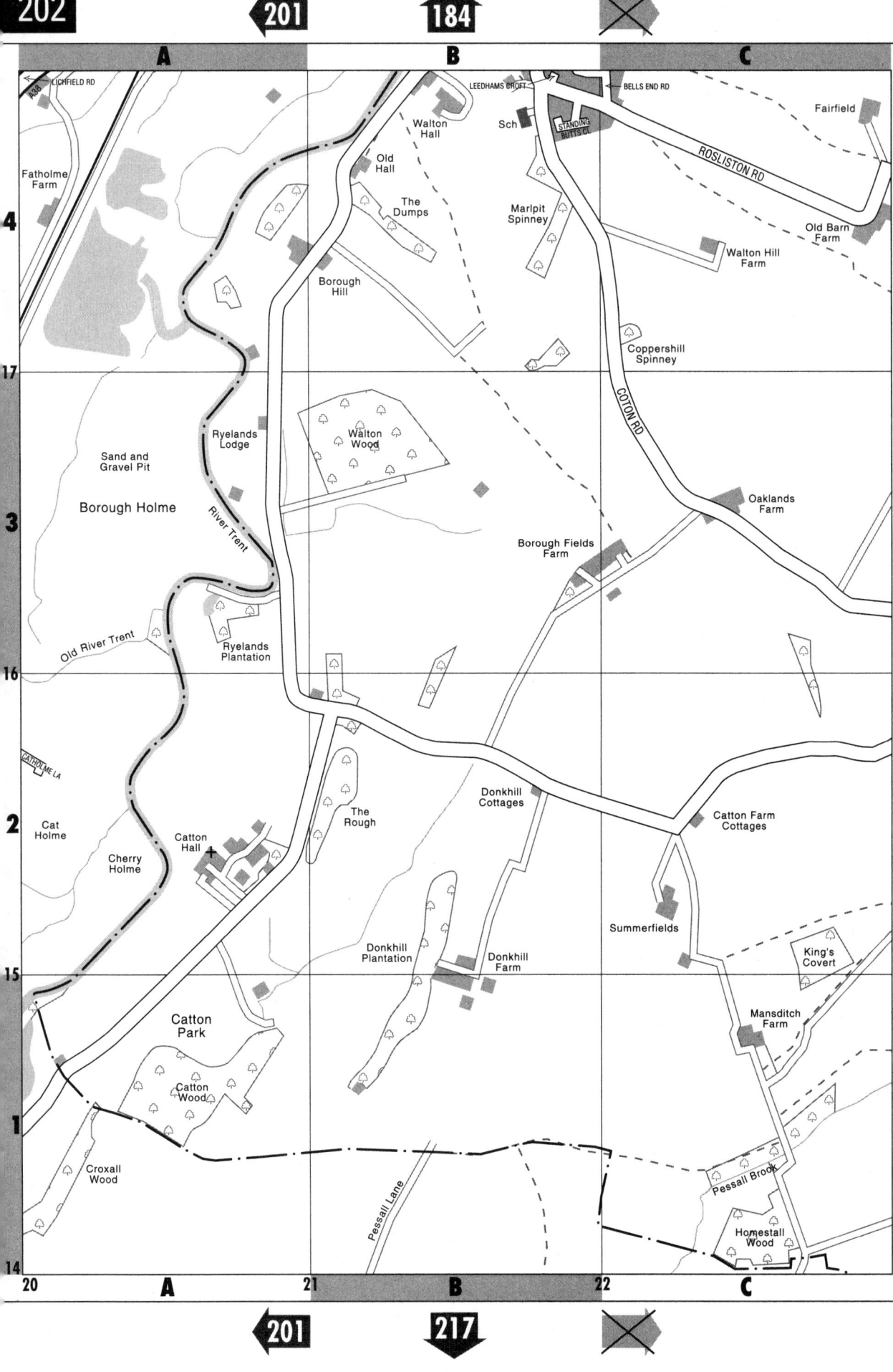

A   B   C

A38 LICHFIELD RD

Fatholme
Farm

4

17

Walton
Hall

Old
Hall

The
Dumps

Borough
Hill

LEEDHAMS CROFT

Sch

STANDING
BUTTS CL

BELLS END RD

Fairfield

ROSLISTON RD

Marlpit
Spinney

Old Barn
Farm

Walton Hill
Farm

Coppershill
Spinney

Sand and
Gravel Pit

Ryelands
Lodge

Walton
Wood

COTON RD

Oaklands
Farm

3

Borough Holme

River Trent

Borough Fields
Farm

Old River Trent

Ryelands
Plantation

16

CATHOLME LA

The
Rough

Donkhill
Cottages

Catton Farm
Cottages

2

Cat
Holme

Cherry
Holme

Catton
Hall

Summerfields

King's
Covert

Donkhill
Plantation

Donkhill
Farm

15

Mansditch
Farm

Catton
Park

Catton
Wood

1

Croxall
Wood

Pessall Lane

Pessall Brook

Homestall
Wood

14

20   A   21   B   22   C

D
E
F

Hoole's
Planting

BUN LA

CHATWELL LA

Chatwell Park
Farm

BS314

A41

4

Brockton
Grange

The Laurels
Farm
Terrace
Farm
Brineton
Farm
Brineton

Villa
Farm
Brineton
House

Blymhill
Marsh

13

Blymhill
Common

GATHERWYND LA

Gatherwynd

Holywell
Plantation

New House
Farm

Cross
Roads

Lower
Beighterton

3

Blymhill

SCHOOL LA

White Sitch

Gorsey
Bank

12

Beighterton
Plantation

Lodge
Farm

Picmoor Wood

HATCH LA

Beighterton
House
Farm

2

The
Big Hythes

The
Little Hythes

Mount
Quarry

Burlington
Pool

A5

The
Mount

Weston-under-Lizard

11

BRIDGEMAN
CT
RECTORY DR

Watling Street

BS314

ROMAN ROAD

A5

Shrewsbury Drive

Weston
Hall

Temple
Wood

1

MILL LA

West
Plantation

Woodlands

Weston Park

New Park Pool

Tong Drive

Woodside
Farm

A41

Lizard
Grange

10

78
D
79
E
80
F

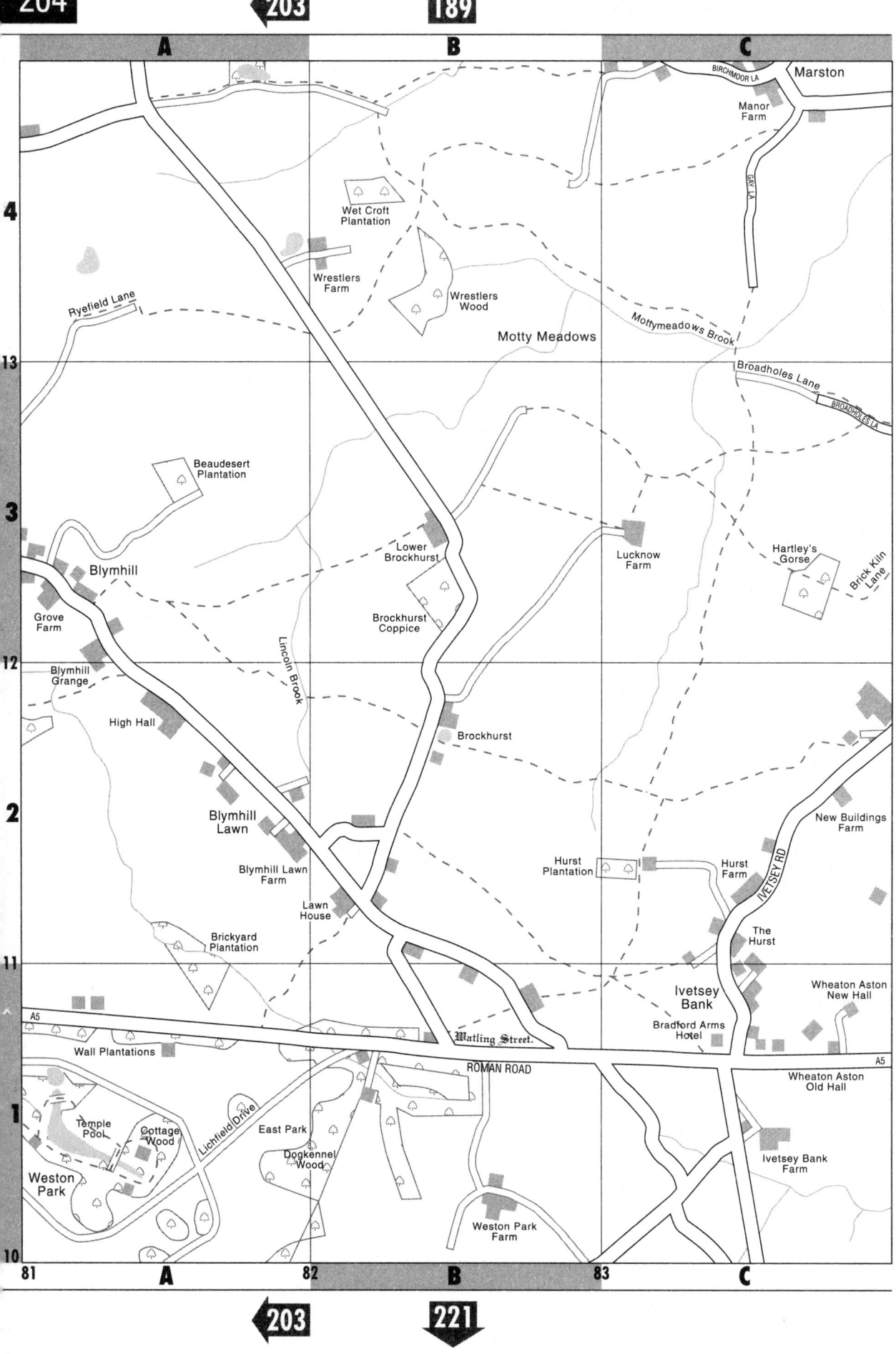

Marston

BIRCHMOOR LA

Manor
Farm

GAY LA

4

Ryefield Lane

Wet Croft
Plantation

Wrestlers
Farm

Wrestlers
Wood

Motty Meadows

Mottymeadows Brook

13

Broadholes Lane

BROADHOLES LA

Beaudesert
Plantation

3

Blymhill

Lower
Brockhurst

Lucknow
Farm

Hartley's
Gorse

Brick Kiln
Lane

Grove
Farm

Brockhurst
Coppice

Lincoln Brook

12

Blymhill
Grange

High Hall

Brockhurst

New Buildings
Farm

2

Blymhill
Lawn

Blymhill Lawn
Farm

Hurst
Plantation

Hurst
Farm

IVETSEY RD

Lawn
House

The
Hurst

Brickyard
Plantation

11

Ivetsey
Bank

Wheaton Aston
New Hall

A5

Wall Plantations

Watling Street.

Bradford Arms
Hotel

A5

ROMAN ROAD

Wheaton Aston
Old Hall

1

Temple
Pool

Cottage
Wood

Lichfield Drive

East Park

Dogkennel
Wood

Ivetsey Bank
Farm

Weston
Park

Weston Park
Farm

10

81

A

82

B

83

C

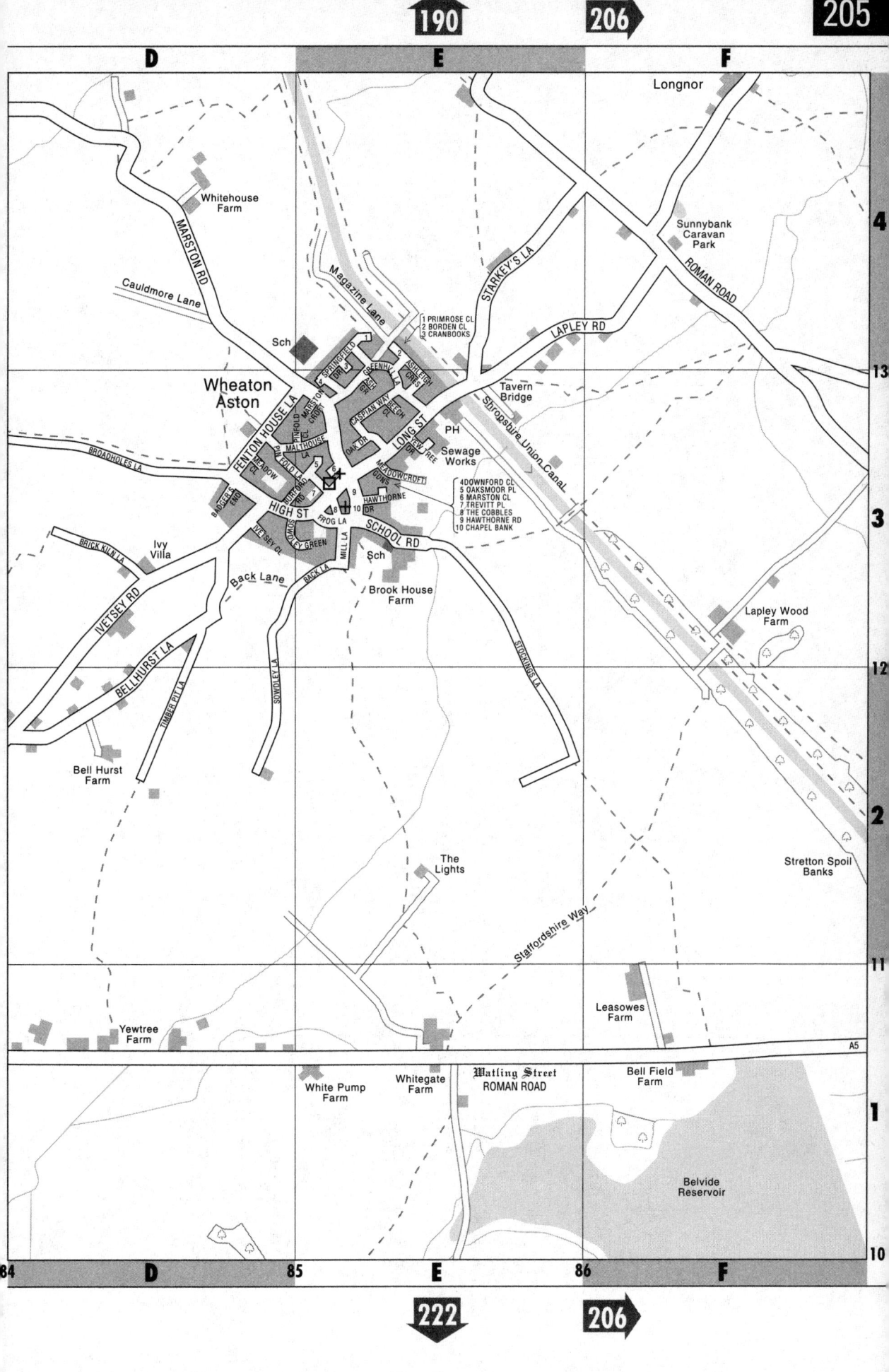

D
E
F

Longnor

Whitehouse
Farm

MARSTON RD

Cauldmore Lane

Magazine Lane

Sunnybank
Caravan
Park

STARKEY'S LA

ROMAN ROAD

4

Sch

1 PRIMROSE CL
2 BORDEN CL
3 CRANBOOKS

LAPLEY RD

Wheaton
Aston

SPRINGFIELD DR

GREENHILL CRES

ASHLEIGH CRES

Tavern
Bridge

13

FENTON HOUSE LA

PINFOLD CL

MARSTON CROFT

CASPIAN WAY

BEECH PL

LONG ST

NEW TREE

Shropshire Union Canal

BROADHOLES LA

MALTHOUSE LA

OAK DR

PH

MEADOW

PILL CROFT

BIRFORD CROFT

MEADOWCROFT

Sewage
Works

4 DOWNFORD CL
5 OAKSMOOR PL
6 MARSTON CL
7 TREVITT PL
8 THE COBBLES
9 HAWTHORNE RD
10 CHAPEL BANK

BADGER'S END

HIGH ST

THOMAS FIELD

IVETSEY CL

IVETSEY GREEN

HAWTHORNE GDNS

FROG LA

3

Ivy
Villa

BRICK KILN LA

BACK LA

MILL LA

Sch

SCHOOL RD

STOCKINGS LA

IVETSEY RD

Back Lane

Brook House
Farm

Lapley Wood
Farm

BELLHURST LA

SOWDLEY LA

TIMBER PIT LA

12

Bell Hurst
Farm

2

The
Lights

Stretton Spoil
Banks

Staffordshire Way

11

Yewtree
Farm

Leasowes
Farm

A5

White Pump
Farm

Whitegate
Farm

Watling Street
ROMAN ROAD

Bell Field
Farm

1

Belvide
Reservoir

10

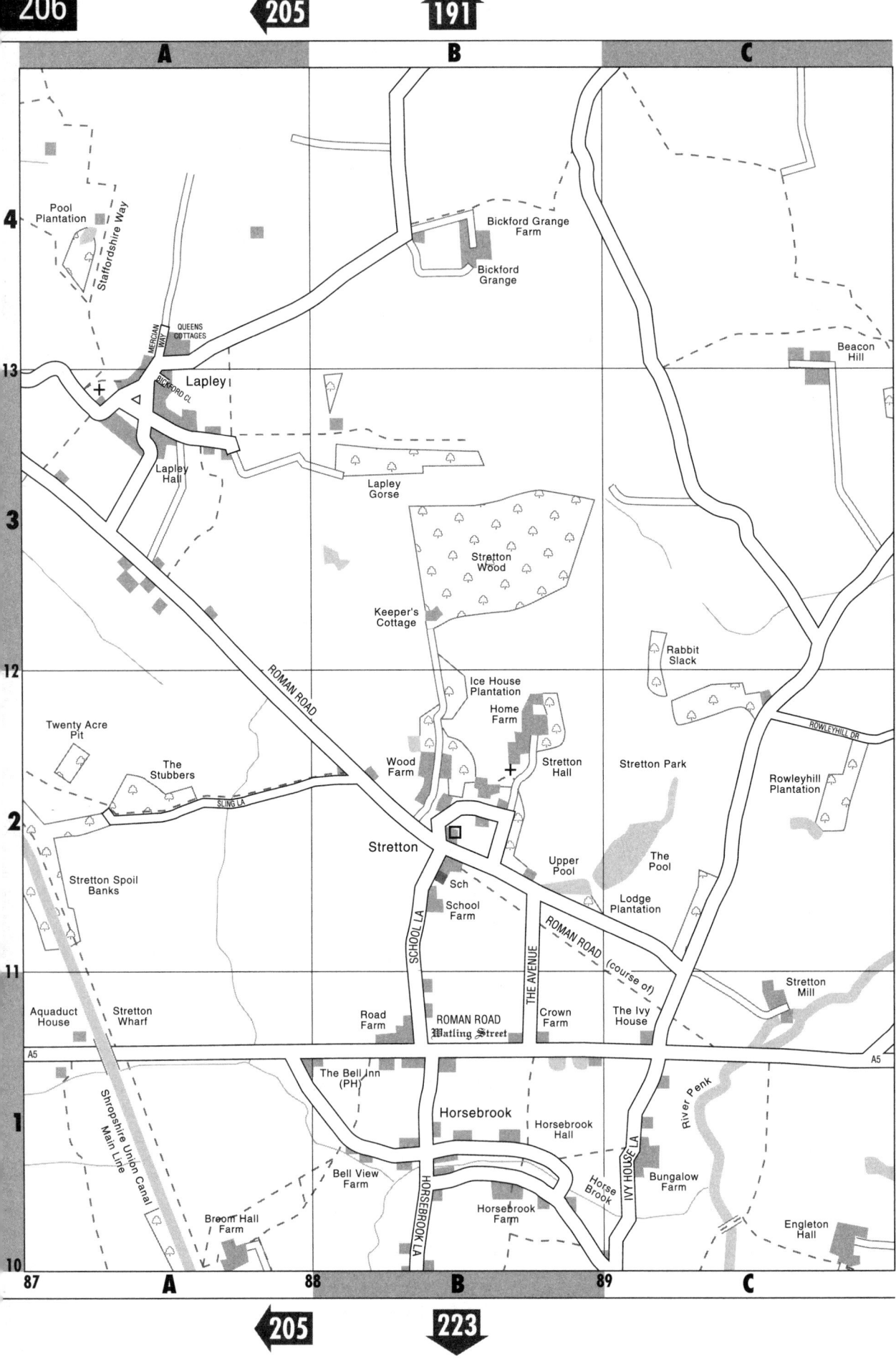

205
191
205
223

A   B   C

4

Pool
Plantation

Bickford Grange
Farm

Bickford
Grange

Beacon
Hill

MERCIAN WAY

Staffordshire Way

QUEENS
COTTAGES

13

Lapley

BICKFORD CL

Lapley
Hall

Lapley
Gorse

Stretton
Wood

Keeper's
Cottage

Rabbit
Slack

3

ROMAN ROAD

12

Ice House
Plantation

Home
Farm

ROWLEYHILL DR

Twenty Acre
Pit

The
Stubbers

SLING LA

Wood
Farm

Stretton
Hall

Stretton Park

Rowleyhill
Plantation

Stretton

Upper
Pool

The
Pool

2

Stretton Spoil
Banks

Sch

School
Farm

Lodge
Plantation

11

Stretton
Mill

Aquaduct
House

Stretton
Wharf

THE AVENUE

ROMAN ROAD (course of)

A5

Road
Farm

ROMAN ROAD
Watling Street

Crown
Farm

The Ivy
House

A5

Shropshire Union Canal Main Line

The Bell Inn
(PH)

Horsebrook

Horsebrook
Hall

River Penk

1

Bell View
Farm

HORSEBROOK LA

Horse
Brook

IVY HOUSE LA

Bungalow
Farm

Broom Hall
Farm

Horsebrook
Farm

Engleton
Hall

10

87   88   89

A   B   C

192
208

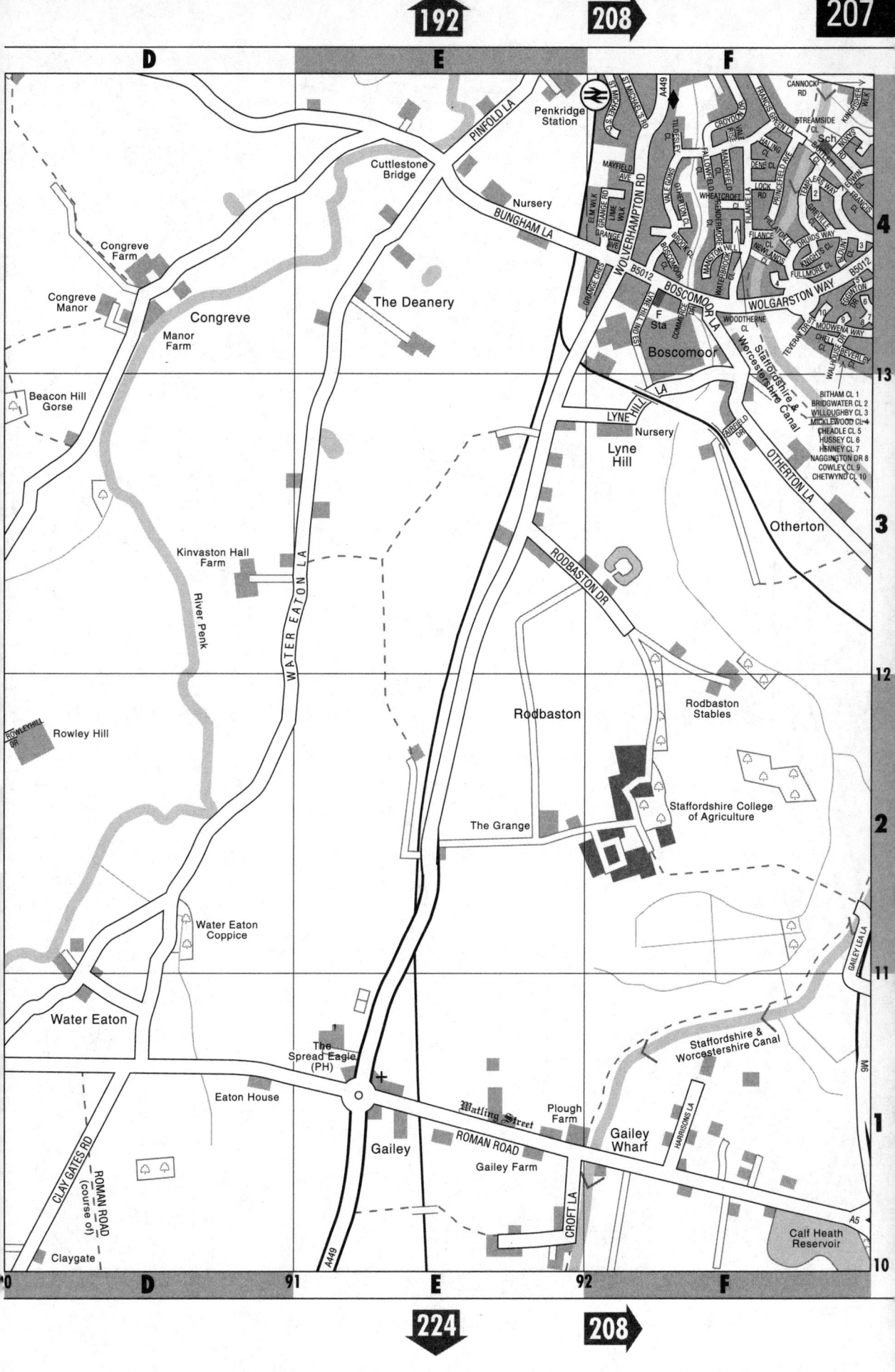

224
208

207
193

A B C

B5012
CANNOK RD
M6
GREENWAYS
ATHELSTAN CL
Sch
PRIC DR
SAXON RD
BROADHEATH
ELMOOR
KENILWORTH CL
WOLGARSTON WAY
FRANCIS CL
DRUIDS WAY
MOOR HALL LA
NAGGINGTON DR
Moor Hall Cottages

Quarry Heath

Pillaton Farm

Pillaton Hall Farm

Pillaton

Newlands Wood

4

ELMCROFT CL
DAMSET CL
RAWNSLEY
ASTON CL
BOYDEN CL

13

Pillaton Old Hall

Mansty Farm

OTHERTON LA

3

Mineral Railway

Mansty Wood

Staffordshire & Worcestershire Canal

12

LC

MICKLEWOOD LA

Horsemoor Wood

B5012

Micklewood

2

Fullmoor Wood

Fullmoor Lodge

Hatherton Wood

11

Gailey Lea Farm

1

GAILEY LEA LA

Gailey Upper Reservoir

Hatherton

Hatherton Hall Farm

M6

A5

Gailey Lower Reservoir

Church Farm

A5

10

93 A 94 B 95 C

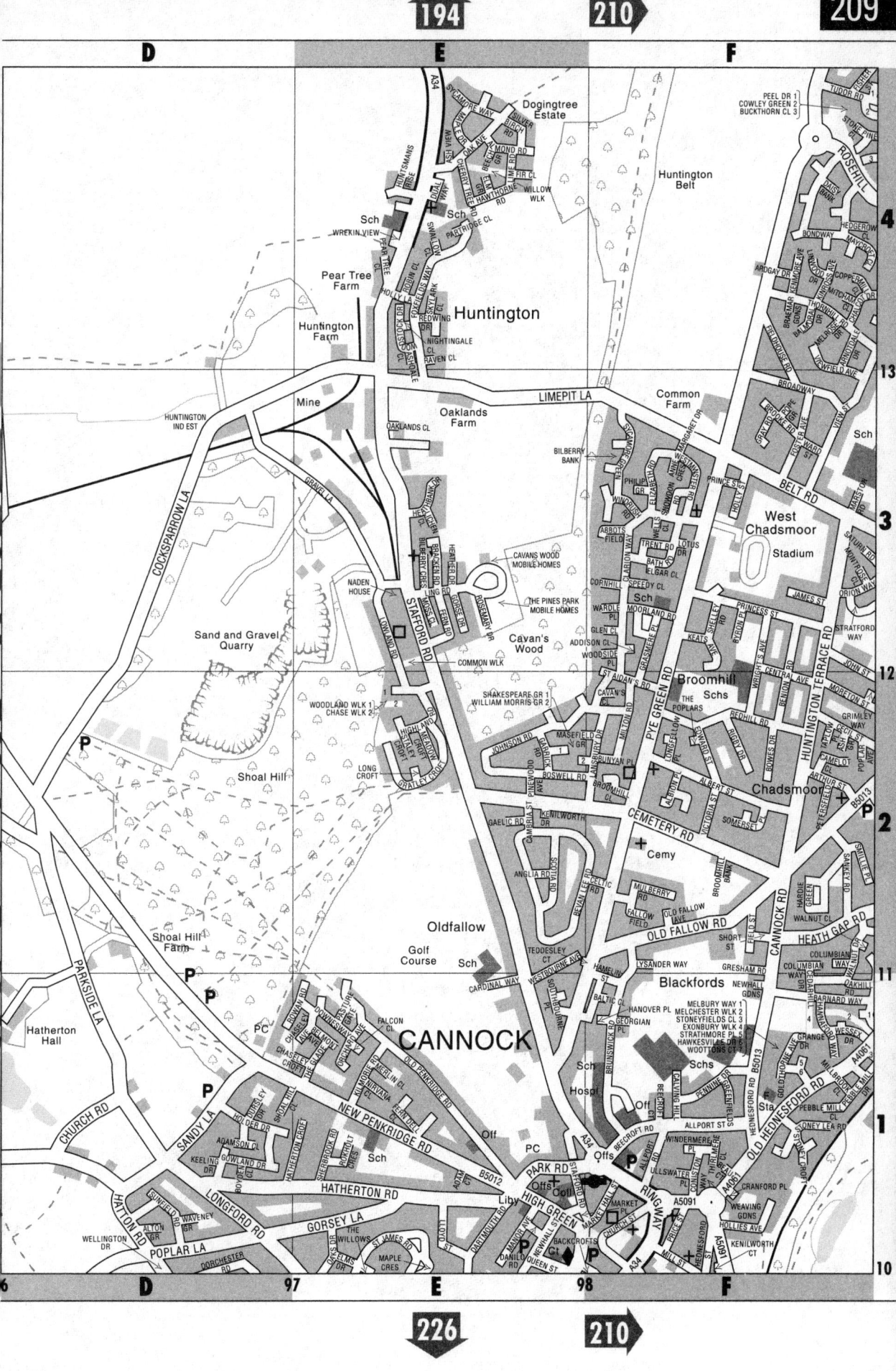

D E F

4

Dogingtree Estate

Huntington Belt

PEEL DR 1
COWLEY GREEN 2
BUCKTHORN CL 3

ROSEHILL

Sch

WREKIN VIEW

Pear Tree Farm

Huntington Farm

Huntington

13

Mine

LIMEPIT LA

Common Farm

BELT RD

Oaklands Farm

HUNTINGTON IND EST

Oaklands CL

Bilberry Bank

West Chadsmoor
Stadium

3

Sch

CAVANS WOOD MOBILE HOMES

NADEN HOUSE

THE PINES PARK MOBILE HOMES

STAFFORD RD

Cavan's Wood

COMMON WLK

Broomhill
Schs

Chadsmoor

12

Sand and Gravel Quarry

WOODLAND WLK 1
CHASE WLK 2

SHAKESPEARE GR 1
WILLIAM MORRIS GR 2

Cavan's

THE POPLARS

P

Shoal Hill

LONG CROFT

PYE GREEN RD

CEMETERY RD

B5013

P

2

Cemy

Shoal Hill Farm

Oldfallow

Golf Course

Sch

OLD FALLOW RD

HEATH GAP RD

Blackfords

MELBURY WAY 1
MELCHESTER WLK 2
STONEYFIELDS CL 3
EXONBURY WLK 4
STRATHMORE PL 5
HAWKESVILLE DR 6
WOOTTONS CT 7

11

Hatherton Hall

P

P

P

CANNOCK

Schs

PARKSIDE LA

CHURCH RD

PC

Hospl

Off

Sta

B5013

1

P

NEW PENKRIDGE RD

Sch

Otf

PC

PARK RD

Offs

Offs

A34

RINGWAY

Sch

CHURCH RD

HATHERTON RD

B5012

HIGH GREEN

Liby

Coll

MARKET HALL

Offs

A5091

Weaving Gdns

HOLLIES AVE

KENILWORTH CT

POPLAR LA

GORSEY LA

ST JAMES RD

MAPLE CRES

BACKCROFTS

QUEEN ST

A34

10

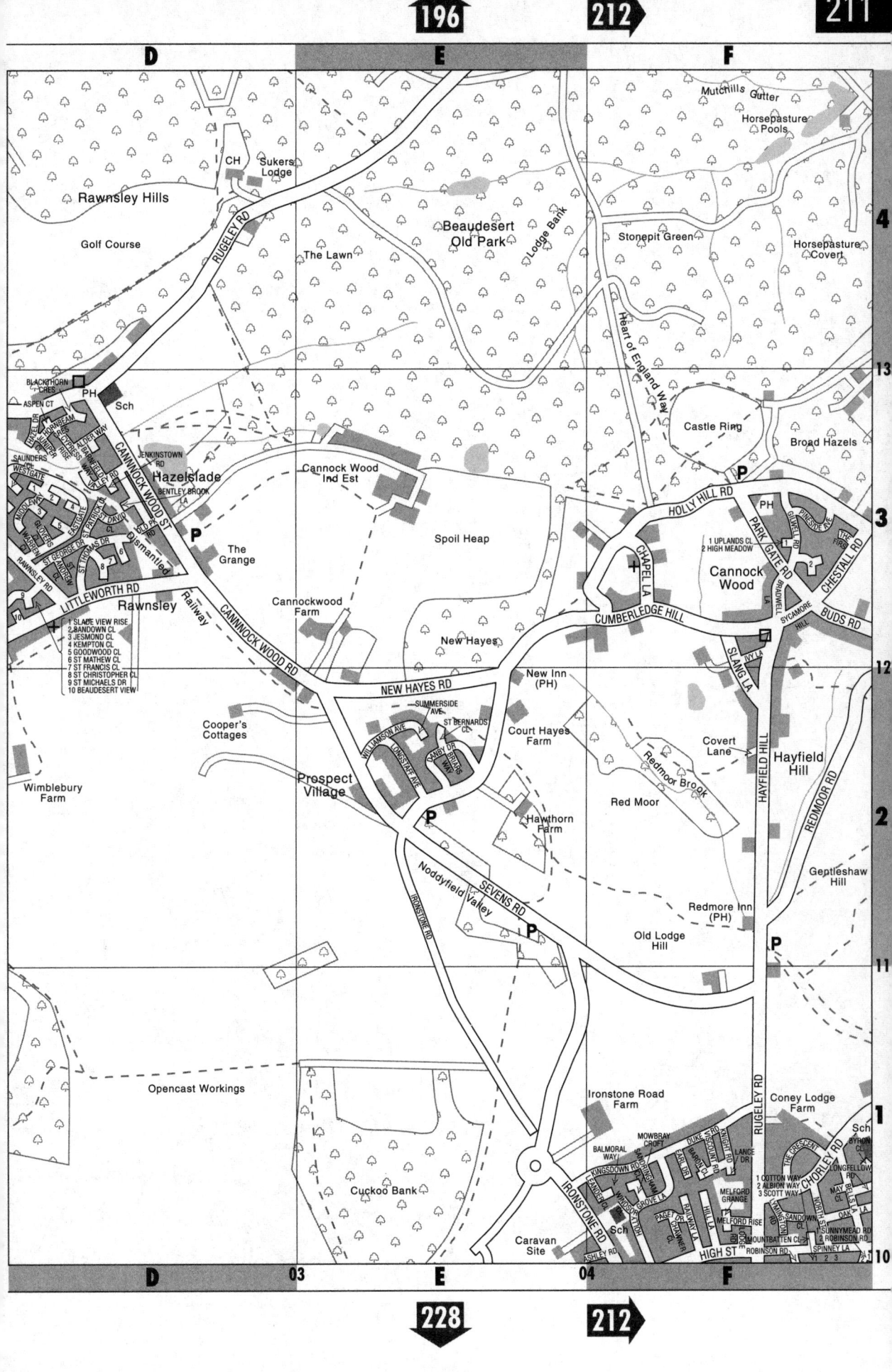

Mutchills Gutter

Horsepasture Pools

Rawnsley Hills

CH   Sukers Lodge

Beaudesert Old Park

Lodge Bank

Stonepit Green

Horsepasture Covert

Golf Course

The Lawn

Heart of England Way

Castle Ring

Broad Hazels

BLACKTHORN CRES
PH
ASPEN CT
Sch

SAUNDERS
WESTGATE

RUGELEY RD

CANNOCK WOOD ST

Hazelslade

JENKINSTOWN RD

BENTLEY BROOK LA

Cannock Wood Ind Est

Spoil Heap

HOLLY HILL RD

CHAPEL LA

1 UPLANDS CL
2 HIGH MEADOW

CHAPELL RD
PINE SIDE AVE
THE FIRS

Cannock Wood

BRADWELL LA
SYCAMORE HILL

CHESTALL RD

P   The Grange

Dismantled Railway

CANNOCK WOOD RD

Cannockwood Farm

New Hayes

CUMBERLEDGE HILL

PH

SLANG LA

BUDS RD

IVY LA

LITTLEWORTH RD

RAWNSLEY RD

ST GEORGE DR
EASTGATE
ST THOMAS CL
ST PATRICK'S
OLD RD

Rawnsley

1 SLADE VIEW RISE
2 SANDOWN CL
3 JESMOND CL
4 KEMPTON CL
5 GOODWOOD CL
6 ST MATHEW CL
7 ST FRANCIS CL
8 ST CHRISTOPHER CL
9 ST MICHAELS DR
10 BEAUDESERT VIEW

NEW HAYES RD

SUMMERSIDE AVE
ST BERNARDS CL

New Inn (PH)

Court Hayes Farm

Covert Lane

Redmoor Brook

Hayfield Hill

HAYFIELD HILL

REDMOOR RD

Wimblebury Farm

Cooper's Cottages

WILLIAMSON AVE
LONGSTAFF AVE
CANBY DR
BRIERS WAY

Prospect Village

P   Hawthorn Farm

Red Moor

Geptleshaw Hill

IRONSTONE RD

SEVENS RD

Noddyfield Valley

P

Redmore Inn (PH)

Old Lodge Hill

P

Opencast Workings

Cuckoo Bank

Ironstone Road Farm

Coney Lodge Farm

MOWBRAY CROFT
BALMORAL WAY
KINGSDOWN RD
DUKE ST
SANDRINGHAM RD
KNIGHT RD
EARL DR
LANCE DR
BARLOW RD

RUGELEY RD

CHORLEY RD

Sch
BYRON CL
LONGFELLOW RD
MAY RD

1 COTTON WAY
2 ALBION WAY
3 SCOTT WAY

THE CRESCENT

MELFORD GRANGE
MELFORD RISE

WINDSOR PL
PAGE DR
RAILWAY HILL
THE CRESCENT

SANDOWN CL
WELLINGTON RD
OAK LA

SUNNYMEAD CL
ROBINSON RD
SPINNEY LA

Sch

Caravan Site

ASHLEY RD

HIGH ST

MOUNTBATTEN CL   ROBINSON RD

03   04

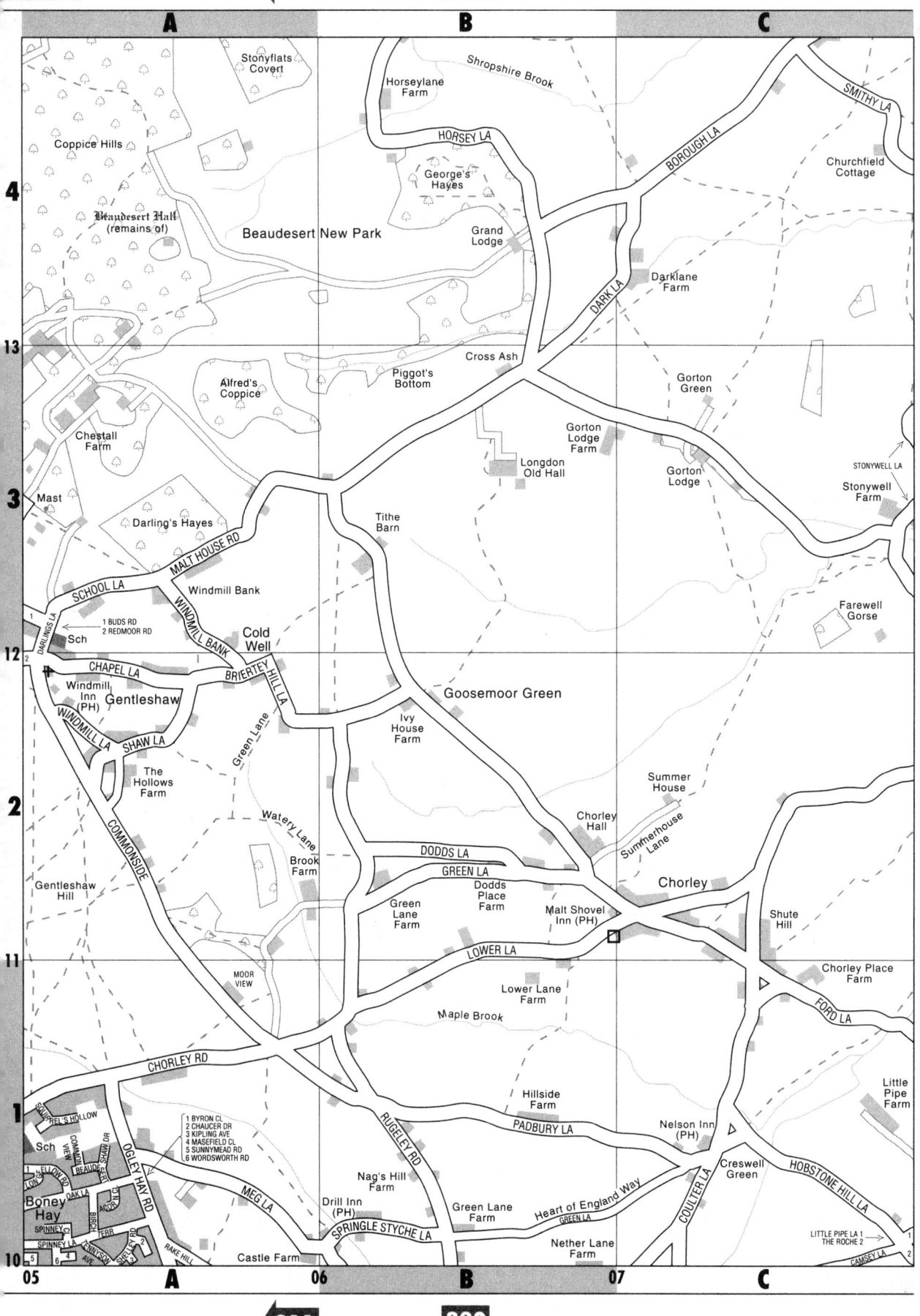

A · B · C

4
Coppice Hills
Stonyflats Covert
Horseylane Farm
Shropshire Brook
Beaudesert Hall (remains of)
George's Hayes
Beaudesert New Park
Grand Lodge
HORSEY LA
BOROUGH LA
SMITHY LA
Churchfield Cottage
DARK LA
Darklane Farm

13
Chestall Farm
Alfred's Coppice
Piggot's Bottom
Cross Ash
Gorton Green
Gorton Lodge Farm
Longdon Old Hall
Gorton Lodge
STONYWELL LA
Stonywell Farm

3
Mast
Darling's Hayes
MALT HOUSE RD
Tithe Barn
Farewell Gorse
SCHOOL LA
Windmill Bank
WINDMILL BANK
DARLINGS LA
1 BUDS RD
2 REDMOOR RD
Sch
Cold Well

12
CHAPEL LA
BRIERTEY HILL LA
Goosemoor Green
Windmill Inn (PH)
Gentleshaw
Green Lane
Ivy House Farm
WINDMILL LA
SHAW LA
The Hollows Farm
Watery Lane
Brook Farm
Summer House

2
COMMONSIDE
Gentleshaw Hill
Chorley Hall
Summerhouse Lane
Chorley
DODDS LA
GREEN LA
Dodds Place Farm
Green Lane Farm
Malt Shovel Inn (PH)
Shute Hill

11
MOOR VIEW
LOWER LA
Lower Lane Farm
Maple Brook
Chorley Place Farm
FORD LA

1
CHORLEY RD
1 BYRON CL
2 CHAUCER DR
3 KIPLING AVE
4 MASEFIELD CL
5 SUNNYMEAD RD
6 WORDSWORTH RD
Hillside Farm
PADBURY LA
Nelson Inn (PH)
Little Pipe Farm
SQUIRREL'S HOLLOW
Sch
COMMON VIEW
OGLEY HAY RD
RUGELEY RD
Nag's Hill Farm
Creswell Green
HOBSTONE HILL LA

10
Boney Hay
SPINNEY
MEG LA
Drill Inn (PH)
SPRINGLE STYCHE LA
Green Lane Farm
Heart of England Way
GREEN LA
Nether Lane Farm
LITTLE PIPE LA 1
THE ROCHE 2
CAMSEY LA
Castle Farm
RAKE HILL

05 · A · 06 · B · 07 · C

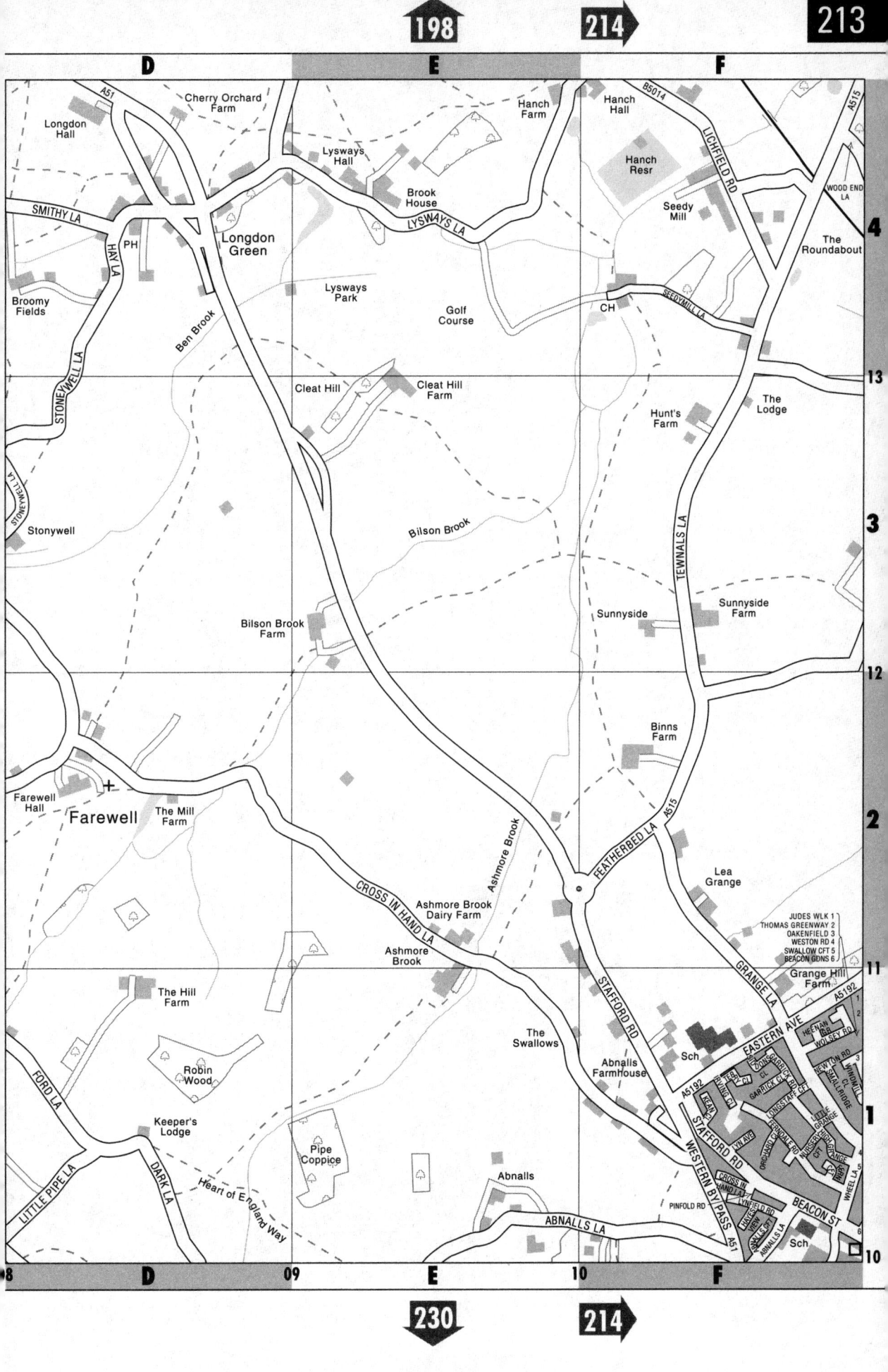

Longdon Hall

Cherry Orchard Farm

A51

SMITHY LA

HAY LA

PH

Longdon Green

Ben Brook

STONEYWELL LA

Broomy Fields

Lysways Hall

Brook House

LYSWAYS LA

Lysways Park

Golf Course

Hanch Farm

Hanch Hall

Hanch Hall

B5014

LICHFIELD RD

A515

WOOD END LA

Hanch Resr

Seedy Mill

The Roundabout

CH

SEEDYMILL LA

4

Cleat Hill

Cleat Hill Farm

Hunt's Farm

The Lodge

13

Stonywell

Bilson Brook

TEWNALS LA

Sunnyside

Sunnyside Farm

3

Bilson Brook Farm

12

Farewell Hall

Farewell

The Mill Farm

CROSS IN HAND LA

Ashmore Brook Dairy Farm

Ashmore Brook

Ashmore Brook

Binns Farm

FEATHERBED LA

A515

Lea Grange

2

Grange Hill Farm

GRANGE LA

11

A5192

The Hill Farm

Robin Wood

Keeper's Lodge

FORD LA

DARK LA

Heart of England Way

Pipe Coppice

The Swallows

STAFFORD RD

Abnalls Farmhouse

Sch

A5192

EASTERN AVE

Sch

1

Abnalls

WESTERN BYPASS

STAFFORD RD

PINFOLD RD

CROSS IN HAND LA

BEACON ST

A51

ABNALLS LA

Sch

10

D
E
F

Fradley Junction

SALE LA

Sale Pit

New Bridge

GORSE LA

HAY END LA

Old Hall Farm

OLD HALL LA

THE MOOR
BROMWICH DR
SHAW CL
STAFFORD LA
TURNER
LONG LA
EDWARDS FARM RD
CHURCH LA

DUMORE HAY LA

LA FOX A38

RODDIGE LA
LC

Fradley

RYKNELD ST

Crown Inn Farm

4

Sch ✝

CHURCH CL

Fradley Bridge

HEATH GAP

Ryecroft

FRADLEY LA

Airfield (disused)

COMMON LA

Bridge Farm

BEECHES CROFT
JORDAN CROFT
OAKLANDS CL
HARVEY RD
FORRESTER CL
JACKMAN RD

WORTHINGTON RD

Hotel

FINE LA
LC

13

Gorse Farm

Bell Bridge

Dunstall

Auction Centre

Industrial Estate

WOOD END LA

West Hill Farm

Roman Road   Ryknild Street

3

IRONSTONE LA
LC

East Hill

Industrial Estate

WELLINGTON CRES

Hilliards Cross

12

Brookhay Bridge   LC

Brookhay Wood

Coventry Canal

Wetleyhay Wood

2

Rough Stockings

Orchard Farm

Bears Hay Farm

Brookhay Farm

Brookhay

BROOKHAY LA

Sennex House

Streethay Bridge

Mare Brook

11

The Manor House

Williford

STOCKFORD LA

Streethay House Farm

King's Orchard Bridge

Thatchmoor Farm

Hurst Farm

Streethay

PH
HOLLAND LG
MEADOW CROFT
BURTON RD
A5127
BURTON OLD RD
LC
DYOTT CL

BROAD LA

BURTON RD

1

Stoney Step Bridge

Whittington Hurst Farm

A38

Hill Farm

Broom Leasoe

The Grove

10

4
D
15
E
16
F

A · B · C

4

13

3

12

2

11

1

10

17 · A · 18 · B · 19 · C

Roddige
Whitemoor Haye
RIDGE LA
BARLEY GREEN LA
RODDIGE LA
STOCKFORD LA

Chetwynd or Salter's Bridge
A513
Brown's Island
Broadfields

Croxall
CROXALL RD
Dovecote
The Hall
Oakley Farm
River Mease
Croxall Mill
A513
New Buildings Farm

River Tame
Lady Walk
Sittles
Elford Park

Sand & Gravel Pit
Bisphill Plantation
Park Farm
The Bungalow

Home Farm
Elford
BRICKHOUSE LA
Greendales Farm
A513
Sch
PH
THE SQUARE
CROFT CL
THE BECK
Raddle Farm
OLD HALL DR
THE GARDENS
CHURCH RD
The Hill
THE SHRUBBERY
BURTON RD
A513
Old Orangery

D   E   F

Pessall Farm

Raddle Farm

The Grange

4

A
Medieval
Village of
Croxall
(site of)

PESSALL LA

13

Wayside

Croxall Mill

Pessall Brook

Brook House Farm

RADDLE LA

CROXALL RD

Broadfield's Farm

3

Edingale

BLAKEWAYS CL

CROXALL RD

PH

TATCHET LA

Sch

SCHOOL LA

MOORES

CHURCH HOLLOW

SCHOFIELD

MAIN RD

LULLINGTON RD

WOODYARD DR

CHURCH LA

HOLLAND CT

12

Crabtree Farm

Poplars Farm

A513

Grange Farm

MILL LA

2

Rose Cottage

River Mease

11

Haselour

MAIN RD

PH

Harlaston

Haselour House

Haselour Hall

MANOR LA

Acacia Grove

Little Harlaston

1

Model Farm

Coppinshill Barn

Well Barn

Twizles Lane

10

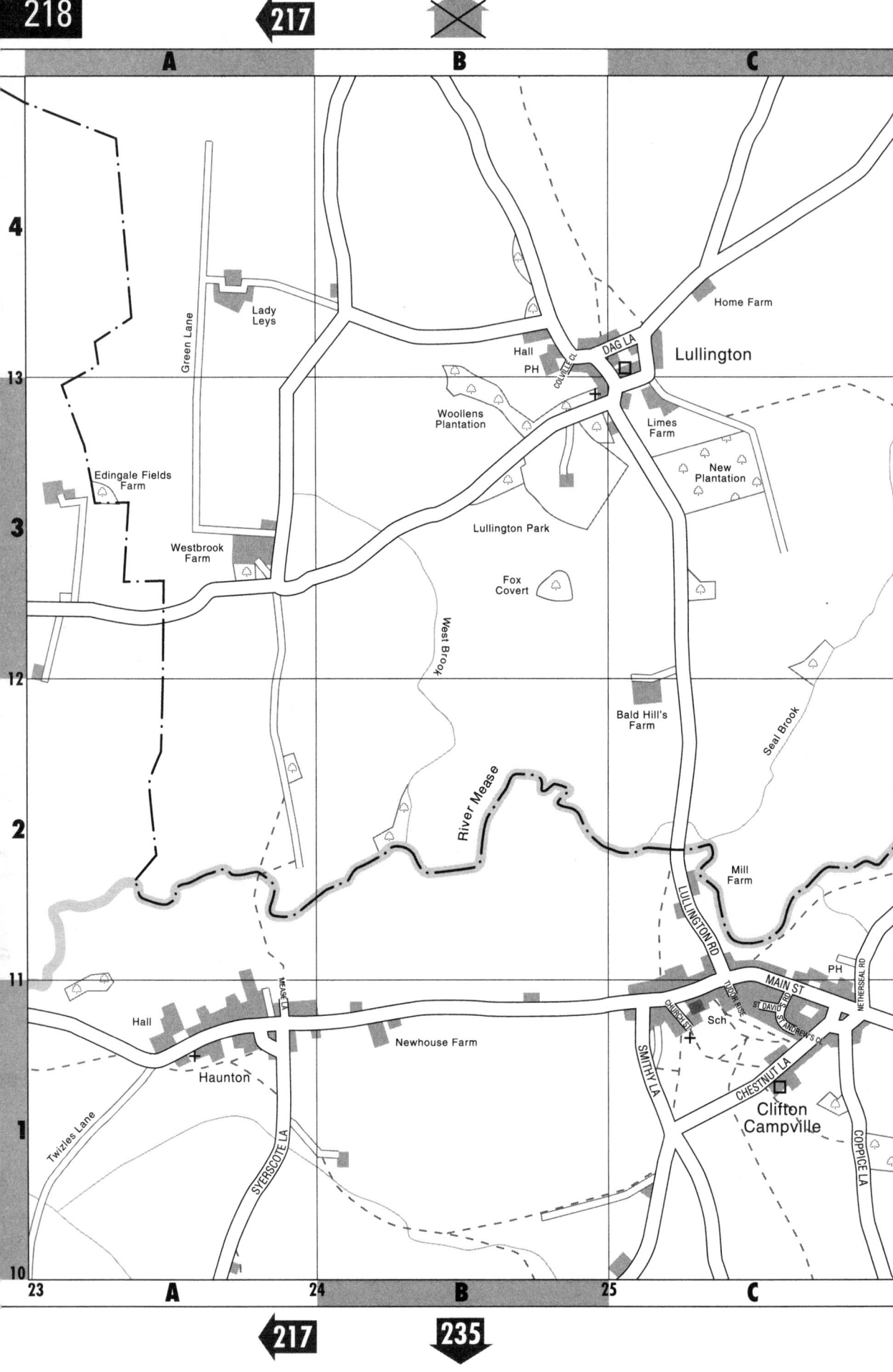

A B C

4

Green Lane

Lady Leys

Home Farm

Hall
PH

DAG LA

COLVILLE CL

Lullington

13

Woollens Plantation

Limes Farm

Edingale Fields Farm

New Plantation

Westbrook Farm

3

Lullington Park

Fox Covert

West Brook

12

Bald Hill's Farm

Seal Brook

River Mease

2

Mill Farm

LULLINGTON RD

11

MAIN ST

PH

Hall

Newhouse Farm

MEASE LA

CHURCH ST

TUDOR RISE

ST DAVID'S

ST ANDREW'S CL

NETHERSEAL RD

Sch

Haunton

SMITHY LA

CHESTNUT LA

Clifton Campville

Twizles Lane

1

SYERSCOTE LA

COPPICE LA

10

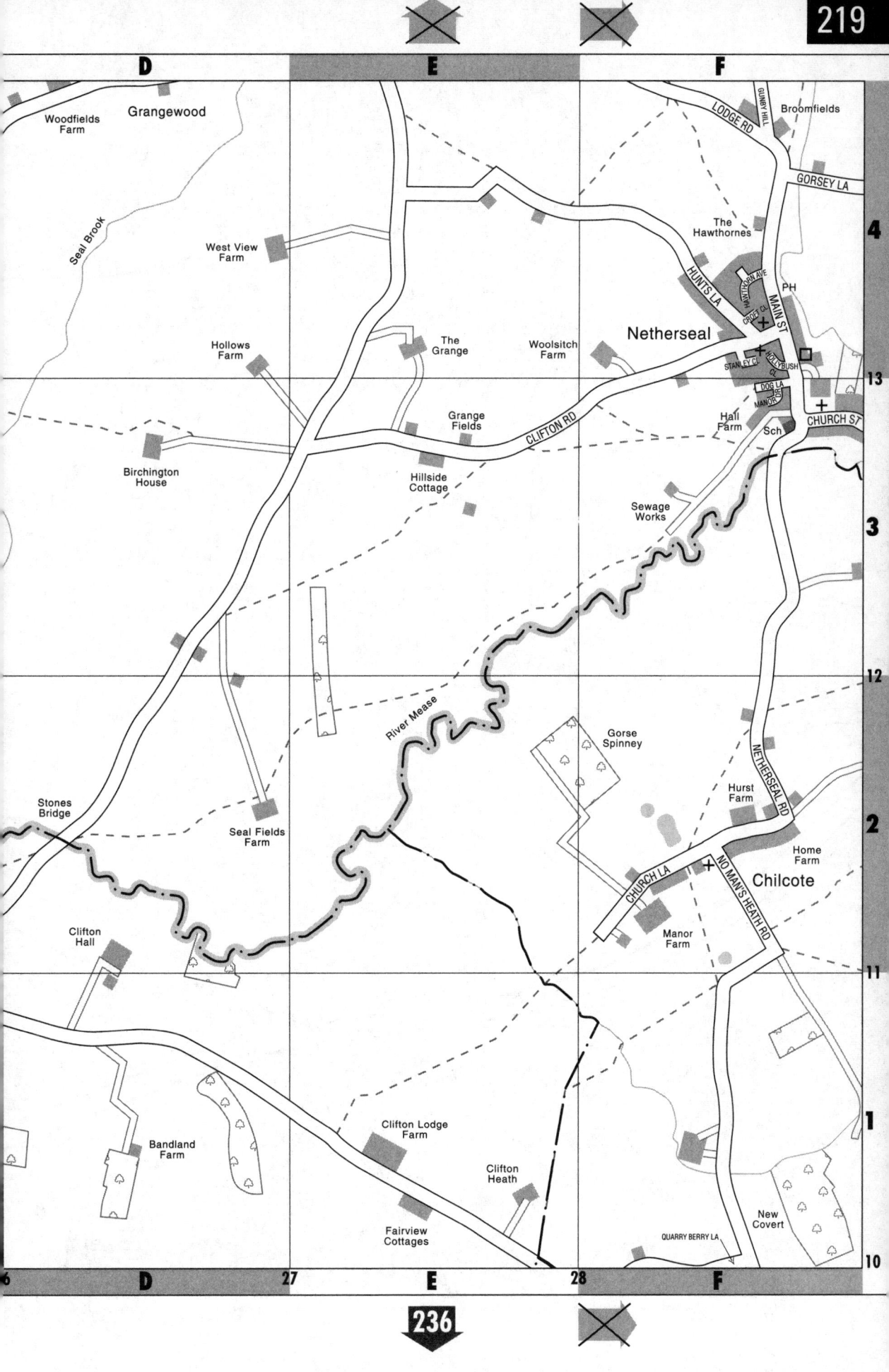

A   **B**   **C**

4

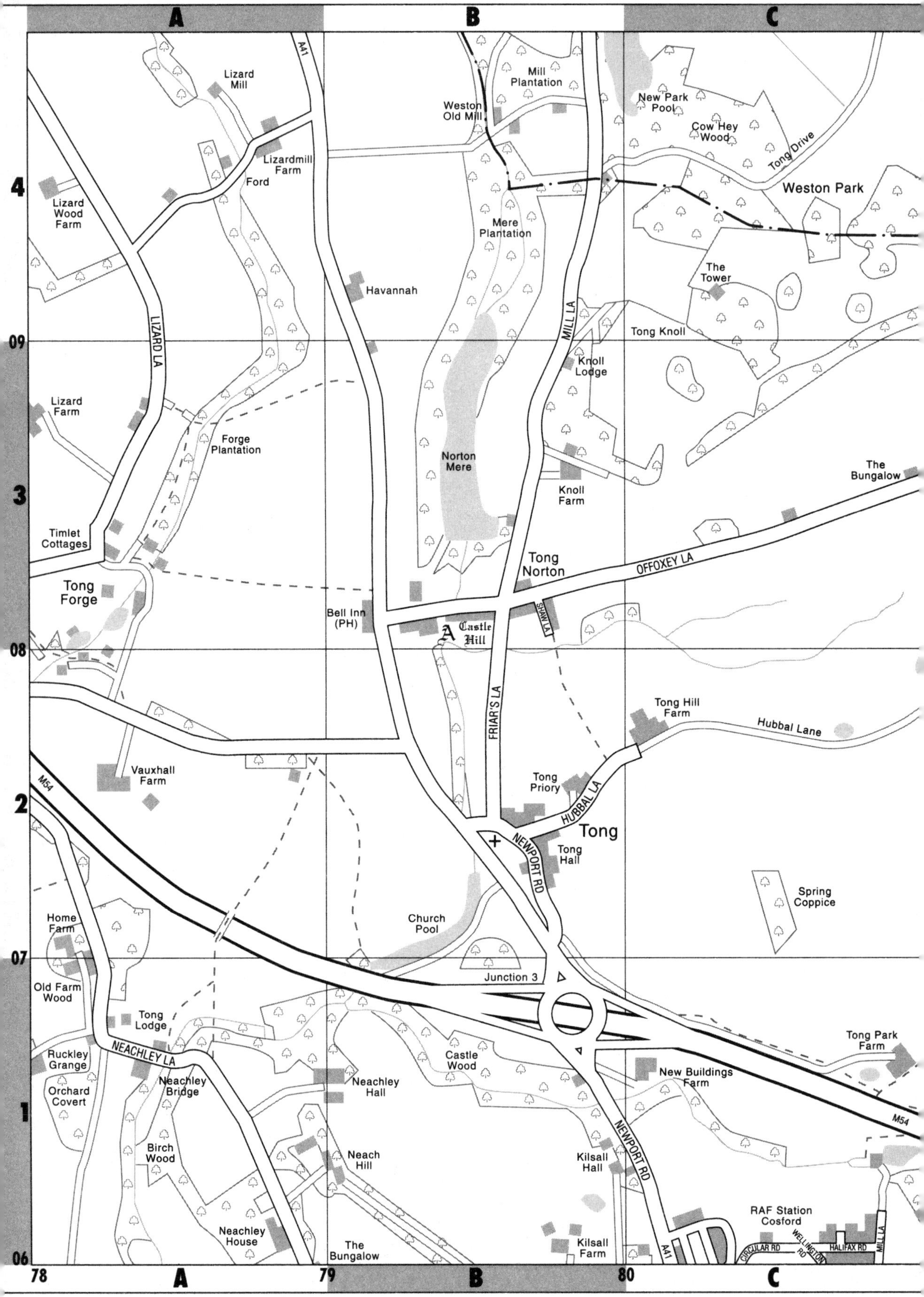

Lizard Mill

Lizardmill Farm

Lizard Ford

Lizard Wood Farm

Mill Plantation

Weston Old Mill

New Park Pool

Cow Hey Wood

Tong Drive

Weston Park

Mere Plantation

The Tower

09

Havannah

LIZARD LA

MILL LA

Tong Knoll

Lizard Farm

Forge Plantation

Knoll Lodge

The Bungalow

3

Norton Mere

Knoll Farm

Timlet Cottages

Tong Forge

Tong Norton

OFFOXEY LA

08

Bell Inn (PH)

Castle Hill

SHAW LA

Tong Hill Farm

Hubbal Lane

FRIAR'S LA

Tong Priory

HUBBAL LA

Tong

M54

Vauxhall Farm

NEWPORT RD

Tong Hall

2

Spring Coppice

Church Pool

Home Farm

Junction 3

Old Farm Wood

Tong Lodge

NEACHLEY LA

Castle Wood

Tong Park Farm

New Buildings Farm

M54

07

Ruckley Grange

Neachley Bridge

Neachley Hall

1

Orchard Covert

Birch Wood

Neach Hill

Kilsall Hall

NEWPORT RD

RAF Station Cosford

Neachley House

The Bungalow

Kilsall Farm

A41

CIRCULAR RD

WELLINGTON RD

HALIFAX RD

MILL LA

06

78   **A**   **79**   **B**   **80**   **C**

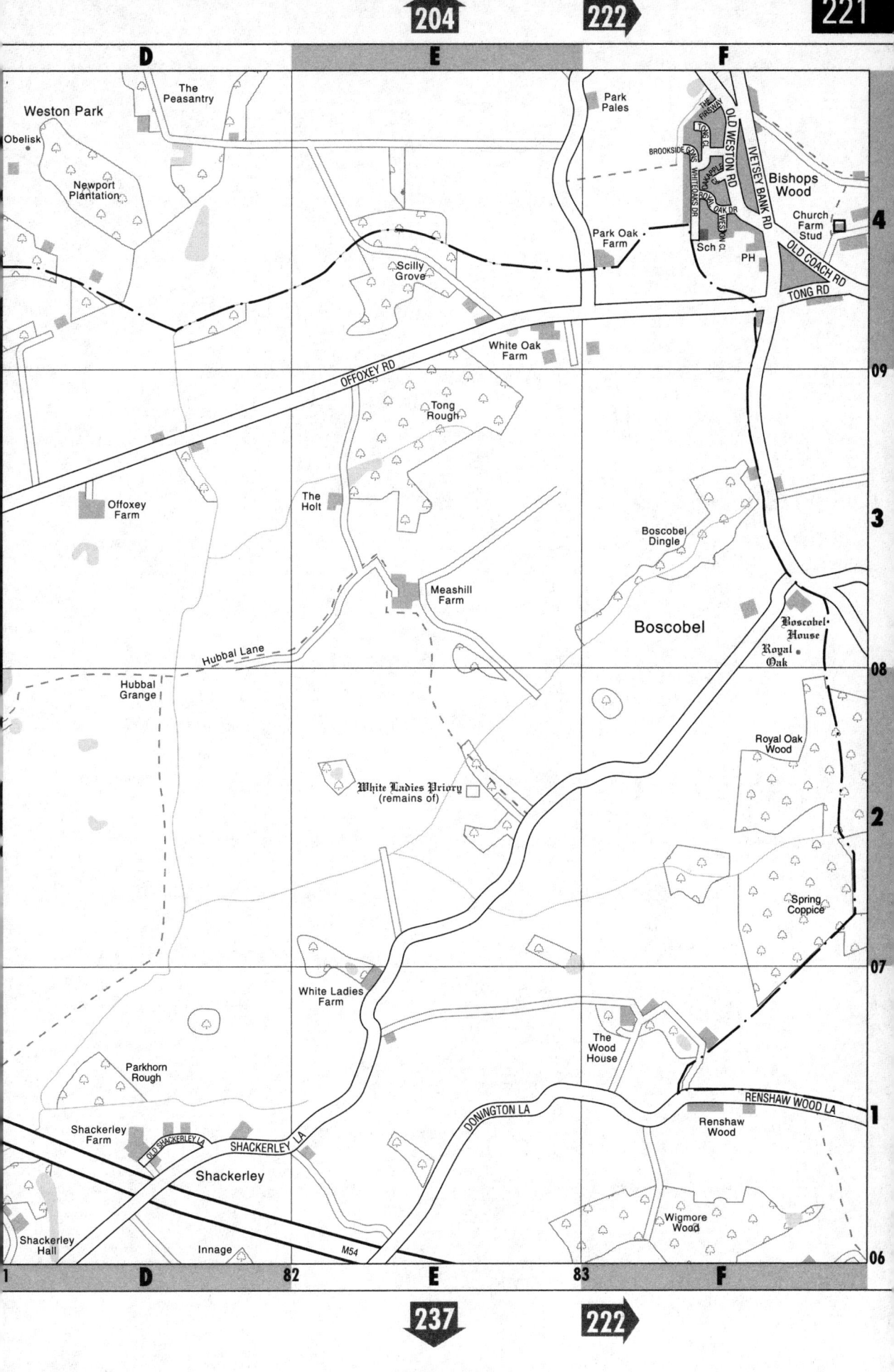

Weston Park

The Peasantry

Obelisk

Newport
Plantation

Park
Pales

THE FIRSWAY
BROOKSIDE GDNS
WHITEOAKS DR
MAPLE CL
TANG CL
OAK DR
WESTON CL
OLD WESTON RD
NETSEY BANK RD

Bishops
Wood

Park Oak
Farm

Sch

PH

Church
Farm
Stud

4

OLD COACH RD

TONG RD

Scilly
Grove

White Oak
Farm

OFFOXEY RD

09

Tong
Rough

Offoxey
Farm

The Holt

Boscobel
Dingle

3

Meashill
Farm

Boscobel

Boscobel
House
Royal
Oak

Hubbal Lane

08

Hubbal
Grange

Royal Oak
Wood

White Ladies Priory
(remains of)

2

Spring
Coppice

07

White Ladies
Farm

The
Wood
House

Parkhorn
Rough

RENSHAW WOOD LA

1

DONINGTON LA

Renshaw
Wood

Shackerley
Farm

OLD SHACKERLEY LA
SHACKERLEY LA

SHACKERLEY LA

Shackerley

Wigmore
Wood

Shackerley
Hall

Innage

M54

06

206
224
239
224

D E F

Broomhall Bridge
Eskew Bridge
SHUTT GREEN LA
Shutt Green
Lea Fields Farm
Staffordshire Way
Cresswell Farmhouse
HORSEBROOK LA
ENGLETON MILL LA
CLAY GATES RD
ENGLETON LA
Somerford Bridge
Brewood Wharf
WEST GATE
CRESSFIELD
Fire Sta
ST MARYS GATE
BLOCKHOUSE PARK
JOHNS GATE
FOUR ASHES RD
Sewage Works
Somerford
Stepping Stone Lane
Sch
SHOP LA
PENDREL PL
DRAYS LA
MICKLE GATE
BISHOPS CT
CHESTER
EAST GATE
DEAN ST FIELD
BOSCOBEL GR
BISHOPS DR
ROWAN GR
PH
Sch
HIGH GREEN
BARGATE ST
THE TORCH
BARGATE
STAFFORD
DEAN
VICARAGE RD
RANSFIELD
CHESHIRE DR
ASH GR
River Penk
KIDDEMORE GREEN RD
Brewood Bridge
Lib y
OAKLEYS
P
OAK RD
Somerford
NEWPORT CROSS
NEWPORT ST
SANDY LA
HALLFARM RD
2 EASTHALL CL
MYRTLE GR
HALLFARM CL
TIMBER GR
School Bridge
SCHOOL RD
CHURCH MARKET
PC
ST CHADS
White House
Hockerhill Farm
DIRTY LA
DEAN ST
THE PAVEMENT
SPARROWS END LA
TINKERS LA
Somerford Hall
Little Hyde Rough
Hill Top
Brewood
Shropshire Union
HYDE MILL LA
Dean's Hall Bridge
Canal
Giffard's Cross Bridge
Brook House
The Woolley
Straasfield House
Hyde Farm
Staffordshire Way
COVEN RD
Avenue Bridge
BREWOOD RD
Giffard's Cross Lodge
Lower Avenue
Pond Bay
Hell Floor
Upper Avenue
Chillington Bridge
Ackbury Heath House
PORT LA
PARK LA
Park Lodge
Dale Flat
Chillington Street
Upper Cottages
Park Bridge
Brewood Park Farm
Staffordshire Way
ROMAN ROAD (course of)

4
09
3
08
2
07
1
06

7 D 88 E 89 F

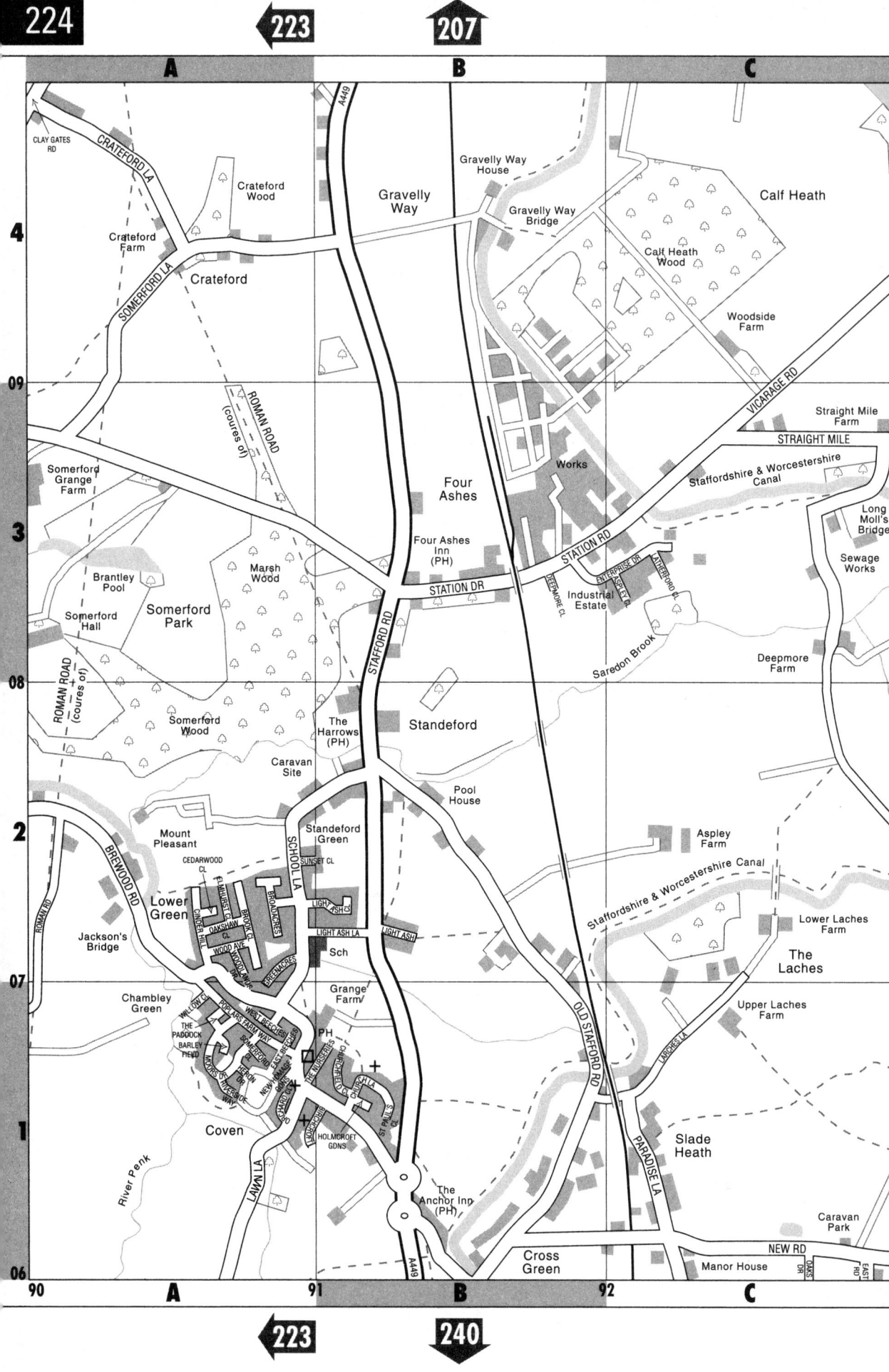

D   E   F

4

09

3

08

2

07

1

06

EASTERN WAY
A460
LICHFIELD RD
HAWK'S GREEN LA
ROCHESTER WAY
TRURO CL
KENSINGTON
HEATH
CANNOCK RD A5190
GORSEMOOR RD
Newlands Lane
CANNOCK RD
B4154
PC
1 HEDNESFORD RD
2 WIMBLEBURY RD
A5190
NORTON RD
WOODFIELD
WOODFIELD HILL
HEDNESFORD RD
NEWLANDS LA
OLD HALL LA
NORTON LA
COAL HAULAGE RD
Newlands Brook
Stoke's Lane
Long Lane
RICHARD
NORTON TERR
BROWNHILLS RD
BROADOAKS
Tip
Leacroft
ORBITAL WAY
Norton Canes
NORTON SPRINGS
HANBURY RD
SPRINGS RD
LEIGHSWOOD
HUSSEY RD
KINGSWOOD
CHAPEL ST
Sch
JEROME RD
Streetway Farm
WASHBROOK LA
BRIDGES RD
BRIDGES CRES
WALLACE
BELLSIZE CL
APEX BSNS PK
1 ROMAN VIEW
2 NUTHURST DR
Sch
POOL VIEW
HUT HILL LA
KINGSWOOD DR
CHURCH VALE
PINFOLD LA
CHURCH RD
CHARTER CL
PENNY CRESS GREEN
NORTON GRANGE
NORTON GREEN LA
WALSALL RD
BETTY'S
CHURCH RD
JACKSON CL
CHURCH RD
BUTTS WAY
BUTTS CL
Watling Street
NORTON LA
ROMAN ROAD
Norton Hall Farm
NORTON HALL LA
BUTTS LA
Works
Norton Green
MANOR AVE
JULIAN CL
TREVOR AVE
LOVE LA
WATLING ST
Swan Farm
ALBUTTS RD
PH
3 SHANKLIN CL
4 ALWYN CL
5 HARTWELL LA
Great Wyrley
Fleur de Lys (PH)
Turf Inn (PH)
A5
FOXLAND AVE
HALL LA
BARN CROFT
ASH LA
APPLEDORE
Liby
JOHNS LA
PARK LA
BROAD MEADOW LA
WALSALL RD
HAZEL LA
Mine (dis)
GAINS LA
Gains Brook
SCHOOL LA
LIME LA
HILTON LA
MOAT
FERN
THE CRESCENT
ESTRIDGE LA
MEADOW GR
WALSALL RD
SAXON CL
SHAW'S LA
BENTON'S LA
JONES LA
GORSEY LA
Gorsey Lane Farm
Tip (dis)
Pelsall Road Bridge
B4154
OAK AVE
ACORN CL
HAWTHORN AVE
WHARWELL LA
Home Farm
WYRLEY LA
Dismantled Railway
Hall Farm
GROVE LA
POPLAR RD
BLUEBELL
FAIR OAKS
A34
JACOB'S HALL LA
Jacob's Hall
PARK LA
Cadman's Lane

227
211

A   B   C

COAL HAULAGE RD
A5190

Cuckoo Bank

CANNOCK RD

No Man's Bank

New Plant Inn (PH)

High St
Chase Terrace
PARK RD
SHAKESPEARE RD
COPPICE
SUNNYMEAD RD
ROBINSON RD
LINDEN AVE
CALVICHDALE
SPENCER DR
EASTGATE ST
CROSS ST
ALDEN HURST
OREGON
DRECHEN GR
REDWOOD DR
COLUMBIAN
Fire Sta
Schs
Libry
SCHOOL LA
IRONSTONE RD
RUGELEY RD
B5011

4

Southacres Farm

Sch
BURNTWOOD RD

Norton East

Sch
School Cl
SCHOOL RD

09

Liby
Recn Gd
RAILWAY ST

Works
JEROME RD
Norton Canes
BELLSIZE CL

Chasetown Ind Est

Chasewater

Chasewater Light Railway

NORTON EAST RD

Sports Stadium

BETTY'S LA
RED LION
Red Lion La
BLENHEIM RD
BRAEMAR RD
CONDUIT RD

ALBUTTS RD

Common Side

Moss Farm
A5

Chasewater

Sailing Club

Sports Ground

Pier

Wyrley and Essington Canal
Anglesey Branch
Anglesey Wharf

Wharf Lane Farm
WHARF LA
Sand Pit

P
PC

Highfields
HIGHFIELDS RD
ANGLESEY

Chasewater Raceway

Anglesey Cres
WYRLEY CL
WHITE HORSE RD
New Town

Mayfields Dr
HEDNESFORD RD
WILKIN RD
Sch

Dismantled Railway

Hotel
A452

Highfield House Farm

WATLING ST ROMAN ROAD

CHESTER RD N

Brownhills Common

Wyrley Common
LIME LA
B4154

Works

THE PARADE

Holland Park

Sch
CHAPEL DR
Sch

TAMWORTH CL
DEAKIN AVE
Sch
OAKENHAYES DR
Dismtd Rly

02   A   03   B   04   C

D
E
F

1 SUNNYMEAD RD
2 SHELLEY RD
3 RYECROFT DR

RAKE HILL
MEG LA
NETHER LA
The Nags Head (PH)

Ryecroft Shopping Centre

BRIDGE CROSS RD
Morley Road Shopping Centre

Coulter Lane Farm

St Matthew's Hospital

St Matthew's Ave

St Matthew's Rd

Glasscroft Cottages

Woodhouses Rd

HIGHFIELD RD

Sch

CANNOCK RD
PC

Gorstey Ley

Church RD

Canterbury Dr

Woodhouses LA
FITCHET'S BANK

09

Burntwood Green

Edial

Sch

1 MOSSBANK AVE
2 FERNDALE CL
Works

LICHFIELD RD
A5190

The Star (PH)

Edial House

3

BURNTWOOD

NORTON LA

Apple Tree Farm

1 ST STEPHEN'S RD
2 STAPLEFORD GDNS
3 BURNTWOOD SHOPPING CENTRE

1 SISKIN CL
2 REDWING CL

Sewage Works

COPPY NOOK LA
Hammerwich Hospital

OVERTON LA

FORGE LA

PINGLE LA

BURNTWOOD RD

08

HIGHFIELDS RD

Overton Farm

Brooklyn Farm

Triangle

Hammerwich Square

Hammerwich

Sun Down

2

WHARF LA

Lamb's Lodge Farm

Brook Farm

MEERASH LA

Meerash Farm

Windmill (dis)

Hammerwich Hall

COPPICE LA

Hammerwich Place Farm

HALL LA

GREEN LA

Sand Pit

STATION RD

Glade Farm

07

Roundhill Farm
ROUNDHILL WAY

Chase Inn (PH)

Crane Brook

ROMAN ROAD

Crane Brook House

LION'S DEN

A5

WATLING ST

New Town

Meadow Farm

B4155

Watling Street

Muckley Corner

A5

1

Wyrley and Essington Canal

Semi-Bungalow Farm

LICHFIELD RD

Wyrley and Essington Canal (dis)

GATEHOUSE TRADING ESTATE

Warrenhouse Farm

Boat Bridge

WALSALL RD

B4155

Boat Inn (PH)
A461
BOAT LA

06

5
D
06
E
07
F
06

A   B   C

THE ROCHE

ABNALLS LA

ST MATTHEW'S RD

Spade Green

Pipe Hall

Jubilee Wood

The Dell

Heart of England Way

A51

WESTERN BY PASS

Wks

P

Golf Course

Pipe Green

The Park

Sch

Maple Hayes

Leamonsley Brook

Sch

CHRIST CHURCH GDNS

4

WOODHOUSES RD

Parker's Plantin

Leamonsley

A51

LEAMONSLEY WICK

LEAMONSLEY WALK

LEAMONSLEY RD

CHRISTCHURCH LA

THE DELL

VICTORIA GDNS

ANCHOR LA

A461

Woodhouses

The Roundabouts

Grange Lane

Sloppy Wood

09

Woodhouses Farm

Edial Farm

Lower Hilltop Farm

Herbert's Spinney

Sandyway

Trunkfields Farm

A5190

Fearn's Farm

LICHFIELD RD

Pipe Grange

Three Tuns (PH)

Sandyway Farm

3

The Meadows

WALSALL RD

Mickle Hills

Sandyway Farm

Broad Lane

Pipe Grange Farm

A5190

Pipehill

Sewage Works

08

Pipehill Wharf (dis)

Pipehill Farm

Fosseway Court

FOSSEWAY LA

LC

Pipe Hill Manor

2

The Lodge

CLAY PIT LA

WALL LA

Aldershawe Hall

Coppice Lane Farm

COPPICE LA

Pipe Place Farm

07

Bridge Farm

Muckley Corner Bridge

Wall Farm

MARKET LA

GREEN LA

Sch

Muckley Corner

Moat Bank House

The Butts

Wall Lane

Wall

Mus

HALL LA

PH

P

THE BUTTS

LETOCETVM ROMAN TOWN

Manor Farm

1

A5

A461

Wall Butts

Wall Lane Farm

Mus

PH

Watling Street ROMAN ROAD

ASHCROFT LA

Ryknild Street ROMAN ROAD (course of)

BOAT LA

CRANEBROOK LA

Hilton House

BULLMOOR LA

The Nurseries

A5

06

08   A   09   B   10   C

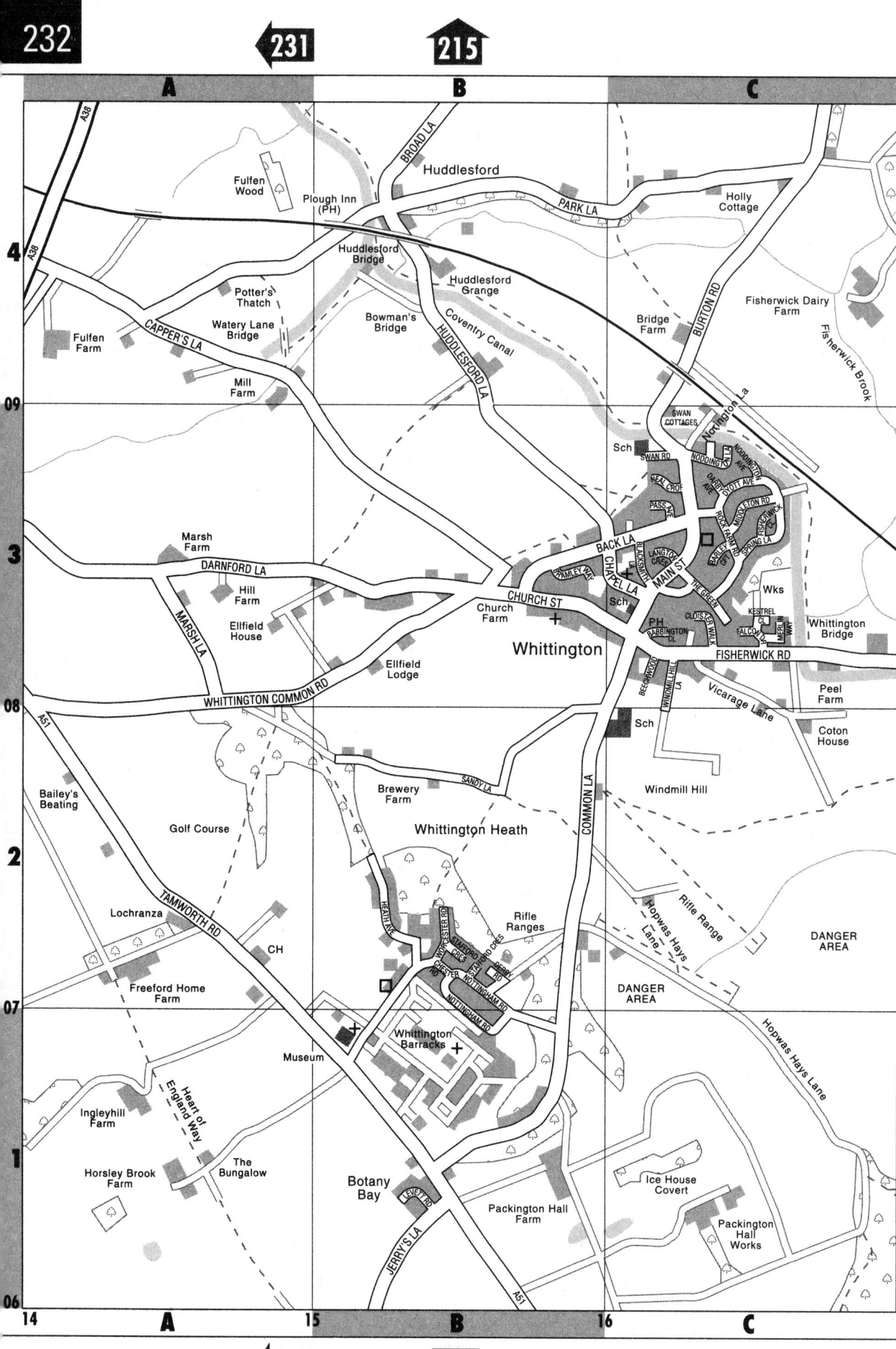

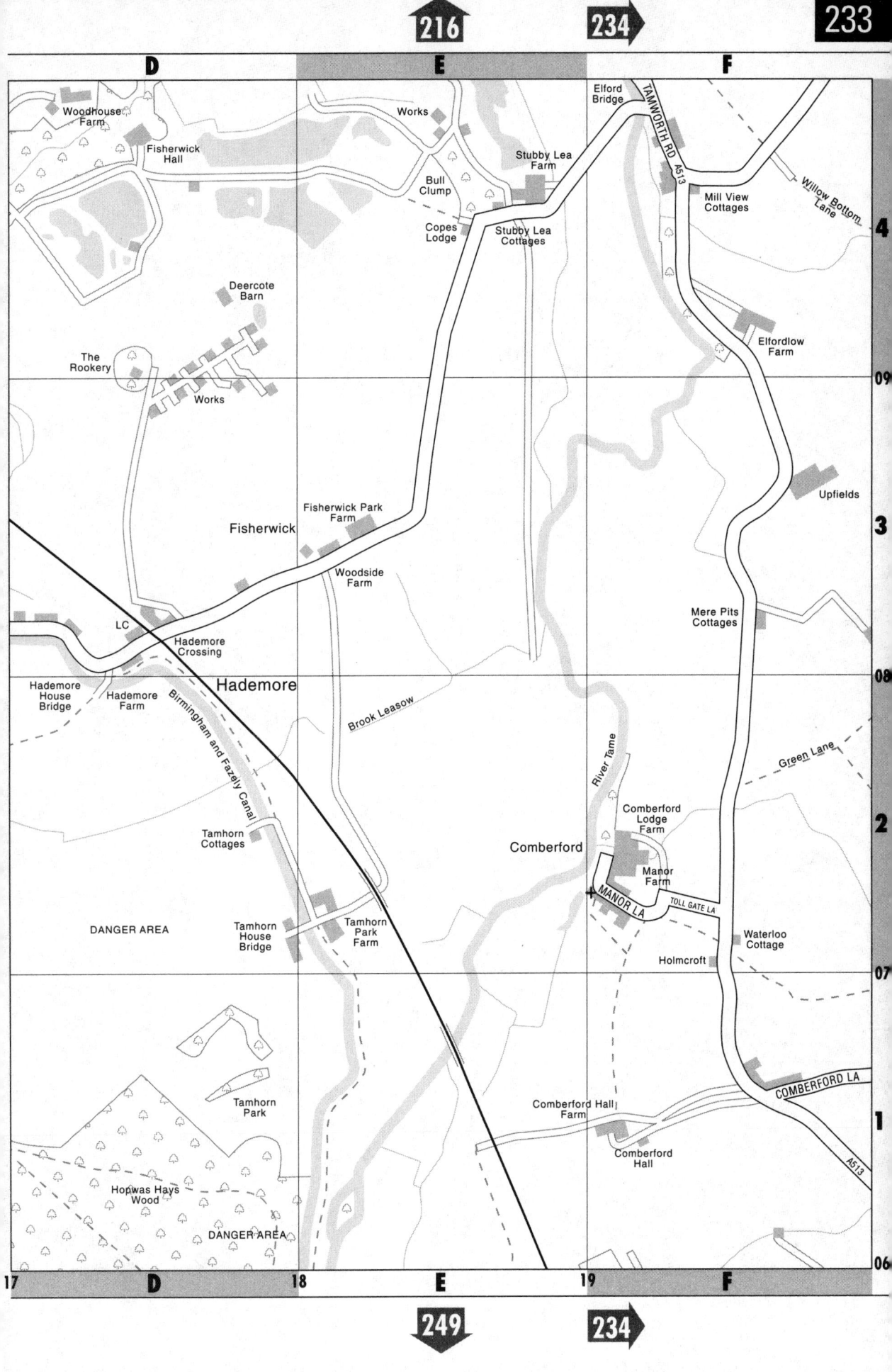

D
E
F

Woodhouse Farm

Fisherwick Hall

Works

Bull Clump

Stubby Lea Farm

Elford Bridge

TAMWORTH RD A513

Mill View Cottages

Willow Bottom Lane

4

Copes Lodge

Stubby Lea Cottages

Deercote Barn

The Rookery

Works

Elfordlow Farm

09

Fisherwick Park Farm

Fisherwick

Upfields

3

Woodside Farm

LC

Hademore Crossing

Mere Pits Cottages

Hademore House Bridge

Hademore Farm

Hademore

Brook Leasow

08

Birmingham and Fazely Canal

River Tame

Green Lane

Tamhorn Cottages

Comberford Lodge Farm

Comberford

2

DANGER AREA

Tamhorn House Bridge

Tamhorn Park Farm

Manor Farm

MANOR LA

TOLL GATE LA

Waterloo Cottage

Holmcroft

07

Tamhorn Park

Comberford Hall Farm

COMBERFORD LA

1

Hopwas Hays Wood

Comberford Hall

A513

DANGER AREA

06

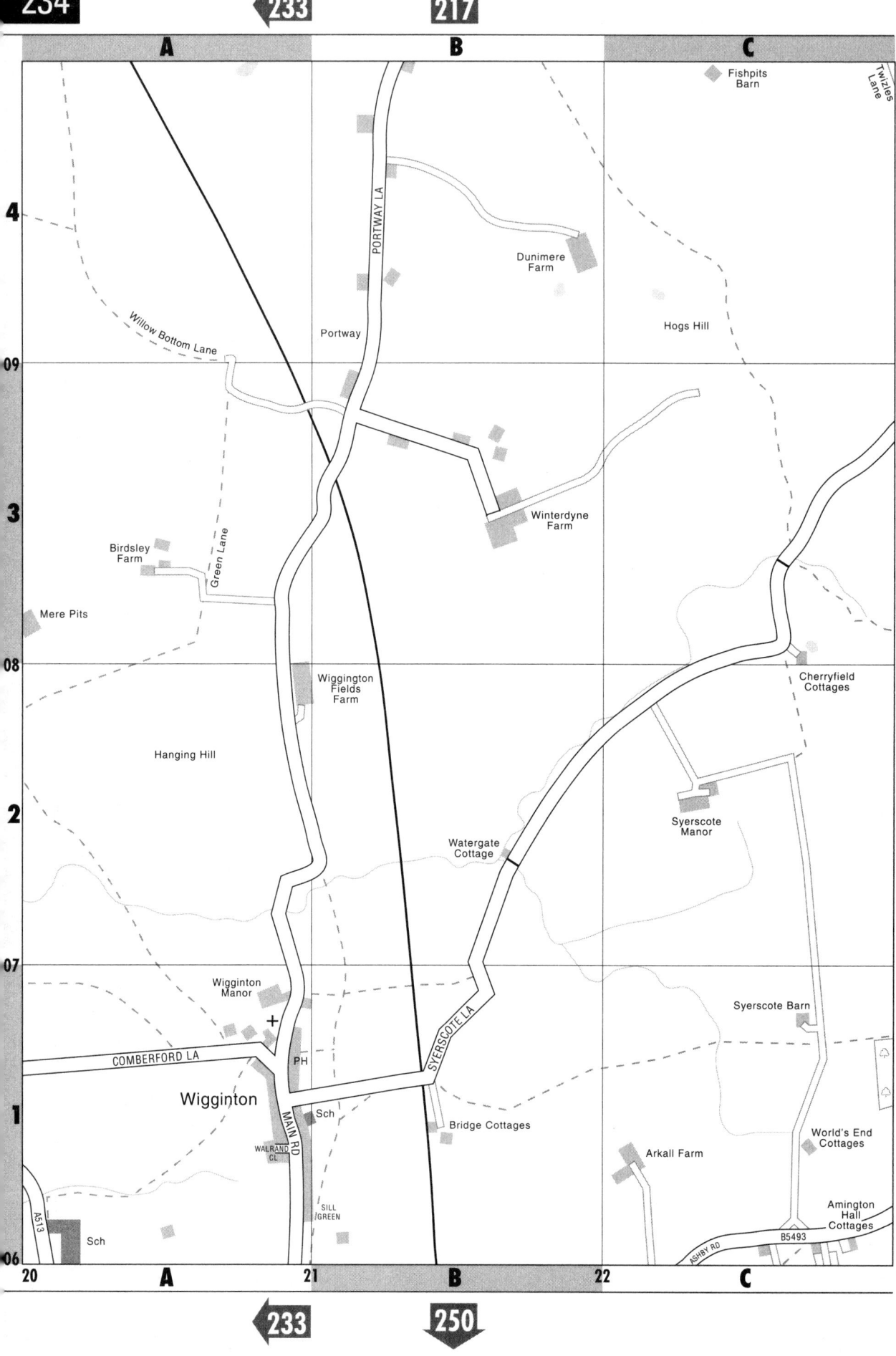

233
217

A
B
C

4

Twizles Lane

Fishpits Barn

PORTWAY LA

Dunimere Farm

Portway

Hogs Hill

09

Willow Bottom Lane

Green Lane

Birdsley Farm

Mere Pits

3

Winterdyne Farm

Cherryfield Cottages

08

Wiggington Fields Farm

Hanging Hill

Syerscote Manor

2

Watergate Cottage

07

Wigginton Manor

Syerscote Barn

+

COMBERFORD LA

SYERSCOTE LA

PH

Wigginton

Sch

World's End Cottages

1

MAIN RD

WALRAND CL

Bridge Cottages

Arkall Farm

SILL GREEN

Amington Hall Cottages

A513

Sch

ASHBY RD

B5493

06

20
A
21
B
22
C

233
250

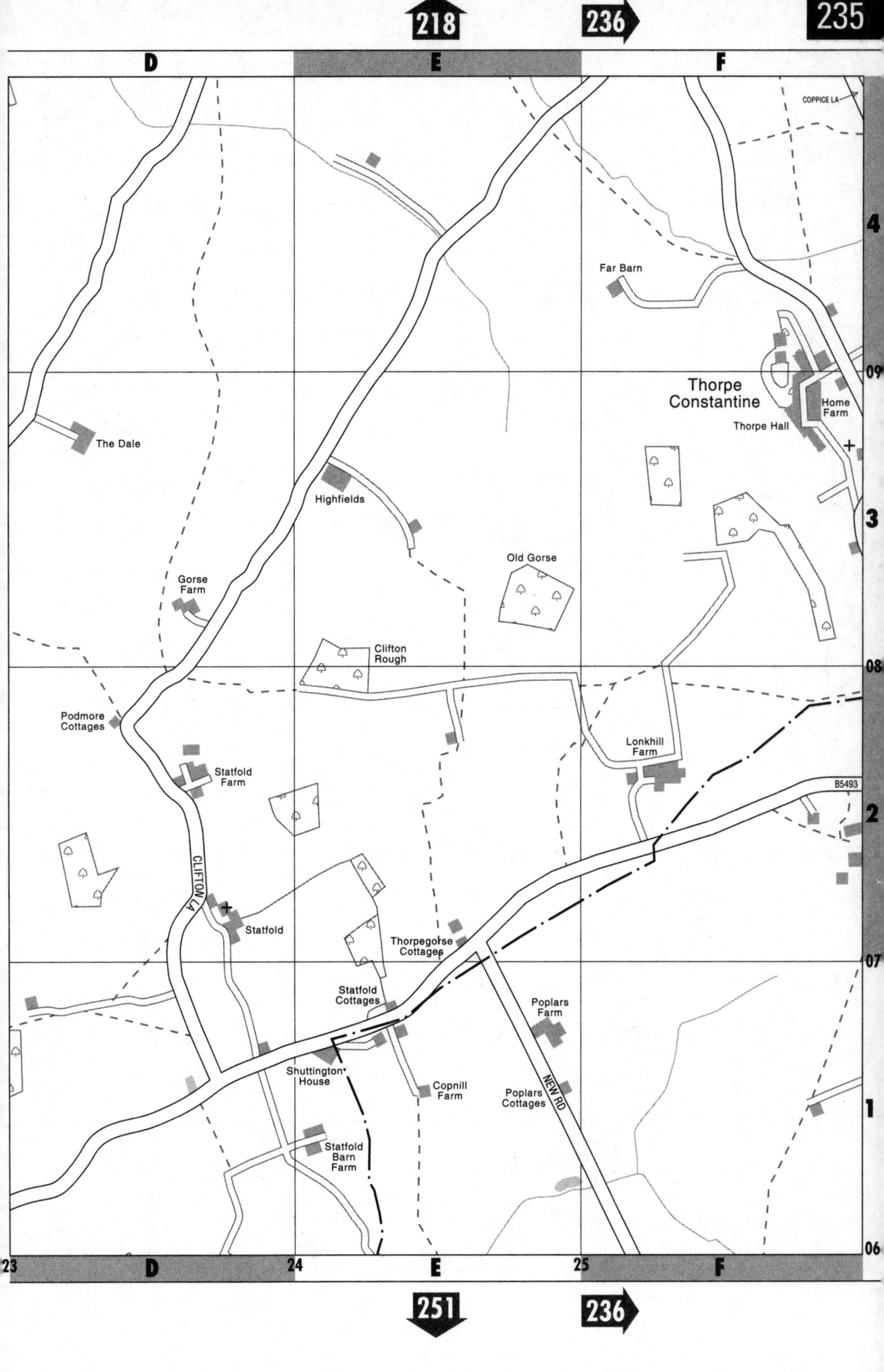

D E F

COPPICE LA

4

Far Barn

09

Thorpe
Constantine

Home
Farm

Thorpe Hall

The Dale

Highfields

3

Old Gorse

Gorse
Farm

Clifton
Rough

08

Podmore
Cottages

Lonkhill
Farm

B5493

Statfold
Farm

2

CLIFTON LA

Statfold

Thorpegorse
Cottages

07

Statfold
Cottages

Poplars
Farm

Shuttington
House

Copnill
Farm

Poplars
Cottages

NEW RD

1

Statfold
Barn
Farm

06

23 D 24 E 25 F

A

B

C

4

Campville
House

Newton
Field

Highfield
Farm

QUARRY BERRY LA
Honeyhill
Farm

Big Meadow
Hovel

09

B5493
ASH LA

AUSTREY LA

No Man's
Heath

Sandy Lane
Barn

SANDY LA

3

Leys Field
Hovel

Sandy Lane
Spinney

Newton Moor
Cottages

The
Grange

KING'S LA

08

Newton
Gorse

2

Newton
Regis

TOWNSEND CL

HAMES LA

Newton
Farm

Newton
Farm

SECKINGTON LA

NEWTON LA

HARRIS GR

PH

Sch

AUSTREY LA

M42

Seckington

OLD HALL FARM

07

MAIN RD

HANGMANS LA

NEWTON LA

1

06

Austrey

M42

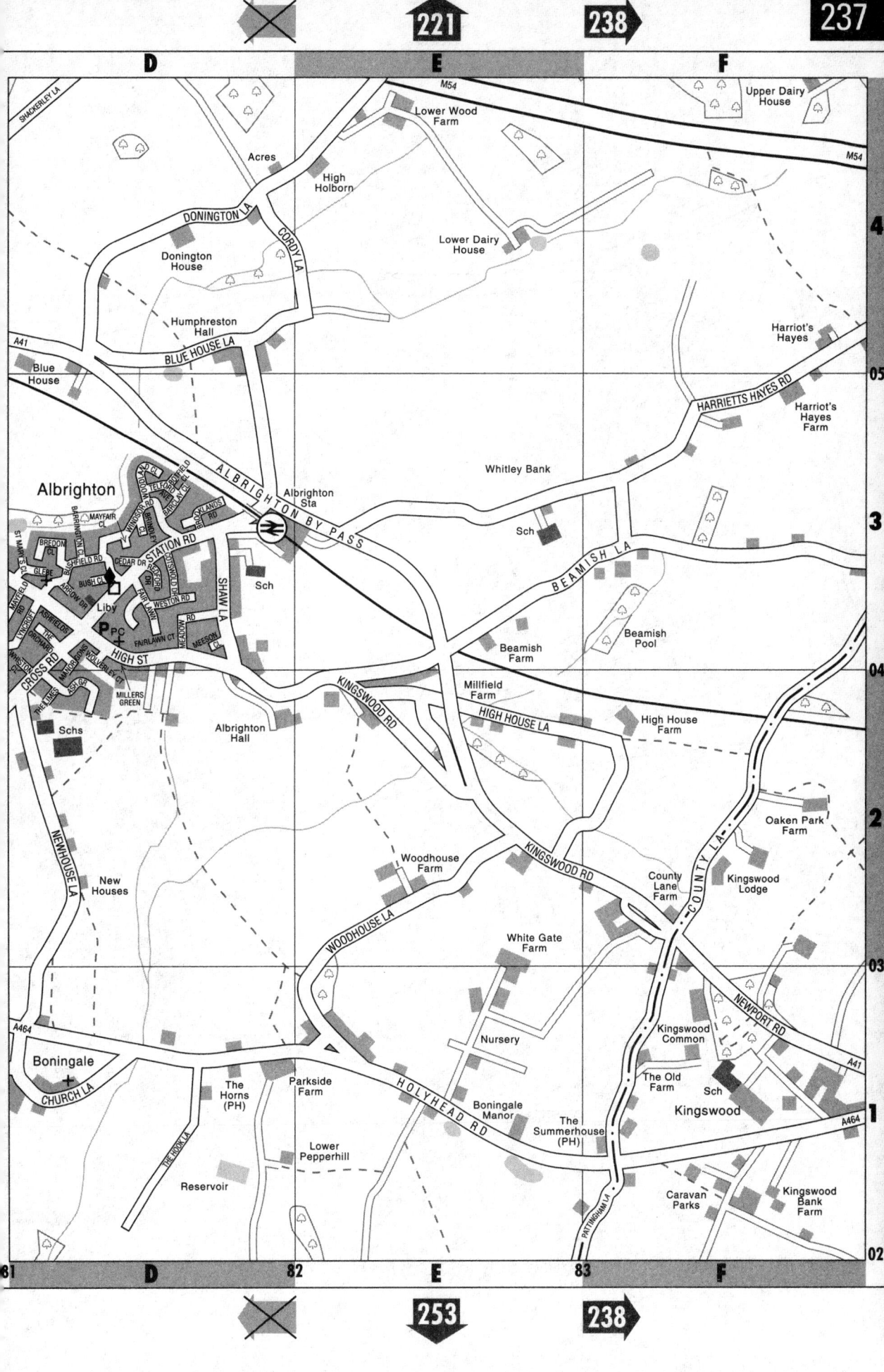

A   B   C

4

Big Wood

M54

The Pool
Payne's Bridge
Gothic Temple
Grecian Temple

The Canal

Old Park Wood

HARRIETS HAYES RD

White House

WHITEHOUSE LA

Leper House

M54

05

Cross Guns (PH)

Codsall Wood

COUNTY LA

Pendrell Hall Coll

Leighton Pool

Moors Farm

Wood Hall Farm

Wheatstone Park

CHILLINGTON LA

Nursery Farm

3

Little Harriot's Hayes Farm

BEAMISH LA

Cemy

Sch

MILL LA
CHURCH HILL

Wheatstone Lodge Farm

HUSPHINS LA

Husphins Farm

SLATE LA

MOATBROOK LA

Codsall

GUNSTONE LA
SANDY LA

04

Husphins Bridge

The Stockings

WOOD RD

Wheeler Cl
Sch
STONELEIGH GDNS

Moor Hall Bridge

MALPASS
BAKERS CL
BAKERS GDNS

STRETTON
WALTON GDNS

CHURCH RD

STONEFIELD DR

BAKERS WAY
The Square
P

MAYBURY
MAYBROOK AVE
WARWICK DR
FLATTING CL

MOUNT CL
BENTLEY DR

STATION RD

WOLVERHAMPTON RD
CODWELL GDNS
ASHFIELD GDNS
ELM TREE DR

2

STRAWMOOR LA

FAIRFIELD DR
SANFORD CRES

WILKES RD
ARPS RD
OVER ROAD
LOVERIDGE CL
STATION CL

RAVENHILL DR

Strawmoor Farm

Springfield House

OAKEN DR

Codsall Station

Liby

Oaken Lawn Farm

OAKEN LA

Staffordshire Way

KINGSLEY GDNS
OAKEN COVERT
OAKEN GR
LONG ACRE
LANSDOWNE AVE

THE DRIVE

CHAPEL LA

WINDSOR
HISTONS HILL

Oaken Lawn

03

Riding School

Kingswood Common

The Terrace

PINE WLK
CHESTNUT CL
POPLARS CL

QUEENS GDNS

WAYSIDE ACRES

Oaken

HOLLYBUSH LA

OAKEN LANES

HISTONS HILL

1

NEWPORT RD
A41
A464

The Foaming Jug (PH)

Garage

HOLYHEAD RD

MIDDLE LA

MANOR FOLD

SHOP LA

STAFFORD LA

MEADOW WLK
HAWTHORNE LA
BEECH GDNS

SUCKLING GREEN LA

HEATH HOUSE LA

WERGS HALL RD

Greenhills

Garden Centre

Lodge

Golf Course

A41

Greenhills Farm

02

84   A   85   B   86   C

D E F

4

The Old
Hattons

Hunting Bridge

Lower
Hattons
Bridge

05

Ash
Coppice

ROMAN ROAD (course of)

The Middle
Hattons

Ring Hill
Covert

The Upper
Hattons

River Penk

LAWN LA

M54

3

PENDEFORD HALL LA

Upper Hattons
Bridge

Gunstone

PORT LA

Long Birch
Farm

Staffordshire
Way

Gunstone Farm

WHITEHOUSE LA

Gunstone
Hall

WATERY LA

MIDDLE LA

04

Moat Brook

Shropshire Union Canal

Caravan
Park

CHILLINGTON DR

SANDY LA

ELLIOTTS LA

Sch

BILBROOK RD

MANOR HOUSE LA

Bilbrook

Sewage
Works

Pendeford
Bridge

WOBASTON RD

Upper
Pendeford
Farm

Pendeford
Business
Park

2

Sch

JOEYS LA

MILL GR

Works

HOMEFIELD RD

PENDEFORD MILL LA

Lane
Green

Balliol
Business
Park

PRINCETON GDNS 1
QUADRILLE LAWNS 2
SOLENT CL 3
EXBURY CL 4
HAYWAIN CL 5

WOLVERHAMPTON RD

Sch

DUCK LA

LANE GREEN
SHOPPING
PARADE

P

BILBROOK
CT

FLORENCE RD

ALEXANDER RD

CLIFTON
GDNS

DOWNIE

BARNHURST LA

03

THE DROVEWAY

Turnover
Bridge

Pendeford

Sta

Bilbrook
Station

LANE GREEN RD

BIRCHES RD

Lane Green
Farm

Bilbrook
Bridge

River Penk

MARKHAM CROFT 1
ASHWELLS GR 2
ALVERSTOKE CL 3

KEEPERS LA

PRINCES DR
PRINCES GDNS

SUCKLING GREEN LA

Oaken Park

MADERA AVE

Sch

EASTWARD GLEN

LANE GREEN AVE

CODSALL RD

Sch

1

Bedford Gorse

THE HAYMARKET

FULLERTON
CL

02

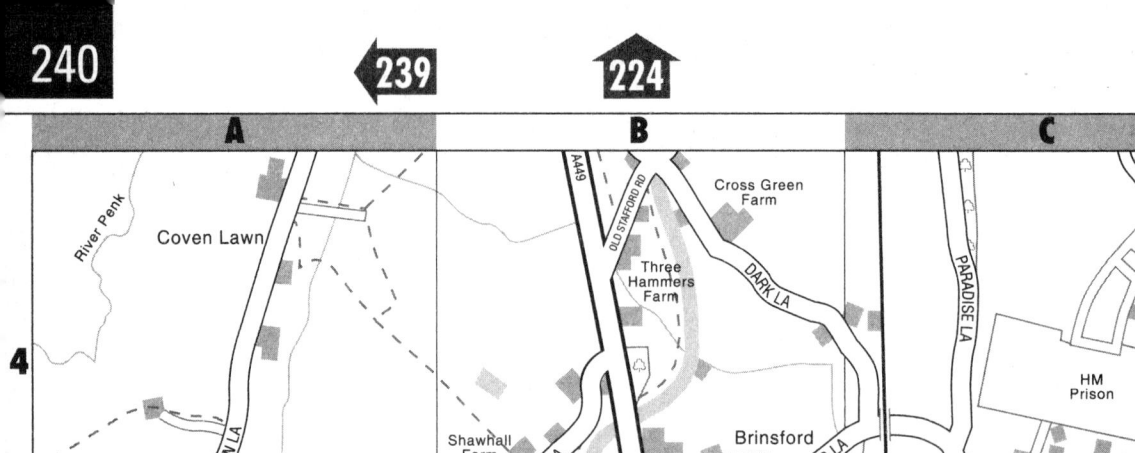

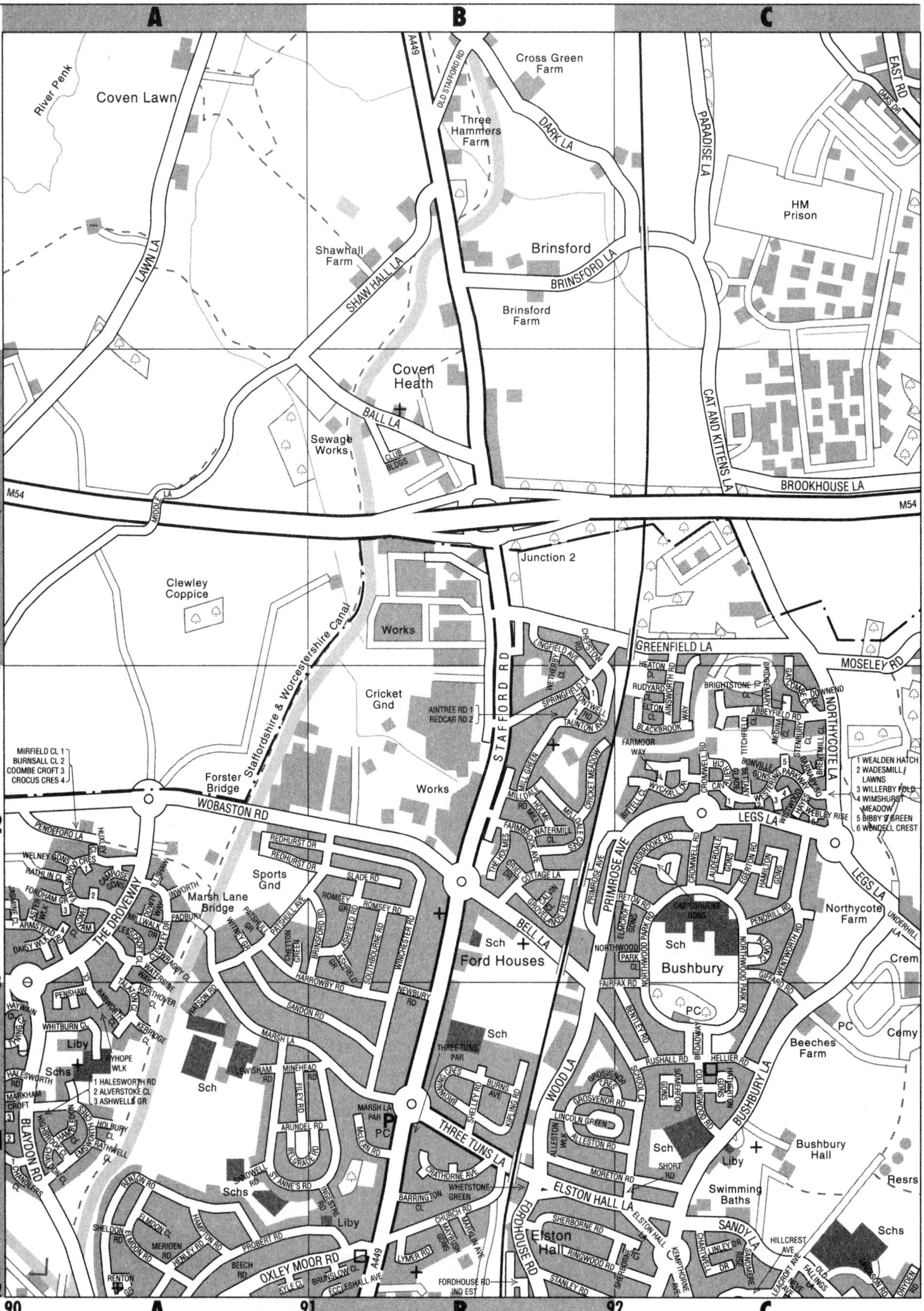

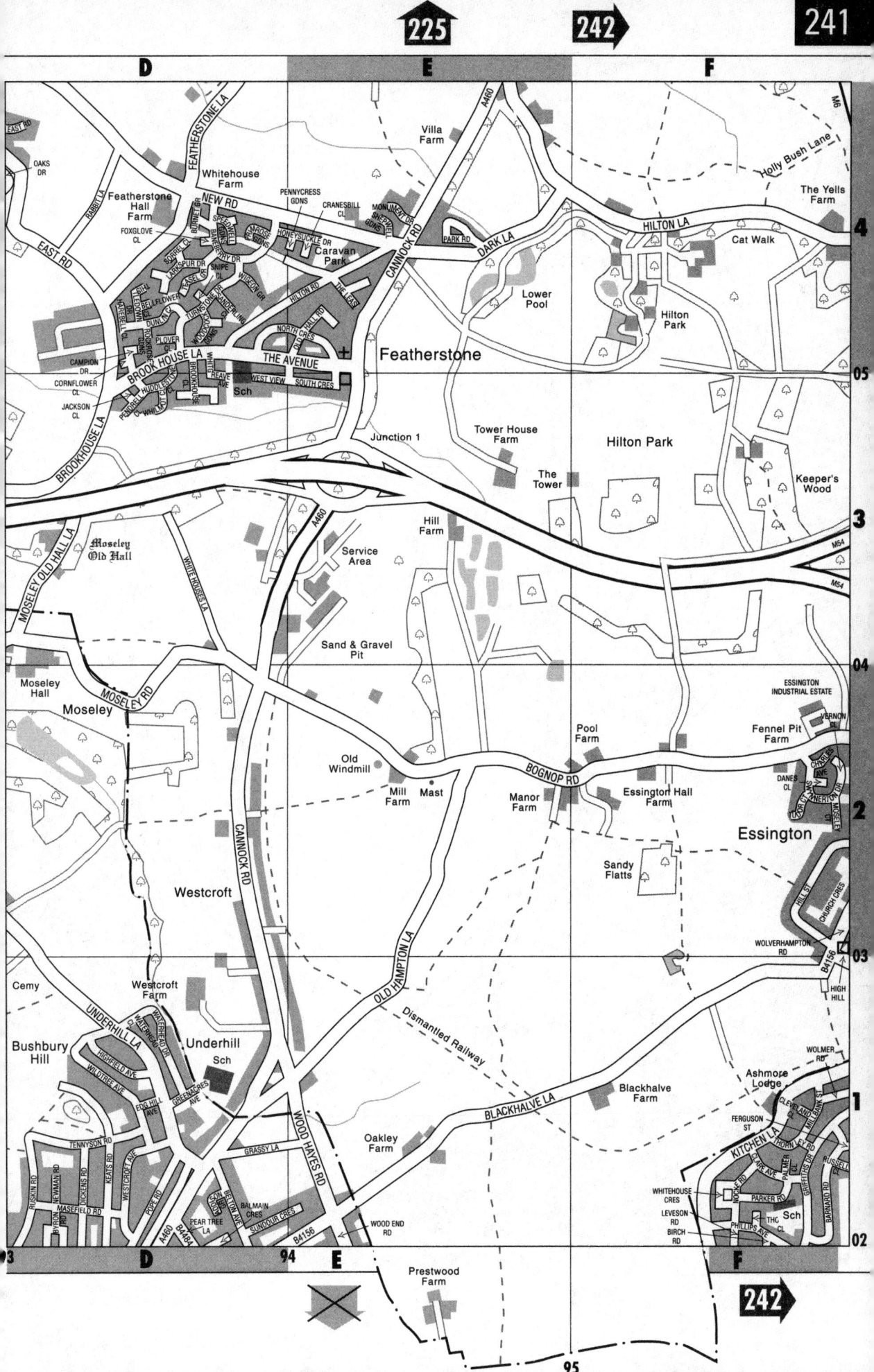

M6

A462

Works

Warstone

SOMERFORD CL

UPPER LANDYWOOD LA

WESTON DR

DUNSTON CL

PENDREL CL

ENTERPRISE PARK

GORSEY LA

TOWER VIEW RD

STREETS LA

HOLLY LA

Sch

4

Sewage Wks

MILTON LA

OLD WARSTONE LA

WARSTONE RD

HOLLY HILL

HOLLY LA

Upper Landywood

LILAC LA 1
PENNY CT 2

Clay Pit

Hilton Park Service Areas

OLD LANDYWOOD LA

STRAWBERRY LA

NEW LANDYWOOD LA

05

The Ride

Burns Wood

Holly Bank Farm

The White House

Long Lane Bridge

LONG LA

B4210

Wyrley and Essington Canal (disused)

3

M54

B4156

Chapel Farm

Springhill

PH

Springhill Covert

M54

04

School Farm

Sch

HOBNOCK RD

Junction 10a

BURSNIPS RD

BROAD LA

Wood Farm Golf Range

BOGNOP RD

FORREST AVE

KINGSWAY

BIRCHWOOD CL

PH

COXMOOR CL 1
TREVOSE CL 2
COALMEADOW CL 3
ROMSEY WAY 4
BOLTON WAY 5
FURNESS CL 6
TURNBERRY RD 7
FOUNTAINS WAY 8
PERSHORE WAY 9
EASBY WAY 10
MARGAM WAY 11
MARGAM TERR 12
GLASTONBURY WAY 13
SNEYD HALL RD 14

P

2

WOLVERHAMPTON RD

BROWNSHORE LA

ST JOHNS RD

MITRE CL

WILLOW GR

GORSEMOOR WAY

Bloxwich North Sta

PERSHORE RD

CRESWELL CRES

B4210

NEW ST

BUTTERMERE DR

THIRLMERE DR

HIGH HILL

P

03

Holly Bank House

Red Lane

Sneyd Farm

Sch

TEWKESBURY RD

FOUNTAINS RD

WAVERLEY RD

TINTERN CRES

KIRKSTALL

UPPER SNEYD RD

WITHYWOOD CL 1
BROCKERIDGE CL 2
FALCONDALE RD 3
CRANLEIGH CL 4
DORCHESTER RD 5
DORCHESTER CL 6
FAIRLAWN WAY 7
BROOKHILLWAY 8
GRIFFITHS RD 9

KITCHEN LA

DRUMMOND CL

Ashmore Park

HEANTON RD

COPPICE FARM WAY

ESSINGTON RD A462

GRANTOCAS

SNEYD LA

Farbrook Farm

VERNON WAY

Sch

NETLEY RD

NEATH WAY

ROCHE RD

LICHFIELD RD

MULBERRY PL

1

WOLMER

Sch

PERKS RD

GRIFFITHS DR

RUSSELL CL

GAIRLOCH RD

ASTORIA

ASTORIA CL

WYCHWOLD WAY

Sch

Sneyd Resr

CRAB LA

M6

LYNWOOD CL

A4124

CHEPSTOW WAY

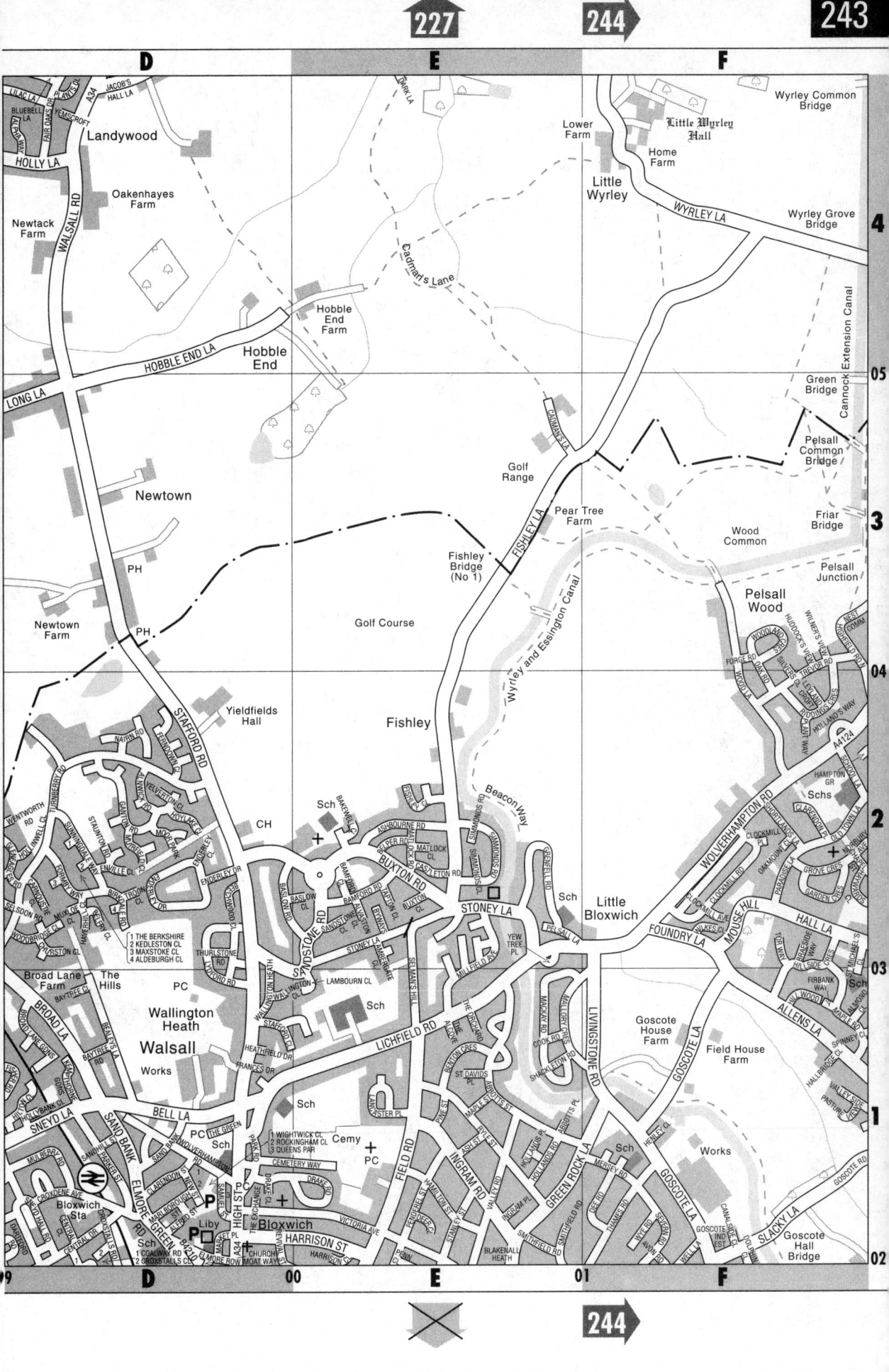

D E F

4

Landywood

HOLLY LA

Newtack Farm

LILAC LA
BLUEBELL LA
FAIR OAK LA

Oakenhayes Farm

WALSALL RD

Hobble End Farm

LONG LA

HOBBLE END LA

Hobble End

05

Cadman's Lane

Little Wyrley Hall

Lower Farm

Home Farm

Little Wyrley

WYRLEY LA

Wyrley Common Bridge

Wyrley Grove Bridge

Cannock Extension Canal

Green Bridge

Pelsall Common Bridge

Friar Bridge

3

Newtown

PH

Golf Range

FISHLEY LA

CADMAN'S LA

Pear Tree Farm

Wood Common

Pelsall Junction

Pelsall Wood

Fishley Bridge (No 1)

Golf Course

Wyrley and Essington Canal

Newtown Farm

PH

04

STAFFORD RD

Yieldfields Hall

Fishley

Beacon Way

WOLVERHAMPTON RD

Schs

HAMPTON GR

A4124

2

Sch

CH

BAKENELL

Buxton Rd

Stoney La

Little Bloxwich

HALL HILL

MOUSE HILL

FOUNDRY LA

ALLENS LA

Sch

03

Broad Lane Farm

The Hills

Wallington Heath

Walsall

Works

PC

1 THE BERKSHIRE
2 KEDLESTON CL
3 MAXSTOKE CL
4 ALDEBURGH CL

Sch

LICHFIELD RD

Lambourn Cl

Yew Tree Pl

PELSALL LA

Sch

LIVINGSTONE RD

Goscote House Farm

GOSCOTE LA

Field House Farm

Sch

BROAD LA

SNEYD LA

BELL LA

SAND BANK

ELMORE GREEN RD

The Green

PC

Sch

Cemy

Sch

1 WIGHTWICK CL
2 ROCKINGHAM CL
3 QUEENS PAR

PC

FIELD RD

INGRAM RD

GREEN ROCK LA

Sch

Works

1

Bloxwich Sta

P

P

Liby

Bloxwich

HARRISON ST

GOSCOTE LA

SLACKY LA

Goscote Hall Bridge

Sch

1 COALWAY RD
2 CROXSTALLS CL

02

9 D 00 E 01 F

244

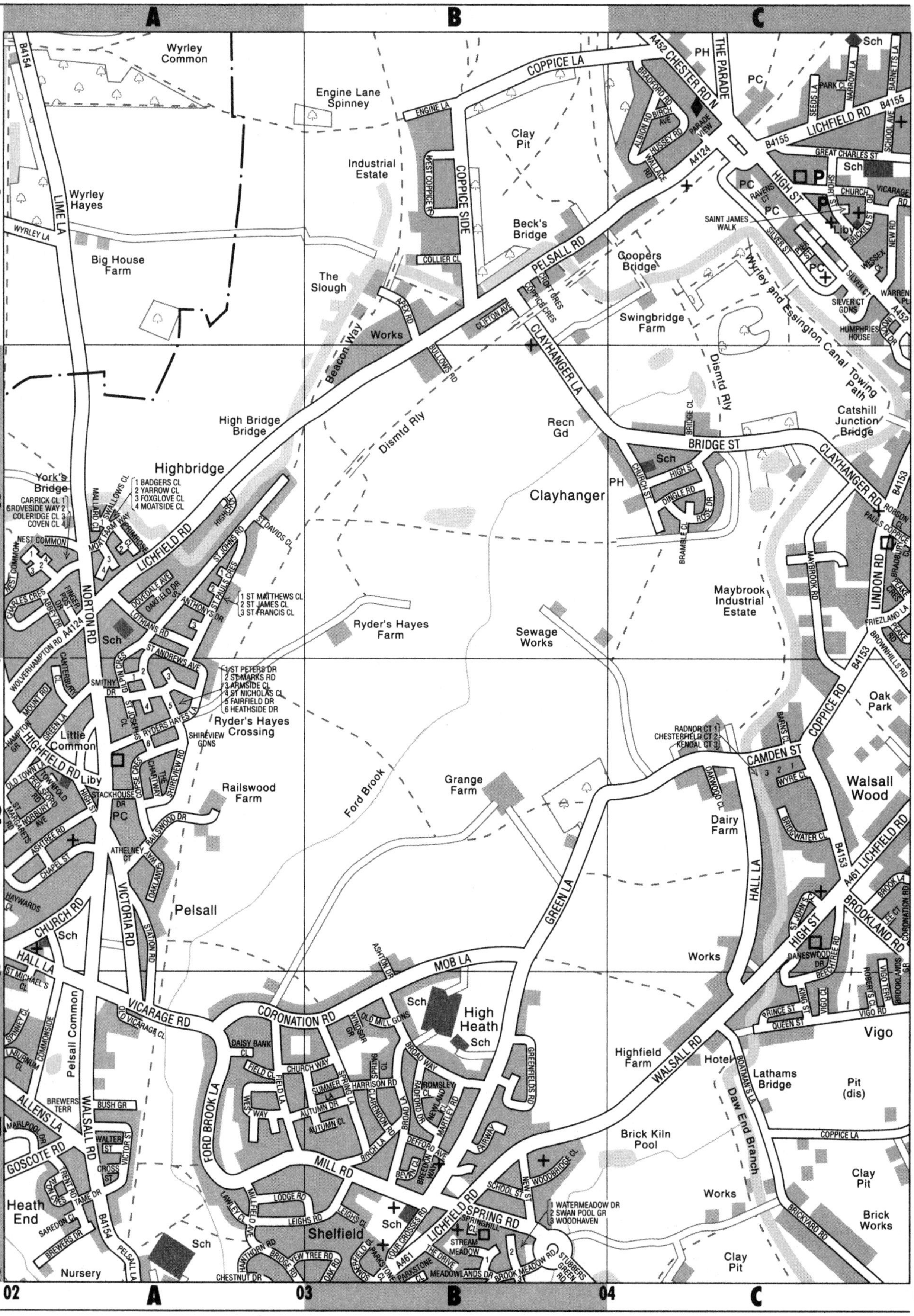

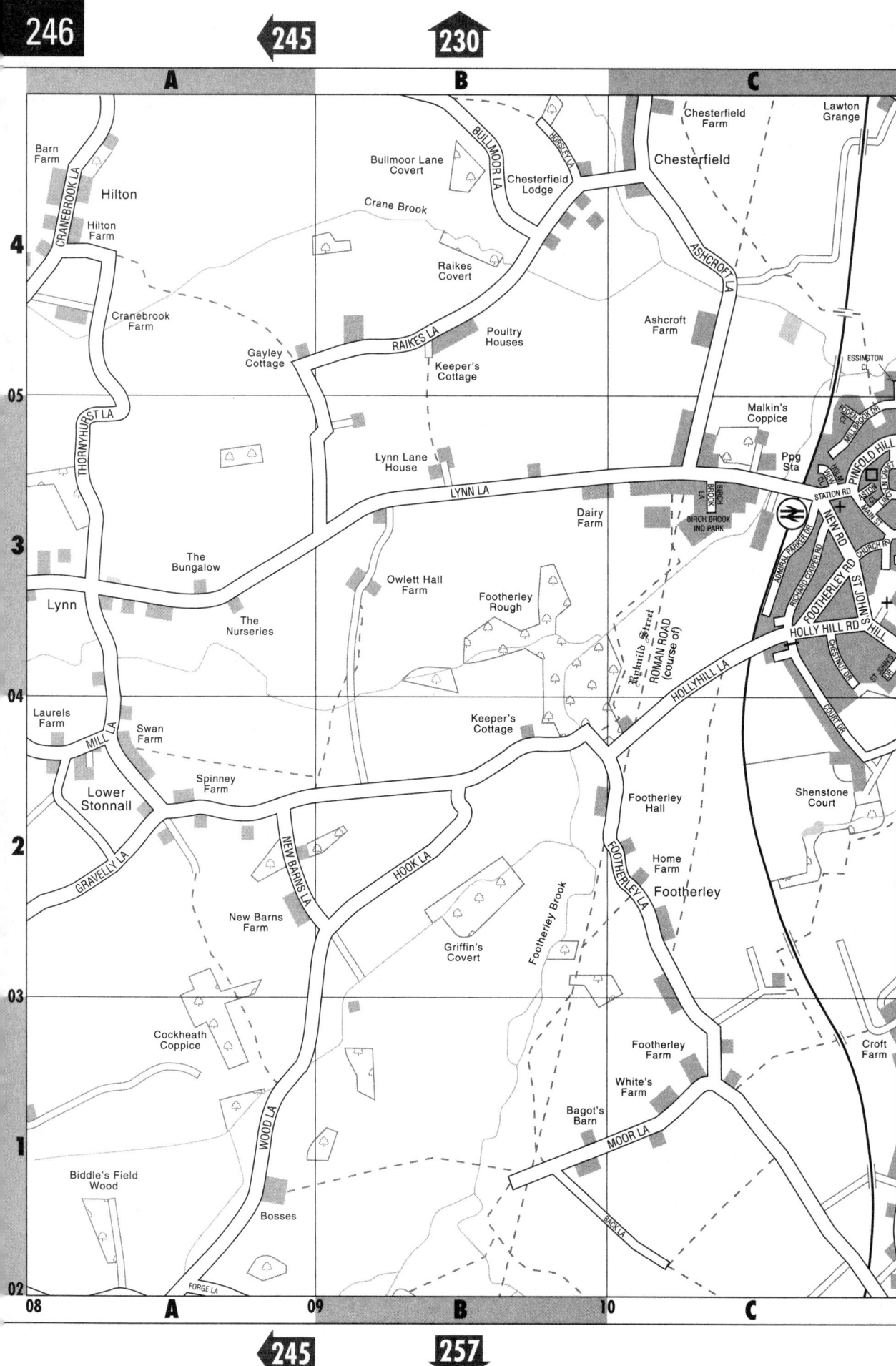

D E F

4

05

3

04

2

03

1

02

A5
A5148
A5127

Nurseries

The Castle

STREETWAY RD

Pinglefield Cottages

Swinfen Lane

Watling Street
ROMAN ROAD

A38

Home Farm

Hotel

Swinfen Hall

The Belt

Keepers

Mascotte Covert

Tamworth Lane

Round Wood

Streetway House

MILL LA

PINFOLD HILL

Shenstone Hall

Bull's Head (PH)

Broad Heath

Shenstone

Liby

Sch

MAIN ST
CHURCHILL RD

ST JOHN'S HILL
ST JOHN'S DR

BIRMINGHAM RD

COURT DR

Sewage Works

Broad Heath Woods

Brick Kiln Covert

HUNGRY LA

A5

04

Thickbroom Barn

Weeford Lodge

Shenstone Court Park

PARK LA

Black Brook

Shenstone Park

Privet Covert

Thickbroom Farm

Blackbrook Farm

The Mount

LITTLE HAY LA

Home Farm

The Grove

Old Plantation

LONDON RD

Sand and Gravel Pit

Oakwood

Sch

Coach and Horses Plantation

Lodge Farm

Holly Bush (PH)

Littlehay Brook

Cottage Farm

Manley Croft

Sand and Gravel Pit

Shenstone Woodend

Little Hay Farm

Little Hay

GREEN BARNS LA

Green Barn

Manley Wood

Moneymore

Wood End Farm

A5127

Windmill (dis)

A38

1 D 12 E 13 F

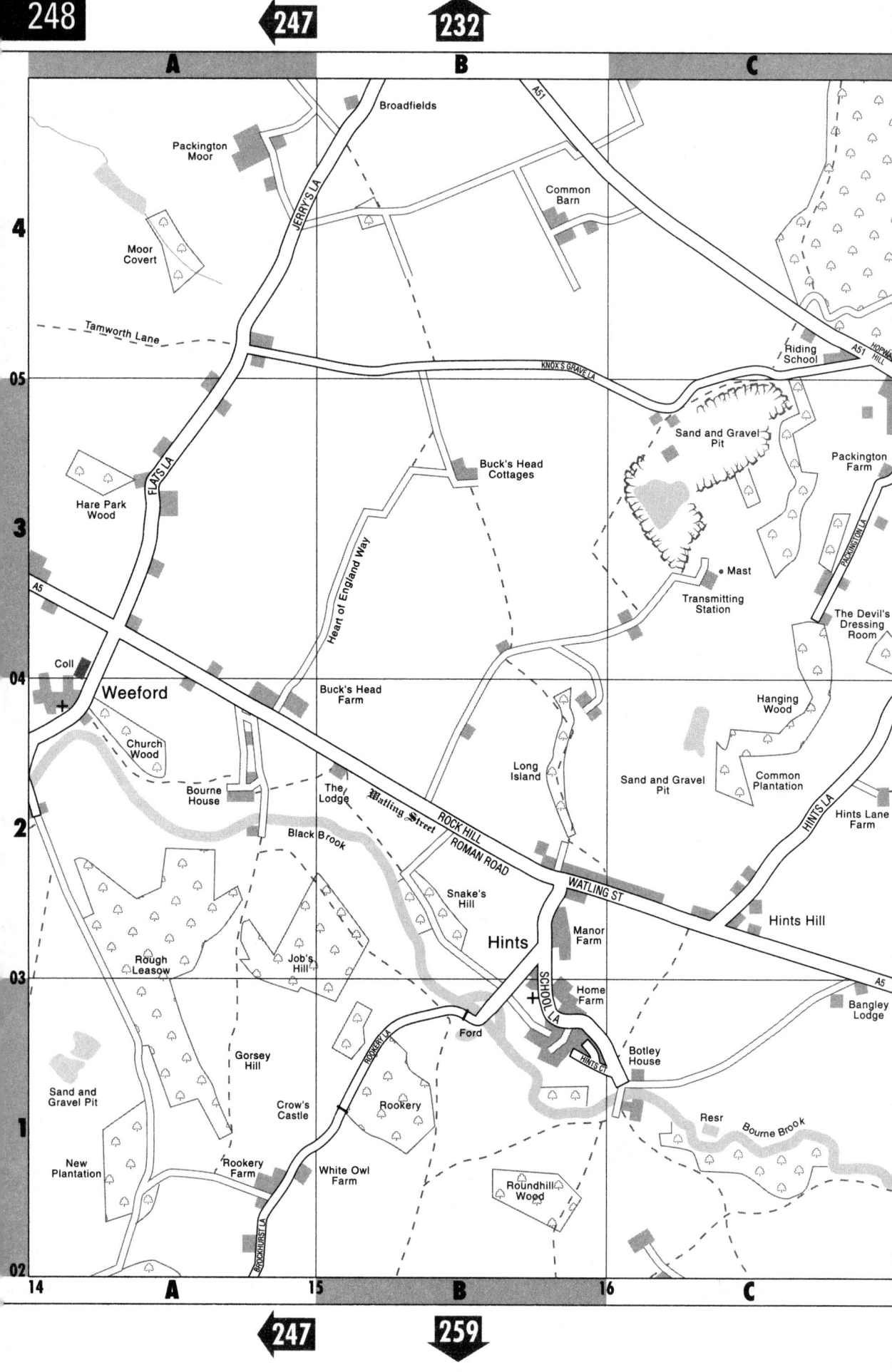

247
232

A   B   C

Broadfields

Packington
Moor

A51

Common
Barn

4

Moor
Covert

JERRY'S LA

Tamworth Lane

Riding
School

HOPWAS HILL

KNOX'S GRAVE LA

A51

05

Sand and Gravel
Pit

Packington
Farm

Buck's Head
Cottages

FLATS LA

Hare Park
Wood

Mast

PACKINGTON LA

The Devil's
Dressing
Room

3

Heart of England Way

A5

Transmitting
Station

Hanging
Wood

Coll

04

Buck's Head
Farm

Common
Plantation

Weeford

+

Sand and Gravel
Pit

Church
Wood

HINTS LA

Long
Island

Hints Lane
Farm

Bourne
House

The
Lodge

Watling Street

ROCK HILL

ROMAN ROAD

WATLING ST

2

Black Brook

Snake's
Hill

Hints Hill

Rough
Leasow

Job's
Hill

Manor
Farm

Hints

A5

03

SCHOOL LA

Home
Farm

+

Bangley
Lodge

Gorsey
Hill

ROOKERY LA

Ford

HINTS CT

Botley
House

Sand and
Gravel Pit

Crow's
Castle

Rookery

Resr

Bourne Brook

1

New
Plantation

Rookery
Farm

White Owl
Farm

Roundhill
Wood

RAVENSHURST LA

02

14   A   15   B   16   C

247
259

D E F

Hopwas Hays Wood

The Woodhouse

Hopwas

Resr

HOPWAS HILL

B5404

Chequers (PH)

Sch

DAINTRY DR

LICHFIELD RD

Coton House Farm

Fox Inn (PH)

Coton

Nursery

NURSERY LA

Ball's Bridge

Hopwas House Farm

HINTS LA

HINTS RD

A51

Birmingham & Fazeley Canal

River Tame

Coton Hall Farm

GAWSWORTH

HELMINGHAM

OSBORNE

CHARTWELL

KENTWELL

CHATSWORTH

UNDERHAVEN

CHURCHILL

GOODALL HILL

LITTLECOTE

BUCKINGHAM

CHALFIELD

BROWNSHOLME

BRAHAM

NEWSTEAD

MELFORD

NORRIS LA

RUFFORD

THORESBY

WYNYATES

WATT LA

LONGLEAT

GERARD

KEPLER

KARAME

CAVENDISH

LARGANGE

MARINER

LANDSEER

MEANDER

Coton Farm

Coton Green

Sewage Works

PEGASUS WLK 1
OAK TREE WLK 2
SHIRLEY WLK 3
COTON GREEN 4
PRECINCT

COTON LA

BROWNING CL

Sch

HANOVER CT

ROBINSON CL

KIPLING RISE

KEATES CL

CARIBER

WILLOUGHBY

ELM TREE WLK

SEMITAR CL

LONGFELLOW

WITNEY

BLOOMFIELD WAY

CHELSEA

LIBRA

ALVIS

FONTENAY RD

ROMAN WAY

COMPTON RD

ATHELSTAN CL

LANCHESTER CL

BOGAN

RANGERS RD

ROBERT CL

PRIORY

1 SHELLEY RD
2 CLIFTON AVE

Wiggington Lodge

Leyfields

Wiggington Park

TA Centre

WAYNFLEET

Industrial Estate

Paper Mills

LICHFIELD RD

ARMSTRONG

APOLLO

LOVELL

BORMAN

CARAVEL

BRADFORD ST

SHAWMOTE

MEADOW PARK

A51

Broad Meadow

Flood Relief Channel

Windmill Farm

Coton Green

LOMOND CL 1
PORTLAND AVE 2

CLAREMONT RD

HAYWORTH CL

BROWNING CL

LICHFIELD ST

A5

PLANTATION LA

Bodnets Farm

The Bodnets

Bodnets Farm

Kendall's Wood

Pipes Wood

Dunstall Farm

Dunstall Bridge

Dunstall Farm Bridge

DUNSTALL LA

Bonehill Farm

BONEHILL RD

BONEHILL RD

A453

Bangley Farm

Mile Oak Farm

Road under Construction

Mile Oak Cross Roads

PH

SUTTON RD

A453

GEORGE AVE

THE ISLAND

FRENCH AVE

ALLTON AVE

ORCHARD

FIRST

CORONATION

Sch

Mile Oak

Watling Street

ROMAN ROAD

B5404

ADDERLEY AVE

PRICE AVE

MANOR RD

BROOKSIDE RD

LONGWOOD PATH

WATLING ST

THE GREEN

Bonehill

STUD FARM COTTS

ALDIN CL

WEST LA

MANOR PARK

BREWSTER CL

DEER PARK RD

REINDEER RD

BOURNE AVE

RANDER RD

SAMBAR RD

REINDEER RD 1
DRAYTON MANOR RD 2

QUARRY DR

LICHFIELD ST

A5

Bourne Brook

4

05

3

04

2

03

1

02

D E F

4

Decoy Barn

Amington Hall

Cow Barn

The Decoy

NEW RD

PEAR TREE CL

MILNER DR

Wolferstan Arms (PH)

Shuttington

CORONATION CTGES

CHURCH LA

SCHOOL LA

Sch

Church Farm

Amington Old Hall

05

Shuttington Bridge

The Pretty Pigs (PH)

SHUTTINGTON RD

Alvecote

ALVECOTE COTTS

MOOR LA

3

LUDGATE CL

TAMWORTH RD (AMINGTON)

BY PASS RD

RISE LA

HODGE LA

Coventry Canal

River Anker

Askew Bridge

REPINGTON RD

ROUND

LEVETT RD

GREENGORE

CHANDLERS DR

Sch

TAMWORTH RD (AMINGTON)

Cemy

MERCIAN WAY

Hodge Lane

TREFOIL

TILIA

WOODS RISE LA

CRESTWOOD

SORREL

LINDERA

Alvecote Priory

04

RIDGEMOUND RISE

ROSEMARY

INGRAM ST

JASMINE RD

HIGHFIELD AVE

HARBELL

SPRUCE

Sch

SPURR

MADRONA

JUNIPER

Amington

BLENCATHRA

YTHAM

TURNBERRY

MOT LAKE

CARNOUSTIE

1 SUNNINGDALE
2 MUIRFIELD

MAGNOLIA

WOODLAND RD

KERRIA CENTRE

NEMESIA

SAFFRON

ST ANDREWS

TROON

CH

ROBEY'S LA

Alvecote Wood

2

FOXGLOVE

GREENHART

P

KERRIA

PEBBLE CL

EAGLE DR

Golf Course

Priory Farm

CLEMATIS

P

MERCIAN WAY

SANDY WAY

Lodge Farm

Works

BROOKWEED

BRIAR

AMBER CL

AMBER CL

BRIAR

B5000

FELSPAR RD

Amington Ind Est

Sch

War Meml

03

Sch

SIGNAL WLK

BEYER CL

STEPHENSON

BRAIN ST

SILICA RD

GLASCOTE RD

MICA CL

Pooley Hall and remains of Hall

POOLEY LA

PULLMAN

SILVER LINK RD

CASTLEHILL

CARLTON

B5080

B5000

CORREEN

CHEVIOT

CRIGDON

DEEPDALE

DOVESTONE

Sports Gnd

TAMWORTH RD

River Anker

1

FARINGDON

PENNINE RD

CRANWELL

CROMWELL

CRAVEN

EALINGTON

AMICOMBE

CHILTERN

BROADLEE

BRINKLOW

TAMWORTH RD

HERMITAGE LA

The Hermitage

Playing Field

Schs

P

BRENDON

BUCKDEN

DARNBROOK

MENDIP

LOWFORCE

M42

THE GULLEY

Stonydelph Lane

LINTLY

WETHERSDALE

MALHAM RD

VICTORIA

LOUGHSAY

MARRICK

SAXON PL

THE LYNCH

02

3 D 24 E 25 F

A

B

C

Beckbury

Rous's Covert

4

Snowdon Pool

01

Lower Snowdon

Burnhill Green

SNOWDON RD

Dartmouth Arms (PH)

Half Moon Plantation

3

Bennetts Wood

Middle Ley

Shepherds Buildings

Shepherds Plantation

Home Farm

FARM RD

RUSHEY LA

Shropshire Lodge

Patshull Park

Bishton Cottages

Bishton Manor

Albrighton Lodge

Wildicote

Wilderness Hill

Monkey Bridge

Monkeybridge Plantation

Decoy Wood

Church Pool

Patshull Hall

Golf Course

Old Park

Old Park Plantation

Cut Spinney

The Great Pool

HOME FARM RD

00

Green's Coppice

Mill Pond

Jubilee Plantation

Far Ley

Oulton Garden

Hotel

Plant's Neck

2

Badger

Bridgenorth Plantation

Stanlow Farm

Pasford Farm

Pasford

99

Kingslow Cottages

Kingslow

Kingslow Farm

Kingslow Hall

Pasford House

1

Chesterton Cottage

Nun Brook

Birchley Farm

98

78

A

79

B

80

C

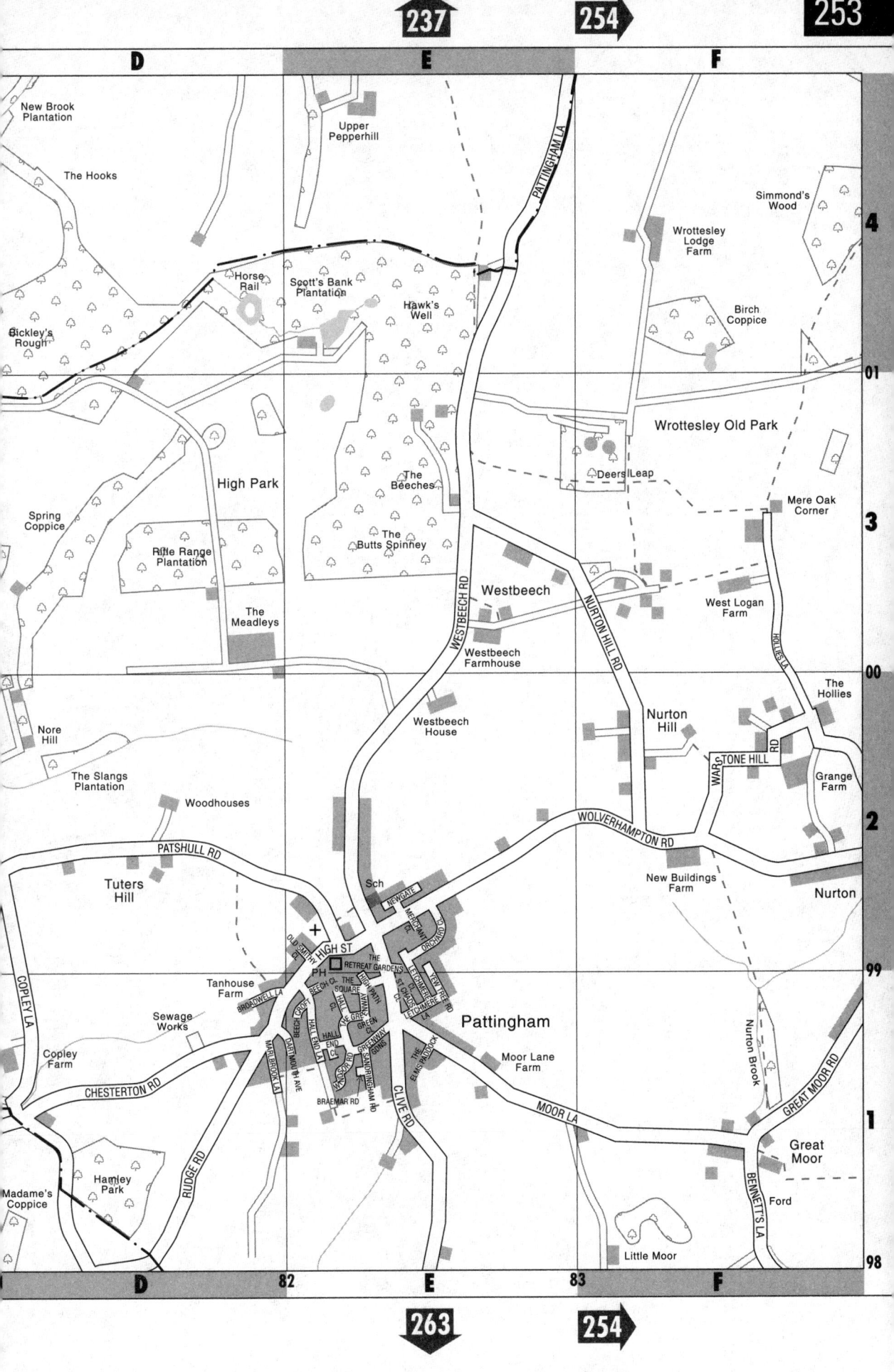

237
254

D
E
F

New Brook Plantation

The Hooks

Upper Pepperhill

Simmond's Wood

4

Horse Rail

Scott's Bank Plantation

Hawk's Well

Wrottesley Lodge Farm

Birch Coppice

Bickley's Rough

01

High Park

The Beeches

Wrottesley Old Park

Deers Leap

Spring Coppice

The Butts Spinney

Mere Oak Corner

3

Rifle Range Plantation

Westbeech

West Logan Farm

WESTBEECH RD

NURTON HILL RD

The Meadleys

Westbeech Farmhouse

The Hollies

00

Nore Hill

Westbeech House

Nurton Hill

HOLLIES LA

The Slangs Plantation

WAR STONE HILL

Grange Farm

WARSTONE HILL RD

Woodhouses

WOLVERHAMPTON RD

2

PATSHULL RD

Nurton

Tuters Hill

Sch

New Buildings Farm

NEWGATE

MERCHANT DR

ORCHARD CL

COPLEY LA

OLD SMITH CR

HIGH ST

THE RETREAT GARDENS

ST CHADS

FIERN TREE RD

FLETCHMERE

FLETCHMERE LA

99

Tanhouse Farm

PH

THE SQUARE

BEECH CL

THE GREEN

BROADWELL LA

Pattingham

Nurton Brook

Sewage Works

HALL END LA

GREENWAY GDNS

THE ELMS PADDOCK

Moor Lane Farm

GREAT MOOR RD

Copley Farm

DARTMOUTH AVE

MARBROOK LA

KESGOT RD

SANDRINGHAM RD

CHESTERTON RD

BRAEMAR RD

CLIVE RD

MOOR LA

1

RUDGE RD

Great Moor

BENNETT'S LA

Madame's Coppice

Hamley Park

Ford

Little Moor

98

D
82
E
83
F

263
254

D

E

F

Brookside
Farm

Palmers
Cross

River Penk

The
Waltons

Wergs
Plantation

Golf
Course

Works

Sewage
Works

1 FULLERTON CL
2 COSGROVE WLK
3 RYEFIELD
4 BARDWELL CL
5 GANTON WLK
6 BURMARSH WLK
7 DANEHILL WLK

Blakeley
Green

4

Aldersley

Wergs
Farm

Wergs

Cemy

Danescourt

CH

Stockwell
End

Claregate

Sch

Stadium

01

Race
Course

3

Woodthorne
Offices

WROTTESLEY RD W

WROTTESLEY RD

Tettenhall

REDHOUSE RD

Sch

Amb
Sta

REGIS RD

Sch

Sch

Malthouse La

LOWLANDS AVE

THE ROOK

Sch

Sch

PC

00

Offices

F Sta

LIMES RD

HIGH ST

PC

P

Coll

Valley Park

NEW HAMPTON RD W

2

NORTHDALE

HAYWOOD DR

Hospl

Tettenhall
Wood

Sch

Sch

Newbridge

Staffordshire and Worcestershire Canal

Smestow Brook

HENWOOD RD

Sch

Schs

St Judes Ct 1
Bromford Dale 2

P

St Mawes
Rd

SCHOOL RD

Sch

Liby

PC

CHURCH RD

ORMES LA

THE HOLLOWAY

WOOD RD

Dismantled Railway

WOLVERHAMPTON

University of
Wolverhampton

Coll

PAGET RD

99

MOUNT RD

Compton

Coll

COMPTON RD

Merridale

Graiseley Brook

Sch

BRIDGENORTH RD

Hospice

COMPTON RD W

FINCHFIELD HILL

Ashfield

Mayfair
Gdns

Richmond

Sch

1

Wightwick
Bridge

WINDMILL LA

Sch

The Pines

YORK AVE

York
Cres

FINCHFIELD RD

Mus

Cemy

98

STUDLEY RD

FINCHFIELD RD W

BROAD LA

D

88

E

89

F

ALDRIDGE

Leighswood

Leighswood Ind Est

Leighwood
Ind Est

Druids Heath
Farm

Golf
Course

Nuttalls
Farm

HOBS HOLE LA

Fairview
Nurseries

Plough
and Harrow
(PH)

Millgreen
Farm

Mill
Green
Farm

Mill
Green

FORGE LA

Aldridge
Court

Fairlawns
Hotel

Old
Irish Harp
(PH)

ALDRIDGE RD

LITTLE ASTON ROAD

Sand
Pit

Branton
Hill

Bourne
Farm

Golf
Course

Lowlands
Wood

1 ANCHOR PAR
2 THE SQUARE
3 ROOKERY PAR

1 DUMBLEDERRY LA
2 WESTBROOK AVE
3 LYNMOUTH CL
4 DARTMOUTH DR

Sch

Daniels Lane

DANIELS LA

Shrubbery
Farm

Corporation
Wood

Tower's
Covert

Waterworks
Farm

Nursery

Hardwick

Lodge
Farm

Bulls Head
Farm

Barr
Common

Bourne
Vale

BOURNE VALE

KESWICK GR

The Dingle

CHESTER RD

HARDWICK RD

Cuckoo's
Nook

LONGWOOD RD

ERDINGTON RD

BARR COMMON RD

LITTLE HARDWICK RD

Cemy

Peronne
Poultry
Farm

Primrose
Farm

Crem

NURSERY VIEW CL 1
BARLEY CL 2
HARVESTERS CL 3

WOOD LA

FOLEY RD E

Beacon Way

Birch
Wood

Potter's
Wood

The Foley Arms
(PH)

FOLEY RD W

Moat
Farm

SUTTON RD

CROOK LA

LITTLE JOHNSON'S LA

BEACON HILL

ALDRIDGE RD

B4151

B4151

246

258

D E F

WOOD LA

French Croft Farm

Forge Farm

Sewage Works

Forge Cottages

Forge Wood

Forge Wood

Riding Stables

Back Lane

FOOTHERLEY LA

FORGE LA

New Wood

4

The Belt

Mill Green

A4026

01

Blake Street Station

MILL LA

FORGE LA

Mill Farm

Home Farm

Sch

Cottage Farm

BLAKE ST

Hill Hook

BYRON CL

SHERLEY DR

TENNYSON

KENT'S CL

BEIGHTON CL

ALDRIDGE RD

LITTLE ASTON LA

Claypit Rough

P

Marlborough CL

STATION APP

CLEEVE DR

VAUGHAN GDNS

CHANNEL WAY

BECKET CL

AUGUSTUS RD

PETERHOUSE DR

A5127

WAY

3

LAKESIDE

THE SPINNEY

A4026

THE GROVE

POPLAR RISE

ROSEMARY NOOK

B4138

LEGENDY WAY

BICKLEY AVE

VERNON AVE

BRADGATE DR

Mill Pond

BALMORAL DR

HILL HOOK RD

WETHERFIELD RD

KESTREL RD

HILL VILLAGE RD

AS127 RD

LICHFIELD RD

Little Aston Hall

Golf Course

Hospl

SQUIRREL WLK

ROMAN RD

WOODSIDE DR

KEEPERS RD

BIRCH CR

SILVER BIRCH COPPICE RD

Hornton Manor

BEECHWOOD CROFT

HORNTON CL

CHERRYWOOD WAY

KENSINGTON RD

Liby

ST GEORGES ST

HARRISON RD

ATTLESFORD DR

SOUTHBOURNE

CHESTERFIELD WRIGHTSBRIDGE DR

WEYMOUTH

CHELSEA DR

FIRS BANK RD

WALL RD

BEECH GATE

KEEPERS RD

WATERMANS LN

00

Little Aston

CH

LONGBRAES

LONGFIELD RD

CHOP VIEW DR

EDGE HILL RD

BLACKBERRY LA

WHITE FARM RD

Schs

Schs

HILLSIDE RD

ROMAN ROAD

PARK DR

ROSEMARY HILL RD

WOODSTOCK DR

WALSALL RD

RUSSELL BANK RD

HOOK DR

HARDWICK DR

CLARENCE RD

HILL MORTON RD

MEADVALE RD

2

Roundabout Wood

Roman Park

CLAVERDON DR

ROMAN LA

ROSEMARY DR

SADDWOOD DR

THE HEADLANDS

WAYSIDE

PINEWAYS

JERVIS CRES

PARK VIEW RD

STREETLY CRES

STREETLY DR

BENNETT RD

MELLOR DR

LONGDON LA

Four Oaks

FOUR OAKS COMMON RD

GROVNES RD

ORCHARD CL

WEEFORD DR

BUTLERS LA

BARRS CROFT

ALDERHYTHE GR

ROYDER RD

VERNON AVE

FALLOW FIELD

NEWICK AVE

LITTLE ASTON PARK RD

GRASMERE

TALBOT AVE

ST MARGARET'S

HIGHFURST RD

BENNETT RD

WATERS DR

HIGHCROFT DR

CROWN LA

WOODSIDE

KNIGHTON DR

EARNFORD DR

ALL SAINTS DR

CLARENCE DR

VESY

Sch

99

LEAFY GLADE

THISTLE DOWN CL

CHESTNUT CL

TIMBERLY CL

HARDWICK RD

BURNETT RD

LESLIE RD

SEYMOUR GDNS

Sch

B4151

Streetly

STREETLY LA

BELWELL LA 1

FOUR OAKS RD 2

PARK DR 3

A454

Sch

1

MARWOOD CROFT

CARLTON CROFT

FEATHERSTON RD

CARLTON AVE

COLEY CHURCH CL

HIGHGATE

EASTMOOR CL

THORNHILL RD

Streetly Lodge

LINKS VIEW

Mayor's Arbour

GUNSLADE

GREENSFIELDS

ROPER CROSS RD

HARTOPP RD

CLIVEDEN COPPICE

LUTTRELL RD

B4151

FOLEY RD E

REDLANDS WAY

FAIRGREEN WAY

MIDDLETON RD

Sch

Streetly Wood

Streetly Belt

Bracebridge Pool

1 THORNEY RD

ASTOR RD

BRIAR AVE

LANGFORD

ICKNIELD CL

CH

Golf Course

MANOR RD

B4138

PARKSIDE WAY

98

D 09 E 10 F

258

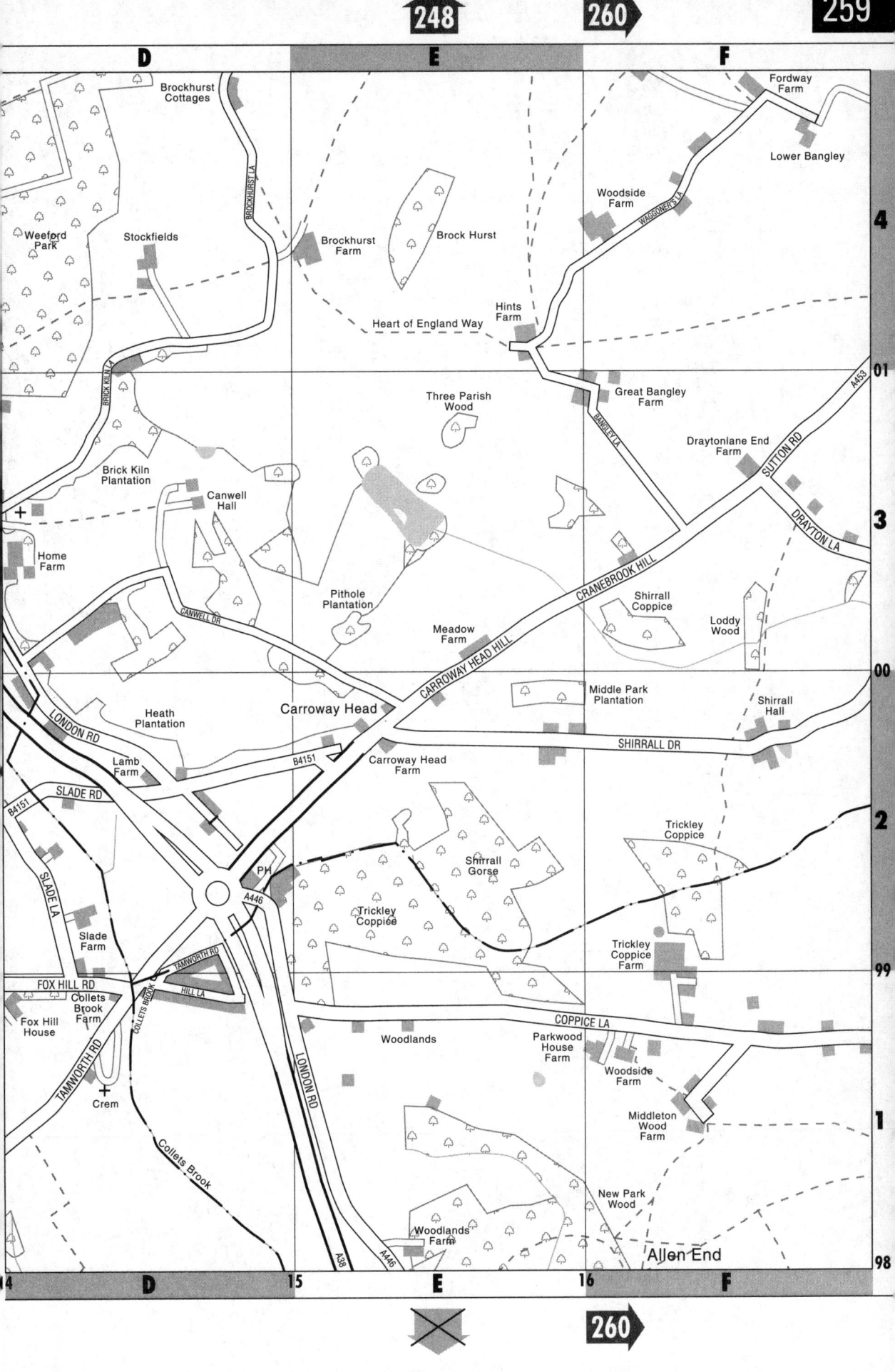

4

New House Farm

BANGLEY LA

SUTTON RD

A453

CANSTON CL

GAINSBOROUGH DR

KIRKLAND WAY

A453

CRANWELL RISE

Bourne Bridge

Alder Wood

Bourne Brook

Bourne Brook Cut

Seventeen Acre Wood

Duck Decoy

Longwood House

YORKSAND RD

REINDEER RD

DAMA RD

Fazeley

MAYAMA RD

DRAYTON MANOR DR

SWISS LODGE DR

Drayton Manor Park

Works

Hill Farm

Lodge Farm

Drayton Park

CH

DRAYTON MANOR DR

01

3

Golf Course

Longwood Stables

COLESHILL RD

A4091

Heathley Farm

HEATHLEY LA

Bullocks End Farm

Drayton Bassett

Edden's Wood

OLD MANOR CL

MOAT DR

CHURCH CL

EDDENS WOOD CL

NEWTON

PEEL CL

Sch

Oak Farm

SHIRRAL DR

Stone House

Heart of England Way

DRAYTON LA

Sewage Works

RECTORY CL

SALTS LA

00

Ashdene Farm

PORTLEYS LA

Brook End Farm

Drayton Brick Bridge

Brook Farm

Heart of England Way

2

Birmingham and Fazeley Canal

Upper House Farm

Gallows Brook

99

COPPICE LA

Quarry

Mill Plantation

1

Middleton

Sch

Highfields Farm

SIMMONS CL

CHURCH LA

Park-gate Farm

Middleton Park

Newhouse Farm

The Green Man (PH)

Walker's Spinney

Sewage Works

Middleton Pool

Middleton Hall

VICARAGE HILL

Langley Brook

CROWBERRY LA

A4091

98

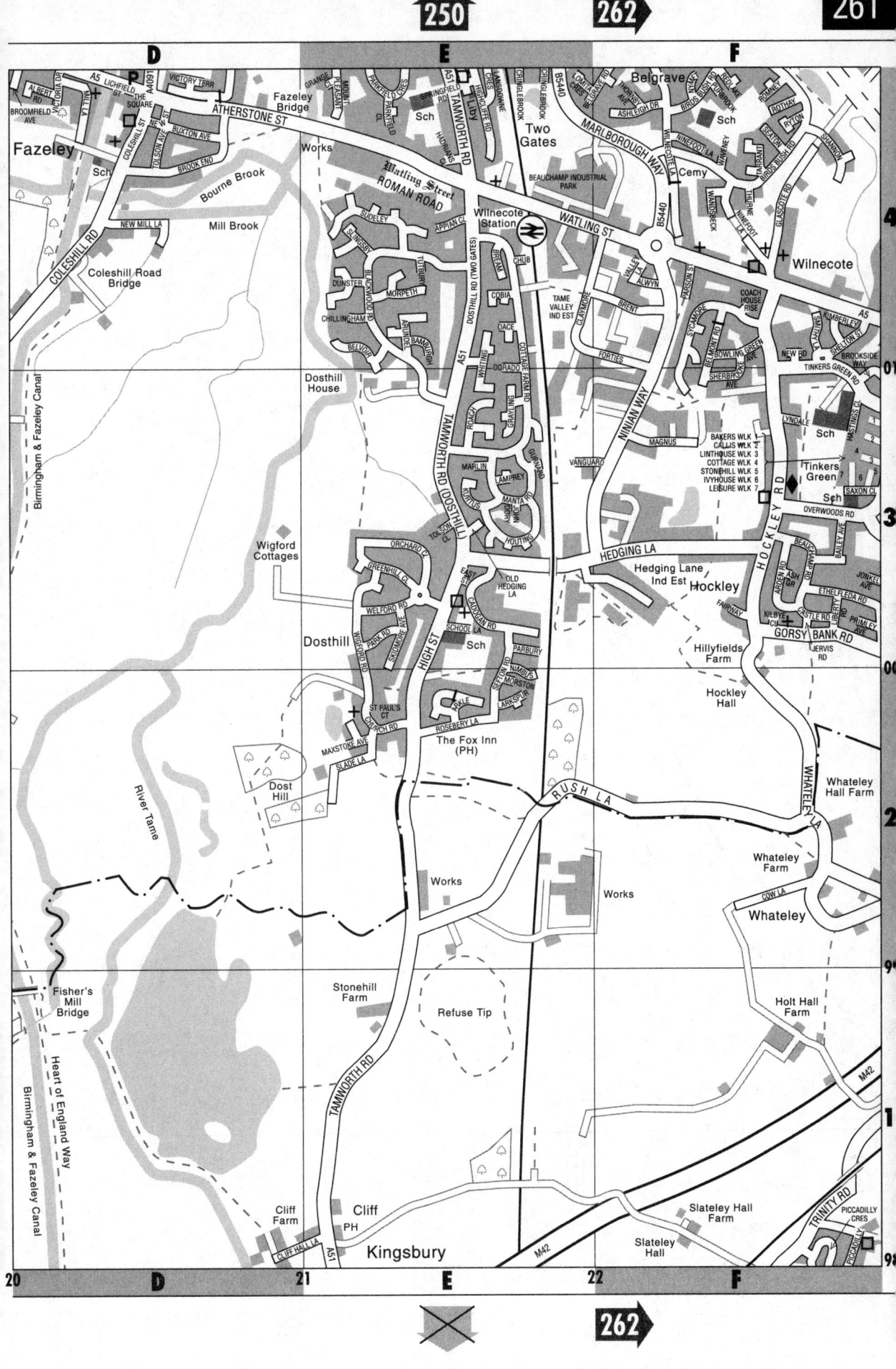

Belgrave

Fazeley

ATHERSTONE ST
Fazeley
Bridge

Two
Gates

Watling Street
ROMAN ROAD

WATLING ST

MARLBOROUGH WAY

Wilnecote
Station

Wilnecote

Coleshill Road
Bridge

Mill Brook

Bourne Brook

NEW MILL LA

Dosthill
House

Wigford
Cottages

TAMWORTH RD (DOSTHILL)

Hedging Lane
Ind Est

Tinkers
Green

Hockley

Dosthill

Old
Hedging La

HIGH ST

The Fox Inn
(PH)

RUSH LA

Hillyfields
Farm

Hockley
Hall

GORSY BANK RD

Whateley
Hall Farm

Dost Hill

River Tame

Whateley
Farm

Whateley

Works

Works

Birmingham & Fazeley Canal

Fisher's
Mill
Bridge

Stonehill
Farm

Refuse Tip

Holt Hall
Farm

Heart of England Way

Birmingham & Fazeley Canal

TAMWORTH RD

Cliff
Farm

Cliff

Kingsbury

Slateley Hall
Farm

Slateley
Hall

TRINITY RD
PICCADILLY
CRES

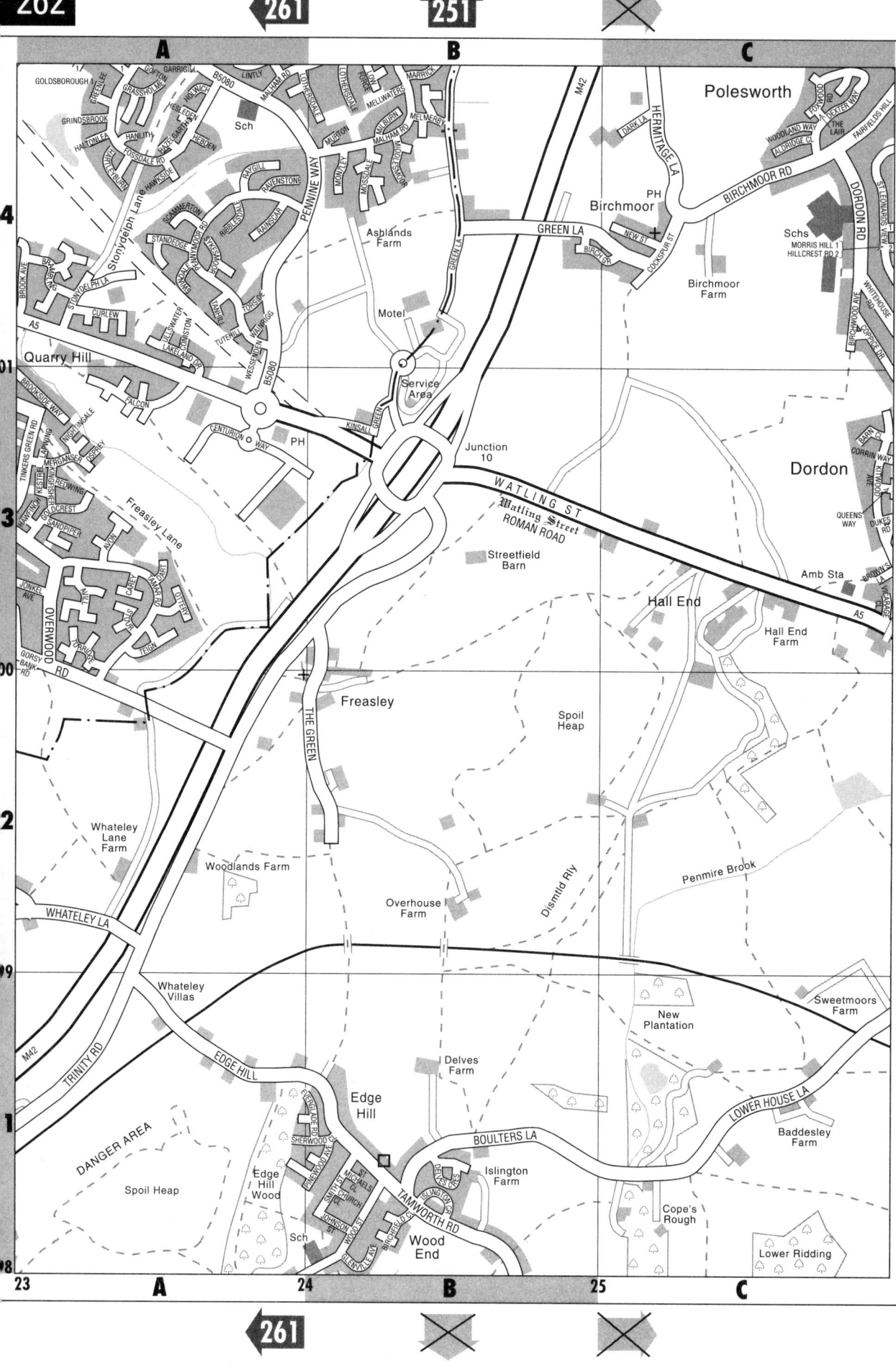

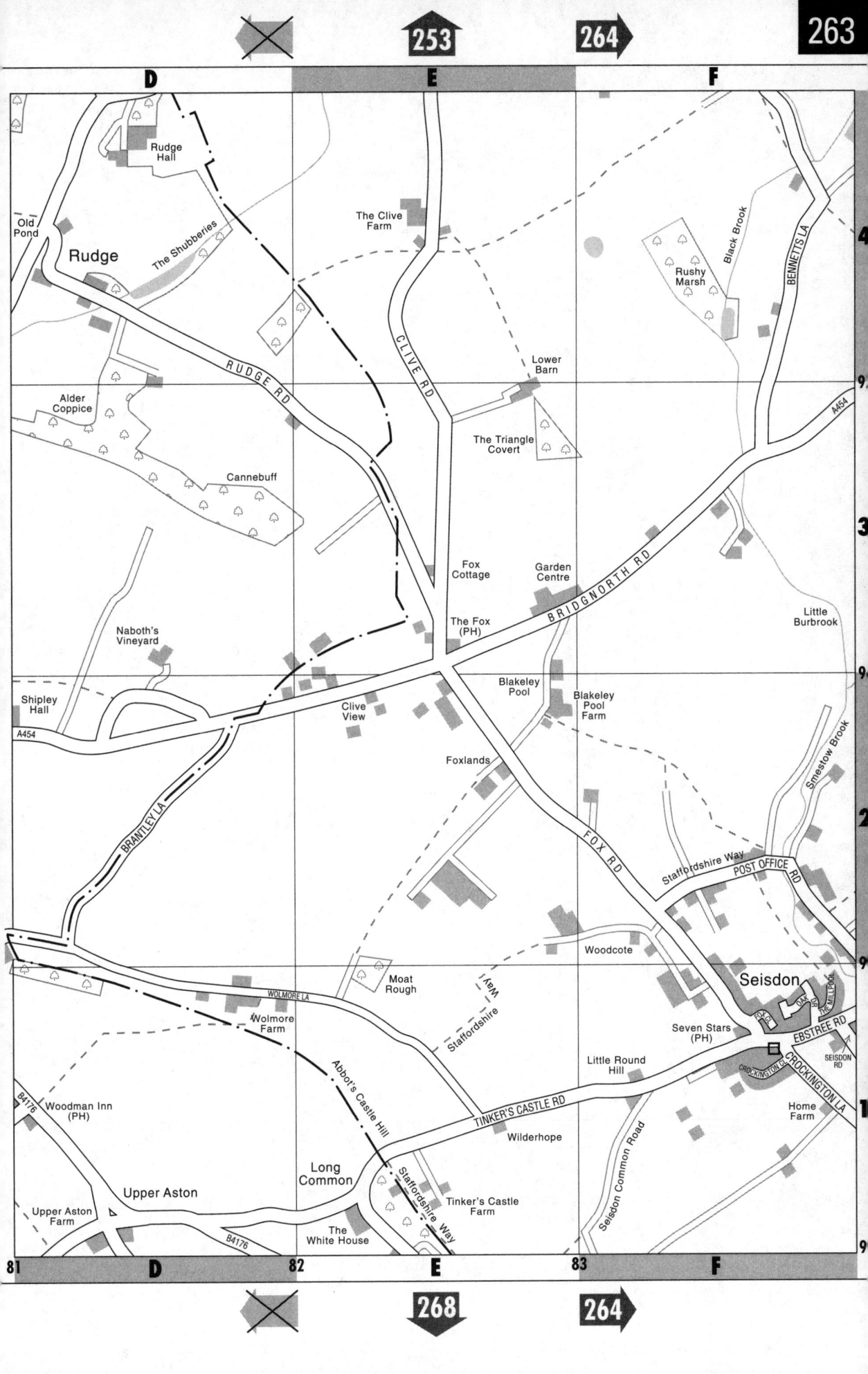

D E F

Rudge Hall

Old Pond

Rudge

The Shubberies

The Clive Farm

CLIVE RD

Black Brook

BENNETTS LA

A454

Rushy Marsh

4

Lower Barn

Alder Coppice

RUDGE RD

The Triangle Covert

9

Cannebuff

Fox Cottage

Garden Centre

BRIDGNORTH RD

Little Burbrook

3

Naboth's Vineyard

The Fox (PH)

Shipley Hall

A454

Clive View

Blakeley Pool

Blakeley Pool Farm

9

BRANTLEY LA

Foxlands

Smestow Brook

FOX RD

2

Staffordshire Way

POST OFFICE RD

Woodcote

Seisdon

9

WOLMORE LA

Moat Rough

Staffordshire Way

Wolmore Farm

Seven Stars (PH)

EBSTREE RD

Seisdon RD

B4176

Woodman Inn (PH)

Abbot's Castle Hill

Little Round Hill

CROCKINGTON LA

Home Farm

1

Staffordshire Way

TINKER'S CASTLE RD

Wilderhope

Seisdon Common Road

Long Common

Upper Aston

Upper Aston Farm

B4176

The White House

Tinker's Castle Farm

9

81 D 82 E 83 F

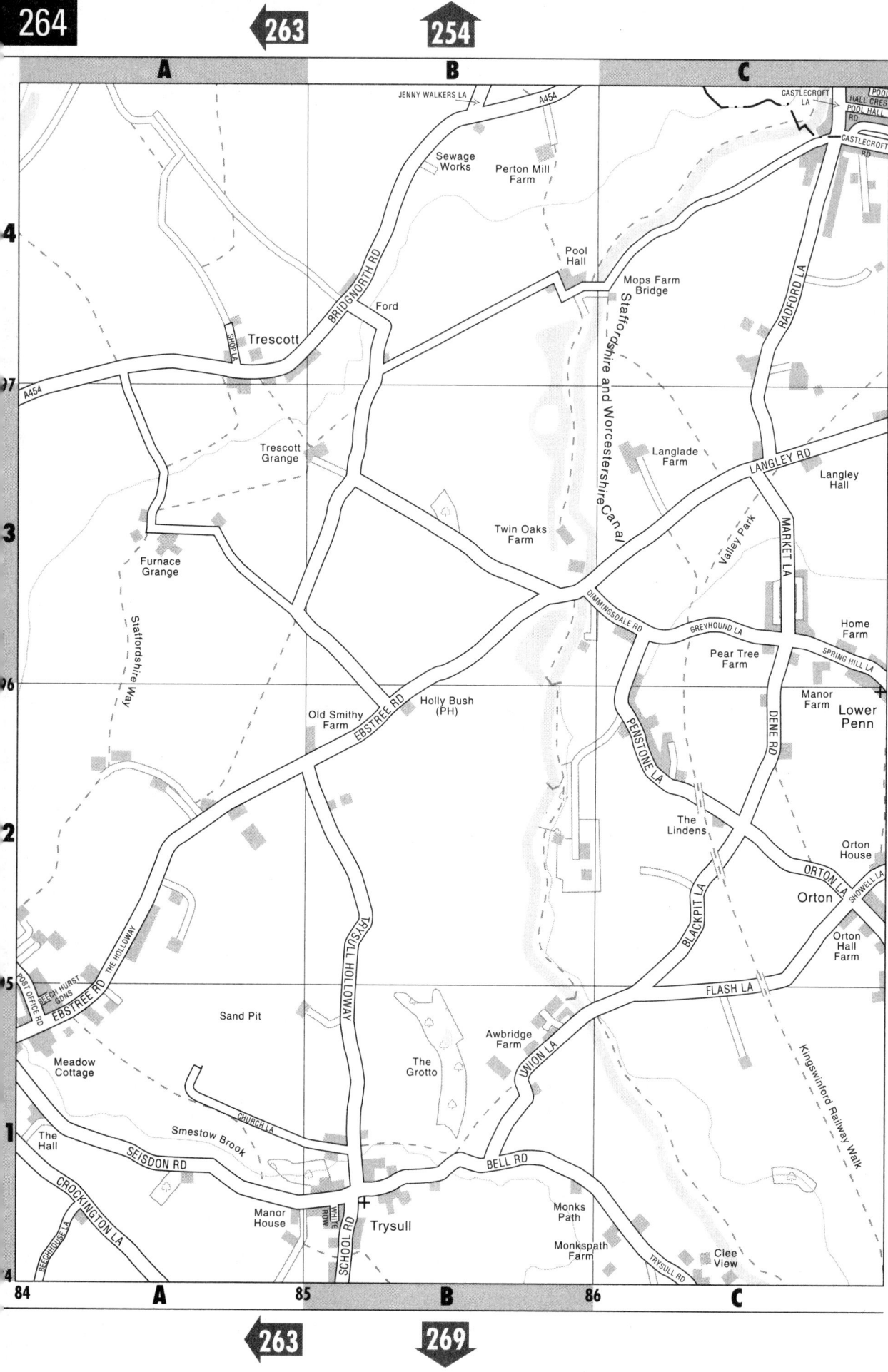

263
254

A   B   C

4

97

3

96

2

'5

1

4

84   A   85   B   86   C

263
269

JENNY WALKERS LA
A454
Sewage Works
Perton Mill Farm
CASTLECROFT LA
POOL HALL CRES
POOL HALL RD
CASTLECROFT RD

BRIDGNORTH RD
Ford
Pool Hall
Mops Farm Bridge
Staffordshire and Worcestershire Canal
RADFORD LA

SHOP LA
Trescott

A454

Trescott Grange
Langlade Farm
LANGLEY RD
Langley Hall

Furnace Grange
Twin Oaks Farm
Valley Park
MARKET LA
Home Farm

Staffordshire Way
DIMMINGSDALE RD
GREYHOUND LA
Pear Tree Farm
SPRING HILL LA

Old Smithy Farm
EBSTREE RD
Holly Bush (PH)
PENSTONE LA
DENE RD
Manor Farm
Lower Penn

The Lindens
Orton House

ORTON LA
SHOWELL LA
Orton

THE HOLLOWAY
BLACKPIT LA
Orton Hall Farm

POST OFFICE RD
BEECH HURST GDNS
EBSTREE RD
FLASH LA

TRYSULL HOLLOWAY
Sand Pit
Kingswinford Railway Walk

Meadow Cottage
Awbridge Farm
UNION LA

The Grotto

CHURCH LA
Smestow Brook

The Hall
SEISDON RD
BELL RD

CROCKINGTON LA
Manor House
WHITE ROW
SCHOOL RD
Trysull
Monks Path

BEECHHOUSE LA
Monkspath Farm
TRYSULL RD
Clee View

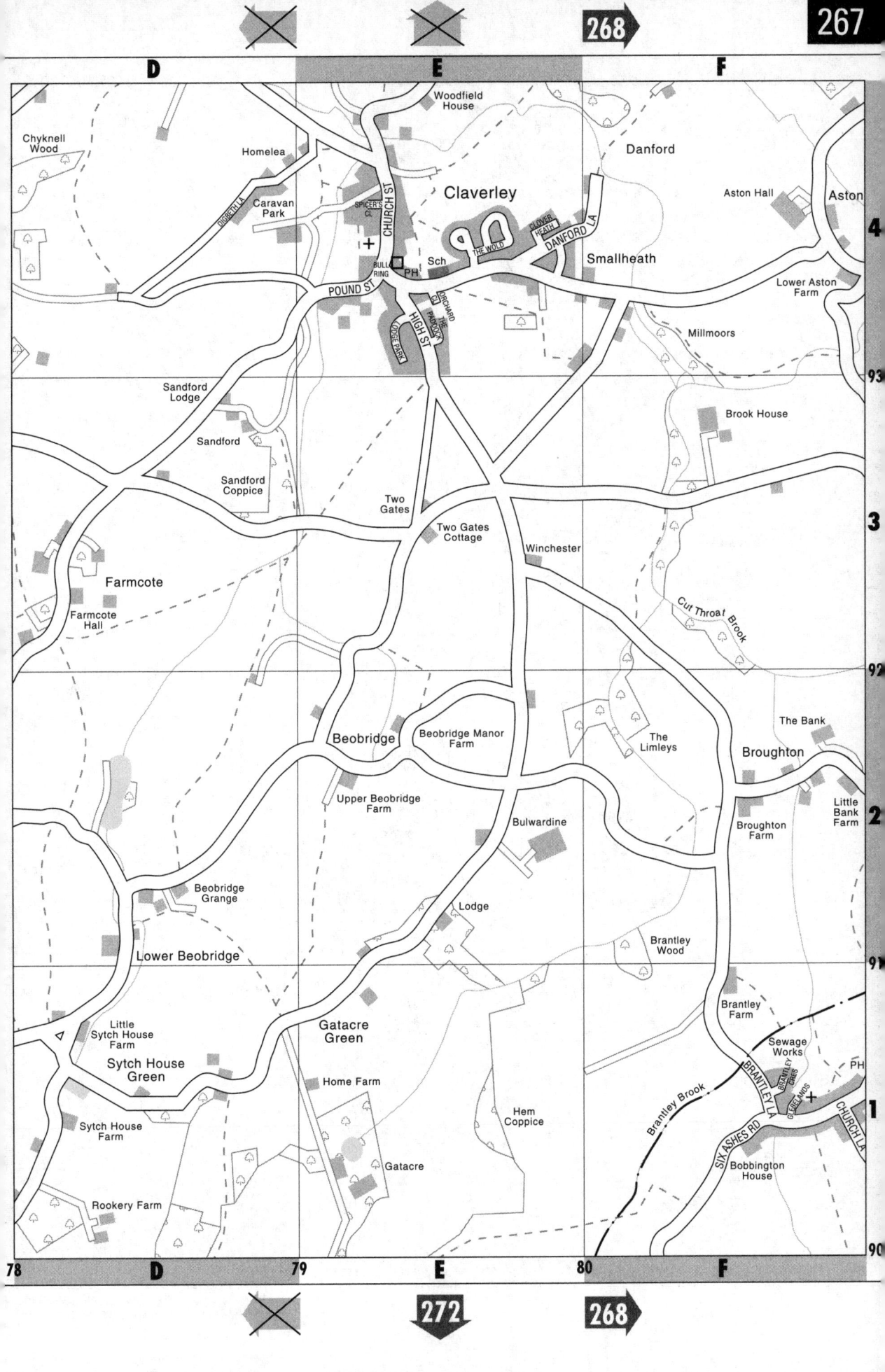

← 267
263 ↑

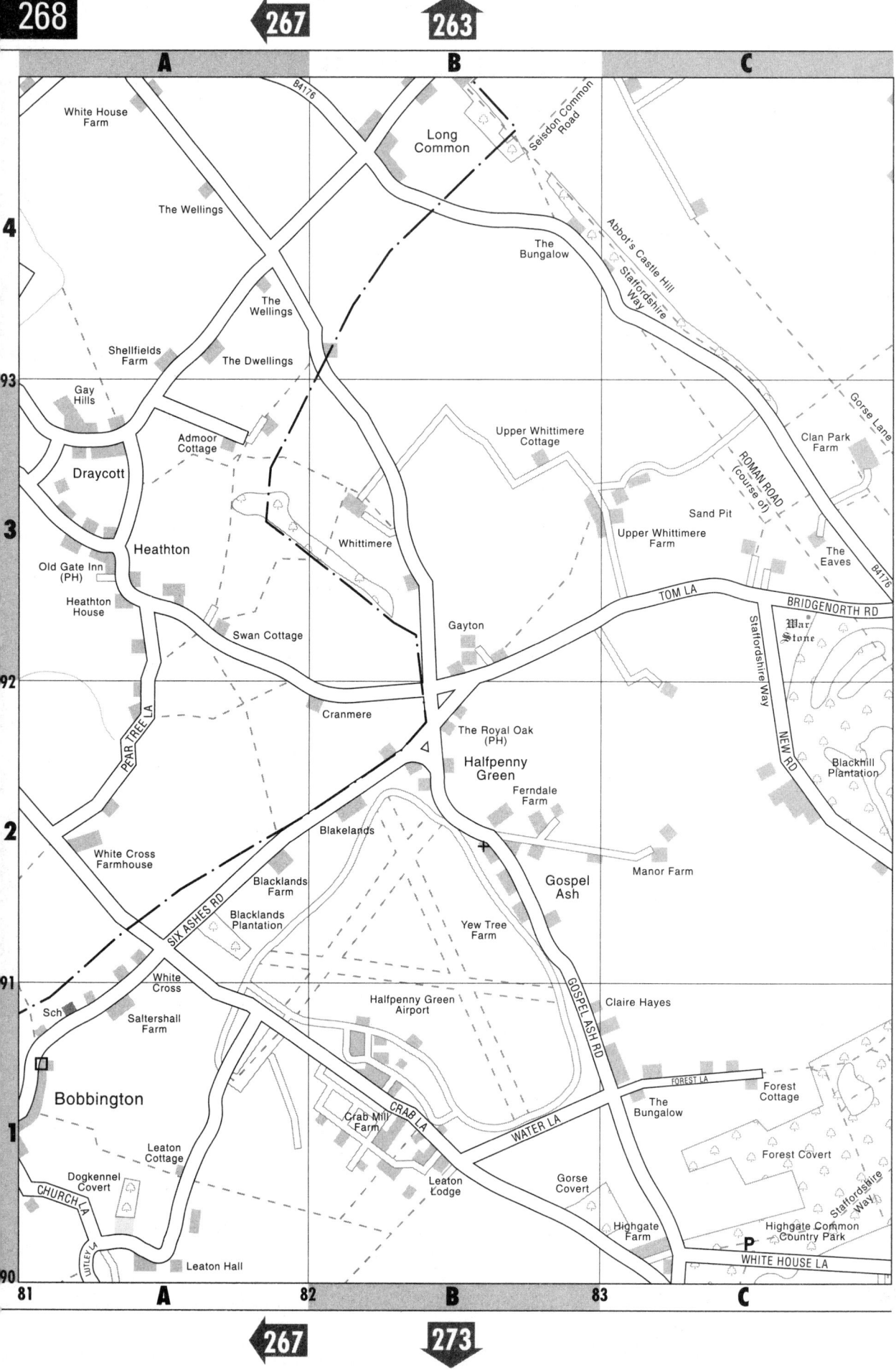

← 267
273 ↓

269
265
269
275

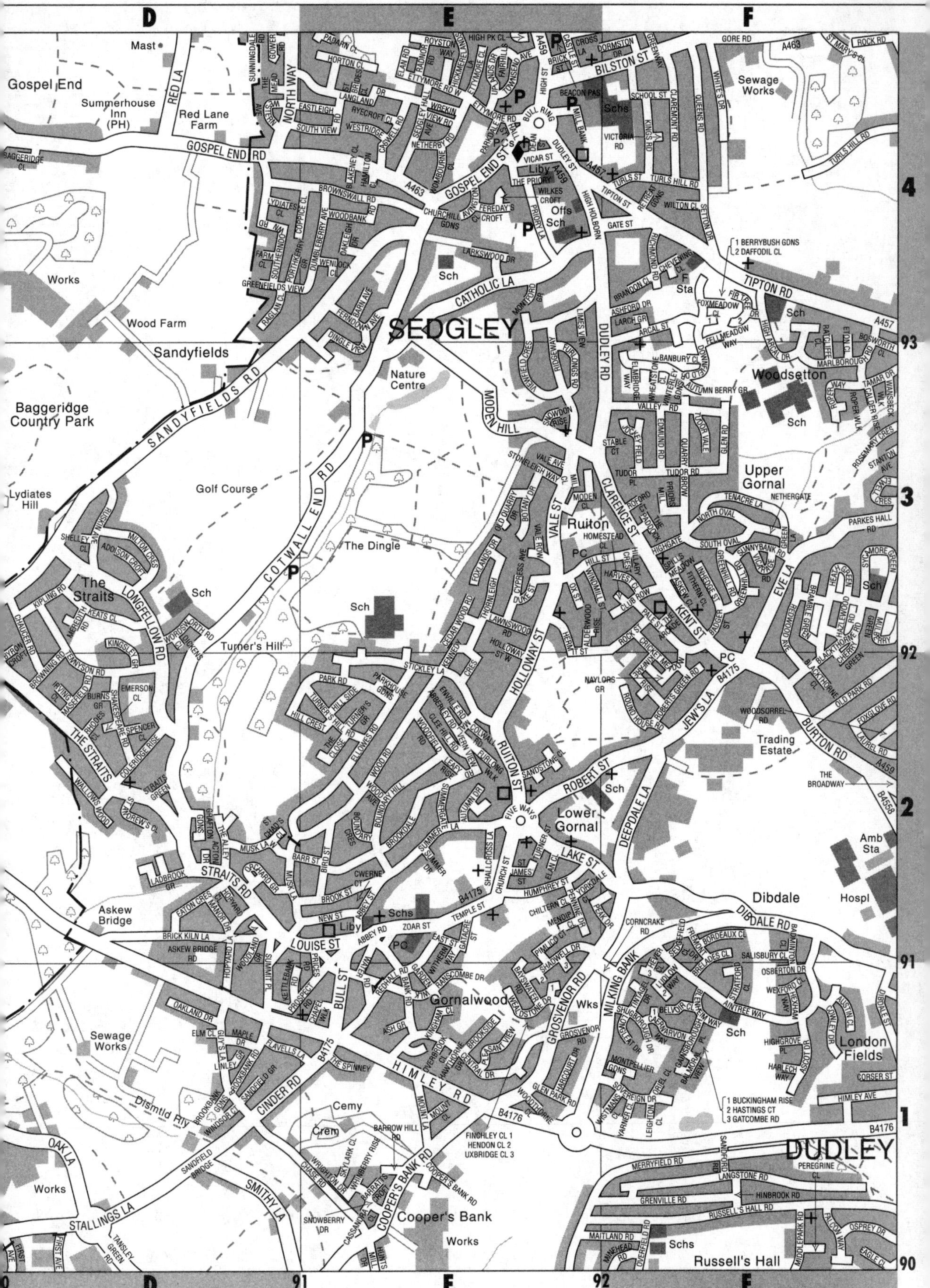

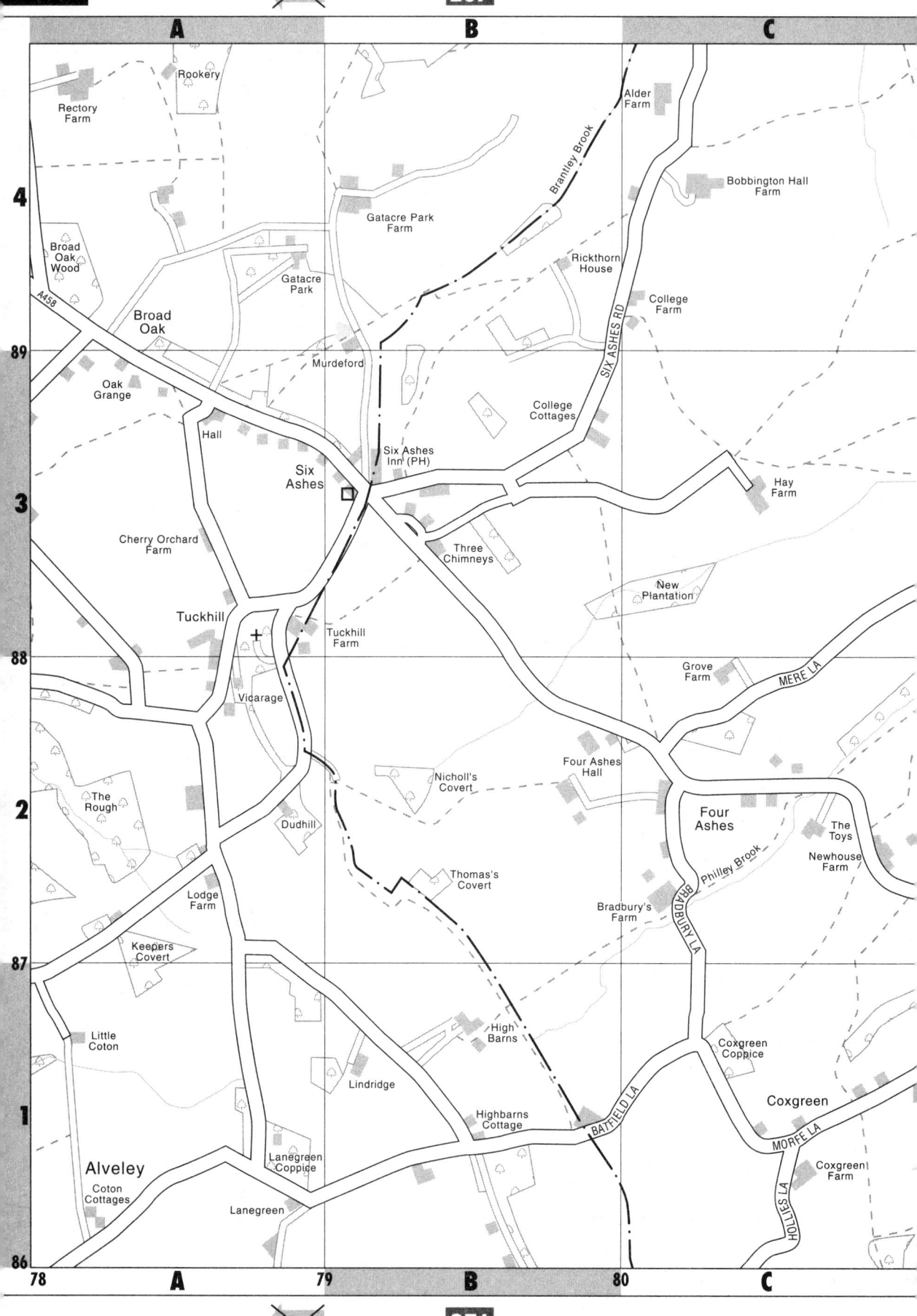

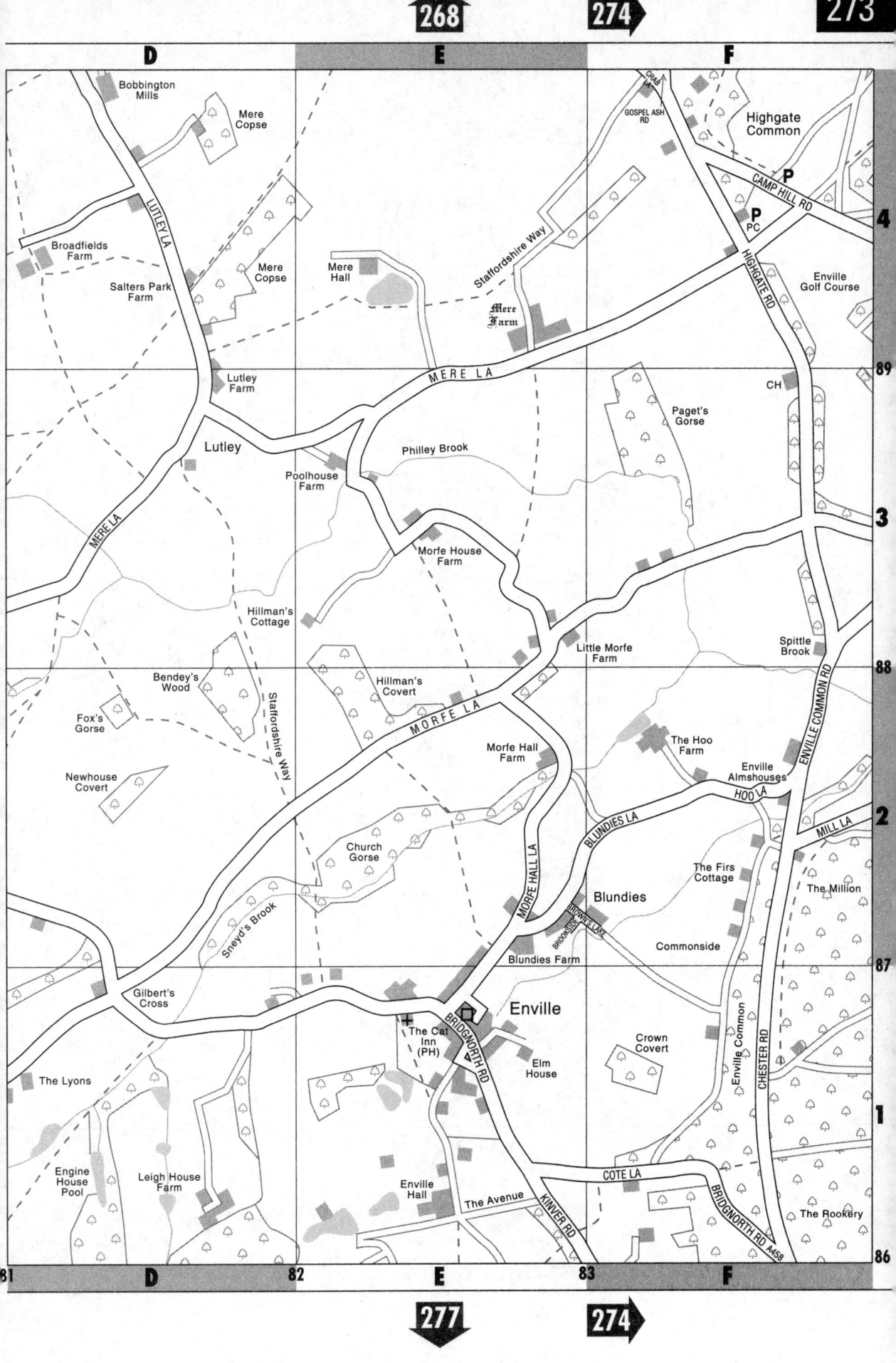

A **B** **C**

Hinksford

Chasepool
Farm

Hollow Mill
Farm

HINKSFORD LA

SWINDON RD

Highgate Common

CHASEPOOL RD

ROMAN ROAD
(course of)

Caravan
Park

Old Bush
(PH)

4

Greensforge
Rough

ROMAN ROAD
(course of)

P

MILE FLAT

Camp
Farm

My Lady's
Farm

89

Camp
Cottages

Bank
Farm

Greensforge
Farm

PH

Ashwood
Lodge

Greensforge

Golf
Course

Smestow Brook

Ashwood

DOCTORS LA

3

ENVILLE COMMON RD

Lodge
Plantation

The
Gorse

P

88

Spittle Brook

Old
Mill
Pond

LITTLE CHECKHILL LA

Waterworks
Cottages

Mill
Farm

GREAT CHECKHILL RD

Staffordshire
and Worcestershire
Canal

ROMAN ROAD

MILL LA

Windmill

Checkhill
Farm

2

Rumford
Hill

GREENSFORGE LA

Holloway
House

Gothersley
Bridge

87

The Million

Radway Hill

Gothersley

GOTHERSLEY LA

Gothersley
Rough

Gothersley
Farm

1

Gothersley
House

Prestwood
Bridge

Prestwood

Hampton Valley

Stourton
Gorse

Nursing
Home

A449

86

84 **A** **85** **B** **86** **C**

A

B

C

4

Astley

Filletts

Chidleys Farm

The Hollies

HOLLIES LA

Barrets

Cains Coppice

Perry House

Leybrook Coppice

85

Perryhouse Dingle

Cains Gorse

No Man's Green

SHEEPWALKS LA

Birch Wood

NO MAN'S GREEN LA

3

Howlet Hall

Herons Gate Farm

HERONS GATE RD

Herons Gate

Square Coppice

Bowhills Dingle

Roughpark Wood

84

New Barns

Lenmores

Hartsgreen

Stoneacre

Heath House Farm

Park Farm

2

Cross Farm

Lower House Farm

BEACON LA

Tucksash

Hightrees Farm

Start's Green

83

Brittle's Farm

Romsley

Tudor House

ROMSLEY LA

Poolhouse Farm

Arley Wood

1

Brittle's Cottages

Castlehill Wood

A442

Hammer Hill Farm

Upper Arley

A442

Coldridge Wood

82

78   **A**   **79**   **B**   **80**   **C**

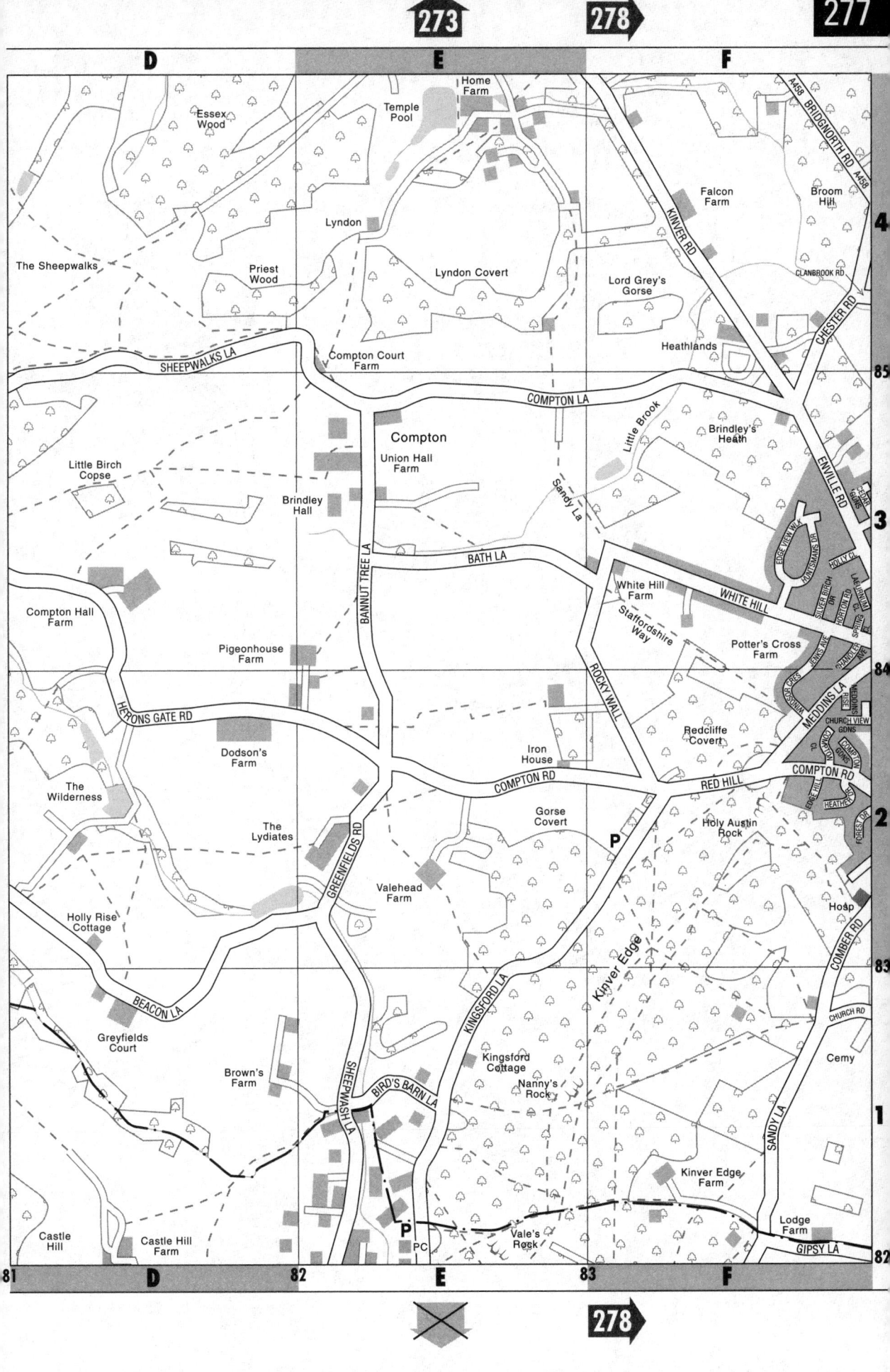

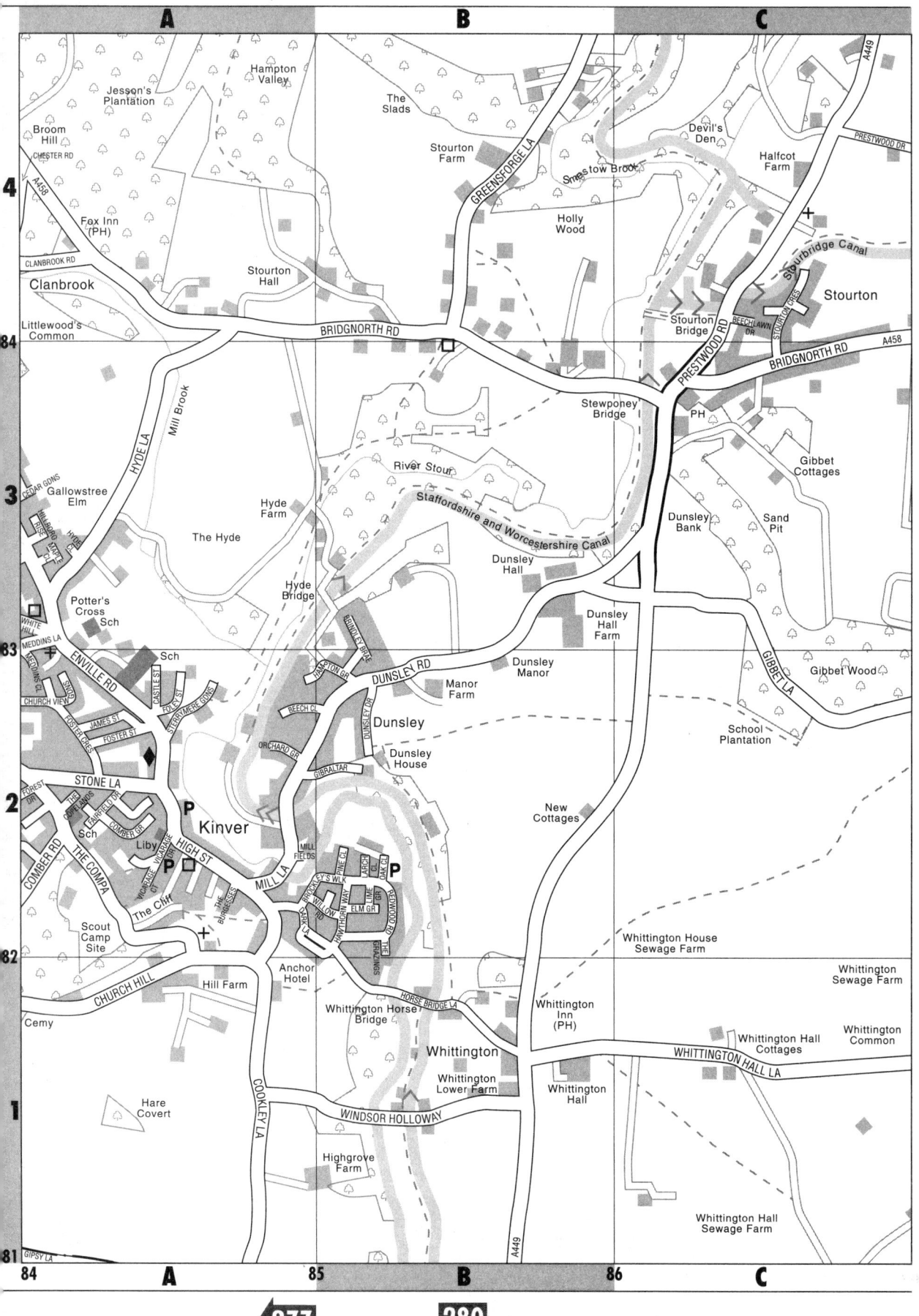

A   B   C

Jesson's
Plantation

Hampton
Valley

The Slads

Stourton
Farm

Devil's
Den

PRESTWOOD DR

Broom
Hill

CHESTER RD

Smestow Brook

Halfcot
Farm

4

Fox Inn
(PH)

A458

Holly
Wood

Stourbridge Canal

CLANBROOK RD

Stourton
Hall

Stourton
Bridge

BEECHLAWN DR

Stourton

Clanbrook

STOURTON CRES

Littlewood's
Common

BRIDGNORTH RD

PRESTWOOD RD

BRIDGNORTH RD

A458

84

Stewponey
Bridge

PH

A449

Mill Brook

HYDE LA

Gibbet
Cottages

River Stour

3

CEDAR GDNS

Gallowstree
Elm

Hyde
Farm

Staffordshire and Worcestershire Canal

Dunsley
Bank

Sand
Pit

HILL

HYDE

The Hyde

Dunsley
Hall

WHITE HILL

MEDDINS LA

Potter's
Cross Sch

Hyde
Bridge

Dunsley
Hall
Farm

GIBBET LA

MEDDINS LA

Sch

BERKLEY BRGE

Sch

Dunsley
Manor

Gibbet Wood

83

CHURCH VIEW

ENVILLE RD

CASTLE ST

HAMPTON GR

DUNSLEY RD

FOLEY ST

STEEPMERE EDNS

BEECH CL

Manor
Farm

School
Plantation

JAMES ST

FOSTER CRES

FOSTER ST

DUNSLEY DR

Dunsley

ORCHARD GR

Dunsley
House

STONE LA

GIBRALTAR

FOREST DR

THE
COPPICE GDNS

P

New
Cottages

2

COMBER RD

Kinver

MILL
FIELDS

SPINE CL

Sch

THE COMPA

Liby

P

HIGH ST

BRICKLEY'S WLK

LARCH CL

OAK CL

COMBER GR

FEARFIELD DR

VICARAGE
DR

MILL LA

HAWTHORN WAY

ELM GR

REDWOOD RD

VICARAGE DR

THE BLIBBERSEE

WILLOW
RD

LIME
TREE

The Cliff

THE
GRAZINGS

Scout
Camp
Site

Whittington House
Sewage Farm

82

Anchor
Hotel

Whittington
Sewage Farm

CHURCH HILL

Hill Farm

HORSE BRIDGE LA

Whittington
Horse
Bridge

Whittington
Inn
(PH)

WHITTINGTON HALL LA

Cemy

Whittington Hall
Cottages

Whittington
Common

Whittington

Whittington
Hall

1

COOKLEY LA

Whittington
Lower Farm

Hare
Covert

WINDSOR HOLLOWAY

Highgrove
Farm

A449

Whittington Hall
Sewage Farm

GIPSY LA

81

84   A   85   B   86   C

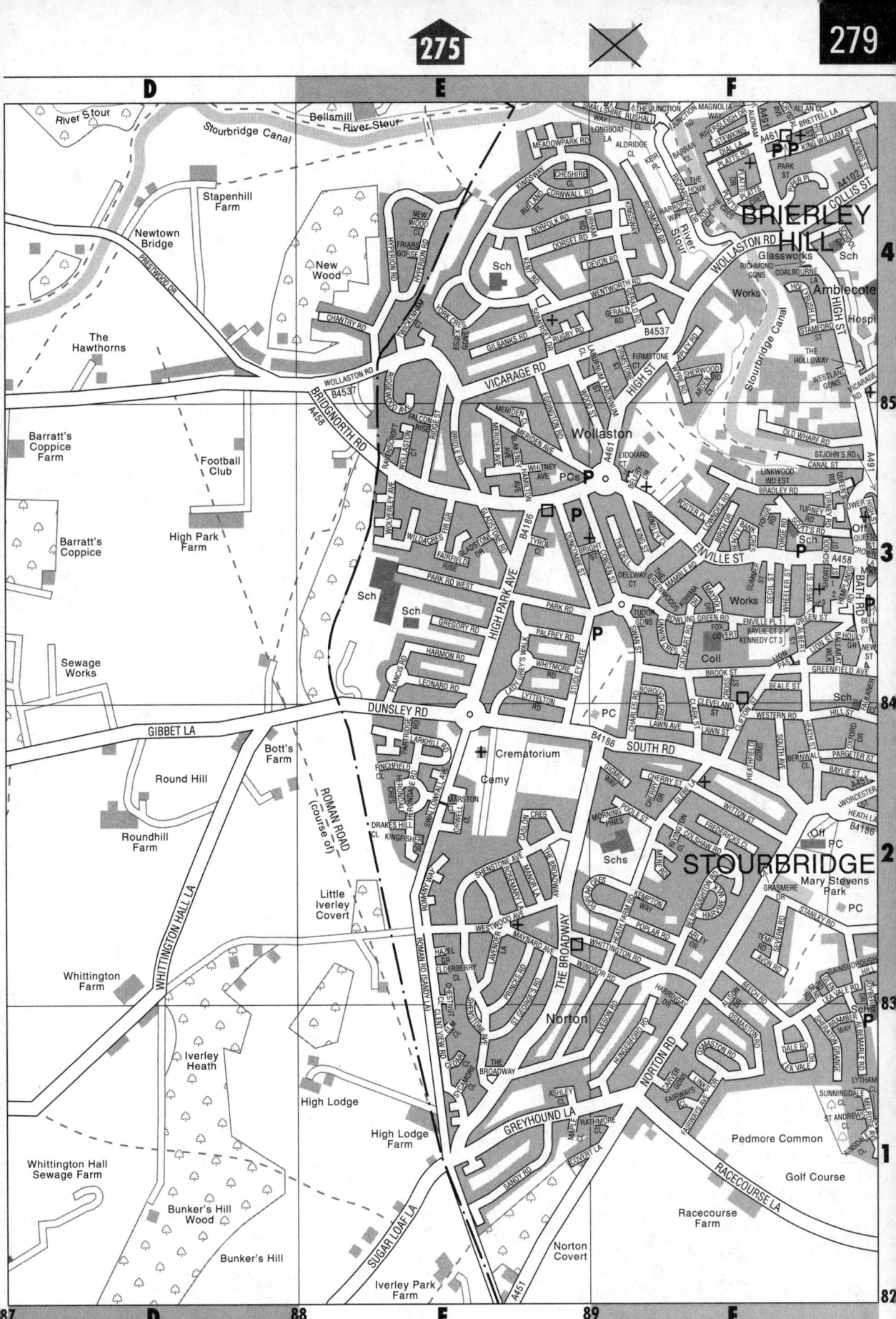

278

A **B** **C**

GIPSY LA

4

Turbine Cottage

Handkerchief Barn

Clouts Covert

North Worcestershire Path

Heath Barn

Whittington Hall Sewage Farm

KINVER LA

KINVER LA

NEW RD

Webb's Caunsall Farm

81

Caunsall

Fairy Glen

ORCHARD GR

WINSTONE DR

CAUNSALL RD

River Stour

Staffordshire and Worcestershire Canal

Beechtree Farm

BEECHTREE LA

Works

BRIDGE RD

Cookley

Austcliffe House Farm

Sleepy Mill (dis)

COMMON BARN LA

Ismere Grange

3

AUSTCLIFFE RD

Bull's Head (PH)

The Island Pool (PH)

Island Pool

Common Barn Farm

A451

Sch

LEA LA

STAITE DR

HIGHFIELD RD

ELEANOR HARRISON DR

SHRUBBERY CL

GATACRE RD

CLEE RD

BEECHERD

Austcliffe

Whitehouse Farm

Waggon and Horses (PH)

Ismere

80

PORTWAY PLACE

LIONFIELDS RD

ELM PL

ELM PL

Ismere Grange Farm

CASTLE RD

WESTHEAD RD NORTH

WOOD KINGS RD

ELAN CLOSE

KIMBERLEY CL

BRAMPTON CL

Wellfield

The Gorse

Ismere House

Parr's Farm

WESTHEAD RD

2

WOLVERHAMPTON RD

Lea Castle Farm

HOO CRESCENT

Talbotshill Coppice

Hospl

AXBOROUGH LA

Axborough Wood

Sch

WAGGON LA

79

Broom Covert

B4189

WOLVERLEY RD

STOURBRIDGE RD

Woodhouse Farm

Wannerton Plantation

PARK GATE RD

Park Gate (PH)

B4189

1

Sch

Sch

CHARLES AVE

Hurcott Kennels

Wood House

ISMERE WAY

WALKER DR

LEONARD AVE

HEATH DR

ROYAL AVE

ASH DR

Wannerton Farm

Broadwaters

SION AVE

DUNNINGTON AVE

CHAPEL CT

KENDLEWOOD RD

HIGHGROVE CT

PITT ST

CHAPEL

DUNNINGTON RD

A451

78

A449

A451

KIDDERMINSTER

Hurcott Wood

A **B** **C**

84 85 86

D E F

4

Sugarloaf Farm

ROMAN ROAD (SANDY LA) NORTON RD

A451

ROMAN ROAD COUNTY LA

COUNTY JOHN LA

Burys Hill

KIDDERMINSTER RD

Crown Inn (PH)

Iverley

SUGAR LOAF LA

Iverley House Farm

Iverley Hay Farm

The Birches

81

Highdown Cottages

STOURBRIDGE RD

North Worcs Path

ROMAN ROAD (course of)

Upper Brake Farm

Sch

BRAKE LA

Common Farm

IVERLEY LA

Palmer's Hill

Hagley

WOODLAND AVE

SWEETPOOL LA

Sch

HAYBRIDGE AVE

HOARSTONE

SUMMERVALE RD

THE CRESCENT

3

Five Ways

Brakemill Plantation

WILLOW CL

THE GREENWAY

Pumping Station

Brakemill Farm

Sewage Works

LONG CL

CAVENDISH DR

MILESTONE

80

SPRING CL

MAYFAIR

PINEWOODS AVE

PINEWOOD CL

A456

KIDDERMINSTER RD S

A450

Stakenbridge Farm

STAKENBRIDGE LA

Stakenbridge

STONEY LA

THICKNALL LA

2

WAGGON LA

CHURCHILL LA

Churchill

Churchill Farm

Bridge Farm

Harborough Hill

Harborough Farm

Nursery

WORCESTER RD

79

Golf Course

SOUTHORPE RD

THE CROFT

WHEATMILL CL

MILL CR

BIRMINGHAM RD

Harborough Hall

Broome Mill

Windmill Pool

BROOME LA

CH

MILL LA

LC

Churchill and Blakedown Station

STATION DR

Blakedown

STOURBRIDGE RD

BROOME LA

1

Wannerton House

Downs Plantation

WANNERTON RD

BROADWOOD DR

LYNWOOD DR

ROAD CL

THE AVENUE

SWAN CL

Schs

B4188

Broome Lodge Farm

Sewage Works

HALESHIRE LA

FORGE LA

Swan Pool

Forge Pool

New House Farm

BELBROUGHTON RD

A456

A450

B4188

Knoll Hill House

Hackman's Gate

Hundred Acre Farm

78

7 D 88 E 89 F

EXPLANATION OF THE STREET INDEX REFERENCE SYSTEM

Street names are listed alphabetically and show the locality, the page number and a reference to the square in which the name falls on the map page.

Example:	Rutland St. Han..57 D3

Rutland St	This is the full street name, which may have been abbreviated on the map.
Han	This is the abbreviation for the town, village or locality in which the street falls.
57	This is the page number of the map on which the street name appears.
D3	The letter and figure indicate the square on the map in which the centre of the street falls. The square can be found at the junction of the vertical column carrying the appropriate letter and the horizontal row carrying the appropriate figure.

ABBREVIATIONS USED IN THE INDEX
Road Names

Approach	App	Grove	Gr
Arcade	Arc	Heights	Hts
Avenue	Ave	Industrial Estate	Ind Est
Boulevard	Bvd	Junction	Junc
Buildings	Bldgs	Lane	La
Business Park	Bsns Pk	North	N
Broadway	Bwy	Orchard	Orch
By-Pass	By-Ps	Parade	Par
Causeway	Cswy	Passage	Pas
Circle	Circ	Place	Pl
Circus	Cir	Pleasant	Plea
Close	Cl	Precinct	Prec
Common	Comm	Promenade	Prom
Corner	Cnr	Road	Rd
Cottages	Cotts	South	S
Court	Ct	Square	Sq
Courtyard	Ctyd	Stairs	Strs
Crescent	Cres	Steps	Stps
Drive	Dri	Street,Saint	St
Drove	Dro	Terrace	Terr
East	E	Walk	Wlk
Embankment	Emb	West	W
Esplanade	Espl	Yard	Yd
Gardens	Gdns		

Key to abbreviations of Town, Village and Rural locality names used in the index of street names.

285

Ash Bank Rd. Cav

Bankhouse Dr. Congle

Ash Bank Rd. Cav 59 D2
Ash Cl. Che 76 C1
Ash Cl. Cod 239 D2
Ash Cl. Utt 126 A4
Ash Cres. Kingsw 275 F3
Ash Dr. Hau 172 C3
Ash Gr. Albr 237 D2
Ash Gr. Barl 88 B1
Ash Gr. Bly 90 B4
Ash Gr. Bre 223 E3
Ash Gr. Cann 209 F2
Ash Gr. Cav 58 C2
Ash Gr. Fen 72 C1
Ash Gr. Lich 231 F4
Ash Gr. N-u-L 55 D1
Ash Gr. Sedg 271 E1
Ash Gr. Tam 261 F3
Ash Gr. Whe As 205 E3
Ash Green Cl. Tren 88 A4
Ash Grove La. Eg 148 B3
Ash Hill. Wolv 255 E1
Ash La. Gr Wyr 227 D2
Ash La. Ne Re 236 C3
Ash La. Swyn 118 C3
Ash Rd. Sto 120 A4
Ash Rise. Staf 174 C2
Ash St. Bu on T 166 A1
Ash St. Wal 243 E1
Ash Tree Cl. Swad 186 C3
Ash Tree Hill. Che 76 B1
Ash Tree La. Stre 215 D1
Ash Tree Rd. Ba-u-Ne 183 E1
Ash View. Hunt 209 E4
Ash Way. Cav 58 C2
Ashbourne Cl. Cann 210 A2
Ashbourne Dr. Ma Dra 97 E1
Ashbourne Dr. N-u-L 55 D1
Ashbourne Dr. Swad 186 C1
Ashbourne Gr. Han 57 E3
Ashbourne La. Alst 35 D1
Ashbourne Rd. Alst 35 D2
Ashbourne Rd. Che 76 C2
Ashbourne Rd. Leek 31 D2
Ashbourne Rd. May 81 E4
Ashbourne Rd. Roc 95 F2
Ashbourne Rd. Utt 111 D1
Ashbourne Rd. Wal 243 E2
Ashbourne Rd. Wolv 266 C2
Ashbrook Cl. Gno 171 E4
Ashbrook Cl. Utt 126 B3
Ashbrook La. Ab Br 161 E3
Ashbrook. Bu on T 167 D1
Ashburton St. Burs 57 D4
Ashby Cres. Lon 72 C1
Ashby Rd E. Bretby 167 F1
Ashby Rd. Bu on T 167 D1
Ashby Rd. Tam 250 B4
Ashby Rd. Wig 250 B4
Ashcombe Gr. Lon 72 C1
Ashcombe Rd. Ched 45 E2
Ashcombe Way. Leek 30 C2
Ashcott Wlk. Buck 58 B1
Ashcroft Ave. S-o-T 71 F1
Ashcroft Cl. N-u-L 56 A3
Ashcroft Gr. N-u-L 56 A3
Ashcroft La. Shen 246 C3
Ashcroft La. Wall 246 C4
Ashcroft Oval. N-u-L 56 A3
Ashcroft Pl. N-u-L 56 A3
Ashcroft Rd. N-u-L 56 A3
Ashdale Cl. Bu on T 186 A4
Ashdale Cl. Kingsw 275 E4
Ashdale Cl. Sto 120 A4
Ashdale Dr. Staf 155 E4
Ashdale Park. Swyn 118 C3
Ashdale Rd. Fen 72 B3
Ashdale Rd. Leek 31 D3
Ashdale Rd. Tam 250 B3
Ashdale Rise. N-u-L 71 D2
Ashdene Gdns. Kingsw 275 E1
Ashdene Gr. Tren 71 F1
Ashdown Dr. Kingsw 275 F2
Ashe's La. Dr in C 144 B4
Ashen Cl. Sedg 266 B2
Ashenden Rise. Wolv 265 D4
Ashendene Gr. Tren 87 F4
Ashenhurst Way. Leek 30 C2
Ashenough Rd. Kids 40 B3
Ashfield Ct. N-u-L 56 A1
Ashfield Gr. Wolv 240 B2
Ashfield Rd. Wolv 240 B2
Ashfield Rd. Wolv 255 E1
Ashfield Sq. Buck 58 A1
Ashfields Grange. N-u-L 56 A1
Ashfields New Rd. N-u-L 56 A1
Ashfields. Albr 237 D3
Ashflats Rd. Brad 174 C2
Ashflats Rd. Staf 174 C2
Ashford Dr. Sedg 271 F4
Ashford Gr. Sto 120 B4
Ashford Rd. Bu on T 166 A3
Ashford St. S-o-T 72 B4
Ashgrove. Burnt 228 C3
Ashland St. Wolv 266 A4
Ashlands Ave. S-o-T 71 F4
Ashlands Cl. Tam 250 B4
Ashlands Cres. S-o-T 71 F4
Ashlands Gr. S-o-T 71 E4
Ashlands Rd. S-o-T 71 F4
Ashlands. Hix 139 E1
Ashlar Cl. Che He 42 A4
Ashlea Dr. May 81 E4
Ashleigh Ave. Swad 186 C3
Ashleigh Cres. Whe As 205 E4
Ashleigh Dr. Tam 261 F4
Ashleigh Dr. Utt 110 C4
Ashleigh Rd. Rug 196 C4
Ashleigh Rd. Up Tea 92 C2
Ashley Cl. Bu on T 167 D2
Ashley Cl. Kingsw 275 E2
Ashley Cl. Staf 155 D2
Ashley Cl. Stour 279 E1
Ashley Croft. Ch Eat 190 A4
Ashley Ct. Bu on T 167 D2
Ashley Gdns. Cod 238 C2
Ashley Gr. N-u-L 56 B2
Ashley Rd. Burnt 211 F1
Ashley Rd. Kid 280 A1
Ashley Rd. Wal 242 C1
Ashley Rd. Wolv 265 F3
Ashley View. Ma Dra 97 E1
Ashman St. Che He 42 B1
Ashmead Rd. Burnt 229 D4
Ashmole Cl. Lich 231 F3
Ashmore Ave. Wolv 242 A1
Ashmore Dr. Gno 171 E4
Ashmore Wlk. Han 57 E2
Ashoale Cl. Hunt 209 E4
Ashover Gr. Che He 41 F4
Ashover Rd. Swad 186 C3
Ashridge Ave. N-u-L 71 D1
Ashridge Gr. Lon 73 E3
Ashridge Wlk. Staf 136 B1
Ashton Cl. Congle 6 A1
Ashton Ct. Cav 59 D2
Ashton Ct. N-u-L 71 E1
Ashton Dr. Brown 244 B2
Ashton St. Lon 73 D2
Ashtree Bank. Rug 197 D3
Ashtree Cl. Col 177 E4
Ashtree Rd. Brown 244 A2
Ashurst Gr. Meir 90 A4
Ashwell Rd. S-o-T 71 E4
Ashwells Gr. Wolv 240 A1
Ashwood Ave. Kingsw 275 E1
Ashwood Cl. Ma Dra 97 D1
Ashwood Gr. Fors 91 D3
Ashwood Gr. Wolv 266 A3
Ashwood Terr. Lon 73 E3
Ashwood. Lon 73 E2
Ashworth Ave. Bu on T 167 E1
Ashworth House. Cann 210 A2
Ashworth St. Fen 72 B3
Ashworth Way. Newp 168 C1
Askerbank La. Wd Gr 8 A1
Askew Bridge Rd. Sedg 271 D2
Askew Cl. Sedg 271 F3
Aspen Cft. Staf 174 A4
Aspen Cl. Kids 26 C2
Aspen Ct. Cann 211 D3
Aspen Gr. Burnt 228 C4
Aspen Rd. Ba-u-Ne 201 E4
Aspen Way. Newp 168 C1
Aspley Cl. Penk 224 C3
Asquith Cl. Bidd 27 F4
Asquith Dr. Cann 210 B1
Astbury Cl. Kids 26 B2
Astbury La Ends. Congle 15 F4
Aster Cl. Meir 74 A3
Aster Wlk. Wolv 240 A2
Astil St. Bu on T 166 C1
Aston Bk. Sei 154 C2
Aston Bk. Staf 154 C2
Aston Cl. Col 177 E4
Aston Cl. Penk 208 A4
Aston Cl. Shen 246 C3
Aston Dr. Newp 168 C1
Aston Hill. Sei 154 C2
Aston La. Maer 83 F4
Aston La. Sto 120 B2
Aston La. Sud 129 D3
Aston La. Woore 67 F1
Aston Lodge Parkway. Sto 120 B3
Aston Rd. N-u-L 40 B1
Aston St. Wolv 266 A4
Aston Terr. Staf 155 F3
Astonfields Rd. Staf 155 F3
Astor Rd. Aldr 257 D1
Astor Rd. Kingsw 275 F3
Astoria Cl. Wal 242 B1
Astoria Dr. Staf 174 C3
Astoria Gdns. Wal 242 B1
Astro Gr. Lon 73 D2
Athelney Ct. Brown 244 A2
Athelstan Cl. Penk 208 A4
Athelstan Gr. Pert 254 C3
Athelstan St. Tuns 41 E2
Athelstan Way. Tam 249 F4
Athena Rd. Han 57 F3
Atherstone Rd. Tren 88 A4
Atherstone St. Faz 261 D4
Athlestan Way. Bu on T 147 E1
Athlone St. Che He 42 B1
Atholl Rd. Lon 73 E1
Atkins Way. Roc 95 F2
Atlam Cl. Buck 58 A2
Atlantic Gr. Tren 88 A4
Atlas St. Fen 72 C3
Attingham Dr. Cann 210 A1
Attlee Cres. Rug 196 C4
Attlee Cres. Staf 174 B4
Attlee Gr. Cann 210 B1
Attlee Rd. Che 76 B1
Attwell Park. Wolv 265 E4
Attwood St. Kids 26 A1
Aubrey St. Tuns 41 D4
Auchinleck Dr. Lich 214 B1
Auckland Rd. Kingsw 275 F2
Auden Ct. Pert 254 C2
Auden Pl. Lon 73 E2
Auden Way. Staf 174 B4
Audlem Rd. Woore 67 D1
Audley Ave Bsns Pk. Newp 169 D1
Audley Ave. Newp 169 D1
Audley House Mews. Newp 169 D1
Audley House. Newp 169 D1
Audley Pl. N-u-L 71 D3
Audley Rd. Alsag 39 E4
Audley Rd. Audley 40 A1
Audley Rd. Barth 38 C3
Audley Rd. Kids 40 A3
Audley Rd. N-u-L 40 A1
Audley Rd. Newp 168 C2
Audley St. N-u-L 55 F2
Audley St. Tuns 41 E2
Audmore Rd. Gno 171 E4
Audnam. Br Hi 275 F1
Augustine Cl. Sto 120 B4
Augustine Gr. Sut C 257 F3
Augustines Wlk. Lich 214 A2
Aukland St. Burs 57 D4
Aulton Rd. Sut Co 258 C1
Austcliffe Rd. Cook 280 A3
Austin Cl. Sedg 271 F1
Austin Cl. Sto 120 A4
Austin Cote La. Lich 231 F4
Austin Friars. Staf 155 F1
Austin St. Han 57 E1
Austrey La. Ne Re 236 C2
Austrey La. Ne Re 236 C3
Austwick Gr. S-o-T 71 F3
Autumn Berry Gr. Sedg 271 F3
Autumn Cl. Brown 244 B1
Autumn Dr. Brown 244 B1
Autumn Dr. Lich 214 B1
Autumn Dr. Sedg 271 E2
Avarne Pl. Staf 155 F2
Aveling Green. Han 57 F4
Aveling Rd. Han 57 F4
Avenue Rd S. Newp 168 C1
Avenue Rd. Cann 210 C1
Avenue Rd. Newp 168 C1
Avenue Rd. S-o-T 57 E1
Avenue Rd. Wolv 255 F1
Avenue The. Bag 43 F2
Avenue The. Bla 281 D1
Avenue The. Che 76 B1
Avenue The. Ched 45 E2
Avenue The. End 43 F4
Avenue The. Feath 241 D4
Avenue The. Fors 91 D4
Avenue The. Kids 25 F1
Avenue The. N-u-L 56 B1
Avenue The. N-u-L 71 E4
Avenue The. Sto 105 D1
Avenue The. Whe As 206 B2
Avenue The. Wolv 265 D4
Avenue The. Wolv 265 F2
Avenue The. Woo 79 F3
Averil Rd. Staf 174 B4
Averill Dr. Rug 178 B1
Aviation La. Bu on T 165 E2
Avill. Tam 262 A3
Avington Cl. Sedg 271 E4
Avion Cl. Meir 90 B4
Avoca St. Han 57 E3
Avocet Cl. Utt 126 B3
Avon Ave. Che He 41 F2
Avon Cl. Kids 26 A1
Avon Cl. N-u-L 71 D2
Avon Cl. Pert 254 C2
Avon Cl. Staf 156 A2
Avon Cres. Brown 244 A1
Avon Dale. Newp 168 C2
Avon Gr. Ashl 99 E3
Avon Gr. Che 76 C1
Avon Gr. Sto 120 A3
Avon Hill. Staf 156 B2
Avon Rd. Burnt 228 C3
Avon Rd. Cann 226 B4
Avon Rd. Stour 279 F2
Avon Rd. Wal 243 F1
Avon Rise. Staf 156 A2
Avon Way. Bu on T 167 D1
Avon. Tam 262 A3
Avondale Cl. Kingsw 275 F4
Avondale Rd. Wolv 255 F2
Avondale St. Burs 56 B4
Avonlea Gdns. Rug 178 B1
Avonwick Gr. Buck 58 A3
Axborough La. Cook 280 B2
Axbridge Wlk. Che He 42 B1
Axon Cres. Meir 74 A2
Aylesbury Rd. Buck 58 B1
Aylesford Cl. Sedg 266 B1
Aylesford Dr. Sut C 257 F3
Aynsley Ave. N-u-L 71 D2
Aynsley Cl. Che 76 B1
Aynsley Rd. S-o-T 57 D1
Aynsley's Dr. Bly 90 C4
Ayr Rd. Kings 76 C3
Ayrshire Way. Congle 6 A1
Ayrton Cl. Pert 255 D2
Ayshford St. Lon 73 D2
Azalea Cl. Cod 239 D2
Babbacombe Ave. Staf 175 F4
Babbington Cl. Tut 146 B3
Babbington Cl. Whit 232 C3
Babworth Cl. Wolv 240 A1
Back Browning St. Staf 155 E2
Back Bunt's La. N-in-M 43 E2
Back Cross La. Congle 16 A4
Back Ford Green Rd. Che He 42 B1
Back Gdn St. N-u-L 71 E4
Back Heathcote St. Kids 26 A1
Back La. Aldr 256 C4
Back La. Alst 35 F2
Back La. Alt 78 C1
Back La. Ash 100 A3
Back La. Betley 53 D4
Back La. Col 177 E4
Back La. Ella 80 A2
Back La. End 28 A1
Back La. End 43 D4
Back La. Gno 171 E3
Back La. Hau 173 D3
Back La. Hix 139 E1
Back La. Leek 30 B3
Back La. Mill 102 B3
Back La. Ran 153 E2
Back La. Shen 246 C1
Back La. Utt 126 B4
Back La. Water 49 F1
Back La. Whe As 205 E3
Back La. Whit 232 B3
Back La. Woo 79 F4
Back La. Woods 151 E4
Back Radfords. Sto 105 D1
Back Rd. Kingsw 275 E4
Back Westlands Rd. Utt 126 A3
Backcester La. Lich 231 D4
Backcrofts. Cann 209 E1
Baddeley Green La. N-in-M 43 D1
Baddeley Hall Rd. N-in-M 43 E2
Baddeley Rd. N-in-M 43 D1
Baddeley St. Burs 41 F1
Baddeley St. Che 76 C1
Baddely's Ct. Newp 168 C1
Baden Rd. Che He 42 B1
Baden St. N-u-L 56 A1
Bader Rd. Pert 254 C2
Badger Brow Rd. Ashl 99 E3
Badger Gr. Meir 90 B4
Badger La. Maer 84 B2
Badger St. Sedg 271 F3
Badger's End. Whe As 205 D3
Badgers Bank Rd. Sut C 257 F3
Badgers Cl. Brown 244 A3
Badgers Croft. Ecc 133 F3
Badgers Croft. Staf 175 E3
Badgers Hollow. Up Tea 93 D1
Badgers Way. Cann 210 B1
Badgery Cl. Utt 111 D1
Badminton Cl. Sedg 271 F2
Badnall Cl. Leek 30 B3
Badnall St. Leek 30 B3
Bag La. Adm 159 E4
Bag La. March 127 F1
Bag La. Rost 96 C4
Baggeridge Cl. Him 271 D4
Baggott Pl. N-u-L 70 C4
Baggott St. Wolv 266 B4
Bagnall Rd. Bag 43 E1
Bagnall Rd. N-in-M 43 E1
Bagnall St. Han 57 E2
Bagot Gr. Han 57 F4
Bagot St. Ab Br 160 C3
Bagots Oak. Staf 174 B4
Bagots View. Ab Br 161 D3
Bagots View. Ch Lei 109 D2
Bagridge Cl. Wolv 265 D4
Bagridge Rd. Wolv 265 D4
Bailey Ave. Tam 261 F3
Bailey Cl. Cann 210 A2
Bailey Cres. Congle 6 A2
Bailey Rd. Fen 72 C2
Bailey St. Bu on T 166 B1
Bailey St. N-u-L 56 A1
Bailey St. S-o-T 56 C1
Bailey St. Staf 155 F1
Bailey's Bank. Bidd 16 B2
Bain House. Staf 174 C3
Bainbridge Rd. Tren 88 A4
Bains Gr. N-u-L 55 F4
Baker Ave. Wolv 266 C1
Baker Cres N. N-in-M 43 E2
Baker Cres S. N-in-M 43 D2
Baker Cres. N-in-M 43 E2
Baker St. Bu on T 185 F4
Baker St. Burnt 228 C3
Baker St. Fen 72 C3
Baker's La. Aldr 256 A3
Baker's La. Lich 231 D4
Baker's La. Norb 150 B2
Bakers Gdns. Cod 238 C2
Bakers Way. Cod 238 C2
Bakers Wlk. Tam 261 F3
Bakewell Cl. N-u-L 55 D1
Bakewell Cl. Wal 243 E2
Bakewell Dr. Sto 120 B3
Bakewell Green. Swad 186 C3
Bakewell St. S-o-T 71 F3
Bala Gr. Che 76 C2
Balaam's La. Sto 106 B3
Balance Hill. Utt 126 B4
Balance St. Utt 126 B4
Baldwin Gr. Cann 210 B1
Baldwin Way. Swi 269 F1
Balfour Cres. Wolv 255 F2
Balfour Gr. Bidd 27 F4
Balfour Rd. Kingsw 275 F4
Balfour St. Bu on T 166 B3
Balfour St. Han 57 E2
Balfour. Tam 250 A2
Balk Pas. Staf 155 E2
Ball Haye Green. Leek 31 D4
Ball Haye Rd. Leek 30 C3
Ball Haye St. Leek 30 C3
Ball Haye Terr. Leek 30 C3
Ball Hayes Rd. Che He 42 B3
Ball La. Bre 240 B3
Ball La. End 43 D3
Ball La. Leek 30 C3
Ball La. N-in-M 43 D3
Ball's Yd. N-u-L 56 A1
Ballarat Wlk. Stour 279 F3
Ballington Gdns. Leek 30 C3
Ballington View. Leek 30 C2
Ballinson Rd. Lon 72 C1
Balloon St. S-o-T 56 B1
Balmain Cres. Ess 241 D1
Balmoral Cl. Lich 231 E3
Balmoral Cl. Sto 120 A3
Balmoral Cl. Tren 72 A1
Balmoral Ct. Cann 210 A3
Balmoral Dr. Cann 209 F4
Balmoral Dr. Ma Dra 97 F1
Balmoral Dr. Wom 265 D1
Balmoral Rd. Bu on T 167 D2
Balmoral Rd. Kingsw 275 E1
Balmoral Rd. Staf 156 B1
Balmoral Rd. Sut C 257 F3
Balmoral Rd. Wolv 266 A3
Balmoral View. Sedg 271 F1
Balmoral Way. Burnt 211 F1
Baltic Cl. Cann 209 F1
Baltic Cl. Tren 88 A4
Bamber Cl. Wolv 265 F4
Bamber Pl. N-u-L 55 F3
Bamber St. S-o-T 72 A4
Bamborough Cl. Bu on T 166 B4
Bamburgh. Tam 261 E4
Bambury St. Fen 73 E3
Bambury St. Lon 73 E3
Bamford Cl. Wal 243 E2
Bamford Gr. Han 57 D3
Bamford Rd. Wal 243 E2
Bamford Rd. Wolv 266 A4
Bamford St. Tam 250 B2
Bampton Ave. Burnt 229 D4
Bampton Cl. End 43 F4
Banbery Dr. Wom 269 F2
Banbury Cl. Sedg 271 F3
Banbury Gr. Bidd 27 E4
Banbury Rd. Cann 226 B4
Banbury St. Kids 25 E1
Bancroft La. Fors 90 C3
Bancroft La. Ha Ri 199 D4
Bancroft. Tam 250 C2
Bandridge La. Wd Gr 18 A4
Baneberry Dr. Feath 241 D4
Bangley La. Dra Ba 260 A4
Bangley La. Hint 259 F3
Bank Cl. Utt 126 B4
Bank Cres. Burnt 228 C3
Bank End. End 43 D4
Bank Hall Rd. Che He 42 A1
Bank House Dr. N-u-L 56 C1
Bank Pas. Staf 155 F2
Bank Rd. Sedg 271 E1
Bank Side. Hartin 24 B3
Bank Side. Sto 119 F3
Bank St. Cann 210 C1
Bank St. Che 76 B2
Bank St. Kids 26 B2
Bank St. Tuns 41 E2
Bank The. Sch Gr 26 A4
Bank Top Ave. Che He 42 A2
Bank Top. Rug 178 B1
Bank Wlk. Bu on T 166 A4
Bankerwall La. Stan 80 B4
Bankfield Gr. Audley 54 C2
Bankfield Rd. Meir 89 F4
Bankhouse Dr. Congle 6 A3

287

Beresford Dell. Made — Brackenfield Way. Staf

Beresford Dell. Made 68 B3
Beresford La. Alst 24 B1
Beresford St. S-o-T 57 D1
Bergamot Dr. Meir 90 A3
Berkeley Cl. Pert 254 C2
Berkeley Dr. Kingsw 275 E4
Berkeley St. Han 57 E2
Berkeley Terr. Sto 104 C1
Berkeley Way. Longd 198 A1
Berkley Cl. Gno 171 F4
Berkshire Gr. N-u-L 71 E3
Berkshire The. Wal 243 D2
Berkswell Cl. Sut C 257 F2
Bernard Cheadle La. Swyn 103 E2
Bernard Gr. Sto 89 F2
Bernard St. Han 57 E2
Berne Ave. N-u-L 70 C3
Bernwall Cl. Stour 279 F2
Berrisford Cl. Ma Dra 97 F1
Berrisford Rd. Ma Dra 97 F1
Berry Gdns. Bu on T 167 E2
Berry Hedge La. Bu on T 167 E2
Berry Hill Rd. S-o-T 57 F1
Berry Hill. Cann 210 B2
Berry La. Lon 73 D2
Berry Rd. Staf 155 D4
Berry St. S-o-T 72 A4
Berrybush Gdns. Sedg 271 F4
Berryfield Gr. Lon 73 F2
Berryfields. Shen 245 F3
Bert Smith Way. Ma Dra 97 E1
Bertlein Rd. Staf 155 F4
Berwick Dr. Cann 226 A4
Berwick Wlks. N-u-L 70 C4
Berwyn Gr. Ches Hay 226 C2
Best Ave. Bu on T 167 D1
Best St. Fen 72 C3
Beswick Cl. Che 76 B1
Beswick Rd. Che He 41 F3
Beswicks La. N in H 82 B1
Bethesda Rd. Han 57 E1
Bethesda St. Han 57 E2
Betjeman Wlk. Staf 174 B4
Betley Hall Gdns. Betley 53 D3
Betley Pl. N-u-L 71 E3
Betlingspring La. Snel 81 E2
Beton Way. Staf 155 E4
Bettany Glade. Wolv 240 C2
Bettany Rd. Burs 57 D4
Betton Rd. Ma Dra 97 F1
Betty's La. Nor Ca 228 A2
Bevan Ave. Kids 40 C3
Bevan Ave. Wolv 266 D2
Bevan Cl. Brown 244 B1
Bevan Lee Rd. Cann 209 E2
Bevan Pl. Made 68 C4
Bevandean Cl. Tren 88 B3
Beveridge Cl. Meir 74 A1
Beverley Cl. Penk 207 F4
Beverley Cres. Fors 91 D4
Beverley Cres. Wolv 266 C2
Beverley Dr. Buck 58 B1
Beverley Dr. Staf 155 E4
Beverley Hill. Cann 210 B3
Beverly Dr. Kingsw 275 E4
Beverston Rd. Pert 255 D2
Beville St. Fen 72 C3
Bevin La. Buck 58 A2
Bew St. N-in-M 42 C3
Bewcastle Gr. Meir 90 A4
Bexhill Gr. Han 57 F3
Bexley St. Han 57 D3
Beyer Cl. Tam 251 D1
Bhylls Cres. Wolv 265 E4
Bhylls La. Wolv 265 E4
Bibby's Green. Wolv 240 C2
Bichall Ave. Tuns 41 E3
Bickford Cl. Whe As 206 A3
Bickley Ave. Sut C 257 F3
Bida La. Congle 16 A4
Biddulph Common Rd. Bidd 17 D3
Biddulph Park Rd. Bidd 17 D3
Biddulph Rd. Bidd 26 C3
Biddulph Rd. Che He 42 A4
Biddulph Rd. Congle 16 A4
Biddulph Rd. Kids 26 C3
Biddulph St. Congle 16 B4
Bideford Ave. Staf 175 E4
Bideford Way. Cann 226 A4
Biggin Cl. Pert 254 C3
Bignall End Rd. Audley 40 A2
Bigsbury Wlk. Burs 56 C4
Bigwood La. Bradl 173 F2
Bigwood La. Copp 173 F2
Bilberry Bank. Cann 209 F3
Bilberry Cl. Rug 178 B1
Bilberry Cres. Hunt 209 E3
Bilbrook Ct. Cod 239 D2
Bilbrook Gr. Cod 239 D2
Bilbrook Rd. Cod 239 D2
Billinge St. Burs 56 C4
Billington Ave. Col 158 B1
Billington Bank. Bradl 173 E3
Billy Buns La. Wom 270 A4
Bilston Rd. Wolv 266 C4
Bilston St. Sedg 271 F4
Bilton St. S-o-T 72 A3
Bingley St. Wolv 266 A4
Birch Ave. Bidd 27 D3
Birch Ave. Brown 244 C4
Birch Ave. Burnt 228 C3
Birch Ave. Cann 226 B4
Birch Ave. Swad 186 C4
Birch Brook Ind Park. Shen 246 C3
Birch Brook La. Shen 246 C3
Birch Cl. Col 158 B1
Birch Cl. Dens 95 E3
Birch Cl. Staf 175 F3
Birch Coppice. Wom 269 F3
Birch Croft. Aldr 256 B4
Birch Dale. Made 68 C3
Birch Dr. Li As 257 E3
Birch Dr. Stour 279 F3
Birch Gr. Bly 90 A2
Birch Gr. Fors 91 D4
Birch Gr. Lich 231 E4
Birch Gr. Pol 262 B4
Birch Green Gr. Han 57 F4
Birch Hill Ave. Wom 269 F3
Birch House Rd. N-u-L 55 E4
Birch La. Aldr 245 E1
Birch La. Brown 244 B1
Birch La. Rug 197 D3
Birch Rd. Audley 39 F1
Birch Rd. Ess 241 F1
Birch Rd. Sedg 266 C1
Birch Rd. Sto 120 A4
Birch Rise. Ashl 99 F2
Birch St. Han 57 F3
Birch Terr. Burnt 212 A1
Birch Terr. Han 57 E2
Birch Tree La. Sch Gr 26 A4
Birch Tree La. Whitm 85 E4
Birch Wlk. Lon 73 D1
Birchall Cl. Leek 30 C1
Birchall La. Leek 30 C1
Birchall Park Ave. Leek 30 C2
Bircham Wlk. N-u-L 71 D1
Birchcroft. Bre 224 B1
Birchdown Ave. Che He 42 A2
Birchendale Cl. Up Tea 92 C1
Birchenfields La. Che 75 F3
Birchenwood Rd. Che He 41 F4
Birchenwood Rd. Kids 26 C1
Birches Ave. Cod 239 E1
Birches Barn Ave. Wolv 265 F4
Birches Barn Rd. Wolv 265 F4
Birches Cl. Bu on T 166 B4
Birches Head Rd. Buck 57 F3
Birches Head Rd. Han 57 F3
Birches Park Rd. Cod 239 D1
Birches Rd. Cod 239 D1
Birches The. Che 76 B1
Birches Valley. Rug 195 E3
Birchfield Ave. Wolv 255 D3
Birchfield Cl. King 262 B1
Birchfield Rd. Bu on T 185 F3
Birchfield Rd. Buck 58 B3
Birchfields Cl. Sto 119 F3
Birchfields Dr. Cann 210 B1
Birchgate Gr. Buck 58 B2
Birchgate. Buck 58 B2
Birchglade. Wolv 255 E1
Birchlands Rd. Han 57 F3
Birchmoor La. Blym 189 E1
Birchmoor La. Ch Eat 189 E1
Birchmoor Rd. Pol 262 C4
Birchover Way. Che He 42 A4
Birchtree La. Rug 196 C3
Birchwood Ave. Dord 262 C4
Birchwood Cl. Ess 242 A2
Birchwood Rd. Lich 231 F4
Birchwood Rd. Wolv 266 A3
Birchwood Rise. Ab Br 161 D3
Birchwood Wlk. Kingsw 275 F4
Bird Rd. Meir 74 A1
Bird St. Lich 231 D4
Bird St. Sedg 271 E2
Bird's Barn La. Cook 277 E1
Bird's Barn La. Kin 277 E1
Birdhope. Tam 251 E1
Birds Bush Rd. Tam 261 F4
Birdsgrove La. May 66 B2
Birdsgrove La. Swin 66 B2
Birkdale Dr. Kids 26 B2
Birkdale Dr. Staf 156 B2
Birkdale Rd. Wal 243 D2
Birks Dr. Ashl 99 E3
Birks St. S-o-T 72 A3
Birmingham New Rd. Wolv 266 C2
Birmingham Rd. Aldr 256 A2
Birmingham Rd. Bla 281 E1
Birmingham Rd. Lich 231 D2
Birmingham Rd. Shen 247 D2
Birmingham St. Wolv 266 B4
Birrell St. Fen 72 C3
Biscay Gr. Tren 88 B4
Bishop Rd. Che He 42 A3
Bishop St. Lon 73 D3
Bishop's Cl. Kids 40 B4
Bishops Ct. Ecc 133 F4
Bishops Dr. Bre 223 E4
Bishops Grange. Rug 178 C1
Bishops La. Ma Dra 97 D1
Bishops Way. Sut C 257 F3
Bishton La. Col 178 A3
Bitham Cl. Penk 207 F4
Bitham Ct. Bu on T 147 E1
Bitham La. Bu on T 147 E1
Bittell Cl. Wolv 240 C2
Bittern La. Che 76 C2
Bitterne Pl. Buck 73 E4
Bitterscote La. Tam 250 A1
Black Bank Rd. Ched 44 B3
Black Dr. Inge 157 E3
Black Horse La. Han 57 E2
Black La. Fort 150 C1
Black La. Kings 62 B2
Blackbank Rd. N-u-L 55 E2
Blackberry La. Brown 245 D2
Blackberry La. Staf 155 E2
Blackberry La. Sut C 257 F2
Blackbird Cl. Utt 126 B3
Blackbrook Way. Wolv 240 C2
Blackburn Ave. Wolv 255 F4
Blackdown. Tam 251 E1
Blackfriar's Rd. N-u-L 71 D4
Blackhalve La. Ess 241 E1
Blackheath La. Hop 156 C2
Blackhole La. Sei 154 B1
Blackies La. Sto 120 C4
Blacklake Dr. Bly 90 A2
Blackmere Cl. Newp 168 B1
Blackpit La. Dove 127 D4
Blackpit La. Wom 264 C2
Blackpool St. Bu on T 185 E4
Blackroot Dr. Burnt 229 E2
Blackshaw Cl. Congle 6 A1
Blacksmith La. Whit 232 C3
Blacksmith's La. Eg 148 A3
Blacksmith's La. N Sol 167 F4
Blackthorn Ave. Burnt 228 C2
Blackthorn Cres. Cann 211 D3
Blackthorn Pl. N-u-L 55 F4
Blackthorn Rd. Br Hi 275 F1
Blackthorn Rd. Bu on T 185 F3
Blackthorne Cl. Dud 271 F2
Blackthorne Rd. Dud 271 F3
Blackthorne Rd. Lich 231 E4
Blackwell's Row. Han 57 D3
Blackwood Pl. Lon 73 F2
Blackwood Rd. Aldr 256 C1
Blackwood Rd. Tam 261 E4
Bladon Ave. N-u-L 71 D2
Bladon Cl. Che He 42 A4
Bladon St. Bu on T 167 E2
Bladon View. Bu on T 148 A1
Blaizefield Cl. Woore 67 E1
Blake Cl. Cann 210 A3
Blake St. Burs 56 C4
Blake St. Li As 257 F3
Blake St. Shen 257 F3
Blakeley Ave. Wolv 255 F4
Blakeley Heath Dr. Wom 270 A3
Blakeley La. Kings 63 D1
Blakeley La. Oak 63 D1
Blakeley Rise. Wolv 255 F4
Blakelow La. Stan 65 D1
Blakelow Rd. Buck 58 A3
Blakemore Rd. Brown 245 D2
Blakenall Heath. Wal 243 E1
Blakeney Ave. N-u-L 71 D2
Blakeney Ave. Stour 279 E3
Blakeney Cl. Sedg 271 E4
Blakenhall Gdns. Wolv 266 B4
Blakeways Cl. Edin 217 E3
Blakiston St. Staf 155 F2
Blanchard Cl. Meir 90 B4
Blandford Dr. Kingsw 275 F2
Blanefield. Wolv 239 F1
Blanford Gdns. Burnt 229 E3
Blantyre St. Lon 73 E1
Blantyre Wlk. Lon 73 E1
Blatchford Cl. Meir 74 A1
Blaydon Ave. Sut Co 258 C1
Blaydon Rd. Wolv 240 A1
Blaze Hill Rd. Kingsw 275 D4
Blaze Park. Kingsw 275 D4
Bleak Pl. Burs 57 D4
Bleak St. N-u-L 56 B2
Bleeding Wolf La. Sch Gr 25 F3
Blencarn Gr. N-in-M 43 E2
Blenheim Cl. Bu on T 167 E2
Blenheim Cl. Tam 250 B2
Blenheim Rd. Burnt 229 D4
Blenheim Rd. Kingsw 275 F3
Blenheim Rd. Nor Ca 228 A2
Blenheim St. Fen 72 B3
Blenheim Way. Sedg 271 F1
Bleriot Cl. Meir 90 B4
Blewitt St. Cann 210 A4
Blithbury Rd. Colt 179 E3
Blithbury Rd. Ha Ri 180 C2
Blithbury Rd. Hi Ri 179 E3
Blithfield Cl. Cav 59 D1
Blithfield House. Staf 174 C3
Blithfield Pl. Cann 210 A1
Blithfield Rd. Brown 228 A1
Bloomfield Cl. Wom 269 E3
Bloomfield Cres. Lich 214 A1
Bloomfield Dr. Wal 242 B1
Bloomfield Way. Tam 249 F4
Bloomsbury St. Wolv 266 B4
Bloomsbury Way. Lich 231 F4
Blore Rd. Blo 98 C1
Blossomfield Cl. Kingsw 275 F4
Blount Cl. Penk 207 F4
Blounts Dr. Utt 126 A3
Blue House Barns. Chet 168 C2
Blue House La. Albr 237 D4
Bluebell Cl. Bidd 27 F4
Bluebell Cl. Cann 210 A3
Bluebell Cl. Kingsw 275 E1
Bluebell La. Gr Wyr 227 D1
Bluebell Rd. Brown 245 D2
Bluebird Cl. Lich 231 E4
Bluemeadow La. Wom 270 A4
Bluestone Ave. Che He 42 A1
Bluestone La. Bu on T 186 A4
Blundies La. Env 273 F2
Blunt St. N-u-L 56 B2
Blunt's Hollow. Ab Br 162 A2
Blurton Rd. Barl 89 D2
Blurton Rd. Fen 72 C2
Blurton Rd. Lon 72 C2
Blythe Ave. Bly 90 A3
Blythe Bridge Rd. Cav 74 C1
Blythe Cl. Bly 90 B4
Blythe Cl. Burnt 229 E3
Blythe Gdns. Cod 238 C2
Blythe Mount Park. Fors 91 D4
Blythe Rd. Fors 91 D4
Blythe Rd. Staf 174 C3
Blythe St. Tam 250 B2
Blythe View. Bly 91 D1
Blythe View. Fors 90 C3
Blythe View. Ha Ri 180 C1
Blythebridge Bank. Kingst 140 C3
Blythfield. Bu on T 166 C2
Boardman Cres. Staf 155 E2
Boardman Rd. Swad 186 C1
Boardmans Bank. End 28 A1
Boat La. Wall 229 F1
Boat La. Wes on Tr 138 B2
Boathorse Rd. Kids 41 D4
Boathorse Rd. Tuns 41 D3
Boatman's La. Brown 244 C1
Bodiam Ct. Pert 255 D2
Bodicote Gr. Sut Co 258 C1
Bodington Rd. Sut Co 258 B2
Bodmin Ave. Staf 175 E4
Bodmin Wlk. Che He 42 B1
Bognop Rd. Ess 241 E2
Bogs La. Fors 90 C3
Bolberry Cl. Meir 73 F1
Bold St. Han 57 F3
Bolebridge Mews. Tam 250 A3
Bolebridge St. Tam 250 B2
Boley Cl. Lich 231 F4
Boley Cottage La. Lich 231 F4
Boley La. Lich 231 E4
Boleyn Cl. Ches Hay 226 B1
Bolina Gr. Fen 73 D3
Bollin Gr. Bidd 16 C1
Bolney Gr. Han 57 F3
Bolsover Cl. Che He 42 A4
Bolton Pl. Meir 89 F4
Bolton Way. Wal 242 C2
Boma Rd. Tren 87 F4
Bond End. Yox 182 A1
Bond St. Bu on T 166 B1
Bond St. Tuns 41 E2
Bondfield La. Yox 181 F1
Bondfield Way. Meir 74 A1
Bondway. Cann 209 F4
Bonehill Rd. Faz 249 F2
Bonehill Rd. Tam 249 F2
Boney Hay Rd. Burnt 229 D4
Boningdale Way. Staf 174 A4
Bonnard Cl. Meir 90 B3
Bonnington Cres. Staf 155 E1
Bonville Gdns. Wolv 240 C2
Boon Ave. S-o-T 72 A4
Boon Gr. Staf 174 C3
Boon Hill Rd. Audley 39 F1
Booth La. Adm 140 C2
Booth La. Kingst 140 C2
Booth St. Audley 39 E1
Booth St. Cann 210 A3
Booth St. N-u-L 55 F3
Booth St. S-o-T 72 A3
Boothen Green. S-o-T 72 A3
Boothen Old Rd. S-o-T 72 A3
Boothen Rd. S-o-T 72 A3
Boothenwood Terr. S-o-T 72 A3
Boothroyd St. Han 57 E2
Bordeaux Cl. Sedg 271 F2
Borden Cl. Whe As 205 E4
Borden Cl. Wolv 255 F4
Border Way. Staf 174 C3
Bore St. Lich 231 D4
Borman. Tam 249 F3
Borough Cres. Stour 279 F3
Borough La. Longd 212 C4
Borough Rd. Bu on T 166 B2
Borough Rd. Tam 250 B4
Borrowcop La. Lich 231 E3
Borrowdale Rd. N-in-M 42 C2
Boscobel Gr. Bre 223 E4
Boscombe Gr. Tren 88 B3
Boscomoor Cl. Penk 207 F4
Boscomoor La. Penk 207 F4
Bosinney Cl. Lon 73 D3
Bosley Gr. Tuns 41 E3
Bosley View. Congle 6 A1
Bostock Cl. Sto 120 B3
Boston Cl. Cann 210 C1
Bosty La. Aldr 256 A2
Boswell Rd. Cann 209 E2
Boswell St. S-o-T 56 C1
Bosworth Cl. Sedg 271 F3
Bosworth Dr. Bu on T 166 A4
Botany Bay Rd. Han 57 F3
Botany Dr. Sedg 271 E3
Botfield Cl. Albr 237 D3
Botham Dr. Ched 45 E3
Botterham La. Wom 269 F2
Botteslow St. Han 57 E2
Bottom La. Ipst 47 E3
Bottom La. Swyn 103 D4
Boucher Rd. Ched 45 E2
Boughey Rd. Audley 39 F1
Boughey Rd. Newp 168 C1
Boughey Rd. S-o-T 72 B4
Boughey St. S-o-T 72 A3
Boulevard The. Tuns 41 F2
Boulters La. King 262 B1
Boulton Cl. Burnt 229 E4
Boulton St. Han 57 E3
Boulton St. N-u-L 56 B3
Boundary Cl. Leek 30 C2
Boundary Cl. Sto 119 F3
Boundary Cres. Sedg 271 E2
Boundary Ct. Han 57 E3
Boundary Hill. Sedg 271 E2
Boundary La. Congle 16 A4
Boundary Rd. Eg 148 B4
Boundary St. Han 57 E3
Boundary St. N-u-L 56 B1
Boundary View. Che 76 A1
Boundary Way. Wolv 254 C1
Boundary Way. Wolv 265 E3
Bourne Ave. Faz 249 F1
Bourne Ave. Ran 153 E3
Bourne Cl. Cann 210 C1
Bourne Pl. Leek 30 B3
Bourne Rd. Kids 25 F1
Bourne St. Fen 72 C2
Bourne St. Sch Gr 26 B4
Bourne Vale. Aldr 256 B2
Bournes Bank S. Burs 57 D4
Bournes Bank. Burs 56 C4
Bouverie Par. Han 57 F4
Bow St. Rug 178 C1
Bowden St. Che He 42 A1
Bowdler Rd. Wolv 266 B4
Bowen St. Wolv 266 C3
Bowen-cooke Ave. Pert 254 C3
Bower Cl. Lich 214 B1
Bower End La. Made 68 B3
Bower La. Rug 178 B2
Bower St. Han 57 E1
Bowers Ct. Sto 120 B4
Bowes Dr. Cann 209 F2
Bowfell Gr. Fen 73 D3
Bowhill La. Betley 53 D3
Bowland Ave. N-u-L 55 F1
Bowling Alley. Act Tru 193 F4
Bowling Green Ave. Tam 261 F4
Bowling Green Rd. Stour 279 F3
Bowman Gr. Che He 42 A4
Bowmead Cl. Tren 88 B3
Bowmere Cl. Bidd 16 B1
Bowness St. Han 57 D3
Bowood Dr. Wolv 255 E3
Bowsey Wood Rd. Made 68 C4
Bowstead St. S-o-T 72 A4
Bowyer Ave. N-in-M 42 C3
Box La. Meir 73 F1
Boxer Cl. Arm 198 B2
Boxwood Pl. N-u-L 55 E4
Boxwood Rd. Up Tea 92 C2
Boyden Cl. Cann 209 D1
Boyden Cl. Penk 208 A4
Boyles Hall Rd. Audley 39 F1
Brabazon Cl. Meir 90 B4
Bracken Ave. Ashl 99 E3
Bracken Cl. Bly 89 F3
Bracken Cl. Burnt 229 E4
Bracken Cl. Cann 210 B4
Bracken Cl. Lich 231 F3
Bracken Cl. Staf 155 D4
Bracken Cl. Titt 88 A1
Bracken Cl. Wolv 239 F1
Bracken Dale. Leek 30 A3
Bracken Park Gdns. Kingsw 275 F1
Bracken Rd. Hunt 209 E3
Bracken St. Fen 72 C2
Bracken View. Broc 176 B2
Bracken Way. Newp 168 C2
Bracken Way. Rug 178 B1
Brackenberry. N-u-L 56 A2
Brackenfield Ave. Buck 58 B1
Brackenfield Way. Staf 155 E4

288
Brackenhill Rd. Burnt
Broomfield Cl. Newp

Brackenhill Rd. Burnt 229 D4
Brackens The. N-u-L 71 E1
Brackenwood Rd. Bu on T 185 F3
Brackley Ave. Che He 42 A1
Bradbury Cl. Brown 244 C3
Bradbury Cl. N-in-M 42 C2
Bradbury La. Cann 210 A4
Bradbury La. Env 272 C2
Bradbury La. Ki Brom 199 E3
Bradbury Rise. Staf 155 D2
Braden Rd. Wolv 265 E2
Bradford Rd. Brown 244 C4
Bradford St. Cann 210 A3
Bradford St. Tam 249 F3
Bradford Terr. Han 57 F3
Bradgate Dr. Sut C 257 F3
Bradley Dr. Mill 117 F2
Bradley La. Brad 174 B3
Bradley La. Bradl 173 D2
Bradley La. Hau 173 D2
Bradley Rd. Stour 279 F3
Bradley Rd. Wolv 266 C4
Bradley St. Bu on T 185 F4
Bradley St. Utt 126 B4
Bradmore Rd. Bu on T 166 A3
Bradmore Rd. Wolv 265 F4
Bradshaw Way. Staf 155 E4
Bradwell Grange. N-u-L 56 A4
Bradwell La. Cann 211 F3
Bradwell La. N-u-L 56 A4
Bradwell St. Burs 56 B4
Braemar Ave. Kingsw 275 E1
Braemar Cl. Buck 58 B2
Braemar Cl. Sedg 266 B1
Braemar Gdns. Cann 209 F4
Braemar Rd. Nor Ca 228 A2
Braemar Rd. Patt 253 E1
Braemore Rd. Buck 58 A3
Braeside Way. Brown 243 F2
Braham. Tam 249 E3
Brain St. Tam 251 D1
Braithwaite Cl. Kingsw 275 E3
Brake La. Hag 281 F3
Brake Level. Sch Gr 26 A4
Brake The. Sch Gr 26 A4
Brake Village. Sch Gr 26 A4
Brakespeare St. Tuns 41 E4
Bramber Way. Stour 279 F1
Bramber. Tam 250 B1
Bramble Cl. Brown 244 C3
Bramble Dr. Cann 210 B4
Bramble Green. Dud 271 F3
Bramble La. Burnt 229 D4
Bramble Lea. Made 68 C3
Bramble Way. Rug 178 B1
Brambles Ct. Bidd 27 E4
Brambles The. Lich 231 E3
Brambles The. N-u-L 71 E1
Brambleside. Br Hi 275 F1
Brambleside. Staf 175 E4
Bramblewood Dr. Wolv 265 F4
Brambling Cl. Utt 126 B3
Brambling. Tam 262 A4
Bramblings The. Staf 175 E3
Bramdean Wlk. Wolv 265 E3
Bramell Cl. Bran 184 C4
Bramfield Dr. N-u-L 56 B1
Bramhall Cl. Sei 154 A4
Bramhall La. Staf 155 E3
Bramley Cl. Che 76 C1
Bramley Dale. Swad 186 C1
Bramley Pl. S-o-T 71 F1
Bramley Way. Whit 232 B3
Brammall Dr. Bly 90 C4
Brammer St. Che He 42 B2
Brampton Cl. Cook 280 A2
Brampton Ct. N-u-L 56 B1
Brampton Dr. Cann 210 C1
Brampton Gdns. N-u-L 56 B2
Brampton Ind Est. N-u-L 56 A1
Brampton Rd. N-u-L 56 B1
Brampton Sidings. N-u-L 56 A1
Brampton Wlk. Lon 73 E1
Bramsgrove Pl. Lon 73 D2
Bramshall Rd. Utt 125 F4
Bramshaws The. Che 76 C1
Bramstead Ave. Wolv 255 D1
Brandon Cl. Aldr 256 C2
Brandon Cl. Sedg 271 F4
Brandon Gr. Tren 87 F4
Brandon Park. Wolv 265 F4
Brandons The. Staf 174 C3
Branson Ave. Lon 73 F2
Branston Rd. Bran 184 B4
Branston Rd. Bu on T 185 E4
Bransty Gr. Tren 88 B3
Brant Ave. N-u-L 56 A2
Brantley Ave. Wolv 255 E1
Brantley Cres. Bobb 267 F1
Brantley La. Bobb 267 F1
Brantley La. Seis 263 D2
Branton Hill La. Aldr 256 B3
Brantwood Ave. Burnt 229 D3
Brassington St. Betley 53 D3
Brassington Way. Buck 58 B1
Bratch Common Rd. Wom 269 F4
Bratch Hollow. Wom 270 A4
Bratch La. Wom 269 F4
Bratch Park. Wom 269 F4
Brattswood Dr. Law-g 25 D3
Braunton Ave. Staf 175 F4
Brawdean Dr. Penk 192 C1
Braystones Cl. Che He 41 F4
Brazenhill La. Hau 172 C4
Breach La. Che 92 B3
Breach La. Dr in M 92 B3
Breach La. Scro 129 E3
Breach Rd. End 43 E4
Breadmarket St. Lich 231 D4
Bream Way. Che He 42 A2
Bream. Tam 261 E4
Brean Rd. Staf 175 E3
Brecon Way. Buck 58 B1
Bredon Cl. Albr 237 D3
Breech Cl. Water 48 C1
Breedon Cl. N-u-L 55 F2
Breedon Way. Brown 244 B1
Breeze Ave. Nor Ca 228 A3
Breeze Ave. Tuns 41 F3
Brelades Cl. Sedg 271 F1
Brendale Cl. Tren 72 A1
Brendon Cl. Staf 175 E4
Brendon. Tam 251 D1
Brent. Tam 261 F4
Brentmill Cl. Wolv 240 C2
Brentnall Dr. Sut Co 258 A2
Brentnor Cl. Lon 73 F2
Brenton Rd. Wolv 265 F2
Brentwood Dr. Cav 59 D2
Brentwood Gr. N-in-M 43 E2
Brenwood Cl. Kingsw 275 D4
Brereton Hill. Rug 197 D3
Brereton Lodge. Rug 197 D3
Brereton Pl. Tuns 41 F1
Brereton Rd. Rug 196 C4
Breretonhill La. Longd 197 E1
Bretby Bsns Pk. Bretby 186 C4
Bretby La. Bretby 167 F2
Bretby La. Bu on T 167 E1
Bretby Rd. Swad 186 C4
Bretherton Pl. Che He 42 A3
Bretlands Way. Bu on T 186 A3
Brettell La. Br Hi 279 F4
Brevitt Rd. Wolv 266 B3
Brewers Dr. Brown 244 A1
Brewers Terr. Brown 244 A1
Brewery La. Col 158 A1
Brewery St. Han 57 E2
Brewery St. Rug 196 C4
Brewester Rd. Buck 57 F2
Brewood Rd. Bre 224 A2
Brewster Cl. Faz 249 F1
Brianson Ave. Han 57 E4
Briar Ave. Aldr 257 D1
Briar Cl. Cann 210 A4
Briar Cl. Rug 178 B1
Briar Cl. Staf 175 F3
Briar Cl. Swad 186 C3
Briar Way. Mill 102 C1
Briar. Tam 251 D2
Briarbank Cl. Tren 71 F1
Briars The. N-u-L 56 A1
Briars Way. Cann 211 E2
Briarsleigh. Staf 175 E4
Briarswood. Kids 26 A1
Briarwood Pl. Meir 74 A1
Brick House St. Burs 56 C4
Brick Kiln La. Broc 175 F2
Brick Kiln La. Hint 259 D3
Brick Kiln La. Rolle 147 D2
Brick Kiln La. S-o-T 56 C1
Brick Kiln La. Salt 137 F1
Brick Kiln La. Sedg 271 D2
Brick Kiln La. Whe As 205 D3
Brick Kiln Way. Rug 196 C3
Brick St. Sedg 271 E4
Brick-kiln La. N-u-L 55 F4
Brickbridge La. Wom 269 F3
Brickfield Cl. Hix 139 E1
Brickfield Pl. Lon 73 E3
Brickhill La. Newb 163 D3
Brickhouse La. Elf 216 B1
Brickiln St. Brown 244 C4
Brickyard Rd. Aldr 244 C1
Brickyard Rd. Aldr 256 A4
Bridal Path. Cav 59 D2
Bridestone Cl. Meir 90 A4
Bridge Ave. Ches Hay 226 C2
Bridge Cl. Audley 39 F1
Bridge Cl. Brown 244 C3
Bridge Cl. Wes on Tr 138 B2
Bridge Cres. Sto 120 A4
Bridge Croft. Che He 42 A3
Bridge Cross Rd. Burnt 229 D4
Bridge Farm. Bu on T 147 F1
Bridge La. Wes on Tr 139 D2
Bridge Rd. Arm 198 B2
Bridge Rd. Brown 244 A1
Bridge Rd. Cook 280 A3
Bridge Rd. S-o-T 71 F2
Bridge Rd. Utt 126 B4
Bridge St Ind Units. Utt 126 B4
Bridge St. Br Hi 275 F1
Bridge St. Brown 244 C3
Bridge St. Bu on T 147 F1
Bridge St. Bu on T 166 C2
Bridge St. Cann 226 C3
Bridge St. Che He 27 D1
Bridge St. N-u-L 55 E1
Bridge St. N-u-L 56 A1
Bridge St. Staf 155 F1
Bridge St. Tam 250 C3
Bridge St. Tut 146 B4
Bridge Terr. Tho 20 C3
Bridgefoot Wlk. Wolv 239 F1
Bridgeman Ct. Wes-u-Liz 203 F1
Bridgemary Cl. Wolv 240 C2
Bridgenorth Rd. Wolv 255 D1
Bridges Cres. Nor Ca 227 F3
Bridges Rd. Nor Ca 227 F3
Bridgeside Trading Est. Tam 250 B1
Bridgeside. Bu on T 147 F1
Bridgetown Bsns Centre. Cann 226 C3
Bridgett Cl. S-o-T 71 F3
Bridgewater Cl. Congle 6 A1
Bridgewater St. Burs 56 B4
Bridgewater St. Tam 250 C3
Bridgewood St. Lon 73 E2
Bridgnorth Ave. Wom 269 F3
Bridgnorth Gr. N-u-L 40 C1
Bridgnorth Rd. Env 273 E1
Bridgnorth Rd. Him 270 A2
Bridgnorth Rd. Kin 278 B4
Bridgnorth Rd. Pert 264 B4
Bridgnorth Rd. Seis 263 F3
Bridgnorth Rd. Seis 269 E3
Bridgnorth Rd. Stour 279 E3
Bridgnorth Rd. Wom 269 E3
Bridgwater Cl. Brown 244 C2
Bridgwater Cl. Penk 207 F4
Bridgwood Rd. Fors 91 D4
Bridg ford Ave. Bran 184 C4
Bridle La. Ell 153 E4
Bridle La. Swad 186 A3
Bridle Path The. Made 68 B3
Bridle Path The. N-u-L 70 C2
Bridle Path. Lon 73 E1
Bridle Rd. Staf 175 E3
Bridle Rd. Stour 279 E3
Bridle Wlk. Rug 178 A1
Bridleway The. Ma Dra 97 D1
Brierley Hill Rd. Kingsw 275 F1
Brierley Rd. Congle 6 A1
Brierley St. Che He 42 B1
Brierlow Bar. Chel 5 D4
Briertey Hill La. Longd 212 A2
Brieryhurst Cl. Buck 58 B3
Brieryhurst Rd. Kids 26 A2
Bright Cres. Tam 250 B1
Bright St. Meir 74 A1
Bright St. Stour 279 E3
Brightgreen St. Lon 73 E3
Brighton St. S-o-T 72 A4
Brighton The. N-u-L 55 D1
Brightstone Cl. Wolv 240 C2
Brindiwell Gr. Tren 88 B3
Brindley Ave. Wolv 242 A1
Brindley Bank Rd. Rug 178 C2
Brindley Brae. Kin 278 B3
Brindley Cl. Albr 237 D3
Brindley Cl. Br Hi 275 F1
Brindley Cl. Kids 25 F1
Brindley Cl. Penk 208 A4
Brindley Cl. Staf 155 F4
Brindley Cl. Wom 269 E3
Brindley Cres. Cann 210 B4
Brindley Cres. Ched 45 E2
Brindley Heath Rd. Cann 210 B4
Brindley Heath Rd. Rug 195 E1
Brindley La. N-in-M 43 E2
Brindley Pl. Che He 42 B3
Brindley Rd. Cann 194 C1
Brindley Rd. Rug 194 C1
Brindley St. N-u-L 56 A1
Brindley Way. Congle 6 A1
Brindleys Way. Audley 39 F1
Brindon Cl. Meir 74 A2
Brinkburn Cl. Rug 178 A1
Brinkholme Dr. Bly 90 A3
Brinley Way. Kingsw 275 E3
Brinscall Green. Che He 42 A4
Brinsford La. Feath 240 B4
Brinsford Rd. Wolv 240 B2
Brinsley Ave. Tren 88 A3
Brisbane Rd. Staf 155 D4
Brisley Hill. S-o-T 71 F3
Bristol Cl. Cann 210 A1
Bristol St. N-u-L 56 B3
Bristol St. Wolv 266 A4
Britannia Park Ind Est. Han 57 D4
Britannia St. Leek 30 C3
Britannia Way. Lich 231 F4
Brittain Ave. N-u-L 55 F4
Brittain Rd. Ched 45 E3
Brittania Dr. Bu on T 166 B4
Brittle Pl. Che He 42 B1
Britton St. S-o-T 56 C1
Brixham Cl. Buck 57 F1
Brizlincote La. Bu on T 167 E1
Brizlincote St. Bu on T 166 C1
Broad Eye. Staf 155 E2
Broad La. Brown 244 B1
Broad La. Ch Eat 171 F1
Broad La. End 43 E4
Broad La. G Wyr 242 C2
Broad La. Lich 231 E3
Broad La. Wal 243 D1
Broad La. Whit 215 F1
Broad La. Wolv 265 F4
Broad Lane Gdns. Wal 243 D1
Broad Meadow Ct. Staf 155 D2
Broad Meadow La. Gr Wyr 227 D1
Broad Meadow. Aldr 256 A4
Broad Oaks. Staf 174 C3
Broad St. Cann 226 C3
Broad St. Han 57 D2
Broad St. Kingsw 275 E3
Broad St. Leek 30 C3
Broad St. N-u-L 56 A1
Broad St. Staf 155 E2
Broad Way. Brown 244 B1
Broadacres. Bre 224 A2
Broadfield Cl. Kingsw 275 E3
Broadfield Rd. Tuns 41 E4
Broadholes La. Whe As 205 D3
Broadhurst Cl. Cann 194 C1
Broadhurst Green Rd. Act Tru 194 B1
Broadhurst Green. Cann 194 C1
Broadhurst St. Che He 42 A1
Broadlands Rise. Lich 231 E4
Broadlands. Bu on T 166 B4
Broadlawns Dr. Fen 73 D3
Broadlee. Tam 251 E1
Broadmeadow. Kingsw 275 F4
Broadmine St. Fen 72 C3
Broadoak Way. Lon 72 C1
Broadoaks Cl. Nor Ca 227 F3
Broadsmeath. Tam 250 B1
Broadstone Cl. Wolv 266 B3
Broadway La. Water 49 D2
Broadway Pl. Meir 73 F1
Broadway St. Bu on T 166 B1
Broadway The. Dud 271 F2
Broadway The. Stour 279 E2
Broadway The. Wom 270 A3
Broadway. Cann 209 F3
Broadway. Cod 238 C2
Broadway. Meir 73 F1
Broadway. Newp 169 D2
Broadway. Wolv 240 C1
Broadway. Wolv 255 E1
Broadwell La. Patt 253 D1
Broc Cl. Penk 208 A4
Brockbank Pl. Che He 42 A3
Brockeridge Cl. Wal 242 B1
Brockhill. Ashl 99 E3
Brockhurst La. Hint 259 D4
Brockhurst Rd. Sut Co 258 B1
Brocklehurst Way. Han 57 F4
Brockley Sq. Han 57 E2
Brockley's Wlk. Kin 278 A2
Brocksford St. Lon 73 D3
Brockton Hts. Broc 176 B2
Brockton La. Ecc 117 E2
Brockton Rd. Broc 176 B3
Brocton Cres. Broc 175 F2
Brocton La. Staf 175 F3
Brogan St. Fen 72 C3
Bromford Dale. Wolv 255 F2
Bromford Rise. Wolv 266 A4
Bromley Ct. Han 57 D3
Bromley Gdns. Cod 239 D2
Bromley Hough. S-o-T 71 F3
Bromley La. Kingsw 275 F2
Bromley St. Han 57 D3
Bromley St. Wolv 266 B4
Bromleyhedge La. Water 48 B2
Brompton Dr. N-in-M 43 D2
Brompton Lawns. Wolv 255 D2
Bromsberrow Way. Meir 90 A4
Bromwich Dr. Alre 215 E4
Bromwynd Cl. Wolv 266 A3
Bronant Wlk. Burs 57 D4
Bronte Cl. Bu on T 166 B4
Bronte Ct. Tam 250 A3
Bronte Dr. Cann 210 B1
Bronte Rd. Wolv 266 C3
Brook Ave. Tam 262 A4
Brook Cl. Bre 224 A2
Brook Cl. Brown 245 D2
Brook Cl. End 44 A4
Brook Cl. Fors 91 D4
Brook Cl. Lich 214 A1
Brook Cl. Penk 207 F4
Brook Cres. Kingsw 275 E4
Brook End. Burnt 229 D2
Brook End. Faz 261 D4
Brook End. Hau 172 C3
Brook End. Longd 197 F1
Brook Gdns. Bidd 16 B1
Brook Glen Rd. Staf 174 C4
Brook Gr. Cod 239 D1
Brook House La. Feath 241 D4
Brook House. Newp 168 C2
Brook La. Broc 176 B2
Brook La. Brown 244 C2
Brook La. Ch Lei 108 C3
Brook La. End 43 F4
Brook La. Gr Wyr 227 D2
Brook La. N-u-L 71 D4
Brook La. Ran 153 E2
Brook Meadow Rd. Brown 244 B1
Brook Pl. N-u-L 71 E3
Brook Pl. S-o-T 56 C1
Brook Rd. Ches Hay 226 C2
Brook Rd. Tren 88 A4
Brook Rd. Wom 269 F3
Brook Sq. Rug 196 C3
Brook St. Br Hi 275 F1
Brook St. Bu on T 166 B2
Brook St. Kids 27 D3
Brook St. Kingsw 270 A1
Brook St. Leek 30 C3
Brook St. N-u-L 55 E1
Brook St. S-o-T 72 A4
Brook St. Sedg 271 E2
Brook St. Stour 279 F3
Brook St. Swad 186 C3
Brookbank Gdns. Sedg 271 D1
Brookbank Rd. Sedg 271 D1
Brookdale Dr. Wolv 265 F3
Brookdale. Sedg 271 E2
Brooke Rd. Cann 209 F3
Brookers Ct. Fen 72 C3
Brookfield Ave. End 43 F4
Brookfield Cl. Kings 62 B2
Brookfield Ct. Han 57 E3
Brookfield Ct. Sto 120 B3
Brookfield Dr. Cann 226 C4
Brookfield Rd. Aldr 245 D1
Brookfield Rd. Cod 239 D2
Brookfield Rd. N-in-M 43 E2
Brookfield Rd. S-o-T 71 F3
Brookfield. Ashl 99 E3
Brookfields Rd. Ipst 62 A4
Brookgate. Fors 91 D4
Brookhay La. Alre 215 F2
Brookhay La. Whit 215 F2
Brookhill Cl. Wal 242 B1
Brookhill Way. Wal 242 B1
Brookhouse Cl. Feath 241 D3
Brookhouse Dr. Barl 88 B1
Brookhouse La. Buck 58 C2
Brookhouse La. Cav 58 C2
Brookhouse La. Ched 45 D2
Brookhouse La. Congle 6 B1
Brookhouse La. Feath 241 D3
Brookhouse Rd. Che 76 A2
Brookhouse Rd. Gno 171 E4
Brookhouse Rd. Meir 74 A1
Brookhouse Rd. N-u-L 55 F4
Brookhouse Way. Che 76 A1
Brookhouse Way. Gno 171 E3
Brookhouses Ind Est. Che 76 A1
Brookland Ave. Lon 73 D1
Brookland Rd. Brown 244 C2
Brookland Rd. Che He 41 F3
Brooklands Ave. Gr Wyr 226 C2
Brooklands Gr. Brown 244 C2
Brooklands Rd. Albr 237 D3
Brooklands Rd. Cann 210 A2
Brooklands The. Swi 269 F1
Brooklands Way. Leek 45 F4
Brooklands. Br Hi 275 F1
Brooklyn Gr. Kingsw 275 D4
Brooklyn Rd. Burnt 229 D2
Brooklyn Rd. Cann 210 B1
Brookmead Gr. Fen 73 D3
Brookside Ave. Newp 168 C1
Brookside Cl. N-u-L 71 D4
Brookside Cl. Wom 269 F3
Brookside Dr. End 44 A4
Brookside Dr. Fen 72 C1
Brookside Gdns. Bre 221 F4
Brookside La. Sto 119 F4
Brookside Rd. Ba-u-Ne 183 E1
Brookside Rd. Faz 249 E1
Brookside Rd. Utt 126 B4
Brookside Way. Bla 281 D1
Brookside Way. Kingsw 275 E4
Brookside Way. Tam 262 A3
Brookside. Bu on T 167 D3
Brookside. Burs 56 B4
Brookside. Env 273 E2
Brookside. Kings 62 A2
Brookside. Ran 153 E3
Brookside. Rolle 147 D2
Brookside. Sedg 271 E1
Brookview Dr. Lon 73 F2
Brookweed. Tam 251 D2
Brookwillows. Staf 175 E4
Brookwood Cl. N-u-L 71 D2
Brookwood Dr. Meir 74 A1
Broom Lea. Ashl 99 E2
Broom St. Han 57 E3
Broom's La. Scro 129 D1
Broome Hill. N-u-L 71 E1
Broome La. Bla 281 F1
Broome La. Hag 281 F1
Broome Wlk. Arm 198 B2
Broomfield Ave. Faz 261 D4
Broomfield Cl. Newp 168 B2

289

Broomfield Cl. Sto

Carroll Dr. Lon

Broomfield Cl. Sto 120 A3
Broomfield Ct. Sto 105 D1
Broomfield La. Ella 79 F1
Broomfield Pl N. Han 57 D2
Broomfield Pl S. Han 57 D2
Broomfield Pl. Newp 168 B2
Broomfield Rd. N-in-M 42 B3
Broomfield Rd. Newp 168 B2
Broomfields. Bidd 17 D1
Broomhill Bank. Cann 209 F2
Broomhill Cl. Cann 209 F2
Broomhill St. Tuns 41 E2
Brooms Rd. Sto 120 A3
Broomstead Cres. Staf 155 D3
Broomyclose La. Utt 111 D2
Brough Cl. Wolv 266 C2
Brough La. Tren 88 A4
Brough Rd. Bu on T 167 E2
Broughton Cl. Staf 155 E4
Broughton Cres. Barl 88 C1
Broughton Ct. Pert 255 D2
Broughton Rd. Buck 57 F2
Broughton Rd. N-u-L 56 B1
Broughton Rd. Wolv 255 E1
Brow Hill. Leek 30 C3
Brown Ave. Law-g 25 D3
Brown Lees Rd. Bidd 27 D2
Brown Lees Rd. Kids 27 D3
Brown St. Burs 57 D4
Brown St. Wolv 266 B4
Brown's La. Tam 250 B4
Brown's La. Yox 182 A1
Brown's Lake. Env 273 E2
Brownfield Rd. Meir 74 A1
Brownhill Rd. End 43 D4
Brownhills Rd. Brown 245 D2
Brownhills Rd. Nor Ca 228 A2
Brownhills Rd. Tuns 41 E1
Browning Cl. Che 76 B1
Browning Cl. Tam 249 F4
Browning Cres. Wolv 240 B1
Browning Gr. Kids 40 B4
Browning Gr. Pert 254 C2
Browning Rd. Burnt 229 E4
Browning Rd. Lon 72 C1
Browning Rd. Sedg 271 D2
Browning St. Staf 155 E2
Brownley Rd. Che He 42 B1
Browns Wlk. Rug 178 B1
Brownsea Pl. Fen 72 C2
Brownsfield Rd. Lich 214 B1
Brownsholme. Tam 249 E3
Brownshore La. Ess 242 A2
Brownswall Rd. Sedg 271 E4
Broxwood Pk. Wolv 255 E2
Bruford Rd. Wolv 266 A4
Brund La. Ched 45 D2
Brundall Oval. Buck 58 B1
Brunel Cl. Burnt 229 D4
Brunel Cl. Staf 155 F4
Brunel Cl. Tam 250 A3
Brunel Gr. Pert 254 C3
Brunel Wlk. Lon 73 E2
Brunslow Cl. Wolv 240 B1
Brunswick Pl. Han 57 E2
Brunswick Rd. Cann 209 F1
Brunswick St. Han 57 E2
Brunswick St. Leek 30 C3
Brunswick St. N-u-L 56 B1
Brunswick Terr. Staf 155 E1
Brunt St. Burs 56 B4
Brutus Rd. N-u-L 55 E3
Bryan Ave. Wolv 265 E2
Bryan St. Han 57 E2
Bryans La. Rug 178 C1
Bryans Way. Cann 210 C2
Bryant Rd. Buck 58 A3
Brymbo Rd. N-u-L 55 F3
Brynmawr Rd. Wolv 266 C2
Buccleuch Rd. Lon 73 E1
Buckden. Tam 251 E1
Buckingham Cl. Bu on T 166 B4
Buckingham Cl. Staf 156 B1
Buckingham Cres. Tren 72 A1
Buckingham Ct. Bu on T 167 E2
Buckingham Dr. Kingsw 275 E3
Buckingham Gdns. Lich 231 D3
Buckingham Gr. Kingsw 275 E4
Buckingham Pl. Cann 210 B1
Buckingham Rd. Tam 249 F4
Buckingham Rd. Wolv 266 A3
Buckingham Rise. Sedg 271 F1
Buckland Cl. Cann 210 B1
Buckland Gr. Tren 88 B3
Buckland Rd. Staf 136 B1
Buckley Rd. Che He 42 B3
Buckley Rd. Wolv 265 E3
Buckley's Row. N-u-L 71 D4
Buckmaster Ave. N-u-L 71 E3
Bucknall New Rd. Han 57 E2
Bucknall Old Rd. Han 57 E2
Bucknall Rd. Buck 57 F2
Bucknall Rd. Han 57 F2
Bucknall Rd. Wolv 242 A1
Buckthorn Cl. Cann 209 F4
Buckton Cl. Sut Co 258 C1
Buds Rd. Cann 211 F3
Buildwas Cl. Wal 242 C1
Bull Hill. Staf 155 F2
Bull La. Che He 27 D1
Bull La. Wom 270 A4
Bull Ring The. Wes on Tr 138 B1
Bull Ring. Clav 267 E4
Bull Ring. Sedg 271 E4
Bull St. Sedg 271 E1
Bulldog La. Lich 214 A1
Buller St. Han 57 E1
Buller St. Wolv 266 C3
Bullgap La. Stan 65 E2
Bullgap La. Swin 65 E2
Bullmoor La. Wall 230 A1
Bullocks House Rd. Kids 26 C2
Bullows Rd. Brown 244 B3
Bulstrode St. Burs 56 C4
Bumblehole Meadows.
Wom 269 F4
Bun La. Blym 188 B1
Bun La. Sher 203 D4
Bungalows The. Adb 131 E2
Bungham La. Penk 207 E4
Bunny Hill. N-u-L 71 E3
Bunt's La. N-in-M 43 E2
Bunting Cl. Utt 126 A3
Bunting The. Ched 60 A4
Bunting The. Kings 61 E2
Buntingdale Rd. Ma Dra 112 A4
Bunyan Pl. Cann 209 F2
Burcham Cl. Staf 155 D4
Burdock Cl. Cann 210 A2
Burford Rd. Staf 156 B1
Burford Rd. Whe As 205 D3
Burford Way. Buck 58 A1
Burgage Cl. Ma Dra 97 E1
Burgage The. Ecc 133 F4
Burgage The. Ma Dra 97 E1
Burgess St. Burs 56 C4
Burgesses The. Kin 278 A2
Burgis Cl. Ched 45 E2
Burgoyne St. Cann 210 A3
Burland Ave. Wolv 255 F3
Burland Rd. N-u-L 40 B1
Burleigh Cl. Cann 210 A4
Burleigh Croft. Burnt 229 D2
Burleigh Gr. N-u-L 56 B2
Burleigh Rd. Wolv 266 A4
Burlidge Rd. Che He 42 A3
Burlington Ave. N-u-L 56 B2
Burlington Dr. Staf 174 A4
Burmarsh Wlk. Burs 56 C4
Burmarsh Wlk. Wolv 255 F4
Burnaby Rd. Tuns 41 E3
Burnell Gdns. Wolv 265 F4
Burnet Gr. Feath 241 D4
Burnett Pl. N-in-M 42 B2
Burnett Rd. Li As 257 D1
Burnfield Dr. Rug 178 B1
Burnfields Cl. Aldr 256 A4
Burnham Cl. Kingsw 275 F2
Burnham Green. Cann 226 A4
Burnham St. Lon 73 D3
Burnhays Rd. Burs 41 F1
Burnley St. Han 57 E3
Burns Ave. Staf 174 A4
Burns Ave. Wolv 240 B1
Burns Cl. Kids 41 D4
Burns Cl. Lich 231 D3
Burns Dr. Burnt 229 E4
Burns Gr. Sedg 271 D2
Burns Rd. Congle 6 A1
Burns Rd. Tam 250 A3
Burns Row. Meir 74 A1
Burns St. Cann 210 A2
Burnsall Cl. Wolv 240 A2
Burnside Cl. Meir 90 A4
Burnside. Rolle 147 D2
Burnthill La. Rug 196 C4
Burntwood Rd. Burnt 229 E3
Burntwood Rd. Nor Ca 228 A4
Burntwood Shopping
Centre. Burnt 229 E3
Burntwood Town Shopping
Centre. Burnt 228 C4
Burnwood Ct. Che He 42 B1
Burnwood Pl. Che He 42 A3
Burrington Dr. Tren 88 B3
Burrows Rd. Kingsw 275 F2
Burrows The. Swad 186 C3
Burslem Enterprise Cen.
Burs 57 D4
Bursley Cl. Staf 174 B3
Bursley Rd. Burs 57 D4
Bursley Way. N-u-L 56 A4
Bursnips Rd. Ess 242 B2
Bursnips Rd. G Wyr 242 B2
Burt St. Meir 74 A2
Burton Bank La. Brad 174 B3
Burton Bank La. Staf 174 C3
Burton Cl. Tam 250 B4
Burton Cres. Han 57 F4
Burton Cres. Kings 76 C4
Burton Ct. Staf 174 C4
Burton Enterprise Park.
Bu on T 166 C3
Burton Manor Rd. Brad 174 B3
Burton Manor Rd. Staf 174 B3
Burton Old Rd E. Lich 231 F4
Burton Old Rd W. Lich 231 E4
Burton Old Rd. Lich 231 F4
Burton Old Rd. Stre 214 C1
Burton Pl. Han 57 E2
Burton Rd. Alre 201 D2
Burton Rd. Bran 185 D4
Burton Rd. Dud 271 F2
Burton Rd. Elf 216 C1
Burton Rd. Linton 186 B1
Burton Rd. Rep 148 C1
Burton Rd. Stre 214 C1
Burton Rd. Tut 146 B2
Burton Rd. Whit 232 C4
Burton Rd. Will 148 C4
Burton Sq. Staf 174 C4
Burton St. Leek 30 B3
Burton St. Tut 146 B3
Bury Ring. Bradl 173 E3
Bush Cl. Albr 237 D3
Bush Dr. Rug 178 C1
Bush Gr. Brown 244 A1
Bushberry Cl. Sto 119 F3
Bushbury La. Wolv 240 C1
Bushey Cl. Aldr 256 C1
Bushfield Rd. Albr 237 D3
Bushton La. Bu on T 146 A1
Bushton La. Tut 146 A1
Business Park. Bu on T 166 C3
Bustomley La. Ch Lei 108 A2
Bute St. Lon 73 D2
Butler Ct. Bu on T 166 A2
Butler St. S-o-T 72 A3
Butlers La. Sut Co 258 A2
Butt La. Ran 153 E1
Butter Bk. Sei 154 C2
Butterbank La. Sei 154 A1
Butterfield Cl. Pert 254 B2
Butterfield Pl. Tuns 41 F2
Butterhill Bank. San 121 D1
Butterhill La. San 121 F3
Buttermere Cl. Burs 56 C4
Buttermere Cl. Cann 210 A2
Buttermere Cl. Wolv 255 E4
Buttermere Ct. Pert 254 C2
Buttermere Dr. Ess 242 A2
Buttermere Gr. Wal 242 A1
Butthouse La. Chap Ch 102 B3
Buttons Farm Rd. Wolv 265 E2
Butts Cl. Nor Ca 227 F2
Butts Croft. Alre 200 C2
Butts Green. Buck 58 B3
Butts La. Nor Ca 227 F2
Butts La. Wars 23 E1
Butts Rd. Ma Dra 97 D1
Butts Rd. Wolv 265 F2
Butts The. Betley 53 D3
Butts The. Wall 230 B1
Butts Way. Nor Ca 227 F2
Butts's La. Water 63 F4
Buxton Ave. Faz 261 D4
Buxton Ave. N-u-L 55 D1
Buxton Cl. Wal 243 E2
Buxton Old Rd. Congle 6 A2
Buxton Rd. Alst 35 D3
Buxton Rd. Congle 6 B3
Buxton Rd. Leek 31 D4
Buxton Rd. Long 13 D4
Buxton Rd. Wal 243 E2
Buxton St. Han 57 E4
By Pass Rd. Tam 251 D3
Byatt's Gr. Lon 73 D1
Bycars La. Burs 42 A1
Bycars La. Che He 42 A1
Bycars Rd. Burs 41 F1
Byland Pl. N-u-L 71 D3
Byland Way. Wal 242 C1
Byland. Tam 250 B2
Byrd's Cl. Utt 125 F4
Byrd's La. Utt 125 F4
Byrkley St. Bu on T 166 B2
Byrne Rd. Wolv 266 B4
Byron Ave. Bu on T 185 F4
Byron Ave. Lich 231 D3
Byron Cl. Burnt 211 F1
Byron Cl. Che 76 A1
Byron Cl. Ma Dra 112 A4
Byron Cl. Staf 156 A3
Byron Croft. Sedg 271 D3
Byron Croft. Sut C 257 F3
Byron Ct. Kids 41 D4
Byron Ct. Sut Co 258 A3
Byron Pl. Cann 209 F3
Byron Pl. Rug 178 B1
Byron Rd. Ess 241 D1
Byron Rd. Tam 250 A4
Byron St. Leek 30 B3
Byron St. S-o-T 56 B1
Bywater Gr. Lon 73 E3
Byways. Wal 243 E2
Cable St. Wolv 266 C4
Cacklehill La. Snel 81 E1
Cadeby Gr. N-in-M 43 D1
Cadley Hill Rd. Swad 186 C2
Cadman Cres. N-in-M 42 C2
Cadman's La. G Wyr 243 E3
Cadogan Rd. Tam 261 E3
Caerdon Dr. Staf 174 A4
Caernarvon Cl. Bu on T 166 B4
Caernarvon Cl. Ma Dra 97 F1
Caernarvon Way. Sedg 271 F1
Cairn Cl. Buck 58 B2
Cairns Dr. Staf 156 A3
Caistor Cl. Faz 260 A4
Caistor Cl. N-in-M 43 D1
Calais Rd. Bu on T 166 A3
Calcot Dr. Wolv 255 F4
Caldbeck Pl. Han 57 E2
Calder Rise. Sedg 271 F3
Calder. Tam 251 D1
Caldercrofts. Newp 168 C2
Caldervale Dr. Staf 175 E3
Caldew Gr. Tren 88 B3
Cale Cl. Tam 250 B1
Caledonia Rd. Han 57 D1
Caledonia Rd. Wolv 266 C4
Caledonian. Tam 250 C1
Calgary Cres. Bu on T 167 E2
California St. Lon 73 D2
Californian Gr. Burnt 228 C4
Callaghan Gr. Cann 210 B1
Callender Pl. Burs 57 D4
Callingwood La. Tate 164 C2
Callis Wlk. Tam 261 F3
Callow Hill La. Dil 75 E2
Calrofold Dr. N-u-L 40 B1
Calvary Cres. Buck 73 E4
Calveley Cl. Swyn 118 C3
Calver St. Tuns 41 E2
Calverley St. Lon 73 E1
Calvert Gr. N-u-L 56 A4
Calvin Cl. Wolv 240 B2
Calvin Cl. Wom 269 F3
Calving Hill. Cann 209 F1
Camberley Cres. Wolv 266 C1
Camberley Dr. Wolv 266 A2
Camberley Rd. Kingsw 275 F2
Camberwell Gr. Tren 88 B3
Camborne Cl. Staf 175 F4
Camborne Cres. N-u-L 71 D3
Cambourne Cl. Congle 15 F4
Cambria St. Cann 209 E2
Cambrian La. Rug 178 B2
Cambrian. Tam 251 D1
Cambridge Cl. Aldr 256 A4
Cambridge Cl. Bidd 16 B1
Cambridge Ct. N-u-L 71 E2
Cambridge Dr. N-u-L 71 E2
Cambridge St. Bu on T 166 A1
Cambridge St. Han 57 D2
Cambridge St. Staf 156 A2
Camden Dr. Tam 250 C2
Camden St. Brown 244 C2
Camden St. Fen 72 C2
Camden Way. Kingsw 270 B1
Camelford Cl. Staf 175 F4
Camelot Cl. Bu on T 147 F1
Camelot Cl. Cann 209 F2
Camelot Cl. Tren 88 B2
Cameo Way. Staf 155 D4
Cameron Cl. Bu on T 167 D1
Camhouses. Tam 251 D1
Camillus Rd. N-u-L 55 F1
Camoys Ct. Burs 57 D4
Camoys Rd. Burs 57 D4
Camp Hill Rd. Env 273 F4
Camp Hill. Br Hi 275 F1
Camp Rd. Broc 194 B3
Camp Rd. Che He 42 B1
Camp Rd. Shen 258 B3
Camp Rd. Weef 258 B3
Campbell Ave. Leek 30 B2
Campbell Cl. Congle 6 A2
Campbell Cl. Rug 178 B1
Campbell Cl. Tam 249 F4
Campbell Pl. S-o-T 72 A4
Campbell Rd. Ma Dra 97 E1
Campbell Rd. S-o-T 72 A3
Campbell Terr. Han 57 F3
Campian's Ave. Ches Hay 226 B1
Campion Ave. N-u-L 56 B2
Campion Cl. Ecc 133 E3
Campion Cl. Wom 269 F3
Campion Dr. Feath 241 D4
Camrose Gdns. Wolv 240 A2
Camsey La. Burnt 229 F4
Canal Cl. Barl 88 B1
Canal La. Tuns 41 E1
Canal Mews The. Tren 88 B3
Canal Rd. Congle 15 F4
Canal Rd. Sto 104 C1
Canal St. Br Hi 279 F3
Canal St. Bu on T 166 B1
Canal St. Burs 56 B4
Canalside Cl. Wal 243 F1
Canaway Wlk. Rug 178 B1
Canberra Cres. Meir 90 B4
Canberra Dr. Staf 156 A2
Canford Cres. Cod 238 C2
Cannel Rd. Burnt 228 B3
Canning Rd. Tam 250 C2
Canning St. Fen 72 C3
Cannnock Wood Rd.
Cann 211 D3
Cannnock Wood St.
Cann 211 D3
Cannock Rd. Broc 176 A2
Cannock Rd. Burnt 228 B4
Cannock Rd. Burnt 229 D4
Cannock Rd. Cann 210 A3
Cannock Rd. Cann 227 E4
Cannock Rd. Feath 241 D2
Cannock Rd. Hunt 208 A4
Cannock Rd. Penk 192 C1
Cannock Rd. Staf 175 E3
Cannock Rd. Wolv 241 D2
Cannon Pl. Han 57 E2
Cannon Rd. Wom 270 A3
Cannon St. Han 57 E2
Canons Cl. Sto 120 A3
Canterbury Cl. Brown 244 A2
Canterbury Cl. Lich 214 B2
Canterbury Dr. Burnt 229 F4
Canterbury Dr. Che He 42 A2
Canterbury Dr. Pert 254 C2
Canterbury Rd. Bu on T 167 E2
Canterbury Rd. Wolv 265 F3
Canterbury Way. Cann 210 A1
Canvey Gr. Meir 90 A4
Canwell Dr. Hint 259 D3
Cape Ave. Staf 174 A4
Cape Cl. Brown 245 D3
Cape St. Han 57 E3
Capesthorne Cl. Cav 59 D2
Capewell St. Lon 73 E2
Capper Cl. Kids 26 A1
Capper St. Tuns 41 F2
Capper's La. Whit 232 A4
Cappers La. Lich 231 F4
Capricorn Way. Che He 41 F3
Captain's Cl. Wolv 255 E1
Captain's La. Ba-u-Ne 201 E4
Caradoc. Tam 251 D1
Caraway Pl. Meir 90 A3
Carberry Way. Lon 74 A2
Card St. Burs 57 D4
Carder Ave. Staf 155 D4
Carder Green. Long 13 D3
Cardiff Gr. Han 57 E1
Cardiff St. Wolv 266 A4
Cardigan Ave. Rug 196 B3
Cardigan Gr. Tren 88 B3
Cardigan Pl. Cann 210 B3
Cardinal Way. Cann 209 E1
Cardington Cl. N-u-L 71 D2
Cardway. N-u-L 56 A4
Cardwell St. Han 57 F3
Carey. Tam 262 A3
Carfax. Cann 226 C4
Carier Ave. Cod 239 D2
Carina Gdns. Che He 42 B1
Carisbrooke Dr. Staf 174 A4
Carisbrooke Gdns. Wolv 240 C2
Carisbrooke Rd. Pert 255 D2
Carisbrooke Rd. Wolv 240 C2
Carisbrooke Way. Tren 88 B3
Carisbrooke. Tam 251 D1
Carlcroft. Tam 251 D1
Carling Cl. Staf 155 D1
Carling Gr. Lon 73 D3
Carlisle Rd. Cann 226 B4
Carlisle St. Lon 73 D1
Carlos Cl. Che 76 B2
Carlos Pl. N-u-L 41 D1
Carlton Ave. Aldr 257 D1
Carlton Ave. Che He 42 A2
Carlton Ave. End 43 D3
Carlton Ave. N-u-L 71 D2
Carlton Cft. Aldr 257 D1
Carlton Cl. Cann 210 B1
Carlton Cl. Che 76 B1
Carlton Cl. End 43 D3
Carlton Cres. Burnt 229 D4
Carlton Cres. Tam 249 F4
Carlton Ct. Bu on T 166 A2
Carlton Rd. S-o-T 72 B4
Carlton Rd. Wolv 266 A4
Carlton Sq. Staf 174 A4
Carlton St. Bu on T 166 A3
Carlton Terr. Leek 31 D3
Carlyon Pl. Han 57 E4
Carmel Cl. Cann 210 B3
Carmichael Cl. Lich 231 E4
Carmount Rd. Buck 58 A4
Carnation Cl. Meir 74 A3
Carnforth Cl. Kingsw 275 D4
Carnforth Gr. Che He 41 F4
Carnoustie Cl. Wal 243 D2
Carnoustie. Tam 251 E3
Caroline Cl. Cav 59 D2
Caroline Cres. End 43 D3
Caroline St. Lon 73 E2
Caroline Terr. Bu on T 166 B1
Carpenter Rd. Lon 73 D2
Carr Bank. Oak 78 A4
Carr La. Audley 39 D1
Carr La. Wet 34 C1
Carr St. Kids 26 C1
Carriage Dr. Bidd 16 C1
Carrick Cl. Brown 244 A3
Carrick Pl. Tren 72 A1
Carriers Fold. Wom 270 A4
Carriers Rd. Eg 148 B3
Carroll Dr. Lon 73 E2

290

Carron St. Lon — Chester Rd. Chet

Carron St. Lon 73 D3
Carroway Head Hill. Hint 259 E3
Carryer Pl. N-u-L 70 C4
Carshalton Gr. Wolv 266 C4
Carson Rd. Che He 41 F2
Carter St. Utt 126 B4
Carters Croft. Up Tea 92 C2
Cartersfield La. Shen 245 E3
Cartlich St. Tuns 41 E3
Cartmel Pl. Che He 42 A2
Cartway The. Pert 254 B2
Cartwright Dr. Gno 171 E4
Cartwright Rd. Sut Co 258 B2
Cartwright St. Lon 73 E2
Cartwright St. Wolv 266 B4
Carver Gdns. Stour 279 F1
Carver Rd. Bu on T 166 B3
Carver Rd. Staf 155 F3
Casa Mia Ct. Cann 210 B3
Casewell Rd. Han 57 E4
Casewell Rd. Kingsw 275 E4
Casey La. Bu on T 166 A2
Casey La. Shav 37 D3
Casey The. Ipst 48 A1
Cash La. Ecc 132 C2
Caslon Cres. Stour 279 E2
Caspian Gr. Tren 88 A4
Caspian Way. Whe As 205 E3
Cassandra Cl. Sedg 271 E1
Castel Cl. N-u-L 70 C2
Castle Acre. Staf 174 A4
Castle Bank. Staf 174 A4
Castle Cl. Brown 228 C1
Castle Cl. Tam 250 C2
Castle Ct. Tut 146 B4
Castle Dyke. Lich 231 D4
Castle Hayes La. Tut 146 A3
Castle Hill Rd. Alt 78 C1
Castle Hill Rd. N-u-L 56 A1
Castle Inn Rd. Congle 16 B4
Castle La. Made 68 C3
Castle Park Rd. Bu on T 166 A4
Castle Rd. Brown 245 D1
Castle Rd. Cook 280 A2
Castle Rd. Kids 26 B4
Castle Rd. Swad 186 C1
Castle Rd. Tam 261 F3
Castle Ridge. N-u-L 70 C4
Castle St. Brown 228 C1
Castle St. Ecc 133 F4
Castle St. Kin 278 A2
Castle St. N-u-L 55 F4
Castle St. N-u-L 56 B1
Castle St. Sedg 271 E4
Castle St. Staf 155 E2
Castle St. Tut 146 B3
Castle View. Bidd 27 E3
Castle View. Sei 154 C1
Castle View. Staf 155 E2
Castle View. Tam 250 B2
Castle Way The. Will 148 C3
Castle Way. Staf 155 E1
Castlecroft Ave. Wolv 265 D4
Castlecroft Gdns. Wolv 265 E4
Castlecroft La. Wolv 254 C1
Castlecroft Rd. Wolv 265 D4
Castledene Dr. Staf 155 E1
Castledine Gr. Lon 73 F2
Castlefield St. Han 57 D1
Castlefields. Staf 155 E1
Castlefort Rd. Brown 245 D2
Castlehall. Tam 251 D1
Castlehill Rd. Brown 245 E2
Castleton Rd. Meir 89 F4
Castleton Rd. Wal 243 E2
Castleview Gr. Che He 41 F4
Castleview Rd. Kids 26 A2
Castleview. Hatton 146 B4
Caswell Rd. Sedg 271 E4
Cat And Kittens La. Wolv 240 C3
Catalina Pl. Meir 90 B3
Caterham Dr. Kingsw 275 F2
Caterham Pl. Meir 90 A3
Catesby Dr. Kingsw 275 E4
Catharine Rd. Che He 42 B3
Cathcart Rd. Stour 279 F3
Cathedral Cl. Lich 231 D4
Cathedral Rise. Lich 231 D4
Catherine St. N-u-L 56 B2
Catholic La. Sedg 271 E4
Catholme La. Ba-u-Ne 201 F3
Catisfield Cres. Wolv 239 F1
Catkin Wlk. Rug 178 B1
Catmeadow La. Longd 197 E1
Caton Cres. N-in-M 42 C1
Catsbridge La. Ches Hay 225 F4
Catshill Rd. Brown 245 D4
Cauldon Ave. Ched 45 E3
Cauldon Ave. N-u-L 56 A4
Cauldon Cl. Leek 30 C2
Cauldon Pl. Han 57 D1
Cauldon Rd. S-o-T 57 E1
Caulton St. Burs 41 F1
Caunsall Rd. Cook 280 A3
Causeley Gdns. Buck 58 A2
Causeley Rd. Buck 58 A2
Cavalier Cir. Wolv 240 C2
Cavan's Cl. Cann 209 F2
Cavans Wood Mobile Homes. Hunt 209 E3
Cavendish Cl. Kingsw 275 E2
Cavendish Dr. Hag 281 F2
Cavendish Gr. N-u-L 71 D2
Cavendish St. Han 57 D2
Cavendish Way. Aldr 256 A3
Cavendish. Tam 249 F4
Caverswall La. Meir 90 B4
Caverswall Old Rd. Fors 90 C4
Caverswall Rd. Dil 75 D2
Caverswall Rd. Fors 90 C4
Caverswall Rd. Meir 74 A2
Cavour St. Han 56 C2
Caxton St. Cann 226 C4
Cayley Pl. Meir 90 B3
Cecil Ave. Han 57 D3
Cecil Payton Cl. Ab Br 160 C3
Cecil Rd. Swad 186 C3
Cecil St. Cann 209 F2
Cecil St. Stour 279 F3
Cecilly St. Che 76 C2
Cecilly Terr. Che 76 C2
Cedar Ave. Brown 245 D4
Cedar Ave. Fors 91 D3
Cedar Ave. Kids 25 E1
Cedar Cl. Burnt 229 D3
Cedar Cl. Cann 195 D1
Cedar Cl. Che 76 C1
Cedar Cl. Lich 231 F4
Cedar Cl. Ma Dra 97 D1
Cedar Cl. Stour 279 E1
Cedar Cl. Utt 110 C4
Cedar Cres. Audley 39 F1
Cedar Cres. End 43 F3
Cedar Cres. Rug 197 D3
Cedar Ct. Congle 15 F4
Cedar Dr. Albr 237 D3
Cedar Dr. Aldr 256 C1
Cedar Dr. Tam 250 A4
Cedar Dr. Utt 111 D2
Cedar Gdns. Kin 277 F3
Cedar Gr. Bidd 17 D1
Cedar Gr. Cod 239 D2
Cedar Gr. Fen 72 C2
Cedar Gr. Wolv 265 F4
Cedar Park Rd. Wal 242 B1
Cedar Park. Sto 120 A4
Cedar Rd. Ba-u-Ne 183 E1
Cedar Rd. Burnt 229 D4
Cedar Rd. N-u-L 40 B1
Cedar Wood Rd. Sedg 271 E3
Cedarhill Dr. Cann 209 F2
Cedarhill. Alt 78 B1
Cedars Ave. Kingsw 275 E2
Cedars Ave. Wom 270 A3
Cedars Dr. Sto 120 A3
Cedarwood Cl. Bre 224 A2
Cedarwood. Sut Co 258 A1
Celandine Cl. Kingsw 275 E2
Celandine Cl. N-in-M 43 D1
Celandines The. Wom 269 F3
Cellarhead Rd. Ched 59 F2
Cellarhead Rd. Ched 60 A4
Celtic Ave. Che He 41 F4
Celtic Rd. Cann 209 F2
Cemetery Ave. Lon 73 D1
Cemetery Rd. Cann 209 F2
Cemetery Rd. Han 57 D1
Cemetery Rd. Ma Dra 97 D1
Cemetery Rd. N-u-L 55 E1
Cemetery Rd. N-u-L 55 F2
Cemetery Rd. Weston 37 D3
Cemetery St. Ches Hay 226 B1
Cemetery View. Lon 73 D1
Cemetery View. N-u-L 55 F2
Cemetery Way. Wal 243 D1
Cemlyn Ave. Fen 72 C2
Central Ave. Buck 58 A2
Central Ave. Cann 209 F3
Central Cl. Wal 243 D1
Central Dr. Fen 72 C2
Central Dr. Sedg 271 E1
Central Dr. Wal 243 D1
Central St. Sch Gr 26 A3
Central Trading Estate. Wolv 266 C4
Central Way. Bu on T 166 A4
Centre Rd. Sto 104 C1
Centurion Way. Tam 262 A3
Century St. Han 57 D2
Chadsfield Rd. Rug 178 C1
Chadswell Hts. Lich 214 B1
Chadwell Gdns. Cod 238 C2
Chadwell Way. Buck 58 B1
Chadwick Cl. Hi Ri 198 A4
Chadwick Cl. Wolv 265 E3
Chadwick Ct. Rug 196 C4
Chadwick St. Lon 73 E2
Chadwyn Dr. N-in-M 43 D1
Chaff La. Stan 65 E1
Chaffinch Cl. Cann 210 A2
Chaffinch Cl. Sedg 266 B1
Chaffinch Dr. Bidd 27 F4
Chaffinch Dr. Utt 126 B3
Chain La. Staf 174 C2
Chain St. Che He 42 B1
Chalcot Dr. Cann 210 A4
Chaldon Cl. Wolv 240 A1
Chalfield. Tam 249 E3
Chalfont Ave. Cann 226 B4
Chalfont Green. Buck 58 B1
Challinor Ave. Leek 30 C3
Challinor St. Tuns 41 F2
Chamberlain Ave. S-o-T 72 A3
Chamberlain St. Han 57 D1
Chamberlain Way. Bidd 27 F4
Chamberlain's La. Wolv 265 F2
Chamberlain's La. Wom 265 F2
Chance Hall La. Sch Gr 25 D4
Chancery Dr. Cann 210 B4
Chancery La. Lon 73 E2
Chandler Ave. Kin 277 F3
Chandler Dr. Wom 265 E2
Chandlers Cl. Wolv 240 A1
Chandlers Dr. Tam 251 D3
Chanterelle Gdns. Wolv 266 A2
Chantry Rd. Kin 279 E4
Chantry Rd. N-u-L 71 D4
Chapel Ave. Brown 228 C1
Chapel Bank. Kids 26 B3
Chapel Bank. Whe As 205 E3
Chapel Cl. Sch Gr 26 A3
Chapel Cl. Wom 269 F3
Chapel Ct. Gno 171 E3
Chapel Ct. Kid 280 A1
Chapel Ct. N-u-L 55 E1
Chapel Dr. Brown 228 C1
Chapel Green. Dove 127 E4
Chapel Hill. Kid 280 A1
Chapel La. Ans 165 D3
Chapel La. Ash 100 A3
Chapel La. Ashl 99 F2
Chapel La. Audley 39 E1
Chapel La. Bidd 17 D1
Chapel La. Bradl 191 D4
Chapel La. Burs 57 D4
Chapel La. Cann 211 F3
Chapel La. Cod 238 C2
Chapel La. End 28 A1
Chapel La. Hanb 144 C1
Chapel La. Kids 26 C2
Chapel La. Kings 62 A1
Chapel La. Lich 231 D3
Chapel La. Longd 212 A2
Chapel La. Mu 83 E3
Chapel La. N in H 82 B1
Chapel La. Newb 162 C4
Chapel La. Rolle 147 D2
Chapel La. Rudy 29 D3
Chapel La. Tate 164 B2
Chapel La. Whit 232 C3
Chapel Rd. Arm 197 F3
Chapel Sq. Ches Hay 226 B2
Chapel St. Audley 39 F2
Chapel St. Brown 228 C1
Chapel St. Brown 244 A2
Chapel St. Buck 58 A2
Chapel St. Burnt 228 C4
Chapel St. Cann 210 C1
Chapel St. Che 76 B2
Chapel St. Fors 91 D4
Chapel St. Kids 25 E1
Chapel St. Kings 61 E2
Chapel St. Kingsw 275 D4
Chapel St. Kingsw 275 E2
Chapel St. Long 13 D3
Chapel St. N-u-L 55 E1
Chapel St. N-u-L 55 F2
Chapel St. N-u-L 56 B2
Chapel St. Nor Ca 227 F3
Chapel St. Sch Gr 26 A3
Chapel St. Staf 155 F2
Chapel St. Swad 186 C3
Chapel St. Wolv 266 B4
Chapel St. Wom 269 F3
Chapel Terr. Staf 155 F2
Chapel Wlk. Sedg 271 E1
Chapelon. Tam 251 D1
Chapelside. Rug 178 B1
Chaplain Rd. Cann 210 C1
Chaplin Rd. Lon 73 E1
Chapter Wlk. Buck 58 A3
Charlemonte Cl. Cann 210 B2
Charles Ave. Ess 241 F2
Charles Ave. Kid 280 A1
Charles Ave. Wolv 266 A3
Charles Cl. Ches Hay 226 B1
Charles Cotton Dr. Made 68 B3
Charles Cotton St. Staf 155 E3
Charles Cres. Brown 244 A3
Charles Rd. Stour 279 F2
Charles St. Bidd 27 E4
Charles St. Che 76 B2
Charles St. Han 57 E2
Charles St. N-u-L 56 B2
Charlesdale Dr. Aldr 256 A2
Charlesway. Ma Dra 112 A4
Charlock Cl. Cann 210 B2
Charlotte Cl. Col 177 E4
Charlotte St. Tuns 41 E4
Charlton St. S-o-T 72 A4
Charminster Rd. Meir 90 A4
Charmouth Cl. Buck 58 A3
Charmwood Cl. Cann 210 B2
Charnes Rd. Ash 100 B3
Charnley Dr. Sut Co 258 C1
Charnley Rd. Staf 155 F3
Charnock Pl. Che He 42 A4
Charnsford La. Ash 100 A2
Charnwood Ave. Sedg 266 B1
Charnwood Cl. Leek 30 B2
Charnwood Cl. Lich 214 B1
Charnwood Cl. Rug 178 B1
Charnwood Rd. Bu on T 166 A4
Charnwood Rd. Meir 73 F1
Charnwood. Kids 26 A1
Charsley Pl. Lon 72 C1
Charter Cl. Nor Ca 227 F2
Charter Ct. Ma Dra 97 E1
Charter Rd. N-u-L 56 A2
Charterfield Dr. Cann 210 B1
Charterfield Dr. Kingsw 275 E4
Charterhouse Dr. Staf 156 A1
Charters Ave. Cod 239 D1
Charters The. Lich 214 A1
Chartley Cl. Bly 90 C3
Chartley Cl. Pert 254 C2
Chartley Cl. Staf 155 E4
Chartley Hall Cottages. Wes on Tr 139 E3
Chartway The. Brown 244 A2
Chartwell Cl. Cav 59 D2
Chartwell Dr. Sut C 257 E2
Chartwell Dr. Wolv 240 C1
Chartwell Dr. Wom 269 F3
Chartwell Rd. Staf 175 E4
Chartwell. Tam 249 E4
Chartwood. Ashl 99 E3
Chase Ave. Ches Hay 226 C2
Chase Cres. Broc 176 A2
Chase La. Titt 103 F3
Chase Park Ind Est. Burnt 228 C4
Chase Rd. Broc 176 B1
Chase Rd. Brown 229 D1
Chase Rd. Burnt 229 D3
Chase Rd. Sedg 271 E1
Chase Vale. Burnt 228 C3
Chase View La. Copp 174 B2
Chase View. Arm 198 A2
Chase View. Wolv 266 C1
Chase Wlk. Hunt 209 E2
Chaseley Ave. Cann 209 E1
Chaseley Cl. Rug 178 A1
Chaseley Croft. Cann 209 E1
Chaseley Gdns. Burnt 229 E4
Chaseley Rd. Rug 178 A1
Chasepool Rd. Swi 274 B4
Chaseside Dr. Cann 210 A2
Chaseside Ind Est. Cann 210 A2
Chaseview Rd. Alre 200 C1
Chasewater Dr. Che 76 C2
Chasewater Way. Nor Ca 227 F3
Chasewood Park Bsns Centre. Cann 210 C1
Chatfield Pl. Lon 73 E1
Chatham St. Han 57 D1
Chatsworth Dr. Cann 210 A2
Chatsworth Dr. Cav 59 D2
Chatsworth Dr. N-in-M 42 C3
Chatsworth Dr. Tut 146 B3
Chatsworth Pl. Meir 73 F1
Chatsworth Pl. N-u-L 55 F4
Chatsworth. Tam 249 E4
Chatteris Cl. Meir 90 A3
Chatterley Cl. N-u-L 56 A4
Chatterley Dr. Kids 41 D4
Chatterley Rd. Tuns 41 E2
Chatterley St. Burs 41 F1
Chatterton Pl. Lon 73 E2
Chatwell La. Blym 188 B1
Chatwell La. Sher 203 D4
Chaucer Cl. Bu on T 166 B3
Chaucer Cl. Lich 231 D3
Chaucer Cl. Tam 250 A3
Chaucer Dr. Burnt 212 A1
Chaucer Rd. Sedg 271 D3
Chaucer Rd. Staf 174 B4
Chaulden Rd. Staf 136 B1
Chawner Cl. Burnt 211 F1
Cheadle Cl. Penk 207 F4
Cheadle Rd. Alt 78 C1
Cheadle Rd. Ched 45 E2
Cheadle Rd. Dr in M 91 F3
Cheadle Rd. Fors 91 D4
Cheadle Rd. Leek 45 F4
Cheadle Rd. Up Tea 92 B3
Cheadle Rd. Utt 111 D1
Cheam Gdns. Wolv 255 F4
Cheapside. Han 57 E2
Cheapside. N-u-L 56 A1
Chebsey Dr. Staf 155 D3
Checkley Dr. Bidd 16 B1
Checkley Gr. Lon 73 E3
Checkley La. Betley 52 C1
Checkley La. Bridge 52 C1
Checkley Rd. N-u-L 40 B1
Chedale Rd. Kings 61 E1
Cheddar Dr. N-u-L 54 C1
Cheddleton Heath Rd. Leek 45 F4
Cheddleton Park Ave. Ched 45 F3
Cheddleton Rd. Leek 30 C2
Cheedale Cl. Bu on T 167 D3
Chelford Cl. Penk 193 D1
Chell Cl. Penk 207 F4
Chell Gr. N-u-L 56 A4
Chell Green Ave. Che He 42 A3
Chell Heath Rd. Che He 42 B2
Chell Rd. Staf 155 E2
Chell St. Han 57 E3
Chelmarsh Ave. Wolv 265 D4
Chelmorton Dr. Meir 73 F1
Chelmsford Dr. Buck 58 B1
Chelmsford Rd. N-u-L 56 B3
Chelsea Cl. Bidd 16 B1
Chelsea Dr. Sut C 257 F2
Chelsea Way. Kingsw 275 E3
Chelsea Way. Staf 155 E1
Chelson St. Lon 73 E2
Chelston Dr. Wolv 255 F2
Cheltenham Ave. Kings 76 C3
Cheltenham Dr. Kingsw 275 D3
Cheltenham Dr. Staf 175 E4
Cheltenham Gr. Han 57 F3
Cheltenham Gr. N-u-L 54 C1
Chelwood St. Han 57 D3
Chemical La. Tuns 41 E1
Chepstow Cl. Bidd 16 B1
Chepstow Cl. Pert 254 C2
Chepstow Dr. Staf 175 E4
Chepstow Rd. Wal 242 C1
Chepstow Rd. Wolv 240 B3
Chepstow Way. Wal 242 C1
Chequer St. Wolv 266 A3
Chequerfield Dr. Wolv 266 A3
Chequers Ave. Wom 265 D1
Chequers The. Lich 231 E4
Cheriton Gr. Pert 254 C2
Cheriton Green. Buck 58 B1
Cherrington Dr. Gr Wyr 226 C2
Cherrington Gdns. Wolv 255 D1
Cherry Bank. Cann 210 B3
Cherry Cl. Bly 106 C4
Cherry Cl. Burnt 228 C3
Cherry Cl. N-u-L 40 B1
Cherry Gr. Fen 72 C2
Cherry Gr. Stour 279 F2
Cherry Green. Dud 271 F2
Cherry Hill Ave. Meir 74 A1
Cherry Hill La. N-u-L 55 F1
Cherry Hill. Made 68 C3
Cherry La. Che 77 D3
Cherry La. Congle 16 C4
Cherry La. Gay 138 C3
Cherry La. Him 270 B2
Cherry La. Sei 135 E2
Cherry Leys. Bu on T 167 E2
Cherry Orch. Lich 231 E4
Cherry Orchard. N-u-L 56 A1
Cherry Orchard. Sto 120 B4
Cherry St. Stour 279 F2
Cherry St. Tam 250 A3
Cherry Tree Ave. Law-g 25 D3
Cherry Tree Cl. Ecc 133 F4
Cherry Tree Cl. Sto 119 F3
Cherry Tree Cl. Swad 186 C3
Cherry Tree Cl. Tren 88 A3
Cherry Tree Gdns. Cod 239 D2
Cherry Tree La. Bidd 17 D1
Cherry Tree La. Cod 239 D2
Cherry Tree Rd. Audley 39 F1
Cherry Tree Rd. Hunt 209 E4
Cherry Tree Rd. Kingsw 275 F4
Cherry Tree Rd. N-u-L 40 C1
Cherry Tree Rd. Nor Ca 228 A3
Cherry Tree Rd. Rug 196 C3
Cherry Tree Wlk. Tam 250 A4
Cherry Way. Ma Dra 97 E1
Cherrybrook Dr. Penk 193 D1
Cherrytree Cres. Sei 135 D1
Cherrytree Rd. Bu on T 185 F4
Cherrywood Cl. Staf 175 E3
Cherrywood Gr. Meir 89 F3
Cherrywood Rd. Aldr 256 B1
Cherrywood Way. Li As 257 E2
Chertsey Pl. Han 57 E4
Chervil Cl. Meir 90 A3
Cherwell Dr. Brown 228 B1
Cherwell. Tam 250 B1
Chesham Gr. Meir 90 A3
Chesham Rd. Staf 155 F3
Cheshire Cl. Stour 279 E4
Cheshire Dr. Bre 223 E3
Cheshire Gdns. Ma Dra 97 E1
Cheshire Gr. Pert 254 C2
Cheshire St. Ma Dra 97 E1
Cheslyn Dr. Ches Hay 226 B1
Chessington Cres. Tren 88 B4
Chestall Rd. Cann 211 F3
Chester Ave. Wolv 255 F4
Chester Cl. Cann 210 A1
Chester Cl. Kids 40 C4
Chester Cl. Lich 214 B2
Chester Cres. N-u-L 71 D3
Chester Rd N. Brown 228 B1
Chester Rd. Aldr 256 C2
Chester Rd. Audley 39 E1
Chester Rd. Brown 245 E2
Chester Rd. Chet 168 B4

291

Chester Rd. Env Coalway Rd. Wal

Chester Rd. Env 273 F1
Chester Rd. Kids 40 B4
Chester Rd. Kin 277 F4
Chester Rd. Whit 232 B2
Chesterfield Ave. Swad 186 C3
Chesterfield Ct. Brown 244 C2
Chesterfield Rd. Lich 231 D3
Chesterton Rd. Bu on T 166 B4
Chesterton Rd. Patt 253 D1
Chesterton Way. Tam 250 A4
Chesterwood Rd. Che He 42 A2
Chestnut Ave. Tam 250 A4
Chestnut Cl. Aldr 257 D2
Chestnut Cl. Arm 198 B2
Chestnut Cl. Cann 210 B1
Chestnut Cl. Gno 171 E4
Chestnut Cl. Sei 154 C1
Chestnut Cl. Stour 279 E1
Chestnut Cl. Up Tea 92 C2
Chestnut Cres. Fors 91 D3
Chestnut Ct. Mill 102 B2
Chestnut Dr. Brown 244 A1
Chestnut Dr. Ches Hay 226 B2
Chestnut Dr. Gr Wyr 226 C2
Chestnut Dr. Shen 246 C3
Chestnut Dr. Wom 270 A3
Chestnut Gr. Kingsw 275 F3
Chestnut Gr. N-u-L 40 C1
Chestnut La. C Camp 218 C1
Chestnut Rd. Ashl 99 E3
Chestnut Rd. Bu on T 185 F4
Chestnut Rd. End 43 E4
Chestnut Rd. Ma Dra 112 A4
Chestnut Way. Wolv 265 E4
Chestow Pl. Lon 73 E3
Cheswardine Rd. N-u-L 56 A4
Cheswell Cl. Wolv 255 D1
Chetton Green. Wolv 240 A2
Chetwode Cl. Mu 83 E3
Chetwynd Ave. Cav 59 D2
Chetwynd Ave. N-in-M 42 C3
Chetwynd Cl. Penk 207 F4
Chetwynd Cl. Rug 196 C3
Chetwynd End. Newp 168 C2
Chetwynd Gr. Newp 168 C2
Chetwynd Park. Chet 168 B4
Chetwynd Rd. Chet 168 B3
Chetwynd Rd. Edg 168 B3
Chetwynd Rd. N-u-L 56 A3
Chetwynd Rd. Newp 168 C2
Chetwynd Rd. Wolv 266 A3
Chetwynd St. Che He 42 B1
Chetwynd St. N-u-L 56 B3
Chevelstone Cl. Tren 88 B3
Chevening Cl. Sedg 271 F4
Chevin The. Bu on T 147 E1
Cheviot Cl. N-u-L 55 F2
Cheviot Dr. Che He 42 B2
Cheviot Dr. Rug 178 B2
Cheviot Rd. Wolv 266 C4
Cheviot Rise. Cann 210 B3
Cheviot. Tam 251 E1
Chichester Dr. Cann 210 B1
Chichester Wlk. Han 57 E3
Chieveley Cl. Rug 178 B1
Childerplay Rd. Bidd 27 E2
Chilgrove Cl. Han 57 F3
Chilgrove Gdns. Wolv 255 E3
Chillingham. Tam 261 E4
Chillington Cl. Gr Wyr 226 C1
Chillington Dr. Cod 238 C2
Chillington La. Cod 238 B3
Chillington St. Wolv 266 C4
Chillwell Ave. Col 177 F4
Chiltern Cl. Sedg 271 E2
Chiltern La. Ecc 133 F3
Chiltern Pl. N-u-L 55 F2
Chiltern Rd. Swad 186 C2
Chiltern Rd. Tam 251 E1
Chilton St. Fen 72 C2
Chilworth Gr. Lon 72 C1
China St. Fen 72 C3
Chingford Cl. Kingsw 275 E2
Cholerton Cl. Fen 72 C3
Chorley Ave. Che He 42 A3
Chorley Rd. Burnt 212 A1
Chorley St. Leek 30 C3
Chorlton La. Ho Co 37 D1
Chorlton Rd. Han 57 E3
Chorlton Terr. Utt 111 E1
Christ Church Gdns. Lich 230 C4
Christ Church La. Ma Dra 112 A4
Christchurch La. Lich 230 C4
Christchurch St. Fen 72 C3
Christie Ave. Staf 155 E2
Christie Pl. Lon 73 F3
Christine St. Buck 58 A2
Christopher Rd. Wolv 266 C4
Christopher Sq. Fen 72 C3
Christopher Terr. Staf 156 A1
Christopher Wlk. Lich 214 A2
Chrystal St. Han 57 D3
Chub. Tam 261 E4
Chubb Way. S-o-T 71 F2
Chumleigh Gr. Che He 42 A1
Church Ave. Grin 34 A1
Church Ave. Hatton 146 B4
Church Ave. N-in-M 43 D1
Church Bank. Audley 39 E1
Church Bank. Keele 69 F4
Church Bank. Oak 78 A3
Church Bank. Water 63 F4
Church Cl. Alre 215 E4
Church Cl. Bidd 27 E3
Church Cl. Bly 89 F3
Church Cl. Bu on T 167 D2
Church Cl. Copp 192 C4
Church Cl. Dra Ba 260 C3
Church Cl. Hau 172 C3
Church Cl. King 262 B1
Church Cl. Kingst 141 E4
Church Cl. March 127 F1
Church Cl. Ran 153 E3
Church Cl. Rug 196 A4
Church Cl. Shen 247 D3
Church Cl. Staf 174 C3
Church Cres. Ess 241 F2
Church Croft. Utt 125 E4
Church Dr. Hopw 249 D4
Church Eaton Rd. Ch Eat 189 D3
Church Eaton Rd. Gno 188 B3
Church Farm. Ash 100 B3
Church Farm. Utt 111 D2
Church Fields. Keele 69 F4
Church Gr. Ecc 133 E4
Church Hill Dr. Wolv 255 F3
Church Hill Rd. Wolv 255 E3
Church Hill St. Bu on T 167 D2
Church Hill. Cann 210 B3
Church Hill. Cod 238 C3
Church Hill. Kin 278 A1
Church Hill. Wolv 265 F2
Church Hollow. Edin 217 E3
Church La. Albr 237 D1
Church La. Alre 215 E4
Church La. Arm 197 F3
Church La. Ba-u-Ne 183 E1
Church La. Betley 53 E3
Church La. Bidd 17 D1
Church La. Bobb 268 A1
Church La. Bradl 173 E1
Church La. Bre 224 A1
Church La. Burnt 229 E2
Church La. Ched 46 C1
Church La. Chil 219 F2
Church La. Cod 238 C2
Church La. Dr in M 91 F3
Church La. Ecc 116 A3
Church La. Edin 217 E3
Church La. Ella 80 A2
Church La. End 43 F4
Church La. Gay 138 B3
Church La. Gno 188 B4
Church La. Han 145 D2
Church La. Hi Ri 198 A4
Church La. Hix 158 B4
Church La. Ipst 46 C1
Church La. Ki Brom 199 E3
Church La. Kids 26 C4
Church La. Kingst 141 E4
Church La. Leek 30 C3
Church La. Lon 73 D1
Church La. March 127 F1
Church La. May 81 E3
Church La. Mid 260 B1
Church La. N Sol 167 E4
Church La. N-u-L 55 F1
Church La. N-u-L 56 B2
Church La. Roc 96 A2
Church La. Rost 96 B4
Church La. Rug 178 B1
Church La. Sch Gr 25 E4
Church La. Sei 154 C1
Church La. Seis 264 A1
Church La. Shen 245 F2
Church La. Shut 251 F4
Church La. Staf 155 F2
Church La. Stand 102 A2
Church La. Sto 105 E2
Church La. Tam 250 A3
Church La. Thorpe 51 E1
Church La. Tren 71 F1
Church La. Up Tea 109 D4
Church La. Utt 125 E4
Church La. Water 63 F4
Church Meadow. Ipst 46 C1
Church Meadow. N in H 82 B1
Church Mews. Act Tru 193 F4
Church Mews. Hatton 146 B4
Church Moat Way. Wal 243 D1
Church Plantation. Keele 70 A4
Church Rd. Alre 200 C2
Church Rd. Ash 100 B3
Church Rd. Bidd 27 E4
Church Rd. Bran 184 C4
Church Rd. Bre 223 E3
Church Rd. Brown 244 A2
Church Rd. Brown 244 C4
Church Rd. Bu on T 147 F1
Church Rd. Burnt 229 E4
Church Rd. Cod 238 C2
Church Rd. Eg 148 A2
Church Rd. Elf 216 B1
Church Rd. End 43 D4
Church Rd. Hix 139 E1
Church Rd. Hunt 209 D1
Church Rd. Kingsw 275 F1
Church Rd. Lon 88 C4
Church Rd. Nor Ca 227 F2
Church Rd. Penk 192 C1
Church Rd. Rolle 147 D2
Church Rd. Shar 225 E1
Church Rd. Shen 245 F2
Church Rd. Shen 246 C3
Church Rd. Snel 81 E2
Church Rd. Swi 269 E1
Church Rd. Tam 261 E2
Church Rd. Wolv 240 B1
Church Rd. Wolv 255 D2
Church Rd. Wolv 255 F3
Church Rd. Wolv 265 F4
Church Rd. Wom 270 A4
Church Sq. Burs 56 C4
Church St. Ab Br 160 C3
Church St. Alst 35 F2
Church St. Audley 40 A1
Church St. Brown 244 C3
Church St. Burnt 228 C3
Church St. C Camp 218 C1
Church St. Cann 209 F1
Church St. Cann 210 A2
Church St. Cann 226 B3
Church St. Che 76 B2
Church St. Clav 267 E4
Church St. Ecc 133 E4
Church St. Hartin 24 B3
Church St. Kids 25 E1
Church St. Kids 26 A2
Church St. Kings 61 F1
Church St. Leek 30 C3
Church St. Lich 231 E4
Church St. Long 13 D3
Church St. Ma Dra 97 E1
Church St. N-u-L 55 D1
Church St. N-u-L 55 F4
Church St. N-u-L 56 A1
Church St. Neth 219 F3
Church St. Rug 178 C1
Church St. S-o-T 72 A4
Church St. Sch Gr 26 B3
Church St. Sedg 271 E2
Church St. Sto 120 A4
Church St. Tam 250 A3
Church St. Tut 146 B4
Church St. Utt 126 B4
Church St. Whit 232 B3
Church Terr. Burs 57 D3
Church Terr. Cav 74 C1
Church Terr. Wars 23 D1
Church Vale. Nor Ca 227 F2
Church View Gdns. Kin 278 A2
Church View. Adb 131 E2
Church View. Audley 54 C2
Church View. Bu on T 166 B4
Church View. Mill 102 C1
Church View. N-u-L 55 F1
Church View. Rug 197 D3
Church Way. Brown 244 A1
Church Way. Longd 198 A1
Church Wlk. N-u-L 55 F4
Church Wlk. Wolv 255 F3
Church Wlk. Wolv 265 F4
Churchcroft Gdns. Rug 178 C1
Churchfield Ave. Lon 73 E1
Churchfield Cl. Bre 224 B1
Churchfield Cl. Staf 156 B1
Churchfield Rd. Ecc 133 E3
Churchfields. Yox 182 A1
Churchill Ave. Ched 45 E3
Churchill Ave. Tren 87 F4
Churchill Cl. Bly 90 C3
Churchill Cres. Alre 200 C1
Churchill Gdns. Sedg 271 E4
Churchill La. Bla 281 D2
Churchill Rd. Che 76 C2
Churchill Rd. Shen 247 D3
Churchill Rd. Sto 119 F4
Churchill Way. Staf 174 C3
Churchill Way. Tren 87 F4
Churchside Way. Aldr 245 D1
Churchward Gr. Wom 270 A4
Churn Hill Rd. Aldr 256 A2
Churnet Cl. Ched 45 D2
Churnet Ct. Bu on T 166 C2
Churnet Gr. Pert 254 C2
Churnet Rd. Che 76 C1
Churnet Rd. Fors 91 D4
Churnet Valley Rd. Kings 62 A1
Churnet View Rd. Oak 78 A4
Churnet View. Leek 31 D4
Churston Cl. N-u-L 71 D1
Churston Cl. Wal 243 D2
Churston Pl. Han 57 E4
Cinder Hill La. Sch Gr 25 F4
Cinder Hill. Bre 224 A2
Cinder Rd. Burnt 228 C4
Cinder Rd. Sedg 271 D1
Cinderhill Ind Est. Lon 73 F2
Circular Rd. Albr 220 C1
City Arcade. Lich 231 D4
City Bank. Bidd 16 B1
City La. Leek 30 A2
City Rd. Fen 72 B3
City Rd. S-o-T 72 B3
Clamgoose La. Che 76 B4
Clanbrook Rd. Kin 278 A4
Clandon Ave. Tuns 41 F2
Clanford Cl. Staf 174 C3
Clanford La. Sei 154 A3
Clanford Rd. Sei 154 A4
Clanway St. Tuns 41 F3
Clap Gate Gr. Wom 269 F3
Clap Gate Rd. Wom 269 F4
Clare Ave. Ess 241 F1
Clare Ave. N-u-L 56 A3
Clare Cres. Wolv 266 C1
Clare Rd. Staf 155 E4
Clare St. Kids 26 C2
Clare St. S-o-T 56 B1
Clare St. Sch Gr 26 B3
Claremont Cl. N-u-L 56 B4
Claremont Cl. Sto 120 A4
Claremont Gr. Staf 174 A4
Claremont Mews. Wolv 266 A4
Claremont Rd. Ecc 133 F3
Claremont Rd. Sedg 271 F4
Claremont Rd. Tam 250 A4
Claremont Rd. Wolv 266 A4
Clarence Gdns. Sut C 257 F1
Clarence Rd. Lon 73 D2
Clarence Rd. Sut C 257 F2
Clarence St. Bu on T 166 B1
Clarence St. Fen 72 C3
Clarence St. N-u-L 56 A3
Clarence St. N-u-L 56 B1
Clarendon Pl. Brown 243 F2
Clarendon Rd. Brown 244 B1
Clarendon Rd. Sut Co 258 B2
Clarendon St. Fen 72 B3
Clarendon St. Wal 243 D1
Claridge Rd. S-o-T 56 C1
Clarion Way. Cann 209 F3
Clark Rd. Wolv 255 F1
Clark St. Staf 155 F2
Clark St. Stour 279 F2
Clark's Cres. Ab Br 161 D3
Clarke Ind Est. Bu on T 166 C2
Clarke St. Han 57 D1
Clarke's Ave. Cann 195 D1
Clarke's Cl. Utt 111 D1
Claud St. Fen 72 B2
Claverdon Dr. Li As 257 D2
Claverhouse Rd. Bu on T 167 D1
Claverley Dr. Wolv 265 E3
Clay Gates Rd. Bre 207 D1
Clay Hills. Tuns 41 E2
Clay La. End 43 F4
Clay Pit La. Lich 230 C2
Clay Pit La. Wall 230 C2
Clay St E. Bu on T 167 D1
Clay St. Bu on T 166 C1
Clay St. Penk 192 C1
Clayalders Bank. Stand 101 E3
Claydon Cres. N-u-L 71 D1
Claydon Rd. Kingsw 270 B1
Clayfield Gr W. Fen 73 E3
Clayfield Gr. Lon 73 E3
Claygate Rd. Cann 210 C2
Clayhanger Cl. N-u-L 56 A4
Clayhanger La. Brown 244 B3
Clayhanger Rd. Brown 244 C3
Clayhanger St. Burs 56 C4
Claymills Rd. Bu on T 148 A1
Claymore. Tam 261 E4
Clays La. Bran 184 C4
Clayton Av. Congle 6 A3
Clayton La. N-u-L 71 E2
Clayton La. S-o-T 71 E2
Clayton Rd. N-u-L 71 E2
Clayton St. Lon 73 D2
Clayton St. Wolv 266 B4
Claytonwood Rd. S-o-T 71 F2
Cleadon Pl. Buck 58 A3
Clear View. Kingsw 275 D3
Cleasby. Tam 251 E1
Clee Hill Dr. Wolv 255 D1
Clee Hill Rd. Sedg 271 E2
Clee Rd. Cook 280 A3
Clee View Rd. Wom 269 F3
Cleeton St. Cann 210 B1
Cleeve Dr. Sut C 257 F3
Cleeve Rd. Wal 242 C2
Cleeve Way. Wal 242 C2
Cleeve. Tam 250 B2
Clematis Ave. Fors 90 C3
Clematis Cl. Sei 135 D1
Clematis Cres. Bu on T 186 A4
Clematis. Tam 250 C2
Clement Cl. Staf 155 F3
Clement Pl. N-in-M 42 C2
Clement Rd. Che He 42 A3
Clent View Rd. Stour 279 E1
Clerk Bank. Leek 30 C3
Clermont Ave. Tren 72 A1
Clevedon Ave. Staf 175 F4
Cleveland Cl. Ess 241 F1
Cleveland Dr. Cann 210 A2
Cleveland Rd. Han 57 E1
Cleveland Rd. N-u-L 55 F2
Cleveland St. Burs 56 C4
Cleveland St. Stour 279 F2
Cleveland Walk. Staf 174 A4
Cleves Cres. Ches Hay 226 B1
Clewley Dr. Wolv 240 A2
Clewley Rd. Bran 184 C4
Clewlow Pl. Lon 73 E3
Clewlows Bank. Bag 43 F2
Clews St. Burs 56 C4
Clews Wlk. N-u-L 56 B3
Cley Gr. N-u-L 71 D1
Cliff Hall La. King 261 D1
Cliff Rd. Col 158 B1
Cliff St. Che He 42 B1
Cliff Vale Pl. S-o-T 56 C1
Cliffe Pl. Che He 42 A2
Clifford Cl. Tam 250 C2
Clifford Rd. Ma Dra 112 A4
Clifford St. Han 57 E1
Clifford St. Tam 250 C2
Cliffs La. Fort 150 C1
Clifton Ave. Aldr 245 E1
Clifton Ave. Brown 244 B4
Clifton Ave. Cann 226 B4
Clifton Ave. Tam 250 A4
Clifton Cl. Fen 72 C3
Clifton Cl. Staf 156 A2
Clifton Cl. Swad 186 C1
Clifton Dr. Staf 156 A2
Clifton Gdns. Cod 239 E2
Clifton La. Th Co 235 D2
Clifton Rd. Clif 81 F4
Clifton Rd. Neth 219 E3
Clifton Rd. Wolv 255 E3
Clifton St. Fen 72 C3
Clifton St. N-u-L 56 B2
Clifton St. Sedg 266 C1
Clifton St. Stour 279 F2
Clinton Cres. Burnt 229 D4
Clinton Gdns. Sto 120 A4
Clinton Sq. Han 57 D2
Clive Ave. N-in-M 43 D2
Clive Cl. Sut Co 258 B1
Clive Rd. Burnt 229 D4
Clive Rd. Ma Dra 97 E1
Clive Rd. N-u-L 56 B3
Clive Rd. Patt 263 E4
Clive St. Tuns 41 F2
Cliveden Ave. Aldr 245 D1
Cliveden Coppice. Sut C 257 F1
Cliveden Pl. Lon 73 E1
Clockmill Ave. Brown 243 F2
Clockmill Pl. Brown 243 F2
Clockmill Rd. Brown 243 F2
Cloister Walk. Whit 232 C3
Cloister Wlk. Buck 58 A3
Cloisters The. Bu on T 166 C1
Cloisters The. Gno 171 F3
Close Bank. Tut 146 B3
Close La. Sch Gr 26 B4
Close The. Made 68 C4
Close The. Meir 74 A3
Close The. Sedg 271 E2
Close The. Staf 155 E1
Close The. Staf 174 C3
Close The. Swi 269 F1
Close The. Tut 146 A3
Cloud View. Congle 6 A1
Clough Hall Dr. Kids 40 C3
Clough Hall Rd. Kids 40 C4
Clough La. Cav 59 D1
Clough St. Han 57 D2
Clovelly Wlk. Burs 56 C4
Clover Heath. Clav 267 E4
Clover La. Kingsw 275 D4
Clover Meadows. Cann 210 B1
Clover Rd. N-u-L 56 B3
Clover Ridge. Ches Hay 226 B2
Cloverdale Pl. Lon 73 F2
Cloverdale Rd. N-u-L 56 A2
Cloverdale. Pert 254 B2
Cloverdale. Staf 175 E4
Clowes Rd. Buck 58 A2
Club Bldgs. Bre 240 B3
Club Row. Sedg 271 F3
Club St. S-o-T 72 A3
Clumber Ave. N-u-L 71 E3
Clumber Gr. N-u-L 71 E3
Cluny Pl. Buck 58 A3
Clyde Ave. Bidd 16 C1
Clyde Pl. N-u-L 71 D2
Clyde Rd. Burs 57 D4
Clyde St. Han 57 D1
Clyde Wlk. Han 57 D2
Clynes Way. Meir 74 A2
Co-operative St. Staf 155 E3
Coach House Rise. Tam 261 F4
Coal Haulage Rd. Nor Ca 227 E4
Coalbourne La. Br Hi 279 F4
Coalmeadow Cl. Wal 242 C2
Coalpit Hill. Kids 40 B4
Coalpit La. Rug 197 D3
Coalpitford La. Ched 44 C2
Coalport Cl. Che 76 B1
Coalville Pl. Meir 74 A3
Coalway Ave. Wolv 266 A3
Coalway Gdns. Wolv 265 E4
Coalway Rd. Rug 197 D3
Coalway Rd. Wal 243 D1

293

Crescent The. N-u-L Dennis St. Fen

Crescent The. N-u-L 55 D1
Crescent The. N-u-L 71 D3
Crescent The. Rudy 18 B1
Crescent The. S-o-T 71 F2
Crescent The. Staf 175 F4
Crescent The. Swad 186 C3
Crescent The. Wolv 255 D2
Cressington Dr. Sut Co 258 A1
Cresswell Ave. N-u-L 40 B1
Cresswell La. Bre 223 E3
Cresswell La. Dr in M 91 E2
Cresswell Old La. Dr in M 91 F2
Cresswell Rd. Han 57 F2
Crest Cl. Bu on T 147 F1
Crestbrook Rd. Buck 58 B3
Crestfield Rd. Meir 89 F4
Crestway Rd. N-in-M 43 E2
Crestwood Cl. Bu on T 166 B4
Crestwood Dr. Sto 119 F3
Crestwood Glen. Wolv 255 F4
Crestwood Park. Bre 223 E4
Crestwood Rise. Rug 178 B1
Crestwood. Tam 251 D3
Creswell Cres. Wal 242 C1
Creswell Dr. Sei 154 C4
Creswell Farm Dr. Staf 155 D4
Creswell Gr. Sei 154 C4
Crewe Rd. Law-g 25 D2
Crich Way. Swad 186 C3
Crichton Ave. Bu on T 166 B4
Crick Rd. Han 57 F1
Cricket Cl. N Sol 167 F4
Cricket La. Lich 231 E3
Cricket Meadow. Sedg 271 F2
Cricket Meadow. Wolv 240 B2
Cricketers Cl. Bu on T 185 F4
Crigdon. Tam 251 E1
Crinan Gr. Staf 174 B3
Cringlebrook. Tam 250 B1
Crispin Cl. Staf 155 E4
Critchlow Gr. Lon 73 D1
Crockford Dr. Sut Co 258 A2
Crockington Cl. Seis 263 F1
Crockington La. Seis 264 A1
Crocus Cres. Wolv 240 A2
Croft Ave. Cann 195 D1
Croft Ave. N-u-L 56 A3
Croft Cl. Elf 216 C1
Croft Cl. Neth 219 F4
Croft Cl. Rolle 147 D2
Croft Cres. Brown 244 B4
Croft Cres. S-o-T 72 A3
Croft Ct. Che He 42 B1
Croft Gdns. Burnt 229 D4
Croft Gr. Utt 111 E1
Croft La. Penk 207 E1
Croft Leys The. Arm 198 B2
Croft Par. Aldr 256 A3
Croft Rd. Che 76 B2
Croft Rd. N-u-L 56 A1
Croft Rd. Sto 119 F3
Croft St. Burs 56 C4
Croft St. Tam 250 A3
Croft The. Bla 281 E1
Croft The. Bu on T 166 C1
Croft The. Che 76 C3
Croft The. Ched 45 E2
Croft The. Col 158 B1
Croft The. Hix 158 B4
Croft The. Ki Brom 199 E3
Croft The. Longd 197 F1
Croft The. Maer 84 B1
Croft The. S-o-T 71 F3
Croft The. Sedg 266 C1
Croft The. Swad 186 C3
Croft The. Wom 269 E3
Croft Way. Ma Dra 97 D1
Crofter Cl. Bidd 27 D4
Crofters Wlk. Wolv 239 F1
Croftfield St. Buck 73 E4
Croftstead Ave. Dens 95 E3
Cromartie St. Lon 73 E1
Cromer Cres. Han 57 F2
Cromer Gdns. Wolv 255 F3
Cromer Rd. Han 57 F2
Cromer St. N-u-L 56 B2
Crompton Cl. Col 177 F4
Crompton Gr. Tren 88 B3
Crompton Rd. Sto 120 A4
Cromwell Cl. Hop 137 E1
Cromwell Cl. Tut 146 B3
Cromwell Rd. Cann 210 C1
Cromwell Rd. Tam 249 F4
Cromwell Rd. Wolv 240 C2
Cromwell St. Bidd 27 E4
Cromwell St. Han 57 E3
Cromwell Terr. Leek 30 C3
Cromwells Meadow. Lich 231 E3
Crony Cl. Ched 45 E2
Crook La. Aldr 256 A1
Crooked Bridge Rd. Staf 155 F2
Crosby Cl. Wolv 255 F3
Crosby Rd. S-o-T 71 F2
Cross Butts. Ecc 133 E3
Cross Edge. End 43 D4
Cross Hill. Burs 56 C4
Cross In Hand La. Fare 213 E2
Cross In Hand La. Lich 213 F1
Cross Keys. Lich 231 D4
Cross La. Audley 39 F3
Cross La. Congle 6 A1
Cross La. Lich 231 E3
Cross La. Rolle 147 D1
Cross La. Sedg 266 B1
Cross La. Sto 105 E3
Cross La. Water 48 C2
Cross May St. N-u-L 71 D4
Cross Of The Hand. Ab Br 161 D1
Cross Pl. Sedg 266 C1
Cross Rd. Albr 237 D2
Cross Rd. Rug 196 C4
Cross Rd. Utt 111 D1
Cross Side. Clif 81 F4
Cross St S. Wolv 266 B4
Cross St. Bidd 27 E4
Cross St. Brown 244 A1
Cross St. Bu on T 166 B2
Cross St. Burnt 228 C4
Cross St. Cann 210 C1
Cross St. Cann 226 C3
Cross St. Che 76 B2
Cross St. Ches Hay 226 B2
Cross St. Gno 171 E3
Cross St. Kings 61 E2
Cross St. Kingsw 275 D4
Cross St. Kingsw 275 E2
Cross St. Kingsw 275 E3
Cross St. Leek 30 C3
Cross St. Lon 73 E2
Cross St. Ma Dra 97 E1
Cross St. Meir 74 A3
Cross St. N-u-L 55 F4
Cross St. Staf 155 E3
Cross St. Stour 279 F3
Cross St. Tam 250 A3
Cross St. Tam 250 B2
Cross St. Tuns 56 B4
Crossdale Ave. N-in-M 43 D1
Crossdale Ave. N-in-M 43 D1
Crossfell. Tam 251 D1
Crossfield Ave. Bidd 27 E3
Crossfield Ave. Fors 90 C3
Crossfield Rd. Lich 231 F4
Crosshill Bank. Mil 122 C3
Crossing La. Sei 154 B1
Crossings The. Lich 231 F4
Crossland Cres. Wolv 255 F4
Crossland Pl E. Meir 90 A4
Crossland Pl W. Meir 74 A1
Crosslands. Congle 6 A1
Crossley Rd. Che He 42 A2
Crossley Stone. Rug 178 C1
Crosslow La. A le Da 36 C3
Crossman St. Bu on T 166 A2
Crossmead Gr. Han 57 F3
Crossway Rd. Han 57 E4
Crossway The. N-u-L 56 B2
Crossway. Staf 156 A2
Crossways Rd. Law-g 25 D2
Crossways. Bidd 16 C1
Croston St. Han 57 D1
Crotia Ave. Weston 37 D3
Crouch Ave. Che He 42 A2
Crouch La. Congle 6 B2
Crowberry La. Ba-u-Ne 183 E1
Crowberry La. Mid 260 B1
Crowborough Rd. Bidd 28 A3
Crowcrofts Rd. Lon 88 C4
Crowden Rd. Tam 251 D1
Crowfoot La. Ch Bro 129 F4
Crowland Ave. Pert 254 C2
Crown Bank Cres. Kids 40 B3
Crown Bridge. Penk 192 C1
Crown Cl. Sedg 266 B1
Crown Ind Est. Bu on T 166 A1
Crown La. Stour 279 F3
Crown La. Sut C 257 F2
Crown St. Han 57 E2
Crown St. N-u-L 55 E1
Crown St. Sto 120 A4
Crowndale Pl. Che He 41 F4
Crowther Gr. Wolv 255 F2
Crowther Rd. Wolv 255 F3
Crowther St. S-o-T 72 B4
Croxall Rd. Edin 217 D3
Croxden Rd. Buck 58 A3
Croxdene Ave. Wal 242 C1
Croxdene Ave. Wal 243 D1
Croxhall Rd. Alre 201 D1
Croxstalls Cl. Wal 243 D1
Croxstalls Rd. Wal 243 D1
Croyde Pl. Meir 90 A3
Croydon Dr. Penk 207 F4
Cruso St. Leek 30 C3
Crutchley Ave. Tam 250 A1
Crystal Ave. Br Hi 275 F1
Cubley La. M Mont 96 C1
Cuckoo Cage La. Tate 164 C1
Cuckoo Cl. Cann 210 B1
Cull Ave. Staf 156 A2
Cullamore La. Utt 126 A2
Cumberland Cl. Kids 40 C4
Cumberland Cl. Kingsw 275 F2
Cumberland Cres. Burnt 229 D4
Cumberland Dr. Tam 250 A1
Cumberland Rd. Bu on T 185 E3
Cumberland Rd. Cann 210 A2
Cumberland St. Fen 72 C3
Cumberland St. N-u-L 56 B1
Cumberledge Hill. Cann 211 F3
Cumberpatch Ave. Che He 42 A4
Cumbers The. Sei 154 A3
Cumming St. S-o-T 71 F4
Cunningham Rd. Pert 254 C2
Curborough Rd. Lich 214 A1
Curland Pl. Lon 73 F1
Curlew Cl. Lich 231 F4
Curlew Cl. Utt 126 B3
Curlew Hill. Cann 210 A2
Curlew. Tam 262 A4
Curtiss Pl. Meir 90 B3
Curzon Pl. Rug 196 C4
Curzon Rd. Che He 42 A1
Curzon Rise. Leek 30 A3
Curzon St W. Bu on T 166 A2
Curzon St. Bu on T 166 B2
Curzon St. N-u-L 56 B1
Curzon St. Wolv 266 B4
Cutts St. Han 57 D1
Cwerne Ct. Sedg 271 E2
Cygnet Cl. Keele 69 D4
Cynthia Gr. Che He 42 A1
Cypress Ave. Sedg 271 E3
Cypress Cl. Ma Dra 97 D1
Cypress Gdns. Kingsw 275 E2
Cypress Gr. Fors 91 D3
Cypress Gr. N-u-L 55 E4
Cypress Rise. Cann 211 D3
Cyprus St. Wolv 266 B3

D'Urberville Cl. Wolv 266 C3
D'Urberville Rd. Wolv 266 C3
D'Urberville Wlk. Cann 210 A1
Dace Gr. Che He 42 A2
Dace. Tam 261 E4
Daffodil Cl. Sedg 271 F4
Daffodil Wlk. Rug 178 B1
Dag La. Lull 218 C4
Dahlia Cl. Meir 74 A3
Dain Pl. N-u-L 56 A3
Dain St. Burs 56 C4
Daintry Cl. Leek 30 C3
Daintry Dr. Hopw 249 D4
Daintry St. Leek 30 C3
Daintry St. S-o-T 71 F2
Dairyhouse La. Che 60 C1
Dairyhouse La. Dil 60 A1
Dairylands Rd. Law-g 25 D2
Daist Bk. Leek 30 C3
Daisy Ave. Ipst 62 A4
Daisy Bank Cl. Brown 244 A1
Daisy Bank. Cann 209 F4
Daisy La. Alre 200 B1
Daisy Pl. Fen 72 C2
Daisy Wlk. Wolv 240 A2
Dalbeg Cl. Wolv 255 F4
Dale Ave. N-in-M 42 C3
Dale Cl. Che 76 C1
Dale Cl. Whitm 85 E3
Dale Cres. Congle 6 A1
Dale Dr. Burnt 229 D4
Dale Gr. Congle 6 A1
Dale La. Hau 173 D4
Dale La. Sei 154 A1
Dale La. Stan 64 C2
Dale Rd. Stour 279 F1
Dale St. Bu on T 166 B1
Dale St. Burs 56 C4
Dale The. Ash 100 A3
Dale The. Bly 90 C1
Dale The. Wars 23 E1
Dale View Dr. N-u-L 55 E1
Dale View. E St 5 D2
Dale View. Meir 74 A2
Dalebrook Rd. Bu on T 167 D3
Dalecot Green. Buck 73 E4
Dalegarth Gr. Meir 89 F4
Dalehall Gdns. Burs 56 C4
Dalehead Ct. Meir 89 F4
Dalehouse Rd. Ched 45 E2
Dalelands Est. Ma Dra 112 A4
Dalelands W. Ma Dra 112 A4
Dales Cl. Bidd 28 A4
Dales Cl. Swad 186 C3
Dales Green Rd. Kids 26 B3
Daleside. Bu on T 167 D1
Dalesman Cl. Kingsw 275 D4
Dallow Cl. Bu on T 166 B3
Dallow Cres. Bu on T 166 B3
Dallow St. Bu on T 166 B3
Dalton Gr. Buck 58 B1
Dalton St. Wolv 266 A4
Daltry Way. Made 68 C4
Daly Cres. N-u-L 55 D1
Dam La. A le Da 36 C2
Dam La. Bidd 17 D1
Dam St. Lich 231 D4
Dama Rd. Faz 260 C4
Dame Paulet Sq. Bu on T 166 B1
Dampier St. Leek 30 C3
Dams The. Cav 74 B1
Danby Crest. Staf 174 A4
Danby Dr. Cann 211 E2
Dandillion Ave. Che 92 B4
Dane Dr. Bidd 16 C1
Dane Gdns. Kids 26 B1
Dane Gr. Che 76 C1
Dane Wlk. Han 57 E2
Danebower Rd. Tren 88 A3
Danebridge Gr. Han 57 F3
Danehill Gr. Tren 71 F1
Danehill Wlk. Wolv 255 F4
Danelagh Cl. Tam 249 F4
Danemead Cl. Meir 90 A4
Danes Cl. Ess 241 F2
Danes Croft. Tren 88 A4
Danescourt Rd. Wolv 255 E3
Danesgate. Leek 30 C3
Daneswood Dr. Brown 244 C2
Danford La. Clav 267 E4
Daniels Cross. Newp 169 D2
Daniels La. Aldr 256 B3
Danilo Rd. Cann 209 E1
Danta Way. Staf 156 B1
Darby Ave. Whit 232 C3
Darges La. Gr Wyr 226 C2
Darius Cl. N-u-L 56 A4
Dark La. Alre 201 D2
Dark La. Dun 184 A4
Dark La. Fare 213 D1
Dark La. Feath 240 B4
Dark La. Feath 241 E4
Dark La. Gr Wyr 227 E1
Dark La. Kin 278 A2
Dark La. Longd 212 B4
Dark La. Newb 162 B4
Dark La. Newp 168 C1
Dark La. Pol 262 C4
Darley Dale. Swad 186 C1
Darley Gr. Che 76 C1
Darlings La. Longd 212 A3
Darnbrook. Tam 251 E1
Darnel Hurst Rd. Sut Co 258 B2
Darnford Cl. Staf 155 E4
Darnford La. Lich 231 F3
Darnford La. Whit 232 A3
Darnford Moors. Lich 231 F3
Darnford View. Lich 214 C1
Darnley St. S-o-T 72 B4
Darrall Gdns. S-o-T 71 F2
Darsham Gdns. N-u-L 71 E1
Dart Ave. Che He 42 A2
Dart Cl. Bidd 16 B1
Dart Gr. Che 76 C1
Dart Pl. N-u-L 71 D2
Dart. Tam 262 A3
Dartford Pl. Che He 42 B2
Dartford Rd. Wal 242 C1
Dartmouth Ave. Cann 226 B4
Dartmouth Ave. Kingsw 275 E2
Dartmouth Ave. N-u-L 71 D3
Dartmouth Ave. Patt 253 E1
Dartmouth Cl. Cann 226 B4
Dartmouth Dr. Aldr 256 A3
Dartmouth Pl. Meir 89 F4
Dartmouth Rd. Cann 209 E1
Dartmouth St. Che He 42 A1
Dartmouth St. Staf 156 A2
Dartmouth St. Wolv 266 B4
Darwin Cl. Burnt 229 D4
Darwin Cl. Cann 210 C1
Darwin Cl. Lich 231 D4
Darwin Cl. Staf 156 B2
Darwin Ct. Pert 254 C2
Dash Gr. Che He 42 B1
Datteln Rd. Cann 210 A2
Davenport Cl. Leek 30 A2
Davenport Rd. Wolv 255 D3
Davenport St. Burs 56 B4
Davenport St. Tuns 41 F1
Daventry Cl. Buck 57 F1
David Garrick Gdns. Lich 214 A1
David Rd. Meir 73 F1
Davidson Ave. Congle 6 A3
Davidson Rd. Lich 231 D4
Davies Dr. Utt 110 C4
Davis Rd. Tam 250 C2
Davis St. Han 57 D1
Davison St. Burs 57 D4
Davy Cl. Buck 58 A2
Davy Pl. Rug 196 B3
Dawes Cl. Arm 197 F2
Dawes La. Brown 229 D1
Dawley Brook Rd. Kingsw 275 E4
Dawley Rd. Kingsw 275 E4
Dawley Trading Est. Kingsw 275 E4
Dawlish Ave. Staf 175 E4
Dawlish Dr. Buck 58 B1
Dawn Ave. Che He 42 A2
Dawn View. Meir 74 A2
Dawney Dr. Sut Co 258 A2
Dawson Ave. Wolv 266 C1
Dayson Pl. N-u-L 56 A4
Dayton Dr. Rug 178 B1
Daywell Rise. Rug 178 B2
De Ferrers Croft. Bu on T 166 B4
De Havilland Dr. Swyn 118 C3
De-wint Rd. Sto 120 A4
Deacon Way. Rug 178 C1
Deakin Ave. Brown 228 C1
Deakin Gr. N-u-L 71 E3
Deakin Rd. Che He 42 A3
Deal Ave. Burnt 229 D4
Dean Ct. Pert 254 C3
Dean Hollow. Audley 39 E1
Dean Pl. Han 57 E1
Dean Rd. Wom 269 F3
Dean St. Bre 223 E3
Dean St. Buck 58 B2
Dean St. Sedg 271 E4
Dean's La. N-u-L 40 B1
Deanery Cl. Rug 178 C1
Deanery Cl. Shar 225 E1
Deans Croft. Lich 231 E4
Deans La. Barth 38 B2
Deansberry Cl. Tren 88 A4
Deanscroft Way. Lon 73 F2
Deansfield Cl. Bre 223 E3
Deansfield Rd. Bre 223 E3
Deanshill Cl. Staf 155 E1
Deansway. Tren 88 A3
Dearnsdale Cl. Staf 155 D4
Deavall Way. Cann 210 A1
Deavall Way. Cann 210 A2
Deaville Rd. Buck 58 B2
Debenham Cres. Buck 58 A1
Deborah Cl. Wolv 266 B3
Dee Cl. Bidd 16 C1
Dee Cl. Kids 40 C4
Dee Gr. Cann 226 B4
Dee La. N-u-L 71 D2
Dee Rd. Wal 243 F1
Deebank Ave. Leek 31 D3
Deeley. Tam 251 D1
Deep Cut Rd. Dr in C 144 A4
Deepdale Cl. Bu on T 167 D3
Deepdale Cl. N-in-M 42 C1
Deepdale La. Sedg 271 F2
Deepdale La. Snel 81 D1
Deepdale. Tam 251 E1
Deepdales. Staf 175 E3
Deepdales. Wom 269 F3
Deepmore Cl. Alre 201 D1
Deepmore Cl. Feath 224 B3
Deer Cl. Nor Ca 228 A4
Deer Cl. Wal 243 E1
Deer Hill. Broc 176 B2
Deer Park Rd. Faz 249 F1
Deer Park. Gno 171 F4
Deer Wlk. Wolv 239 F1
Deerfold Cres. Burnt 229 D4
Deerhill. Tam 251 E1
Deerhurst Rise. Cann 210 C3
Deerleap Way. Rug 178 B1
Defford Ave. Brown 244 B1
Defoe Dr. Lon 73 F2
Delafield Way. Rug 178 B1
Delamere Gr. N-u-L 56 A1
Delamere Gr. Tren 88 A4
Delamere La. Staf 174 A4
Delaney Dr. Lon 73 F2
Delhurst Ave. Wolv 266 C2
Delius Gr. Han 57 F3
Dell Cl. Staf 155 D4
Dell The. Cann 210 C2
Dell The. Lich 230 C4
Dell The. N-u-L 55 E1
Dell The. Stour 279 F3
Dell The. Tam 250 A3
Dellway Ct. Stour 279 F3
Dellwood Gr. Lon 73 E3
Delph Wlk. Fen 72 C3
Delphouse Rd. Che 76 A1
Delphouse Rd. Fors 75 F1
Delphside. Audley 39 F1
Delta Way Bsns Centre. Cann 226 B3
Delta Way. Cann 226 C4
Deltic. Tam 251 D1
Delves Cres. King 262 B1
Delves Pl. N-u-L 71 D3
Den La. Betley 52 B2
Den La. Blake 52 B2
Denbigh Cl. Bidd 27 E3
Denbigh Cl. Bu on T 166 B4
Denbigh Cl. N-u-L 71 E2
Denbigh St. Han 57 D3
Denbury Cl. Cann 210 B1
Denby Ave. Lon 73 E3
Dency Gr. Che He 42 A2
Dene Ave. Kingsw 275 E2
Dene Cl. Penk 207 F4
Dene Rd. Low Pen 264 C2
Dene Rd. Stour 279 F2
Dene Side. N-u-L 71 D4
Denehurst Cl. Meir 74 A1
Denewood Pl. Meir 74 A1
Denford Rd. Longs 44 C4
Denham Gdns. Wolv 265 D4
Denham Sq. Lon 72 C1
Denleigh Rd. Kingsw 275 F2
Denmark Rise. Cann 210 B4
Dennington Cres. Lon 72 C1
Dennis St. Br Hi 279 F4
Dennis St. Fen 72 C3

295

Eaton Cres. Sedg Farm Gr. Newp

Eaton Cres. Sedg 271 D2
Eaton Pl. Kingsw 275 F3
Eaton Rd. Roc 95 F2
Eaton St. Han 57 E2
Eaton St. Utt 111 E1
Eaves Ct Rd. Sedg 266 B1
Eaves La. Buck 58 B3
Eaves La. Che 76 C1
Eaves La. Oak 78 A4
Eaveswood Rd. Buck 58 B3
Ebenezer St. Cann 210 A4
Ebor St. Lon 73 E1
Ebstree Rd. Seis 264 A2
Ebury Gr. Meir 73 F1
Eccleshall Ave. Wolv 240 B1
Eccleshall Rd. Ashl 99 F2
Eccleshall Rd. Mu 99 D3
Eccleshall Rd. Sei 135 E1
Eccleshall Rd. Staf 155 E3
Eccleshall Rd. Sto 119 F3
Eccleston Pl. Che He 42 A3
Edale Cl. Kingsw 275 D4
Edale Cl. N-u-L 55 D1
Edale Cl. Tuns 41 D4
Edale Cl. Wolv 266 C2
Edale. Tam 251 D1
Eddens Wood Cl. Dra Ba 260 C3
Eddisbury Dr. N-u-L 40 B1
Eden Cl. Bidd 16 C1
Eden Cl. Cann 210 C1
Eden Cl. Kids 26 A1
Eden Gr. Ashl 99 E3
Eden Gr. Che 76 C1
Eden Gr. Meir 73 F1
Edenhurst Ave. Meir 74 B1
Edensor Ct. N-u-L 55 F4
Edensor Rd. Lon 73 D2
Edensor St. N-u-L 55 F4
Edensor Terr. Lon 73 D1
Edgar Cl. Tam 249 F4
Edgar Pl. Fen 73 E3
Edge Ave. Che He 42 A3
Edge Hill Ave. Ess 241 D1
Edge Hill Dr. Pert 254 C2
Edge Hill Dr. Sedg 266 B1
Edge Hill Rd. Sut C 257 E2
Edge Hill. Kin 277 F2
Edge Hill. King 262 A1
Edge La. End 43 E4
Edge St. Burs 41 F1
Edge View Cl. N-in-M 43 E1
Edge View Ct. Bidd 27 E4
Edge View Rd. N-in-M 43 E1
Edge View Wlk. Kin 277 F3
Edgefield La. End 43 E3
Edgefield Rd. Lon 73 E3
Edgeley Rd. Bidd 27 E4
Edgemoor Meadow. Cann 210 B1
Edgeview Rd. Congle 16 A4
Edgeware St. Han 57 D3
Edghill Rd. Leek 30 B3
Edgmond Rd. Newp 168 C2
Edinburgh Cres. Kingsw 275 E1
Edinburgh Rd. Congle 6 A1
Edinburgh Way. Bu on T 166 B4
Edision St. Fen 72 B3
Edison Cl. Cann 210 B4
Edison Rd. Staf 155 F3
Edmonton Cl. Cann 210 A1
Edmonton Gr. N-in-M 42 C1
Edmonton Pl. Bu on T 167 E1
Edmund Ave. Staf 174 A4
Edmund Rd. Sedg 271 F3
Ednam Gr. Wom 265 D1
Ednam Pl. Meir 74 A1
Ednam Rd. Wolv 266 B3
Edwal Rd. Meir 74 A2
Edward Ave. Aldr 256 A4
Edward Ave. N-u-L 71 D3
Edward Ave. Tren 88 A4
Edward Ave. Wolv 266 C3
Edward Ct. Tam 250 C2
Edward Davies Rd. Che He 42 B1
Edward Rd. Pert 254 C3
Edward St. Audley 39 F2
Edward St. Bu on T 166 B2
Edward St. Cann 209 F2
Edward St. Fen 72 C4
Edward St. N-u-L 56 B2
Edward St. Sto 105 D1
Edward St. Tam 250 A3
Edwards Farm Rd. Alre 215 F4
Edwards Rd. Burnt 228 C3
Edwards Rd. Sut Co 258 B2
Edwin Cl. Penk 207 F4
Edwin Cl. Staf 155 D1
Efflinch La. Ba-u-Ne 201 F4
Egal St. Wolv 266 A4
Egelwin Cl. Pert 254 C3
Egerton Rd. Aldr 256 C1
Egerton Rd. S-o-T 71 F4
Egerton Rd. Wolv 240 C2
Egerton St. Han 57 E1
Egg La. Hix 158 C4
Eggington Rd. Hilton 147 F4
Eggington Rd. Stour 279 E3
Egginton Dr. Penk 207 F4
Egginton Rd. Etwall 148 A4
Elan Cl. Cook 280 A2
Elan Cl. Sedg 271 E2
Elan Rd. Sedg 271 E4
Elburton Rd. Fen 73 D3
Elder Cl. Cann 210 B1
Elder Gr. Wom 269 F3
Elder La. Burnt 229 E4
Elder Pl. Burs 57 D3
Elder Rd. Burs 57 D3
Elderberry Cl. Stour 279 E2
Eldertree La. Ash 100 A4
Eldertree La. Ash 100 B3
Eldon St. Bu on T 167 D2
Eldon St. Han 57 E3
Eldridge Cl. Wolv 239 F1
Eleanor Cres. N-u-L 71 D3
Eleanor Harrison Dr. Cook 280 A3
Eleanor Pl. N-u-L 71 D3
Eleanor View. N-u-L 71 D3
Electric Ind Est. Bu on T 166 C3
Electric St. Bu on T 166 C3
Elenora St. S-o-T 72 A4
Elford Cl. Staf 155 E4
Elgar Cl. Cann 209 F3
Elgar Cl. Lich 214 A1
Elgar Cres. Buck 58 A3
Elgin Cl. Sedg 266 C1
Elgin Ct. Pert 254 C2
Elgin St. S-o-T 57 D1
Elgood La. Tuns 41 E4
Elias Cl. Lich 231 F3
Eliases La. Bidd 17 D1
Eliot Cl. Tam 250 A4
Eliot Way. Staf 155 E1
Elizabeth Ave. Rolle 147 D2
Elizabeth Ave. Wolv 266 A3
Elizabeth Ct. Kids 40 B3
Elizabeth Ct. Ma Dra 112 B4
Elizabeth Dr. N-u-L 55 F4
Elizabeth Dr. Tam 250 A3
Elizabeth Rd. Cann 209 F3
Elizabeth St. Han 57 F2
Elkington Cl. Newp 168 C1
Elkington Rise. Made 68 C4
Elkstone Cl. Tuns 41 F2
Ellam's Pl. N-u-L 55 F1
Ellastone Gr. S-o-T 71 F3
Ellastone Road. Cot 63 E3
Elldawn Ave. N-in-M 42 C1
Ellerbeck. Tam 251 D1
Ellerby Rd. Lon 88 C4
Ellers Gr. Burs 56 C4
Ellesmere Ct. Newp 168 C1
Ellesmere Gr. Ma Dra 112 A4
Ellesmere Rd. Cann 226 A4
Ellgreave St. Burs 56 C4
Ellington Ave. Staf 156 A3
Ellington Cl. Buck 58 A1
Elliot Cl. Arm 198 A2
Elliot Dr. Cav 59 D2
Elliot Rd. Fen 72 C3
Elliott St. N-u-L 56 B1
Elliotts La. Cod 239 D2
Ellis St. Han 57 E4
Ellis Wlk. Cann 226 C4
Ellison St. N-u-L 56 B3
Ellowes Rd. Sedg 271 E2
Elm Ave. Staf 175 F3
Elm Cl. Col 158 A1
Elm Cl. Dove 127 E4
Elm Cl. Kids 41 D4
Elm Cl. Leek 30 B3
Elm Cl. Newp 168 C1
Elm Cl. Sedg 271 D1
Elm Cl. Stour 279 E1
Elm Ct. Brad 174 B3
Elm Dr. Bla 281 D1
Elm Dr. Bradl 191 E4
Elm Dr. Che 76 C1
Elm Dr. Ma Dra 112 A4
Elm Farm Rd. Wolv 266 B4
Elm Gdns. Lich 231 E4
Elm Gr. Cod 239 D2
Elm Gr. Hunt 209 E4
Elm Gr. Kin 278 A2
Elm Pl. Cook 280 A2
Elm Pl. Lon 72 C1
Elm Rd. Kingsw 275 F3
Elm Rd. Nor Ca 228 A3
Elm Rd. Sto 120 A4
Elm St. Burs 57 D4
Elm St. N-u-L 56 B1
Elm Tree Cl. Wom 269 F3
Elm Tree Dr. Audley 39 F1
Elm Tree Wlk. Tam 249 F4
Elm View. Dens 95 F3
Elm Wlk. Penk 207 F4
Elmbridge Way. Sedg 271 F3
Elmbrook Cl. Meir 89 F4
Elmcroft Gdns. Wolv 240 C2
Elmcroft Rd. Buck 58 A3
Elmdale Dr. Aldr 256 B4
Elmdon Cl. Penk 208 A4
Elmdon Cl. Wolv 240 A1
Elmdon Pl. Meir 90 A4
Elmdon Rd. Wolv 240 A1
Elmhurst Cl. Bre 224 A2
Elmhurst Cl. Buck 57 F1
Elmhurst Cl. Staf 155 E4
Elmhurst Dr. Burnt 229 D2
Elmhurst Dr. Kingsw 275 F2
Elmhurst. Eg 148 A3
Elmley Gr. Pert 254 C2
Elmore Green Rd. Wal 243 D1
Elmore House. Rug 178 C1
Elmore La. Rug 178 C1
Elmore Row. Wal 243 D1
Elms Cl. Shar 225 E1
Elms Dr. Cann 209 E1
Elms La. Shar 225 E1
Elms Paddock The. Patt 253 E1
Elms Rd. Bu on T 166 C1
Elms The. N-u-L 56 B4
Elms Way. Meir 74 A1
Elmsdale. Wolv 255 D1
Elmsmere Rd. Buck 58 A3
Elmstead Cl. Tren 71 F1
Elmstone Cl. Staf 175 F3
Elmtree Rd. Aldr 256 B1
Elmwood Ave. Ess 242 A2
Elmwood Cl. Cann 210 A2
Elmwood Cl. Fors 91 D3
Elmwood Cl. Gno 171 E4
Elmwood Cl. Law-g 25 D2
Elmwood Dr. Fors 91 D3
Elmwood Gr. Utt 110 C4
Elmwood Rd. Kingsw 275 E1
Elmwood Rise. Sedg 266 A1
Elphinstone Rd. S-o-T 71 F2
Elsby Pl. Che He 42 A3
Elsdon Rd. Staf 174 B3
Elsing St. Fen 72 B3
Elsmere Ave. Lon 73 D1
Elston Hall La. Wolv 240 B1
Elstree Cl. Meir 73 F1
Elstree Gr. Buck 58 A3
Elswick Rd. Buck 72 C4
Eltham Gdns. N-u-L 56 B2
Elton Cl. Newb 162 C4
Elton Cl. Wolv 240 C2
Elton La. Newb 162 C4
Elton Terr. Tuns 41 E4
Elton Way. Gno 171 E4
Elunda Gr. Burnt 228 C3
Elviron Dr. Wolv 255 D3
Elwell Cres. Sedg 271 F3
Elworthy Cl. Staf 156 A3
Elwyn Cl. Bu on T 147 E1
Ely Cl. Cann 210 A1
Ely Wlk. Lon 73 E2
Embers Way. End 44 A4
Emberton St. N-u-L 55 F3
Emberton St. N-u-L 56 B3
Embleton Wlk. Burs 56 C4
Embry Ave. Staf 156 A3
Emerald Way. Sto 120 A2
Emerson Cl. Sedg 271 D2
Emerson Rd. Burs 57 D3
Emerson Rd. Wolv 240 C1
Emery Ave. Han 57 F4
Emery Ave. N-u-L 71 D4
Emery St. Burs 57 D3
Emmanuel Rd. Burnt 229 D4
Empire Pas. S-o-T 72 A3
Empire Rd. Bu on T 167 E2
Empire St. S-o-T 72 A3
Emstone Cl. Lon 88 C4
Emsworth Cres. Wolv 240 A1
Emsworth Rd. Lon 88 C4
Encounter Pl. Han 57 F3
End Hall Rd. Wolv 255 D2
End The. N Sol 167 F4
Enderby Dr. Wolv 266 A3
Enderby Rise. Bu on T 166 A4
Enderley Cl. Wal 243 D2
Enderley Dr. Wal 243 D2
Enderley St. N-u-L 56 A1
Endon Dr. Bidd 27 D3
Endon Rd. N-in-M 42 C2
Endon Rd. N-in-M 42 C3
Endwood Dr. Li As 257 E2
Engelsea Brook La. Weston 38 A2
Engine La. Brown 244 B4
Engine La. Tam 251 D1
Englesea Ave. Meir 74 A3
Engleton La. Bre 223 E4
Engleton Mill La. Bre 223 F4
Ennerdale Cl. Burs 56 C4
Ennerdale Dr. Pert 254 C2
Ennerdale Rd. Wolv 255 E4
Enoch St. Burs 56 C4
Ensall Dr. Br Hi 275 F1
Ensford Cl. Sut C 257 F3
Enson La. Mar 137 D4
Enson La. Salt 137 D4
Ensor Dr. Pol 251 F1
Enstone Ct. N-u-L 71 D2
Enterprise Dr. Feath 224 B3
Enville Cl. Wal 243 D2
Enville Common Rd. Env 273 F2
Enville Pl. Stour 279 F3
Enville Rd. Kin 278 A2
Enville Rd. Kingsw 275 D4
Enville Rd. Sedg 271 E2
Enville Rd. Wolv 265 E2
Enville St. Stour 279 F3
Ephraim St. Han 57 E1
Epping Rd. S-o-T 71 F2
Epsley's Yd. Staf 155 F1
Epsom Cl. Kings 76 C3
Epsom Cl. Lich 231 E4
Epsom Cl. Pert 254 C2
Epsom Dr. Staf 175 E4
Epworth St. S-o-T 72 A4
Erasmus Way. Lich 231 D4
Erdington Rd. Aldr 256 B2
Eringden. Tam 251 D1
Ermington Rd. Wolv 266 C2
Ernald Gdns. Sto 120 A4
Eros Cres. Han 57 F3
Errill Cl. Fen 72 B3
Erskine St. Lon 73 E1
Eskdale Pl. N-u-L 71 D3
Eskdale Pl. Tren 88 A4
Eskrett St. Cann 210 B3
Esperanto Way. Che He 57 E4
Esselie Ave. Ash 100 B3
Essex Ave. Kingsw 275 D3
Essex Dr. Bidd 16 B1
Essex Dr. Cann 210 A2
Essex Dr. Col 158 B1
Essex Dr. Kids 25 F1
Essex Dr. Rug 196 B3
Essex Dr. Sto 119 F3
Essex Gdns. Stour 279 E4
Essex Pl. N-u-L 71 D3
Essex Rd. Bu on T 185 E3
Essex Rd. Sut Co 258 B1
Essington Cl. Alre 201 D2
Essington Cl. Br Hi 275 F1
Essington Cl. Lich 231 D3
Essington Cl. Shen 247 D3
Essington Ind Est. Ess 241 F2
Essington Rd. Wal 242 A1
Estridge La. Gr Wyr 227 D1
Etching Hill Rd. Rug 178 A1
Ethelfleda Rd. Tam 261 F3
Ethelred Cl. Sut Co 258 A2
Eton Ave. N-u-L 70 C2
Eton Cl. Bu on T 166 C3
Eton Cl. Sedg 271 F3
Eton Cl. Staf 156 A1
Eton Park. Bu on T 166 C3
Eton Rd. Bu on T 166 B3
Etruria Old Rd. Han 56 C2
Etruria Rd. Han 57 D2
Etruria Vale Rd. Han 57 D2
Etruria Way. N-u-L 56 C2
Etruscan St. Han 56 C1
Etruscan Wlk. Barl 88 C2
Ettingshall Park Farm La. Wolv 266 C2
Ettymore Cl. Sedg 271 E4
Ettymore Rd W. Sedg 271 E4
Ettymore Rd. Sedg 271 E4
Etwall Rd. Eg 148 A4
Europa Way. Lich 231 F4
Eva Gr. Titt 87 E4
Evans Croft. Faz 250 A1
Evans St. Burs 41 F1
Evans St. Wolv 266 C1
Eve La. Dud 271 F3
Evelyn St. Fen 72 B3
Everest Rd. Kids 26 B2
Everglade Rd. King 262 B1
Eversley Ave. Leek 30 C3
Eversley Gr. Sedg 266 B1
Eversley Rd. Lon 73 F1
Evesham Cres. Wal 242 C2
Evesham Way. Lon 73 F2
Eveson Rd. Stour 279 F1
Ewe Dale La. Alst 35 D2
Exbury Cl. Wolv 239 F1
Exchange Ind Est The. Cann 226 C3
Exchange Rd. Alre 201 D2
Exchange The. Wal 243 D1
Exeter Green. Buck 58 B1
Exeter Rd. Cann 226 A4
Exeter St. Staf 174 C4
Exley. Tam 250 B1
Exmouth Gr. Burs 57 D4
Exonbury Wlk. Cann 209 F1
Eynsham Ct. Wolv 255 F3
Eyre St. Burs 56 C4
Eyrie The. Bu on T 167 E2
Faceby Gr. Meir 90 B4
Fair Lawn. Albr 237 D3
Fair Oak Rd. N-u-L 40 B1
Fair Oak. Newp 168 C2
Fair Oaks Dr. G Wyr 243 D4
Fair View Rd. Leek 31 D2
Fair View. Arm 198 B2
Fair View. May 81 E4
Fairbank Ave. S-o-T 72 A3
Fairbanks Wlk. Swyn 103 D2
Fairclough Pl. Che He 42 A2
Fairfax Rd. Wolv 240 C2
Fairfax St. Han 57 E3
Fairfield Ave. End 43 D4
Fairfield Ave. Lon 89 E4
Fairfield Ave. N-u-L 56 B2
Fairfield Ave. Rolle 147 E2
Fairfield Cl. Cann 210 B1
Fairfield Cres. Swad 186 C3
Fairfield Ct. Staf 155 F3
Fairfield Dr. Brown 244 A2
Fairfield Dr. Cod 238 C2
Fairfield Dr. Kin 278 A2
Fairfield Dr. Penk 207 F3
Fairfield Rd. Br Hi 275 F1
Fairfield Rd. Utt 126 A4
Fairfield Rise. Stour 279 E3
Fairfields Hill. Pol 262 C4
Fairfields Rd. Bidd 17 D1
Fairfields Rd. Ma Dra 97 E1
Fairfields. Audley 39 F1
Fairford Gdns. Burnt 229 E3
Fairford Gdns. Kingsw 275 F2
Fairgreen Way. Aldr 257 D1
Fairham Rd. Bu on T 147 F1
Fairhaven Gr. Han 57 F3
Fairhills. Sedg 271 E4
Fairlawn Cl. Meir 89 F4
Fairlawn Cl. Wal 242 B1
Fairlawn Ct. Albr 237 D3
Fairlawn Dr. Kingsw 275 E2
Fairlawn Way. Wal 242 B1
Fairlawns. N-u-L 56 A1
Fairlight Gr. Meir 90 A4
Fairmead Cl. Staf 175 E3
Fairmount Way. Rug 178 B1
Fairoak Ave. Staf 155 E4
Fairoak Dr. Wolv 255 D2
Fairview Ave. Weston 37 D3
Fairview Cl. Ches Hay 226 B1
Fairview Cl. Tam 250 C3
Fairview Cres. Kingsw 275 F3
Fairview Rd. Wolv 265 E2
Fairview Way. Staf 156 B1
Fairway Rd. Che He 42 A2
Fairway The. Swad 186 C3
Fairway. Bran 185 D4
Fairway. Brown 244 B1
Fairway. Cann 226 B3
Fairway. Staf 156 A1
Fairway. Tam 261 F3
Fairway. Tren 87 F4
Fairways Ave. Stour 279 F1
Fairways Cl. Stour 279 F1
Falcon Cl. Bu on T 166 C3
Falcon Cl. Cann 209 E1
Falcon Cl. Ches Hay 226 B1
Falcon Cres. Wolv 266 C1
Falcon Dr. Whit 232 C3
Falcon Rd. Meir 90 A3
Falcon Rise. Stour 279 E3
Falcon Way. Dud 271 F1
Falcon. Tam 262 A3
Falcondale Rd. Wal 242 B1
Falkirk Grange. N-u-L 70 C4
Falklands Cl. Swi 269 F1
Fallow Field. Cann 209 F2
Fallow Field. Li As 257 D2
Fallow Field. Lich 214 A2
Fallow Rd. Faz 249 F1
Fallowfield Cl. Penk 207 F4
Fallowfield. Lon 88 C4
Fallowfield. Pert 254 B2
Fallowfield. Staf 175 E3
Fallowfield. Wolv 239 F1
Fallowfields Dr. Ba-u-Ne 183 E1
Falmouth Ave. Staf 175 F4
Falmouth Cl. Staf 175 F4
Falmouth Ct. N-u-L 71 E3
Falmouth Rd. Congle 15 F4
Falna Cres. Tam 249 F4
Fancourt Ave. Wolv 265 E2
Fancy Wlk. Staf 155 E3
Fane Rd. Wolv 242 A1
Fanlizard La. Gno 171 E2
Far Green Ind Est. Han 57 E3
Far Ridding. Gno 171 E3
Far View. Aldr 245 D1
Faraday Ave. Bu on T 147 E1
Faraday Pl. S-o-T 71 F4
Faraday Rd. Staf 155 F3
Farcroft Ave. N-u-L 55 F3
Farcroft Dr. Ma Dra 97 D1
Fareham Cres. Wolv 265 E3
Fareham Gr. Meir 89 F4
Farewell La. Burnt 229 F3
Faringdon. Tam 251 D1
Farington Pl. Che He 42 A3
Farland Gr. Che He 42 A4
Farleigh Dr. Wolv 265 D4
Farleigh Gr. Buck 58 B1
Farleigh Rd. Pert 255 D2
Farley La. Oak 78 B2
Farley Rd. Oak 78 A3
Farm Cl. Bu on T 166 A4
Farm Cl. Cann 210 B2
Farm Cl. Cod 239 D1
Farm Cl. Rug 178 B1
Farm Cl. Sedg 271 D4
Farm Cl. Tam 250 B4
Farm Gr. Newp 168 B2

297
Freshwater Gr. Buck
Grange Rd. Ched

Freshwater Gr. Buck 57 F2
Freville Gdns. Tam 250 A3
Friar St. Lon 73 E2
Friar St. Staf 155 E3
Friar's Alley. Lich 231 D4
Friar's La. Tong 220 B2
Friar's St. N-u-L 71 D4
Friars Ave. Sto 120 A4
Friars Cl. Che 76 B2
Friars Cl. Kingsw 275 E2
Friars Gorse. Kin 279 E4
Friars Pl. Buck 58 A4
Friars Rd. Buck 58 A4
Friars' Rd. Staf 155 F1
Friars' Terr. Staf 155 F1
Friars' Wlk. N-u-L 71 D3
Friars' Wlk. Staf 155 F1
Friarswood Rd. N-u-L 71 D4
Friary Ave. Ab Br 160 C3
Friary Ave. Lich 231 D3
Friary Gdns. Lich 231 D4
Friary Rd. Lich 231 D4
Friary The. Lich 231 D4
Friday Acre. Lich 214 A1
Friezland La. Brown 245 D3
Friezland Way. Brown 245 D3
Frinton Cl. Staf 155 F3
Frith St. Leek 30 B3
Frobisher Dr. Swyn 103 E2
Frobisher St. N-in-M 43 D3
Frodingham Rd. Buck 58 B1
Frog La. Lich 231 D4
Frog La. Whe As 205 E3
Froghall Rd. Che 76 C3
Froghall Rd. Ipst 62 A3
Froghall Rd. Kings 76 C3
Froghall. N-u-L 56 A1
Frogmore Rd. Ma Dra 97 E1
Frome Wlk. Che He 42 A2
Froyle Cl. Wolv 255 E3
Fulford Rd. Bly 106 C4
Fullbrook Ave. Ba-u-Ne 201 F4
Fullelove Rd. Brown 245 D4
Fuller St. Tuns 41 F2
Fullerton Cl. Wolv 239 F1
Fullmore Cl. Penk 207 F4
Fullwood Wlk. Buck 58 B1
Fulmer Pl. Meir 90 A4
Furber Pl. Kingsw 275 F3
Furguson St. Wolv 242 A1
Furlong Ave. Up Tea 92 C2
Furlong Cl. Alre 201 D1
Furlong Cl. Up Tea 92 C2
Furlong Cl. Wes on Tr 138 B1
Furlong Dr. Up Tea 92 C2
Furlong La. Alre 201 D1
Furlong La. Alst 35 E2
Furlong La. Bradl 173 E2
Furlong La. Burs 56 C4
Furlong Par. Burs 56 C4
Furlong Pas. Burs 56 C4
Furlong Rd. Tuns 41 F2
Furlong The. Swyn 118 C3
Furlong Wlk. Sedg 271 E2
Furlongs Rd. Sedg 271 E3
Furmston Pl. Leek 31 D4
Furnace Cl. Wom 269 F3
Furnace La. Made 68 C4
Furnace Rd. Lon 73 E1
Furness Cl. Wal 242 C2
Furness Gr. Staf 174 A4
Furness. Tam 250 B2
Furnival St. Han 57 D3
Furnivall Cres. Lich 214 B1
Furst St. Brown 245 E4
Fyfield Rd. Bu on T 185 F3
Fynney St. Leek 30 C3

Gable Croft. Lich 231 F3
Gable St. S-o-T 72 A3
Gaelic Rd. Cann 209 E2
Gag La. Tiss 51 E3
Gagarin. Tam 249 F3
Gaia La. Lich 231 D4
Gaia Stowe. Lich 214 A1
Gaiafields Rd. Lich 214 A1
Gaialands Cres. Lich 214 A1
Gail Cl. Brown 245 D2
Gail Park. Wolv 265 E4
Gailey Lea La. Hunt 208 A1
Gailey Lea La. Penk 207 F2
Gainford Cl. Wolv 239 F1
Gains La. Nor Ca 227 E2
Gainsborough Dr. Faz 260 A4
Gainsborough Dr. Pert 255 D2
Gainsborough Hill. Stour 279 F2
Gainsborough Pl. Sedg 271 F1
Gainsborough Rd. Lon 88 C4
Gainsborough Rd. N-u-L 55 F3
Gainsborough Way.
Bu on T 167 D2
Gainsbrook Cres. Nor Ca 227 F3
Gairloch Rd. Wal 242 A1
Galahad Dr. Bu on T 147 F1
Galleys Bank. Kids 26 A2
Galloway Rd. Buck 73 F4
Gallowstree La. May 81 E4
Gallowstree La. N-u-L 70 C4
Galsworthy Rd. Fen 73 D3
Galway Rd. Burnt 229 D4
Gamesfield Green. Wolv 255 F1
Ganton Rd. Wal 243 D2
Ganton Wlk. Wolv 255 F4
Gaol Butts. Ecc 133 E3
Gaol Rd. Staf 155 F2
Gaol Sq. Staf 155 F2
Gaolgate St. Staf 155 F2
Garage Cl. Tam 250 B3
Garbett St. Tuns 41 E4
Garden Cotts. Gno 171 E3
Garden Cres. Brown 243 F2
Garden Croft. Aldr 256 A4
Garden Dr. Rug 197 D4
Garden Pl. S-o-T 71 F4
Garden Pl. Staf 155 F1
Garden St. Leek 30 B3
Garden St. N-u-L 71 E4
Garden St. S-o-T 71 F3
Garden St. Staf 155 F1
Garden View. Rug 178 B1
Garden Wlk. Sedg 271 E1
Gardeners Cl. Bidd 27 D3
Gardeners Way. Wom 269 F2
Gardenholm Cl. Meir 89 F4
Gardens The. Elf 216 B1
Gardiner Dr. Lon 73 D1
Gardner Pl. Utt 111 D1
Garfield Ave. Tren 71 F1
Garfield Cres. Tren 71 F1
Garfield St. Han 57 D1
Garibaldi St. Han 56 C2
Garlick St. Che He 42 A1
Garner St. Burs 56 C2
Garner St. S-o-T 56 C1
Garners Way. Made 68 C4
Garnet St. Han 57 D2
Garnett Rd E. N-u-L 56 A3
Garnett Rd W. N-u-L 56 A3
Garnham Pl. Lon 73 E2
Garret Cl. Kingsw 275 E4
Garrick Cl. Lich 213 F1
Garrick Rd. Cann 209 E2
Garrick Rd. Lich 213 F1
Garrick Rise. Burnt 229 D4
Garrick Rise. Rug 197 D3
Garrigill. Tam 251 D1
Garrod Sq. Staf 156 A3
Garsdale Cres. Lon 88 C4
Garth Cl. Staf 174 C3
Garth Rd. Staf 174 C3
Garth St. Han 57 E2
Garth The. Lich 214 A1
Gas St. Utt 111 E1
Gaskell Rd. Buck 58 B2
Gatacre St. Sedg 271 E2
Gatcombe Cl. Bu on T 147 E1
Gatcombe Cl. Wolv 240 C2
Gatcombe Rd. Sedg 271 F1
Gate St. Meir 74 A3
Gate St. Sedg 271 F4
Gatehouse Trading Estate.
Brown 229 D1
Gateway Ave. Whitm 85 E3
Gatherwynd La. Blym 203 F3
Gatley Gr. Meir 90 A3
Gauledge La. Long 13 D3
Gaunt St. Leek 30 B3
Gawain Gr. Bu on T 147 F1
Gawsworth Cl. Lon 73 E3
Gawsworth. Tam 249 E4
Gay La. Ch Eat 204 C4
Gaydon Rd. Aldr 256 A2
Gayle. Tam 251 D1
Gaymore Rd. Cook 280 A3
Gayton Ave. N-in-M 43 D1
Geary La. Bretby 167 F1
Gedney Gr. N-u-L 71 D1
Geen St. S-o-T 72 A4
Gemini Dr. Nor Ca 226 C3
Gemini Gr. Che He 41 F3
Geneshall Cl. Gno 171 E4
Geneva Dr. Han 57 F3
Geneva Dr. N-u-L 70 C3
Genge Ave. Wolv 266 C2
Genista Cl. Bu on T 186 A4
Genthorne Cl. Wolv 266 C2
Geoffrey Ave. Leek 30 B3
Geoffrey Gr. Meir 74 A2
George Ave. Faz 249 E1
George Ave. Meir 74 A1
George Baily Ct. Staf 155 F1
George Brealey Cl. Rug 196 C4
George Elliott Cl. Utt 126 B3
George La. Lich 231 E4
George La. Sto 120 B4
George St. Audley 39 E1
George St. Br Hi 275 F1
George St. Bu on T 166 B2
George St. Cann 210 B2
George St. Fen 72 C4
George St. N-u-L 55 D1
George St. N-u-L 55 F4
George St. N-u-L 56 B1
George St. N-u-L 56 B3
George St. Staf 155 E3
George St. Tam 250 A2
George Walker Ct.
Bu on T 166 B2
Georges Ct. Lon 73 D2
Georges Way. Audley 39 F1
Georgian Pl. Cann 209 F1
Gerald Rd. Stour 279 F4
Gerard. Tam 249 F4
Gerards Way. Ash 100 B3
Gerrard St. S-o-T 72 A4
Gibb La. Sud 128 C3
Gibbet La. Kin 279 D2
Gibbins St. Han 57 E3
Gibbons Gr. Wolv 255 F2
Gibbons Hill Rd. Sedg 266 B1
Gibbons Rd. Sut Co 258 A2
Gibbons Rd. Wolv 255 F2
Gibraltar. Kin 278 B2
Gibson Gr. N-u-L 55 E4
Gibson Pl. Meir 74 A1
Gibson Rd. Pert 254 C2
Gibson St. Tuns 41 F1
Giddywell La. Longd 197 F1
Giffard Rd. Wolv 240 C1
Gifford Pl. S-o-T 71 F3
Giffords Croft. Lich 214 A1
Giffords Croft. Lich 214 A1
Giggetty La. Wom 269 F3
Gigmill Way. Stour 279 F2
Gilbanks Rd. Stour 279 E4
Gilbern Dr. Bidd 27 D3
Gilbert Cl. Kids 26 A1
Gilbert Cl. Newp 168 B1
Gilbert La. Wom 270 A4
Gilbert Rd. Lich 214 B1
Gilbert St. Tuns 41 E4
Gilbert Wlk. Lich 214 B1
Gilbeys Cl. Br Hi 275 F1
Gilchrist Pl. Burs 57 D4
Giles Cl. Che 76 B2
Giles Rd. Lich 214 A2
Giles Wlk. Han 57 F3
Gill Bank Rd. Kids 41 D4
Gill Bank Rd. Tuns 41 D4
Gill Wlk. Han 57 D2
Gilliard's Croft. Ki Brom 199 E3
Gilliat Wlk. Buck 58 B1
Gillingham Cres. Staf 155 D1
Gillway. Tam 250 A4
Gilman Ave. N-in-M 43 D1
Gilman Pl. Han 57 E2
Gilman St. Han 57 E2
Gilmour La. Ba-u-Ne 183 F1
Gilpin Cres. Brown 244 A2
Gilwell Rd. Cann 211 F3
Gimson St. Fen 72 C3
Ginger Hill. Gno 171 E3
Ginger La. Ecc 116 A2
Gipsy La. Alst 35 F2
Gipsy La. Cook 280 A4
Girsby Cl. Tren 88 B3
Girton Rd. Cann 226 C4
Gisbourne Cl. Yox 182 A2
Gitana St. Han 57 E2
Glade The. Cann 209 E1
Glade The. N-u-L 71 D1
Glade The. Staf 175 D4
Glade The. Wolv 239 F1
Glades The. Aldr 256 A4
Glades The. Aldr 256 C1
Gladstone Dr. Stour 279 E3
Gladstone Gr. Bidd 27 E4
Gladstone Gr. Kingsw 275 E4
Gladstone Pl. S-o-T 71 F3
Gladstone Rd. Cann 210 C1
Gladstone Rd. Stour 279 E3
Gladstone St. Leek 30 C3
Gladstone St. S-o-T 56 C1
Gladstone Way. Staf 156 A3
Gladwyn St. Buck 58 B2
Glaisher Dr. Meir 90 B4
Glamis Cl. Bu on T 166 B4
Glamis Dr. Sto 120 B3
Glandore Rd. Lon 73 F2
Glanville Dr. Sut Co 258 A2
Glascote Ct. Tam 250 C2
Glascote Rd. Tam 250 C2
Glascote Rd. Tam 261 F4
Glass La. Ab Br 161 F1
Glass St. Han 57 E2
Glasscroft Cottages.
Burnt 229 F4
Glastonbury Cl. N-in-M 43 E2
Glastonbury Cl. Staf 175 E3
Glastonbury Cres. Wal 242 C1
Glastonbury Way. Wal 242 C1
Glebe Ave. Staf 155 E3
Glebe Cl. Chesw 130 A4
Glebe Cl. Dove 127 D4
Glebe Cl. Fors 91 D3
Glebe Cl. Rolle 147 D2
Glebe Ct. S-o-T 72 B4
Glebe La. Gno 171 F4
Glebe La. Stour 279 F2
Glebe Rd. Arm 198 B3
Glebe Rd. Che 76 A1
Glebe Rd. Che 76 B2
Glebe St. Kids 25 E1
Glebe St. S-o-T 72 A4
Glebe St. S-o-T 72 B4
Glebe The. Cheb 135 D4
Glebe. Albr 237 D3
Glebedale Rd. Fen 72 C3
Glebefields. Woods 151 E4
Glebelands. Bobb 267 F1
Glebelands. Staf 174 C3
Glebeville. Leek 30 C2
Gledhill Park. Lich 231 E3
Glen Cl. Cann 209 F3
Glen Ct. Cod 239 D2
Glen Ct. Wolv 255 F1
Glen Dr. Alt 94 C4
Glen Park Rd. Sedg 271 E1
Glen Rd. Sedg 271 F3
Glen Rd. Stour 279 F2
Glen Rise. Bu on T 166 A4
Glen The. Sto 120 A4
Glencastle Way. Tren 88 B3
Glencoe Rd. Cann 210 A2
Glencoe St. Lon 73 D1
Glendale Cl. Wolv 265 E4
Glendale Ct. N-u-L 71 E1
Glendale Dr. Wom 270 A3
Glendale St. Burs 57 D4
Glendawn Cl. Cann 210 A2
Glendene Rd. Cann 210 B3
Glendon Cl. Ma Dra 112 A4
Glendower Cl. Gno 171 E3
Glendower Rd. Aldr 245 D1
Glendue Gr. Tren 88 B3
Gleneagles Cres. Han 57 F3
Gleneagles Dr. Bu on T 147 E1
Gleneagles Dr. Staf 156 B2
Gleneagles Rd. Pert 254 B3
Gleneagles Rd. Wal 242 C2
Gleneagles. Tam 251 D3
Glenfield Rise. Bu on T 166 A4
Glenfield Way. Buck 73 F4
Glenfield. Wolv 239 F1
Glengarry Gdns. Wolv 255 F1
Glenhaven. Rug 178 B1
Glenmore Ave. Burnt 229 D3
Glenmore Cl. Wolv 265 F4
Glenroyd Ave. Buck 58 A1
Glenroyd Wlk. Buck 58 B1
Glenthorne Cl. Staf 175 E3
Glenthorne Dr. Ches Hay 226 C2
Glenville Ave. King 262 B1
Glenwood Cl. Lon 73 D2
Glenwood Cl. N-u-L 55 E1
Glenwood Rise. Shen 245 E2
Globe Ave. Staf 174 C3
Globe St. Burs 56 C4
Gloucester Cl. Lich 214 A2
Gloucester Grange. N-u-L 71 E3
Gloucester Rd. Kids 25 F1
Gloucester Way. Bu on T 167 D1
Gloucester Way. Cann 210 A1
Glover St. Cann 210 C2
Glover St. Han 57 E3
Glover St. Staf 155 E2
Glovers Cl. Cann 211 D3
Glyme Dr. Wolv 255 F3
Glyn Pl. Che He 41 F2
Glyndebourne. Tam 249 E4
Glynne Ave. Kingsw 275 E3
Gnosall Rd. Gno 152 A2
Gnosall Rd. Gno 170 B1
Goddard St. Lon 73 E2
Godfrey Rd. Buck 58 A2
Godley La. Dil 75 E3
Godleybarn La. Dil 75 F3
Godolphin. Tam 249 E4
Godsall Gdns. Cod 238 C2
Gofton. Tam 262 A4
Golborn Ave. Bly 90 A2
Golborn Cl. Bly 90 A2
Gold St. Lon 73 D2
Goldcrest Way. Bidd 27 F4
Goldcrest. Tam 262 A3
Goldenhill Rd. Lon 73 D3
Goldfinch View. Ashl 99 E2
Goldhurst Dr. Up Tea 92 C1
Goldsborough. Tam 251 D1
Goldsmith Pl. Lon 73 E2
Goldsmith Pl. Tam 250 A4
Goldthorn Ave. Wolv 266 A3
Goldthorn Cres. Wolv 266 A3
Goldthorn Hill. Wom 266 B3
Goldthorn Rd. Wolv 266 A4
Goldthorne Ave. Cann 209 F1
Golf Links Cl. Tuns 41 E4
Goms Mill Rd. Lon 73 D1
Goodel Cl. Sto 119 F3
Goodfellow St. Tuns 41 E2
Goodman St. Bu on T 166 B3
Goodrich Ave. Pert 255 D2
Goods Station La. Penk 192 C1
Goodson St. Han 57 E2
Goodwick Cl. Tren 88 B3
Goodwin Ave. N-u-L 56 A1
Goodwin Rd. Meir 74 A1
Goodwood Ave. Che 76 C2
Goodwood Cl. Bu on T 147 E1
Goodwood Cl. Cann 211 D3
Goodwood Cl. Lich 231 E4
Goodwood Pl. Tren 88 A4
Goose La. Ab Br 160 C3
Goose St. N-u-L 71 D4
Goosefield Cl. Ma Dra 97 D1
Goosemoor Gr. Meir 90 A4
Goostry Cl. Tam 250 B3
Goostry Rd. Tam 250 B3
Gordale Cl. Congle 6 A3
Gordon Ave. Che 76 A2
Gordon Ave. Han 57 E4
Gordon Ave. Staf 155 E4
Gordon Ave. Wolv 266 C2
Gordon Cl. Leek 30 B2
Gordon Cres. Han 57 E4
Gordon Rd. Tuns 41 E3
Gordon St. Bu on T 166 B2
Gordon St. Che He 42 A1
Gordon St. N-u-L 55 F2
Gordon St. Wolv 266 B4
Gore Rd. Sedg 271 F4
Gorse Cres. Ashl 99 E3
Gorse Dr. Hunt 209 E3
Gorse La. Alre 215 D4
Gorse La. Astb 15 E3
Gorse La. Gno 152 A4
Gorse La. Lich 231 F3
Gorse La. Rug 196 C3
Gorse La. Seis 269 D3
Gorse Rd. Rug 196 C3
Gorse St. Fen 72 C2
Gorse Way. Cann 210 B4
Gorsebrook Leys. Staf 155 D3
Gorseburn Way. Rug 178 B1
Gorsemoor Rd. Cann 210 B1
Gorsemoor Way. Ess 242 A2
Gorseway. Burnt 229 D3
Gorsey Bank. N-in-M 42 C3
Gorsey La. Cann 209 E1
Gorsey La. Gr Wyr 226 C1
Gorsey La. Mill 102 B2
Gorsey La. Neth 219 F4
Gorsey La. Nor Ca 227 F1
Gorsley Dale. Staf 175 E3
Gorstey Lea. Burnt 229 E4
Gorsty Bank. Lich 231 F4
Gorsty Hayes. Cod 238 C2
Gorsty Hill Rd. Up Tea 92 C3
Gorsy Bank Rd. Tam 261 F3
Gorsy La. Norb 150 A2
Gort Rd. N-u-L 55 F2
Gosberryhole La. Congle 7 D1
Goscote Ind Est. Wal 243 F1
Goscote La. Wal 243 F1
Goscote Rd. Brown 244 A1
Gosforth Gr. Meir 90 B4
Gospel Ash Rd. Bobb 268 B1
Gospel Ash Rd. Env 268 B1
Gospel End Rd. Him 271 D4
Gospel End Rd. Sedg 271 D4
Gospel End St. Sedg 271 E4
Gothersley La. Kin 274 B1
Gough Cl. Staf 155 E4
Gould Firm La. Aldr 256 C3
Govan Rd. Buck 72 C4
Gowan Ave. Che He 42 A2
Gower Ave. Kingsw 275 F2
Gower Rd. Sedg 266 A1
Gower Rd. Sto 120 A4
Gower St. Lon 73 E2
Gower St. N-u-L 56 B1
Gower St. Wolv 266 C4
Gowland Dr. Cann 209 D1
Goya Cl. Cann 210 B1
Grace St. Leek 30 B3
Graffam Gr. Che 76 C2
Grafton Ave. Che He 42 A1
Grafton Gdns. Sedg 271 D2
Grafton Rd. Bu on T 167 D1
Grafton Rd. Lon 73 E2
Grafton St. Han 57 E2
Graham Cl. Bu on T 185 E4
Graham Rd. Kingsw 275 E2
Graham St. Buck 58 A2
Graiseley Hill. Wolv 266 B4
Graiseley Row. Wolv 266 B4
Granary Cl. Kingsw 275 D4
Granary Rd. Wolv 239 F1
Granary The. Aldr 256 A3
Granby Wlk. S-o-T 71 F3
Granchester Cl. Meir 90 A3
Grange Ave. Aldr 245 D1
Grange Ave. Burnt 229 D4
Grange Ave. Penk 207 F4
Grange Ave. Sut Co 258 B2
Grange Cl. Bu on T 166 A2
Grange Cl. Ell 134 A1
Grange Cl. Tam 261 E4
Grange Cres. Penk 207 F4
Grange Ct. Bidd 16 B1
Grange Ct. Eg 148 A3
Grange Dr. Cann 209 F1
Grange Gdns. Leek 30 B2
Grange La. Kingsw 275 F2
Grange La. Lich 213 F1
Grange La. N-u-L 56 B3
Grange La. Sut Co 258 B2
Grange Rd. Bidd 16 C2
Grange Rd. Burnt 229 D3
Grange Rd. Ched 45 E2

298
Grange Rd. Gno
Hampshire Cl. End

Grange Rd. Gno 151 F3
Grange Rd. Meir 90 A3
Grange Rd. Nor Ca 228 A3
Grange Rd. Penk 207 F4
Grange Rd. Sto 120 B4
Grange Rd. Swad 186 C3
Grange Rd. Utt 111 D1
Grange Rd. Wolv 255 E2
Grange Rd. Wolv 266 A3
Grange St. Bu on T 166 A2
Grange St. Burs 57 D3
Grange The. Bu on T 166 A2
Grange The. Ki Brom 199 E3
Grange The. Longd 197 E1
Grange The. Meir 74 A1
Grange The. Wom 270 A4
Grange. Lich 213 F1
Grangefield Cl. Ched 45 E2
Grangefield Cl. Wolv 239 F1
Grangefields. Bidd 16 C2
Grangewood Ave. Meir 89 E3
Grangewood Rd. Meir 74 A1
Granstone Cl. Che He 42 A4
Grant Cl. Kingsw 275 E4
Grant St. S-o-T 72 B4
Grantham Pl. Buck 58 A3
Grantley Cl. Lon 73 D1
Grantley Cres. Kingsw 275 E4
Granville Ave. Han 57 E4
Granville Ave. N-u-L 56 B1
Granville Ave. Newp 168 C1
Granville Cl. Newp 168 C1
Granville Dr. Kingsw 275 F3
Granville Rd. Buck 58 A3
Granville Rd. Newp 168 C1
Granville Sq. Sto 105 D1
Granville St. Wolv 266 B4
Granville Terr. Sto 105 D1
Granville Vilas. Newp 168 C1
Granville. Tam 250 C1
Granwood Rd. Titt 88 A1
Grasmere Ave. Li As 257 D1
Grasmere Ave. N-u-L 71 D2
Grasmere Ave. Pert 254 C2
Grasmere Cl. Bu on T 167 D1
Grasmere Cl. Kingsw 275 D4
Grasmere Cl. Wolv 255 F4
Grasmere Dr. Stour 279 F2
Grasmere Pl. Cann 209 F3
Grasmere Terr. Che He 42 A2
Grassholme. Tam 262 A4
Grassmere Ct. Ches Hay 226 B2
Grassmere Hollow. Staf 154 C3
Grassy La. Ess 241 D1
Grassygreen La. Audley 39 F1
Gratley Croft. Hunt 209 E2
Gratton La. End 29 D2
Gratton La. Rudy 29 D2
Gratton Rd. Buck 58 B2
Gravel Hill. Wom 270 A3
Gravel La. Hunt 209 E3
Gravel La. Staf 174 C3
Gravelly Bank. Meir 89 F4
Gravelly Dr. Newp 168 C1
Gravelly Hill. Ash 100 A3
Gravelly La. Shen 245 F2
Gray Rd. Cann 209 F3
Gray's Cl. Sch Gr 26 A4
Grayling Gr. Che He 42 A2
Grayling Willows. Made 68 C3
Grayling. Tam 261 E3
Grayshott Rd. Tuns 41 F3
Grayston Ave. Tam 250 C2
Grazings The. Kin 278 B2
Greasley Rd. Buck 58 A3
Great Charles St. Brown 244 C4
Great Checkhill Rd. Kin 274 B2
Great Furlong. Alre 201 D1
Great Hales St. Ma Dra 97 E1
Great Moor Rd. Patt 253 F1
Great Wood Rd. Up Tea 92 C2
Greatbatch Ave. S-o-T 71 F4
Greatmead. Tam 250 B1
Greatoak Rd. Audley 39 F2
Greaves La. Hanb 144 C2
Green Acres. Wom 269 F3
Green Barns La. Shen 258 B4
Green Barns La. Weef 258 B4
Green Brook Ct. N-u-L 56 A2
Green Cl. Barl 88 B1
Green Cl. Bly 90 B4
Green Cl. Patt 253 E1
Green Cl. Sto 119 F4
Green Gore La. Staf 175 F4
Green Heath Rd. Cann 210 A4
Green La. Aldr 256 C3
Green La. Ash 100 B3
Green La. Brown 244 A2
Green La. Brown 244 B2
Green La. Burnt 212 B1
Green La. Burnt 229 D1
Green La. Cann 226 C3
Green La. Clif 81 F4
Green La. Dord 262 B4
Green La. Ecc 133 F3
Green La. Fare 212 B2
Green La. Fors 91 D3
Green La. Fort 150 C1
Green La. Ha Ri 181 D2
Green La. Heat 18 C1
Green La. Kingsw 275 E4
Green La. March 127 F2
Green La. Newp 168 C2
Green La. Pol 262 B4
Green La. Rost 96 C4
Green La. Rug 178 B1
Green La. Sedg 271 F3
Green La. Tiss 36 B1
Green La. Tut 146 B3
Green La. Wall 230 B1
Green La. Water 65 D4
Green La. Whitg 135 F4
Green La. Wolv 255 F4
Green Lane Venture Centre. Cann 226 C3
Green Meadow Cl. Wom 269 F3
Green Meadows. Cann 210 B1
Green Oak Rd. Cod 239 D1
Green Park. Bly 90 C1
Green Park. Ecc 133 F3
Green Rd. S-o-T 71 F2
Green Rd. Wes on Tr 138 B1
Green Rock La. Wal 243 E1
Green Slade Gr. Cann 210 B4
Green St. Bu on T 166 B1
Green St. Stour 279 F3
Green The. Aldr 256 B3
Green The. Arm 198 B3
Green The. Ba-u-Ne 183 E1
Green The. Broc 176 A2
Green The. Broc 176 B4
Green The. Bu on T 147 F1
Green The. Cav 74 B2
Green The. Che 76 A1
Green The. Cheb 134 C3
Green The. Dord 262 B2
Green The. End 43 D4
Green The. Faz 249 F1
Green The. Kings 61 E1
Green The. Kingsw 275 E1
Green The. Law-g 25 D2
Green The. N-u-L 71 E2
Green The. N-u-L 71 F4
Green The. Rug 197 D3
Green The. Tam 251 D3
Green The. Wal 243 D1
Green The. Wes on Tr 138 B1
Green The. Whit 232 C3
Green Way. Aldr 245 D1
Green Way. Bu on T 166 A4
Green Way. Utt 126 A4
Green's La. Cav 58 C2
Greenacre Cl. Tam 251 D3
Greenacre Dr. Cod 239 D1
Greenacre The. Clif 81 F4
Greenacres Ave. Bly 90 B4
Greenacres Ave. Ess 241 D1
Greenacres Cl. Aldr 256 C1
Greenacres Dr. Utt 111 D1
Greenacres Way. Newp 168 B2
Greenacres. Bre 224 A2
Greenacres. Sedg 266 A1
Greenacres. Wolv 255 D3
Greenbank Rd. Che He 42 A2
Greenbank Rd. N-u-L 56 B2
Greencroft. Kingsw 275 E2
Greencroft. Lich 214 A1
Greendale Dr. N-u-L 40 B1
Greendale La. Che 77 E2
Greendock St. Lon 73 D2
Greenfield Ave. Arm 198 A2
Greenfield Ave. End 43 E4
Greenfield Ave. Stour 279 F3
Greenfield Cl. End 43 E4
Greenfield Cres. Che 76 C2
Greenfield Dr. Utt 126 A4
Greenfield La. Wolv 240 C3
Greenfield Pl. End 43 E4
Greenfield Rd. Staf 175 E3
Greenfield Rd. Tuns 41 F3
Greenfield. Bidd 27 E3
Greenfields Dr. Rug 178 B1
Greenfields La. Ma Dra 97 D1
Greenfields Rd. Brown 244 B1
Greenfields Rd. End 43 F4
Greenfields Rd. Hix 139 E1
Greenfields Rd. Kin 277 E2
Greenfields Rd. Kingsw 275 F3
Greenfields Rd. Wom 270 A3
Greenfields View. Sedg 271 D4
Greenfields. Aldr 256 A4
Greenfields. Cann 209 F1
Greenfields. Dens 95 E3
Greenfields. Gno 171 F4
Greenfinch Cl. Utt 126 B3
Greengate St. Staf 155 F2
Greengates St. Tuns 41 F2
Greenhart. Tam 251 D2
Greenhead St. Burs 56 C4
Greenhill Cl. Tam 261 E3
Greenhill Ct. Wom 270 A3
Greenhill Gdns. Wom 270 A3
Greenhill La. Whe As 205 E4
Greenhill Rd. N-in-M 42 C3
Greenhill Rd. Sedg 271 F3
Greenhill Way. Aldr 245 D1
Greenhill. Lich 231 E4
Greenhill. Wom 270 A3
Greenhough Rd. Lich 231 D4
Greenland Cl. Kingsw 275 F4
Greenlands. Wom 269 F4
Greenlea Cl. Tren 88 B3
Greenlee. Tam 262 A4
Greenleighs. Sedg 266 B2
Greenly Rd. Wolv 266 B3
Greenmeadow Gr. End 43 F3
Greenmeadows Rd. Made 68 C4
Greenmoor Ave. Che He 42 A4
Greenock Cl. N-u-L 70 C4
Greensforge La. Kin 274 C2
Greenside Ave. N-in-M 43 E2
Greenside Cl. Kids 41 D4
Greenside. N-u-L 56 A1
Greenside. Swyn 118 C3
Greenslade Rd. Sedg 266 A1
Greensome Cl. Staf 155 D2
Greensome Cres. Staf 155 D3
Greensome Ct. Staf 155 D2
Greensome La. Staf 155 D3
Greenvale Cl. Bu on T 185 F4
Greenway Ave. Br Hi 275 F1
Greenway Ave. Che He 42 A1
Greenway Ave. Sto 120 A3
Greenway Bank. Bidd 27 E2
Greenway Bank. N-in-M 43 E1
Greenway Gdns. Patt 253 E1
Greenway Gdns. Sedg 266 C1
Greenway Hall Rd. N-in-M 43 E2
Greenway Pl. Buck 58 A4
Greenway Rd. Bidd 16 C1
Greenway The. Hag 281 F3
Greenway The. N-u-L 56 B2
Greenway The. Patt 253 E1
Greenway The. Tren 87 F4
Greenway. Ecc 133 F3
Greenway. Fen 72 C2
Greenway. Sedg 266 C1
Greenway. Staf 156 A2
Greenways Dr. Che 76 B2
Greenways. Audley 39 F1
Greenways. Brad 174 B3
Greenways. Kingsw 275 E1
Greenways. Penk 208 A4
Greenwood Ave. S-o-T 71 F1
Greenwood Dr. Lich 231 E3
Greenwood Gr. Staf 174 B4
Greenwood Park. Aldr 245 E1
Greenwood Park. Cann 210 A4
Greenwood Rd. Aldr 245 D1
Greenwood Rd. Bu on T 185 F4
Greenwood Rd. Fors 91 D4
Greenwoods The. Stour 279 F3
Gregory La. Norb 150 B3
Gregory La. Woods 150 B3
Gregory Rd. Stour 279 E3
Gregory St. Lon 73 D2
Gregson Cl. Lon 73 D2
Greig Ct. Cann 210 B1
Grenadier Cl. Tren 88 B2
Grendon Gdns. Wolv 265 E3
Grendon Green. Buck 58 B1
Grenfell Rd. Wal 243 E2
Grenville Cl. Utt 110 C4
Grenville Rd. Dud 271 F1
Grenville St. Han 57 E3
Gresham Rd. Cann 209 F2
Gresley Cl. Sut Co 258 A2
Gresley Row. Lich 231 E4
Gresley Way. Audley 39 F1
Gresley Wood Rd. Swad 186 C1
Gresley. Tam 250 C1
Gresty St. S-o-T 72 A4
Gretton Ave. Bu on T 147 F1
Greville Cl. Penk 207 F4
Grey Friars Way. Staf 155 E3
Grey Friars' Pl. Staf 155 E2
Grey Friars. Staf 155 E3
Grey Walk. Staf 174 B4
Greyfriars Rd. Buck 58 A3
Greyhound La. Low Pen 264 C3
Greyhound La. Stour 279 E1
Greylarch La. Staf 175 E4
Greysan Ave. Che He 41 F4
Greysbrooke. Shen 247 D3
Greystoke Dr. Kingsw 275 E3
Greyswood Rd. S-o-T 71 F2
Grice Rd. S-o-T 71 F4
Griffin Cl. Burnt 228 C4
Griffin Cl. N in H 82 B1
Griffin St. Lon 73 D2
Griffiths Dr. Wolv 242 A1
Griffiths Dr. Wom 270 A3
Griffiths Rd. Wal 242 B1
Griffiths Way. Sto 120 B3
Grimley Way. Cann 209 F2
Grindcobbe Gr. Rug 178 B2
Grindley Bank. Hix 140 C3
Grindley La. Bly 90 A3
Grindley Pl. S-o-T 71 F3
Grindsbrook. Tam 262 A4
Grisedale Cl. Meir 90 A4
Grissom Cl. Staf 156 A3
Gristhorpe Way. Buck 58 B1
Gritton St. Tuns 41 E1
Grocott Cl. Penk 192 C1
Grosvenor Ave. Aldr 256 C1
Grosvenor Ave. S-o-T 71 F2
Grosvenor Cl. End 43 F4
Grosvenor Cl. Lich 231 E3
Grosvenor Cl. Penk 192 C1
Grosvenor Cl. Sut Co 258 B1
Grosvenor Cres. Wolv 240 B1
Grosvenor Gdns. N-u-L 71 E4
Grosvenor Park. Wolv 265 F3
Grosvenor Pl. N-u-L 56 B3
Grosvenor Pl. Tuns 41 E2
Grosvenor Rd. Ma Dra 97 E1
Grosvenor Rd. Meir 73 F1
Grosvenor Rd. N-u-L 71 E4
Grosvenor Rd. Sedg 271 E1
Grosvenor Rd. Wolv 240 B1
Grosvenor Rd. Wolv 266 C2
Grosvenor St. Leek 30 C3
Grosvenor St. Lon 73 D2
Grosvenor Way. Staf 175 F3
Grotto La. Wolv 255 F3
Grotto Rd. Ma Dra 112 A4
Grounds Dr. Sut C 257 F2
Grounds Rd. Sut C 257 F2
Grove Ave. Fen 72 C2
Grove Ave. Kids 25 F1
Grove Ave. Law-g 25 D2
Grove Cl. Nor Ca 227 F3
Grove Cres. Brown 243 F2
Grove Cres. Woore 83 E4
Grove Gdns. Ma Dra 97 E1
Grove La. Dove 127 F4
Grove La. Nor Ca 227 F1
Grove La. Wolv 255 D1
Grove Park Ave. Law-g 25 D2
Grove Park. Kingsw 275 E4
Grove Pl. Han 57 D1
Grove Rd. Fen 72 B2
Grove Rd. Sto 119 F4
Grove St. Burs 57 D3
Grove St. Leek 30 B3
Grove St. N-u-L 55 F2
Grove St. Wolv 266 B4
Grove The. Bly 90 C3
Grove The. Che He 42 A1
Grove The. Law-g 25 D2
Grove The. Li As 257 E3
Grove The. N-u-L 71 D3
Grove The. Wolv 266 C3
Grovebank Rd. S-o-T 71 F2
Grovelands Cres. Wolv 240 B2
Groveside Way. Brown 244 A3
Grub St. Norb 151 D3
Grub St. Woods 151 D3
Grunmore Dr. Bu on T 147 F1
Guernsey Cl. Congle 6 A1
Guernsey Dr. N-u-L 70 C2
Guernsey Wlk. Lon 73 D2
Guild La. Fort 169 F4
Guild St. Bu on T 166 B2
Guildford St. S-o-T 72 B4
Guinevere Ave. Bu on T 147 F1
Gullet The. Pol 251 F1
Gun Battery La. Bidd 28 A4
Gunby Hill. Neth 219 F4
Gungate. Tam 250 A3
Gunn St. Bidd 27 E4
Gunstone La. Cod 238 C3
Gurnard Cl. Wolv 242 A1
Gurnard. Tam 261 E3
Guthrum Cl. Pert 254 C1
Guy St. Buck 58 A2
Guy's La. Sedg 271 D1
Guys Cl. Tam 249 F4
Gwendoline Way. Brown 245 D2
Gwenys Cres. Fen 72 C2
Gwyn Ave. Bidd 27 E3
Gypsum Way. Dr in C 144 B3
Hackett Cl. Lon 73 E2
Hackford Rd. Wolv 266 C2
Hackwood Cl. Barl 88 C2
Hadden Cl. Cav 59 D1
Haddon Gr. N-u-L 55 F3
Haddon La. Chap Ch 85 F1
Haddon Pl. Buck 58 B3
Haddon Pl. Sto 120 B4
Haden Cl. Kingsw 275 E1
Hadfield Gn. Che He 42 B1
Hadleigh Cl. N-u-L 71 D1
Hadleigh Rd. Buck 58 A3
Hadley Park Gdns. Rug 196 B4
Hadley St. Yox 181 F2
Hadrian Way. N-u-L 55 E3
Hadrians Cl. Tam 261 E4
Haggar St. Wolv 266 B3
Hagley Dr. Rug 178 B1
Hagley Rd. Rug 178 B1
Haig Cl. Cann 210 A3
Haig Rd. Leek 31 D4
Haig St. Lon 73 E1
Haigh Cl. Ched 45 E3
Hailes Park Cl. Wolv 266 C3
Hailsham Cl. Tuns 41 F3
Hainult Cl. Kingsw 275 E2
Halcyon Way. Bu on T 166 A2
Haldale. Tam 251 E1
Hales Hall Rd. Che 76 C2
Hales Pl. Lon 73 E1
Halesworth Cres. N-u-L 71 D1
Halesworth Rd. Wolv 239 F1
Halford Ave. Han 57 E4
Halford St. Tam 250 A3
Halfshire La. Bla 281 D1
Halfway Pl. N-u-L 55 F1
Halifax Cl. Meir 90 B4
Halifax Rd. Albr 220 C1
Haling Cl. Penk 207 F4
Haling Rd. Penk 192 C1
Hall Ave. Leek 31 D4
Hall Bank. Hartin 24 C3
Hall Cl. Patt 253 E1
Hall Cl. Staf 175 D4
Hall Dr. Meir 74 A2
Hall End Cl. Patt 253 E1
Hall End La. Patt 253 E1
Hall Farm Cres. Salt 137 F2
Hall Green Ave. Bu on T 147 F1
Hall Hill Dr. Buck 73 E4
Hall La. Brown 243 F2
Hall La. Burnt 229 F2
Hall La. Dove 127 D4
Hall La. Gr Wyr 227 D2
Hall La. Stan 80 A3
Hall La. Wolv 266 C1
Hall Meadow. Ches Hay 226 A3
Hall Orch. Che 76 B2
Hall Orchard. Utt 125 D4
Hall Pl. N-u-L 56 B3
Hall Rd. Arm 198 B3
Hall Rd. March 127 F1
Hall Rd. Rolle 146 C2
Hall Rd. Utt 126 A4
Hall St. Audley 39 E1
Hall St. Burs 56 C4
Hall St. N-u-L 56 A1
Hall St. Sedg 271 E4
Hall Yd. Up Tea 92 C2
Hallahan Cl. Sto 120 B3
Hallahan Gr. S-o-T 72 A4
Hallam Rd. Utt 110 C4
Hallam St. Fen 72 B3
Hallams Row. Bu on T 166 B2
Hallbridge Cl. Brown 243 F1
Hallcourt Cl. Cann 226 C4
Hallcourt Cres. Cann 226 C4
Hallcourt La. Cann 226 C4
Hallcroft Cl. Newp 168 C2
Hallcroft Gdns. Newp 168 C2
Hallcroft Way. Aldr 256 B3
Halldearn Ave. Cav 74 B2
Hallfarm Cl. Bre 223 E3
Hallfarm Rd. Bre 223 E3
Hallfield Gr. Tuns 41 F3
Hallfields Rd. Swad 186 B2
Hallfields Rd. Swad 186 C2
Hallhill La. Ab Br 161 D3
Halls Rd. Bidd 16 B1
Halls Rd. Sch Gr 26 B4
Halston Rd. Burnt 229 D4
Halton Green. Lon 88 C4
Haltonlea. Tam 262 A4
Ham La. Kingsw 270 C1
Hamble Gr. Pert 254 C2
Hamble Rd. Wolv 265 E3
Hamble Way. Buck 58 B1
Hamble. Tam 250 B1
Hambledon Cl. Wolv 240 A1
Hambleton Pl. Bidd 27 D3
Hambridge Cl. Staf 174 B4
Hambro Pl. Che He 42 A4
Hamelin St. Cann 209 F2
Hames La. Ne Re 236 B2
Hamil Dr. Leek 30 B3
Hamil Rd. Burs 42 A1
Hamil Rd. Burs 57 D4
Hamil Rd. Che He 42 A1
Hamilton Ave. Stour 279 E3
Hamilton Cl. Cann 210 C2
Hamilton Cl. Kingsw 275 E1
Hamilton Cl. Sedg 271 E4
Hamilton Ct. N-u-L 71 E1
Hamilton Dr. Kingsw 275 E1
Hamilton Fields. Bu on T 167 D1
Hamilton Gdns. Wolv 240 C2
Hamilton Rd. Bu on T 167 D1
Hamilton Rd. Lon 73 E1
Hamilton Rise. N-in-M 43 D1
Hamilton St. Fen 72 B3
Hamilton St. Wal 243 E1
Hamlett Pl. N-in-M 42 C2
Hammersley Hayes Rd. Che 76 C3
Hammersley St. Han 57 F3
Hammerton Ave. Buck 57 F1
Hammerwich La. Burnt 229 F2
Hammerwich Rd. Burnt 229 E3
Hammond Ave. End 43 D4
Hammond Rd. N-u-L 55 F4
Hammonds Cl. Hix 158 B4
Hammoon Gr. Buck 58 A1
Hamner Green. Buck 73 E4
Hamps Cl. Burnt 229 E4
Hamps Valley Rd. Water 48 C1
Hampshire Cl. End 43 F4

Jubilee Cl. Gr Wyr

Lanchester Cl. Tam

303

Lancia Cl. Bidd — Lingfield Gr. Pert

Lancia Cl. Bidd 27 D3
Lancing Ave. Staf 175 D4
Lander Pl. Che He 42 A3
Landon St. Lon 73 E2
Landor Cres. Rug 196 C4
Landport Rd. Wolv 266 C4
Landrake Gr. Che He 41 F4
Landsberg. Tam 249 F3
Landseer Pl. N-u-L 55 F3
Landywood Enterprise Park. G Wyr 242 C4
Landywood La. Ches Hay 226 C1
Lane Farm Gr. Han 57 F4
Lane Green Ave. Cod 239 E1
Lane Green Rd. Cod 239 E1
Lane Green Shopping Parade. Cod 239 D2
Lane Head. Long 13 D4
Lane's Cl. Ki Brom 199 E3
Lane. Ella 80 A2
Lanehead Rd. Han 56 C2
Lanehead Wlk. Rug 178 B1
Lanes Cl. Wom 269 F3
Langdale Cres. Han 57 E4
Langdale Dr. Cann 226 B4
Langdale Green. Cann 226 B4
Langdale Rd. N-u-L 71 D3
Langford Rd. Buck 58 B2
Langford Rd. N-u-L 71 D2
Langford St. Leek 30 B3
Langham Green. Aldr 256 C1
Langham Rd. N-in-M 43 D1
Langholm Dr. Cann 210 C1
Langland Dr. Lon 73 D1
Langland Dr. Sedg 271 E4
Langley Gdns. Wolv 265 E4
Langley Rd. Low Pen 265 D4
Langley Rd. Wolv 265 D4
Langley St. S-o-T 56 B1
Langot La. Ecc 115 E2
Langstone Rd. Dud 271 F1
Langton Cres. Whit 232 C3
Langton Ct. Cav 59 D2
Langton Ct. Lich 214 A1
Langtree Cl. Cann 210 B1
Lanrick Gdns. Rug 178 C1
Lansbury Cl. Staf 174 C4
Lansbury Dr. Cann 209 F2
Lansbury Gr. Meir 74 A2
Lansbury Rd. Rug 196 C3
Lansdell Ave. N-u-L 56 A3
Lansdown Cl. Sto 119 F3
Lansdowne Ave. Cod 238 C1
Lansdowne Cl. Leek 30 B3
Lansdowne Cres. Cav 59 D2
Lansdowne Cres. Tam 261 E4
Lansdowne Rd. Bran 184 C4
Lansdowne Rd. S-o-T 56 C1
Lansdowne St. Lon 73 D1
Lansdowne Terr. Bu on T 166 B3
Lansdowne Way. Rug 178 B1
Lansdowne Way. Staf 175 E3
Lant Cl. Ki Brom 199 E3
Lapley Ave. Staf 155 D4
Lapley Rd. Whe As 205 E4
Lapper Ave. Wolv 266 C1
Lapwing Cl. Ches Hay 226 B1
Lapwing. Tam 262 A3
Lapwood Ave. Kingsw 275 F3
Lapworth Way. Newp 169 D2
Larch Cl. Kids 41 D4
Larch Cl. Kin 278 B2
Larch Cl. Lich 231 F4
Larch Gr. Fen 72 C1
Larch Gr. Sedg 271 F4
Larch Pl. N-u-L 55 F4
Larch Rd. Kingsw 275 F4
Larch Rd. Rug 196 C3
Larch Rd. Swad 186 C3
Larches La. Feath 224 C1
Larches The. Newp 168 C1
Larchfields. Sto 120 A3
Larchmere Dr. Ess 242 A2
Larchmount Cl. Tren 88 A4
Larchwood Dr. Cann 210 A2
Larchwood. Keele 70 A3
Larchwood. Staf 175 E3
Larcombe Dr. Wolv 266 B3
Lark Rise. Utt 126 A3
Larkfield. Kids 26 A1
Larkhill La. Ash 100 A2
Larkhill Rd. Stour 279 E2
Larkholme Cl. Rug 178 A1
Larkin Ave. Lon 73 E2
Larkin Cl. Staf 174 B4
Larksfield Rd. Che He 42 B1
Larksmeadow Vale. Staf 175 E3
Larkspur Ave. Burnt 229 D2
Larkspur Dr. Feath 241 D4
Larkspur Gr. N-u-L 56 B1
Larkspur. Tam 261 E2
Larkstone La. Wet 34 C1
Larkswood Dr. Sedg 271 E4
Larkswood Dr. Wolv 265 E2
Lascelles St. Tuns 41 E1
Lask Edge Rd. Bidd 28 B4
Laski Cres. Meir 74 A1
Latebrook Cl. Tuns 41 E4
Latham Cl. Bu on T 167 E1
Latham Gr. Che He 42 A4
Latherford Cl. Penk 224 C3
Latherford La. Shar 225 D2
Lathkill Dale. Swad 186 C1
Latimer Way. Buck 58 B1
Lauder Cl. Sedg 266 B1
Lauder Pl N. Buck 73 F4
Lauder Pl S. Buck 73 F4
Lauderdale Gdns. Wolv 240 C2
Launceston Cl. Tam 250 B1
Laurel Cl. Lich 231 E4
Laurel Cres. Cav 59 D2
Laurel Dr. Burnt 229 E4
Laurel Dr. Cann 210 C2
Laurel Dr. Kids 26 C2
Laurel Dr. Newp 168 C2
Laurel Gr. Bu on T 185 F3
Laurel Gr. Fen 72 B1
Laurel Gr. Staf 174 C4
Laurel Gr. Wolv 265 F3
Laurel Rd. Dud 271 F2
Laurels The. Rug 196 C4
Lauren Cl. Fen 72 C3
Laurence Gr. Wolv 255 F4
Lavender Ave. Fors 90 C3
Lavender Cl. Meir 74 B3
Lavender Cl. Sei 135 E1
Lavender La. Stour 279 E2
Lavender Lodge. Col 177 F4
Lavender Rd. Tam 250 C2
Laverock Gr. Made 68 C3
Lawford Ave. Lich 231 F4
Lawley Cl. Brown 244 A1
Lawley St. Lon 73 E2
Lawn Ave. Stour 279 F2
Lawn La. Bre 240 A4
Lawn La. Chesw 113 F1
Lawn Rd. Staf 155 E1
Lawn Rd. Wolv 266 C3
Lawn St. Stour 279 F2
Lawnoaks Cl. Brown 228 B1
Lawns The. Ma Dra 97 E1
Lawns The. Rolle 147 D2
Lawns The. Utt 111 D1
Lawnsfield Wlk. Staf 136 B1
Lawnswood Ave. Burnt 228 C3
Lawnswood Ave. Kingsw 275 E2
Lawnswood Ave. Wolv 255 F4
Lawnswood Ave. Wolv 266 C2
Lawnswood Cl. Cann 210 B1
Lawnswood Dr. Brown 245 D2
Lawnswood Dr. Kin 275 D1
Lawnswood Rd. Kingsw 275 E2
Lawnswood Rd. Sedg 271 E3
Lawnswood Rise. Wolv 255 F4
Lawnswood. Kin 275 D2
Lawrence Ct. Tam 250 A3
Lawrence Dr. Swyn 103 D2
Lawrence St. Han 57 D1
Lawrence St. Staf 155 F1
Lawson Cl. Aldr 256 A2
Lawton Ave. Law-g 25 E2
Lawton Coppice. Law-g 25 F2
Lawton Cres. Bidd 27 E4
Lawton St. Bidd 27 E4
Lawton St. Che He 42 A1
Lawton St. Kids 26 B2
Lawtongate Estate. Law-g 25 D2
Laxey Rd. N-u-L 56 A2
Laxton Gr. Tren 88 B2
Lazy Hill. Aldr 245 E1
Le More. Sut Co 258 A1
Lea Cl. Whitm 85 E3
Lea Cres. Staf 174 B4
Lea Green. Staf 155 E4
Lea Hall La. Rug 197 D3
Lea La. Colt 159 F1
Lea La. Cook 280 A3
Lea La. Gr Wyr 227 D2
Lea Manor Dr. Wolv 265 F2
Lea Pl. Meir 74 A1
Lea Rd. Hix 139 E1
Lea Rd. Sto 119 F3
Lea Rd. Wolv 266 A4
Lea The. Tren 88 A4
Lea Vale Rd. Stour 279 F1
Lea Wlk. Cann 210 A2
Leacliffe Way. Aldr 256 C2
Leacote Dr. Wolv 255 E2
Leacroft Ave. Wolv 240 C1
Leacroft Cl. Aldr 245 D1
Leacroft La. Gr Wyr 226 C3
Leacroft Rd. Kingsw 275 F4
Leacroft Rd. Meir 90 A4
Leacroft Rd. Penk 193 D1
Leadbeater Ave. S-o-T 71 F3
Leadendale La. Sto 89 F2
Leafdown Cl. Cann 210 B2
Leafenden Ave. Burnt 229 D3
Leaford Way. Kingsw 275 F3
Leaford Wlk. Buck 57 F1
Leafy Glade. Aldr 257 D2
Leafy Rise. Sedg 271 E2
Leahurst cl. Staf 175 E3
Leaks Alley. Lon 73 D1
Leam Dr. Burnt 229 E4
Leamington Cl. Cann 226 B4
Leamington Gdns. N-u-L 56 C2
Leamington Rd. Bran 184 C4
Leander Cl. Burnt 211 F1
Leander Cl. Gr Wyr 226 C1
Leander Rise. Bu on T 186 A4
Lear Rd. Wom 270 A4
Leas The. Feath 241 E4
Leasawe Cl. Col 158 B1
Leaside Ave. Arm 198 B3
Leaside Rd. S-o-T 71 F3
Leason Rd. Meir 74 A1
Leason St. S-o-T 72 A4
Leasowe Rd. Rug 197 D3
Leasowe The. Lich 214 A1
Leasowes Dr. Pert 254 B2
Leasowes Dr. Wolv 265 E3
Leaswood Cl. N-u-L 71 E1
Leaswood Pl. N-u-L 71 E1
Leathermill La. Rug 178 C1
Leathersley La. Scro 129 E1
Leathersley La. Sud 129 E1
Leawood Rd. S-o-T 71 F2
Lebanon Gr. Burnt 228 C4
Ledbury Cl. Aldr 245 E1
Ledbury Cres. Han 57 F3
Ledstone Way. Lon 73 F2
Lee Ct. Brown 244 C2
Lee Gr. N-u-L 71 D2
Leech Ave. N-u-L 55 F3
Leech St. N-u-L 71 E4
Leedham Ave. Tam 250 B3
Leedhams Croft. Wa on T 202 B4
Leeds St. Fen 72 C3
Leek La. Bidd 28 A4
Leek New Rd. Che He 57 E4
Leek New Rd. N-in-M 42 C1
Leek Rd. Buck 58 A4
Leek Rd. Cav 59 F2
Leek Rd. Che 76 B3
Leek Rd. Ched 45 E4
Leek Rd. Ched 59 F2
Leek Rd. Congle 16 A4
Leek Rd. Cons 60 B2
Leek Rd. End 43 E4
Leek Rd. End 43 F3
Leek Rd. Han 57 F1
Leek Rd. Kings 60 B2
Leek Rd. Long 13 D3
Leek Rd. N-in-M 42 C2
Leek Rd. N-in-M 58 A4
Leek Rd. S-o-T 72 B4
Leek Rd. Wet 34 B2
Leekbrook Way. Leek 30 C1
Lees Cl. Rug 197 D3
Lees La. Ch Lei 108 C1
Leese La. Act Tru 175 D1
Leese St. S-o-T 72 A4
Leet Ct. Arm 198 A2
Legge La. Hix 139 E1
Legge St. N-u-L 71 E4
Legge St. Wolv 266 C3
Legion Cl. Nor Ca 228 A3
Legs La. Wolv 240 C2
Leicester Cl. N-u-L 71 E3
Leicester Pl. Buck 58 B1
Leicester St. Bu on T 185 E4
Leigh Ave. Burnt 229 D4
Leigh Bank. Ch Lei 108 C4
Leigh Cl. Staf 174 C3
Leigh La. Ch Lei 108 B3
Leigh La. Tuns 41 E1
Leigh La. Utt 125 D4
Leigh Rd. Congle 6 A3
Leigh Rd. Newp 168 C1
Leigh St. Che He 42 A1
Leighs Cl. Brown 244 B1
Leighs Rd. Brown 244 A1
Leighswood Ave. Aldr 256 A4
Leighswood Cl. Nor Ca 227 F3
Leighswood Gr. Aldr 256 A4
Leighswood Rd. Aldr 256 A3
Leighswood. Staf 175 E4
Leighton Cl. N-in-M 43 E2
Leighton Cl. Sedg 271 F1
Leighton Cl. Utt 126 B3
Leighton Rd. Utt 126 B3
Leighton Rd. Wolv 265 F3
Leisure La. Hartin 24 C3
Leisure Wlk. Tam 261 F3
Lema Way. Staf 156 B2
Lennox Gdns. Wolv 266 A4
Lennox Rd. Lon 73 E1
Lenthall Ave. Congle 15 F4
Leofric Cl. Ki Brom 199 E3
Leomansley Cl. Lich 230 C4
Leomansley Rd. Lich 230 C4
Leomansley View. Lich 230 C4
Leonard Ave. Kid 280 A1
Leonard Ave. N-in-M 43 D2
Leonard Dr. End 43 D4
Leonard Rd. Stour 279 E3
Leonard St. Che He 42 A1
Leonard St. Leek 30 C3
Leonora St. Burs 56 C4
Leopold St. Fen 72 C3
Lerridge La. Adb 131 F3
Lerryn Cl. Kingsw 275 F3
Lerwick Cl. Kingsw 275 F3
Lesley Dr. Kingsw 275 F2
Leslie Rd. Li As 257 D1
Lesscroft Cl. Wolv 240 A2
Lessways Cl. N-u-L 56 A4
Lessways Wlk. Burs 56 C4
Lester Gr. Aldr 256 C1
Letchmere Cl. Patt 253 E1
Letchmere La. Patt 253 E1
Letheridge Gdns. Staf 174 A4
Levedale Cl. Staf 155 D4
Levedale Rd. Bradl 191 E4
Levedale Rd. Penk 192 C1
Levels The. Rug 196 C3
Leven Dr. Wal 242 A1
Lever St. Wolv 266 B4
Leveson Ave. Ches Hay 226 C1
Leveson Rd. Ess 241 F1
Leveson Rd. Tren 71 F1
Levett Rd. Hopw 232 B1
Levett Rd. Tam 251 D3
Levetts Fields. Lich 231 E4
Levetts Sq. Lich 231 D4
Levington Cl. Pert 254 C2
Levita Rd. S-o-T 71 F2
Lewis Cl. Lich 231 F4
Lewis Dr. Bu on T 166 A4
Lewis St. S-o-T 72 A4
Lewis's La. Ki Brom 199 E3
Lewisham Dr. Tuns 41 E4
Lewisham Rd. Wolv 240 A1
Lewthorne Rise. Wolv 266 B2
Lexham Pl. Lon 73 F1
Lexington Green. Staf 174 A4
Ley Gdns. Lon 73 D1
Ley Hill Rd. Sut Co 258 B1
Ley Rise. Sedg 266 B1
Leybourne Cres. Wolv 239 F1
Leycett La. Keele 54 B1
Leycett Rd. Audley 54 C2
Leyfield Rd. Tren 88 A3
Leyfields. Lich 214 A1
Leyland Ave. Wolv 255 F1
Leyland Croft. Brown 243 F2
Leyland Dr. Rug 178 C1
Leyland Green. Che He 42 A3
Leyland Rd. Tam 250 C2
Leys Dr. N-u-L 70 C2
Leys La. N-in-M 43 E2
Leys The. Swad 186 C3
Liberty Park Staf 174 A4
Liberty Rd. Tam 261 F3
Libra Cl. Tam 249 F4
Libra Pl. Che He 41 F3
Lichen Cl. Hunt 209 E3
Lichfield Bsns Centre. Lich 214 B1
Lichfield Cl. N-u-L 55 E1
Lichfield Ct. Staf 155 F1
Lichfield Dr. Col 158 A1
Lichfield Dr. Hopw 249 D4
Lichfield Rd. Ab Br 161 D2
Lichfield Rd. Arm 198 B2
Lichfield Rd. B-u-Ne 184 B2
Lichfield Rd. Bran 184 B2
Lichfield Rd. Brown 244 A3
Lichfield Rd. Brown 244 B1
Lichfield Rd. Brown 245 D4
Lichfield Rd. Burnt 229 E1
Lichfield Rd. Burnt 229 E3
Lichfield Rd. Cann 226 C4
Lichfield Rd. Cann 227 D4
Lichfield Rd. Dun 184 B2
Lichfield Rd. Ha Ri 180 C1
Lichfield Rd. Ki Brom 198 B2
Lichfield Rd. Ki Brom 199 D3
Lichfield Rd. Kids 40 B4
Lichfield Rd. San 137 E4
Lichfield Rd. Staf 155 F1
Lichfield Rd. Sto 120 A4
Lichfield Rd. Sut Co 258 A2
Lichfield Rd. Tam 249 F3
Lichfield Rd. Wal 242 C1
Lichfield Rd. Wal 243 E1
Lichfield St. Bu on T 166 B1
Lichfield St. Faz 249 F1
Lichfield St. Han 57 E1
Lichfield St. Rug 196 C4
Lichfield St. Sto 120 A4
Lid La. Che 76 B2
Lid La. Rost 96 C4
Liddiard Ct. Stour 279 F3
Liddle St. S-o-T 72 A3
Lidgate Wlk. N-u-L 71 D1
Liffs Rd. A le Da 36 B4
Lifton Croft. Kingsw 275 F3
Light Ash Cl. Bre 224 B2
Light Ash La. Bre 224 B2
Light Ash. Feath 224 B2
Light Oaks Ave. N-in-M 43 E1
Lightfoot Rd. Utt 110 C4
Lightwater Gr. N-in-M 42 C1
Lightwood Rd. Lon 73 E1
Lightwood Rd. Meir 89 E3
Lightwood Rd. N-u-L 40 B1
Lightwood Rd. Yox 181 F1
Lilac Ave. Cann 226 B4
Lilac Cl. Meir 74 B3
Lilac Cl. N-u-L 40 B1
Lilac Cl. Sei 135 E1
Lilac Dr. Wom 269 F3
Lilac Gr. Bu on T 185 F3
Lilac Gr. Burnt 228 C4
Lilac Gr. Fen 72 C2
Lilac Gr. Staf 174 C4
Lilac La. G Wyr 243 D4
Lilac Rd. Tam 250 A4
Lilleshall Cres. Wolv 266 B4
Lilleshall Rd. N-u-L 71 E3
Lilleshall St. Lon 73 E1
Lilleshall Way. Staf 174 B4
Lillington Cl. Lich 231 D4
Lillydale Rd. Buck 58 A2
Lily St. N-u-L 56 B3
Limbrick Rd. Audley 39 D1
Lime Cl. Ch Lei 109 D3
Lime Cl. Dove 127 D4
Lime Cl. Gr Wyr 226 C2
Lime Cl. Meir 74 B3
Lime Gr. Barl 88 C2
Lime Gr. Bu on T 185 F3
Lime Gr. Burnt 229 E3
Lime Gr. Kin 278 A2
Lime Gr. Lich 231 E4
Lime Gr. Water 48 C2
Lime Kiln La. Alt 78 C1
Lime Kiln La. Kids 25 E1
Lime La. Nor Ca 244 A4
Lime Rd. Hunt 209 E4
Lime Rd. Sedg 266 C1
Lime St. S-o-T 72 A3
Lime St. Wolv 266 A4
Lime Tree Ave. Wolv 255 D2
Lime Tree Gdns. Cod 239 D2
Lime Tree Rd. Cod 239 D2
Lime Wlk. Penk 207 F4
Limeheath Pl. Tuns 41 F3
Limehurst Ave. Wolv 255 E1
Limepit La. Cann 209 E3
Limepit La. Hunt 209 E3
Limes Ave. Longs 30 A1
Limes Rd. Wolv 255 E2
Limes The. Albr 237 D2
Limes The. N-u-L 56 B4
Limes View. Sedg 271 E4
Limetree Ave. Staf 155 E3
Limetree Rd. Aldr 256 B1
Limewood Cl. Fors 91 D3
Linacre Rd. Ecc 133 F3
Linacre Way. Lon 73 F3
Lincoln Ave. N-u-L 71 E3
Lincoln Cl. Lich 214 B2
Lincoln Croft. Shen 247 D3
Lincoln Dr. Cann 226 C4
Lincoln Gr. N-u-L 71 E3
Lincoln Green. Wolv 240 B1
Lincoln Meadow. Staf 174 A4
Lincoln Rd. Bu on T 185 E4
Lincoln Rd. Burs 57 D4
Lincoln Rd. Kids 25 F1
Lincoln St. Han 57 E2
Linda Rd. Tuns 41 F3
Lindale Cl. Congle 6 A3
Lindale Dr. Wom 269 F3
Lindale Gr. Meir 90 A4
Linden Ave. Burnt 229 D4
Linden Cl. Congle 16 A4
Linden Cl. N-u-L 56 A2
Linden Cl. Staf 174 A4
Linden Cl. Tam 250 C2
Linden Dr. Bidd 16 B1
Linden Gr. N-u-L 56 A2
Linden Lea. Wolv 255 E1
Linden Pl. Lon 72 C1
Linden Rd. Ba-u-Ne 183 E1
Linden View. Cann 210 A2
Linden Way. Ma Dra 97 E1
Lindenbrook Vale. Staf 175 E4
Lindens The. Sto 120 A3
Lindens The. Wolv 255 F2
Lindera. Tam 251 D2
Lindisfarne. Tam 250 B2
Lindley Pl. Bly 90 A2
Lindley St. Han 57 D4
Lindon Dr. Brown 245 D3
Lindon Rd. Brown 244 C3
Lindon View. Brown 245 D3
Lindop Ct. Han 57 E2
Lindop St. Han 57 E2
Lindops La. Made 68 C4
Lindrick Cl. Wal 242 C2
Lindrosa Rd. Aldr 256 C2
Lindsay St. Han 57 D2
Lindum Ave. Tren 88 B4
Lineker Cl. Staf 155 D2
Linfield Gdns. Sedg 266 B1
Linfield Rd. Han 57 E2
Linford Cl. Arm 198 B2
Ling Rd. Hunt 209 E3
Lingard St. Burs 57 D4
Lingfield Ave. End 43 D4
Lingfield Ave. Wolv 240 B3
Lingfield Cl. Gr Wyr 226 C1
Lingfield Dr. Gr Wyr 226 C1
Lingfield Gr. Pert 254 C2

309

Ox-Hey Cres. Bidd

Pimlico Ct. Sedg

Ox-Hey Cres. Bidd 16 B1
Ox-Hey Dr. Bidd 16 B1
Oxbarn Ave. Wolv 265 F4
Oxbarn Rd. Staf 174 B3
Oxclose La. A le Da 36 B1
Oxford Ave. Han 57 E4
Oxford Cl. Gr Wyr 226 C2
Oxford Cres. S-o-T 72 A4
Oxford Dr. Stour 279 F2
Oxford Gdns. Staf 155 F3
Oxford Green. Cann 226 C4
Oxford Rd. Cann 226 C4
Oxford Rd. Che He 42 A4
Oxford Rd. N-u-L 56 B1
Oxford Rd. N-u-L 56 B2
Oxford St. Bu on T 166 A1
Oxford St. S-o-T 72 A4
Oxhay Ct. N-u-L 56 B2
Oxhay View. N-u-L 56 B2
Oxleathers Ct. Staf 174 A4
Oxley Cl. Gr Wyr 226 C1
Oxley Moor Rd. Wolv 240 A1
Oxley Moor Rd. Wolv 255 F4
Oxley Rd. Bu on T 167 D2
Oxmead. May 81 E4

Pacific Rd. Tren 88 A4
Pack Horse La. Burs 56 C4
Packett St. Lon 73 D2
Packington La. Hopw 248 C3
Padarn Cl. Sedg 266 B1
Padbury La. Burnt 212 B1
Padbury. Wolv 240 A2
Paddock Cl. Staf 155 E4
Paddock La. Aldr 256 A3
Paddock La. Gr Wyr 227 D2
Paddock Rise. Tren 88 A3
Paddock The. Bre 224 A1
Paddock The. Bu on T 167 D2
Paddock The. Che 76 B1
Paddock The. Clav 267 E4
Paddock The. Cod 238 C1
Paddock The. Lich 231 E3
Paddock The. Pert 254 B2
Paddock The. Rolle 147 D2
Paddock The. Sedg 271 F3
Paddock The. Sei 154 B3
Paddock The. Wom 269 F3
Paddocks Cl. Pol 251 F1
Paddocks Green. Congle 15 F4
Paddocks The. Ma Dra 97 D1
Paddocks The. Swad 186 C3
Paddocks The. Swyn 118 C3
Padstow Way. Tren 88 B3
Padworth St. Meir 74 A2
Paget Cl. Penk 208 A4
Paget Dr. Burnt 211 F1
Paget Rd. Wolv 255 F2
Paget Rise. Ab Br 160 C3
Paget St. Bu on T 166 B1
Pagham Cl. Wolv 239 F1
Paisley Cl. Buck 73 F4
Paladin Ave. Meir 74 A2
Palatine Dr. N-u-L 55 E3
Pale St. Sedg 271 F3
Palfrey Rd. Stour 279 E3
Pall Mall. Han 57 E2
Palmbourne Ind Pk. Staf 155 E2
Palmer Cl. Ba-u-Ne 183 E1
Palmer Cl. Bran 185 D4
Palmer Cl. Ess 241 F1
Palmer Cl. Staf 156 A2
Palmer St. Lon 73 E2
Palmers Green. S-o-T 71 E4
Palmers Way. Cod 239 E1
Palmers Way. N-u-L 71 E4
Palmerston St. Han 57 E1
Palmerston St. N-u-L 56 B3
Pandora Gr. Han 57 F3
Panton Cl. Staf 156 A2
Pantulf Cl. Staf 155 D1
Parade The. Brown 228 C1
Parade The. Kingsw 275 D4
Parade The. N-u-L 55 E1
Parade View. Brown 244 C4
Paradise La. Brown 243 F2
Paradise La. Feath 224 C1
Paradise St. Tuns 41 E2
Paragon Ave. N-u-L 71 D2
Paragon Cl. Che 76 B1
Paragon Rd. Lon 73 E2
Parbury. Tam 261 E3
Parchments The. Lich 214 A1
Pargeter St. Stour 279 F2
Paris Ave. N-u-L 70 C3
Park Ave W. N-u-L 56 A3
Park Ave. Burnt 229 D3
Park Ave. Che 76 C1
Park Ave. Kids 40 C4
Park Ave. Meir 74 A3
Park Ave. N-u-L 56 B3
Park Ave. Nor Ca 228 A3
Park Ave. Staf 174 B4
Park Ave. Sto 119 F4
Park Ave. Utt 111 D1
Park Ave. Wolv 266 B3
Park Ave. Wom 269 F3
Park Cl. Ba-u-Ne 183 E1
Park Cl. Brown 244 C4
Park Cl. Ches Hay 226 C2
Park Cl. Made 68 C4
Park Cres. Staf 155 F1
Park Ct. N-u-L 55 F4
Park Dr. Barl 104 B4
Park Dr. Cav 59 E2
Park Dr. Che 76 B2
Park Dr. Li As 257 E2
Park Dr. Sut C 257 F1
Park Dr. Tren 87 F4
Park Dr. Wolv 266 B3
Park End. Lich 231 F4
Park Farm Rd. Tam 250 B1
Park Farm View. Tuns 41 E4
Park Gate Rd. Cann 211 F3
Park Gate Rd. Kid 280 A1
Park Hall Ave. Meir 74 A2
Park Hall Cl. Rug 178 B2
Park Hall Cres. Meir 74 A2
Park Hall Ind Est. Lon 73 F3
Park Hall Rd. Buck 73 F3
Park Hall Rd. Lon 73 F3
Park Hall Rd. Wolv 266 B3
Park Hall St. Lon 73 E2
Park House Dr. Sto 120 B4
Park La. Ash 100 A4
Park La. Audley 39 D2
Park La. Bidd 27 E3
Park La. Blo 99 D1
Park La. Bre 223 E1
Park La. Broc 176 A2
Park La. Che 76 B2
Park La. Ched 45 D3
Park La. Colt 179 D4
Park La. Congle 6 A1
Park La. End 44 A4
Park La. Faz 249 F1
Park La. Fen 72 C3
Park La. Gr Wyr 227 D2
Park La. Hau 172 C3
Park La. Ipst 47 D1
Park La. Kingsw 275 F4
Park La. Shen 247 D2
Park La. Tut 146 A3
Park La. Whit 232 B4
Park La. Woods 132 A1
Park Lane Cl. Che 76 B2
Park Pale The. Tut 146 B3
Park Pl. Fen 72 C3
Park Pl. Utt 126 B4
Park Rd West. Stour 279 E3
Park Rd. Alre 201 D2
Park Rd. Ba-u-Ne 183 E1
Park Rd. Burnt 228 C4
Park Rd. Burnt 229 D3
Park Rd. Cann 209 E1
Park Rd. Cav 59 E2
Park Rd. Che He 42 A1
Park Rd. Feath 241 E4
Park Rd. Leek 30 C4
Park Rd. N-u-L 55 E1
Park Rd. Nor Ca 228 A3
Park Rd. Sedg 271 E2
Park Rd. Stour 279 E3
Park Rd. Swad 186 B3
Park Rd. Tam 261 E3
Park Rd. Wal 243 D1
Park Rd. Whitm 70 C1
Park Rise. Wolv 255 F1
Park St S. Wolv 266 B3
Park St. Br Hi 279 F4
Park St. Bu on T 166 B1
Park St. Cann 226 C3
Park St. Ches Hay 226 C2
Park St. Fen 72 C3
Park St. Kingsw 275 E3
Park St. Staf 155 F1
Park St. Tam 250 A3
Park St. Utt 111 E1
Park Terr. Tuns 41 F2
Park The. May 81 E4
Park Venture Centre. Cann 226 C3
Park View Rd. Kids 26 A2
Park View Rd. Sut C 257 E2
Park View Terr. Rug 178 B1
Park View. Bly 90 C3
Park View. Swyn 103 D2
Park Way. Fors 91 D4
Park Way. Wolv 242 A1
Park Wood Dr. Whitm 85 D4
Parkdale. Sedg 271 E4
Parkend. Fors 91 D4
Parker Bowles Dr.
Ma Dra 112 A4
Parker Rd. Ess 241 F1
Parker St. Bu on T 166 B3
Parker St. Han 57 D2
Parker St. Leek 31 D3
Parker St. Wal 243 D1
Parker's Croft Rd. Staf 155 F1
Parker-Jervis Rd. Lon 73 F2
Parkers Cl. Ch Eat 190 A4
Parkes Ave. Cod 239 D1
Parkes Hall Rd. Dud 271 F3
Parkfield Ave. Tam 250 B1
Parkfield Cl. Barl 88 B1
Parkfield Cl. Tam 261 E4
Parkfield Cres. Tam 261 E4
Parkfield Cres. Wolv 266 C3
Parkfield Gr. Wolv 266 C3
Parkfield La. Snel 81 E2
Parkfield Rd. Lon 73 E1
Parkfield Rd. Wolv 266 C3
Parkfields Cl. N-u-L 55 D1
Parkfields. End 43 F4
Parkfields. Staf 174 B4
Parkgate La. Ella 79 F3
Parkhall La. Ch Lei 109 D3
Parkhead Cres. Meir 74 A2
Parkhead Dr. Meir 74 A2
Parkhead Gr. Meir 74 A2
Parkhill Rd. Burnt 229 D4
Parkhouse Gdns. Sedg 271 E2
Parkhouse Rd E. N-u-L 41 D1
Parkhouse Rd W. N-u-L 40 C1
Parkhouse St. Han 57 D1
Parklands Rd. Up Tea 92 C2
Parklands The. Congle 6 A1
Parklands. Bidd 17 D1
Parklands. Kids 26 A1
Parklands. Wolv 255 E1
Parks Cres. Ess 242 A2
Parkside Ave. Staf 155 E4
Parkside Cres. End 43 F4
Parkside Dr. N-u-L 56 B2
Parkside Gr. N-u-L 56 B2
Parkside Ind Est. Wolv 266 C4
Parkside La. Gay 139 D4
Parkside La. Hunt 209 D1
Parkside Way. Aldr 257 D1
Parkside. Tam 250 C1
Parkside. Tren 88 A4
Parkstone Ave. N-u-L 71 E4
Parkstone Cl. Brown 244 B1
Parkway The. Han 57 E1
Parkway The. Pert 254 C2
Parkway The. Tren 87 F4
Parkway. Sto 120 B4
Parkwood Ave. Tren 87 F4
Parkwood Cl. Brown 245 D3
Parkyn St. Wolv 266 C4
Parliament Row. Han 57 E2
Parliament Sq. Han 57 E2
Parliament St. Swad 186 C3
Parnell Sq. Congle 6 A1
Parson St. Tam 261 F4
Parsonage St. Tuns 41 E2
Parsons Cl. Hartin 24 B3
Parsons Dr. Gno 171 F3
Parsons La. Butter 33 E2
Parsons La. Grin 33 E2
Parton Gr. Meir 74 A2
Partridge Cl. Hunt 209 E4
Partridge Cl. Meir 90 A4
Partridge Croft. Lich 231 E4
Partridge Dr. Utt 126 B3
Partridge Rd. Stour 279 E2
Partridge Ride. Ashl 99 E2
Parva Ct. Utt 110 C4
Paskin Cl. Alre 215 E4
Pass Ave. Whit 232 C3
Passfield Ave. Cann 210 B4
Pastoral Cl. Made 68 C3
Pasture Cl. Whitm 85 E3
Pasture Gate. Cann 209 E1
Pasture View. Brown 243 F1
Pasturefields La. Hix 158 A3
Pastures The. Pert 254 B2
Pastures The. Swad 186 C3
Patch Cl. Bu on T 166 A3
Patch Meadow Rd. Che 76 A2
Paterson Ave. Mill 117 F2
Paterson Pl. Brown 245 D3
Patricia Ave. Wolv 266 B3
Patrick Pl. Che He 27 D1
Patshull Ave. Wolv 240 A2
Patshull Gr. Wolv 240 A2
Patshull Rd. Patt 253 D2
Patterdale Rd. Cann 210 A2
Patterdale St. Che He 42 A2
Pattingham La. Patt 253 E4
Pattingham Rd. Pert 254 B1
Paul St. Wolv 266 B4
Pauls Coppice. Brown 245 D3
Pauls Wlk. Lich 214 A2
Pavement The. Bre 223 E3
Pavilion Cl. Aldr 256 B4
Pavior's Rd. Burnt 228 C2
Paxton Ave. Pert 254 C2
Paxton St. Han 57 E1
Paynter St. Fen 72 C3
Peace Cl. Ches Hay 226 C2
Peacehaven Gr. Tren 88 B3
Peach Ave. Staf 174 C4
Peacock Hay Rd. Kids 40 C2
Peacock La. Swyn 87 D4
Peacock La. Whitm 87 D4
Peacock Rd. N-u-L 55 F3
Peacock View. Buck 57 F1
Peak Cl. Arm 198 A2
Peak Dale Ave. Tuns 41 E4
Peak Dr. Sedg 271 F2
Peak View. Leek 31 D3
Peake Cres. Brown 244 C3
Peake Rd. Brown 245 D3
Peake St. N-u-L 55 F2
Peakes Rd. Rug 178 A1
Pear Tree Ave. Swad 186 C4
Pear Tree Cl. Barl 88 B1
Pear Tree Cl. Gno 171 F3
Pear Tree Cl. Hunt 209 E4
Pear Tree Cl. Shut 251 F4
Pear Tree Dr. Made 68 B4
Pear Tree La. Brown 228 B1
Pear Tree La. Clav 268 A2
Pear Tree La. Ess 241 D1
Pear Tree La. N-u-L 55 E4
Pear Tree Rd. Audley 39 F1
Pearson Dr. Sto 120 B4
Pearsons St. Wolv 266 B4
Peartree La. Hi Ri 180 A3
Peascroft Rd. N-in-M 42 B2
Pebble Cl. Tam 251 D2
Pebble Mill Cl. Cann 209 F1
Pebble Mill Dr. Cann 210 A1
Pebble Mill St. Burs 56 C2
Peck Mill La. Che He 27 E1
Peckforton View. Kids 41 D4
Pedley Gr. Che He 42 B1
Pedley La. Congle 6 C2
Peebles Rd. N-u-L 54 C1
Peel Cl. Dra Ba 260 C3
Peel Dr. Astb 15 D4
Peel Dr. Cann 209 F4
Peel Hollow. Audley 39 D1
Peel La. Astb 15 E4
Peel St. Bu on T 166 B1
Peel St. Lon 73 E1
Peel St. N-u-L 56 B3
Peel St. Staf 155 E2
Peel St. Tuns 56 B4
Peel Terr. Staf 155 F3
Pegasus Gr. Che He 42 B1
Pegasus Wlk. Tam 249 F4
Peggs La. Woods 150 C4
Peggy's Bank. Audley 54 C4
Pegroy Gr. Che He 42 B1
Pelham St. Han 57 E1
Pellfield Ct. Wes on Tr 138 B1
Pelsall La. Brown 244 A1
Pelsall La. Wal 243 E2
Pelsall Rd. Brown 244 B4
Pemberton Dr. Bly 90 A3
Pembridge Rd. Lon 88 C4
Pembroke Dr. N-u-L 71 D4
Pembroke Dr. Sto 120 B4
Pembroke Gdns. Kingsw 275 E1
Pembroke Rd. N-in-M 43 D1
Pen-y-bryn Way. Newp 168 C1
Penarth Gr. Han 57 E3
Penarth Pl. N-u-L 71 D4
Pencombe Dr. Wolv 266 B3
Penda Gr. Pert 254 C3
Pendeford Ave. Wolv 255 F4
Pendeford Cl. Wolv 255 F4
Pendeford Hall La. Cod 239 E3
Pendeford La. Wolv 240 A2
Pendeford Mill La. Cod 239 E2
Penderel St. Wal 243 E1
Pendinas Dr. Cod 239 D2
Pendine Gr. Fen 73 D3
Pendle Hill. Cann 210 B2
Pendrel Cl. G Wyr 242 C4
Pendrell Cl. Cod 239 D2
Pendrell Cl. Feath 241 D3
Pendrill Rd. Wolv 240 C2
Pendryl Cl. Bre 223 E4
Penfleet Ave. Meir 74 A1
Pengrove Cl. Che He 41 F4
Penhallow Dr. Wolv 266 C3
Penk Dr N. Rug 178 B1
Penk Dr S. Rug 178 B1
Penk Dr. Burnt 229 E3
Penk Rd. Fors 91 D4
Penk Rise. Wolv 255 D2
Penkhull New Rd. S-o-T 72 A3
Penkhull Terr. S-o-T 72 A3
Penkridge Bank. Rug 195 E3
Penkridge Rd. Act Tru 193 D4
Penkvale Rd. Staf 174 C3
Penkville St. S-o-T 72 A3
Penleigh Gdns. Wom 269 F4
Penmere Dr. Cav 59 D2
Penmere Dr. N-u-L 71 E1
Penn Cl. Wal 243 E1
Penn Croft La. Wom 266 A1
Penn Croft. Col 177 E4
Penn Rd. Him 270 C4
Penn Rd. Wolv 266 A3
Penn St. Wolv 266 A4
Pennell St. Buck 58 A2
Pennhouse Ave. Wolv 265 F3
Pennine Dr. Cann 209 F1
Pennine Dr. Sedg 271 E2
Pennine Way. Bidd 16 C1
Pennine Way. N-u-L 55 F2
Pennine Way. Tam 262 A4
Pennington Cl. Meir 74 B1
Penns Wood Cl. Sedg 266 B1
Pennwood La. Wolv 265 F2
Pennwood La. Wom 265 F2
Penny Cress Green.
Nor Ca 227 F2
Penny Ct. G Wyr 242 C4
Pennycress Gdns. Feath 241 E4
Pennycroft La. Utt 111 E1
Pennycroft Rd. Utt 111 D1
Pennycrofts. Staf 155 F2
Pennyfields Rd. Kids 26 B1
Pennymoor Rd. Tam 262 A4
Pennymore Cl. Tren 88 A4
Pennys Croft. Lich 214 C1
Penport Gr. Lon 73 D1
Penrhyn Ave. Che He 42 A1
Penrith Cl. Tren 88 B3
Penrith Ct. N-u-L 71 D3
Pensford Gr. Han 57 F3
Pensgreave Rd. Bu on T 166 A3
Penshaw Cl. Wolv 240 A1
Penstone La. Low Pen 264 C2
Pentire Rd. Lich 231 E3
Pentland Gdns. Wolv 255 F1
Pentland Gr. N-u-L 55 F2
Penton Pl. Lon 88 C4
Penton Wlk. Lon 88 C4
Penzer St. Kingsw 275 E4
Peolsford Rd. Brown 244 A2
Peover La. Congle 6 C3
Pepper St. Keele 54 C1
Pepper St. Keele 69 F4
Pepper St. N-u-L 71 E4
Perceval St. Han 57 F3
Percival Dr. N-in-M 43 E2
Percy St. Han 57 E2
Peregrine Cl. Bu on T 167 E2
Peregrine Cl. Dud 271 F1
Perivale Cl. Buck 58 A3
Perkins St. Tuns 41 E4
Perks Rd. Wolv 242 A1
Perle Brook. Ecc 133 E4
Perott Dr. Sut Co 258 B1
Perrin Cl. Staf 174 C3
Perry Cl. Han 57 E2
Perrycrofts Cres. Tam 250 B4
Pershore Cl. Wal 242 C1
Pershore Rd. Wal 242 C1
Pershore Way. Wal 242 C1
Perth Cl. Bu on T 167 E1
Perth St. Lon 73 D3
Perthy Gr. Tren 87 F4
Perton Brook Vale. Wolv 254 C1
Perton Gr. Wolv 254 C1
Perton Rd. Wolv 254 C1
Pessall La. Edin 217 E4
Peter James Ct. Staf 155 F3
Peter's La. Burnt 230 A3
Peterborough Dr. Cann 210 B1
Peterdale Dr. Wolv 265 F2
Peters Wlk. Lich 214 A1
Petersfield Rd. Che He 42 A4
Petersfield. Cann 209 F2
Petershouse Dr. Sut C 257 F3
Pethills La. One 48 B3
Petrel Gr. Meir 90 A4
Pevensey Gr. Lon 73 E3
Peverill Rd. Pert 254 C2
Peverill Rd. Wolv 266 C2
Pheasant Wlk. Ashl 99 E2
Philip Gr. Cann 209 F3
Philip La. Cav 59 D2
Philip St. Fen 72 C3
Phillips Ave. Ess 241 F1
Phillipson Way. Che He 57 E4
Phoenix Bank. Ma Dra 97 E1
Phoenix Centre. Cann 226 C3
Phoenix Cl. Rug 178 C1
Phoenix Rd. Cann 210 A1
Phoenix St. Tuns 41 E2
Phoenix St. Wolv 266 B3
Picasso Cl. Cann 210 B1
Piccadilly Arc. Han 57 E2
Piccadilly La. May 66 B1
Piccadilly St. Tuns 41 E2
Piccadilly. Han 57 E2
Pickering Cl. Lon 73 D1
Pickford Pl. Meir 74 A1
Pickleys La. Dove 127 E4
Pickmere Cl. N-in-M 43 D2
Picknal La. Utt 126 A4
Picknals. Utt 126 A4
Pickwick Pl. Kids 25 E1
Pickwood Ave. Leek 31 D3
Pickwood Cl. Leek 31 D3
Picton St. Han 57 E2
Picton St. Leek 30 B3
Piddocks Rd. Swad 186 A3
Pidduck St. Burs 56 C4
Pier St. Brown 244 C4
Pierce St. Tuns 41 E2
Pigeonhay La. Utt 110 B1
Piggott Gr. Buck 58 A2
Pike Cl. Staf 156 A3
Pike La. Arm 198 A2
Pikelow La. Water 49 D2
Pilgrim Pl. Staf 155 F1
Pilgrim St. Staf 155 F1
Pilkington Ave. N-u-L 71 D3
Pillaton Cl. Penk 207 F4
Pilsbury St. N-u-L 56 B3
Pilsden Pl. Meir 90 B4
Pimlico Ct. Sedg 271 E2

311

Radmore La. Ab Br
Rose Bay Meadow. Cann

316

Sunningdale Way. Wal Tittensor Rd. Barl

Sunningdale Way. Wal 243 D2
Sunningdale. Sto 120 A4
Sunningdale. Tam 251 E3
Sunny Hill Cl. Wom 270 A3
Sunny Hollow. N-u-L 56 B2
Sunny Side. Kings 61 E2
Sunnybank Cl. Aldr 256 C1
Sunnycroft Ave. Lon 73 D1
Sunnyfield Oval. N-in-M 43 E1
Sunnyhills Rd. Leek 30 B2
Sunnymead Rd. Burnt 212 A1
Sunnymede Rd. Kingsw 275 F2
Sunnyside Ave. Tuns 41 F2
Sunnyside Rd. Utt 111 D1
Sunnyside. Brown 245 D1
Sunnyside. Swad 186 C4
Sunridge Ave. Wom 270 A4
Sunridge Cl. N-in-M 43 D1
Sunrise Hill. Cann 210 A3
Sunset Cl. Bre 224 A2
Sunset Cl. Gr Wyr 226 C2
Sunset Cl. Tam 250 A3
Sunset Pl. Wolv 266 C2
Surrey Cl. Cann 226 C4
Surrey Cl. Rug 196 B3
Surrey Dr. Kingsw 275 F2
Surrey Dr. Tam 250 A1
Surrey Dr. Wolv 255 F1
Surrey Rd. Kids 26 A1
Surrey Rd. Staf 174 B4
Surrey Wlk. Aldr 245 D1
Surtees Gr. Lon 73 D3
Sussex Ave. Aldr 256 A4
Sussex Dr. Cann 210 A3
Sussex Dr. Kids 25 F1
Sussex Dr. Wolv 255 F1
Sussex Rd. Bu on T 185 F3
Sutherland Ave. Lon 73 D1
Sutherland Ave. Wolv 266 C4
Sutherland Cres. Bly 90 C3
Sutherland Dr. N-u-L 70 C3
Sutherland Dr. Wom 265 D1
Sutherland Gr. Pert 254 C2
Sutherland Pl. Lon 73 E1
Sutherland Rd.
Ches Hay 226 C1
Sutherland Rd. Lon 73 E2
Sutherland Rd. Longs 30 A1
Sutherland Rd. Sto 120 B4
Sutherland Rd. Titt 88 A1
Sutherland Rd. Wolv 266 A3
Sutherland St. Fen 72 B3
Sutton Ave. Tam 250 A1
Sutton Cl. Rug 196 C3
Sutton Ct. Wolv 266 C1
Sutton Dr. S-o-T 71 F2
Sutton Dr. S-o-T 71 F3
Sutton Pl. Che He 42 A3
Sutton Rd. Aldr 256 A1
Sutton Rd. Dra Ba 260 A4
Sutton Rd. Faz 249 E1
Sutton Rd. Hint 259 F3
Sutton St. Br Hi 275 F1
Sutton St. N-u-L 55 F3
Sutton Way. Ma Dra 112 A4
Swadlincote La. Swad 186 C1
Swaffham Way. Buck 58 B1
Swainsfield Rd. Yox 182 A1
Swainsley Cl. Burs 57 D4
Swaledale Ave. Congle 6 A3
Swallow Cl. Hunt 209 E4
Swallow Cl. Kids 26 A1
Swallow Cl. Meir 90 A4
Swallow Cl. Rug 178 B1
Swallow Cl. Utt 126 A3
Swallow Croft. Leek 30 B2
Swallow Croft. Lich 214 A1
Swallow Wlk. Bidd 27 E4
Swallowdale. Brown 245 D2
Swallowdale. Staf 175 E3
Swallowdale. Wolv 254 C1
Swallowfall Ave. Stour 279 E2
Swallowfield. Tam 249 F3
Swallowfields Dr. Cann 210 A2
Swallowfields Rd. Sedg 266 B1
Swallows Cl. Brown 244 A3
Swan Bank. Kids 40 B4
Swan Bank. Wolv 265 F2
Swan Bank. Woore 67 D1
Swan Cl. Bla 281 D1
Swan Cl. Ches Hay 226 B1
Swan Cl. Kids 40 B4
Swan Cl. Longd 197 F1
Swan Cl. Rug 197 D3
Swan Cl. Staf 155 E1
Swan Cottages. Whit 232 C3
Swan La. Ab Br 161 D3
Swan La. Br Hi 275 F1
Swan La. Kingsw 275 F1
Swan La. Penk 192 C3
Swan La. S-o-T 71 F2
Swan La. Shar 225 E1
Swan Mews. Lich 231 D4
Swan Pas. Bly 90 C4
Swan Pool Gr. Brown 244 B1
Swan Rd. Dr in C 144 B3
Swan Rd. Lich 231 D4
Swan Rd. Whit 232 C3
Swan Sq. Burs 56 C4
Swan St. S-o-T 72 A4
Swan St. Stour 279 F3
Swan Wlk. Bu on T 166 B1
Swanage Cl. Meir 90 A4
Swancote Dr. Wolv 265 E3
Swanfield Rd. Br Hi 275 F1
Swanfields. Burnt 229 E3
Swanland Gr. Lon 73 E2
Swanmere. Newp 168 C3
Swanmore Cl. Wolv 265 F4
Swanmote. Tam 249 F3
Swannington St. Bu on T 166 A3
Swanton Pl. Tren 87 F4
Swarbourn Cl. Yox 182 A1
Swaythling Gr. Buck 58 B1
Sweetbriar Way. Staf 175 E3
Sweetbrier Dr. Br Hi 275 F1
Sweetman St. Wolv 255 F2
Sweetplace La. Ch Eat 189 F1
Sweetpool La. Hag 281 F3
Swift Cl. Kids 26 A1
Swift Pl. Lon 73 F3
Swift. Tam 250 C2
Swin Forge Way. Swi 269 F1
Swinburne Cl. Lon 72 C1
Swinburne Cl. Staf 174 B4
Swindale. Tam 262 A4
Swindon Rd. Kingsw 275 D4
Swinfen Broun Rd. Lich 231 D4
Swinford Leys. Wom 269 E3
Swingle Hill Rd. Lon 72 C2
Swinscoe Hill. May 66 A1
Swinson Cl. Roc 96 A2
Swiss Dr. Kingsw 275 F1
Swiss Lodge Dr. Faz 260 C4
Swithin Dr. Fen 73 D3
Swynnerton Dr. Ess 241 F2
Sycamore Cl. Bidd 16 C1
Sycamore Cl. Bly 90 A3
Sycamore Cl. Kids 40 C4
Sycamore Cl. Stour 279 E1
Sycamore Cl. Utt 125 F4
Sycamore Cres. Rug 197 D3
Sycamore Dr. Wolv 255 E1
Sycamore Gr. Fen 72 C2
Sycamore Gr. N-u-L 56 B2
Sycamore Green. Cann 209 F3
Sycamore Green. Dud 271 F3
Sycamore Hill. Cann 211 F3
Sycamore La. Staf 174 A4
Sycamore Rd. Bu on T 185 F3
Sycamore Rd. Burnt 228 C4
Sycamore Rd. Cann 210 C2
Sycamore Rd. Kingsw 275 F3
Sycamore Rd. May 81 E4
Sycamore Rd. Sto 120 A4
Sycamore Way. Hunt 209 E4
Sycamore Way. Ma Dra 97 E1
Sycamore. Tam 261 F4
Sycamores The. Lich 231 D3
Sydenham Pl. Buck 73 E4
Sydnall La. Sut 112 C1
Sydney St. Bu on T 166 B3
Sydney St. N-u-L 56 B1
Syerscote La. C Camp 218 A1
Syerscote La. Wig 234 B1
Sykesmoor. Tam 262 A4
Sylvan Gr. S-o-T 71 F2
Sylvan Way. Staf 175 E3
Sytch La. Wom 270 A3
Sytch Rd. End 43 D4

Tabor St. Fen 72 C3
Tack Farm Rd. Kingsw 275 E1
Tadgedale Ave. Ashl 99 E3
Tag La. Chesw 113 F2
Tagg La. Mo 14 C4
Talaton Cl. Wolv 240 A1
Talbot Ave. Li As 257 D2
Talbot Cl. Newp 168 B1
Talbot Rd. Rug 196 C3
Talbot Rd. Staf 155 F1
Talbot Rd. Wolv 266 B3
Talbot St. Han 57 E2
Talbot St. Leek 30 C3
Talbot St. Rug 196 C4
Talbot. Tam 250 C2
Talke Rd. Audley 40 B2
Talke Rd. Audley 40 C2
Talke Rd. Kids 40 B2
Talke Rd. N-u-L 40 B2
Tall Ash Ave. Congle 6 A2
Tallis Gr. Han 57 F3
Tallpines. Staf 175 E4
Talsarn Gr. Tren 88 B3
Tamar Cl. Brown 228 B1
Tamar Dr. Sedg 271 F3
Tamar Gr. Che 76 C1
Tamar Gr. Staf 174 A4
Tamar Rd. Kids 26 A1
Tamar Rd. Tam 262 A3
Tame Ave. Burnt 229 E3
Tame Cl. Bidd 16 B1
Tame Ct. Tam 250 A3
Tame Dr. Brown 244 A1
Tame Gr. Cann 226 B4
Tame St. Tam 250 B2
Tame Valley Ind Est.
Tam 261 E4
Tame Wlk. Lon 74 A2
Tamedrive. Tam 250 A2
Tamworth Cl. Brown 228 C1
Tamworth Rd (Amington).
Tam 250 C3
Tamworth Rd (Dosthill).
Tam 261 E3
Tamworth Rd. Al En 259 D1
Tamworth Rd. Elf 233 F4
Tamworth Rd. Faz 261 D4
Tamworth Rd. King 262 B1
Tamworth Rd. Lich 231 F3
Tamworth Rd. Pol 251 F1
Tamworth Rd. Sut C 259 D1
Tamworth Rd. Tam 250 B1
Tamworth Rd. Whit 232 A2
Tamworth St. Lich 231 D4
Tan Bank. Newp 168 C2
Tanfield Cl. Wolv 255 D2
Tanglewood Gr. Sedg 266 B1
Tangmere Cl. Pert 254 C3
Tanhill. Tam 262 A4
Tanners Rd. Buck 58 A4
Tannery Cl. Rug 178 C1
Tansey Cl. Buck 58 A2
Tansley Green Rd. Sedg 271 D1
Tansley View. Wolv 266 B4
Tanyard. Lich 231 E4
Tape St. Che 76 C2
Taplin Cl. Staf 155 E4
Taplow Pl. Cann 209 F2
Tapton Cl. Wal 243 E2
Targate Ct. Arm 198 A3
Target Cl. Kids 40 C3
Tarleton Rd. Han 57 F2
Tarporley Gr. S-o-T 71 F3
Tarragon Dr. Meir 90 A3
Tarrant. Tam 261 F4
Tarvin Gr. Che He 41 F3
Tasman Dr. Staf 156 A3
Tasman Gr. Pert 254 C3
Tasman Sq. Han 57 F3
Tatenhill Comm. Tate 164 C1
Tatenhill La. Bran 184 B4
Tatenhill La. Dun 184 A4
Tatenhill La. Tate 164 B1
Tatlowfold La. Water 48 C2
Tatton Cl. Leek 30 A3
Tatton St. Lon 73 E1
Taunton Ave. Wolv 240 B2
Taunton Pl. N-u-L 55 F4
Taunton Way. Buck 58 B1
Taurus Gr. Che He 41 F3
Taverners Cl. Wal 242 B1
Tavistock Ave. Staf 156 B1
Tavistock Cl. Tam 250 B4
Tavistock Cres. N-u-L 71 D3
Tavistock Pl. S-o-T 56 C1
Tawney Cl. Kids 26 A1
Tawney Cres. Meir 74 A1
Tay Cl. Bidd 16 C1
Tay Cl. Kings 76 C3
Taylor Ave. N-u-L 56 B2
Taylor Rd. Buck 58 A3
Taylor Rd. Wolv 266 C3
Taylor St. N-u-L 56 B2
Taylor St. Tuns 41 E4
Taylor Walk. Staf 174 B4
Taylor's La. Rug 178 C1
Taynton Cl. Che He 42 A4
Tean Cl. Bu on T 167 D1
Tean Cl. Burnt 229 E3
Tean Rd. Che 76 B1
Teanhurst Cl. Up Tea 92 C1
Teanhurst Rd. Up Tea 92 C1
Teasel Gr. Feath 241 D4
Tebworth Cl. Wolv 239 F1
Tedder Rd. Staf 156 A3
Teddesley Ct. Cann 209 F2
Teddesley Rd. Act Tru 193 D3
Teddesley Rd. Penk 192 C1
Teign. Tam 262 A3
Telegraph St. Staf 155 F1
Telford Ave. Albr 237 D3
Telford Ave. Gr Wyr 226 C2
Telford Cl. Burnt 229 D4
Telford Cl. Congle 6 A1
Telford Cl. Kids 40 C4
Telford Dr. Staf 155 F4
Telford Gdns. Bre 223 E4
Telford Gdns. Wolv 265 E4
Telford Gr. Cann 210 A4
Telford La. Gno 171 E3
Telford Rd. Tam 249 F4
Telford Way. N-in-M 42 A2
Tellwright Gr. N-u-L 56 A4
Tellwright St. Che He 42 A1
Telmah Cl. Bu on T 147 E1
Teme Rd. Stour 279 F2
Temperence Pl. Tuns 41 E4
Tempest St. Tam 250 A3
Templar Cres. N-u-L 56 A3
Templar Terr. N-u-L 56 A3
Temple St. Fen 72 B3
Temple St. Sedg 271 E2
Templers Way. Penk 207 F4
Templeton Ave. Buck 73 E4
Ten Butts Cres. Staf 174 C3
Tenacre La. Sedg 271 F3
Tenbury Ct. Wolv 265 E3
Tenbury Dr. Aldr 256 B4
Tenbury Gdns. Wolv 265 E3
Tenbury Green. Buck 58 B1
Tenby Dr. Staf 155 F3
Tenby Gr. N-u-L 55 F4
Tenford La. Che 92 B3
Tennant Pl. N-u-L 56 A4
Tennscore Ave.
Ches Hay 226 C2
Tennyson Ave. Burnt 212 A1
Tennyson Ave. Kids 41 D4
Tennyson Ave. Sut C 257 F3
Tennyson Ave. Tam 250 A3
Tennyson Cl. Che 76 A1
Tennyson Cl. Ma Dra 112 A4
Tennyson Gdns. Lon 72 C1
Tennyson Rd. Bu on T 166 B4
Tennyson Rd. Ess 241 D1
Tennyson Rd. Sedg 271 D2
Tennyson Rd. Staf 174 B4
Tenterbanks. Staf 155 E2
Tercel Gr. Meir 90 A4
Terence Wlk. Che He 27 D1
Tern Ave. Kids 26 B1
Tern Cl. Bidd 27 F4
Tern Cl. Wolv 266 B2
Tern Gr. Ashl 99 E3
Tern View. Ma Dra 112 A4
Terrace The. Che 76 B2
Terrace The. Wolv 255 E1
Terrington Dr. N-u-L 71 D1
Terry Cl. Lich 213 F1
Terry Cl. Meir 74 A2
Terson Way. Lon 73 F2
Tettenhall Rd. Wolv 255 F2
Teveray Dr. Penk 207 F4
Tewkesbury Gr. Buck 58 A2
Tewkesbury Rd. Wal 242 C1
Tewnals La. Elm 213 F3
Tewson Green. Han 57 E4
Thackeray Dr. Lon 73 D1
Thackeray Dr. Tam 250 A4
Thackeray Walk. Staf 174 B4
Thames Dr. Bidd 27 F4
Thames Dr. Che 76 C1
Thames Rd. N-u-L 71 D2
Thames Rd. Wal 243 F1
Thames Way. Staf 174 A4
Thanet Cl. Kingsw 275 E4
Thanet Gr. Lon 73 D2
Thatcham Green. Lon 88 C4
Thatcher Gr. Bidd 27 D4
Thatchmoor La. Ba-u-Ne 182 B4
Thelma Ave. End 43 D4
Theodore Rd. Buck 58 A2
Thereas Cl. Tren 72 A1
Thicknall La. Hag 281 F2
Third Ave. Brown 229 D1
Third Ave. Buck 58 B2
Third Ave. Kids 25 F1
Third Ave. Kingsw 275 F4
Thirlmere Cl. Cann 209 F1
Thirlmere Cl. Wolv 255 E4
Thirlmere Dr. Wolv 242 A1
Thirlmere Gr. Lon 73 F2
Thirlmere Gr. Pert 254 C2
Thirlmere Pl. N-u-L 71 D3
Thirlmere Rd. Wolv 255 E4
Thirlmere Way. Staf 174 C4
Thirsk Pl. N-u-L 55 D1
Thistle Cl. Rug 178 B1
Thistle Down Cl. Aldr 257 D1
Thistleberry Ave. N-u-L 70 C4
Thistledown Ave. Burnt 229 D3
Thistledown Dr. Cann 210 B1
Thistledown Rd. Feath 241 D4
Thistledown Wlk. Sedg 266 B1
Thistley Hough. S-o-T 71 F3
Thistley Nook. Lich 214 A1
Thomas Ave. N-u-L 56 A2
Thomas Ave. Staf 155 D2
Thomas Ave. Sto 120 B3
Thomas Greenway. Lich 214 A1
Thomas St. Bidd 16 B1
Thomas St. Kids 26 C1
Thomas St. Kids 40 B4
Thomas St. Leek 30 B3
Thomas St. Tam 250 B2
Thomas St. Wolv 266 B4
Thompson Ave. Wolv 266 C3
Thompson Cl. Staf 174 B4
Thompson Rd. Rug 197 D3
Thompstone Ave. N-u-L 55 F2
Thor Cl. Cann 210 A3
Thoresby. Tam 249 F3
Thorn Tree La. Bretby 186 C4
Thorn Tree La. Swad 186 C4
Thornburrow Dr. S-o-T 71 F4
Thornbury Ct. Pert 255 D2
Thornby Ave. Tam 261 F4
Thorncliff Gr. Han 57 F3
Thorncliff Rd. Leek 31 E4
Thorncliffe View. Leek 31 D4
Thorndyke St. Han 57 D1
Thorne Pl. Meir 74 A2
Thornes Croft. Shen 245 F2
Thornescroft Gdns. Bran 185 D4
Thornewill Dr. Bu on T 147 F1
Thorney Cl. Ess 241 F1
Thorney Lanes. March 142 C3
Thorney Rd. Aldr 256 C1
Thorneycroft Ave. Che He 42 A1
Thornfield Ave. Leek 31 D3
Thornfield Cres. Burnt 229 D4
Thornham Cl. N-u-L 71 D1
Thornham Green. Buck 58 B1
Thornhill Cl. Ba-u-Ne 183 E1
Thornhill Dr. Made 68 C4
Thornhill Rd. Aldr 257 D1
Thornhill Rd. Buck 73 F4
Thornhill Rd. Cann 209 F4
Thornhill Rd. Leek 30 B2
Thornhill Rd. Li As 257 D1
Thornleigh. Sedg 271 E3
Thornley Dr. Che 76 C1
Thornley Rd. Che He 42 A2
Thornley Rd. Ess 241 F1
Thornley St. Bu on T 166 B3
Thornton Rd. S-o-T 72 B4
Thorny Lanes. Newb 143 D1
Thornyedge Rd. Bag 44 A1
Thornyedge Rd. Bag 44 B1
Thornyfields La. Brad 174 A4
Thornyfields La. Staf 174 A4
Thornyhurst La. Shen 246 A3
Thorpe Ave. Burnt 228 B4
Thorpe Cl. Burnt 228 B4
Thorpe Green. Lon 88 C4
Thorpe Rise. Che 76 C3
Thorpe St. Burnt 228 B4
Thorswood La. Stan 65 D1
Three Tuns La. Wolv 240 B1
Three Tuns Par. Wolv 240 B1
Thurlstone Dr. Wolv 265 F2
Thurlstone Rd. Wal 243 D2
Thurlwood Dr. N-in-M 42 C1
Thurne. Tam 261 F4
Thursfield Ave. Kids 26 A2
Thursfield Pl. N-in-M 42 B2
Thursfield Wlk. N-in-M 42 B3
Thurston Way. Buck 73 E4
Thurvaston Rd. M Mont 96 C1
Thyme Gr. Meir 90 A3
Tibb St. Audley 39 F1
Tibberton Cl. Wolv 265 E4
Tiber Dr. N-u-L 55 E3
Tickhill La. Dil 75 D4
Tidebrook Pl. Che He 41 F4
Tideswell Green. Swad 186 C3
Tideswell Rd. Lon 73 E3
Tierney St. Han 57 E3
Tiffany La. Wolv 239 F1
Tilbrook Cl. Buck 73 E4
Tilbury Cl. Wolv 265 D4
Tilcon Ave. Staf 156 B1
Tildesley Cl. Penk 207 F4
Tilehurst Pl. Lon 72 C1
Tilery La. Lon 88 B4
Tilewright Cl. Kids 26 A1
Tilia Rd. Tam 251 D3
Till Wlk. Lon 73 E3
Tillet Green. Meir 74 A2
Tilling Dr. Sto 120 A3
Tillington St. Staf 155 E3
Tilson Ave. S-o-T 71 F4
Tilstone Cl. Kids 41 D4
Timber Gr. Bre 223 E3
Timber La. Utt 126 A3
Timber Pit La. Whe As 205 D2
Timberfields. Swyn 118 C3
Timble Cl. Buck 73 E4
Times Sq. Lon 73 D2
Timmis St. Han 57 D1
Timor Gr. Tren 88 A4
Timothy Cl. Fen 73 E3
Tinacre Hill. Wolv 254 C1
Tinker's Castle Rd. Seis 263 E1
Tinker's La. March 143 D4
Tinkers Green Rd. Tam 262 A3
Tinkers La. Ash 100 A2
Tinkers La. Bre 223 F3
Tintagel Cl. Bu on T 147 F1
Tintagel Cl. Pert 254 C2
Tintagel Dr. Sedg 271 F1
Tintagel Pl. Buck 73 E4
Tintern Cres. Wal 242 C1
Tintern Ct. Pert 254 C2
Tintern Pl. N-u-L' 55 F4
Tintern St. Han 57 F2
Tintern Way. Wal 242 C1
Tipping Ave. Meir 74 A1
Tipping St. Staf 155 F2
Tipton Rd. Sedg 271 F4
Tipton St. Sedg 271 F4
Tirley St. Fen 72 C3
Tissington Pl. Meir 90 B4
Titan Way. Lich 231 F4
Titchfield Cl. Wolv 240 C2
Tithe Barn Ct. Staf 156 A2
Tithe Barn Rd. Staf 156 A2
Tithebarn Rd. Rug 178 C1
Tittensor Rd. Barl 104 A4

318
Victoria Ct. N-u-L
Wesley Pl. Cann

Victoria Ct. N-u-L 56 B2
Victoria Dr. Faz 261 D4
Victoria Gdns. Lich 230 C4
Victoria Gr. Wom 270 A4
Victoria Meadow. Ki Brom 199 E3
Victoria Park Rd. Tuns 41 F2
Victoria Park. Newp 168 C2
Victoria Pl. Fen 72 C3
Victoria Pl. N-u-L 55 F4
Victoria Pl. N-u-L 56 B3
Victoria Rd. Brown 244 A2
Victoria Rd. Bu on T 166 B2
Victoria Rd. Fen 72 C4
Victoria Rd. Ma Dra 97 D1
Victoria Rd. N-u-L 71 E4
Victoria Rd. Sedg 271 F4
Victoria Rd. Staf 155 E2
Victoria Rd. Tam 250 B3
Victoria Rd. Wolv 255 F3
Victoria Rd. Wolv 265 F4
Victoria Row. Bidd 27 E2
Victoria Sq. Han 57 D2
Victoria St. Cann 209 F2
Victoria St. Cann 210 B3
Victoria St. Cann 226 B4
Victoria St. Che 76 C2
Victoria St. Kingsw 270 A1
Victoria St. Leek 31 D3
Victoria St. N-u-L 55 E1
Victoria St. N-u-L 55 F4
Victoria St. N-u-L 71 E4
Victoria St. S-o-T 56 B1
Victoria St. Staf 155 F2
Victoria St. Sto 105 D1
Victoria St. Yox 182 A2
Victoria Terr. Staf 155 F3
Victoria Way. Staf 175 F3
Victory Ave. Burnt 228 C4
Victory Cres. Che 76 C2
Victory Terr. Faz 261 D4
Vienna Pl. N-u-L 70 C3
View St. Cann 209 F3
Viewfield Ave. Cann 209 F4
Viewfield Cres. Sedg 271 E3
Viewlands Dr. Wolv 255 D1
Viggars Pl. N-u-L 55 F1
Vigo Cl. Brown 244 C1
Vigo Pl. Aldr 256 A4
Vigo Rd. Brown 244 C1
Vigo Terr. Brown 244 C1
Villa Cl. Bidd 27 E4
Villa Cl. Shar 225 E1
Villa Rd. Ched 45 E4
Villa St. S-o-T 72 A3
Village Gdns. Staf 175 F4
Village The. Astb 15 D4
Village The. End 29 D1
Village The. Kingsw 275 F4
Village The. Staf 175 F3
Villas The. Ipst 62 B3
Villas The. S-o-T 72 A3
Villiers St. Lon 73 D1
Vincent St. Han 57 F3
Vine Bank Rd. Kids 26 A1
Vine La. Cann 226 B3
Vine Row. S-o-T 72 A3
Vine St. Br Hi 275 F1
Vinebank St. S-o-T 72 A3
Vineyard Dr. Newp 168 C2
Vineyard Rd. Newp 168 C2
Violet La. Bu on T 185 F4
Violet Way. Bu on T 186 A4
Virginsalley La. Snel 81 E1
Viscount Rd. Burnt 211 F1
Viscount Wlk. Meir 90 A4
Vista The. Sedg 266 B1
Vivian Rd. Fen 72 C3
Vowchurch Way. Buck 58 B1
Voyager Dr. Nor Ca 226 C3
Vulcan Rd. Lich 214 C1

Waddell Cl. Wolv 266 C1
Wadden La. Gay 138 C2
Wade Ave. N-u-L 56 B3
Wade Cl. Che 76 B1
Wade Cl. Hi Ri 197 F4
Wade La. Hi Ri 197 F4
Wade St. Che He 42 A1
Wade St. Lich 231 D4
Wadebridge Rd. Buck 58 A1
Wadesmill Lawns. Wolv 240 C2
Wadham St. S-o-T 72 A4
Waggon La. Bla 280 C2
Waggoner's La. Hint 259 F4
Wain Ave. N-in-M 42 C3
Wain Ave. N-u-L 70 C4
Wain Dr. S-o-T 71 F3
Wain St. Burs 41 F1
Wainrigg. Tam 262 A4
Wainwood Rise. S-o-T 71 F3
Wainwright Wlk. Han 57 E2
Wakefield Ave. Tut 146 A3
Wakefield Rd. S-o-T 71 F2
Wakeley Hill. Wolv 265 F2
Wakeley Hill. Wom 266 B2
Walcot Cl. Sut Co 258 A2
Walcot Gr. Buck 58 A1
Waldale Cl. Wal 242 B1
Walden Ave. Staf 155 E3
Walden Gdns. Wolv 265 F3
Wales La. Ba-u-Ne 183 E1
Walford Ave. Wolv 265 F4
Walford Rd. Rolle 147 E2
Walhouse Dr. Penk 207 F4
Walhouse St. Cann 226 C4
Walk La. Wom 270 A3
Walk The. Sedg 266 B1
Walker Dr. Kid 280 A1
Walker Rd. Che He 41 F2
Walker St. Bu on T 166 A1
Walker St. Tuns 41 E1
Walkers Croft. Lich 214 B1
Walkers Rise. Rug 210 B4
Walkersgreen Rd. N-u-L 40 B1
Walkfield Rd. Alre 200 C1
Walklate Ave. N-u-L 56 B2
Walkley Bank. Fort 169 E2
Walkmill Bsns Pk. Cann 226 B3
Walkmill La. Cann 226 B3
Walkmill Rd. Ma Dra 112 B4
Walks The. Leek 30 B3
Wall Croft. Aldr 256 A4
Wall Ditch. Alst 35 D1
Wall Dr. Sut C 257 F2
Wall Heath La. Shen 245 F3
Wall La Terr. Ched 45 E3
Wall La. Wall 230 B2
Wallace Cl. Nor Ca 227 F3
Wallace Rd. Brown 244 C4
Wallbridge Cl. Leek 30 B2
Wallbridge Dr. Leek 30 B2
Wallbridge Precinct. Leek 30 B2
Wallbrook Rd. Frad 122 C2
Wallbrook Rd. Mil 122 C2
Walley Dr. Tuns 41 E3
Walley Pl. Burs 57 D4
Walley St. Bidd 27 E4
Walley St. Burs 57 D4
Walley's Dr. N-u-L 56 B1
Wallfield Cl. Up Tea 92 B2
Wallheath Cres. Shen 245 F3
Wallington Cl. Wal 243 D1
Wallington Heath. Wal 243 D1
Wallis Pl. Buck 58 A3
Wallis St. Fen 72 C3
Wallis Way. N-in-M 43 D1
Wallows Wood. Sedg 271 D2
Wallshead Way. Newp 168 C1
Walmer Meadow. Aldr 256 A4
Walmer Pl. Lon 73 D3
Walmers The. Aldr 256 A4
Walney Gr. Han 57 E3
Walnut Ave. Cod 239 D2
Walnut Cl. Cann 209 F2
Walnut Cl. Newp 168 C1
Walnut Cres. Hix 158 B4
Walnut Ct. Rug 197 D3
Walnut Dr. Cann 209 F2
Walnut Dr. Wolv 255 E1
Walnut Gr. Lich 231 F4
Walnut Gr. N-u-L 55 E4
Walnut Tree La. Gno 188 A4
Walpole St. Lon 73 E3
Walrand Cl. Wig 234 A1
Walsall Rd. Aldr 256 A3
Walsall Rd. Brown 244 A1
Walsall Rd. Brown 244 C1
Walsall Rd. Cann 226 C4
Walsall Rd. Gr Wyr 227 D1
Walsall Rd. Li As 257 E2
Walsall Rd. Lich 230 B3
Walsall Rd. Nor Ca 227 F2
Walsall Rd. Shen 245 F4
Walsall Rd. Sut C 257 E2
Walsall Rd. Wall 230 B3
Walsall Wood Rd. Aldr 256 A4
Walsingham Gdns. N-u-L 71 D1
Walter St. Brown 244 A1
Walton Cres. Fen 72 B3
Walton Cres. Wolv 266 C3
Walton Gdns. Cod 238 C2
Walton Gr. Kids 40 B4
Walton Grange. Sto 120 A4
Walton Heath. Wal 242 C2
Walton Ind Est. Sto 119 F3
Walton La. Broc 176 A3
Walton Lodge. Staf 175 F3
Walton Mead Cl. Staf 175 F4
Walton Pl. N-u-L 55 F3
Walton Rd. Aldr 245 D1
Walton Rd. Aldr 245 D1
Walton Rd. S-o-T 71 F2
Walton Rd. Wa on T 185 E3
Walton Rd. Wolv 266 C3
Walton Way. Kids 40 B4
Walton Way. Sto 119 F4
Waltonbury Cl. Staf 175 F3
Wanderers Ave. Wolv 266 B3
Wandsbeck. Tam 261 F4
Wannerton Rd. Bla 281 D1
Wansbeck Wlk. Sedg 271 F3
Warburton St. Burs 57 D4
Ward Grove. Wolv 266 C2
Ward Pl. Che He 42 A3
Ward Rd. Cod 238 C2
Ward Rd. Wolv 266 B3
Ward St. Cann 209 F3
Wardel Cres. Leek 30 C2
Wardel La. N-in-M 43 E1
Wardle Cl. Sut Co 258 A2
Wardle Pl. Cann 209 F3
Wardle St. Tam 250 A3
Wardle St. Tuns 41 F2
Wardles La. Gr Wyr 226 C1
Wardlow Cl. Wolv 266 A3
Wards La. Congle 16 B4
Warings The. Wom 269 F2
Warm Croft. Sto 120 B4
Warminster Pl. Lon 73 D2
Warmson Cl. Fen 73 E3
Warner Rd. Cod 238 C2
Warner St. Han 57 E2
Warnford Wlk. Wolv 265 E3
Warren Cl. Cann 211 D3
Warren Cl. Lich 231 F4
Warren Croft. Arm 198 B2
Warren Ct. Ma Dra 97 E1
Warren Dr. Sedg 266 B1
Warren Gdns. Kingsw 275 E3
Warren La. Bran 184 C4
Warren Pl. Brown 245 D4
Warren Pl. Lon 73 E1
Warren Rd. Burnt 229 D3
Warren Rd. Che He 42 A3
Warren St. Lon 73 E1
Warrens La. Staf 155 D3
Warrilow Heath Rd. N-u-L 40 B1
Warrington Dr. Leek 30 B3
Warrington Rd. Han 57 E1
Warrington St. Fen 72 C3
Warsill Gr. Lon 73 E2
Warstone Hill Rd. Patt 253 F2
Warstone Rd. Ches Hay 242 B4
Warstones Cres. Wolv 265 E3
Warstones Dr. Wolv 265 E3
Warstones Gdns. Wolv 265 E3
Warstones Rd. Wolv 265 E3
Wartell Bank. Kingsw 275 E4
Warwick Ave. Meir 73 F1
Warwick Ave. N-u-L 71 E2
Warwick Ave. Pert 254 C2
Warwick Cl. Bran 184 C4
Warwick Cl. Cann 226 C4
Warwick Cl. Kids 26 A2
Warwick Cl. Ma Dra 97 F1
Warwick Dr. Cod 238 C2
Warwick Gr. N-u-L 56 C2
Warwick Rd. Kingsw 275 E1
Warwick Rd. Staf 175 D4
Warwick Rd. Tam 250 C2
Warwick St. Bidd 27 E4
Warwick St. Bu on T 166 B3
Warwick St. Han 57 D2
Warwick St. N-u-L 55 F4
Warwick Way. Aldr 245 D1
Wasdale Dr. Kingsw 275 F3
Wash Dale La. Sto 105 D3
Washbrook La. Nor Ca 227 E3
Washbrook La. Tiss 51 F2
Washerwall La. Cav 59 D2
Washerwall St. Buck 73 E4
Washington Cl. Bidd 16 B1
Washington St. Tuns 41 F1
Waste La. Woo 79 E2
Wastwater Ct. Pert 254 C2
Wat Tyler Cl. Rug 178 B2
Watchfield Cl. Meir 73 F1
Water Dale. Wolv 255 F1
Water Eaton La. Penk 207 E3
Water La. Env 268 B1
Water La. Newp 168 C2
Water Rd. Sedg 271 E1
Water St. Burnt 228 C4
Water St. Kingsw 275 E4
Water St. N-u-L 40 B1
Water St. N-u-L 56 B1
Water St. S-o-T 72 A3
Water St. Staf 155 F2
Waterbeck Gr. Tren 88 B3
Waterbrook Cl. Penk 207 F4
Waterdale Gr. Lon 73 F2
Waterdale. Wom 269 F3
Waterfall La. Water 48 C1
Waterford Dr. Newp 168 C1
Waterford Rd. Kingsw 275 E4
Watergate St. Tuns 41 E2
Waterhead Cl. Ess 241 D1
Waterhead Dr. Ess 241 D1
Waterhead Rd. Meir 73 F1
Watering Trough Bank. Keele 69 D4
Waterloo Bvd. Cann 210 C2
Waterloo Gr. Kids 26 A1
Waterloo Rd. Burs 57 D3
Waterloo Rd. Edg 168 A3
Waterloo Rd. Han 57 D3
Waterloo St. Bu on T 166 B2
Waterloo St. Han 57 E2
Waterloo St. Leek 30 B3
Watermeadow Dr. Brown 244 B1
Waterpark Rd. Dove 127 D4
Waters Dr. Sut C 257 E2
Waters Rd. Ab Br 160 C2
Waterside Ct. Gno 171 E3
Waterside Dr. Lon 88 C4
Waterside Mews. Newp 168 C2
Waterside Rd. Bu on T 185 E4
Waterside Rd. Wa on T 185 E4
Waterside Way. Brown 228 B1
Waterside Way. Wolv 240 A2
Waterside. Bu on T 185 F4
Waterside. Rug 196 C3
Waterways Gdns. Kingsw 275 F1
Watery La. Ab Br 160 B2
Watery La. Ashb 81 F4
Watery La. Astb 15 E3
Watery La. Clif 81 F4
Watery La. Cod 239 D3
Watery La. Ella 80 A2
Watery La. Hau 172 C3
Watery La. Kingsw 275 F1
Watery La. Lich 214 B2
Watery La. Meir 73 E1
Watery La. Scro 129 F1
Watery La. Swad 186 B3
Watford Gap Rd. Shen 258 A4
Watford St. S-o-T 72 B4
Wathan Ave. Wolv 266 C1
Watkin St. Fen 72 B3
Watkiss Dr. Rug 178 B1
Watlands Ave. N-u-L 56 B3
Watlands Rd. Audley 39 F1
Watlands View. N-u-L 56 B3
Watling St. Brown 228 B1
Watling St. Cann 226 B3
Watling St. Dord 262 B3
Watling St. Faz 249 F1
Watling St. Gr Wyr 226 B3
Watling St. Gre 262 B3
Watling St. Hint 248 B2
Watling St. Nor Ca 227 E2
Watling St. Tam 262 B3
Watson Cl. Rug 178 B2
Watson Rd. S-o-T 71 F2
Watson Rd. Wolv 240 A1
Watson Rd. Wolv 266 C1
Watson St. Bu on T 166 B1
Watson St. S-o-T 71 F4
Watt Pl. Che 76 B2
Wattfield Cl. Rug 197 D3
Wattles La. Act Tru 175 D1
Waveney Ave. Pert 254 C2
Waveney Gr. Cann 209 D1
Waveney Gr. N-u-L 71 D2
Waveney Wlk N. Che He 42 A2
Waveney Wlk S. Che He 42 A2
Waveney. Tam 261 F4
Wavenham Cl. Sut C 257 F3
Waverley Cres. Wolv 266 A3
Waverley Cres. Wolv 266 C2
Waverley Gdns. Rug 178 A1
Waverley Gdns. Wom 270 A4
Waverley La. Bu on T 166 A2
Waverley Pl. N-u-L 71 D3
Waverley Rd. Wal 242 C1
Waverton Rd. Buck 73 F4
Wavertree Ave. Sch Gr 25 F4
Waybutt La. Betley 52 B4
Waybutt La. Ho Co 52 B4
Wayfield Dr. Staf 155 E4
Wayfield Gr. N-u-L 71 E4
Wayside Acres. Cod 238 C1
Wayside Ave. N-u-L 56 B2
Wayside Dr. Li As 257 E2
Wayside. Wolv 239 F1
Wayte St. Han 57 D3
Wealden Hatch. Wolv 240 C2
Wealdstone Dr. Sedg 271 E1
Weathercock La. Congle 6 C2
Weatheroaks. Brown 245 D2
Weaver Cl. Bidd 16 B1
Weaver Cl. Che 76 C3
Weaver Dr. Staf 174 A4
Weaver Pl. N-u-L 71 D2
Weaver Rd. Utt 111 D1
Weaver St. Han 57 E2
Weaver Wlk. Swyn 103 E2
Weavers La. Sto 120 B4
Weavers The. Dens 95 E3
Weaving Gdns. Cann 209 F1
Webb St. Meir 74 A2
Webberley La. Lon 73 E2
Webley Rise. Wolv 240 C2
Webster Ave. Lon 73 F3
Webster St. N-u-L 71 E4
Webster Wlk. Cann 210 A2
Wedgewood Cl. Bu on T 167 D1
Wedgewood Cl. Burnt 229 E4
Wedgewood Rd. Hop 156 A4
Wedgwood Ave. Audley 40 A1
Wedgwood Ave. N-u-L 71 D4
Wedgwood Ct. Han 57 D2
Wedgwood Dr. Barl 88 C2
Wedgwood La. Barl 88 C2
Wedgwood La. Bidd 16 B1
Wedgwood Pl. Burs 56 C4
Wedgwood Rd. Che 76 B1
Wedgwood Rd. Fen 72 C3
Wedgwood Rd. Kids 40 B4
Wedgwood St. Burs 56 C4
Wedgwood St. N-u-L 56 B3
Weeford Rd. Sut Co 258 C2
Weeping Cross. Staf 175 E4
Weetman Cl. Tuns 41 E4
Weighton Gr. Buck 58 C1
Weir Bank. Bu on T 185 F3
Weir Gr. Kids 26 A1
Weirside. May 81 E4
Welbeck Pl. Buck 58 B3
Welbury Gdns. Wolv 255 F3
Welby St. Fen 72 B3
Welch St. S-o-T 72 A4
Weldon Ave. Meir 74 A2
Welford Gr. Sut C 257 F2
Welford Rd. Tam 261 E3
Welford Rise. Bu on T 166 A3
Well La. Bidd 16 B2
Well La. Gr Wyr 227 D1
Well La. Norb 150 B2
Well La. Wal 243 F1
Well La. Wars 22 A1
Well St. Bidd 27 E4
Well St. Che 76 C2
Well St. Fors 91 D4
Well St. Han 57 E2
Well St. Leek 30 C3
Well St. N-u-L 71 E4
Well St. Sch Gr 26 B4
Welland Cl. Bu on T 167 D3
Welland Gr. N-u-L 71 D2
Wellbury Cl. Tren 88 B3
Weller St. S-o-T 71 F4
Wellesbourne Cl. Wolv 265 D4
Wellesbourne. Tam 250 B4
Wellesley St. Han 57 D1
Wellfield Cl. Cann 226 A4
Wellfield Rd. Aldr 256 A4
Wellfield Rd. Alre 201 D1
Wellfield Rd. Buck 58 B1
Wellington Ave. Wolv 265 F4
Wellington Cl. Kingsw 275 F2
Wellington Cres. Alre 215 D2
Wellington Ct. Han 57 E2
Wellington Dr. Cann 209 D1
Wellington Dr. Cann 226 A4
Wellington Dr. Rug 196 C4
Wellington Rd. Albr 220 C1
Wellington Rd. Bran 166 A1
Wellington Rd. Bu on T 166 A1
Wellington Rd. Han 57 E2
Wellington Rd. Kids 26 A1
Wellington Rd. Newp 168 C1
Wellington St E. Bu on T 166 A2
Wellington St W. Bu on T 166 A2
Wellington St. Bu on T 166 A2
Wellington St. Han 57 E2
Wellington St. Leek 30 C3
Wellington St. N-u-L 56 B3
Wellington Terr. Han 57 E2
Wells Cl. Bidd 27 E4
Wells Cl. Cann 209 F3
Wells Cl. Pert 254 B2
Wells Dr. Staf 175 F4
Wells La. Bradl 191 E4
Wells Rd. Wolv 265 F3
Wellyards Cl. Wes on Tr 138 B1
Welney Gdns. Wolv 240 A2
Wendell Crest. Wolv 240 C2
Wendling Cl. Buck 58 B1
Wendover Gr. Buck 58 B1
Wendover Rd. Wolv 266 C1
Wendy Cl. Buck 58 A1
Wenger Cres. Tren 88 A4
Wenham Dr. Meir 90 A4
Wenlock Ave. Wolv 265 F4
Wenlock Cl. Che He 42 A4
Wenlock Cl. N-u-L 40 C1
Wenlock Cl. Sedg 271 E4
Wenlock Dr. Newp 168 C1
Wenlock. Tam 250 B2
Wensleydale Av. Congle 6 A3
Wentlows Ave. Up Tea 92 B3
Wentlows Rd. Up Tea 92 B3
Wentworth Cl. Burnt 229 E4
Wentworth Ct. Sut Co 258 A1
Wentworth Dr. Bu on T 147 E1
Wentworth Dr. Kids 26 B2
Wentworth Dr. Lich 231 E3
Wentworth Dr. Staf 156 B2
Wentworth Gr. Han 57 F4
Wentworth Gr. Pert 254 B3
Wentworth Rd. Stour 279 F4
Wentworth Rd. Wal 242 C2
Wentworth Rd. Wolv 240 C2
Werburgh Dr. Tren 88 A4
Wereton Rd. Audley 39 E1
Wergs Dr. Wolv 255 D4
Wergs Hall Rd. Cod 254 C4
Wergs Hall Rd. Wolv 255 D4
Wergs Rd. Cod 254 C4
Wergs Rd. Wolv 255 D3
Werrington Rd. Buck 58 A2
Wesker Pl. Lon 73 F2
Wesley Ave. Ches Hay 226 B2
Wesley Ave. Cod 239 D1
Wesley Dr. Sto 120 B3
Wesley Gdns. Kids 26 A1
Wesley Pl. Audley 54 B4
Wesley Pl. Cann 210 B4

ORDNANCE SURVEY

STREET ATLASES

The Ordnance Survey / Philip's Street Atlases provide unique and definitive mapping of entire counties

Street Atlases available

- **Berkshire**
- **Bristol and Avon**
- **Buckinghamshire**
- **Cheshire**
- **Derbyshire**
- **East Essex**
- **West Essex**
- **North Hampshire**
- **South Hampshire**
- **Hertfordshire**
- **East Kent**
- **West Kent**
- **Nottinghamshire**
- **Oxfordshire**
- **Staffordshire**
- **Surrey**
- **East Sussex**
- **West Sussex**
- **Warwickshire**

The Street Atlases are revised and updated on a regular basis and new titles are added to the series. Many counties are now available in full-size hardback and softback editions as well as handy pocket-size versions. All contain Ordnance Survey mapping except Surrey which is by Philip's

The series is available from all good bookshops or by mail order direct from the publisher. However, the order form opposite may not reflect the complete range of titles available so it is advisable to check by telephone before placing your order. Payment can be made by credit card or cheque / postal order in the following ways:

By phone
Phone your order through on our special Credit Card Hotline on 01933 414000. Speak to our customer service team during office hours (9am to 5pm) or leave a message on the answering machine, quoting T506N99CO1, your full credit card number plus expiry date and your full name and address

By post
Simply fill out the order form opposite (you may photocopy it) and send it to: Cash Sales Department, Reed Book Services, PO Box 5, Rushden, Northants, NN10 6YX

OS STREET ATLASES ORDER FORM

Registered office: Michelin House, 81 Fulham Road, London SW3 6RB. Registered in England No 1974080

T506N99CO1

	Hardback		Softback		Pocket		
	QUANTITY	TOTAL	QUANTITY	TOTAL	QUANTITY	TOTAL	
	£12.99		£8.99		£4.99		
Berkshire							➤
	ISBN 0-540-05992-7		ISBN 0-540-05993-5		ISBN 0-540-05994-3		
Buckinghamshire							➤
	ISBN 0-540-05989-7		ISBN 0-540-05990-0		ISBN 0-540-05991-9		
East Essex							➤
	ISBN 0-540-05848-3		ISBN 0-540-05866-1		ISBN 0-540-05850-5		
West Essex							➤
	ISBN 0-540-05849-1		ISBN 0-540-05867-X		ISBN 0-540-05851-3		
North Hampshire							➤
	ISBN 0-540-05852-1		ISBN 0-540-05853-X		ISBN 0-540-05854-8		
South Hampshire							➤
	ISBN 0-540-05855-6		ISBN 0-540-05856-4		ISBN 0-540-05857-2		
Hertfordshire							➤
	ISBN 0-540-05995-1		ISBN 0-540-05996-X		ISBN 0-540-05997-8		
East Kent							➤
	ISBN 0-540-06026-7		ISBN 0-540-06027-5		ISBN 0-540-06028-3		
West Kent							➤
	ISBN 0-540-06029-1		ISBN 0-540-06031-3		ISBN 0-540-06030-5		
Nottinghamshire							➤
	ISBN 0-540-05858-0		ISBN 0-540-05859-9		ISBN 0-540-05860-2		
Oxfordshire							➤
	ISBN 0-540-05986-2		ISBN 0-540-05987-0		ISBN 0-540-05988-9		
Surrey							➤
	ISBN 0-540-05983-8		ISBN 0-540-05984-6		ISBN 0-540-05985-4		
East Sussex							➤
	ISBN 0-540-05875-0		ISBN 0-540-05874-2		ISBN 0-540-05873-4		
West Sussex							➤
	ISBN 0-540-05876-9		ISBN 0-540-05877-7		ISBN 0-540-05878-5		
	£12.99		£9.99		£4.99		
Bristol and Avon							➤
	ISBN 0-540-06140-9		ISBN 0-540-06141-7		ISBN 0-540-06142-5		
Cheshire							➤
	ISBN 0-540-06143-3		ISBN 0-540-06144-1		ISBN 0-540-06145-X		
Derbyshire							➤
	ISBN 0-540-06137-9		ISBN 0-540-06138-7		ISBN 0-540-06139-5		
Staffordshire							➤
	ISBN 0-540-06134-4		ISBN 0-540-06135-2		ISBN 0-540-06136-0		
	£10.99						
Warwickshire							➤
	ISBN 0-540-05642-1						⬇

Name_____

Address_____

_____

_____ Postcode

◆ **Free postage and packing** ◆ *All available titles will normally be dispatched within 5 working days of receipt of order but please allow up to 28 days for delivery*
☐ *Please tick this box if you do not wish your name to be used by other carefully selected organisations that may wish to send you information about other products and services*

*I enclose a cheque / postal order, for a **total** of* [____]

made payable to **Reed Book Services,** *or please debit my*

☐ Access ☐ American Express ☐ Visa

account by [____]

Account no ☐☐☐☐ ☐☐☐☐ ☐☐☐☐ ☐☐☐☐

Expiry date ☐☐ ☐☐

Signature_____